# 501

## MUST-VISIT CITIES

# 501

## MUST-VISIT CITIES

**B** **Bounty**
Books

**Publisher:** Polly Manguel

**Project Editor:** Emma Beare

**Publishing Assistant:** Sarah Marling

**Designer:** Ron Callow/Design 23

**Picture Researchers:** Jennifer Veall, Vickie Walters

**Production Manager:** Neil Randles

**Production Assistant:** Pauline LeNavenec


This edition first published in Great Britain in 2008 by
Bounty Books, a division of Octopus Publishing Group Limited
2-4 Heron Quays, London E14 4JP


Copyright © 2008 Octopus Publishing Group Limited

A CIP catalogue record is available from the British Library


ISBN: 978-0-753716-03-8


Printed and bound in Italy

**Please note:** We now know that political situations arise very quickly and a city or country that was quite safe a short time ago can suddenly become a 'no-go' area. Please check with the relevant authorities before booking tickets and travelling if you think there could be a problem.

The seasons given in this book relate to the relevant hemisphere. Be sure to check that you visit at the correct time.

# Contents

# Introduction

There are about 6.4 billion of us humans living on this planet. At some stage early in 2007 something extremely noteworthy – though little reported – took place: from inhabiting a world in which most people lived in the countryside we moved to a world where the majority of us now live in cities.

The UN estimates that some 180,000 people are added to the world's urban population *every day*. There are now 300 cities with populations of over 1 million. The rate of growth in population of some cities is extraordinary – while it took 130 years for London's population to grow from 1 million to 8 million, it took Seoul only 25 years to do the same. There are no less than 90 cities in China with over a million inhabitants and each year a staggering 8.5 million rural Chinese peasants move to the cities. Though the world's most populous city at the moment is less than 20 million, it seems entirely possible that in a few decades we shall see 'megacities' with 50 million or more inhabitants.

Men and women have been living in cities for some 12,000 years. There were human settlements then in what are now Damascus and Jericho, the two oldest continuously inhabited cities in this book. Harappa and Mohenjo-daro, the once famous, now destroyed cities of the Indus Valley civilization around 2,000-3,000 BC, each with about 35,000 residents, were forerunners of many modern cities – they had planned layouts based on grids of streets, the world's first urban sanitation systems as well as bathhouses, swimming pools and market squares. In comparison many cities included here are quite recent, and some are positively new – Brazil's capital Brasilia, though it's already home to around 2.4 million people, is only 50 years old.

You will find most of the world's largest cities, such as Mexico City, Tokyo, Mumbai and New York, featured in this book, yet you can also read about many cities which are on a very different scale altogether: St David's in Wales (with a population of only 1,600 it seems more of a village than a city), Bulgaria's 'Pearl of the Black Sea' Nessebar (population 10,000) or Colonia del Sacramento, Uruguay's oldest city (population 22,000). Not surprisingly though, some of the 501 cities are a lot more 'must-visit' places than others! While Vancouver is, according to a recent survey, the world's most liveable city, Algiers is ranked as one of the worst cities in the world for crime, instability and poor infrastructure.

Many cities are packed with all types of restaurants and hotels and have entertainments of every description. Most have fascinating histories, with museums, art galleries and all manner of sights to inform, delight and entertain. Yet you will find others with few obvious sights to attract visitors. Such cities require you to soak up the atmosphere, take in the style of daily life and go with the flow before you can fully appreciate them. If you decide to visit the entrancing Ethiopian city of Harar or legendary Timbuktu in Mali or the Shangri-la city of Thimpu, capital of Bhutan, you should not go expecting to find five-star hotels, night-clubs or burger bars. The experience and pleasure to be gained from visiting cities in the developing world is a very different one from going to San Francisco or Venice or Paris – almost certainly more challenging but potentially just as rewarding and enjoyable.

Whichever cities you put on your own must-visit list, make sure you do your research and read as much as you can about your chosen destination before you make the final decision to go. Gain some knowledge of the customs, culture, history and layout of your cities and try to learn some of the language. Just knowing how to say 'Good Morning' and 'Thank You' in the local language can often help to get you off on the right footing. Don't forget that cities can be dangerous places – indeed included in this book are some cities you would probably be unwise to visit at present. So always consult your government's official advice about whether to travel and what precautions to take. Make sure you have travel insurance, pack the right clothes for the time of year, have the appropriate vaccinations, obtain your visas, if required…

As with all travelling, you should of course keep your wits about you while visiting your chosen cities. Don't go expecting the same attitudes, the same food, the same accommodation etc. as you would find at home. Go prepared but go with an open mind. Be sensible. Have fun!

7

# EUROPE & THE MIDDLE EAST

# Copenhagen

**WHEN TO GO:**
Explore Copenhagen in summer, when the weather is pleasant and evenings are light and long.
**DON'T MISS:**
The spectacular Øresund Bridge, which opened in 2000 and connects Copenhagen to Malmø in Sweden.
Gefion Fountain, Copenhagen's largest monument showing the goddess Gefion ploughing with four oxen, which has become a wishing well.
The Church of our Saviour in Christian's Harbour, with an extraordinary golden staircase winding up the outside of the spire.
Rosenborg Castle, in the centre of Copenhagen, a grand summerhouse containing the Danish royal collections, including the crown jewels.
Free entertainment in the late afternoon and evening, when a variety of street performers come out to play on the Strøget.
**YOU SHOULD KNOW:**
Quite a few of Denmark's 40 cricket clubs are in Copenhagen.

*Strøget - Europe's longest pedestrian shopping street*

Wonderful, wonderful . . . Thanks to the Danny Kaye song, you know the rest. Copenhagen is a city that should be visited at least once in a lifetime, because the Danish capital has special charm. Denmark has the world's oldest monarchy, and the royal family lives in the middle of the city at the Amalienborg Palace. Don't be surprised to see Queen Margrethe out and about, as the royals are famously egalitarian.

A sense of history is everywhere as you stroll through cobbled squares and narrow streets lined with old buildings, before finding the vast City Hall Square, bounded on one side by the renowned Tivoli Gardens with Strøget (the straight), Europe's longest pedestrian shopping street, on the other. The square was constructed around 1900 in romantic style and revamped when Copenhagen was Cultural Capital of Europe in 1996. Walk down the broad Strøget and find Gammel Square, with an exquisite bronze fountain erected in 1608, then take a break at an open-air café in Gråbrødre Square in the heart of this trendy shopping area.

There are excellent green parks in Copenhagen, and the Tivoli pleasure gardens offer all sorts of entertaining experiences (especially for those who like roller coasters). You must not miss the Little Mermaid, sculpted by Edward Eriksen in 1913, and doomed to sit on her rock in Copenhagen harbour for 300 years before entering the human world (just a couple of centuries to wait, then). She isn't lonely, though, with a million visitors a year.

The New Harbour (Nyhavn, built in the 17th century) is a picturesque waterside area, with mouth-watering restaurants and lively bars. Danish fairy-tale author Hans Christian Andersen lived here for some years. It serves as a starting point for water tours that give a wonderfully different view of this special city.

# Aalborg

This northern Danish city is on the Limfjord, and became well established as a harbour and trading centre in the Middle Ages. It later developed as a hard-working industrial city. Though many traditional heavy industries have declined, it remains an important centre of commerce.

However, the old town centre beside the water is picturesque, with narrow cobbled streets, 17th century houses, the half-timbered Aalborghus Castle and Jens Bang's establishment, the finest example of ostentatious 17th century mercantile

*Jens Bang's house*

architecture in northern Europe (don't miss the grotesque carvings on the façade, said to represent the enemies of Jens Bang). Keeping it in the family, another well-preserved merchant's house is that of Bang's half brother, Jørgen Olufsen. The Budolfi Cathedral with its colourful interior is mostly 18th century with older elements. Beneath the main shopping street is an unusual museum created from the excavation of an 11th century Franciscan Friary.

Aalborg offers quality shopping, with a variety of interesting and unusual shops in side streets and courtyards. The place to enjoy the bustle of city life whilst relaxing with a coffee or drink is undoubtedly the famous Jomfru Ane Gade (Virgin Anne Street), where visitors are encouraged to take a guided tour of great Danish beers. After tourists and workers have departed for the day, it turns into the centre of Aalborg's nightlife.

Culture is well served, too. The North Jutland Museum of Art is a striking modern building designed by renowned Finnish architect Alvar Aalto. The Historical Museum recreates the city's history over the past millennium, whilst the 17th century House of Crafts houses a variety of workers exercising traditional skills. Another local delight is the Jako Bole Theatre for children, with a constantly changing repertoire to delight the youngsters. The Spring Carnival is an annual highlight.

**POPULATION:**
122,000 (2006)
**WHEN TO GO:**
If possible (the city gets crowded then) take in carnival week at the end of May.
**DON'T MISS:**
The site of two ancient settlements and the remains of a Viking burial ground, with an associated museum, on Lindholm Høje, a hill above the city.
Africa – Aalborg Zoo has created an African village complete with houses, trees, savannah and animals. Oh, and there are polar bears just around the corner!
A charming windmill at Vester Mariendel, built in the 1750s and moved to its present site in 1893.
Bustling Rosdahl's Saturday food market down by the harbour, for delicious local produce.
The lofty view from the top of the Aalborgtårnet tripod tower, 105 m (345 ft) above sea level.
**YOU SHOULD KNOW:**
Most of the world's supply of the fiery Scandanavian spirit known as *akvavit* (literally 'water of life') is distilled here.

*St Angsar church in Odense*

# Odense

Danish author and poet Hans Christian Andersen was born in Odense in 1805, and the city is proud of its famous son, with a dedicated museum and his childhood home preserved for posterity. A new cultural centre called Fyrtøjet (tinder box) brings his fairy tales to life, and there is a festival held in his honour in Funen village, usually in July or August. The composer Carl Nielsen was also a local lad, and has his own museum.

If Andersen could return today, he would recognize many buildings, including fine half-timbered houses and, of course, St Canute's Cathedral, erected in brick on earlier foundations in the 13th century. This is one of the finest gothic buildings in Denmark, named after the saintly King Canute (not the one of tide-commanding fame) slain here in 1086. Also notable is St Hans Church, whilst the 19th century town hall continues the tradition of monumental architecture.

Odense is on Funen Island close to the fjord of the same name and linked to the sea by a deep canal. Ease of access was greatly improved in the late 1990s with the opening of Great Belt Bridge, the second-longest suspension bridge in the world, joining Funen to Zealand, Denmark's other main island. Formerly a tough shipbuilding city, Odense is making a real effort to adapt to a world where traditional industries are no longer enough – take a walk to the harbour and see how well the major transformation from industrial port to waterside leisure area is going. The city has retained some industry but is now focusing on service industries (especially tourism).

This has resulted in added emphasis on the city's cultural heritage, plus a real effort to create a much brighter, livelier city centre, with picturesque pedestrian shopping streets, a wealth of restaurants and bars and the constant buzz that comes from a large student population.

**POPULATION:**
147,000 (2007)

**WHEN TO GO:**
Unless you like cold, short days and long dark nights it's best to visit between May and September.

**DON'T MISS:**
The races – horse, trotting and greyhound races at Denmark's only race track (Væddeløbsbane Fyns), with a children's playground for the youngsters.
The Funen Village, an open-air museum where old rural buildings from all over the country have been reconstructed to illustrate country life around 1850.
Oceanium at the zoo, beside the river – offering an amazing journey through the flora and fauna of South America, including underwater sections.
Vintage trains and ferries going back 150 years at the Danish Railway Museum, along with a mini-railway, model railways and a play area for children.
A small replica of the Odin Tower in Odinsparken, where it once stood – built in 1935 to rival the Eiffel Tower, but blown up in 1944.

**YOU SHOULD KNOW:**
St Canute's Cathedral has the skeletons of both the eponymous Canute and his brother on display.

# Aarhus

Denmark's second-largest city and principal port (often known by the contemporary Danish name of Ärhus) is on the Jutland peninsula and lies at the heart of a huge urban conurbation. Founded in Viking times, this is the oldest city in Scandinavia. Aarhus takes pride in its heritage, but also in being a thoroughly modern city when it comes to commerce, culture and quality of life.

There is much to admire about the old. The 15th century cathedral, dedicated to patron saint of sailors St Clemens, is the tallest, longest church in the country. It has the most frescoes, the biggest organ and Denmark's largest medieval artwork, a triptych. There are fine tombs, early choir stalls and a wonderful altar. It's an experience to remember, worth a morning of anyone's time. Another splendid church is that of Our Lady, the city's oldest (one up on the cathedral!). It dates from 1100 with a recently discovered 11th century crypt. In the Botanical Gardens may be found Den Gamle By (The Old Town), an atmospheric collection of half-timbered town houses and shops from all over Denmark dating from the 17th to 19th centuries.

Ancient and modern come together in some of the city's oldest areas, which are atmospheric, trend-setting centres for shopping, relaxing at pavement cafés or eating out. This is especially true of the Latin Quarter beyond the cathedral, a warren of historic streets centred on Pustervig Torv Square. Another lively place is the colourful Spanish Steps on a waterfront that serves as a magnet for locals (including 40,000 students) and tourists alike. There are numerous safe beaches nearby, whilst parks and open spaces abound within the city. The annual summer Aarhus Festuge (Aarhus Party Week) features a different theme each year.

**POPULATION:**
296,000 (2006)
**WHEN TO GO:**
In summer, when the city buzzes with open-air life and its green spaces are at their best.
**DON'T MISS:**
Tivoli Friheden amusement park on the south side, and the tranquil adjacent wooded World War I memorial park.
The royal summer residence at Marselisborg, with its superb rose garden (unfortunately closed if the Queen is in residence).
Aros Aarhus Kunstmuseum – a magnificent modern city gallery opened in 2004, that attracted its one millionth visitor two years later.
Moesgård Manor House, south of town, an exceptional museum of prehistory that includes the mummified Grauballe Man from 55 BC (whose throat was cut!).
The modern Aarhus City Hall by architect Arne Jacobsen, recognized as one of the most important modern buildings in Denmark.
**YOU SHOULD KNOW:**
Due for completion in 2010, the Light House on the harbour will be Denmark's tallest building at 142 m (465 ft).

*The view across the pond at the Old Town Museum*

# Turku

**POPULATION:**
175,000 (2006)
**WHEN TO GO:**
July, for the Medieval Market festival (and because it's the warmest month).
**DON'T MISS:**
Two three-masted museum ships, *Suomen Joutsen* and *Sigyn* (this is also the name of the glass-walled modern concert hall in town).
The Aboa Vetus Museum, built over a fascinating 14th century archaeological site in the 1990s, and the adjoining Ars Nova modern art museum.
A ride on the small passenger ferry Föri across the Aura River.
Ruissalo Island in the Archipelago Sea, with ancient oak forests and the University of Turku's botanical garden.
The diverse Hansa shopping mall in the centre of town, for everything you could ever want to buy.
**YOU SHOULD KNOW:**
Turku is Finland's official 'Christmas City' and the traditional Declaration of Christmas Peace is made there every Christmas Eve at noon.

The country's original capital is its oldest city, and the very name Finland used to refer only to the southern area around Turku. Today, it is Finland's third-largest city and a hive of activity, being the country's most important year-round ice-free port, handling millions of passengers and huge quantities of freight. As a traditional 'gateway to Sweden', Swedish influence is significant with the language widely spoken and one of the two universities teaching in Swedish.

Following a common Scandinavian pattern, the city has been extensively redeveloped over the years, often starting when the old wooden town went up in flames. In this case, Turku was almost completely destroyed by fire in 1827, with few buildings surviving. Turku Cathedral did, but was damaged and rebuilt. There is an exceptional 13th century castle overlooking the harbour that has seen much military action over the centuries and now serves as a museum. Another magical survivor is Luostarinmäki, an area of late 18th century housing and now a handicrafts museum.

For all its commercial and economic importance, Turku is a restful place. The River Aura winds through the city centre, crossed by nine bridges, lined with small boats and surrounded by green parks. The river also passes some of the best modern buildings – the Sibelius Museum, City Theatre and Wäinö Aaltonen Museum of Art, dedicated to Finland's most famous sculptor. These are a formal expression of the city's vibrant cultural life, with its emphasis on music and theatre. Indeed, Turku is pitching to become a European Capital of Culture in 2011.

But more mundane needs are not neglected, with plenty of good restaurants, coffee houses and bars. A morning market is held on the big square at Kauppatori, a flea market in Aninkaistentori and a lively Medieval Market festival is held every July.

*The Castle walls*

# Oulu

This lively northern city has a strong industrial and commercial tradition, growing up around the Merikoski rapids that today feed a striking power station designed by avant-garde architect Alvar Aalto. This constant supply of cheap energy supports timber, paper and chemical industries, but there is still plenty of original charm and character about the place, which is a centre of cultural life.

In common with many Finnish cities, Oulu is an intriguing mixture of old and new. This contrast is powerfully made in the busy riverside Market Square, shared by ancient preserved salt houses and the city's ultramodern theatre. After a disastrous fire, much of the city centre was rebuilt in the 1820s in the neoclassical style also seen in Helsinki, designed by the same architect, Carl Ludvig Engel. He also planned the rebuilding of Oulu Cathedral, completed in 1845. It contains a notable curiosity – the oldest-known Finnish portrait painting.

There are plenty of worthwhile attractions in and around the city, such as a vehicle museum, old sawmill or Finland's first interactive science facility, Tietomaa, said to offer something for the whole family. The Rapids Centre in the river estuary is worth a visit, with its interconnecting islands, spectacular fountains and modern architecture. Those with cultural interests will find plenty to please them, with conventional museums, galleries and a thriving classical music scene. The Oulu Music Centre is home to the city's symphony orchestra and annual winter music festival. The Oulunsalo Music Festival is in summer and the International Children's Film Festival in November.

Other festivals are less genteel, with a strong emphasis on contemporary rock music. Prominent among them is the annual outing of the World Air Guitar Championships. But there is also a constant programme of concerts of every sort encompassing rock, jazz and classical music.

*Baskets for sale in Market Square*

**POPULATION:**
118,000 (2007)
**WHEN TO GO:**
Unless you're determined to see the Northern Lights, Finland is an ideal summer destination.
**DON'T MISS:**
The open-air museum of Finnish life on Turkansaario Island, on the river close to the city.
Recently renovated North Ostrobothnia Museum in Ainola Park, illustrating the lives of Oulu's people over the centuries.
The oldest wooden house in Oulu, dating from the early 18th century, to be found on Pikisaari Island. Now a sailors' museum.
The University Botanical Gardens with glass pyramids known as Romeo and Juliet, housing thousands of plants from warmer climes.
**YOU SHOULD KNOW:**
In the 19th century, Oulu had the world's most important tar-exporting harbour.

15

# Helsinki

**POPULATION:**
565,000 (2007)
**WHEN TO GO:**
Summer is perfect – unless you're a fan of continuous darkness!
**DON'T MISS:**
An outing to Tapiola Garden City in the suburbs, one of the best examples of integrated modern architecture in the city.
Linnanmäki Amusement Park, with many rides including the new (and fearsome!) ZacSpin rollercoaster.
The Suomenlinna fortress complex, built on six islands in the 18th century and now a UNESCO World Heritage Site.
An imposing monument for Finnish composer Jean Sibelius in the park that bears his name.
Helsinki Zoo, located on a rocky island reached by a bridge from the mainland.
**YOU SHOULD KNOW:**
Helsinki (rather reluctantly) stood in for Russia in several movies of the cold war era, such as *The Kremlin Letter* and *Gorky Park*.

*The Great Church in Helsinki*

Until the early 19th century, Helsinki (known by the Swedish name of Helsingfors) was an insignificant market town near the mouth of the River Vantaa. Finland was then seized from Sweden by Russia, and Tzar Alexander I made Helsinki its capital. Finland remained under Russian rule until 1918. In 1940 Russia attempted an invasion but troops only got as far as the Mannheim Line.

The elegant old city dates from the 1830s, when it was built in neoclassical style to resemble St Petersburg, becoming known as 'the white city of the north'. It is largely on a peninsula linked to widespread suburbs by bridges, causeways and ferries and the sea seems to be around every corner, with trees and rocks forming part of the urban scene.

Helsinki is a rich city, generating about a third of the country's wealth, but despite the high level of economic activity remains a perfect destination for visitors. The old city seems to offer everything – it is small and intimate with a lively atmosphere, but the pace of life remains relaxed. There are elegant buildings aplenty. Start with those around the central Senate Square, including the magnificent Lutheran cathedral. The South Harbour should be the next port of call, with its bustling daily market, cafés and the offer of sightseeing boat trips. From the harbour, walk up the grand Esplanaadikatu boulevard with its excellent shops and find Mannerheimintie, a main artery giving access to theatres, galleries, museums and concert halls.

Modern architecture is a major feature of the city, starting with art nouveau buildings from the early 1900s through sports venues built for the aborted 1940 Olympic Games to the loved (or hated!) works of renowned Finnish architect Alvar Aalto, such as Finlandia Hall. Don't miss the extraordinary Temppeliaukio Church, built into the living rock and lit by a glazed dome.

# Vaasa

This is the main west-coast centre for sea and air travel from Finland across the Gulf of Bothnia to Sweden. Ties between Vaasa and its neighbour are close, with roughly a quarter of the population speaking Swedish as a first language. The old town was destroyed by fire in 1852 and a new one constructed closer to the sea. The ruins may still be seen at the original site, Mustasaari, with surviving buildings including churches, a castle and the 18th century Falander-Wasastjerna House, now housing the Old Vaasa Museum. In the civil war of 1918, Vaasa was the headquarters of the communist-hating White Guards (they won!) and the temporary capital of Finland.

The modern city was planned by Carl Axel Setterberg in Empire style, around five broad avenues joined by narrow streets and alleys to reduce the risk of another city-wide fire. Leafy avenues, generous parks surrounding public buildings and the extensive shoreline combine to create a relaxed atmosphere. At the centre of city life is the busy market square, which contains Finland's own Statue of Liberty (a man!), erected in 1938. Between the market place and the sea is the Rewell Centre, a large mall guaranteed to satisfy shopaholics.

Most of the summer recreational activities in Vaasa are of the open-air variety, mostly associated with water – walking along the shore, swimming, wildlife watching (birds and seals), fishing, sailing and boat excursions around the many islands in the Kvarken Archipelago off Vaasa, which became a UNESCO World Natural Heritage Site in 2006, the first in Finland.

Vaasa has an active cultural life, with frequent concerts of all sorts. There are good museums including the Kuntsi Museum of Modern Art, opened in 2007, and Brage Open-Air Museum at Hietalahti (a collection of old farm buildings).

**POPULATION:**
57,000 (2005)
**WHEN TO GO:**
Make it summertime, when the living is easy.
**DON'T MISS:**
The harbour – sit at a café table watching all the comings and goings.
Tropiclandia, a water park with indoor and outdoor wild water slides, waterfalls, bubble baths and saunas.
The magnificent Court of Appeal building – a survivior of Old Vaasa, now a church.
Waslandia Amusement Park, offering a full day's action for all the family with dozens of rides and other activities.
The fine regional collections at the Ostrobothian museum.
The waterside Finnish aviation monument, sculpted in bronze in the form of a sea eagle.
**YOU SHOULD KNOW:**
Vaasa's proudest boast is that it's Finland's sunniest city.

# Tromsø

**POPULATION:**
64,000 (2004)
**WHEN TO GO:**
November to March for the Northern
Lights and a winter wonderland.
**DON'T MISS:**
The cable car ride up to Mount
Storsteinen for a dramatic panoramic
view of Tromsø.
Tromsø Museum's display on the
Lapps (Sami people), the indigenous
inhabitants of the Scandinavian and
Russian Arctic.
Polaria Aquarium – you guessed it, the
world's most northerly aquarium, with
performing seals and comprehensive
additional displays illustrating every
aspect of polar life.
The *Polstjeme*, a famous seal-hunting
ship, preserved in a museum close to
Polaria that serves as a reminder of
the Arctic hunting that served Tromsø
so well in the past.
Tromsø Military Museum in a wartime
German bunker (summer only).
**YOU SHOULD KNOW:**
The German pocket battleship *Tirpitz*
was sunk off Tromsø in 1944, with the
loss of a thousand German sailors.

Anyone with ambitions to see the spectacular Northern Lights (Aurora Borealis) before they die should head for Tromsø. They periodically shimmer above Norway's arctic city on clear nights, and may be enjoyed in conjunction with traditional activities like dog sledding, horse-drawn sleigh rides or ice fishing. At just 2,000 km (1,240 mi) from the North Pole, this is also the land of the midnight sun, where summer days are literally endless (as are winter nights!). Tromsø is located amidst wonderful coastal and mountain scenery and was originally confined to Tromsøya Island, but it has spread to the mainland and part of adjacent Kvaløya Island, each with a soaring bridge connection.

One of the city's claims to fame is that it has the world's most northerly, well, nearly everything . . . cathedral, nunnery, Catholic bishop, brewery, botanical garden, planetarium, league soccer team, university and more. In truth, its very character has been forged by its location within the Arctic Circle. It came to prominence in the 19th century as a centre for Arctic hunting, becoming known as 'The Paris of the North' for the surprising level of sophistication and cultural awareness shown in such a rugged outpost – an aura that remains to this day. It was also the starting point for the pioneering expeditions of Arctic explorers such as Amundsen and Nansen.

This compact island city retains considerable original charm, with the best collection of old wooden houses north of Trondheim. There is also a great deal of modern building, to meet the needs of a city that has expanded dramatically since World War II. One of the most striking examples of this is the much-photographed Arctic Cathedral, completed in 1965. By way of typical Scandinavian old-new contrast, the Lutheran Cathedral dating from 1861 is one of Norway's most important wooden churches.

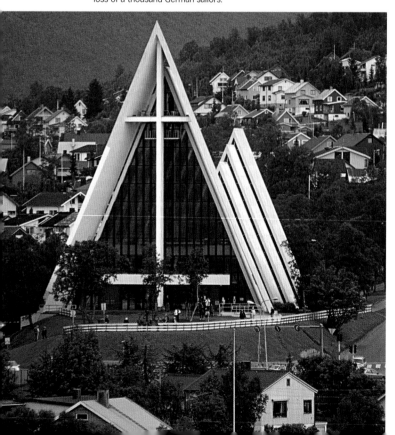

*The façade of the Arctic Cathedral, a Lutheran church*

# Ålesund

This small but perfectly formed fishing port sits on islands connected by bridges in the northern part of Norway's fjord area, and is an ideal base for exploring this spectacular area of coastal scenery. Ålesund is a major fishing port and the commercial centre of the Sunnmøre district, with picturesque quays that bustle with activity all day long as fish catches are landed, cargo shifted and the coastal ferry comes and goes. It's all too easy to sit there all day, relaxing amidst all that fascinating activity as others do the hard work!

The town was almost totally destroyed by fire in 1904 and rebuilt in record time. The architects chose a version of the then-popular Art Nouveau style, but gave it a distinctive local look. Wander round the town and spot incredible turrets, towers, spires, dragons, human faces, figures from folklore and medieval detail. This is the most complete example of coherent art nouveau construction in the world.

From the top of the Aksla Mountain, rising almost vertically from the town, are coastal views considered to be among the best in Norway. The 418 steps may be testing, but the effort is worthwhile – especially as there's a restaurant waiting. At its base is a 19th century park containing a statue of Gange Rolf (Rollo). He was a colourful saga figure from the locality who became feudal lord of Normandy and ancestor of William the Conqueror.

From Ålesund it is possible to visit Sunnmøre's wonderful fjords, fishing villages, islands and mountains. Many people explore on foot, but a car helps cast the net wider. There are also organized trips available by land and sea. The town is adjacent to the Hjørund and Geiranger fjords, which are must-see tourist destinations.

*The small fishing port of Ålesund*

**POPULATION:**
41,000 (2006)
**WHEN TO GO:**
With its mild maritime climate, winters are not severe, though most organized activities are in summer.
**DON'T MISS:**
The Atlantic Sea Park just outside town – an extraordinary aquarium built into the natural coastline, facing the open sea.
Nearby Runde Island, a rocky refuge for hundreds of thousands of seabirds.
The Art Nouveau Centre of Norway (Jugendstil Senteret), for real insight into this influential movement.
Alnes lighthouse and fishing village on the outer island of Giske.
The view from the top of nearby Skjerdingen Mountain, the highest in the area.
Sunnmøre Museum, with 50 old buildings, boats, Middle Ages display and nature park.
**YOU SHOULD KNOW:**
The only person killed in the great conflagration of 1904 lived next to the fire station.

19

*The old harbour*

# Stavanger

In typical Norwegian fashion this is a city of contrasts, with the old and picturesque rubbing shoulders with the new and striking. Stavanger has experienced many ups and downs since its foundation in the 12th century, the latest upswing coming since it became the main on-shore base for the country's booming North Sea oil and gas industry in the 1970s. For all its industrial past and present, Stavanger was selected as a European Capital of Culture for 2008, an honour shared with Liverpool.

Old Stavanger is part of the city centre, and possesses one of the most charming collections of 18th and 19th century wooden buildings in Scandinavia. Stavanger Cathedral, dedicated to St Swithin, was consecrated in the 12th century and, despite various alterations and renovations since, remains a well-preserved example of Gothic architecture. Old Stavanger hosts the city museum, showcasing Stavanger's history as' the herring capital of Norway'.

Vågen, the old harbour, has also retained much of its original character, including the town watchman's tower. This is the perfect place to sit at a quayside table in summer, eating fresh prawns and watching comings and goings in the busy harbour. Then find the pedestrian shopping streets behind the restaurants and bars on the harbour's east side, or take a leisurely evening stroll along the Blue Promenade, named after blue lights embedded in the ground, which passes several small docks and other interesting sights like the new concert hall. There are two colourful markets to visit – a food market by the cathedral selling the produce of local farmers, and the indoor fish market at harbour's end.

Stavanger's citizens love festivals and there's something happening all the time, usually on the themes of music, eating and drinking or maritime life. Not to mention the beach volleyball tournament in June or July!

**POPULATION:**
115,000 (2006)
**WHEN TO GO:**
Definitely a summer destination, with a host of outdoor attractions and activities to enjoy.
**DON'T MISS:**
The Jernaldergarden reconstructed Iron Age village, not far from the centre, incongruously sited close to modern apartment blocks.
Ullandhaug telecomms tower for wonderful views, plus peaceful woodland walks and the nearby Botanical Gardens.
The Norwegian Petroleum Museum on the waterfront, opened in 1999, with its seaward aspect cunningly designed to look like an oil platform.
The Swords in Rock monument at the Møllebukta recreation area on the south side of the fjord, commemorating the Battle of Hafrsfjord in 872.
**YOU SHOULD KNOW:**
The average monthly temperature in Stavanger never drops below freezing point.

# Oslo

Once called Christiania, then Kristiania, Oslo is Norway's capital and largest city. It lies at the head of the Oslofjord, spreading down either side to form a huge 'U'. The inevitable Scandinavian fire (actually Oslo's unlucky 14th) destroyed the medieval town in 1624 and a new town sprang up around the Akershus Fortress across the water (still a military area today, but open to the public). Oslo is such a force in Norwegian life that it faces criticism for depopulating rural areas by attracting the young – which does, however, help make it a lively place. Oslo regards itself as the party capital of Norway and has an enormous selection of restaurants, bars and clubs.

It is also the excuse for popular resistance to extensive further development, ensuring that the city remains surrounded at close quarters by unspoiled wilderness. By way of contrast, Oslo is a major cultural capital, with world-class museums, galleries, sculpture parks and music venues. Take a ferry to the Bygdøy Peninsula to see superb maritime museums – of Viking ships, *Kon-Tiki* and *Fram*, the latter pair celebrating great Norwegian seafarers Thor Heyerdahl and Roald Amundsen.

Oslo is a place of visual contrasts, with a lot of modern architecture some of which, from the 1960s, is frankly hideous. But the overall effect is not displeasing and there are many interesting vistas. Walk along Karl Johans Gate through the heart of the city, from the Royal Palace to the railway station, for a flavour of Oslo at its best (and that includes shops!). For charming original wooden houses find your way to areas like Kampen, Rodeløkka or Vålerenga. The 17th century cathedral (Oslo's third) is definitely worth visiting, whilst those with grand designs will love a tour of the sumptuous Royal Palace.

**POPULATION:**
552,000 (2007)
**WHEN TO GO:**
Late spring/summer/early autumn (winters are long and very cold).
**DON'T MISS:**
The Nobel Peace Centre, which has an exhibit for every single winner of the prestigious prize.
A visit to the City Hall on the waterfront, site of the annual Nobel Prize ceremony, for huge murals in its spectacular main hall.
The view from the top of the Holmenkollen ski jump opened in 1892, and a trip round the accompanying skiing museum.
The Munch Museum, for hundreds of paintings by Norway's tortured genius.
A walk down beside Oslo's tumbling River Akerselva from rural Frysja to the centre, for a unique experience of the city.
Vigeland Sculpture Park, within Frogner Park, for over 200 bronze and granite sculptures by Norwegian master Gustav Vigeland.
**YOU SHOULD KNOW:**
Oslo is one of the world's largest capitals by area, much of it forest, with 40 islands and 343 lakes within city limits.

*The 17th century Cathedral*

# Bergen

Despite its status as one of Norway's leading centres for the offshore oil and gas industry, this is one of the country's most beautiful cities. It is built round scenic Vågen Bay on the country's south-west coast, surrounded by De Syv Fjell (the seven mountains). Bergen's wealth was established in early medieval times with the trade in dried cod, and the picturesque quayside of Bryggen is a reminder of this, though the colourful houses that make up this UNESCO World Heritage Site actually date from a later period – 1702, being rebuilt after one of the fires that inevitably ravaged Scandinavia's wooden towns over the centuries.

Bergen has been burned slightly less completely than most, and there are many old quarters of quaint wooden houses scattered around the city. But there was another fire in 1916, after which the central shopping area around the main Torgallmenningen Square was rebuilt in the Art Nouveau and functionalist styles then popular in Scandinavia. Another architecturally interesting area is Nygårdshøyden with its 19th century neo-classical look. There was considerable damage in World War II (Bergen was occupied on the first day of the German invasion in 1940) and much post-war building took place. But the many styles combine harmoniously and the overall effect is pleasing.

A large open-air fish market (that nowadays sells a lot more than fish) is held along the harbour and live examples of the fishermen's quarry can be seen at nearby Bergen Aquarium. The fish market is an ideal starting point for an exploration of the old city. Within walking distance may be found Bergen's oldest building – the 12th century St Mary's Church with an extraordinary decorated pulpit. Not far away is the medieval Rosenkrantz Tower that offers a wonderful view of the scenic sea front.

*An eclectic mix of buildings in Bergen*

# Trondheim

This ancient place has been at the centre of Norse culture since the Dark Ages, when its location at the mouth of the River Nidelva was the site where kings of Norway were hailed by all free men and true. The fires that ravaged every Scandinavian medieval wooden town over the centuries were particularly active here. Trondheim was almost completely rebuilt after the fire of 1681, with broad avenues to act as firebreaks, but the city still went up in flames several more times.

A strong flavour of the old may be found in Bakklandet, a lively area on the east side of the river full of wooden buildings, once working-class homes of but now restored as a mixture of houses, shops and cafés. The city centre has broad tree-lined avenues and fine 19th century brick buildings, but there are still plenty of charming narrow streets and alleys lined with wooden buildings that echo Trondheim's true architectural heritage.

Unwilling to cede northernmost everything to rival Tromsø, Trondheim has the world's most northerly medieval cathedral. Nidaros Cathedral is said to be the most important church in Norway, and is a fine example of Romanesque and Gothic architecture. It was the country's coronation church from 1400 to the early 1900s, when the ceremony was discontinued. But new monarchs still receive a blessing here and the royal regalia are on show. Beside the cathedral is the beautifully preserved 12th century Archbishop's Palace.

The Market Square (still with regular open-air markets) is a good place to start exploring, handily located in the centre of town between cathedral and harbour. The main shopping area may be found around the pedestrianized Nordre Gate and nearby Olav Tryggvason Gate, whilst the trendiest place to shop is the recently redeveloped Nedre Elvehavn docks complex.

**POPULATION:**
162,000 (2007)
**WHEN TO GO:**
Summer (almost all attractions are closed out of season).
**DON'T MISS:**
The view from the quaint old town bridge, looking downstream at the jumble of 18th century warehouses that line the river.
DORA 1, the massively constructed German submarine base from World War II, now a civilian installation that includes a bowling alley.
The bicycle lift up Brubakken Hill to the Kristiansten Fortress – if you haven't got a bike walk up anyway for the wonderful view from the top!
Monks' Island (Munkholmen) in the harbour, an intriguing old fort and prison steeped in history – take a boat from Ravnkloa, the city's fish market area.
A meal in the revolving restaurant at the top of the Tyholt Telecomms Tower, or simply savour the all-round view from the lookout gallery.
**YOU SHOULD KNOW:**
Riots followed the government's attempt to change Trondheim's name to Nidaros in the late 1920s.

*The Nidelva River and Solsiden area*

*Typical store fronts in the centre of Malmö*

# Malmö

The commercial centre of southern Sweden, Malmö – like many blue-collar cities in Europe – is having to adjust to the modern reality that old-style heavy industries are in decline, requiring a switch to more knowledge-based activities. A good example of this process is the creation of Västra Hamnen (The city of tomorrow) on the site of a former shipyard, now becoming a lively commercial and university centre with striking up-market architect-designed houses.

Malmö's oldest areas go back to the 14th and 15th centuries. The layout of the centre and some of the original buildings date back to this time, including typical small timbered houses of the period. A 'must see' is the 13th century St Peter's Church. Major expansion took place from the mid-1800s into the 20th century, with the Art Nouveau style so popular in Nordic countries a significant part of the process. Intensive redevelopment from the 1960s onwards has reshaped the city centre, with much of the historic core lost for ever.

The places to shop (and enjoy a drink or cup of coffee) are the Lilla Torg and Möllevångstorget pedestrian areas. Most shops are open on Sundays. For the culturally inclined, theatres, museums and art galleries are within comfortable walking distance. The Stortoget (big square) houses the historic Town Hall and a massive equestrian statue of King Karl X, not to mention a square well.

The waterfront of the Western Harbour is a popular summer spot, with an artificial sandy beach and a long boardwalk. There is also an open-air swimming pool that the hardy Swedes use all year round. Other open-air activities include strolling through many beautiful parks such as the Pildammsparken or seeing the city from the unique perspective of a canal boat ride.

**POPULATION:**
258,000 (2005)
**WHEN TO GO:**
Winters are biting; summers are therefore recommended.
**DON'T MISS:**
The Turning Torso, a spectacular new residential skyscraper that has quickly become a city landmark.
Malmö city library by night – a soaring glass-fronted building overlooking a lake with a stunning light show.
The curving Öresund Bridge that connects Malmö to Copenhagen by road and rail.
Traditional midsummer celebrations at the splendid Renaissance castle of Malmöhus Slott (actually worth visiting at any time).
The romantic Tragos sculpture and fountain, representing 22 theatrical characters, located outside the opera house.
**YOU SHOULD KNOW:**
Malmö is closer to Italy than it is to the northern tip of Sweden.

# Gothenburg

Sweden's second-largest city sits astride the Göta Älv River, facing the North Sea across the northern tip of Denmark, and was planned by Dutch engineers in the 17th century. Gothenburg then became a significant trading harbour and home to the Swedish East India Company. Heavy industry followed in the late 19th and early 20th centuries, though this has declined with consequent economic and social problems. The city is now looking to high-tech industries and tourism, with considerable success.

There are few reminders of the original town, which was largely built in wood. Exceptions are two fortresses – the Skansen Crown in the centre, now a military museum, and the New Älvsborg Fort on an offshore island, a popular tourist attraction. There are splendid 18th century merchants' houses along the canals, including the East India House (now Gothenburg City Museum). The 19th century saw the introduction of Landshövdingehusen, unique to Gothenburg. These three-storey buildings have a ground floor built in brick and two upper floors in wood. The first one ever built was demolished as recently as 1975, which says something else about the city.

Though the Landshövdingehusen evolved to reflect increasing wealth and movements like Art Nouveau, Gothenburg – in common with much of Scandinavia – embraced modern architecture in the 20th century, often at the expense of the old. It is this progression and the pleasing mixture of architectural styles that gives the city its special visual character.

Gothenburg's main street is known as Avenyn (The Avenue, though officially it's Kungsportsavenyn after a long-demolished city gate). It buzzes with life and is an excellent starting point for shopping, eating or simply relaxing in one of the many bars and cafés for which the street – and city – are famous.

*A striking building in Gothenberg's harbour area*

**POPULATION:**
490,000 (2006)
**WHEN TO GO:**
The city has a maritime climate but winters are best avoided.
**DON'T MISS:**
Masthugget Church in its dominant position, a fine example of Nordic romantic architecture completed in 1914.
The Feskekôrka ('Fish Church', after the building's Gothic exterior), a bustling indoor fish market.
Gothenburg Museum of Art, fronted by the famous fountain statue of Poseidon, standing in a commanding position looking down the broad main street.
A boat trip to the craggy Southern Gothenburg Archipelago.
Liseberg Amusement Park, Scandinavia's largest by the number of different rides.
The Gothenburg Botanical Gardens, one of the finest to be found in Europe.
**YOU SHOULD KNOW:**
The 17th century Dutch blueprints for Gothenburg's city canals were also used in Jakarta, Indonesia.

*The view of Riddarholmen and
Riddarholm Church from
Soder Malarstrand*

# Stockholm

Located on the east coast of Sweden at the mouth of Lake Mälaren, Stockholm is widely renowned for its natural beauty. The city is built on a group of fourteen islands in the Stockholm Archipelago, making a wonderful location for this, Sweden's capital city.

The Swedish statesman Birger Jarl erected a fortress on the small island of Gamla Stan in 1252 to help defend the narrow passage of water leading from the Baltic to Lake Mälaren. It is said that he chose the spot by pushing a log into the water to see where the currents would take it ashore, showing him the best location for a harbour for returning ships. The city's name derives from this spot: log (*stock*) and islet (*holm*). The settlement that grew up around the fortress eventually became the Stockholm of today. By the middle of the fifteenth century it became the capital of the Scandinavian kingdom, which then encompassed modern-day Sweden, Norway, Denmark, Finland, Iceland and Greenland. The first independent King of Sweden, Gustav Vasa, was crowned in 1523 so Stockholm became home to the royal family as it still is today.

Stockholm's old town is on the island of Gamla Stan and still retains its medieval street plan, with buildings in almost every western European style. The city is fresh and colourful as most houses are still painted in their original colours: seventeenth-century buildings are red, eighteenth-century buildings are yellow, more recent buildings are off-white or grey.

Stockholm boasts several royal palaces which are interesting to explore. The largest is the Baroque Drottningholm, originally built in the late sixteenth century. The palace is still the private residency of the Swedish royal family, but it is also a popular tourist attraction with wonderful gardens. There are over 70 museums in the city. The National Museet has a wide range of fine art, with 16,000 paintings (some by Rembrandt) and 30,000 other works. The Modern Museet features more contemporary works, including those by Picasso and Dalí. The Nordiska Museet is an ethnographical museum dedicated to the culture of Sweden, while Vasamuseet has the famous reconstruction of an ancient ship.

**POPULATION**:
787,000 (2007)
**WHEN TO GO**:
May to October.
**DON'T MISS**:
Kungliga Slottet – the Royal Palace of Stockholm and the king's official residence.
Gamla Stan – the old town; an area of medieval alleyways and cobbled streets dating back to the 13th century.
Stadshuset – the red-bricked City Hall which dominates Kungsholmen.
Vasamuseet – this maritime museum displays the only fully intact 17th century ship ever salvaged.
**YOU SHOULD KNOW**:
In winter there are only six hours of daylight per day.

# Reykjavik

The world's northernmost capital city is wet and windy but – thanks to the Gulf Stream – surprisingly warm. Reykjavik is built on the site of Iceland's first human settlement, established by Vikings in the 9th century. It remained a trading settlement until the 18th century, thereafter developing to become the national centre of government, commerce and population. The process accelerated in the second half of the 20th century to create today's ultra-modern waterside city.

Reykjavik lies on Faxaflói Bay in an area of superb coastal scenery, overlooked by Mount Esja with the sparkling Snaefellsjokull Glacier on the horizon. It is a neat low-rise city with a large central lake – a compact place clean enough to belong in Switzerland. It has a buzzing cultural scene, built around two summer events – the Arts Festival in May and June presents concerts, theatre, dance, opera and art exhibitions. Reykjavik Culture Night in August involves the whole city celebrating wildly, culminating in a spectacular firework display over the harbour.

Iceland's past is celebrated at the open-air Reykjavik City Museum, whilst its Viking heritage is explored at the new Reykjavik 871 +/— 2 Settlement Exhibition in the city centre, containing the oldest settlement remains in the country, including a Viking longhouse. The National Gallery is worth a visit, as is the Art Museum at its three locations.

But this is a two-faced city – with good shopping, endless coffee shops, good restaurants and a very relaxed atmosphere by day . . . and a vibrant, pulsing nightlife that starts around midnight and lasts far into the small hours.

If you can bear to leave, a trip out from the city will deliver spectacular natural wonders like Gulfoss Waterfall, those famous hot springs, the mineral-rich Blue Lagoon and Thingvellir National Park (a World Heritage Site).

**POPULATION:**
117,000 (2007)
**WHEN TO GO:**
Summer, when the nights are nearly as bright as the days.
**DON'T MISS:**
Videy Island, a few minutes from town by boat – a unique place, combining nature, history and culture.
The Hub of Reykjavik – a metal insert in stone captioned 'Hence and hither and thither', from which point every house number in the city is arranged.
Seeing a tree in the countryside (if you can find one). The local joke goes "How does an Icelander lost in a forest find his way out?" – the answer being "Stands up". You heard it here first!
A ride on a sturdy Icelandic horse at the city's family-friendly zoo.
One of Iceland's tallest buildings – the amazing modern Hallgrimur's Church with its landmark tower.
Bæjarins beztu, the best hotdog stand in Europe (nominated by *The Guardian* newspaper), as patronized by former President Bill Clinton.
**YOU SHOULD KNOW:**
Beer was banned in Iceland until first orders were called in 1989.

*Reykjavik and surrounding mountains*

# Tallinn

The capital and largest city of Estonia, Tallinn lies on the northern coast along the Gulf of Finland. Throughout history the city has been repeatedly invaded, most recently by Soviet air forces during the latter stages of World War II, yet still much of the medieval old town remains and is today popular with tourists.

The city has historically consisted of two parts. At the top of the hill is the Toompea (Domberg), the seat of power, inhabited first by Danish captains, then the komturs of the Teutonic Order, and finally by the Swedish and then Russian governors. It was, until 1877, a separate town occupying an easily defensible site overlooking the surrounding districts and divided off with a defensive wall. The best way to enter Toompea is through the Pikk Jalg gate tower, built in 1380. Another must-see is the Alexander Nevsky Cathedral, its distinctive onion domes denoting its Russian Orthodoxy. Its beautiful icons and mosaics were imported from St Petersburg. The fourteenth-century Lutheran cathedral (Toomkirik), Estonia's oldest church, contains some magnificently carved tombs.

Tallinn's old town, lower down the hill, was not united with Toompea until the late nineteenth century. Inhabited by merchants and craftsmen, it was a member of the Hanseatic League, a trade alliance operating in the Baltic in medieval times, and grew prosperous and powerful through trade. This area is a well-preserved mass of winding, cobbled streets and arches, and pretty pastel houses, which is still undergoing renovation.

The main sights of the old town include the Town Hall square, containing merchants' houses dating from the 15th century, and some splendid guildhalls such as the Great Guild, now housing part of the State History Museum. The town walls and towers are well worth exploring, as is St Olaf's church, which was the tallest building in medieval Europe. To the east is Kadriorg Palace which houses the national collection of foreign art.

*The old town of Tallinn*

# Liepaja

This city, built on a strip of land between the Baltic Sea and Tosmare Lake, is an important ice-free port and naval centre – nowadays for the NATO nation of Latvia, but previously for the Tsarist navy and then that of the Soviet Union, which established its major Baltic naval base here in the 1960s. The Soviets ended all commercial traffic and turned Liepaja into a closed city dominated by over 25,000 Soviet military personnel. Even out-of-town Latvians needed a permit to enter the place.

Liepaja, in common with most of Latvia, suffered terrible damage in World War II and was occupied by the Soviet Union until 1990, when the country regained independence, although the last Russian troops didn't leave until 1994. The vast but crumbling Soviet base at Karosta can be visited and serves as an eerie and atmospheric reminder of the Cold War.

In common with many Scandinavian and Baltic towns, Liepaja has some splendid examples of Art Nouveau architecture, but here a variety of different styles in a relatively confined area creates an atmosphere unique to the city, underlined by the fact that the central area is dominated by small wooden and stone houses.

Though still somewhat run down, the city is working hard to reinvent itself, with the port in full swing again, a special economic zone and various industries such as ship building and paper milling. It remains an uncrowded and unfussy destination, with beautiful architecture and a pristine beach. Liepaja is fast gaining a reputation as a centre of popular culture, with a symphony orchestra, galleries appearing all over town, regular concerts and musicians playing in most bars and clubs. Tirgonu Street is an excellent pedestrian precinct, with the most lively cafés and interesting shops.

*St Nicholas Orthodox Cathedral – Liepaja's finest building*

**POPULATION:**
86,000 (2006)
**WHEN TO GO:**
This is a summer destination, allowing the many open-air activities to be enjoyed.
**DON'T MISS:**
Liepaja's finest building – St Nicholas Orthodox Cathedral, built in 1900 - 1903, with Tsar Nicholas II laying the first stone.
The Holocaust Memorial in the Jewish Cemetery, a moving reminder of Liepaja's many Holocaust victims.
The hugely impressive wood carving in Holy Trinity Church that belies the bland exterior.
St Anne's Lutheran Church, the oldest in Liepaja, first mentioned in records in 1508.
**YOU SHOULD KNOW:**
It's possible to spend time (even a night!) locked in a cell at the old Russian military prison.

# Riga

**POPULATION:**
727,000 (2006)
**WHEN TO GO:**
May to September.
**DON'T MISS:**
Riga Castle – located on the banks of
the River Daugava, it is now the
official residence of the President of
Latvia as well as home to
a number of museums.
St Peter's Church – one of the best
examples of Gothic architecture in
the Baltics.
The Three Brothers – medieval
dwelling houses, the oldest of which
(the White Brother) dates back to the
15th century. The Latvian Museum of
Architecture is housed here.
St John's Church – dating back to the
13th century, was famous for its
wooden tower (unfortunately the
wood was replaced by metal in
recent restoration), the highest in
Europe at that time. From the tower,
you can enjoy a stunning panoramic
view of the city.
**YOU SHOULD KNOW:**
This is a Unesco World Heritage Site.

*St John's Church and medieval
houses in the pedestrian area*

Situated on Latvia's Baltic Sea coast at the mouth of the River Daugava, Riga is the largest city in the Baltic states. It was founded in 1201, and has since been occupied by many powers, including the Poles, Germans, Swedes and Russians. Many years of Soviet domination finally came to an end in 1991 when Latvia became an independent country. Riga quickly became the Baltic's most cosmopolitan city, and its historic centre has been designated a UNESCO World Heritage Site. The city is known for its wonderful Art Nouveau buildings, some of the best in the world.

The Art Nouveau buildings are in Central Riga, where there are whole streets of wonderfully decorative houses. Elizabetes Iela has some gorgeous examples but perhaps the very best are on Alberta Iela where there is a whole row designed by Mikhail Eisenstein, father of the Russian film-maker Sergei Eisenstein. Another Art Nouveau highlight is the façade of the School of Economics.

Riga also boasts architectural gems from other eras. The Three Brothers are perfect examples of medieval residential buildings, a picturesque row of houses, the oldest of which was built in the fifteenth century. Riga Cathedral dominates the old town. Built near the river in 1211 by Albrecht von Buxthoeven, it is probably the largest medieval church in the Baltic states. Another notable sight, Riga Castle is the official residence of the President of Latvia as well as home to the Museum of Latvian History and the Museum of Foreign Art. Also worth a look are St. Peter's Church, with its 123-metre tower, and St. John's Church, a small thirteenth-century chapel just behind it. The city's old centre contains handsome streets and squares built in the 16th and 17th centuries by the Germans. Many are decorated with intricate carvings and statues, and it is a joy to wander here.

# Siauliai

This Baltic country's fourth-largest city is the unofficial capital of Northern Lithuania and was founded in the 13th century, since when it has experienced many turbulent times. It was redeveloped along classical lines in the 18th century after a violent peasants' revolt. Following partition of Poland in the 1800s, the city grew rapidly as an industrial and cultural centre. It was largely destroyed in World War 1. Newly independent Lithuania struggled to rebuild, but was devastated again in World War II, when Siauliai was again severely damaged.

*The Hill of Crosses*

One of the most moving places that should be visited is the Hill of Crosses, north of the city. It was established in the early 19th century as a site of catholic pilgrimage, and over the years thousands upon thousands of crosses, crucifixes, statues of the Virgin Mary, effigies and rosaries have been left there. But perhaps its true national significance is the role it served during the Soviet occupation (1944-1990), when it became a focal point for peaceful resistance by the Lithuanians.

Very little of old Siauliai remains, though the 18th century grid pattern is still apparent. The vast majority of buildings were put up after World War II and are of no particular architectural distinction. One notable survivor is the St Peter and Paul Cathedral from the early 1600s, built on the site of an earlier wooden church. The town hall is another, actually consisting of two linked buildings. Also worth a look is the 17th century Zubov's Palace, now part of the new city university.

Siauliai is full of life, with organized activities and festivals happening all summer long. There is a pedestrian boulevard in the city centre, decorated with the sort of modern sculptures found everywhere, with numerous shops, cafés and bars.

**POPULATION:**
129,000 (2005)
**WHEN TO GO:**
Summer and autumn unless you like winter wonderlands – Baltic winters can be harsh.
**DON'T MISS:**
Siauliai's symbol – the Golden Archer, atop his column beside the cathedral.
A performance by the city's world-famous Polifonija State Chamber Choir.
Birchwood Leisure Park, a family leisure centre in the southern part of the city with a host of attractions.
Prisikelimo Square, that has served as the city's centre for fairs, markets and trade for hundreds of years.
The old city cemetery beside Lake Talsa – atmospheric and peaceful.
Saules Laikrodzio Square, containing a wonderfully artistic sun dial created in 1981 to celebrate the city's 750th anniversary.
**YOU SHOULD KNOW:**
There is a magic arch on Vilniaus Street – walk under it and a wish comes true, but go back and the wish vanishes.

*A view of the town from the Hill of the Three Crosses*

# Vilnius

This is Lithuania's capital and largest city. The Grand Duchy of Lithuania had gained great importance by the 16th century, but the country was then squabbled over for centuries (and occupied, in no particular order and often more than once) by Russia, Poland, France and Germany. It was only with the collapse of the Soviet Union in 1990 that it regained independence, though occupying Russians briefly tried to retain control by force. This explains why Vilnius is in a hurry to create a new, ultra-modern identity. Between the wars, under Polish rule, less than one per cent of the population was of ethnic Lithuanian origin, so the Lithuanians are determined to create a distinctive city that's all their own.

These efforts have been rewarded by the fact that Vilnius will be a European Capital of Culture in 2009. Despite the constant ravages of war, the city has retained a historic centre that's a UNESCO World Heritage Site. This large area has diverse architectural styles, though the overall flavour is baroque. Its centre is Cathedral Square, and a stroll from there down Pilies Street to the Dawn Gate (the last remaining fortified city gate) will provide an excellent introduction to the higgledy-piggledy old city. Wander off down narrow side streets and find craftsmen's workshops and intriguing courtyards. Check out some of the 40 churches and 1,500 historic buildings.

But – after being trapped in a timewarp for decades – there is a new city centre with striking buildings and Vilnius is fast developing the sort of hotels, restaurants, shops and museums expected of a modern capital city. Happily, it's not quite there yet. Despite the undoubted energy that pulses through the place, it still has a slightly old-fashioned feel that is charming.

**POPULATION:**
554,000 (2005)
**WHEN TO GO:**
Unless you like ice fishing (lakes and rivers freeze for the long winter), make this a summer destination.
**DON'T MISS:**
The view of Vilnius old town from the hilltop Gedimas Tower, the only substantial remnant of the once-mighty 14th century Upper Castle.
Europa Tower in the new city centre – at 146 m (480 ft) high it's the tallest building in the Baltic states.
The Days of the Capital City festival, in September with many cultural activities and the wonderful Francis Handicraft Market in City Hall Square.
The Amber Museum and Gallery, showing (and selling) amber containing insects and leaves, and in many unusual colours such as blue, green and black.
Vilnius Cathedral, Lithuania's spiritual centre, and especially the baroque chapel of St Casimir (built 1623-1636).
The Grand Courtyard and other magnificent old buildings at the ancient University of Vilnius.
**YOU SHOULD KNOW:**
There is a park north of Vilnius containing a monument that is claimed to be at the geographical centre of Europe.

# Kaunas

Lithuania's second city is also its industrial powerhouse, located at the confluence of the country's main rivers (the Nemunas and the Neris), and close to the vast Kaunas Lagoon. Kaunas is not over-endowed with picturesque buildings and tourist attractions, and has not recovered from Russian rule as quickly as some, but this somewhat shabby low-rise city is nonetheless fascinating, with a variety of offbeat curiosities and oddities.

For a start, it is the most authentically Lithuanian city. Centuries of foreign occupation have left the country with an ethnically mixed population, but native Lithuanians make up 93 per cent of the inhabitants of Kaunas, compared with just 58 per cent in the capital, Vilnius. Walk down one of Europe's longest pedestrian streets, Liberty Avenue with its fine linden trees, for a flavour of the city, continuing along Vilnius Street to the oldest part of town.

There are interesting historic buildings to see. Kaunas is particularly rich in churches – don't miss the early 15th century Church of Vytautas the Great, the monastery and church of Pazaislis, one of the best examples of Italian Baroque architecture in Eastern Europe, St George Church (1487) and the garrison church of St Michael the Archangel. Other notable buildings include the 15th century red-brick merchant's house of Perkunas and Kaunas Town Hall (nicknamed 'The White Swan') in its old city square.

Kaunas has many museums, some rather quirky. These include the Devil's Museum with its thousands of images of Old Nick, the medical and pharmacy museum and one for folk music. There are also more conventional art galleries and museums, along with those celebrating specific areas of local interest.

One decided advantage of this bustling city's workaday character is that living costs are very reasonable, with restaurants, bars and clubs offering incredibly low prices. Enjoy!

**POPULATION:**
361,000 (2005)
**WHEN TO GO:**
Winters are hard, summers warm.
**DON'T MISS**
The Vytautas – houses the Great War Museum, showcasing the history of Lithuania and Kaunas, with an incomparable display of artefacts and weaponry.
The Russian fortifications throughout the town, built in the 19th century after uprisings by the local population.
The preserved ruins of the 14th century Kaunas Castle, with an art gallery in the round tower.
A superb panoramic view of the city from the tower of the brand new Resurrection Church, after riding up the funicular railway to the church.
The vast Kaunas Botanical Garden, serving as a showcase for both local plant life and interesting research projects.
Lithuania's only state-run zoo.
**YOU SHOULD KNOW:**
Kaunas welcomed Napoleon's arrival in 1812, hoping it would free Lithuania from Russian rule, and named a local hill after him.

*Archangel Michael looks towards the garrison church of St Michael the Archangel.*

*Hohensalzburg Fortress dominates the Salzburg skyline.*

# Salzburg

Salzburg, with its world-famous baroque architecture, has one of the best-preserved city centres in the German-speaking world, and was listed as a UNESCO World Heritage Site in 1997. It is the fourth largest city in Austria, set between the Salzach River and the Mönchsberg in a wonderful mountainous area at the northern boundary of the Alps. The mountains to the south of the city make a fine contrast to the rolling plains to the north. The closest alpine peak – the Untersbergat at 1,972 m (6,470 ft) – is only a few kilometres from the city centre and makes a fine backdrop to the beautiful architecture.

Salzburg started out as a Roman town; the first Christian kingdom was established here by St Rupert in the late seventh century. During the following centuries, the Archbishops of Salzburg became more and more powerful and were given the title of Prince of the Holy Roman Empire. The 17th-century baroque cathedral, the Salzburger Dom, is one of several wonderful churches in the city. Dedicated to Saint Rupert of Salzburg, this is where Mozart was baptized.

Mozart was born in Salzburg, a fact which is impossible to miss when visiting. The city was not generous towards him during his lifetime but it does its level best to make the most of him now. Everywhere you go his music is being played, and there are two Mozart museums and even chocolate balls called Mozart Kugeln.

The Hohensalzburg Fortress was built for the prince-archbishops. It sits sedately on Festungberg Hill and is one of the largest medieval castles in Europe. It is fascinating to see the lavish lifestyle that was led here, but perhaps even better to see the truly astonishing views from the fortress over the Alps and the city. On the other side of the river, the Schloss Mirabell was built in 1606 by Prince-Archbishop Wolf Dietrich for his mistress. It is surrounded by lovely formal gardens. The marble hall is covered with Baroque reliefs and lit by magnificent chandeliers.

**POPULATION:**
150,000 (2007)
**WHEN TO GO:**
May to June, or September to October.
**DON'T MISS:**
The Mozart museums.
Views from the Hohensalzburg Fortress.
The Residenz - this Baroque palace is one of the most important historic buildings of Salzburg. The current building dates back to around 1600 when Prince Archbishop Wolf Dietrich von Raitenau made major changes to the original Residenz buildings.
Schloss Hellbrunn - an early Baroque castle built in the early 17th century. The castle is also famous for its watergames held in the grounds in the summer months. These games were conceived by Markus Sittikus as a series of practical jokes to be performed on guests!
A horse-drawn carriage ride around the city.
**YOU SHOULD KNOW:**
Salzburg is the birthplace of Mozart.

# Graz

On the banks of the River Mur in the forested area of Styria, Graz is Austria's second largest city, a picturesque place of cultural interest and wonderful architecture. The old town was designated a UNESCO World Heritage Site in 1999 because of its harmonious mixture of buildings of different styles from Gothic to contemporary. As it lies in the cultural borders between Central Europe, Italy and the Balkan States, Graz has absorbed influences from all neighbouring regions to make it what it is today.

The city is overshadowed by the Schlossberg, the small wooded hill rising over it. The Stallbastei fortress on the hill was built by Domenico dell'Aglio, an Italian architect. No one could take the fortress, though many tried, including Napoleon. However, after a victory over the ruling Hapsburgs in 1809, Napoleon demanded the demolition of the fortress. The inhabitants of Graz paid a huge sum of money to the French to prevent the Clock Tower and Bell Tower from being destroyed, and these are well worth a visit today.

The architecture of Graz is its main attraction. In the 16th century, Italian Renaissance architects and artists came to Graz and controlled its design and construction. The best known building in this style is the Landhaus, with its fabulous Italian Renaissance courtyard, designed by Domenico dell'Allio. The Burg (castle complex), with Gothic double staircase, was built 1438–1453 by Emperor Frederick III because the old castle on the Schlossberg was too small.

The Schloss Eggenberg, a Baroque palace built in the 17th century, has an extraordinary interior dedicated to astronomical and mythological themes. There is also a fine cathedral, the Domkirche, a rare monument of Gothic architecture, next to which stands the Baroque mausoleum of Ferdinand II.

Graz is nowadays just as famous for its ground-breakingly modern new buildings, including the Kunsthaus (house of modern art), right next to the river. Just as impressive is the Murinsel, a fake island made of steel in the river which functions as a trendy café with a bridge.

Graz is home to a multitude of museums, with themes as diverse as folklore, the visual arts, contemporary photography, locks and keys, criminology, aviation, the Catholic Church and German literature. The Landesmuseum Joanneum is a vast natural history museum, but perhaps a more obviously Austrian museum is the Landeszeughaus, an amazing collection of over 30,000 items of armour and weapons largely from the 17th century.

**POPULATION:**
250,000 (2006)
**WHEN TO GO:**
April to September.
**DON'T MISS:**
The Murinsel - an artifical island in the Mur.
The Schlossbergbahn - a funicular railway up the Schloßberg.
The Landhaus - a palace in Lombardic style, this is one of the most important examples of Renaissance architecture in Austria and was built by the Italian architect Domenico dell'Allio between 1557 and 1565.
**YOU SHOULD KNOW:**
Graz has a spectacular mix of architecture dating back to the 1480s.

*The wonderful new Kunsthaus with the Bell Tower in the background*

# Linz

**POPULATION:**
189,000 (2006)
**WHEN TO GO:**
Visit from Whitsun to September
to enjoy a wide range of
cultural activities.
**DON'T MISS:**
The twin-spired pilgrimage church on
the Pöstlingberg hill above the city,
reached by Europe's steepest tram
route that still operates with
romantic Victorian cars.
One of the many river excursions
and cruises on the mighty Danube.
The 'Linz Window' in the New
Cathedral, a stained glass
masterpiece with scenes from the
city's past.
A ride on the Grotto Railway, located
in old fortifications, where a 'dragon
train' whisks you though a world of
fairy tales.
Seriously beautiful botanical gardens
with many thousands of different
plants to enjoy.
**YOU SHOULD KNOW:**
Adolf Hitler regarded Linz as his
home town.

The thing to do upon arrival in Linz is to find a café and order Linzer Torte, so you can say you have partaken of the world's oldest cake – or, more accurately, one made to the world's oldest named cake recipe, first described in 1653.

This bustling city straddles the River Danube (Donau) in the north-east of Austria near the Czech border. A major industrial centre, the country's third-largest city lacks the picture-postcard charm of Graz or Salzburg but more than holds its own when it comes to cultural activities, then and now. Mozart wrote his Symphony No. 36 (the Linz Symphony) here in a house that may still be seen, and composer Anton Bruckner was a local church organist. This proud tradition has been developed to the point where Linz is famous as a centre for the arts. The open-air Linz Festival takes place beside the Danube at Whitsun. July sees hundreds of clowns, acrobats and mime artists performing on the streets.

In September, there is a music festival in the Donaupark, the annual Bruckner season and a spectacular Ars Electronica Festival at the city's interactive 'Museum of the Future'. There are eleven more museums, ranging from the striking new Lentos Museum of Modern Art to the unmissable Museum of the History of Dentistry in Upper Austria (no appointment needed). In recognition of its vibrant cultural life, Linz has been nominated as a European Capital of Culture for 2009. There is a somewhat run-down old town, beneath the castle, serving as a reminder of the city's ancient origins. This has plenty of places to eat and drink (except on Sunday nights) and is worth exploring, offering fascinating buildings including many churches, one of which – St Martin's, dating from the 8th century – is Austria's oldest.

*The Oberosterreich Fountain and Old Cathederal in the Hauptplatz*

# Vienna

No Grand Tour of Europe is complete without seeing Austria's capital, where people still dance the night away to the haunting strains of Strauss waltzes. This fine city sits astride the 'Blue Danube' and in 2001 the old city centre became a UNESCO World Heritage Site, reflecting its historical importance.

Vienna was at the heart of the medieval Holy Roman Empire, and later the mighty Hapsburg Austro-Hungarian Empire. Reminders of the city's illustrious past are everywhere – from the Imperial Palace itself to the Hapsburg burial vault and palaces of Belvedere and Schönbrunn, the latter home to Europe's oldest zoo. Indeed, Vienna has many famous sights, including the Spanish Riding School, St Stephen's Cathedral and the Ring Boulevard with its imposing public buildings. Then, of course, there's the Prater pleasure garden, boasting more than 250 attractions dominated by the giant ferris wheel that featured in the iconic Orson Welles film *The Third Man*.

With many parks and open spaces, Vienna is one of the 'greenest' cities in Europe. It is also renowned for culture, with splendid theatres, an opera house, museums and a musical tradition that goes far beyond those stirring Strauss Viennese waltzes, with Beethoven and Mozart amongst illustrious former resident composers. Adolf Hitler also lived here, from 1907 to 1913, trying and failing to enter the Academy of Fine Arts. But he's no more than an unhappy memory, and today's visitors can not only sample the city's traditional and modern architecture and many cultural opportunities, but also enjoy the fine food, vibrant café society and nightlife for which the city is justly famous.

To enjoy Vienna at its most laid back, a visit to Danube Island is a must, with its countless bars, restaurants, night clubs, sports opportunities and sandy beach.

**POPULATION:**
1,661,000 (2005)
**WHEN TO GO:**
Vienna is a year-round destination but some attractions (like the Spanish Riding School and Vienna Boys' Choir) take a summer break.
**DON'T MISS:**
The Hofberg, an old treasury that holds the imperial jewels of the Hapsbury dynasty.
Hundertwasser House, an amazing modern apartment building with a grass roof and trees growing out of the windows.
The museum quarter in magnificent converted imperial stables, with a number of different museums including the Museum of Modern Art.
The Art Nouveau Anchor Clock, forming a bridge between two buildings in Hoher Markt, Vienna's oldest square.
Rococo Belvedere Palaces in their park setting, with collections of Austrian painting and a stunning alpine garden (best in spring).
A panoramic view from the top of the soaring 352-m (1,155-ft) high Danube Tower with its revolving café-restaurant.
**YOU SHOULD KNOW:**
Sigmund Freud discovered what makes us tick in Vienna.

*Domes of the Hofburg Chapel*

# Innsbruck

Innsbruck and winter sports go hand in ski glove, but there's more than sliding on snow to this ancient settlement in Western Austria's mountainous Tyrol region. Innsbruck enjoyed great strategic importance long before it became famous as a winter sports centre that has twice hosted the Winter Olympic Games, being close to the Brenner Pass that connects Italy with the north via the easiest route over the Alps.

The area has been fought over since Roman times, often changing hands, and in the late 15th century Innsbruck became a major European centre when Emperor Maximilian 1 moved his court there. This heritage is expressed in some fine early buildings such as the impressive Schloss Ambras castle, the baroque cathedral of Dom zu St Jakob, the Kaiserliche Hoffe (Imperial Palace), civic buildings, churches and a triumphal arch erected in 1765. Other notable sights include the Golden Roof building, constructed under gilded copper tiles in 1500 for Maximilian, whose impressive tomb monument may be found in the Hofkirche. Tourism now provides the mainstay of the local economy all year round, and Innsbruck is geared to providing for the every need of its visitors. The old town is a delight for sightseers, shoppers and leisurely café frequenters alike.

The surrounding countryside and mountains offer superb facilities for winter sports, and in summer become a picture-postcard Alpine scene straight from *The Sound of Music*, offering a range of open-air activities, including a visit by cable car to the spectacular Alpine Garden south of the city. There are several interesting and unusual museums in town, one of which – the Bell Museum – has been in the same family for many generations. Another is the Riesenrundgemälde, which houses a massive panoramic painting of the Battle of Bergisel in the Napoleonic Wars.

*Innsbruck and its backdrop*
*of mountains*

# Liège

Liège is a city that is both ancient and modern, with an emphasis on the latter. It lies on the River Meuse in eastern Belgium, close to Germany and the Netherlands. Once a major industrial centre, the city suffered when its core coal mining and steel-making activities declined drastically. It became a byword for urban depression and decay, but has reinvented itself as a modern manufacturing city and important logistical centre, with Europe's third-largest river port connecting Germany with Antwerp and Rotterdam. This revival has led to much modern redevelopment. But a surprising number of fine old buildings have survived this modernizing zeal, not to mention artillery pounding in 1914 and a barrage of V1 flying bombs after liberation in 1944.

*The rooftops of Liège*

The historical Market Square is surrounded by 17th century buildings and contains the 13th century structure know as Le perron, a symbol of the city upon whose steps justice was once dispensed. The extraordinary 16th century gothic palace of the ruling prince-bishops may still be seen, but the adjacent St Lambert Cathedral was destroyed by French revolutionaries in the 1790s. Happily, many interesting churches remain – Liège has been called' City of a Hundred Spires' – and there are a number of interesting museums and good city walks.

But above all Liège is known for its lively quality of life. La Batte is a huge market along the river every Sunday and there are numerous festivals, including the 15 August folk festival when the medieval quarter of Outre-Meuse comes alive with eating, drinking and general merriment. There is also an annual jazz festival and renowned night life centred on an area known as Le Carré where bars stay open until the last customers stagger out at dawn.

**POPULATION:**
187,000 (2006)
**WHEN TO GO:**
Visit for the 15 August festival or any Sunday market.
**DON'T MISS:**
Archeoforum, an underground tour presenting a fascinating account of city history, on the excavated site of St Lambert Cathedral.
The famous Liège Waffle (*Gaufre de Liège*) available from all bakers or street stands.
Climb all 406 steps up the Bueren Mountain for a panoramic view of the city.
Regular shows featuring the ancient folklore puppet Tchantches, said to personify the rebellious character of the Liègeois.
Domaine de Blegny near the city, a preserved coal mine with underground tours, celebrating the city's now-defunct mining industry.
**YOU SHOULD KNOW:**
Famous detective Maigret was born in Liège, in the imagination of prolific writer (and legendary lover) Georges Simenon.

*Bruges, the 'Venice of the north'*

# Bruges

Bruges, the capital city of the West Flanders area of Flemish-speaking Belgium, is one of the most beautiful and best-preserved medieval cities in Europe. Its historic centre has been designated a UNESCO World Heritage Site. Known as Brugge by the locals, the city is criss-crossed by canals edged with cobbled streets and pretty gabled houses.

During the eleventh century, wool became an important industry in Bruges, and there were strong trade links with England and Scotland's wool-producing districts. English tradesmen introduced Norman grain and Gascon wines to the city. By the late thirteenth century Bruges was the main link to Mediterranean trade. This opened not only the trade in spices from the Levant, but introduced commercial and financial techniques to Bruges which resulted in a flood of capital into the city. The Bourse opened in 1309 and became the most important money market in the region at the time. By the sixteenth century, however, Bruges' importance waned. It split from the Netherlands, and the port of Antwerp took over much of its trade. Bruges declined into a quiet provincial city.

There is plenty of architecture and art to keep the visitor busy. The Church of Our Lady (Onze Lieve Vrouwekerk) has the highest brick tower in Europe and contains a white marble sculpture of the Madonna and Child by Michelangelo. Bruges is also famous for its 13th-century Belfry, which houses a municipal Carillon comprising 47 bells. The city still employs a full-time bell ringer who gives recitals. The Basilica of the Holy Blood (Heilig Bloed Basiliek) is another of the city's famous churches; it contains a phial said to contain the blood of Christ. The Groeninge Museum displays Flemish and Belgian paintings spanning six centuries, including works by Hans Memling and Jan Van Eyck, who lived and worked here.

Don't forget to enjoy the open spaces of this beautiful city. Take a boat trip on the canals or just sit in a café and sip one of the 350 or more beers for which Belgium is famous. *Moules frites* and chocolate are Belgian specialities well worth indulging in.

**POPULATION:**
117,000
**WHEN TO GO:**
May to October
**DON'T MISS:**
A canal trip.
The Groeninge Museum - houses a wide range of Renaissance and Baroque masters, masterpieces of Flemish Expressionism and many items from the city's collection of modern art.
The Memling Museum - formerly the Sint-Jans hospitaal (Hospital of St. John), where the earliest wards date from the 13th century. Nowadays visitors come to see typical medieval hospital buildings filled with furniture and other objects that illustrate their history, as well as the magnificent collection of paintings by the German-born artist Hans Memling.
The Church of Our Lady - a beautiful medieval building with a brick spire of 122m (400 ft).
The Beguinage (the Market Place).
**YOU SHOULD KNOW:**
Chocolate, lace and beer are specialities of the city.

# Namur

The regional capital of Belgium's federal region of Wallonia grew up where the Rivers Meuse and Sambre merge and has been a settlement since ancient times. It really came into its own in the early Middle Ages with the construction of a massive fortified citadel that dominated the two rivers. This – rebuilt several times over the centuries – is still a dominant landmark above the town, now open to the public and reached on foot or by cable car.

Namur was originally confined to the north bank of the Meuse, and is now an important industrial and commercial centre with a main railway junction. Despite suffering considerable damage in World War 1 (briefly sieged and quickly captured by the Germans in 1914) and World War II (Battles of the Ardennes and the Bulge) it retains a lot of character with some fine waterfront architecture, narrow cobbled streets and worthwhile old buildings. One such is the Italianate 18th century St Aubain's Cathedral, and the Belfry of St James in the Place des Armes features on the list collectively designated by UNESCO as a World Heritage Site. The historic 16th century Meat Hall on the banks of the Sambra is now an archeological museum. Other museums of note are the Museum of Ancient Arts (11th to 17th centuries) and the Groesbeeck De Croix, a museum of decorative arts and craftsmanship from Namur, housed in a beautiful 18th century mansion.

The city prides itself on a lively atmosphere coupled with a good quality of life. There are plenty of pedestrian areas for shoppers or those who simply want to relax with a drink or consume a leisurely meal. Shops are mostly old-fashioned, and for now, at least, there are no malls or large supermarkets.

**POPULATION:**
107,000 (2006)
**WHEN TO GO:**
The city claims to be an all-season destination, but winters can be very cold.
**DON'T MISS:**
The Treasure of Hugo d'Oignies, a magnificent collection of religious artefacts at the Convent of the Sisters of Notre Dame.
One of the many boat trips available on the two rivers, to see outstanding views of the city, surrounding countryside and dramatic riverscapes.
The Grognon (pig's head), with its stony ruins, thought to be where the very first pre-Roman settlement was located.
A spin of the wheel at the casino on the left bank of the Meuse (strictly for those feeling lucky!).
The Church of St Loup, a former Jesuit establishment built in the 17th century with rich Baroque decoration.
**YOU SHOULD KNOW:**
There is a curious event in September – The Fight for the Golden Stilt, where two teams in medieval dress do battle . . . on stilts!

*The old town of Namur*

41

# Antwerp

**POPULATION:**
461,000 (2006)
**WHEN TO GO:**
With no tourist high season,
Antwerp can be a year-round
destination, though some
attractions close in winter.
**DON'T MISS:**
The waterside Steen fort, the only
remnant of once extensive city
fortifications.
A preserved house used by the
pioneering printer Christoffel Plantijn
and his successor Jan Morteus in the
16th century.
Three religious paintings by Peter Paul
Rubens in the Cathedral of Our Lady.
The Augustinus Music Centre, opened
in a converted Baroque church in 2005.
The diamond quarter around the
railway station, with its traditional
Jewish character.
Antwerp's fashion centre around Meir
Street, showcasing the work of young
Flemish designers.
**YOU SHOULD KNOW:**
Most of the locals speak a distinctive
dialect called Antverpian.

Diamonds are forever as far as Antwerp is concerned, because the city is famous as the centre of the world's trade in those most glitzy of stones. It lies on the right bank of the River Scheldt, which links to the North Sea and has allowed the city to become Europe's second-largest port.

Antwerp developed as a major international trading centre in the 16th century, and has remained a thriving working city ever since, now with some 5.5 km (3.5 mi) of quays along the river and a huge volume of container shipping and petrochemical traffic. Although not a natural tourist destination, Antwerp is a lively city that offers varied shopping opportunities, great nightlife and serious gourmet eating, with a surprising number of worthwhile heritage features for the more serious minded.

Despite massive damage in World War II and constant redevelopment, culminating in the spectacular law courts building, completed in 2006, it is still possible to see many medieval houses built by merchants in an interesting old quarter. At its centre is the 14th century Cathedral of Our Lady, which remains the tallest building in a largely low-rise city. The ornate Church of St James contains the tomb of the painter Rubens and St Paul's Church is notable for a superb Baroque interior. There is an impressive main square with a fine town hall and superb 16th century guild houses. The city's Central Station is a monumental example of railway architecture, with neo-classical facades and a huge glass dome. For art lovers, the Royal Fine Arts Museum near the southern quays has a superb collection of paintings by Dutch masters. The city zoo, established in 1843 and now home to over 4,000 animals, is also a popular attraction.

*The cathedral*

*Guild houses along the Groslei*

# Ghent

Try not to wear out the camera in Ghent, where lovers of romantic architecture tend to get over-excited. St Armand founded abbeys here in the 7th century but this settlement, at the confluence of the Scheldt and Lys rivers, was pillaged by Vikings in the 9th century. It recovered to become, until the 13th century, a major European city second only to Paris.

This is one of several splendid medieval towns in Belgium that have survived the ravages of time and war – the very best of them say proud locals, with good reason . . . Ghent has more listed structures than the rest of Belgium put together. It is impossible to remain unmoved by so many seriously beautiful old buildings, lanes, cobbled streets and beautiful waterways, all providing a showcase of medieval wealth and success based on wool imported from England. The run of guild houses known as the Graslei along the old waterfront is ultra-scenic. There are many churches, with St Jacob's and St Nicholas' being particularly noteworthy. Three *béguinages* (which housed orders of nuns), together with the belfry and adjacent cloth hall, are UNESCO World Heritage Sites. The trio of ancient towers that dominate the city's skyline belong to St Bavo Cathedral, St Nicholas and the belfry. A view that should not be missed is that from the Grasburg Bridge by night, looking towards the floodlit St Michael's Church.

There are fine restaurants, interesting shops and pavement cafés aplenty, but Ghent is really about culture. In addition to picturesque buildings, it has excellent museums and lively annual festivals, though a reminder of the city's commercial past and continuing present is provided by a large port to the north of the city, with access to the sea via the River Scheldt.

**POPULATION:**
233,000 (2006)
**WHEN TO GO:**
The unique medieval atmosphere of Ghent is best appreciated in warm summer sunlight.
**DON'T MISS:**
The stunning Ghent Altarpiece in St Bavo Cathedral entitled *The Adoration of the Mystic Lamb*, largely attributed to Jan van Eyck.
Picturebook Gravensteen Castle, the 'castle of the counts' rebuilt in 1180, with its collection of torture instruments.
The spectacular Ghent flower show – but plan ahead, because it only happens every five years.
The ancient city roofscape seen from the top of the 90-m (295-ft) belfry tower.
The 10-day Ghent Festival, at the end of July, for free music, parties, fireworks, street theatre and markets.
**YOU SHOULD KNOW:**
Ghent bakers sell a bun called a *mastle*, said to immunize against rabies.

43

*The old Flemish townhall in the market square*

# Mechelen

Mechelen is in the Dutch-speaking north of Belgium between Antwerp and Brussels. This working Flanders city has industrial estates to the south and office complexes to the north, but don't be fooled – it retains a charming and compact medieval city centre, huddled beneath the soaring tower of St Rumbold's Cathedral (for the best view in town, climb 514 steps to the top!).

Traffic is restricted on the atmospheric market square and within easy walking distance there are over 300 listed monuments, including eight historic churches and some incredibly impressive buildings that serve as a reminder of the city's importance in the early Middle Ages – Mechelen gained city status in 1303, prospered from the wool trade and briefly became capital of the Low Countries. There are museums for everyone, some surprising. For example, there is an enchanting toy museum sure to appeal to people large and small, and on Saturdays it is possible to tour the De Wit Royal Tapestry Manufactory, a fascinating reminder of the city's continuing textile heritage. For serious drinkers a visit to the Het Anker Brewery is essential – it still produces Gouden Carolus, the favourite ale of Renaissance Emperor Charles V, who took it with him when he became Charles I of Spain.

For the modern-minded, Technopolis is an interactive centre where the action exhibits make your hair stand on end . . . literally. For the traditional, a visit to the family-run De Beck horse milk dairy is an eye-opener. Horse milk? There's a first time for everything! Still on the animal front, Planckendael – a large and imaginative safari park – can be reached from the city by boat. Anyone who visits Belgium should be sure to include Mechelen on the itinerary, as it's a city full of delightful surprises.

**POPULATION:**
78,000 (2006)
**WHEN TO GO:**
See the splendid old buildings any time, but some of the many attractions are closed in winter.
**DON'T MISS:**
One of the most beautifully decorated churches you'll ever see – the wonderful Basilica of Our Lady of Hanswijk.
The huge De Nekker sports and recreation centre for family fun, with every possible watersport and beaches for the less active.
Mechelen's city museum, housed in the Court of Busleyden, a truly imposing early 16th century building.
The breathtaking *Adoration of the Magi* triptych by Peter Paul Rubens, in St John's Church.
Sending a postcard from a main post office unlike any other, being a magnificent edifice that was once the 15th century town hall.
St Peter and St Paul, a church that contains some wonderful wood carving and a collection of 17th century paintings.
**YOU SHOULD KNOW:**
Take cotton wool – Mechelen, with its carillon school, claims to be a world centre for bell ringing

# Brussels

Brussels punches above its weight – not only is this cosmopolitan city Belgium's capital, but also the political headquarters of both the North Atlantic Treaty Organisation (NATO) and the European Union (EU).

Brussels flourished from the 15th century as Princely Capital of the Low Countries, an integral and important part of the mighty Holy Roman Empire. After various alarms, including the destruction of much of the city by the French in 1695, the revolution that brought Belgian independence took place in Brussels in 1830. There is a strong sense of historical tradition, though the city was largely redeveloped at the end of the 19th century with few original buildings surviving. The shining exception at the city's heart is a magnificent cobbled market square, the Grand Place, which features some wonderful old guild houses and the extraordinary Gothic city hall, all spectacularly lit at night.

Other worthwhile historic buildings include two Royal Palaces (of Laeken and Brussels), the Cathedral of Saint Michael and Saint Gudula, the Basilica of the Sacred Heart and the classically-fronted Stock Exchange. And of course no traveller can ever leave Brussels without seeing the world's most famous bronze statue – that slightly naughty and permanently tinkling Manneken Pis. Another well-known icon is the recently renovated Atomium, representing an iron crystal, dating from the World Expo of 1958.

With over a hundred museums, the strength of Brussels is cultural rather than architectural, though visitors interested in neither will not be disappointed. Shoppers can visit the elegant Galeries Saint Hubert, a superb early Victorian shopping arcade, dedicated drinkers can sample hundreds of different beers and anyone who likes chocolate will soon be dieting. Brussels is officially bi-lingual, reflecting Belgium's complicated indigenous ethnic make-up, but French is the preferred language with Dutch a poor second.

**POPULATION:**
142,000 (2006)
**WHEN TO GO:**
With few outdoor attractions, Brussels is an all-year-round destination, though winter weather can be raw.
**DON'T MISS:**
Mini-Europe, next to the Atomium, that features miniature replicas of many famous European buildings.
Free summer parties in the central Brussels Park, close to the Belgian parliament.
The Belgian Centre for Comic Strip Art, covering a full range of comic art, especially locals like Tintin and Snowy or the Smurfs.
Maxim's Restaurant in the Grand Place, where much of the cult UK TV series 'Secret Army' was filmed in the 1970s.
**YOU SHOULD KNOW:**
Love them or hate them, those sprouts really did originally come from Brussels.

*The Grand Place in the centre of Brussels*

# Dublin

**POPULATION:**
506,000 (2006)
**WHEN TO GO:**
Any time – the city never sleeps and is popular for weekend breaks, but St Patrick's Day (17 March) is very special.
**DON'T MISS:**
Dublin's Main Post Office on O'Connell Street, where Patrick Pearse proclaimed Irish independence on Easter Day in 1916 – and the bullet holes that sum up the British response.
The Chester Beatty Library at Dublin Castle (itself a 'must see'), with an astonishing collection of manuscripts and ancient art.
Packed Grafton Street with its buskers, artists and tourists, symbolizing the vibrant character of this 'young' city.
An expensive visit to the Guinness Storehouse in St James's Gate, to worship at the temple of the black stuff (and visit the Gravity Bar).
The Dublin Writers' Museum in Parnell Square, dedicated to the city's incomparable literary history.
Trinity College's 16th century precinct, with the Old Library containing Ireland's most famous book, the illuminated 8th century manuscript known as the Book of Kells.
**YOU SHOULD KNOW:**
In modern Irish Dublin is Baile Átha Cliath (Settlement at the reed hurdle ford) after a 10th century settlement of King Mael Sechnaill II.

*The Ha'penny Bridge over the River Liffey*

In Dublin's fair city, the girls are still pretty . . . and that's true of Dublin itself, despite the somewhat ill-considered regeneration from the 1930s onwards that swept away and renewed much of the Irish Republic's then-run-down but charming capital. In recent years economic growth has rocketed, creating additional redevelopment pressures.

For all that, the place that reached its peak as the second city of the British Empire in the late 18th century retains some of the finest collective Georgian architecture ever built. If you doubt that, just walk down Henrietta Street to the nearby King's Inns building. But to see the story of Dublin's development at a glance, go to St Stephen's Green and look at the wonderful Georgian house sandwiched between a fancy Victorian building and an uninspiring 1960s office block. It is generally accepted that the demolition of so much of Georgian Dublin was a serious mistake, with the stunning quality of what remains merely serving to illustrate what has been lost.

The River Liffey divides the city centre into Northside (traditionally working class) and Southside (middle and upper classes), in practice a distinction that has long been blurred. Though the city is rich in the museums and galleries that properly reflect a strong cultural heritage, the area around the river and the famous O'Connell Bridge summarizes the one unarguable truth about modern Dublin – with more than half the population under 25, fun-lovers jetting in from all over Europe and a thriving tourist industry, this is a place that simply pulses with energy and life by day and night. Notable areas in this context are Temple Bar with its winding, cobbled thoroughfares, and the streets around St Stephen's Green. Never forget that Dublin was voted 'friendliest city in Europe' in 2007 (it's true, too!).

*Waterford skyline*

# Waterford

Forever synonymous with quality glass making, Waterford is Ireland's oldest city, founded by Vikings in 914. They settled beside a natural harbour, and the city has long been a major port and trading centre, becoming wealthy in the 18th and 19th centuries through commerce and industry. Three important rivers known as the Three Sisters (Suir, Barrow and Nore) merge near Waterford before flowing into the harbour.

The old city is delightful. The long run of quays from Grattan Quay to Adelphi Quay remains a colourful focal point. The ancient heart of Waterford is known as the Viking Triangle, within the original fortified area, which has become a tranquil place with narrow streets, medieval buildings and green spaces. New walls were constructed in the 15th century, most of which remain and are impressive. Don't miss The Mall – a broad street containing some of Waterford's finest Georgian buildings. Be sure also to see the elegant Chamber of Commerce building, City Hall and the Bishop's Palace – prime examples of fine 18th century architecture.

Two splendid cathedrals – Christ Church (Church of Ireland) and Most Holy Trinity (Catholic) were both designed by prominent Waterford architect John Roberts in the 1700s. The city has named a new square after its even-handed cathedral builder (unofficially known as its own Red Square after red paving used when it was created by pedestrianizing the junction of three main thoroughfares). This, along with nearby Arundel Square, is an important commercial area. Beside the city walls is an inner city area with a long market tradition centred on Ballybricken Hill, now an open space but once a thriving livestock market. Waterford is a popular base for tourists seeking to explore the mountainous interior with its numerous lakes, or the rugged coastline with cliffs and sandy bays.

**POPULATION:**
46,000 (2006)
**WHEN TO GO:**
With a long waterside and easy access to wonderful coastline, Waterford is a good summer destination.
**DON'T MISS:**
Waterford Municipal Art Gallery, housed in historic Greyfriars since 2001, with its large collection of pictures by Irish and international artists.
The Waterford Crystal visitor centre, offering fascinating insight into the hand crafting of this world-famous glass.
The Manifesto Gallery in George Street's splendid Port of Waterford building, selling modern pictures and the best of local craft work.
Waterford Treasures at the old Granary, for an atmospheric journey through a thousand years of city history.
The massive City Square Shopping Centre, sure to delight confirmed shopaholics.
Dyehouse Gallery, an art gallery and pottery works operated by renowned local potter Liz McKay.
**YOU SHOULD KNOW:**
Reginald's Tower, Ireland's oldest civic building, is named after Waterford's 10th century founder, the Viking Regnall.

# Cork

*The River Lee in Cork*

The city centre is located on an island in the River Lee, and Cork was granted its charter by King John in 1185. As it spread up the banks, it became a city of bridges. It was once walled, and substantial remnants may still be seen. The river flows into Lough Mahon and thence to the world's second-largest natural harbour (after Sydney). Cork Harbour helped the city become a major seaport, with quays and docks along the wide river on the east side of town.

Cork – Eire's second-largest city – has been a vibrant beneficiary of the Irish Republic's' tiger economy', becoming the major industrial centre in southern Ireland with an influx of modern industries, especially pharmaceuticals and computers, replacing older manufacturing businesses that declined. This led to a great deal of modern development, including infrastructure improvements and massive expansion of the central shopping area, centred on the remodelled St Patrick Street. The place positively hums with life, catering for every taste.

But there are wonderful buildings from times past, starting with the city's lone medieval building – Red Abbey. Much of the centre was burned by the infamous Black and Tans in 1920 during the Irish War of Independence, but rebuilt in Georgian style to match originals that survived. The neo-classical City Hall by the river is one such, paid for by Britain as a gesture of reconciliation. The city's icon is Shandon church tower, with two sides faced in red sandstone, two sides faced white limestone, a huge salmon weather vane and four clock faces that each appear to tell a different time. Ireland's longest building – a Victorian mental hospital – is another impressive sight, now converted to residential use. Cork has two fine cathedrals – St Mary's (Catholic) and St Finn Barre's (Church of Ireland).

# Galway

This west coast city is Ireland's most Irish city (if that's not too Irish), with over half the population fluent in Gaeilge (the Irish language), bilingual signs everywhere and great pride taken in its status as the capital of traditional culture. This is expressed in numerous festivals, events and celebrations, supported by a plethora of creative arts venues and organisations.

Galway's importance as an international trading centre beside the fast-flowing River Corrib came to an abrupt end when it supported King James II against William of Orange, being sieged and captured in 1691. Thereafter, revival had to await Ireland's rapid expansion towards the end of the 20th century, since when Galway has seen phenomenal growth and major redevelopment.

A stroll down the town's cobbled main thoroughfare – imaginatively named Shop Street – serves as a reminder of an old-fashioned Ireland that is fast vanishing, here as elsewhere. One of Galway's medieval laneways has been restored – the charming Kirwan's Lane. The city also has a rather special branch of the Allied Irish Bank – the country's finest surviving medieval town house, known as Lynch's Castle. The Church of Ireland's pleasing St Nicholas' Collegiate Church is the largest medieval church still used in Ireland. A somewhat eclectic Catholic Cathedral is larger still, completed in 1965 to a design somewhat reminiscent of old Spanish architecture. Nearby is the ivy-clad 19th century quadrangle of the National University of Ireland, built as one of three colleges of the Queen's University of Ireland. The university holds UNESCO's archive of spoken material for Celtic languages.

A final word of warning – if anyone should mention a 'Galway hooker', don't blush . . . it's not what you might think, but both a traditional local boat and a regional beer.

**POPULATION:**
73,000 (2006)
**WHEN TO GO:**
Take your pick – winters are mild and rather wet, summers cool and rather wet.
**DON'T MISS:**
The famous 16th century Spanish Arch on the left bank of the River Corrib where it meets the sea.
Two-part Galway City Museum, featuring both the city's history and modern Irish artists of distinction.
The fishing village of Claddagh, just outside Galway's old city walls – home of the famous Claddagh friendship or wedding ring, first produced in the 17th century.
Those stone structures standing in the river – at first sight castle ruins, in fact remnants of the Galway to Clifden railway bridge.
The Saturday market beside St Nicholas' Church, near Shop Street.
Lynch's Window, also beside St Nicholas' Church, where (according to legend) a 15th century mayor hanged his own son for murdering a Spanish guest.
**YOU SHOULD KNOW:**
Galway is nicknamed 'City of the Tribes' after Norman and Irish families (tribes) who ruled the place from the 13th century.

*The Long Walk looking across the harbour.*

# Marseille

**POPULATION:**
1,604,500 (2007)
**WHEN TO GO:**
April to June, or September
to November.
**DON'T MISS:**
The Quai des Belges fish market.
The Maghrebi quarter - a colourful
area that hosts a number of markets
selling everything from exotic
vegetables to African fabrics.
The Musée Cantini - a museum of
modern art near the Palais de Justice
housing several works by Picasso.
**YOU SHOULD KNOW:**
The TGV train link from Paris has
really opened up the city and made it
more accessible.

Set on the Mediterranean coast, Marseille is France's second-largest city and its most important port. Many travellers consider it to be dirty, rough and even downright dangerous, but it is an exciting, colourful place, with a long history. After decades of decay, it is now smartening up its image – buildings are being renovated and there is a new TGV train link to Paris.

Marseille may come as something of a shock to the first-time visitor. The noise, smells, heat and markets can remind you more of Africa than Europe, and there's a tension in the air. This is the oldest city in France by far. Founded around 2,500 years ago, it has always been a lively, rowdy gateway between Europe and the rest of the world. Its character is definitely Mediterranean rather then French, and it is a less visited but worthy rival to Athens, Barcelona or Naples.

The city's main thoroughfare, La Canebière, stretches eastwards from the old port. Once a seedy red light district, known to visiting English sailors as the 'Can o' Beer', it is now a shopping street, surrounded by the colourful Maghrebi quarter, full of markets selling exotic vegetables, colourful African fabrics and spices. The area around the old port is the true heart of Marseille, and this is where the marina and fish market can be found. At the entrance to the port are two large forts standing guard over the harbour: Fort St Nicholas on the south side and Fort St Jean on the other.

Probably Marseille's best-known landmark is the Basilica of Notre-Dame de la Garde standing high above the city to the south of the port. The enormous gilded statue of the Madonna and Child that stands on top of the tower can be seen far out to sea.

Le Panier is the oldest part of Marseille, a warren of narrow streets and stone stairways. During World War II some of it was demolished by the Nazis who used dynamite to clear the area of 'undesirables', such as Jews and resistance fighters. However, much of the district's spirit and architecture survived, including the seventeeth-century Hotel de Ville. There is also the fascinating Musée de Marseille, recounting the city's long and eventful history, as well as what must be the city's most beautiful building, the Hospice de la Vielle Charité. Its three-storey cloisters and gorgeous Baroque chapel were built to house paupers in the late seventeenth century.

*The Old Port of Marseille*

# Rouen

Despite sustaining shocking damage during the Allied invasion of Europe in 1944, Rouen retained enough exceptional old buildings to show what a wonderful medieval town it once was and underlined the point by painstakingly rebuilding many casualties of war. It was a capital of the Anglo-Norman dynasties that ruled England and much of France from the 11th to 15th centuries and was therefore one of the largest and most prosperous European cities in the Middle Ages, with the Exchequer of Normandy located in the Rouen Tourist Office (or Hôtel des Généraux de Finances, as it was called when built, back in 1509).

*An example of some of the beautiful architecture to be seen in Rouen.*

Sitting proudly beside the River Seine, Rouen's town centre is largely given over to pedestrian streets, some narrow and cobbled, lined with old buildings. There are plenty of typically Norman half-timbered houses and some splendid churches. The Palais de Justice is an important example of civic architecture from the late Middle Ages, the vast New Market Hall being the oldest part. Rouen Cathedral is a superb Gothic edifice with a famous 'butter tower'. It contains one of Richard the Lionheart's tombs (there are three in France – this one claiming the best bit, his eponymous heart). Monet did a famous series of paintings of the Cathedral, some of which may be seen in the Musée d'Orsay in Paris. The Gros Horloge is an intriguing 16th-century astronomical clock, recently restored.

But Rouen is more than just a pretty face. To those who have been enjoying the atmospheric city centre, it may come as a surprise to be reminded that this is France's fourth-largest port city. It's the closest that container ships can get to Paris and is busy, but well worth seeing after a pleasant stroll along the riverside.

**POPULATION:**
107,000 (1999)

**WHEN TO GO:**
Summer, for the amazing light show called From Monet to Pixels, projected onto the Cathedral's façade.

**DON'T MISS:**
A charming reminder of Rouen's former cloth industry – old watermills along Rue Eau de Robec.
The panoramic view of the city and winding River Seine from the top of St Catherine's Hill.
The Museum of Fine Arts and Ceramics, with an eye-catching collection of the characteristic Norman faïence pottery for which Rouen was renowned from the 16th to 18th centuries.
A ride round the city's best sights in a horse-drawn carriage.
The Aître Saint-Maclou, an extraordinary Plague Cemetery built in 1348, with galleries added in the 16th century – now home to the regional fine arts school.

**YOU SHOULD KNOW:**
Joan of Arc was only 19 years old when she was burnt at the stake in Rouen in 1431 by the British.

# Avignon

**POPULATION:**
90,000 (2007)
**WHEN TO GO:**
In summer for the Avignon Festival of theatre, dance, music and cinema.
**DON'T MISS:**
Palais du Roure Museum.
Palais des Papes - an imposing Gothic palace begun in 1316 by John XXII and continued by succeeding popes until 1370.
Notre Dame des Doms - a Romanesque building housing many beautiful works of art including the stunning mausoleum of Pope John XXII, a masterpiece of Gothic carving of the 14th century.
Botticelli's *Virgin and Child* at the Petit Palais.
Musée Carnavalet - houses an exceptional collection of Renaissance paintings of the Avignon school.
**YOU SHOULD KNOW:**
Avignon is also known as the City of the Popes.

The capital of the Vaucluse *département*, Avignon stands on the left bank of the River Rhône in the south of France. Known as 'the City of the Popes', Avignon was a major papal city. The city was chosen by Pope Clement V as his residence when Avignon was ruled by the kings of Sicily from the house of Anjou, and from 1309 until 1377 was the seat of the Papacy instead of Eternal Rome.

The ramparts built by the popes are well preserved. As they were not particularly strong, the Popes relied instead on the fortifications of their palace, the Palais des Papes. It was started by the third pope of Avignon, Benedict XII, and completed by his successor, Clement VI. This Gothic building has walls up to five metres thick and was built in 1335–1364 on a natural spur of rock, rendering it all but impregnable. It is divided by the Great Court – to one side the building is austere while to the other it retains evidence of the lavish lifestyle of Clement VI. After being expropriated following the French Revolution, the palace was used as a barracks and prison, and the fine apartments were ruthlessly adapted. It is now municipal property and houses a museum.

Next to the palace stands the cathedral of Notre-Dame-des-Doms, a Romanesque building mainly constructed in the 12th century. Don't miss the gilded statue of the Virgin which surmounts the western tower. Among the many works of art inside, the most beautiful is the mausoleum of Pope John XXII, a masterpiece of Gothic carving.

At the end of the square overlooked by the Palais des Papes is the Petit Palais, where the Pope and his entourage lived before the palace was built. This now houses the Musée Carnavalet which has an exceptional collection of Renaissance paintings of the Avignon school as well as from Italy, including Botticelli's *Virgin and Child*.

The Calvet Museum, so named after F. Calvet, physician, who in 1810 left his collections to the town, is rich in inscriptions, bronzes, glass and other antiquities and in sculptures and paintings.

From the town's low ramparts you can reach what is left of the Pont Saint-Bénézet. Only four of the eighteen piles are left; on one of them stands the small Romanesque chapel of Saint-Bénézet. But the bridge is best known for the famous French song 'Sur le Pont d'Avignon'.

*The ruins of Pont Saint Bénézet partially cross the Rhone at Avignon.*

# Strasbourg

*Les Ponts Couverts*

You may want to visit the capital of the Alsace region for pleasurable purposes – but the army of politicians and bureaucrats who are forced to decamp en masse from Brussels to Strasbourg for regular sittings of the European Parliament are not quite so enamoured with this appealing city on France's border with Germany. Perhaps employees of European Union institutions actually based in the city are more forgiving.

This busy commercial and industrial centre is the second-largest river port on the Rhine (after Duisburg in Germany). For all that it is a large and successful modern working city, Strasbourg is also a popular tourist destination, thanks mainly to a pedestrianized historic centre, part of which – the Grand Île – is a UNESCO World Heritage Site.

This medieval island enclave has wonderful old churches, including the Cathedral of Notre Dame, France's tallest and the world's fourth-tallest church, an ornate example of 15th-century Gothic architecture. Close by is the Petite France area, with a canal and concentration of picturesque half-timbered houses leaning out over uneven cobbled streets.

The wealth of early buildings in the city owes a debt to German origins (Strasbourg was seized for France by Sun King Louis XIV in 1681). There is also some monumental architecture from the period after the Franco-Prussian War, when Germany grabbed Strasbourg back. The Germans also built massive defensive fortifications around the city, most of which are still standing. The city was retrieved by France after World War I, lost to the Nazis and retrieved again after World War II.

Strasbourg has many excellent museums and parks, and one unique claim to patriotic fame – 'La Marseillaise', France's stirring national anthem, was composed here in 1792 by Claude de Lisle during a civic dinner.

**POPULATION:**
273,000 (2004)
**WHEN TO GO:**
Any time – summers can be very hot, and a huge Christmas Market makes up for any chill in the winter air.
**DON'T MISS:**
The Musée de l'Oeuvre on Place du Château near the Cathedral – a showcase for some splendid medieval religious art.
An interesting flea market on Rue du Vieil Höpital on Wednesdays and Saturdays.
The Baroque Palais Rohan, housing three museums – Fine Arts, Decorative Arts and Archaeology.
The view from the 17th-century Barrage Vauban (weir) on the River Ill, for as pretty a medieval picture as you will ever see.
The 15th-century Maison Kammerzell, a famous Strasbourg sight – one of the most ornate and best-preserved medieval houses in the former Holy Roman Empire.
The Museum of Modern and Contemporary Art – one of the biggest of its kind in France.
**YOU SHOULD KNOW:**
The city celebrated its 2,000th birthday (lots of candles) in 1988 (first mentioned in 12 BC).

*The Espéluque Fountain at the Archbishop's Palace*

# Aix-en-Provence

Founded by Romans who were drawn by the thermal springs, Aix-en-Provence is famous for water, water everywhere – it's known as 'the city of a thousand fountains'. Noteworthy examples are the Great Fountain of 1860 on La Rotonde in the town centre, the hot-water fountain from 1734, the Fontaine des Quatre Dauphins (1667) and the 19th century Fontaine du Bon Roi René.

You may not find them all, but you'll certainly pass several as you explore the ancient core of this captivating place. The Cours Mirabeau is a wide avenue dividing the city into old and new with the old town's irregular streets and heritage buildings to the north, and that's the direction to go. On the site of the Roman town is Bourg-Saint-Sauveur, stretching from the Cathédrale-Saint-Sauveur to the Italianate Town Hall on the picturesque Place de la Mairie. The Cathedral summarizes Aix's history in a single building. Begun in the 5th century on Roman foundations, this magnificent edifice was added to over many centuries in three styles (Romanesque, Gothic and Baroque) before work ceased in the 18th century. The Archbishop's Palace dates from the 16th/17th centuries and is now a tapestry museum and cultural venue.

Other highlights include the clock tower, a former 16th-century belfry, spanning the street on Roman foundations with an astronomical clock containing four wooden statues. The Four Seasons fountain contains a Roman column. The pedestrian Cité Comtale is a delightful shopping area, whilst Rue Gaston de Saporta is an ancient street with wonderful buildings. The Corn Exchange is a bold 18th-century statement with a fine pediment and decorative motifs. The Place and Hôtel d'Albertas were created by a prominent Aixois family in the 18th century, and are magical (the inevitable fountain came later!).

**POPULATION:**
140,000 (2005)
**WHEN TO GO:**
June, for the free Street Music Festival, or July for the city's Festival of Lyric Art – the weather should be hot and dry, but with a cooling breeze.
**DON'T MISS:**
A stunning triptych of the 'Burning Bush' in the Cathedral, painted around 1476 for King René (he's on the left, surrounded by saints) – see also some amazing woodcarving.
The Madeleine Church – a former 13th-century convent rebuilt around 1700, now a museum with works by local artists.
The simple, but beautiful 15th-century Espéluque Fountain, moved to the square of the Archbishop's Palace in 1756.
Aix's famous brasserie, Les Deux Garçons (built in 1792) – ask to be shown to Ernest Hemingway's table . . . or Cézanne's (he was born and buried in Aix – you can do a Cézanne tour).
The dinosaurs (or their last remains) – a splendid collection of fossils found around the Saint Victoire Mountain, displayed in the stately Hôtel Boyer D'Eguilles.
**YOU SHOULD KNOW:**
The bathing establishment at Aix's hot springs was built in 1705, but traces of the original Roman baths remain.

# Nantes

The most important city in historic Brittany (from which it has been separated since 1941) has an enviable reputation as one of the most pleasant places to live in France. Nantes is located where the Loire, Erdre and Sèvre Rivers merge, close to the Atlantic, and was at the centre of the French colonial trade – historic Quai de la Fosse still serving as a reminder of those prosperous days. When that trade declined, the city industrialized through the 19th century and was quite badly damaged in World War II.

France's sixth-largest city is a clean, well-run place with beautiful cobbled streets, numerous fine buildings, interesting monuments, great museums, refreshing parks and a lively arts scene . . . all energized by the large student population. Intense postwar redevelopment (some of it rather too ordinary) has somewhat diluted the character of the old city, but there is still plenty to admire.

The stunning Château des Ducs de Bretagne is everything a feudal French castle should be, then some. The well-restored Gothic Cathedral of Saints Peter and Paul is close by (be sure to see the black-and-white marble tomb within). Bouffay is the ancient medieval quarter close to the Cathedral. The area around the Place du Commerce shows French 19th-century architecture at its best, whilst the semicircular Place Graslin contains a recently renovated neoclassical opera house.

The smart shopping area in and around Rue Crébillon has the unique Passage Pommeraya as its star item – an extraordinary three-level 19th-century arcade. A symbol of 21st-century urban regeneration is the Île de Nantes, a former shipyard and dockland on a Loire river island, now being redeveloped as the new civic centre with older warehouse buildings converted into visitor attractions.

**POPULATION:**
790,300 (2007)
**WHEN TO GO:**
The end of March (or thereabouts) for the floats, dancers and street artists of the Nantes Carnival.
**DON'T MISS:**
The Jules Verne Museum that pays homage to the vivid imagination of this 19th-century writer, a son of Nantes.
Contemporary arts centre Le Lieu Unique, in an old biscuit factory – with great views from the tower.
The Brasserie la Cigale, renowned as one of the most beautiful restaurant bars in France.
The Jardin des Plantes (Botanical Garden) for an immaculate example of a formal French city park.
Traditional chocolatier Gautier Debotté in Rue de la Foss – it has an amazing interior that is now a national monument.
The Musée des Beaux-Arts with paintings by Courbet, Ingres, Georges de la Tour and others.
**YOU SHOULD KNOW:**
The Nantes omnibus service, launched in 1826, is thought to be the first-ever public transport system (quickly copied by many of the world's great cities).

*The Cathedral of Nantes was started in 1434, but was completed four centries later.*

# Nîmes

The old road from Italy to Spain, Via Domitia, passed through the Roman settlement of Nemausus, named after a spring, and it became one of the richest and finest towns in Gaul. Today, though somewhat run down, modern Nîmes is a popular tourist destination, with its convenient location between the Cévennes hills to the north and Camargue to the south, not too far from the Mediterranean.

It has exceptional Roman remains. The amphitheatre is the best-preserved Roman arena in France, and still used for bullfights. This was once filled with medieval buildings, cleared by Napoleon. The amazing Pont du Gard is an aqueduct that carried water across a small river valley. The Maison Carrée is one of the finest small temples to be found anywhere. There are two surviving city gates and nearby Mount Cavalier is crowned by the Great Tower, a ruined Roman fort.

The spring that gave the city its name still exists, now surrounded by the elegant 18th-century Jardins de la Fontaine, which contain more Roman relics, the so-called Temple of Diana and stunning water features, including the shady Canal de la Fontaine. The old town has plenty of intriguing narrow streets and unexpected squares, to be found around the main boulevards (Libération, Gambetta, Victor-Hugo and Amiral-Courbet). The Cathedral is one of the few surviving medieval buildings, but is not particularly distinguished following 19th-century alterations (the Protestant Grand Temple is more interesting). There are numerous fine town houses around the Cathedral.

Nîmes is making a determined effort to shake off its sleepy image, with some stunning new buildings by the most prestigious architects – like Norman Foster's daring Carrée d'Art, a museum of contemporary art. Another notable example is the magnificent new sports stadium, Stades de Costières.

*The best-preserved Roman arena in France*

# Carcassonne

This is a tale of two cities in the Languedoc – Carcassonne (the walled city on a rocky outcrop) and . . . Carcassonne (the modern city). Actually, they count as one, despite the fact that they are clearly separate entities.

The fortified city – Cité de Caracssonne – is a UNESCO World Heritage Site. It has a double ring of massive ramparts with 53 towers. Medieval walls are built on Roman foundations, emphasizing the importance of Carcassonne in historical times, standing as it does in a gap between the Massif Central and the Pyrenees, where two roads cross (Atlantic to Mediterranean, Massif Central to Spain). It became an important trading centre that changed hands frequently by marriage or force of arms.

The UNESCO citation recognizes pioneering conservation work done in the 19th century by architect Eugène Viollet-le-Duc. The old city was scheduled for demolition, but saved after a local campaign and restored over many years, not altogether authentically. Even so, the effect is stunning. Only a few hundred people live there now, many of them traditional craftpeople. Just walk around, enjoying the walls, towers, 12th-century castle, Cathedral (Basilica-Saint-Nazarius, begun in the 11th century) and ancient streets.

The lower city (Ville Basse) across the River Aude was founded by King Louis IX in 1247, after Carcassonne submitted to French rule. This medieval city grew rich on the manufacture of shoes and textiles, declined in the 17th century and nowadays thrives on tourism – three million visitors arrive to see the old city each year, supplemented by those cruising the wonderful Canal du Midi (also a UNESCO World Heritage Site). The medieval heart of modern Carcassonne (Bastide Saint-Louis) is itself a delightful enclave centred on Place Carnot with its Fountain of Neptune (1770) and traditional market.

*The ramparts of the old city of Carcassonne*

**POPULATION:**
44,000 (1999)
**WHEN TO GO:**
July, for the Cité Festival, with performances held in the extraordinary open-air theatre in the old city.
**DON'T MISS:**
Jacobins' Gate – built on the site of one of the lower town's four 13th-century gates in 1779.
The Memorial House, an ancient merchant establishment where poet Joë Bousquet lived – he was wounded and paralysed in 1918, and his house is now a museum and cultural centre.
St Vincent's Church, begun in the 13th century – a fine example of 'Languedoc Gothic' architecture with a rich interior.
The harbour area on the Canal du Midi – the original canal ran just outside the town, but was brought into Carcassonne between 1787 and 1810.
The André Chénier Garden, created in the 1820s around a memorial to executed King Louis XVI following the restoration of the French monarchy.
St Michael's Cathedral, begun in the 13th century, updated in the 17th century, restored in the 19th century – and still impressive.
**YOU SHOULD KNOW:**
St Gimer's Church is one of only three ever built by architect Viollet-le-Duc, who restored the old city.

*Reims Cathedral*

# Reims

The largest city in the sparkling Champagne region, Reims is rich in heritage architecture and should be enjoyed for its old-fashioned character. The city has an honourable place in French history, for here Kings of France were anointed, notably Charles VII in the company of Joan of Arc after she helped to expel English besiegers in 1429. Coronations took place in the magnificent 13th-century Cathedral of Notre-Dame, built on the site of earlier churches going back to the 5th century.

The Cathedral was damaged by German shellfire in 1914, but has been painstakingly restored – to such good effect that, along with the Palace of Tau and the former Abbey of Saint-Remi, it became a UNESCO World Heritage Site in 1991. The Palace was the Archbishop's residence, dating back to the 13th century, though the present Baroque appearance results from late 17th-century 'improvements'. It is now a museum with statues and tapestries from the Cathedral, plus coronation relics. The Abbey of Saint-Remi is also a museum, though the adjacent basilica is still an ancient place of worship (it dates from the 11th century).

That's relatively new by Reims standards – among many well-preserved Roman remains is the Porte de Mars, a triumphal arch that is 33 m (108 ft) long and 13 m (43 ft) tall. The Church of St Jacques dates from the 13th century, and is now the centre of a lively shopping area. The old Jesuit College has become a museum. The Town Hall (17th century, enlarged in the 19th century) has a decorative bell tower. The Place Royale is the main square, and the Place Cardinal-Luçon has an equestrian statue of Joan of Arc. There are few green spaces in Reims, but the wooded Léo Lagrane Park in the centre is a welcome exception.

**POPULATION:**
187,000 (1999)
**WHEN TO GO:**
The heritage can be enjoyed at any time of year, and a Christmas Fair rewards hardy December visitors.
**DON'T MISS:**
A 'bubbly' experience – most of the Grand Marque champagne houses have premises in Reims, many offering tours that can include cellars and tunnels dug by the Romans.
A chain of imposing forts around the city's outer perimeter, constructed in 1874 after the Franco-Prussian War – 22 km (14 mi) long and roughly 6 km (4 mi) from the city centre.
The old covered market on Rue du Temple in the heart of the city, for traditional produce and just about everything else.
A slice of medieval Reims life – the 13th- to 16th-century Hôtel le Vergeur, a town house that is now a museum furnished as it would have been in its heyday.
The Roman crypt (Cryptoportique) under the beautiful Place de Forum, for insight into Roman Reims.
**YOU SHOULD KNOW:**
US General Eisenhower received the surrender of the German Army in Reims on 7 May 1945.

# Orléans

Situated on a sweeping bend of the river, Orléans is the most northerly of the Loire Valley's historic towns. Despite serious damage in World War II and recent (successful) efforts to attract new industries to the town, with associated modern development, this is still a quiet but handsome city with an attractive old centre.

It was here that Joan of Arc made her name by lifting a long siege just nine days after arriving in 1429, earning her nickname 'The Maid of Orléans'. This was the moment that marked the beginning of the end of the 116-year Hundred Years' War, with the English finally being expelled from France in 1453.

Though she wasn't around to savour the English rout, Joan is still everywhere in Orléans. The grand 19th-century boulevard Rue Jeanne d'Arc runs to the Cathédrale-Saint-Croix, where there is a monumental altar carved with scenes from her life, with stained glass windows expanding the story. The Maison de Jeanne d'Arc on Place General de Gaulle (heroine meets hero) tells you all you need to know about the saint. Her equestrian statue is in the large central square, Place du Martroi, and another may be found in Place d'Étape, this time pocked with World War II bullet holes.

Orléans is well worth exploring in its own right, with the banks of the untamed Loire a particular delight. Near the Cathedral, the red-brick Renaissance Hôtel Groslot (the old Town Hall) is worth visiting. The Place de la République has a wonderful 15th-century bell tower. The old industrial area's attractive narrow streets slope down to the river, with two important early churches there – St-Aignan and St-Pierre-le-Puellier. Here also is the White Tower, once part of the city walls.

**POPULATION:**
113,000 (1999)
**WHEN TO GO:**
The first week in May, when the city honours (you guessed it) St Joan with parades, a medieval market and fireworks.
**DON'T MISS:**
The extensive Musée des Beaux-Arts, with a collection of extraordinary variety, including French and foreign paintings from several eras.
A small museum in the delightful Hôtel Cabu – housing the fabulous Treasure of Neuvy-en-Sullias, a collection of bronze animals and figures from the 3rd century AD.
The lively market in covered halls off Place du Châtelet, near the river bridge.
A choice of cuisine in Rue de Bourgogne, with its many ethnic restaurants – also the centre of the city's limited nightlife.
The ruined 15th-century Chapel of St Jacques in a small but very pretty garden behind Hôtel Groslot.
**YOU SHOULD KNOW:**
Despite reservations because it contains a nuclear power station, the Loire Valley is now a UNESCO World Heritage Site.

*St Croix cathedral*

*The sweeping bay at Biarritz*

# Biarritz

**WHEN TO GO:**
May, June or September – Biarritz gets horribly crowded in high summer, especially during the July surf festival.
**DON'T MISS:**
A visit to the beachfront Casino, that inevitable adjunct to resort life in the south of France – it has bars and restaurants for those who look after their cents so the euros look after themselves.
Three fine Biarritz churches – the Orthodox Russian with its famous blue dome (built for all those visiting grandees from Tsarist Russia), the 12th-century St Martin's and St Charles.
The Musée de la Mer, containing a fascinating aquarium plus turtles, sharks and seals (riotously fed at 10.30 and 17.00).
The Chapelle Impériale, built for Empress Eugénie, with its intricately decorated roof and stylish wall tiles.
Chocoholic Central – the Musée du Chocolat describes the Basque love affair with the cocoa bean and offers serious tasting possibilities.
A trip inland to see typical Basque villages like Ainhoa, Ascain, Espelette or Sare, with their large red-and-white houses and old galleried churches.
**YOU SHOULD KNOW:**
Biarritz was originally a whaling village founded by Vikings, until 18th-century doctors recommended it as an ideal place to 'take the waters'.

This seaside resort lies on the Atlantic coast, facing the Bay of Biscay on the Côte des Basques, close to the Spanish border. It is popular with tourists and surfers alike, offering some of the best beaches in Europe. In 1854 Empress Eugénie, wife of Napoleon III, built a summer palace here (now simply the very grand Hôtel du Palais). After that, European royalty were frequent visitors and the prestigious status of Biarritz was assured. Happily, those of lesser pedigree are now welcomed, though this does remain a distinctly classy place.

The architecture of Biarritz is not typically that of the Basque country, but rather reflects the taste of the well-heeled Belle Époque aristos who spent their summers here. Art deco villas rub shoulders with mock châteaux and romantically gabled houses. But when all is said and done, Biarritz is about sand and sea.

The sweeping Grand Plage runs on to the Plage Miramar. A walk around the rocky headland will reveal the old fishing port with its tiny cottages, the impressive Rocher de la Vierge (Virgin's Rock), the small and sheltered Plage du Port Vieux . . . and those majestic Atlantic breakers crashing onto the exposed Plage de la Côte des Basques, which attracts the world's best surfers for an annual festival.

There is a strong English connection, remembered in the immaculate golf courses and thriving professional rugby club. There is also a little museum of local history in the former Anglican church, featuring photographs of all the British aristocrats who helped to establish the reputation of Biarritz. Open-air activities such as horse riding and tennis are widely available, and the spa element has not been forgotten – there are a number of pampering establishments offering thalassotherapy (as you ask, it's the noble process of applying marine benefits to the cause of health and beauty). Enjoy!

*The harbour in Cannes*

# Cannes

This Riviera city on the Côte d'Azur hosts Europe's most famous annual Film Festival, and has long been a playground for sophisticated pleasure seekers. Cannes is noted for beautiful sandy beaches, most of which charge an entry fee to keep out the riff-raff. It's a far cry from the early 19th century, when this was a small fishing and agricultural village. But then the place was discovered by the aristocracy, who built exclusive holiday villas, and it was only a matter of time before Cannes became a seriously classy resort.

Nowadays, there are high-tech industries clustered in the hills, but tourism and servicing the rich remains the main economic activity, supported by the regular festivals and exhibitions that take place throughout the year. Cannes is centred on the old port. Harbour-watching is free, and fun, as is car-spotting – set a figure in millions and see how quickly you reach it by totting up the value of expensive cars seen, which won't take long. From the harbour, the famous Croisette Boulevard and beach extends around the bay, in the iconic Rade de Cannes. The Boulevard Jean Hibert goes the other way, past some of the best beaches.

The nearest thing to an old town is Le Suquet, overlooking the west end of the port. This has a medieval flavour, with narrow streets rambling around the hill. From the top, there are sweeping views. Standing on the rampart wall in front of the church, it is possible to see the city, port, bay and Cap de la Croisette, and to the west the Gulf de la Napoule and Massif de l'Esterel mountains.

Cannes is paradise for shoppers who are looking for (and able to afford) the most chic of items. But window-shopping is free, and the streets to cruise enviously are the Rue d'Antibes, Rue Félix Faure and the Boulevard de la Croisette.

**POPULATION:**
70,000 (2004)
**WHEN TO GO:**
May, for a bit of celeb-spotting at the Film Festival . . . if you can fight your way into town (or find a berth for the yacht).
**DON'T MISS:**
The markets, for a slice of the nearest thing to real life Cannes provides – the covered market at Forville, open-air Place Gambetta or Saturday flea market at Sur Les Alées near the port.
A boat excursion to the îles de Lérin, a group of four islands off Cannes – don't miss the cell where the Man in the Iron Mask was incarcerated (on Île-Sainte-Margaret).
The Cimetière du Grand Jas on Avenue de Grasse – a cemetery with some wonderful statuary and funerary monuments.
Interesting churches – Notre Dame de Bon Voyage (18th century), Notre Dame de l'Esperance and the Russian Church of Alexander III.
A lingering look at the Palais des Festivals (where the film stars gather) and the Carlton Hotel (where they stay) – as the saying goes: if you have to ask the price of a room, you can't afford it.
**YOU SHOULD KNOW:**
The driving force behind the 19th-century development of Cannes was an English politician – Lord Henry Peter Brougham.

# Tours

This fine city is on the lower River Loire at its confluence with the River Cher, between Orléans and the Atlantic coast. Tours has a long and sometimes turbulent history – it was here that the Battle of Tours was fought in 732, a decisive encounter that resulted in the defeat of invading Muslim forces, who were pushed back beyond the Pyrenees and never came north again. Sadly, that didn't stop the Vikings looting and pillaging in the 9th and 10th centuries. Tours was the temporary capital of France in 1871-79 during the Franco-Prussian War, when Paris was under siege.

Tours is a popular jumping-off point for the Loire Valley, with bus or train connections to many of the great châteaux. But this pretty place merits considerable attention in its own right. The modern city has spread along the rivers but there is a wonderful old quarter (Le Vieux Tours) that has superb medieval half-timbered houses and Place Plumereau, as nice an old French square as you could ever hope to find.

The city has a reputation for being rather staid, but has become livelier of late with an influx of students and young commuters who can reach Paris in an hour on the high-speed TGV. There are 30 markets throughout Tours – at least one every day – specializing in traditional produce, flowers, antiques, crafts, gourmet food and fleas (as in flea markets).

The surrounding Touraine area produces good wine and Tours is sometimes called 'The Garden of France' – whether for the fine produce grown locally or the city's large number of excellent parks isn't clear. The latter include the impressive Botanic Garden, Jardin des Prébendes d'Oé with grand gates on rue Roger Salengro and the historic François Sicard Square.

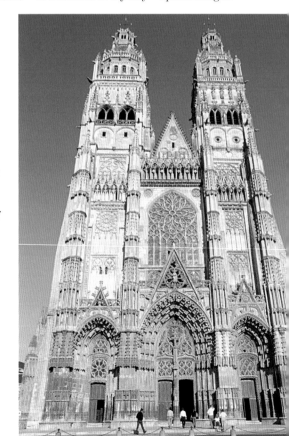

*St Gatien Cathedral*

# Arles

Arles, on the banks of the River Rhône in the south of France, was established by the Greeks in the 6th century BC under the name of Theline. But it wasn't until the first century when Julius Caesar conquered Marseille and Arles was appointed a Roman colony, that it became a wealthy prospect. The city profited from its position on the river and became a main trade route through France. As the Roman empire declined, Arles became less important, which may be why its Roman monuments remain intact and draw so many visitors today. Don't miss the Roman theatre, the arena, the thermae of Constantine and the necropolis (les Alyscamps).

In its day, the impressive Roman theatre held 20,000 spectators; today it is used as a venue for concerts in the summer months. The real gem, however, is the Roman arena (les Arènes), dating from the first century. Today bullfights are conducted there, including Provencal-style bullfights (*courses camarguaises*) in which a team of men attempt to remove a tassel from the bull's horn without getting injured. Every Easter and in September, Arles also holds Spanish-style *corridas* (in which the bulls are killed) with bull-running in the streets before each fight.

Arles has an outstanding museum of ancient history, the Musée de l'Arles Antique. The museum features one of the best collections of Roman sarcophagi anywhere outside Rome itself.

It's not only the Roman remains which are worth a visit, however. The Church of St. Trophime, formerly a cathedral, is one of the finest examples of Romanesque architecture. Be sure to see the representation of the Last Judgment on its portal, and the columns in the adjacent cloister as fine works of Romanesque sculpture.

Vincent van Gogh, who arrived in Arles in 1888, was fascinated by the Provençal landscapes and produced over 300 paintings and drawings during his time there. A famous photography festival takes place in Arles every year.

*The Roman amphitheatre*

**POPULATION:**
53,000 (2005)
**WHEN TO GO:**
In summer for the bull fights in the Roman arena.
**DON'T MISS:**
The Roman theatre and arena – the arena is the best preserved of all the Roman monuments here.
The Thermae of Constantine – these thermal baths were once part of Constantine's grand palace.
Les Alyscamps – a large Roman necropolis located a short distance outside the walls of the old town of Arles. It was one of the most famous necropolises of the ancient world.
The annual photography festival.
**YOU SHOULD KNOW:**
Roman Arles is a UNESCO World Heritage Site.

# Paris

**POPULATION:**
2,153,000 (2005)
**WHEN TO GO:**
In the springtime, of course . . . but canny crowd-haters know the city gets emptier for a month from 15 July for annual holidays.
**DON'T MISS:**
Leonardo Da Vinci's enigmatic Mona Lisa (*La Gioconda*) in the Louvre, if only to smile back personally at the world's most famous picture.
A stroll down Avenue Montaigne, to see the fabulous designer shops.
The foundation stone of modern France – Place de la Bastille where the infamous jail was stormed to mark the start of the French Revolution in 1789 (it only contained seven prisoners).

This global city sits astride the River Seine – whose banks are a UNESCO World Heritage Site – in the middle of a vast urban conurbation that is home to 12 million people, underlining the huge national and international significance of Paris.

As might be expected of the world's most popular tourist destination, Paris tests the superlatives with amazing architecture, incredible museums, world-class galleries, fabulous parks, great theatres, elegant boulevards, classy shops, gourmet restaurants, lively cafés . . . and the iconic Eiffel Tower.

Despite its relative youth, this has become the city's symbol, and those willing to climb 700-odd stairs (and travel on by lift) see a stunning city panorama that has been enjoyed by over 200 million people since the tower opened in 1887. It is the tallest structure in Paris, though it lost the world title to New York's Chrysler Building in 1930.

Paris has a list of landmarks that goes on and on – Cathédrale-Notre-Dame (of Hunchback fame), Arc de Triomphe, Champs-Elysées, Sacré Coeur, Les Invalides, Panthéon, Opéra Garnier, Grande Arche . . . and many more. To those may be added museums like the Louvre, Musée National d'Art Moderne, Musée d'Orsay . . . and many more. Then there are famous quarters like the Rive Gauche, Faubourg Saint-Honairé, L'Opéra, Montmartre, Les Halles, Quartier Latin, Montparnasse . . . and many more.

Yes, it's overwhelming – but actually that doesn't matter. There's so much to see, do and enjoy that it would be impossible to cram everything into a lifetime, let alone one visit. So the answer is simple – go with the flow in the knowledge that wherever it takes you will provide a rewarding experience. Then promise to come back next year.

Parks like the Tuileries Garden (created in the 16th century for a riverside palace) and the Luxembourg Garden on the Left Bank (another former château garden).
The famous Catacombs – mass tombs in underground limestone passages that were the city's late 18th-century solution to overcrowded cemeteries.
The very heart of the ancient city – Île de la Cité, one of the city's two river islands, now home to important civic buildings as well as Notre-Dame.

**YOU SHOULD KNOW:**
Gustave Eiffel first offered his tower to Barcelona . . . but the Spanish city rejected it.

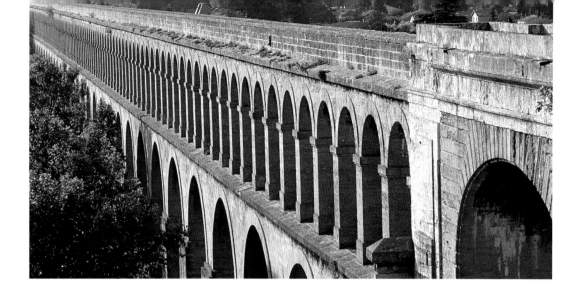

*The 18th-century St Clément Aqueduct*

# Montpellier

The capital of the Languedoc-Roussillon region in southern France is on hilly ground 10 km (6 mi) inland from the sea. Montpellier was founded in the 11th century, soon becoming an important trading centre – and by 1220 it had a university noted for the teaching of medicine. The city was much improved in the 17th century, and by the 19th century was developing a strong industrial base.

The last great change came in the 1960s, with a huge influx of French settlers who were repatriated after Algeria gained independence. Montpellier expanded rapidly thereafter, a process that continues today with its transformation into the country's fastest-growing city and the powerhouse of Mediterranean France.

For all the city's burgeoning suburbs, modern architecture and new infrastructure, a wonderful old walled town lurks in the civilized heart of Montpellier, known as the Ecusson. The 14th-century St Peter's Cathedral broods over a labyrinth of steep, picturesque medieval streets, and there are many fine churches, hidden squares, private mansion houses and intriguing courtyards dating from the 15th to the 17th centuries. The Rue Foch leads to an ornate triumphal arch (Porte de Peyrou of 1691) from whence the terraced Promenade de Peyrou, laid out in 1689, provides far-reaching views. It leads eventually to the 18th-century St Clément Aqueduct modelled on the Roman Ponte du Gard at Nîmes.

Close to the Ecusson, the spacious pedestrianized Place de la Comédie and leafy Esplanade Charles de Gaulle are home to cafés, street entertainers and busy markets. There are some very good museums in Montpellier – like the recently refurbished Musée Fabre with a wonderful picture collection, the Atger Collection inside the medical faculty (a former monastery) and the Musée du Vieux Montpellier with traditional crafts, costumes and furniture.

**POPULATION:**
245,000 (2004)
**WHEN TO GO:**
July – it will be hot, but there's a terrific music festival featuring classical music and jazz, with most events free.
**DON'T MISS:**
The seductive Three Graces fountain – find them tinkling away outside the grand opera house (they're even better by night).
Two towers left of the original 25 that guarded the city walls – the rather threatening Tour de la Babote, converted to an observatory in 1739, and the Tour de Pins.
The Jardin des Plantes, one of Europe's oldest botanical gardens (established in 1593).
The essence of modern Montpellier – two recent developments (Antigone and Hôtel de la Région on the opposite bank of the River Lez) together forming a striking visual axis.
Montpellier's covered market, Halles Castellane near the sturdy Préfecture, for an excellent selection of traditional produce along with the modern stuff.
**YOU SHOULD KNOW:**
Nostradamus (of scary predictions fame) enrolled at Montpellier University in 1529 – but was soon expelled for being a frowned-upon apothecary.

# Toulouse

Home to Airbus Industries, Boeing's international rival in the lucrative airliner manufacturing stakes, Toulouse is the fastest-growing metropolitan area in Europe. It is situated on the Garonne River, midway between the Atlantic Ocean and the Mediterranean Sea. The Industrial Revolution passed the city by, allowing it to become a leading player in cutting-edge modern technologies without the social and economic difficulties that dogged so many northern European cities when their traditional heavy industries declined.

Toulouse is a lively centre of art and culture, but has many of the problems associated with rapid growth, including serious pressure on the infrastructure. Yet this is a super-confident place, with a highly skilled young workforce and large student population contributing to vibrant street life and an energetic atmosphere.

Known as 'The Pink City' after the colour of many buildings, Toulouse has a fine old town, centred on the vast, arcaded Place du Capitole – the grandiose Town Hall is here, complete with huge 19th-century paintings and a wonderful opera house. Close by is the magnificent 12th-century Romanesque Basilica of St Sernin with its multi-arched Italianate bell tower. Toulouse also has the early Cathedral of St Étienne. The medieval quarter has many historic churches, including Les Jacobins where the Dominican Order was founded. There are some impressive 15th-century houses, like Hôtel du Bernuy and Hôtel d'Assézat, the latter with paintings by Bonnard, Matisse, Monet and Pissarro.

But for all its wonderful heritage, the thing that perhaps best represents modern Toulouse is the gigantic Cité de l'espace (Space City) – a high-tech celebration of the city's central role in aerospace and the European space programme, complete with a state-of-the-art planetarium, interactive exhibits and replicas of the Ariane 5 rocket and Mir space station.

**POPULATION:**
435,000 (2005)
**WHEN TO GO:**
April to October (winters can be surprisingly cold).
**DON'T MISS:**
The Donjon du Capitale, a 16th-century keep in Charles de Gaulle Square – once a repository for the city archives, now the Tourist Office.
The amphitheatre, dating from around the middle of the 1st century AD – the city's best-preserved Roman monument.
The Jacobins Monastery, an incomparable example of 13th- and 14th-century monastic architecture, with a wonderful vault, cloister and refectory.
The Saint-Raymond Museum for France's best (and largest) collection of Roman sculpture.
A wonderful Carmelite chapel with remarkable 17th- and 18th-century murals – all that remains of a convent destroyed during the French Revolution.
The former Abbatoirs, now a stunning museum of modern art leading the development of the river's left bank as a cultural centre – see Picasso's monumental theatre curtain from 1936.
**YOU SHOULD KNOW:**
The famously louche fin de siècle painter Henri de Toulouse-Lautrec had absolutely nothing to do with Toulouse – he was born in Albi and worked in Paris.

*The Town Hall forms one side of the Place du Capitole.*

# Grenoble

*The Quartier St Laurent and cable cars crossing the River Isère.*

Situated beneath mountains where the Drac and Isère Rivers meet, Grenoble has been called 'The Capital of the Alps'. The most famous event in its history is the Day of the Tiles (7 June 1788, when roof tiles were the citizens' weapon of choice), which saw an uprising against the troops of Louis XVI, an event credited with being the first 'action' of the French Revolution.

A reminder of historic Grenoble is the La Bastille fortification overlooking the city. Medieval in origin, it became the most extensive 19th-century defence work in France. It is reached by a quirky cable car system across the Isère River, and offers a superb view of city and mountains.

Grenoble is a university city renowned for scientific excellence, but also has heavy industries. Ironically, this isn't the place to sip clean mountain air – the valley location traps pollution. Winter activities centre on snow sports in the surrounding mountains, whilst in summer hiking is the norm.

The heart of the city is Place-Saint-André, containing the former parliament building (the ancient Palais de Justice) and France's second-oldest coffee shop – the Café de la Table Rond, established in 1739. The square hosts regular markets and is surrounded by a network of narrow streets and more intimate squares. The elegant Place du Verdun is what one would expect to receive from central casting if 'a perfect French provincial square' was ordered. It has trees, a circular fountain, the occasional cyclist and grand buildings, notably the old city library.

But this is a lively modern city of culture. The Musée de Grenoble has an extensive art collection (paintings and sculpture) in an impressive purpose-designed building. In the former 19th century warehouse known as Le Magazin, contemporary artists push the boundaries . . . hard!

# Lyon

Habitually anglicized to Lyons, France's third-largest city is in the east, between Paris (a long-time rival) and Marseille. It was an important Roman settlement, a financial centre in the Middle Ages, saw a massacre of Huguenots on St Bartholomew's Day in 1572 and was the scene of uprisings by silk workers in the 19th century. Today, the city's energy is channelled into a frenetic pace of life.

The Rhône and Saône Rivers converge to the south of the old centre, forming a peninsula known as the presqu'île. This is home to one of France's largest squares – Place Bellecour, the hub of smart Lyon and often the scene of special events. A hill to the west is known as Fourvière (the Hill that Prays). To the north, Croix-Rousse (the Hill that Works) housed the numerous silk workshops that produced Lyon's most famous product. Lyon's historic centre with its Italianate look is one of Europe's largest Renaissance quarters – a UNESCO World Heritage Site.

It is a delightful surprise to find that the old part of this sprawling (and rather dirty) modern city is so charming. On the Fourvière is the ornate landmark Basilica Notre-Dame, dating from the 19th century. The hill is also home to convents, the Archbishop's Palace, a soaring mini-Eiffel tower and funicular. In Croix-Rousse and Vieux Lyon (the old town), a unique feature is the network of *traboules*. These ancient passageways run through buildings and were used as shortcuts for transporting goods around town, ensuring that they never got wet. Many are now private but around 40 are still in use, including the rather special Traboule de la cour des Voraces.

In keeping with best French practice, the historic rubs shoulders with the ultra-modern, and Lyon has many examples of daring, attention-grabbing architecture.

**POPULATION:**
1,340,000 (1999)
**WHEN TO GO:**
June to September for the best weather (warm and not often wet).
**DON'T MISS:**
The Parc de la Tête d'Or -- Lyon has few parks, but perhaps doesn't need many – this is the largest urban park in France, complete with large boating lake and small zoo.
The reasonably well-preserved Roman-era Amphithéâtre des Trois Gaules.
The Institut Lumière, where the brothers who invented moving pictures grew up and did their thing – now a museum.
The Place-Saint-Jean, with its huge Gothic Cathedral (begun in the 13th century and completed in 1476) – look for the marvellous Bourbon Chapel and astrological clock.
The entrance of St Nizier's Church, finely carved by Philibert Delorme in the 16th century.
A river cruise to see the best of waterside Lyon – embankments, 28 bridges, monuments and the delightful Île Barbe with its Norman abbey church.
**YOU SHOULD KNOW:**
The headquarters of Interpol, the international crime-fighting organization with 186 member states, is in Lyon.

*Lyon illuminated at twilight*

# Monte Carlo

**POPULATION:**
30,000 (1999)
**WHEN TO GO:**
Best avoid Grand Prix week (in May)
unless that's your reason for going.
**DON'T MISS:**
The burial place of the Grimaldis,
including Princess Grace (the former
actress Grace Kelly) – St Nicholas
Cathedral, consecrated in 1875 but
with much earlier elements.
A flutter in the Casino's fabulous
interior (if you can meet the dress
code, produce a passport and pay an
entry fee) – or simply stand in the
foyer watching the money go by.

To clear up any Monte Carlo/Monaco confusion straight away, Monte Carlo is one of four quarters of the small principality of Monaco, but not the capital (Monaco doesn't have one). It is the richest area, with the famous Casino (no, the bank was never broken) and the neighbourhoods of St Michel, St Roman and the Lavotto beach community. Most of the Monaco Grand Prix circuit is in Monte Carlo, and the Monte Carlo Rally – one of the oldest and most prestigious in the car rallying calendar – starts from here.

The most famous attraction is the Casino complex and Grand Théâtre de Monte Carlo, an opera and ballet theatre. The gambling concession is operated by the Société des Bains de Mer (Sea-bathing Society, though they may have another kind of soaking in mind). This

is majority-owned by the state, helping to free Monégasques from income tax. In return, they may not use the Casino. Monte Carlo is a haunt of the rich and famous, who frequent the place in large numbers. In addition, many rich tax exiles choose Monaco as their international base. But ordinary people are allowed in, if only to see how the other one percent live.

The ruling Grimaldi family have their residence in Monte Carlo. The Prince's Palace started life as a Genoese fortress in 1191. The Grimaldis captured it in 1297 and have been in charge ever since, with the occasional short intermission. They haven't moved house in 700 years, merely altering and adding to the original structure as funds permitted. The Napoleon Museum is attached to the Palace and has many artefacts associated with 'Le Petit Caporal', as well as Monaco's Charter of Independence granted by King Louis XII of France.

A walk along the coastal Avenue Saint-Martin, with its beautiful cliff-side gardens and the Oceanographic Museum and Aquarium (well worth visiting).
Changing of the Guard at the Prince's Palace – be sure to get there for 11.55 sharp on any morning.
The fascinating Jardin Exotique with its hot, dry microclimate, memorable plants and amazing views.
A stroll round the harbour to see who is winning the 'my yacht's bigger than your yacht' game.
**YOU SHOULD KNOW:**
Monaco was the model for Ian Fleming's fictional Royal-Les-Eaux in his first James Bond novel, *Casino Royale* (1953).

# Rennes

*Examples of the highly decorative Breton style*

The capital of Brittany is an inland city, located at the meeting point of two rivers, the Vilaine and the Ille. The ancient centre of Rennes is on a hillside and there are plenty of reminders of the city's historic past. Brittany was the last Roman stronghold in Western Europe after the fall of the Roman Empire, and thereafter proved hard to subdue – Rennes withstood several sieges and Brittany only became part of France in the 16th century.

Rennes expanded after the railway arrived in 1857, becoming a significant industrial city that was badly damaged (by both sides in turn) during World War II. Major regeneration sought to make the city a major growth area, with considerable success. This has not resulted in a natural tourist destination, but Rennes has a large student population and lively nightlife, plus some very fine architecture in the compact old town (though many buildings are actually faithful reconstructions following war damage).

The Place de la République is a square in the grandest French tradition, housing the impressive 'Palace of Commerce'. Though the Parliament of Brittany dates from the 17th century, the city's rather monumental character was established by ambitious rebuilding after a fire in 1720 that destroyed most of the city.

The picturesque Les Lices area happily survived, to become the core of the old town. Roman fortifications from the 3rd century remain, along with sections of 15th-century defensive walls like Duchesne Tower or the Portes Mordelaises, a twin-towered gateway complete with drawbridge that used to be the town's main entrance. There are also cobbled streets of tall timber-framed houses constructed in the highly decorative Breton style. Notre-Dame en Saint-Mélaine is a church dating from the 11th century, with 14th, 17th and 19th century additions.

*The harbour at Nice*

# Nice

This city on the French Riviera (Cote d'Azur) was founded by Greeks around 350 BC and changed hands many times before finally becoming part of France in 1860. Once the preserve of the rich and sometimes infamous, Nice has proved an enormous draw to incomers of many nationalities as well as a multitude of holidaymakers, making it a cosmopolitan place.

Despite some reminders of its long pre-tourist history, Nice is not a destination heritage lovers place top of their list, though the lively old town above the harbour is a picturesque maze of jumbled streets and alleys with many interesting houses. Other notable features include the Baroque Chapelle de la Miséricorde, the 17th-century Cathedral with its unusual bell tower and the quirky Italianate Liscaris Palace.

No, the true raison d'être of Nice is simple – to offer people the pleasurable chance to experience a spicy Mediterranean resort. Before wading in, two 'do nots' are worth mentioning – don't expect to enjoy the Nice experience on the cheap (everything's expensive) and don't expect to find any sandy beaches (there are none). The city does have a wonderful touch of sophistication, though, with grand hotels, classic 19th-century villas, garden squares with fountains, the famous Promenade des Anglais running along the horseshoe of the Baie des Anges, terraced cafés and classy restaurants. But it definitely isn't as exclusive as it once was.

For those with cultural leanings, Nice has plentiful offerings. The Musée Chagall has stained glass by the famous artist. There is a Matisse Museum and the Musée des Beaux-Arts, with the original plaster cast of Rodin's *The Kiss*. The Museum of Modern and Contemporary Art near the bus station is housed in a suitably dramatic set of four connected towers. Then it's back to the seafront!

**POPULATION:**
347,000 (2004)
**WHEN TO GO:**
Any time except mid-July to mid-August, when the place is very hot and extremely crowded.
**DON'T MISS:**
The view from the ruined castle overlooking the harbour – it's a stiff climb, but worth the effort.
A busy daily market on Cours Saleya selling fresh produce and a great selection of flowers (antiques on Mondays).
The Cathedral of St Nicholas – an impressive Russian orthodox church built in 1859, now a French national monument.
The hilltop quarter of Cimiez that is definitely the classiest area in Nice.
Local speciality pissaladière – a savoury tart with onions, anchovies and olives.
An ice cream or 70 (that's how many flavours there are) from the famous Glacier Fenocchio opposite the Cathedral.
**YOU SHOULD KNOW:**
That huge yellow villa on the top of Mount Alban belongs to singer Elton John.

*The Pont de Pierre spans the River Garonne.*

# Bordeaux

The historic centre of Bordeaux, the 'Port of the Moon', is France's most recent UNESCO World Heritage Site, listed in 2007 as "an outstanding urban and architectural ensemble, created in the Age of Enlightenment, whose values continued up to the first half of the 20th century, with more protected buildings than any other French city, except Paris". This supplemented UNESCO's earlier inclusion of three churches in the Pilgrim Routes of Santiago de Compostela Site.

This important city in south-west France on both banks of the River Garonne, with access to the Bay of Biscay, has developed harmoniously over the centuries. But don't expect to find a picturesque time warp – despite its eminence as a capital of traditional fine wine, this is very much a modern working city that is forever sprawling outwards, with an active port and high-tech industries.

Yet the old town has one of the largest concentrations of 18th-century structures in Europe, as it was one of the first French cities to embrace the idea of large-scale urban redevelopment, in this case overseen by Jacques Gabriel, then his son Ange-Jacques, architects to King Louis XV. Some 5,000 buildings survive from the 1700s. Despite this glorious legacy, Bordeaux had become seriously run down, but a determined effort to clean up the city and make the most of its heritage was aimed at making the place more tourist-friendly to increase annual numbers beyond the current 2,500,000.

The effort has certainly paid dividends. For a delicious taste of the architectural feast of Old Bordeaux, just stroll along the river at the Quai de la Douane, see the monumental Place de la Bourse, then find the cobbled Place du Parliament and the maze of narrow lanes and small squares around the Gothic St Peter's Church.

# Munich

Germany's third-largest city lies on the River Isar north of the Bavarian Alps. It began with a monastery and river crossing in the 12th century, with the Dukes of Bavaria ruling continuously until 1918. Munich's history after World War 1 was turbulent, starting with a Communist uprising and ending in domination by Hitler's Nazi party, which regarded the city as its heartland. Several so-called' Führer buildings' were erected around Königsplatz, where rallies were held (two are still there). The infamous Dachau concentration camp was nearby.

Following World War 2, traditional rebuilding left this monumental city looking much as it had done before, with a compact but stunning inner city. Spacious Marienplatz lies at the centre, containing old and new town halls. Three medieval city gates survive, one – Karlstor – being the oldest structure in Stachus, a square that contains the Palace of Justice. There are splendid churches to be found, like the Romanesque St Peter's, Munich's oldest, or the 15th century Cathedral of Our Lady (Frauenkirche). On the edge of the old town is the magnificent Royal Residence (Residenz), now a fabulous museum.

Four grand 19th century avenues run out from the centre. The neoclassical Brienner Strasse opens into the imposing Königsplatz, now a gallery and museum quarter. The Italianate Ludwigstrasse has many fine public buildings. Neo-Gothic Maximilianstrasse encompasses some of Munich's most expensive shops. Lastly, Prinzregentenstrasse with its many museums sweeps across the river. Away from the centre, several palaces are to be found.

In fact, Munich has attractions too numerous to list, including many parks, wonderful buildings, interesting museums and lively street life. If you only visit one German city, make it this one . . . and stay for a week. Munich may be the country's most expensive city, but is worth every penny.

**POPULATION:**
1,337,000 (2007)
**WHEN TO GO:**
Alpine weather is unpredictable, but the summer months (May to September) are pretty good.
**DON'T MISS:**
The Alte Pinakothek with its extraordinary collection of European art.
The view from the south tower of the Cathedral, which can never be spoiled – no taller building may ever be erected in the city.
Nymphenburg Palace, 6 km (4 mi) from the city centre – a 17th century Baroque royal summer residence surrounded by a wonderful park.
Munich's most famous beer hall, Hofbräuhaus am Platz, located in the city centre – bring on the lederhosen and oompah band!
The Christmas Market – takes place from early December until Christmas Eve in Marienplatz and consists of all manner of stalls selling  festive delights.
Oktoberfest - a two week festival held each year, known as the 'largest people's fair in the world'. The Mayor of Munich opens each festival by tapping a keg and declaring 'O 'zapft ist!' ('it's tapped!')
**YOU SHOULD KNOW:**
Munich recently changed its motto from 'The world city with a heart' to the bolder 'Munich loves you' – and the feeling will surely be mutual.

*The Christmas Market in Marienplatz*

# Potsdam

**POPULATION:**
149,000 (2006)
**WHEN TO GO:**
This is a summer destination, with all those wide-open green spaces to enjoy.
**DON'T MISS:**
The Celienhof Palace, close to Lake Jungfernsee, now a hotel and museum, scene of the famous post-war conference between victorious Allies Truman, Churchill and Stalin.
The picture-postcard Babelsberg Castle in its attractive riverside park, created by some of Germany's most famous 19th century architects and garden designers.
The lakeside Marble Palace, built in the late 18th century – guided tours of house and gardens available.
The Potsdam Film Museum, housed in the Old Stables – all that remains of the once-mighty Royal Stadtschloss.
The lighthouse-like Einstein Tower – an astrophysical observatory in the Albert Einstein Science Park, built in the Expressionist style between 1920 and 1924.
The Belvedere lookout tower, on the edge of Sans Souci Park, – as an example of Germany's meticulous rebuilding of monuments destroyed in World War II (as this was).
**YOU SHOULD KNOW:**
The Glienicke Bridge over the River Havel was the scene of real and fictional Cold War spy exchanges, as in the 1966 film *Funeral in Berlin*, starring Michael Caine as Harry Palmer.

*The Sans Souci Park*

This leafy city near Berlin has just a quarter of its area covered with buildings and streets – the remainder consisting of lakes and wide green spaces. Frederick the Great, the 18th century King of Prussia, chose Potsdam for both his court and summer residence. The magnificent Sans Souci Park with its formal gardens, fountains and delightful buildings is a highlight of modern Potsdam, though it seems rather grand for the literal meaning, 'without worries'. This was Frederick's idea of a little place to get away from the cares of state, perhaps explaining why he was called 'Great'.

Potsdam inevitably suffered serious damage in World War II, and afterwards the Communist government of East Germany (GDR) flattened many monuments, damaged or otherwise, that stemmed from the city's long association with Prussian militarism. Since reunification in 1990, there have been a number of historic reconstructions of the sort that have worked well elsewhere, though some major schemes (like that to rebuild the imposing Stadtschloss, former winter residence of the Kaiser) are on hold, though its Fortunaportal (Gate of Fortune) was rebuilt in 2002.

The old town was centred on the Stadtschloss, beside an Old Market Square now dominated by the dome of classical St Nicholas Church. The 18th century Old Town Hall crowned with a gilded Atlas is also here. Other worthwhile sights include the oval French Church, an 18th century Dutch quarter with its red-brick houses, built to remind craftsmen from the Netherlands of home, and Potsdam's version of Berlin's more famous Brandenburg Gate. There is also a Russian quarter built by émigrés in 1825.

The importance – and appeal – of Potsdam may be judged by the fact that its palaces and parks have three UNESCO World Heritage Site listings (1990, 1992 and 1999).

# Cologne

The night of 31 May 1942 was not a good one for Cologne, the major industrial city on the River Rhine. That was when the Royal Air Force hit the city with the first thousand-bomber raid launched on Germany, killing nearly 500 people, making tens of thousands homeless and flattening a large part of the city. And that wasn't the worst of it, for Cologne suffered over 250 air raids in World War II and the city centre was completely destroyed.

*A view of the Cathedral across the River Rhine*

This devastating experience explains why modern Cologne, whilst respecting pre-war street layouts and names, is largely built in a not-altogether-pleasing 1950s architectural style. When older buildings are seen, they have been entirely reconstructed to resemble the originals because of their historical importance. Included on the list are a dozen important Romanesque churches and landmarks like the Gürzenich Hall, and this rebuilding process was not completed until the 1990s.

Miraculously, the magnificent Cologne Cathedral – though hit 14 times by bombs – did not collapse and now, fully restored, has become a UNESCO World Heritage Site. Begun in the 13th century, this massive church with enormous twin spires was not finally completed until 1880, when it was briefly the world's tallest building. Within may be found the extraordinary 13th century golden sarcophagus believed to contain the remains of the Three Wise Men. Other treasures include the large 10th century crucifix carved for Bishop Gero and the 13th century Milan Madonna sculpture.

Of course bland 1950s buildings and reconstructed monuments are not all Germany's oldest city has to offer. There is some striking modern architecture like the square Köln Turm, a prominent high-rise building. And Cologne remains a cultural powerhouse, with a vibrant arts scene, renowned annual carnival, over 30 museums and hundreds of galleries.

**POPULATION:**
990,000 (2006)

**WHEN TO GO:**
July is the warmest month – but consider visiting for the amazing Carnival (seven weeks before Easter), for incredible processions and the legendary 'Crazy Days'.

**DON'T MISS:**
A stein or two of the famous local beer, Kölsch, available at any one of a few thousand lively bars and beer gardens.
The excellent view of modern Cologne for those willing to climb 509 spiral steps up to the Cathedral's viewing platform.
An imposing remnant of the old medieval city walls – Potter's Gate (Ulrepforte).
A ride on the Rheinseilbahn – an aerial tramway crossing the Rhine.
The EL-DE Haus, the city's Gestapo HQ during the Third Reich, now a museum documenting Nazi persecution of minorities and political dissenters.

**YOU SHOULD KNOW:**
In 1945, architect Rudolf Schwarz described Cologne as 'the world's greatest heap of rubble', before planning its reconstruction.

*The old bridge, the River Neckar and the city*

# Heidelberg

There was a time when it was de rigeur amongst the German aristocracy to have a duelling scar on the cheek, earned in single combat at Heidelberg's ancient university. Even now, looking across the River Neckar past the glorious Old Bridge (18th century) to the castle on the wooded hills of Odenwald (Odin's Forest) beyond, one might still be in that vanished era.

In fact, Heidelberg owes its historic character to the fact that it wasn't bombed in World War II, because the Americans had earmarked this city in the south west of Germany as a desirable base when hostilities ceased (they still have a military presence in and around the city today). Since the war, the city has developed rapidly, spreading out from the old centre, but it is the old town that everyone wants to see.

It crouches along the river bank, beneath the not-to-be-missed castle (started in the 14th century, added to periodically until its abandonment in the 17th century). Old Heidelberg has a Baroque charm all its own with narrow streets and picturesque houses. Look out for Karlstor, a triumphal gate completed in 1781, the fine Heiliggeistkirche (Cathedral) and very old Zum Ritter Sankt Georg (House of the Knight of St George). Since the 18th century, Heidelberg has enjoyed a cultural reputation as the centre of German Romanticism. Across the river is Philosophers' Walk, where Heidelberg's thinkers and university lecturers once walked and talked, gazing at the romantic Schloss Heidelberg on Königstuhl (King's Throne Hill) as they did so.

Heidelberg's economy is now based on the university and tourism, the latter exploiting the city's rich heritage to attract millions of visitors each year. To support this activity, there are numerous festivals, frequent firework displays, musical performances and markets . . . even a half marathon.

# Leipzig

Like all major German cities, Leipzig took a fearful pounding from Allied bombers in World War II, before becoming incorporated into the GDR (East Germany). The peaceful Monday demonstrations that marked the beginning of the end for the Iron Curtain and the East German Communist regime began here in 1989, filling Karl Marx Platz after prayers at the Nikolai Church.

The Leipzig Trade Fair was an important annual event during the Communist years, providing a contact point between east and west, but was actually the continuation of a much older tradition – this Saxon city was granted two annual market fairs back in the 12th century, contributing mightily to Leipzig's importance and success as a trading centre over the centuries.

It might be supposed that war damage and subsequent neglect left the city with a huge and burdensome legacy at the time of German reunification in 1990, but to everyone's surprise Leipzig hit the ground running and has quickly established itself as a place that is well worth visiting – regaining its traditional status as a stylish regional centre of trade, education and culture, with excellent shops and a vibrant social scene.

Though plenty of buildings date from both before and after the fall of Communism (the former rather dull, the latter often ultra-modern), with more on the way, the compact city centre seems remarkably unspoiled. There are fine churches, covered market passages (Mädler-Passage is especially good), one of Germany's oldest universities and the medieval Renaissance Market Square, overlooked by a splendid 16th century Old Town Hall (now a fascinating museum). Here also you will find the Gothic Church of St Thomas (Thomaskirche) where the great composer Johann Sebastian Bach served as cantor and was buried. There's even an adjacent Bach Museum for serious musicologists.

*A view across the rooftops of Leipzig*

**POPULATION:**
507,000 (2007)
**WHEN TO GO:**
Summer is the time to make the most of the city and its many open-air attractions.
**DON'T MISS:**
The tongue-twisting Völkerschlachtdenkmal (Battle of Nations Monument), said to be Europe's largest victory monument, built to commemorate a successful battle against Napoleon's troops.
Leipzig Zoo – founded in the 19th century, but now offering state-of-the-art enclosures showing animals in a suitable habitat.
The slightly chilling Museum in der Runden Ecke, formerly HQ of the dreaded Stasi secret police, converted to a museum of bad old GDR days.
The recently opened and futuristically housed Museum der Bildenden Künste, an art gallery with a magnificent collection of pictures.
Auerbach's Cellar – Leipzig's oldest restaurant, where Goethe drank as a student . . . including the place in his play *Faust I*, where it was visited by Mephistopheles and Faust.
**YOU SHOULD KNOW:**
The railway arrived in 1839, and Leipzig became an important hub with the largest terminus in Europe – it's vast!

*Statue of the 'City's Protector' in the Marktplatz*

# Bremen

Germany's oldest coastal city, Bremen started out as a fishing village but has developed to be second only to Hamburg among the country's ports. The Marktplatz (Market Square) is surrounded by important 13th-century buildings, many of which were restored after World War II by the citizens of Bremen themselves.

During the Middle Ages, Bremen was one of the strongest members of the Hanseatic League, an alliance of trading guilds that established and maintained a trade monopoly over most of Northern Europe between the 13th and 17th centuries. In 1646 it became a free imperial city.

Many of Bremen's tourist attractions are found in the Altstadt (Old Town), an historic area surrounded by the Weser River to the southwest and the the moats of the medieval city to the northeast. The town centre is protected by an enormous statue known as Roland, who carries the 'sword of justice' and a shield decorated with an imperial eagle. The townspeople believe that as long as the statue stands in the market place, Bremen will survive as a free city. During bombing raids in World War II, great measures were taken to keep the statue safe.

The Marktplatz is dominated by the opulent façade of the Town Hall (Rathaus). The building was erected between 1405 and 1410 in Gothic style, but the façade was built two centuries later (1609–12) in the local 'Weser Renaissance' style. Across the square from the Rathaus is the Schötting. This magnificent 16th-century guildhall features both Gothic and Renaissance architectural styles.

The Böttcherstrasse, running from Marktplatz to the river, is a medieval alley with a difference. In 1926, local artists renovated the narrow street into a fascinating mixture of Gothic and Art Nouveau. Today it has a good range of boutiques, cafés, a museum and art galleries. Nearby are two adjoining buildings of note: the Roselius-Haus, a 16th-century merchant's house containing mediaeval objets d'art and furniture; and the Paula Modersohn-Becker Museum, containing many of her most famous works. The museum also contains sculptures and paintings by Bernard Hoetger. Between the Cathedral and the river is the Schnoor, a small area of crooked mediaeval lanes and fishing houses, now occupied by cafés, craft shops and galleries.

Since 1036, every year in October Bremen has hosted Freimarkt, one of the world's oldest and in Germany one of the biggest continuously celebrated fairground festivals.

**POPULATION:**
547,000 (2006)
**WHEN TO GO:**
In October for Freimarkt.
**DON'T MISS:**
Marktplatz - dominated by the opulent town hall. Two statues stand in the square; the 'City's Protector' bearing *Durendart* (The Sword of Justice) and *Die Stadtmusikanten* which portrays the donkey, cat, dog and rooster of the Grimm brothers' fairytales.
The Rathaus – the town hall located in Marktplatz. Built in the Gothic style it is over 600 years old and is still in use today – the senate meet here every Tuesday.
Böttcherstrasse – a 'secret' street where you are greeted by 'The Bringer of Light', a gold leaved wall sculpture.
**YOU SHOULD KNOW:**
Bremen's Marktplatz is a UNESCO World Heritage Site.

# Wiesbaden

The state capital of Hesse is Wiesbaden on the north bank of the River Rhine, though nearby Frankfurt am Main is a larger city. To add to local rivalries, Mainz – just across the river – is the capital of Rhineland-Palatinate. A local saying goes "Work in Frankfurt, live in Wiesbaden", and it is true that Wiesbaden has long enjoyed a reputation for healthy living. The Romans appreciated its hot springs, and bathing became big business from the Middle Ages.

The Old Town Hall of 1610 is the city's oldest survivor, following destructive fires. Many monumental buildings date from after the Napoleonic Wars, when the ruling Duke of Nassau moved to Wiesbaden and the city started growing rapidly. Dating from this period are the Schlossplatz (Palace Square), containing the ducal residence, Luisenplatz, named after the Duke's wife and surrounded by Neoclassical buildings, with the magnificent Market Church marking its architectural climax.

After 1866, the city developed further under Prussian rule, attracting the cream of German society (Emperor Wilhelm II was a regular visitor). Wiesbaden became known as the 'Nice of the North', with villas, grand buildings in the mineral spring area (Quellengebiet), a beautiful spa house, magnificent theatre, generous parks and wide tree-lined boulevards. These combined to give the city an elegant character it retains, despite rapid economic growth throughout the 20th century.

Today, there is plenty of commercial and industrial activity, plus a large American military base, but this pretty city is all about pampering visitors, with spas, pedestrianized shopping areas and a dozen annual events spread through the year that have earned Wiesbaden the title of ' The Festival City'. Don't come here for museums and culture, but to relax in the manner to which you'd very much like to become accustomed.

*Schloss Wiesbaden Biebrich*

**POPULATION:**
287,000 (2006)
**WHEN TO GO:**
Winter – Wiesbaden looks wonderful in the snow and there is a great Christmas Fair.
**DON'T MISS:**
The Mosburg Gardens, containing a romantic old ruin that was built as . . . a romantic old ruin.
A pleasurable encounter with water therapy – at the luxurious Kaiser-Friedrich Therme or one of many other spas.
The picturesque Heidenmauer (Heathen Wall) – the last remnant of the Roman fortifications of the place they knew as Aquae Mattiacorum.
The memorial obelisk in Luisenplatz for local soldiers who died helping to defeat Napoleon at the Battle of Waterloo.
The rather grand railway station
**YOU SHOULD KNOW:**
The grave of famous World War I German fighter ace The Red Baron (Manfred von Richthofen) is here, in the Sudfriedhof Cemetery.

# Hamburg

*The town sits on
Lake Binnenalster*

This port is surely one of the liveliest places in Germany. The country's second-largest city is strategically placed on the Jutland Peninsula with continental Europe to the south, Scandinavia to the north, the Baltic Sea to the east and the North Sea to the west. Hamburg lies at the junction of the Rivers Elbe, Alster and Bille and is the commercial and cultural capital of northern Germany.

Although founded as a defensive settlement by Charlemagne in the 9th century, Hamburg didn't really take off for another thousand years, expanding rapidly in the 19th century to become Europe's third-largest port (nowadays second-largest), even though it is 90 km (56 mi) from the sea up the navigable Elbe. With its three rivers, canals and two lakes, water is never far away in Hamburg.

This is a tough working city that would not appear to be a natural tourist destination, though efforts are being made to increase the city's appeal. Many people already come here for specific activities, like concerts, sports events, congresses or fairs, and Hamburg actually contains two of Germany's most popular attractions. The harbour area has a wonderful promenade, the Landungsbrücken. Then there's the (in)famous Reeperbahn, Europe's largest red light district and centre of the city's nightlife, with endless theatres, bars and clubs.

Hamburg is not over-endowed with spectacular heritage buildings, as a result of a destructive fire in 1842, subsequent redevelopment and World War II bomb damage. But there is still plenty to see, including the old warehouse district (Speicherstadt), Hamburg Museum, the Art Hall (Kunsthalle) Museum, a magnificent Town Hall (Rathaus), the ship-like Kontorhaus from 1922, one of the few remaining medieval streets (Krameramtsstuben), Wallanlagen Park (containing some remnants of town ramparts), long-established Hamburg Zoo and Deichtor Halls (a former market now showcasing modern art and photography).

# Nuremberg

The word 'Nuremberg' will be forever linked with 'Rallies' and 'Trials'. It is perhaps appropriate that Germany's Nazi era began and ended in this ancient Bavarian city, because of its traditional importance within the Holy Roman Empire – the Greater German 'Reich' that fired Hitler's ambitions – and cultural significance as a centre of the German Renaissance in the 15th and 16th centuries.

Nuremberg paid a heavy price – it was systematically bombed in World War II and the medieval centre was largely destroyed by an attack in 1945. However, much of the damaged old town was sympathetically rebuilt, which went a long way towards restoring the city's romantic character.

The Gothic Church of St Lorenz is one of Nuremberg's most important buildings, and there are other fine churches. Three castles tower above the city, notably the magnificent Kaiserburg Castle. The Hauptmarkt is the picturesque main market square, containing the much-photographed 14th century Schöner Brunnen (Beautiful Fountain) – actually a replica (the original may be found in the nearby German National Museum). There are stone merchants' houses and timber-framed artisans' houses. On the river bank is the 14th century Hospital of the Holy Spirit, once a leper colony. A medieval cemetery (Johannisfriedhof) contains many interesting monuments and graves, including that of Albrech Dürer (died 1528), the brilliant creator of old master prints. The southern part of the old town (Lorenzer Seite) is bounded by the River Pegnitz and also by long city walls with numerous towers. This is the principal shopping area. There is a medieval marketplace by the walls, now selling handicrafts.

Of course there's a bustling modern city out there, too, with all the amenities you would expect . . . but there's so much to explore in Old Nuremberg that it's hard to leave its encircling walls.

*Schöner Brunnen (Beautiful fountain) and Frauenkirche (Church of Our Lady)*

**POPULATION:**
500,000 (2007)
**WHEN TO GO:**
Winters are hard – and the many green spaces in the city are geared to summer living.
**DON'T MISS:**
Nuremberg Palace of Justice on Fürtherstrasse, where the trials of Nazi war criminals were held after World War II.
The local delicacy, Lebkuchen (gingerbread) – buy it from the small bakeries and ask for the best quality Elisenlebkuchen.
Albrech Dürer's House, where the master lived and worked from 1509 to 1528, now a museum.
The golden Nuremberg Ring within its ornate iron railings at Schöner Brunnen – touch it three times for any wish to come true!
The Nazi Party rally grounds, a vast open area with monumental examples of architecture from the Third Reich.
**YOU SHOULD KNOW:**
The widely reviled medieval torture device known as the Iron Maiden (a metal cabinet with internal spikes) was actually a hoax invented in Nuremberg in 1793.

*The interior of the
Gothic Cathedral*

# Magdeburg

This important medieval city on the River Elbe, where the first Holy Roman Emperor lived in the 10th century, should be a historical treasure house. Sadly, Magdeburg was destroyed by Allied bombing in World War II, with only Dresden suffering worse damage. A few old buildings were reconstructed, but most were demolished or left to decay. The city is therefore largely rebuilt, and only now starting to emerge from decades of neglect under the East German Communist regime.

This was (and is) an industrial city and also a large river port, road and rail junction. Manufacturing industries include metal, textiles and chemicals. Food processing is a significant industry and there are lignite and potash mines close by.

Following German reunification, Magdeburg became capital of the new state of Saxony-Anhalt and rapid regeneration began. At the heart of the city stands a notable survivor – the Gothic Cathedral of Saints Catherine and Maurice, the highest church building in eastern Germany with soaring twin towers and wonderful statuary. The 12th century Romanesque Monastery of Our Lady (now a museum and concert hall) serves as another reminder of the city's former glory, as does the equestrian statue of the Magdeburg Rider from 1240 (possibly representing that aforementioned Holy Roman Emperor, Otto I).

Since 1990, more of the city centre has been rebuilt in period style, an ongoing process that is recreating the feel of the old Magdeburg. The beautifully restored Hasselbachplatz and surrounding streets are a good example of this process – looking just as they once did and bustling with street life. The tree-lined Hegelstrasse leading to the Cathedral is another, an elegant boulevard reconstructed in the 1990s. Magdeburg may have started slowly, but is catching up fast in the race to become a city fit for the 21st century.

**POPULATION:**
230,000 (2006)
**WHEN TO GO:**
Spring or summer to let this city that is striving to enhance its green credentials show itself off.
**DON'T MISS:**
The Green Citadel of Magdeburg – an extraordinary pink residential and commercial building designed by Austrian master Friedensreich Hundertwasser before his death in 2000.
The exhibition in the Lukasklause, celebrating the life and times of local celebrity Otto von Guericke, who conducted 17th century experiments to prove that vacuums exist.
The Old Town Hall – erected in the 17th century, extended in the 19th, destroyed in 1945, rebuilt in 1965 and restored to its former glory.
St John's Church – originally erected in the 12th century but rebuilt several times, most recently completed in 1999 (the Protestant reformer Martin Luther preached here in 1524).
The Elbauenpark, a wonderful green area created in 1999, containing a new city landmark in the conical 'helter-skelter' Millennium Tower.
A tour of the massive infrastructure project designed to connect the canal systems of Hannover, Magdeburg and Berlin, including Europe's longest canal bridge, across the Elbe.
**YOU SHOULD KNOW:**
Magdeburg has been rebuilt from scratch before – it was razed to the ground in 1631 during the Thirty Years' War.

# Berlin

First documented in the 13th century, Berlin has always been at the centre of things. It was the capital of the Kingdom of Prussia (1701–1918), the German Empire (1871–1918), the Weimar Republic (1919–1933) and the Third Reich (1933–1945). After World War II, the city was divided: East Berlin became the capital of East Germany, while West Berlin was surrounded by the Berlin Wall from 1961–1989. Following reunification in 1990, the city regained its status as the capital of all Germany. It has emerged from its dark past and become one of the most vibrant, forward-looking and modern centres of culture in Europe.

All of Berlin's past dynasties have left their mark on the city and there is today a wealth of architecture of various periods. Among those worthy of a visit are the rebuilt Schloss Charlottenburg, the Brandenburg Gate, and the Bundeskanzleramt, the seat of the German Chancellor and just one stunning example of modern architecture. The Reichstag building is the traditional seat of the German Parliament. It was remodeled by British architect Norman Foster in the 1990s and features a glass dome over the session area, which allows free public access and magnificent views of the city. Unter Den Linden is a tree-lined avenue from the Brandenburg Gate to the site of the former Berliner Stadtschloss, and was once Berlin's premier promenade. Many Classical buildings line the street and part of Humboldt University is located there.

The city is also home to hundreds of art galleries. It hosts the annual Art Forum, an international art fair, which focuses on contemporary art. The area around Hackescher Markt is home to fashionable culture, with countless clothing outlets, clubs, bars, and galleries. Berlin is also a magnet for the young and its vibrant nightlife and club scene are second to none. Among its many annual festivals are PopKomm, Myfest and Christopher Street Day, Europe's largest gay pride festival.

Berlin boasts 153 museums, covering subjects as diverse as fine and contemporary art, ancient Egypt, Berlin's past, Bauhaus design, Jewish culture, erotica, ancient Greek architecture, natural history and Indian art, as well as Checkpoint Charlie and the Berlin Wall Memorial. Those on the Museum Island have been designated a UNESCO World Heritage Site.

**POPULATION:**
3,405,000 (2006)
**WHEN TO GO:**
In summer for the festivals.
**DON'T MISS:**
The Berlin Wall memorial – the memorial uses remnants of the original wall. Visitors can light candles in memory of the 'wall's victims'.
The Brandenburg Gate – constructed in 1971 to represent peace it now stands as a symbol of reunification. The design is based upon the gateway to the Acropolis in Athens.
The Reichstag Building – the seat of the German parliament, constructed between 1884 and 1894. The more recently completed glass dome was opened to visitors in 1999.
The UNESCO World Heritage Site of Museum Island – lies between the River Spree and Kupfergraben. The buildings on the island house a number of archaeological collections and art of the 19th century.
**YOU SHOULD KNOW:**
Berlin is in north-east Germany on the River Spree.

*The Reichstag*

# Trier

**POPULATION:**
102,000 (2007)
**WHEN TO GO:**
Slightly off-season (June or September) to avoid the high summer crush.
**DON'T MISS:**
The Landesmuseum (State Museum) – for an incomparable collection of Roman artefacts.
A wonderful old medieval crane on the river bank, built in 1413 on a round base with swivelling top – called The Old Crane to distinguish it from two other ancient cranes.
A superb view of the river, valley and city from the soaring 19th century Mariensäule Monument on a wooded hill across the Moselle.
The Bishop's Museum near the Cathedral, in a former Prussian prison, now housing a collection that includes much early Christian art.
A cruise up or down the river for fairytale castles and magnificent scenery.
**YOU SHOULD KNOW:**
Karl Marx, writer of *Das Kapital* and philosophical father of Communism, was born in Trier (1818).

Among many cities claiming to be Germany's oldest, Trier has better credentials than most, because it was founded in or before 16 BC as a town rather than a settlement or military camp. It lies mainly on the Moselle River's right bank, near Luxembourg, between low hills covered with the vines that produce the famous local white wine.

Trier was founded by Romans (several Emperors lived here) and there is still ample evidence of their presence, like the amazingly well preserved Porta Nigra city gate, the river bridge (still in use), an amphitheatre, a section of town wall and ruins of Roman baths. In addition, there are Roman elements in two great churches – Trier Cathedral (Dom St Peter) and the massive Constantine Basilica dating from around 300 AD. The Roman structures and Cathedral are a collective UNESCO World Heritage Site.

There are other significant churches in Trier, which became a hugely important religious centre in the Middle Ages. The Church of Our Lady (Liebfrauenkirche) is one of the most important early Gothic churches in Germany, and follows the French style. The city's market church, St Gangolph's, stands in one of Germany's finest old market squares and once rivalled the Cathedral. The Church of St Paulin is a fine Baroque edifice. St Matthew's Abbey is still a monastery, where the eponymous apostle is said to be buried. Many Catholic pilgrims visit Trier to honour the relic of the Holy Robe in the Cathedral.

The appeal of this wonderful small city may be judged by the fact that some three million tourists pass through every year. Trier is well able to cater for their needs, with open-air café tables, a wide choice of restaurants and a lively street life. There are several festivals, like the Altstadtfest when the whole city parties.

*Trier Town Square Fountain with the Basilica of St Matthias in the background*

# Lübeck

*Lübeck sits on the Trave River*

Situated on the Trave River in Schleswig-Holstein, northern Germany, Lübeck is the largest German port on the Baltic Sea. Its old town is a charming collection of well-preserved churches, merchants' homes, narrow alleyways and warehouses that have been designated by UNESCO as a World Heritage Site.

In the fourteenth century, Lübeck was the 'Queen of the Hanseatic League', the largest and most powerful member of the trade alliance which operated a monopoly over the Baltic Sea and much of Europe. In 1375, Emperor Charles IV named Lübeck one of the five 'Glories of the Empire'; the other four being Venice, Rome, Pisa and Florence. In the 15th and 16th centuries, Lübeck and the Hanseatic League had a series of successful conflicts with Denmark and Norway over trade rights. However, they were defeated when they became involved in the Count's Feud, a civil war that raged in Denmark from 1534–6. After this defeat, Lübeck's power slowly declined.

The old town, in the heart of the city, is dominated by church steeples, including that of the Cathedral (Lübecker Dom). Started in 1173 by Henry the Lion as a cathedral for the Bishop of Lübeck, it was partly destroyed by bombing in World War II but later reconstructed. Constructed from 1250 to 1350, St Mary's (Marienkirche) is also a dominant presence in the old town. It is the third largest church in Germany, and the tallest building of the old part of Lübeck.

Lubeck's old town also boasts an impressive Town Hall (Rathaus), still in use, and the Art Nouveau Stadttheater, the Heiligen-Geist-Hospital and the Schiffergesellschaft can also be found here. The narrow lanes and alleyways of Lübeck's old town are lined with Gothic, Renaissance, Baroque and Classical town houses with red-brick, gabled façades. There is a multitude of interesting museums, with themes including the history of art, ethnology, fine art, the history of the city, theatre puppets and nature and the environment. One of the best ways to enjoy this lovely city is to take a boat trip around the harbour, leaving from the Holsten Bridge.

**POPULATION:**
213,000 (2005)
**WHEN TO GO:**
May to October.
**DON'T MISS:**
Lübecker Dom – was started in 1173 by Henry the Lion and completed in 1230. The Eastern Vault was destroyed on Palm Sunday 1942 by a bombing raid.
Marienkirche – the tallest church in the city, it was constructed in 1250 and was seen as a symbol of power and prosperity.
The Stadttheater, a listed Art Noveau playhouse.
A stroll in the old town, which is home to over 1,000 listed buildings.
A boat trip along the Trave Canal – take in old city fortresses, mills, the medieval city walls before passing the scenic 'Painter's Corner' and Holsten Gate.
**YOU SHOULD KNOW:**
Lübeck is famous for its marzipan.

# Hannover

Starting life as a small village of ferrymen and fishermen beside the River Leine in northern Germany, Hannover had become a thriving town by the 14th century, when important churches and city walls were built. The Electors (rulers) of Hannover eventually became the Kings of Great Britain, starting with George I in 1714. The association ended with Queen Victoria, as only males could succeed in Hannover.

The modern city is most famous for hosting trade fairs and exhibitions, and its exposition centre (EXPO-Park) is the largest in the world. Most of Hannover was reduced to rubble by intensive bombing in World War II, so don't go looking for a host of wonderful historical edifices.

There is a charming old town full of picturesque corners, together with some splendid buildings – the Old Town Hall (in its way much nicer than the super-grand 1900s 'wedding cake' that superseded it), the huge Market Church, Liebniz House, Nolte House and the Beguine Tower. The quarter around the Kreuz Church has appealing narrow lanes, and close by may be found the ruined Aegidien Church, left as a stark reminder of war. Speaking of which, don't be fooled – much of the 'old' town consists of ancient buildings from all over the city that survived the bombing, brought together in one place for effect, plus some that were reconstructed in situ.

Hannover has wonderful parks and gardens, especially the world-famous Great Garden of Herrenhausen, a Baroque masterpiece created in the 17th century to imitate the gardens at Versailles.

There are plenty of other attractions, too. Hannover Zoo is one of Europe's best. Of the city's 23 museums, the Landesmuseum, Historical Museum and Kestner Museum are notable (free entry on Fridays). There are numerous galleries and theatres, plus a lively music scene – both classical and modern.

*The new Town Hall*

# Regensburg

Here is Bavaria's medieval gem. Unlike most German cities, Regensburg was spared the worst excesses of Allied bombing and did not have to rebuild lost architectural heritage. It did lose the Romanesque Obermünster Church (the belfry survives), but otherwise the old town (Altstadt) remained remarkably intact, a fact reflected in its status as a UNESCO World Heritage Site.

This ancient settlement lies at the confluence of the Danube and Regen rivers, close to the Bavarian Forest. The view across the river to the old town would surely have been recognised by long-ago inhabitants, with the 12th century stone bridge and jumble of colourful waterfront buildings presenting a timeless picture – everything that a medieval town should be.

In truth, those former inhabitants might have been puzzled by the Cathedral's appearance. This Gothic masterpiece was begun in 1275 and added to for another four centuries . . . but the twin spires were not completed until 1869. But then again there's an earlier cloister going back to the 8th century. Many historical structures have been preserved, starting with Roman remains like the east tower of the Praetorian Gate. A wealth of 11th to 13th century architecture defines the character of Old Regensburg, where notable buildings like early churches, towers and the 14th century Town Hall stand proud in a warren of narrow lanes, tall houses, monastic remains and strong fortifications.

But don't arrive expecting to find no more than a Disney-style fairytale medieval town. Regensburg is also a thoroughly modern city that has spread far beyond the old centre, serving as a busy river port and motorway hub, with plenty of industrial activity. If you doubt its 21st century credentials, just take a look at the state-of-the-art BMW factory.

**POPULATION:**
130,000 (2006)
**WHEN TO GO:**
Spring, summer, autumn or even winter (for an enchanting Christmas Fair in the Altstadt)
**DON'T MISS:**
The Historic Shipping Museum on the north bank of the Danube, opposite the old town – spot the paddle steamers.
The underground Document Neupfarrplatz museum, showing Roman remains and those of Regensburg's medieval Jewish quarter, discovered in the 1990s.
The Golf Museum with over a thousand items of equipment and memorabilia from the very first missed putts through to the 1930s.
The extraordinary grotesque carvings on the main doorway of the 12th century Church of St James.
A boat trip to Walhalla, outside the city, an amazing mock Grecian temple built in the early 19th century as a hall of fame for German cultural figures – or any Danube river cruise.
St Emmeram's Abbey (now known as Schloss Thurn und Taxis), a huge castle converted from an abbey founded in the 8th century – museums and guided tours.
**YOU SHOULD KNOW:**
Pope Benedict XVI was Professor of Theology at Regensburg University from 1969 to 1977.

*The Old Town with the Cathedral and bridge over the Danube*

# Dresden

**POPULATION:**
505,000 (2006)
**WHEN TO GO:**
Visit in July and August and take an umbrella (these are Dresden's warmest but wettest months).
**DON'T MISS:**
The wonderful 18th century Frauenkirche, destroyed by bombing and recently restored as a symbol of post-unification reconstruction.
The rebuilt Dresden Castle, centred on a medieval keep and home of the famous Green Vault (Grünes Gewölbe) containing treasures of the Saxon monarchy.
The magnificent Semperoper opera house, a great survivor – built 1841, rebuilt 1869 (fire), rebuilt 1985 (World War II damage), refurbished 2002 (Elbe flood).
All or some of the 11 museums containing the Dresden State Art Collections, one of the world's most important cultural resources.
Dresden's Catholic Cathedral, the Hofkirche, originally built in the 18th century because the Elector of Saxony had to become a Catholic to rule Poland.
The bridge over the moat and well-known Kronentor (crowned gate) of the reconstructed Zwinger Palace.
**YOU SHOULD KNOW:**
Future Russian President Vladimir Putin was stationed in Dresden as a KGB officer in the 1980s, witnessing the collapse of East Germany first hand.

*The city on the River Elbe is enjoying a renaissance.*

Once a beautiful medieval city noted for the manufacture of porcelain, Dresden was destroyed in 1945 by British and American bombs, creating a horrifying firestorm that claimed tens of thousands of lives. It remains the most controversial Allied action of World War II, with subsequent justifications hard to understand.

The remains of Dresden vanished behind the Iron Curtain, emerging as a very different place upon German reunification in 1990. Districts of the outer city that survived the bombing were run-down, much bomb damage remained and there had been massive industrialization. Many important buildings had been reconstructed, some damaged monuments had been demolished and lots of historic ruins remained. But the city's modern appearance had been indelibly set by wholesale building in the brutal 'socialist modern' style, softened only by its many green spaces.

Today, Dresden still has the social problems that afflict so many parts of former East Germany, but this great city on the River Elbe in the south east of Germany is undergoing physical renaissance and striving to recreate its former cultural eminence. There has been massive redevelopment, a process likely to last for decades. Reconstructed historic buildings, Communist post-war structures and some striking post-unification architecture have combined to give the city its distinctive look, but that process is far from over. Indeed, the UNESCO World Heritage Site, an 18-km (11-mi) run of river valley, may enjoy only a brief tenure because an intrusive modern bridge is being constructed.

First-time visitors may be surprised by how 'normal' Dresden seems, but in truth almost all the imposing historic buildings are reconstructed carbon copies. For all that, this interesting city provides fascinating insight into the history of Germany since the beginning of World War II . . . and points hopefully towards the country's future.

# Luxembourg City

The City of Luxembourg is the capital of the wealthy but small Grand Duchy of Luxembourg, an independent survivor of the Low Countries' turbulent past that somehow escaped being taken over by one of its neighbours – Belgium, France and Germany. Luxembourg City is located in the south of the country, where the Rivers Alzette and Pétrusse meet.

This has been an important strategic site since Roman times, and by the 16th century it had become one of the strongest fortifications in Europe. By the 18th century, the defences had been further developed and Luxembourg was thought to be impregnable, becoming known as 'The Gibraltar of the North'. The city's Old Quarters and Fortifications may still be seen, and have become a UNESCO World Heritage Site.

The present city seems complicated, because it sits on rocky upland, straddling several outcrops, ridges and the steep valleys of its two rivers. In consequence, it is a city of bridges, viaducts and wonderful views. It is not densely populated, with plenty of parks and green spaces – even farmland within city limits.

The main shopping areas are in the newer part of the city, around the station. The old town, across the Pétrusse Valley, has some fine old

buildings and a real sense of history. In recent years the city's reputation – as a sober place where nothing much happened after 6 o'clock – has been overtaken by an explosion in the number of bars, clubs and restaurants.

A twice-weekly food market is held on William Square (every Wednesday and Saturday) and a flea market every second and fourth Saturday on the Place d'Armes. From the end of August to mid-September there's Schueberfouer in the vast Glacis Square, continuing the tradition of an itinerant folk fair founded in the 14th century. At Easter, there are long-established religious festivals.

*The River Alzette flows between houses in the Grund district.*

**POPULATION:**
76,000 (2005)
**WHEN TO GO:**
There's something to do and see in every season, but the leaves are spectacular in autumn.
**DON'T MISS:**
A visit to the grave of the legendary US World War II commander General George S. Patton, in Luxembourg's American Military Cemetery.
Notre-Dame Cathedral, a fine example of late Gothic architecture dating from the early 17th century.
The impressive street façade of the Grand Ducal Palace (state visitors only!).
The great arched Adolphe Bridge across the Pétrusse Valley, which is an unofficial symbol of the city – best seen from the park below.
The modern European Court of Justice building – but only if you've got a serious grievance and lots of time to spare!
A stunning panoramic view from the Boulevard Roosevelt on the edge of the old town.
**YOU SHOULD KNOW:**
Luxembourg's communist revolution in 1918 lasted . . . a few hours.

*Erasmus Bridge*

# Rotterdam

Europe's greatest port city – Rotterdam, on the Rhine river's vast delta – may not sound like a promising destination but actually has much to offer, as four million visitors a year attest. It is the cosmopolitan second city of the Netherlands, divided by the New Maas River with the centre on the north bank.

The port now stretches from the old city towards the North Sea for some 40 km (20 mi). The original historic harbour is part of the town centre, but has long been eclipsed by new development, with further port expansion currently under way. Much of the area is on reclaimed land behind dykes. A gritty working city that was almost completely destroyed at the beginning of World War 2, Rotterdam nonetheless has some impressive industrial heritage, notably bridges, tunnels and canals. But it also has a variety of museums, an internationally famous orchestra and many theatres. In fact, it is an important cultural centre, sharing the accolade of European Capital of Culture with Porto in 2001. This is in part due to strenuous efforts to regenerate the city, with some striking modern architecture, many new festivals and a focus on better shopping and nightlife.

Do visit the Linjbaan pedestrian shopping centre, and sample some of the speciality restaurants that abound. There is plenty to do and see in Rotterdam. As well as museums (especially maritime) there's an excellent zoo that includes Oceanium, a fascinating sea aquarium with a scary shark tunnel. But perhaps the city's special quality is the striking modern architecture made possible by post-war reconstruction. Rotterdam has the tallest office and residential buildings in the Netherlands, and is proud of striking landmarks like the 186-m (610-ft) tall Euromast and soaring cable-stay Erasmus Bridge.

**POPULATION:**
589,000 (2006)
**WHEN TO GO:**
Rotterdam is not the ideal place to be on a cold, wet, windy winter day.
**DON'T MISS:**
Famous footsteps – the Walk of Fame commemorates 200 international celebrities, set forever in concrete along 'Star Boulevard'.
The spectacularly lit Waalhaven port, viewed across the water by night.
Europe's then-tallest office building, the White House, built in 1898.
An outing in the colourful 'pancake boat', where as many pancakes as you can eat are served on a cruise past the city's imposing skyline.
The lovely gardens of the Trompenburg Arboretum, for a change of pace and a few peaceful moments.
The Maritime Museum, with over half a million exhibits – large and small.
**YOU SHOULD KNOW:**
The lowest point in the Netherlands at 6.76 m (22.2 ft) below sea level is just east of Rotterdam.

# Arnhem

Arnhem is not a favourite dropping off point for parachutists, being the site of one of the most notorious airborne disasters in World War II. The city stands on the Lower Rhine, and capture of its strategic river bridge was the objective of British and Polish paratroops and glider-borne soldiers in September 1944. After intense fighting, the attack failed and shortly afterwards the bridge was destroyed by American bombers.

That era is long gone, though not forgotten. Despite serious war damage, Arnhem was sympathetically reconstructed and remains an attractive place with many historic buildings and a vibrant centre, concentrated around the old corn market (Korenmarkt), very much the place to eat, drink and sit in a pavement café watching the world go by. The bustling shopping centre is atmospheric, with all sorts of interesting little shops down side alleys off the main streets. Arnhem has a genteel reputation as a 'green and pleasant city' renowned for its parks and open spaces, and also for hilly wooded terrain to the north which is unique in the flat countryside of the Netherlands. In the 19th century it became a picturesque resort much favoured by the Dutch elite, with many rich colonial merchants taking up residence.

Notable tourist sights include the St Eusebius Church (partially destroyed in World War II and rebuilt), the octagonal Koepelchurch, the medieval Saint Peter's Guesthouse, the 16th century Devil's House (now the Mayor's office) and the impressive Sabelspoort, the sole remnant of the old town fortifications. Other attractions include the open air National Heritage Museum just outside the city, which features historic buildings brought to the site from all over the Netherlands, and Burgers' Zoo, the largest and most popular zoo in the country.

**POPULATION:**
143,000 (2007)
**WHEN TO GO:**
With its open-air attractions, Arnhem is ideal for a summer visit.
**DON'T MISS:**
The Airborne Museum at Oosterbeek, keeping alive the memory of the Battle of Arnhem in 1944.
A network of historic cellars from the 12th and 13th centuries, beneath the Rijnstraat.
The panoramic view of the green city from the top of the Eusebius tower.
Park Sonsbeek, formerly a country estate, now Arnhem's largest and best-known park.
The innovative Gelredome, home of the city's football club, Vitesse, which has a slide-out grass pitch and a moveable roof.
The gable of the neo-Gothic main post office, incorporating a number of terracotta monkeys.
**YOU SHOULD KNOW:**
Arnhem has the only trolley-bus system in the Netherlands.

*The Rathaus (town hall)*

# Leiden

**POPULATION:**
118,000 (2007)
**WHEN TO GO:**
Leiden is a city for all seasons, but is perhaps at its best in spring and summer.
**DON'T MISS:**
The large general market held on the banks of the Rhine every Wednesday and Saturday, following a 900-year-old tradition.
The many groups of almshouses in the city centre, peaceful enclaves where time seems to have stood still.
Surprising wall poems that have been placed all over town in recent times.
The Pest House, built to house bubonic plague sufferers but never used; now the entrance to the vast Naturalis natural history museum.
An old corn-grinding windmill (Molen de Valk); now a museum.
Hortus Botanicus, the oldest botanical garden in the Netherlands and one of the oldest in the world.
**YOU SHOULD KNOW:**
The Dutch mania for tulips in the 17th century began here, where Carolus Clusius brought the first examples to flower.

This ancient city is centred on a defensive mound where the Old and New Rhine rivers meet. Leiden was sacked in 1047 and besieged several times before developing into a prosperous cloth town. The people were offered a university or exemption from taxes as a reward for defying the Spanish in 1574, and gallantly chose the former. That triumph is celebrated on 3 October each year with a parade, fair and mass consumption of *hutspot* (a dish of mashed potato, carrots and onions invented after the siege).

Leiden declined as its cloth industry waned, with the happy result that much of the old town has survived. Exceptions are an area where 220 houses were destroyed by a gunpowder blast in 1807 (now Van der Werff Park) and bomb damage in World War II. But it remains a place of compelling charm. With two river branches, a network of canals and many tree-lined quays, the overall effect is delightful. A morning's walk around the streets and along the waterways (boat cruises available for the lazy!) is essential, revealing picturesque townscapes and architectural gems at every turn. Rembrandt was born here, and would still recognize the place.

Among historic buildings too numerous to list, look out for the De Burcht Castle, two old city gates (Zijlpoort and Morspoort), the 13th century Gravensteen fortress, the imposing 15th century St Pancras' Church, St Peter's Church, the old Waag (weighing house), the Latin School of 1599 and the 17th century Stadstimmerwerf (city carpenter's yard and wharf).

But Leiden is not just about fascinating buildings. There is a wealth of interesting shops, plus endless places to eat and drink. One such is Oudt Leyden, the world's oldest pancake house with its signature Delftware crockery (off which Winston Churchill once enjoyed a giant pancake!).

*De Valk windmill with Beestenmarkt in the foreground*

# Amsterdam

Amsterdam started out in the 13th century as a small fishing village. According to legend, it was founded by two Frisian fishermen, who landed on the shores of the Amstel river in a small boat with their dog. The damming of the river gave the village its name. Today it is the capital of the Netherlands, known for its liberal attitudes, rich culture and history. The city has kilometres of attractive canals, some truly great art collections, stunning architecture and fascinating museums.

*An aerial view of Amsterdam*

Few early buildings survive, except the mediaeval Oude Kerk (the Old Church, with little houses on its sides), the Neuwe Kerk (New Church) and the Houten Huis (Wooden House). The historical centre was largely built during the Golden Age in the 17th century, when Amsterdam was one of the wealthiest cities in the world, with trade links to the Baltic, North America, Africa, Indonesia and Brazil. Its stock exchange was the first to trade continuously. This period saw the building of the classical Royal Palace on Damplein, the Westerkerk, Zuiderkerk, and many canal houses, including De Dolfijn (Dolphin) and De Gecroonde Raep (the Crowned Turnip).

Amsterdam has many outstanding museums, including the Rijksmuseum, the Stedelijk Museum and the Rembrandt House Museum. The Van Gogh Museum houses the largest collection of the artist's work in the world. Anne Frank House on the Prinsengracht is where the Jewish diarist hid during World War II to avoid Nazi persecution, and is well worth a visit.

Amsterdam is famous for its canals. The three main canals extend from the IJ Lake, and each of these marks the position of the city walls and moat at different periods in time. The innermost is the Herengracht (Lord's Canal). Beyond it lie the Keizersgracht (Emperor's Canal) and the Prinsengracht (Prince's canal). They are best enjoyed by boat, or by bicycle along the surrounding streets. Smaller canals intersect the main canals, dividing the city into a number of islands, and nearly 1,300 bridges criss-cross the waterways of this beautiful city, known as 'Venice of the North'.

Amsterdam is also known for its nightlife, with its bustling cafés, restaurants, clubs, traditional 'brown' bars, cinemas and theatres. These are mainly centred around the Leidseplein, the Jordaan and Rembrandtplein. Many visitors go for the infamous Red Light District, with its legalized prostitution, strip joints and sex shops.

**POPULATION:**
743,000 (2006)
**WHEN TO GO:**
Between May and September
**DON'T MISS:**
Boat tour of the canals – a great way to see the city's best sights.
Oude Kerk – the oldest church in Amsterdam. The roof is the largest medieval wooden vault in Europe.
Anne Frank House on the Prinsengracht – the former hiding place where Anne wrote her famous diary tells the history of the eight people who were in hiding here. Her diary is among the original objects on display.
Van Gogh Museum – exhibits the largest collection of his paintings in the world.
The nightlife – Amsterdam is one of Europe's premier party cities and offers something for every taste!
**YOU SHOULD KNOW:**
The city has an amazing diversity of cultural and historical attractions.

# Basel

**POPULATION:**
172,000 (2006)
**WHEN TO GO:**
Basel is best enjoyed on foot, for which the summer months are preferable.
**DON'T MISS:**
The panoramic view from the top of St Martin's Tower at the twin-towered Münster, after enjoying sensational stone carving over the St Gallus Door.
Various medieval city gates such as Spalentor, St Johanns Tor and St Alban Tor.
A leisurely stroll along the river promenade on the Lesser Basel side of the Rhine.
Amazing animated mechanical sculptures by Jean Tinguely and like-minded kinetic artists (kids love them) at the museum that bears his name.
Monkeys solving problems to earn their food at the city centre zoo.
The free opening hour that many museums have at the end of the day.
**YOU SHOULD KNOW:**
Most Swiss homes harbour an assault rifle, in case the citizen army is needed to repel surprise invaders (tourists excepted).

*The River Rhine divides the city.*

Switzerland's third-largest city lies on the River Rhine, close to both Germany and France, and is a major industrial centre. It is a railway hub, with three main stations – one each for the Swiss, German and French networks. Five bridges connect the two halves of the city (known as Greater and Lesser Basel), but it's well worth crossing on one of the old-fashioned cable ferries.

A stroll round the city reveals many stunning examples of modern architecture, including the Messeturm, Switzerland's tallest building. But there is historic character aplenty. The medieval town centre in Greater Basel is a delight, and contains splendid buildings like the red sandstone Minster Church on impressive Minster Square (minster is an alternative term for cathedral). This early gothic building was reconstructed after the great earthquake of 1356. The grand Renaissance town hall on the market square (Marktplatz, where there's still a daily market) is also noteworthy. A maze of narrow traffic-free cobbled streets demands to be explored, though fitness is required – they're steep! And be warned that most shops shut on Sundays. The best nightlife is over the river in Lesser Basel.

Basel prides itself as a city of culture, with some 40 museums, a dozen theatres and regular concerts in churches and the open air. But the city is really famous for the Basel Carnival (Fasnacht), the country's largest and one of the world's best. It starts at precisely four o'clock in the morning on the Monday after Ash Wednesday, the first day of Lent, and lasts 72 hours to the minute (they're Swiss, after all). Up to 20,000 revellers wear masks and colourful costumes and there are numerous parades, marching bands, concerts and lantern displays, and all the while a huge amount of confetti rains down. Extraordinary!

# Geneva

Lake Geneva (Lac Léman), one of the largest lakes in Western Europe, lies on the Rhône River on the border between France and Switzerland, between the Jura mountains and the Alps. For many years, visitors have come to marvel at the beauty of the lake, including Jean-Jacques Rousseau, Lord Byron and Shelley. On the shores of the azure lake, in the shadow of the Alps, is the city of Geneva, an historical town filled with many interesting attractions.

The nicest way to explore the lake is by boat, on one of the many steam ships which travel up and down the shores to the towns and villages there. Services usually run from Easter through to October. One of the most famous sights of Geneva is the incredible Jet d'Eau, which spurts lake water an impressive 140 m (459 ft) into the air. Once an overflow valve for a hydroelectric plant, the Jet was turned into a fountain in 1891.

As well as its wonderful scenery, the city is known for a range of diverse things, including its quality watches, knives and cutlery, its fine chocolate, cheese fondues and for being the site of several UN agencies. However, there are plenty of historical sites to occupy the visitor. Built as a base for the League of Nations, the Palais des Nations boasts an awe-inspiring Assembly Hall, interesting library and landscaped grounds. It also houses a fine art collection. Also worth a visit is the medieval cathedral of St. Pierre.

Geneva boasts a wide range of museums, on subjects as diverse as ethnography, horology, the Red Cross, natural history, Voltaire, the Reformation, and modern art. The city spends around 20 per cent of its annual budget on its cultural department, so most of the museums are free.

The city is well-known for its parks and gardens. The Parc des Eaux Vives is a lovely place for a stroll, with views over the lake to the UN campus and the Palais des Nations. For those with a little more energy, there is a beach resort on the lakeside just outside the city where you can swim and try out various beach and water sports.

*The Altstadt is on both banks of the Limmat River.*

# Zürich

**POPULATION:**
372,000 (2007)
**WHEN TO GO:**
Unless you're winter sporty and like the cold, the city only warms up from June to September.
**DON'T MISS:**
Artist Marc Chagall's five stained glass windows in the 13th century Fraumünster Church in the city centre.
Sihlcity in the southern part of town – a vast new shopping and entertainment complex with restaurants, clubs and cinemas.
Le Corbusier Pavilion in Zürichhorn Park, the last building designed by the revered modern architect before he died in 1965.
Writer James Joyce's grave and statue in Fluntern Cemetery – he wrote his masterpiece *Ulysses* here in World War I and returned to Zurich to die in 1941.
The splendid zoo, with a new outdoor lion enclosure and amazing enclosed re-creation of tropical Masoala rainforest.
**YOU SHOULD KNOW:**
Zürich has a well-known red light district.

This is the country where it's an offence to put your rubbish out for collection on the wrong day, so no jokes about gnomes when you arrive in the Swiss financial capital – the straight-laced Swiss do not regard bankers or banking as a humorous matter. That said, Zürich is frequently named as the city with the best quality of life in the world, so those gnomes must know a thing or two about gracious living. The city certainly appears to be a clean, orderly and efficient place, with church spires rising from a pleasing array of traditional buildings beside an impossibly clear blue lake and river.

The city grew up where the River Limmat leaves Lake Zürich. The well-preserved Altstadt (old town) on both banks of the river is a great starting point, with countless places of interest waiting to be discovered in the narrow, winding streets. Another essential experience is window shopping in Bahnhofstrasse (Station Street), one of the most exclusive, longest and expensive shopping streets in Switzerland, running down to the lake from the main station. Stop half way for coffee in the Confiserie Sprüngli café and chocolate shop on Paradeplatz, one of the country's most famous squares.

Zürich is also a city of culture with fine churches, interesting buildings, over 50 museums and festivals throughout the summer. But by now it will be apparent to visitors that first impressions are not necessarily accurate. A recent easing of restrictions has allowed many new bars, clubs and restaurants to open, and the area around the lake shore positively buzzes with life. Indeed, Zürich turns out to be a place where people enjoy themselves in a lively and relaxed way.

# Bern

Duke Berthold V of Zähringen founded the city of Bern on the River Aare in 1191 and is said to have named it after a bear (*bär* in German) he had killed while out hunting. The bear featured on the city's coat of arms first appeared in 1224 and has continued to be the symbol of Bern to this day. The city is situated on a picturesque promontory surrounded on three sides by a bend in the river. The old battlements of the city, converted into promenades, command a magnificent view of the surrounding alpine scenery. Today the old town is a UNESCO World Heritage Site because its architecture and street plan are essentially unchanged since the late Middle Ages. Largely restored in the eighteenth century, Bern has retained all its original charm.

The most famous attraction in Bern is the Zytglogge, a tower in the centre of the old town. Since it was built at the turn of the 13th century, it has served as guard tower, prison, clock tower, centre of urban life and civic memorial. Today it is most famous for its 15th century astronomical clock, both the benchmark of official Bern time as well as the point from which all distances in the canton are measured. It features an intricate astronomical and astrological device, which displays a 24-hour clock, the 12 hours of daylight, the position of the sun in the zodiac, the day of the week, the date and the month, the phases of the moon and the elevation of the sun above the horizon throughout the year.

Just before each hour is struck, mechanical figures appear, including a crowing cock, a parade of bears, Chronos with his hourglass and a dancing jester. There are guided tours to see the internal workings of the clock, and visitors can explore the spire and enjoy the rooftop view.

Other buildings of note in Bern include the 15th century town hall and the Gothic cathedral, the Berner Münster, with the tallest tower in Switzerland. The Rosengarten, a former cemetery on a hill overlooking the old town, offers panoramic views of this beautiful, atmospheric city. Since the 16th century, the city has had a bear pit (the Bärengraben), which can be visited off the far end of the Nydeggbrücke. Nowadays the Bärengraben is part of the Bernese zoo – Dählhölzli.

**POPULATION:**
127,000 (2006)
**WHEN TO GO:**
April to October.
**DON'T MISS:**
The beautiful old city which was founded in 1191 on a hill surrounded by the Aare River. Most of it was restored in the 18th century but it has retained its original charcter and charm.
The Berner Münster – an impressive Gothic church dating back to 1421 that is home to 'the cathedral masters', a married couple who look after it.
The bear pits – these are in the process of being turned into a bear park.
The astronomical clock – this dates back to 1530 and displays the time, day of the week, position of the planets and the signs of the zodiac.
Shopping in the vast covered markets
**YOU SHOULD KNOW:**
The city centre remains largely unchanged since the 12th century

*The Old Town*

# Oxford

*The Radcliffe Camera*

Described as the 'city of dreaming spires' by Matthew Arnold, the nineteenth-century English poet and cultural critic, in reference to its harmonious college buildings, Oxford is home to the oldest university in the English-speaking world. It stands at the meeting point of two rivers: the Cherwell and the Isis, as the Thames is known at this point. The city dates back to Saxon times, but it was not until the twelfth century that its Augustinian abbey began to take and educate students. A century later, the first colleges were founded; others followed as the student population grew.

Most tourists come to Oxford to see the colleges. Among the best are Magdalen College with its beautiful grounds and the distinctive Magdalen Tower, and Christ Church, a grand collection of buildings around an enormous courtyard founded by Cardinal Thomas Woolsey, with its tower built by Sir Christopher Wren.

Oxford also boasts some of the best-known museums in the world. The Ashmolean Museum of Art and Archaeology is noted for its collections of Pre-Raphaelite paintings, Majolica pottery and English silver. The archaeology department has an excellent collection of Greek and Minoan pottery, and some important antiquities from Ancient Egypt. The Pitt Rivers museum is also world famous, with its wonderful archaeological and anthropological collections.

The circular dome and drum of the Radcliffe Camera is one of the most distinctive landmarks in Oxford. Built in the eighteenth century to house a new library, the Camera is today used as the main reading room of the Bodleian Library. The Sheldonian Theatre also warrants a visit. Built in 1667, it was the first major commission for Christopher Wren. Then Professor of Astronomy at Oxford, Wren designed the Sheldonian to imitate a classical Roman theatre.

As well as its dreaming spires, Oxford is known for its rivers. These offer beautiful riverbank walks and the opportunity to hire a punt and spend a lazy afternoon messing about on the river.

*Merchants Bridge in Castlefield*

# Manchester

The great north-western rivalry of Liverpool (commerce) and Manchester (industry) will never be resolved, though the latter is sometimes described as 'the capital of the North', and even claims to be overtaking Birmingham for the nebulous title of 'England's second city'.

Manchester has come through hard times after its traditional manufacturing base collapsed – especially the textile industry that earned Manchester's 19th-century soubriquet 'Cottonopolis'. The dark satanic mills mentioned in William Blake's famous hymn *Jerusalem* are still there, but are nowadays likely to be divided into trendy loft apartments, galleries or interesting shops. The extensive canal system that facilitated the city's development during the Industrial Revolution is being revitalized as desirable real estate after decades of neglect.

Though Manchester has a long history, little remains of the medieval town. The centre was badly damaged in World War II and again by an IRA bomb in 1996, which has allowed extensive redevelopment – often sweeping away second-rate postwar buildings. The result is a pleasing mix of old and new, with some splendid modern architecture rubbing shoulders with sturdy Victorian edifices (Manchester Town Hall is a superb example of Victorian Gothic Revival architecture) to give the city its distinctive character.

Manchester has a strong cultural tradition, and today boasts annual festivals, great galleries, excellent museums (Imperial War Museum North is a wonderful new one, and Manchester Art Gallery a fine example of the old). There is also a very active music scene. But in truth, though Manchester is well worth visiting for its cultural attractions, the city's real strength is its cosmopolitan character, with all sorts of interesting quarters like Chinatown, The Village and the Northern Quarter. Along with that goes the vibrant street life and pulsing nightlife that truly represents this go-ahead city's modern character.

**POPULATION:**
441,000 (2005)
**WHEN TO GO:**
June and July (warm and dry) – though contrary to popular belief, Manchester's rainfall is below the national average.
**DON'T MISS:**
Manchester Cathedral, begun in the 13th century, the oldest building in the city and the country's widest cathedral – damaged in World War II and subsequently repaired.
Castlefield, England's first Urban Heritage site – at the centre of the canal network, now a fascinating place to enjoy a waterside drink.
*B of the Bang* by Thomas Heatherwick, the UK's tallest self-supporting sculpture at 80 m (262ft – constructed to celebrate the 2002 Commonwealth Games.
Salford – a separate city just a few steps from the city centre across the River Irwell, with splendid attractions such as the Lowry Art Gallery on Salford Quays.
St Mary's The Hidden Gem, the oldest post-Reformation Catholic Church in Britain, founded in 1794 and containing the masterful Stations of the Cross paintings by Norman Adams.
**YOU SHOULD KNOW:**
Manchester United, one of the world's richest, most popular soccer clubs, nearly went bankrupt and ceased to be in 1902 (when known as Newton Heath).

*The House that Moved*

# Exeter

With a dash of big city atmosphere, thriving arts scene, bright cafés and bars, large student population and bustling street life, Devon's county town is one of the West Country's livelier cities. Exeter is on the River Exe, historically located at the lowest bridging and highest navigable point. It was an important regional centre from Roman times, declining in the 19th century as the Industrial Revolution passed it by. This preserved character made Exeter second only to Bath as 'a perfect English city'.

Unfortunately, a wealth of historic buildings was lost in World War II when the centre was almost completely destroyed by intensive bombing. Subsequent redevelopment was not sensitive by modern (or even post-war German) standards, as there was virtually no attempt to rebuild damaged buildings, which were swept away to be replaced with undistinguished modern architecture.

Despite this, there are survivors – especially the splendid St Peter's Cathedral, dating from 1050 with later additions. With no central tower, it has the longest uninterrupted vaulted ceiling in England and fascinating internal features like the great clock, minstrels' gallery and a ceiling boss showing the murder of St Thomas à Becket (take binoculars!). The remains of the Norman Rougemont Castle are extant. Exeter's Guildhall is the oldest civic building in England still in use. Other noteworthy buildings are St Nicholas Priory in Mint Lane, the Church of St Mary Steps with its wonderfully elaborate clock and the old Custom House.

In truth, Exeter is a city with some beautiful buildings, but it is not a beautiful city. As such, it is not instantly appealing to tourists. However, efforts are being made to get across the message that what Exeter lacks in looks it makes up for in character, with areas like the Quayside becoming genuine visitor attractions.

**POPULATION:**
118,000 (2005)
**WHEN TO GO:**
Summer, when the students have gone home and the pace of city life slows.
**DON'T MISS:**
The fine old hall of the Guild of Tuckers and Weavers – a poignant reminder of the medieval splendour of Old Exeter before the bombs fell.
The House that Moved – a 14th century building relocated in 1961 to make way for road widening.
Recently redeveloped Princesshay shopping centre, designed to keep Exeter competitive in the all-important retail sales sector.
Northernhay Gardens, England's oldest purpose-made public open space, laid out in 1612.
Wonderful half-timbered houses on the steep, cobbled Stepcote Hill.
The University of Exeter's parkland grounds and interesting sculpture trail.
**YOU SHOULD KNOW:**
Parliament Street is claimed to be the world's narrowest city street, at one point no wider than 0.64 m (25 in).

# Chester

Cheshire's county town is on the River Dee, close to Wales – though traditionally there is no love lost between Chester's inhabitants (Cestrians) and the Welsh. The city is one of the best-preserved walled cities in England. The walls are almost complete – constructed from as early as 120 AD, they enclose the inner city with only two short breaks.

Chester was a significant Roman centre, and evidence of their presence may still be seen – notably the amphitheatre and reconstructed Roman Garden complete with hypocaust (heating system). The city remained important because of its strategic location close to Wales and as a jumping-off point for Ireland. It was a river port and trading centre until overtaken by Liverpool, after which it became a fashionable Georgian retreat from the industrial north-west of England.

The word 'Grosvenor' appears frequently in Chester, being the family name of the Dukes of Westminster who own a considerable amount of property here. Chester's characteristic medieval half-timbered appearance was enhanced by the Victorian remodelling instituted by the first duke, though many 17th century originals remain. Distinctive features of estate-owned buildings are twisted chimneys and grey-brick diamonds within red brickwork, which are still much in evidence.

In common with many British cities, there was rapid development after World War II, often at the expense of historic buildings. This process saw considerable changes in central Chester, but ended with a switch of emphasis to conservation in the late 1960s. Though now surrounded by extensive suburbs, the bustling centre retains a very pleasing variety of architecture, including the unique Rows – a series of half-timbered buildings joined with long galleries, looking for all the world like Tudor shopping malls, with splendid examples to be seen in Watergate, Eastgate and Bridge Street.

*Half-timbered buildings on Eastgate Street*

**POPULATION:**
77,000 (2001)
**WHEN TO GO:**
Summer, to enjoy the walk around those famous city walls in the best possible weather.
**DON'T MISS:**
Chester Cathedral, completed around 1250 and 'modernized' in Victorian times, originally a great Benedictine monastery dedicated to St Werburgh, the city's patron saint.
The Norman Castle, dating from 1069 (rebuilt in the late 18th century) and still occupied by the army.
The much-photographed Eastgate Clock, an extraordinary ornate metal structure erected in 1897 to celebrate Queen Victoria's Diamond Jubilee.
The award-winning Grosvenor Museum, covering a wide range of subjects and including a reconstructed Georgian house.
**YOU SHOULD KNOW:**
In 1656 three witches (Ellen Beech, Anne Osboston and Ann Thornton) were hanged on Gallows Hill and buried in St Mary's-on-the-Hill churchyard.

# Newcastle upon Tyne

**POPULATION:**
277,000 (1995)
**WHEN TO GO:**
The last week in June, for the travelling
Hoppings funfair, said to be the largest
in Europe – held on Town Moor.
**DON'T MISS:**
A stroll across the Millennium Bridge to
Gateshead, to enjoy the fabulous
BALTIC Centre for Contemporary Art
and Norman Foster's The Sage
Gateshead music centre.
Newcastle's Chinatown, with its own
Chinese arch, centred on Stowell Street
in the city centre.
Alderman Fenwick's House, an
important merchant's house dating
from the 17th century on earlier
foundations.
Blackfriars, a former 13th century
monastery, now housing shops and a
restaurant, with outdoor space.
Bessie Surtees House, one of a group
of 18th century timber-framed buildings
with principal rooms on view.
A day trip to the extensive Beamish
open-air museum, south of Gateshead,
for an evocative journey back to life in
the north as lived in the 19th and early
20th centuries.
**YOU SHOULD KNOW:**
Traces of Hadrian's Wall are visible in
Newcastle (along the West Road),
continuing eastwards to a Roman fort
at Wallsend . . . where (of course) the
wall ends!

*The Millennium Bridge*

Residents of Newcastle could call themselves Novocastrians, as their city is a former Roman settlement. Former pupils of the Royal Grammar School do, but most prefer the more down-to-earth 'Geordie', uttered in one of the country's most melodic regional accents. Newcastle's prosperity was initially based on coal exports, but industries like shipbuilding and heavy engineering soon developed.

This compact, friendly and attractive city has a wonderful neo-classical centre, built in the 1830s and recently refurbished. One of the finest streets of its type, Grey Street, curves down from Grey's Monument towards the River Tyne (the second Earl Grey, now atop his tall column, commissioned the redevelopment).

Newcastle is a green city, with splendid parks and open spaces. Town Moor is huge, and freemen of Newcastle graze livestock right up to the Newcastle Civic Centre. In theory, they could also invade the pitch at Newcastle's secular cathedral, the mighty St James' Park, home of Newcastle United Football Club. In reality, they accept a small rent in lieu. Leazes Park was established in Victorian times and Jesmond Dene (the wooded valley of the Ouseburn) is a popular recreational area. The real Cathedral, St Nicholas, is a fine building dating from the 14th century with an unusual lantern spire. The Catholic Cathedral Church of St Mary (1844) is a Pugin masterpiece.

The Tyne is spanned by a number of bridges, including the iconic semicircular iron Tyne Bridge of 1928 and Robert Stephenson's High Level Bridge of 1849. A welcome addition is the tilting Gateshead Millennium Bridge, connecting Gateshead on the south bank to Newcastle on the north. In common with many British cities recovering from the industrial slump, the waterfront has played an important part in the regeneration, and the thriving, cosmopolitan Newcastle-Gateshead quayside area is no exception.

# Canterbury

Situated on the River Great Stour and Watling Street, the Roman route from the coast to London, this ancient city is the seat of the Archbishop of Canterbury, Primate of All England and leader of the worldwide Anglican community. The great Cathedral has been the scene of many significant moments in British history, including the murder of Archbishop Thomas à Becket in 1170.

That infamous event made Canterbury – already England's most significant religious centre – a major medieval pilgrimage site, inspiring Geoffrey Chaucer to write his *Canterbury Tales* in 1387. Christ Church Cathedral, begun in the 7th century and constantly rebuilt and extended until early Norman times, is a breathtaking mixture of Perpendicular and Gothic architecture that is the impressive heart of a UNESCO World Heritage Site. The Cathedral remains a potent draw, attracting well over a million visitors every year (don't forget the crypt).

The small city of Canterbury was heavily bombed in World War II and was subsequently redeveloped. A wander round the partly pedestrianized historic walled centre therefore reveals a mix of old and not-always-pleasing new, though the overall impression is excellent, with a treasure trove of fine buildings and medieval delights at every turn. Part of the city's appeal lies in the number of workaday buildings that have survived, but there are notable monuments too.

The 12th century Eastbridge Hospital for pilgrims is still a Christian foundation, with visitors welcome. Fyndon's Gate is the surviving main entrance to the ruins of St Augustine's Abbey, part of the World Heritage Site – as is the 6th century Church of St Martin, said to be the oldest parish church in England that has been in constant use. Museums include the Sidney Cooper Gallery, Canterbury Royal Museum and Art Gallery (with The Buffs Regimental Museum) and Canterbury Roman Museum.

**POPULATION:**
42,000 (2001)
**WHEN TO GO:**
April to September for the better weather – but you'll never have the place to yourself.
**DON'T MISS:**
Ruined Canterbury Castle, constructed by King Henry I soon after the Norman Conquest – in an excellent park.
An historic river trip revealing fascinating parts of the old city that can be seen no other way – or simply stand on the bridges and enjoy views of old houses backing onto the river.
Greyfriars Chapel, an unusual 13th century structure spanning the river, which is built over the oldest Franciscan building in Britain – now housing a Franciscan exhibition.
A swift drink in the pub, though not just any pub – Simple Simon's is located in one of Canterbury's oldest and most interesting houses.
Medieval Misadventures – a re-creation of 14th century England in St Margaret's Church, focusing on characters from Chaucer's *Canterbury Tales*.
West Gate Museum, with an interesting historical display and a fine view up the High Street to the Cathedral.
**YOU SHOULD KNOW:**
The head of Sir Thomas More, executed by Henry VIII, is buried at St Dunstan's Church in Canterbury (his body stayed at the Tower of London).

*An aerial view of the Cathedral*

*Historic houses and shops on Elm Hill, one of the oldest streets in Norwich*

**POPULATION:**
128,000 (2005)
**WHEN TO GO:**
September, when the four-day Heritage Open Day programme sees a huge number of interesting properties opened for viewing.
**DON'T MISS:**
The Riverside Walk along the River Wensum, or even a boat trip to see the same sights.
Norwich Town Hall on the Market Square – love it or loathe it, you'll never see a better example of 1930s architecture.
The Forum, a striking modern building that replaced the old library, which burnt down in 1994 – if you go in winter, you'll find a small ice rink outside.
Dragon Hall, a beautifully restored medieval trading hall, said to be unique in England.
The Norman Foster-designed Sainsbury Centre for Visual Arts on the university campus, with its permanent collection and changing exhibitions in the underground gallery.
The Roman Catholic Cathedral of St John the Baptist – England's second-largest Catholic cathedral and a delicious feast of Victorian architecture.
**YOU SHOULD KNOW:**
The famous Norwich Canary was brought by Flemish refugees in the 1500s and bred intensively – now Norwich City Football Club's nickname is 'The Canaries'.

# Norwich

Norfolk's county town on the River Wensum bills itself as 'A Fine City', though 'An Ancient City' would be equally appropriate. Norwich was thriving when sacked by the Viking Sven Forkbeard in 1004. Despite the setback, it was one of the largest cities in England by the Norman Conquest. The Normans swiftly left their mark, building a cathedral on Tombland (the old Saxon market place), erecting a castle and establishing their own marketplace (still in use today, six days a week).

Although Norwich has spread far beyond its original boundaries, those were impressive in their time – medieval walls (large sections survive) enclosed an area larger than the City of London. Wool brought wealth, allowing construction of many fine churches – Norwich has more medieval churches than anywhere in Western Europe north of the Alps. The wool trade also saw an influx of Walloons and Huguenots, remembered at the aptly named Strangers Hall, one of their first bases.

The Industrial Revolution passed Norwich by, thanks to its remote East Anglian location. The centre was damaged by bombing in World War II but retains much of its former character. The castle is a dominant feature, and has been a museum since 1895. The cathedral, begun in the 11th century, dominates the city skyline – its spire is the second-tallest in England, after Salisbury. It also has England's only two-storey cloister and a thousand wonderful roof bosses. Many medieval buildings remain in the city centre, where exploration will reveal all sorts of quaint nooks and corners like the atmospheric Elm Hill or Cathedral Close.

Norwich really comes into its own as a shoppers' paradise, with two major malls (The Castle Mall and Chapelfields) plus the bustling Lanes area or the elegant Art Nouveau Royal Arcade.

# London

The United Kingdom's capital is one of the world's largest cities – a place redolent with history. London is a renowned global centre of business, finance and culture, with huge influence over international affairs.

It is also a major tourist destination, with four UNESCO World Heritage Sites (the Tower of London, Maritime Greenwich, the Royal Botanic Gardens at Kew and Westminster Abbey/Palace with St Margaret's Church). In addition, it has numerous iconic sights such as Buckingham Palace, Tower Bridge, Big Ben, the Houses of Parliament, the London Eye (ride it!), Nelson's Column in Trafalgar Square, St Paul's Cathedral, Marble Arch and Piccadilly Circus. There are a host of significant civic buildings, wonderful churches and magnificent Georgian and Victorian architecture.

The city was destroyed by the Great Fire of 1666, that began in Pudding Lane, so few earlier buildings remain. Extensive bomb damage was sustained in World War II, and piecemeal postwar development has resulted in mixed architectural styles that give London its special character. The original City of London, the financial district, is home to striking modern buildings, as is the Isle of Dogs beyond – formerly derelict dockland that now rivals the old City. Further east, massive regeneration was triggered by the award of the 2012 Olympic Games.

World-class cultural facilities include the British Museum, Natural History Museum, Science Museum, Victoria and Albert Museum, National Gallery, National Portrait Gallery, Tate Britain and Tate Modern. London is also the country's entertainment capital, with numerous theatres and concert halls. It's a retail therapist's paradise, too, as the West End (including Oxford Street and Regent Street) vies with classy Knightsbridge to offer the ultimate shopping experience. With endless choice of places to sleep, eat, drink and be merry only one question needs answering – "how much time can you spare?".

**POPULATION:**
7,700,000 (2007)
**WHEN TO GO:**
London is an all-year destination, but not at its best in the dreary winter months (November-March).
**DON'T MISS:**
Beautiful parks, including Regent's Park with its impressive zoo and Hyde Park with the slightly contentious Princess Diana Memorial.
A ride on the traditional open-platform London Routemaster red bus, now during the day only on heritage routes 9 and 15, or one of many sightseeing open-topped bus tours.
Shakespeare's Globe Theatre, a magnificent reconstruction on the South Bank of the River Thames.
A river trip down the Thames – from Westminster to Greenwich.
The Imperial War Museum – also responsible for *HMS Belfast*, a World War II cruiser moored near Tower Bridge.
Somerset House, a fine 18th century building fronting the river, with the Courtauld Institute of Art, Gilbert Collection and Hermitage Rooms.
**YOU SHOULD KNOW:**
It may not be true that the American who purchased London Bridge in 1962 to be rebuilt in Arizona thought he was buying Tower Bridge . . . but it's a good story!

*Big Ben and the Houses of Parliament seen through the London Eye.*

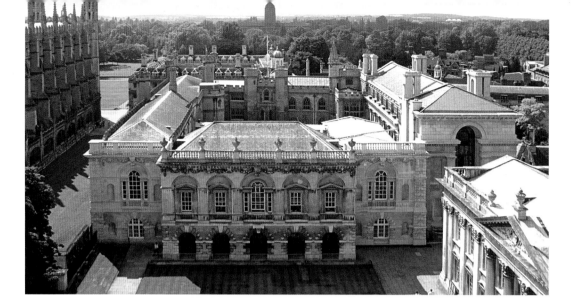

*King's College and the Senate House*

# Cambridge

This old Roman and Saxon settlement expanded under Viking rule from the 9th century, and William the Conqueror built a castle here in 1068, two years after arriving in England. But the fame of Cambridge rests on its ancient university, founded in 1209. The oldest college that still exists, Peterhouse, was formed in 1280. Its hall, dating from 1286, is the oldest university building in Cambridge.

The character of Cambridge – a city that has spread far beyond its original boundaries – is still set by magnificent medieval college buildings, including the landmark King's College Chapel, one of the finest Perpendicular religious structures in Britain (built between 1446 and 1515). The historic university quarter is seen at its best from The Backs, a scenic section of the River Cam. Because Cambridge has a large number of churches and college chapels, but no cathedral, it did not attain city status until 1951.

There are many good museums associated with the university, notably the Fitzwilliam in its grand neoclassical building, which has been described as 'the finest small museum in Europe'. The university's marvellous Botanic Garden has been open to the public since 1846 and displays over 8,000 plant species. Several colleges, including Christ's, Emmanuel and Clare have peaceful gardens.

Thanks to the university, this city full of impressive old buildings is also one of the most forward-looking in Britain, with a cutting-edge presence in the technologies of the future that has earned the nickname Silicon Fen for the Cambridge area.

Approximately one fifth of the city's population consists of students which – together with its popularity as a tourist destination – make Cambridge a very busy place, where the traditional student bicycles are usually a much swifter form of transport than the car.

# York

Recently expanded by boundary changes, York lies at the confluence of the Rivers Ouse and Fosse. This Roman settlement was subsequently occupied by Anglo-Saxons and Vikings. It remained an important religious and commercial centre throughout the Middle Ages, declining only when the Industrial Revolution passed it by.

This has proved a blessing, as York kept much of its medieval heritage, unlike many northern towns that were intensively redeveloped in the 19th century to serve the burgeoning needs of industry. York is therefore one of the most stunning medieval cities in England, reaping a huge tourist dividend as a result.

York Minster, seat of England's second Archbishop, is the largest Gothic cathedral in northern Europe. There has been a church on the site since the seventh century, though the cathedral was largely rebuilt from the 13th century. It was consecrated in 1472, serving as a reminder that the great cathedrals we so admire sometimes took several lifetimes to complete. Since then, York Minster has suffered several disastrous fires and renovation continues. Its Great East Window contains the largest expanse of medieval stained glass in the world.

The compact old city, enclosed by well-preserved gated walls that may be walked for excellent city views, is a delight to explore. A medieval centre has charming streets like the famous Shambles and numerous pedestrian alleys called snickelways. These often have eccentric names like Lady Peckett's Yard or Mad Alice Lane. York's Norman castle has been dismantled, but Clifford's Tower (a quatrefoil keep) remains atop the original motte and the site contains later buildings – courts, a former prison and an interesting museum. York has many old churches, mostly medieval, and a large number of pubs. For those into organized activities, one of York's many regular festivals is usually in progress.

**POPULATION:**
187,000 (2005)
**WHEN TO GO:**
The city is geared to visitors, but April to October is the best period when all the attractions are open.
**DON'T MISS:**
Barley Hall, a gem of a restored medieval house in Coffee Yard, a snickelway off Stonegate.
Eboracum Roman Bathhouse – fascinating remains with a café and restaurant.
Jorvik Viking Centre, an extraordinary recreation of York's Viking settlement on the site of archaeological excavations in Coppergate.
A stroll along the extensive waterfront, perhaps followed by a river cruise that reveals another facet of the city.
Merchant Adventurers' Hall, said to be Europe's finest medieval guildhall, containing a hospital and chapel in the undercroft with a magnificent timbered Great Hall above.
**YOU SHOULD KNOW:**
York's city gates are called bars, its streets are called gates and its bars are called public houses – you heard it here first.

*The east front of York Minster*

*Truro Cathedral*

# Truro

The only city in Cornwall, Truro is an historic centre of a mining industry that was a major feature of Cornish life since prehistoric times, with status as a Stannary town (where locally mined copper and tin were assayed and stamped). It also prospered as an inland port in medieval times, thanks to fishing and trade, with access via the Truro River to the broad River Fal estuary.

By the 18th century, Truro had become the town for wealthy merchants and mine owners, earning the nickname 'London in Cornwall'. Many fine Georgian houses were built, and many remain – Lemon Street and Walsingham Place contain excellent examples. Its importance increased in the second half of the 19th century with the arrival of the Great Western Railway, and Queen Victoria granted city status in 1876. Work on the first cathedral to be built in England since the Middle Ages began in 1880, though this ambitious Gothic Revival building was not completed until the early 1900s – but well worth the wait!

With the decline of both mining and fishing industries, Truro has remained prosperous, seamlessly moving on to the role of Cornwall's administrative centre, whilst maintaining its traditional appeal as a market town that serves as the shopping centre for a wide area of the surrounding countryside (some of which is an Area of Outstanding Natural Beauty). The city is a pleasing hive of activity, with a vast selection of shops and markets. It has also developed as a social centre, with numerous cafés, bars, bistros and restaurants, plus lively nightlife.

This is a delightful small city with good parks like Victoria Gardens (summer bandstand concerts), Boscawen Park beside the Truro River and Bosvigo Gardens with an exotic plant collection.

**POPULATION:**
21,000 (2001)
**WHEN TO GO:**
Everyone else visits in summer – join them or miss the tourist attractions.
**DON'T MISS:**
The Royal Cornwall Museum, Cornwall's oldest museum (founded in 1818) and a leading showcase for Cornish culture..
Lemon Quay piazza, hosting numerous events and serving as a magnet for visitors – with a Farmers' Market every Wednesday and Saturday and the city carnival in September.
The Old Assembly Rooms on the north side of High Cross, built in 1780 and now a bakery where the mandatory Cornish pasty may be purchased (delicious!).
A scenic river trip to Falmouth and back, with stops at Malpas, Trelissick, Tolverne and St Mawes.
**YOU SHOULD KNOW:**
Charles I set up his mint in Truro during the English Civil War, but had to make a rapid escape via Falmouth when the town fell to the Parliamentary Army.

# Bath

The City of Bath is founded around the only naturally occurring hot springs in the United Kingdom. It was first documented as a Roman spa in around 43 AD, although tradition suggests that it was founded earlier. The waters from its spring were believed to have medicinal properties. During the Roman period increasingly grand temples and bathing complexes were built around the springs, including the Great Bath. Rediscovered gradually from the eighteenth century onwards, they have become one of the city's main attractions. The Roman Baths Museum gives a fascinating insight into the Roman complex that was here – you can see the ruins of the 2,000 year old temple or drink the waters in the Pump Room. Part of the complex has recently been refurbished to provide a modern spa.

In the tenth century a monastery was founded at Bath, but the Abbey as it is today was not built until the sixteenth century. Medieval Bath was a prosperous wool-trading town, but it was not until the eighteenth century that Bath became the leading centre of fashionable life in England. It was during this time that Bath's Theatre Royal was built, as well as architectural triumphs such as the Royal Crescent, Lansdown Crescent, the Circus and Pulteney Bridge. Master of Ceremonies Beau Nash, who presided over the city's social life from 1705 until his death in 1761, drew up a code of behaviour for public entertainments.

Today Bath is known for its Georgian architectural gems which are still beautifully preserved. The Royal Crescent is a magnificent curve of Georgian houses built between 1767 and 1775, only a short walk from the Circus, a circle of 30 beautiful town houses. Many famous people have lived here, including David Livingstone and Clive of India.

**POPULATION:**
90,000 (2006)
**WHEN TO GO:**
Any time of year.
**DON'T MISS:**
The Roman baths
Museum of Costume
The Assembly Rooms
The Royal Crescent
Jane Austen Centre
Castle Combe
Lacock Abbey
**YOU SHOULD KNOW:**
The city is a UNESCO World Heritage Site.

*The Royal Crescent*

# Liverpool

**POPULATION:**
448,000 (2005)
**WHEN TO GO:**
August Bank Holiday (at the end of the month) for the Matthew Street Festival, Europe's largest free city centre music festival.
**DON'T MISS:**
The most iconic view in Liverpool – the Pierhead and city skyline with the soaring Liver Building at its centre, viewed from across the River Mersey (spectacular by night, too!).
Two wonderful 20th century cathedrals connected by Hope Street – Anglican Liverpool Cathedral (designed by Catholic Giles Gilbert Scott) and the Catholic Metropolitan Cathedral (original design by Anglican Sir Edwin Lutyens).
A trip on the Mersey Ferry (immortalized in the hit song *Ferry 'cross the Mersey* by Gerry and The Pacemakers).

This northern city is experiencing the sort of renaissance to be expected of a European Capital of Culture for 2008. Like so many British cities, Liverpool's dependence on traditional industries that declined sharply from the 1970s led to economic decay and social problems. However, that has now been reversed and Liverpool is experiencing rapid regeneration. Happily one thing never changes, and that's the legendary Liverpudlians – Scousers with sharp humour, irreverent attitudes and general disregard for authority, making this a lively place to be.

Liverpool is full of reminders of its maritime heritage, and the wealth generated thereby. The docks became a UNESCO World Heritage Site in 2004, and are fast becoming a centrepiece of city life. To show what can be achieved, Albert Dock's warehouses

*The Liver Building dominates the waterfront.*

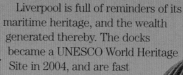

have been converted into shops, apartments, restaurants and bars, with accompanying attractions like the Beatles Story and Merseyside Maritime Museum.

In fact, Liverpool has more national museums and galleries than any other English city except London. The Walker Gallery has a great collection of Pre-Raphaelite paintings. Sudley House is a Victorian mansion housing the collection of ship owner George Holt. The comprehensive World Museum is worth a day in itself. Tate Liverpool has a wonderful modern art collection. The city's strong musical tradition is sustained by regular performances of both classical and popular music.

Some of Liverpool's Georgian architecture rivals that to be found anywhere (it has more Georgian houses than Bath), and there are more listed buildings than any other city in Britain, again with the exception of London. There is an abundance of public sculptures and impressive civic and commercial buildings, plus some splendid modern architecture like the Atlantic Tower Hotel, designed to resemble a ship's prow. Liverpool is rediscovering itself, and the experience is worth sharing.

The Williamson Tunnels Heritage Centre – the eccentric Joseph Williamson constructed a large network of apparently pointless underground tunnels in the early 19th century.
The Philharmonic Dining Rooms – mainly for the pleasure of inspecting the elaborate Victorian toilets, now a major tourist attraction!
**YOU SHOULD KNOW:**
The city celebrated its 800th birthday in 2007 (founded with letters patent granted by King John of Magna Carta fame).

# Brighton

**POPULATION:**
156,000 (2007)
**WHEN TO GO:**
Spring to autumn for the best weather,
though the city never sleeps.
**DON'T MISS:**
The Lanes, the only area retaining its
original layout after the French burned
Brighthelmstone in 1514 – once the
haunt of disreputable antique dealers,
now full of fashionable shops.
St Nicholas Church, the oldest surviving
building in Brighton, dating from around
1350 with a wonderful carved font.
A ride on the world's oldest operating
electric railway –
Volk's Electric Railway – along the
seafront from Palace Pier to Black Rock.
The Brunswick Estate, on the eastern
fringe of Hove – a speculative venture in
1825 that remains a fine example of the
Regency architecture so typical
of Brighton.
Preston Park, a typical Victorian city
park for those who wish to escape the
city scrum.
St Paul's Church in the city centre –
opened in 1848, the fourth
commissioned by vicar Henry Wagner
but the only one still in use as an
Anglican place of worship.
**YOU SHOULD KNOW:**
Before divorce laws were liberalized,
one of Brighton's many hotels was the
place to go to create grounds needed to
secure a divorce.

*Brighton Pier*

Brighhelmstone village emerged as a resort in the 18th century, gained cachet as Brighton when the Prince Regent gave his seal of approval, and took off after the railway arrived in 1841. In 2000, Brighton and Hove was granted city status as part of millennium celebrations. Today, this vibrant place lies at the heart of a sprawling coastal conurbation.

Helped by a large population of students, Brighton is beloved by the young and full of hotels, trendy shops, restaurants and entertainment facilities. This isn't the place for a beach holiday, though the shingle beach gets crowded when the sun shines. It is rather a place to have fun beside the sea – a fact appreciated by Londoners, for whom Brighton is one of the easiest seaside places to reach.

Brighton is forever symbolized by the Royal Pavilion, purchased by the town for £53,000 in 1849 after Queen Victoria decided she didn't need a seaside pleasure palace. The Pavilion was built on the site of a farmhouse rented by the Prince Regent (later George IV) on his first visit in 1786, as a place where he could take seawater for the gout and enjoy his liaison with Mrs Fitzherbert. The extraordinary Indian design was by John Nash and the building is open to the public – for a fee.

There are plenty of fine Regency terraces dating from this period, together with the fruits of Victorian building that created larger edifices like the Grand Hotel and extensive housing. Notable Victorian structures are Brighton's two piers. Brighton Pier (formerly Palace Pier) features arcades, restaurants and a funfair. The West Pier burned in 2003, and plans to replace it with the futuristic i360 observation tower have been approved. This is appropriate – the face of Brighton has constantly changed over the years, and the city is currently experiencing another phase of intensive development.

# Leeds

Situated on the River Aire, Leeds is fast becoming a 21st century success story. This city in West Yorkshire has been there before – it expanded throughout the Industrial Revolution, becoming a major manufacturing base. It suffered when its core industries went into decline, but has reinvented itself as a major financial and commercial centre.

This is an exciting modern city, with universities, wide-ranging cultural opportunities, prestigious festivals, wonderful shopping facilities, a huge variety of restaurants and vibrant nightlife. With good reason, Leeds has become a popular tourist destination, both in its own right and as an exciting base from which to sally forth into the beautiful Yorkshire countryside.

Exploring the city on foot is rewarding. There are plenty of highlights like the magnificent Town Hall, symbol of Victorian civic pride. See also the Grand Theatre, unspoiled City Varieties Music Hall, stunning shopping arcades in the Victoria Quarter, Kirkgate Market, the Corn Exchange, Park Square, Millennium Square, the Waterfront and much more. But the true beauty of Leeds is that it has a delightful mix of architecture old and new, representing the living history of a typical northern industrial town as well as anywhere.

There is a wide choice of things to do on a rainy (or even sunny!) day, for Leeds has excellent museums. The Royal Armories Museum in its striking modern building contains part of the national collection of weaponry moved from the Tower of London. Leeds Art Gallery has recently been completely renovated. Thwaite Mill Museum is a restored water-powered textile mill. Armley Mills Industrial Museum houses industrial machinery and railway locomotives. Abbey House Museum is in the gatehouse of Kirkstall Abbey (well-preserved ruins in the adjacent park) and features historical displays. The Thackray Museum in a former workhouse showcases medical history.

*The view up Woodhouse Lane to the Parkinson Building*

**POPULATION:**
443,000 (2001)
**WHEN TO GO:**
Try a winter break in December for the stunning Christmas Lights.
**DON'T MISS:**
Vast Roundhay Park, the Tropical World visitor attraction and the formal Canal Gardens.
Ride the historic Middleton Railway (the world's oldest) from Moor Road Station, and the scenic Settle-Carlisle line, easily accessed from Leeds Station.
The Henry Moore Sculpture Centre, for a stunning tribute to one of the city's favourite sons.
Harewood House, high on the list of England's finest stately homes – an award-winning visitor experience.
Temple Newsam House, an early 16th century gem with extensive gardens, Capability Brown grounds and a rare breeds farm.
St Anne's Cathedral – a unique Roman Catholic cathedral that is a fascinating example of the Arts and Crafts style.
**YOU SHOULD KNOW:**
Some of the world's first moving pictures were taken here by Louis le Prince in 1888.

# Winchester

**POPULATION:**
40,000 (2005)
**WHEN TO GO:**
April to September
**DON'T MISS:**
Winchester City Mill, a restored mill on the River Itchen, originally mentioned in the Domesday Book of 1086, rebuilt in 1744 and now grinding corn again.
Westgate, one of two surviving city gates, now a fascinating museum with unusual exhibits chronicling local life over the ages.
King Arthur's Round Table in Winchester Castle – actually a 12th century table, lavishly painted with the names of King Arthur and his knights by order of King Henry VIII.
Dean Garnier's Garden in Cathedral Close, on the site of the monastery dormitory.
**YOU SHOULD KNOW:**
Jane Austen moved to Winchester from nearby Chawton in 1817, but died that same year (aged just 41) and was buried in the Cathedral.

Historic Winchester is the county town of Hampshire – something of a comedown from its 10th and 11th century status as England's capital under King Alfred the Great of burnt cakes fame. Located at the western end of the South Downs and the pretty River Itchen runs through the city.

The city's glory is the magnificent Winchester Cathedral, begun in 1079 and with later additions. It housed the shrine of St Swithun and was an important pilgrimage centre (linked to Canterbury by the ancient Pilgrims' Way). The Cathedral Close contains many fine buildings, including the 13th century Deanery, timber-framed Cheyney Court (15th century) and Pilgrims' Hall, the earliest hammer-beamed building in England.

There are many other notable buildings. Winchester College has a 14th century gatehouse, cloister, courtyards, hall and magnificent chapel. Winchester Castle (actually its Great Hall only) dates from the 12th century and is home to a recreated medieval garden. Extensive Wolvesey Castle is a ruined Norman Bishop's Palace. The almshouses and great chapel of the Hospital of St Cross date from the early 12th century, and modern-day travellers can still request (and receive) a' wayfarer's dole' of bread and ale.

The compact city centre can easily be explored on foot and is

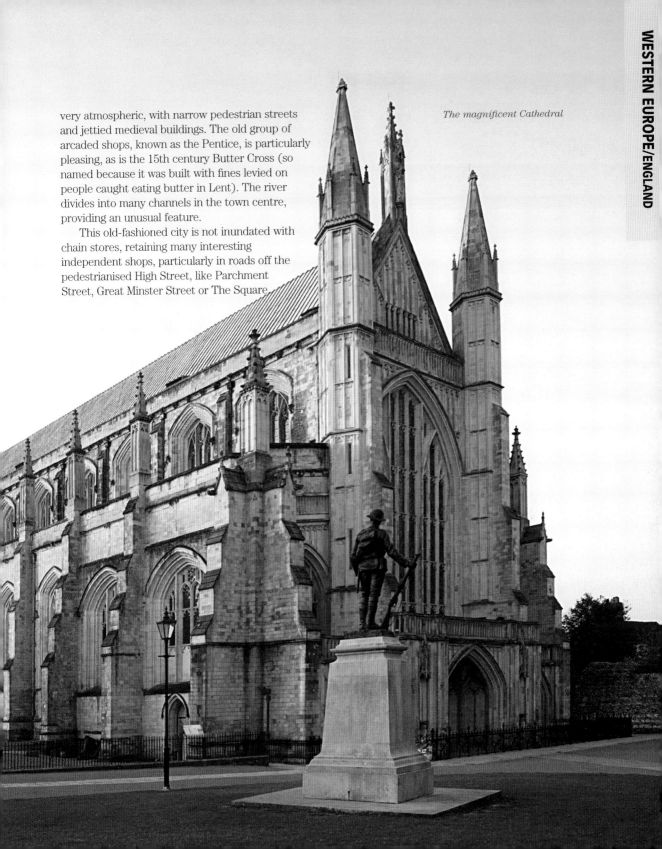

very atmospheric, with narrow pedestrian streets and jettied medieval buildings. The old group of arcaded shops, known as the Pentice, is particularly pleasing, as is the 15th century Butter Cross (so named because it was built with fines levied on people caught eating butter in Lent). The river divides into many channels in the town centre, providing an unusual feature.

This old-fashioned city is not inundated with chain stores, retaining many interesting independent shops, particularly in roads off the pedestrianised High Street, like Parchment Street, Great Minster Street or The Square.

*The magnificent Cathedral*

# Bristol

**POPULATION:**
398,000 (2005)

**WHEN TO GO:**
Summer is a good time to appreciate Bristol's waterside attractions.

**DON'T MISS:**
The Georgian House in Robert Adam's urban masterpiece, Charlotte Square – believed to be the very house where poets Wordsworth and Coleridge first met.
The Seven Stars public house, where anti-slavery campaigner Thomas Clarkson gathered information on Bristol's lucrative slave trade in the late 1700s.
Brunel's restored iron passenger ship SS *Great Britain*, now an award-winning attraction in the dock where she was originally built in 1843.
College Green, a public open space surrounded by interesting buildings, including Bristol's fine 12th century Cathedral.
The New Room, the oldest Methodist chapel in the world – built by the movement's founder John Wesley in 1739.
Bristol City Museum and Art Gallery, with an outstanding general collection in a fine building donated by the prominent local Wills tobacco family.

**YOU SHOULD KNOW:**
Master mariner John Cabot made his voyage of discovery on *Matthew* from Bristol to North America in 1497, financed by local merchants.

*The Brunel-designed Clifton Suspension Bridge*

Like other British port cities, Bristol experienced difficult times when its traditional role declined. The city's famous Floating Harbour on the River Avon fell out of use and commercial port activity moved to Avonmouth and Royal Portbury Dock on the estuary of the River Severn.

Bristol thrived from the 12th century as a port for Irish trade, but it was the 18th century 'triangle trade' that made the city's fortune (Bristol to Africa to pick up slaves, Africa to the Americas with the slaves, the Americas to Bristol with the fruits of slave labour like sugar, tobacco and cotton). Abolition of the slave trade in 1807 was a blow, but the city adapted and played a part in the Industrial Revolution. It is indelibly associated with the great engineer Isambard Kingdom Brunel, who designed the Clifton Suspension Bridge, built two pioneering iron steamships here and created the Great Western Railway between Bristol and London.

The wealthy residential areas like Clifton, where merchants chose to live, are still rich in the finest Georgian architecture, but the old city centre was destroyed by bombing in World War II and is now a park containing two ruined churches and fragmentary remains of Bristol Castle. The bomb-damaged areas were redeveloped with high-rise blocks, cheap modern architecture and an expanded road network. This process is slowly being reversed with road closures, the demolition of high rises and rebuilding of the Broadmead Shopping Centre. But happily, enough of Old Bristol has survived to retain a strong sense of the city's historic character.

With a large student population and strong commercial life, Bristol is a bustling city with lively street life that is reinventing itself for the 21st century, whilst also paying more attention to preserving a heritage that was, until quite recently, under threat.

# St David's

Britain's smallest city lies in the wild and beautiful Pembrokeshire Coast National Park – the rugged area where the patron saint of Wales was born around the year 500 and chose to establish a strict monastic order, which survived numerous Viking attacks. His birthplace and the cathedral built in his honour became an important medieval shrine, with two pilgrimages to St David's equalling one to Rome.

The idyllically situated St Non's Chapel, now a ruin, sits above the sea at St Non's Bay and according to legend marks the spot where St Non gave birth to David. It fell out of use after the Reformation, though the accompanying holy well continued to attract those in hope of a miracle. David is said to have been baptized at Porthclais, the nearby fishing harbour.

The large 12th century Cathedral with its squat tower nestles in a tree-lined hollow on the edge of this tiny city, which in truth is no larger than many villages. It has been repaired and renewed many times over the centuries, but remains a very special place with a wonderful interior. The bells (removed from the Cathedral in 1730 for fear the main tower would collapse) are housed in a detached former gateway known as the Tower Gate (Port-yr-Twr).

The Cathedral – with its active musical life and renowned choir drawn from the city's small population – hosts an annual music festival in May and June. Indeed, this is no lifeless monument, but remains at the very heart of community life.

The city – actually reaffirmed as such only in 1995 – doesn't take long to explore, but has various galleries and (though the Saint might not have approved) several pubs. It serves as a base for coastal walking and watersports in St Bride's Bay.

**POPULATION:**
2,000 (2001)
**WHEN TO GO:**
Spring or autumn to avoid crowds, and soak up the undisturbed essence of Welsh history and culture.
**DON'T MISS:**
An informative exhibition in the Tower Gate, that includes the Abraham Stone, the intricately carved Celtic memorial to an 11th century bishop killed in a Viking raid.
The early 16th century roof and wonderful Irish oak ceiling of the Cathedral nave.
The intricately carved misericords (folding seats) in the Cathedral choir stalls, showing that medieval craftsmen had a lively sense of humour . . . even in church.
The impressive tombs and effigies lining the Cathedral's aisles, including those of the important Bishop Henry Gower and Edmund Tudor, father of King Henry VII.
A boat trip to the RSPB's bird sanctuary on Ramsey Island, a mile off shore.
Whale and dolphin watching trips – nothing guaranteed, but there are frequent sightings of harbour porpoises, dolphins and several species of whale.
**YOU SHOULD KNOW:**
In Welsh, St David's becomes Tyddewi and the man himself is Dewi Sant.

*St. David's Cathedral*

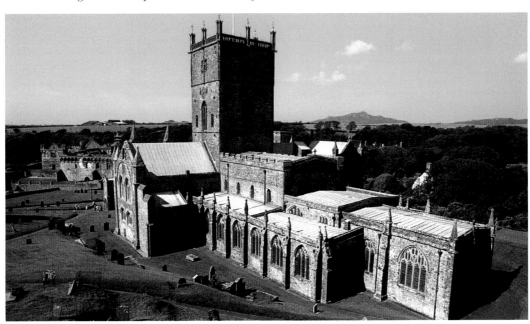

*The Welsh Assembly building*

# Cardiff

Until development of the South Wales coal industry from the beginning of the 19th century, Cardiff was a small coastal town with modest trading and fishing interests. That soon changed, with the town becoming a major port, a city in 1905 and capital of Wales in 1955.

Cardiff has expanded continuously for two centuries, and now includes extensive suburbs, which have contributed to social deprivation in the old inner-city working-class area in the south of the city. But Cardiff is the political, cultural, sporting and economic centre of Wales, and has recently experienced a significant (and ongoing) regeneration programme that aims to revitalize a somewhat run-down place.

It is succeeding. Sparkling modern architecture is springing up everywhere – just look at the Welsh Assembly, Wales Millennium Centre, Millennium Stadium or the extraordinary 'Tube', actually the Cardiff Bay Visitor Centre, where it's possible to see a scale model of the evolving city. These and other developments reinforce Cardiff's credentials as a vibrant modern city that's going places fast, and the energy is palpable.

But there's plenty of heritage for those who prefer more traditional attractions. Llandaff Cathedral has been a focal point since it was begun in the 12th century, and now sits at the heart of a peaceful conservation area close to the River Taff. Cardiff's splendid Catholic Cathedral dates from 1887. Cardiff Castle incorporates Roman remains, a Norman keep and lavish interiors created during 19th century refurbishment for the ultra-rich Marquis of Bute. He also donated the park named after him, adjacent to the castle, which is a large green area at the heart of the city.

Those of athletic bent may be interested in the Taff Trail, a scenic off-road cycleway connecting Cardiff to Brecon.

# Bangor

This city in Gwynedd is one of the smallest in the UK, seeming more like a sleepy market town, though it does have the longest main street in Wales. Half the population consists of students at the university, the other half speaks Welsh as a first or second language. The city's origins date back to the arrival of the Celtic Saint Deiniol early in the 6th century. He founded the monastic settlement that became the abbey that became the cathedral that gave Bangor its city status. The Cathedral – dating from the 12th century but much altered and extended since – remains the major focal point it has always been.

Bangor developed from sleepy village to bustling town when the post road to Holyhead arrived, and later when the Bethesda slate quarries opened. Tourism became important in the 19th century and Bangor became the most important town in North Wales, with a bustling quayside, busy railway junction and local industries like shipbuilding, sawmilling and foundry work. Today, physical evidence of that Victorian heyday remains, but the city is much quieter.

It is contained to the south by Bangor Mountain – actually a steep hillside that appears more imposing than its height should allow. It casts a shadow that means some areas of that long High Street are never bathed in winter sunlight. The city seems even smaller than it really is because a large proportion of the population live in a massive housing estate called Maesgeirchen (colloquially 'Maes-G'), separated from town by Bangor Mountain with but a single access road.

For the energetic, Bangor lies at the end (or beginning) of the 95-km (60-mi) North Wales Path, a long-distance walk that begins (or ends) at Prestatyn, providing some of the most dramatic coastal scenery imaginable.

**POPULATION:**
14,000 (2001)
**WHEN TO GO:**
July and August, for wonderful walks amidst great scenery and a student-free city.
**DON'T MISS:**
The panoramic views of the city, Menai Strait and island of Anglesey from the top of Bangor Mountain.
Bangor's long pier, one of the finest in Britain, saved from demolition in the 1970s and now fully refurbished.
The Norman Penrhyn Castle, containing a collection of early furniture and old master paintings.
Gwynedd Museum and Art Gallery, telling the story of Bangor and its people over the years – and a rattling good yarn it is.
A train ride to scenic Llanberis, beside its clear mountain lake – gateway to Snowdonia National Park.
Port Penrhyn east of town at the mouth of the River Cegin, still in use but no longer of the importance it enjoyed when the slate industry was in full swing.
**YOU SHOULD KNOW:**
The Beatles came to Bangor in 1967 to meet Maharishi Mahesh Yogi for the first time – and learned of manager Brian Epstein's death while they were here.

*Bangor Pier and port*

# Glasgow

**POPULATION:**
579,000 (2001)
**WHEN TO GO:**
During the warmer months – May to September – but be prepared for rain.
**DON'T MISS:**
Kelvingrove Art Gallery and Museum, on Argyle Street, opened in 1901 to house one of Europe's finest civic art collections.
The atmospheric Glasgow Necropolis, a cemetery containing an array of wonderful monuments and a huge statue of John Knox.
The extraordinary Burrell Collection, donated by a Glasgow shipping magnate, in a striking modern building in Pollok Country Park.
The Provand's Lordship in Castle Street, one of the few remaining medieval buildings, now a museum.

In the eternal rivalry between Scotland's two greatest cities, Glasgow in the wild west claims commercial superiority over Edinburgh in the elegant east. As a main hub for American trade, Glasgow prospered from the 18th century, going on to become a world leader in engineering and shipbuilding during the Industrial Revolution and earning the title 'Second City of the British Empire'.

Today, this sprawling city on the River Clyde has half the population it once boasted, thanks to slum clearances and the creation of overspill towns – a policy that has not been altogether successful. The decline of traditional heavy industries led to serious deprivation and urban decay, but a vigorous regeneration programme, beginning with Glasgow's status as a European Capital of Culture in 1990, turned the tide.

Historic Glasgow was focused on St Mungo's Cathedral, one of Scotland's few medieval churches, and the old High Street down

past Glasgow Cross intersection to the river. This fell into decay as the centre moved westwards. It is now bounded by the High Street, the river and the intrusive M8 motorway, based on a grid system. George Square is at the heart, surrounded by Scotland's most important retail area – Argyle, Buchanan and Sauchiehall Streets, sometimes known as 'The Golden Z'.

Most of Glasgow's cultural venues may be found in the centre of this monumental Victorian city, though the old town is being developed as a trendy Arts Quarter, with luxury apartments, warehouse conversions, cafés and restaurants. It hosts the annual Merchant City Festival. The city's better residential areas are to the west, as those who were able to get upwind of the industrial city moved outwards. Today, the West End is a bohemian area of cafés, bars and clubs, though it also contains some of the most expensive residential addresses in Scotland.

Glasgow School of Art in the Garnethill area – one of the most famous creations of favourite son Charles Rennie Mackintosh. GoMA (Gallery of Modern Art) – ironically housed in a fine 18th century building, it is a highly regarded and much-visited gallery.
**YOU SHOULD KNOW:**
Daniel Defoe of *Robinson Crusoe* fame called Glasgow 'the cleanest and beautifullest and best built city in Britain, London excepted'.

*The view from Queen's Park across the city*

# Aberdeen

**POPULATION:**
202,000 (2005)
**WHEN TO GO:**
June, July and August are the months
for those who like a little warmth on
their backs.
**DON'T MISS:**
The splendid view from Torry Battery,
an ancient defence site – over the
bustling harbour to the modern city,
with Old Aberdeen beyond.
Aberdeen Maritime Museum in the
delightful Shiprow, occupying the
House of Provost Ross (1593), telling
the long story of the city's
association with the sea.
A trip inland up the scenic Dee valley
to Balmoral, the Queen's summer
residence.
Fittie (or Footdee) – a charmingly
preserved fishing village at the
mouth of the Dee.
The city's three fine cathedrals – St
Andrew's (Episcopal), St Machar's
(Presbyterian) and St Mary's (Roman
Catholic).
Picturesque Brig o' Balgownie in Old
Aberdeen, the single-arch 14th
century bridge across the dark
waters of the River Don.
**YOU SHOULD KNOW:**
Aberdeen Heliport, serving the oil
industry, is the world's busiest
commercial heliport.

*The view out towards the
harbour and docks*

When it rains, Scotland's famous Granite City looks decidedly dour. When the sun shines, the Silver City with the Golden Sands positively sparkles. Either way, Aberdeen is always the Offshore Oil Capital, despite a gradual slowing of the North Sea oil bonanza.

In fact, this is a tale of two cities – Old Aberdeen and New Aberdeen, though today they are as one. Old Aberdeen was at the mouth of the River Don, New Aberdeen a fishing and trading settlement where the Denburn entered the Dee estuary. The turbulent history of Scotland surged around the city for centuries, culminating in looting after the Battle of Aberdeen in 1644, during the Scottish Civil War.

Today's fine city started taking shape in the 18th century, with further development like the extended harbour following in the 19th century. It has always been an industrial centre, but old industries such as textiles and papermaking have been replaced by oil. Despite industrial activity and modern development, Aberdeen remains an enchanting city, with a striking skyline and historic old town.

Old Aberdeen has vernacular houses and cobbled streets, together with grand monuments like the ancient university's King's College around its famous quadrangle. The High Street is delightful, and within a short walk are almost all the places of interest. The grand Union Street runs from Castle Street to the imposing Town House (town hall). The Marischal College is the second-largest granite building in the world. A wonderful Mercat Cross (market cross) was erected in 1686. Provost Skene's House (more like a mansion!) dates from 1545.

The city is famous for parks, gardens and extensive floral displays (it frequently wins the Britain in Bloom Best City award). It has a number of interesting museums and is a centre for the performing arts.

# Stirling

After the elegant grandeur of Edinburgh and monumental Victorian character of Glasgow, Scotland's smallest city is something completely different. Stirling is clustered around the medieval old town, beneath the commanding presence of one of Western Europe's largest and most important castles.

Once capital of the Kingdom of Scotland, the city is beside the River Forth, in a strategic location aptly described by its nickname – 'Gateway to the Highlands'. It consequently featured in almost all the conflicts that raged through Scotland, with the last of several local battles being fought in 1648, within the town itself, during the Scottish Civil War. It saw further action in the Jacobite rebellion.

The castle stands on top of Castle Hill, a volcanic crag, surrounded on three sides by steep cliffs that made it hard to attack. Most of its buildings date from the 15th and 16th centuries, though there are older elements. The Palace block, begun by James IV and completed by James V, has fine stonework, and the recently restored Great Hall of James IV has two magnificent oriel windows. In 1543, Mary Queen of Scots was crowned at Stirling Castle.

Close by the castle is the Church of the Holy Rood, surrounded by monumental graves. It is one of Scotland's finest medieval parish churches, mercifully escaping the wholesale destruction heaped on Scottish churches in the Reformation. The infant son of Mary Queen of Scots was crowned here in 1567, as James VI.

The old town beneath the castle, called Top o' the Town by locals, is full of character. Noteworthy buildings include Argyl's Lodgings, a wonderful example of a 17th century town house and the 19th century Old Town Jail that replaced the notorious Tolbooth Gaol, which still stands. The Smith Art Gallery is a showcase for local history.

*The Wallace Monument*

**POPULATION:**
41,000 (2001)
**WHEN TO GO:**
Summer, when the attractions are open and Stirling provides the perfect starting point for a raid into the Highlands.
**DON'T MISS:**
The wonderful stone façade of Mars Walk, a Renaissance town house commissioned by the Earl of Mar around 1570.
A trip out to Inchmahome Island with its priory, once a retreat for Mary Queen of Scots.
The National Wallace Monument, completed in 1869 on Abbey Craig, just north of the city, in honour of the legendary Braveheart.
Cambuskenneth Abbey, beside the river just outside town – an historic 12th century ruin.
Bannockburn Heritage Centre, to find out all you need to know about the famous battle in 1314, when Robert the Bruce thrashed the larger English army.
**YOU SHOULD KNOW:**
Warwolf, the largest trebuchet (siege engine) ever made, was used by Edward I of England to breach the walls of Stirling Castle in the 13th century.

# Edinburgh

In the eternal rivalry between Scotland's two greatest cities, Edinburgh in the elegant east claims cultural superiority over Glasgow in the wild west. The nation's capital and seat of the Scottish Parliament sits beside the Firth of Forth. This dramatic city has a rugged location and huge collection of wonderful old buildings. The Old and New Town districts are a UNESCO World Heritage Site, attracting some thirteen million visitors a year, who rarely feel the need to stray far from the historic centre into the wider city beyond.

As a centre of the 18th century Age of Enlightenment, Edinburgh was nicknamed 'Athens of the North', also earning the soubriquet Auld Reekie for its belching chimneys and insanitary living conditions. Historic Edinburgh is divided by Princes Street Gardens, reclaimed in the early 19th century from boggy land that was once a finger of the loch.

To one side Edinburgh Castle perches on its volcanic crag, with the Old Town trailing down the ridge. The medieval plan is preserved and many buildings date from the 16th and 17th centuries. The Royal Mile leads away from the castle. There are market squares and squares surrounding major structures such as St Giles Cathedral, begun in the 12th century. The Law Courts, McEwan Hall, Surgeons' Hall and Royal Museum of Scotland are also noteworthy.

On the other side of Princes Gardens is the New Town, an 18th century response to overcrowding in the constricted Old Town. It started life to a grid design, around George Street, Princes Street and Queen Street, but soon expanded in a less structured manner to become a splendid example of Georgian architecture and planning. Robert Adam's Charlotte Square is considered by many to be the finest Georgian square in the world. It contains Bute House, the residence of Scotland's First Minister.

**POPULATION:**
449,000 (2001)
**WHEN TO GO:**
Spring to autumn, omitting August unless you specifically want to experience the Edinburgh Festival buzz.
**DON'T MISS:**
The Mound, an artifical hill that is now home to both the 19th century Royal Scottish Academy and National Gallery of Scotland.
The former Royal Yacht Britannia, moored behind the Ocean Terminal shopping centre at Edinburgh's port, Leith.
Holyroodhouse, the ancient palace of Kings and Queens of Scotland, now the British monarch's official Scottish residence.
A wonderful panoramic view of the city from the top of Arthur's Seat in Holyrood Park.
Calton Hill, a viewpoint topped by various structures including a Nelson momument, observatories and the unfinished mini-Parthenon known as 'Edinburgh's disgrace'.
The Gothic monument to romantic author Sir Walter Scott in Princes Street Gardens – with a viewing platform reached by 287 spiral steps.
**YOU SHOULD KNOW:**
There are three 'Hearts of Midlothian' – the Walter Scott novel, one of the city's football clubs and a cobbled pavement mosaic in the Royal Mile.

*Belfast City Hall*

# Belfast

Northern Ireland's principal city is situated on the east coast, at the end of Belfast Lough beside the River Lagan, surrounded by scenic hills. If ever a place benefited from the end of troubled times, it's Belfast – capital of Northern Ireland since partition in 1920 and seat of Ulster's new power-sharing government. In the 17th century, settlement of English and Scottish incomers for political reasons divided the population of the north into native Catholics and immigrant Protestants (the majority), leading ultimately to the partition of Ireland in 1920 and subsequent violent Troubles. But the recent 'peace dividend' has seen decades of stagnation end and rapid regeneration begin.

The sort of developments that are transforming the city include the Cathedral Quarter (centred on St Anne's Cathedral and becoming Belfast's main tourist and cultural area), the circular Waterfront Hall and Odyssey complex beside the river, Victoria Square and the soaring Obel Tower. The ill-fated Titanic was built at Harland and Wolff's shipyard, but only the Irish would call the revitalized locality 'The Titanic Quarter'.

Whilst lacking Dublin's Georgian splendour, Belfast has imposing Victorian and Edwardian buildings like the grand City Hall, copied throughout the British Empire. There are two splendid bank buildings (the Northern Bank and Ulster Bank). The Royal Courts of Justice building is very impressive. It is also a city of parks, notable among them the Botanic Gardens containing the Palm House, one of the earliest cast-iron glasshouses ever built (1840).

Belfast is the newly self-confident commercial and educational hub of Northern Ireland, and it is a city going places in a hurry. For all that, the inner city is still divided by 'peace lines' erected at the start of the Troubles in the late 1960s, dividing Unionist and Nationalist areas – old memories die hard.

**POPULATION:**
277,000 (2001)
**WHEN TO GO:**
Now a popular all-year-round weekend break destination, Belfast looks its best in summer.
**DON'T MISS:**
The vast Sir Thomas and Lady Dixon Park, to the south of the city, with a stunning rose garden containing over 20,000 blooms in season.
Striking Unionist and Nationalist murals painted on the gable ends of houses, before they all fade and vanish.
Samson and Goliath, the twin shipbuilding gantry cranes at the dry dock and repair yard on Queen's Island.
The National Trust-owned Crown Liquor Saloon in Great Victoria Street for a genuine reminder of Old Ireland.
Belfast Castle in Cavehill Country Park, offering far-reaching views of Belfast Lough and the city.
The Lagan Weir, a major engineering work beside the old Customs House, completed in 1994 to control the level of the river.
**YOU SHOULD KNOW:**
The oldest daily newspaper in the world is Belfast-based – *The News Letter*, first published in 1737.

# Londonderry

The old walled city of Londonderry (Derry to its large Catholic population and by general usage) is on the west bank of the sinuous River Foyle (City Side), though the modern city has spread to the other bank (Waterside). The Nationalist Bogside area – scene of so many dramatic events during Northern Ireland's sectarian Troubles, is just outside the city walls. Those walls were completed in 1618, to a defensive plan of a central diamond within a walled city with four gates, a layout that remains today. The four gates are Butcher's, Bishop's, Shipquay and Ferryquay, each at the end of one of the city's main streets. The soaring Gothic St Columb's Cathedral (Church of Ireland) dates from slightly later (1633).

Today's walled city has a pleasing mix of Georgian, Victorian and Edwardian buildings, many of which are being restored. Though there are some rather indifferent modern structures throughout the city, often erected hastily after bomb damage, Derry has some wonderful modern architecture too – like the 1970s church on Steelstown Road, the Collon Bar, Creggan Country Park and technology pavilions on the University of Ulster's Magee Campus with its contrasting neo-gothic magnificence.

Old-fashioned character is likely to become Derry's salvation. After becoming run-down during the Troubles, a process accelerated by the collapse of traditional industries like shirt making, the city is seeking to reinvent itself as an important tourist destination. It already serves as the shopping focus for the isolated north west, with two large malls and a host of smaller shops. The new City Hotel has recently opened and it is intended that the famous walls should become a world-renowned tourist attraction. Close to the sea, full of character and surrounded by breathtaking natural beauty, Londonderry will surely succeed in that objective.

**POPULATION:**
84,000 (2001)
**WHEN TO GO:**
Summer for impossibly romantic misty mountains.
**DON'T MISS:**
Various interesting museums like the Workhouse Museum, Harbour Museum, Tower Museum and Foyle Valley Railway Centre.
A visit to Austin's, the world's oldest independent department store (established 1830), located in the central diamond.
The Amy Earhart Centre at Ballyarnet, just north of Derry, where the pioneering 1930s American pilot landed in Ireland.
A trip up the Faughan Valley to Ness Wood to see Ulster's highest waterfall, and enjoy peaceful nature trails.
The original keys of the city, now kept in St Columb's Cathedral, used by the legendary Protestant Apprentice Boys to bar the city to approaching Catholic forces in 1688.
**YOU SHOULD KNOW:**
Derry is nicknamed 'The Maiden City' because the walls were never breached.

*The walled city of Londonderry*

# Andorra la Vella

**POPULATION:**
22,000 (2004)
**WHEN TO GO:**
Winter, for the superb skiing, or any time for duty-free shopping.
**DON'T MISS:**
The striking modern Caldea with its soaring spike, for a thorough pampering – it's Europe's largest spa with all sorts of water-based treats.
A night time stroll along the illuminated Rec del Solà and Rec de l'Obac walkways, starting from Col.legi Sant Ermengol Road and Tarragona Avenue respectively.
La Margineda Bridge – a wonderful medieval structure counterpointed by a striking sculpture by Valencian sculptor Andreu Alfaro.
The rather dourly named Government Exhibition Hall, which stages a rolling programme of exhibitions and displays.
The shop-till-you-drop streets of Avinguda de Meritxell and Avinguda del Princep Benlloch.
**YOU SHOULD KNOW:**
Andorra didn't actually acquire a formal democratic constitution until 1993.

This is the land time almost forgot. Andorra la Vella is the capital city of the principality of Andorra, high in the eastern Pyrenees between France and Spain. As the name suggests – it means 'Andorra the old' – this was a settlement in late Neolithic times and the principality was created as an independent state by Charlemagne back in the 8th century. But until recently Andorra remained a feudal fiefdom, isolated from mainstream European life. The Madriu-Perafita-Claror Valley is a World Heritage Site, representing traditional pastoral life in the high Pyrenees.

But post-World War II development has created a modern city in the mountains – one that swiftly grew to absorb the surrounding villages of Santa Coloma, Escaldes and Engordany. It is very apparent how the principality makes its money as a tax haven and tourist destination, with a preponderance of commercial buildings and hotels, plus endless opportunities for duty-free shopping. Of greater visual interest is the surrounding scenery. Andorra la Vella lies at the confluence of three rushing mountain streams – the Gran Valira, Valira del Oriente and Valira del Norte – and is set beneath towering snow-capped peaks that are a winter skiing paradise.

However, the old town of Andorra la Vella (the Barri Antic) does contain some interesting cobbled medieval streets and characterful stone buildings, the most impressive of which is the early 16th century Casa de la Vall, used since 1707 as the principality's state house, parliament and sole court. The oldest building in the city is the Santa Coloma Church (9th century, with a 12th century tower). The 11th century Romanesque Church of Sant Esteve with its 13th century paintings is at the heart of the picturesque old town (which was, in truth, never much more than a large village).

*The 11th century Church of St Esteve*

# Barcelona

The second largest city in Spain and capital of Catalonia, Barcelona is situated on the Mediterranean coast and makes a vibrant and exciting place to visit. The Barri Gòtic (Gothic Quarter in Catalan) is the splendid mediaeval centre of the old city of Barcelona, including the well-known Las Ramblas. Many of the buildings date from medival times, others from as far back as the Roman settlement of Barcelona. Catalan Modernisme architecture (known as Art Nouveau in the rest of Europe), developed between 1885 and 1950 and left an important legacy in Barcelona. Many of these buildings are World Heritage Sites. Especially remarkable is the work of architect Antoni Gaudí (1852–1926), which can be seen throughout the city.

The most famous of Gaudí's domestic works, the Casa Milà is an apartment block whose undulating façade was inspired by the rock face of Catalonia's sacred mountain. It was nicknamed La Pedrera ('the quarry') by the Barcelonese of the time when it was built (1905–1907), who considered it ugly.

It is Gaudí's church, however, that is perhaps his greatest achievement. From 1884 La Sagrada Família became Gaudí's obsession which he worked on for 40 years and is still unfinished today. It has four spires, each of them topped with coloured ceramics, and stone porches that look as though they are made of dripping wax. Other Gaudí works include the Casa Batlló and the Palau and Park Güell. Other UNESCO World Heritage Sites in Barcelona are Lluis Domènech i Montaner's Palau de la Música Catalana and Hospital de Sant Pau.

Barcelona has a wide variety of museums to visit. The National Museum of Art of Catalonia possesses a well-known collection of Romanesque art, while the Fundació Joan Miró, Picasso Museum and Fundació Antoni Tàpies hold important collections of works by these world-renowned artists. The city has several history and archaeology museums, such as the City History Museum, the Museum of the History of Catalonia, the Archaeology Museum of Catalonia and the Barcelona Maritime Museum.

*Looking out over the Barri Gòtic (Gothic Quarter)*

**POPULATION:**
1,670,000 (2006)
**WHEN TO GO:**
Any time of year.
**DON'T MISS:**
Palau and Park Güell – the mansion was designed by Gaudi for industrial tycoon Eusebi Güell to entertain his high-society guests. The park was also designed by Gaudi who, in this instance, took his inspiration from English gardens, hence the name 'Park'. From here, there are stunning views of Barcelona and the Bay.
Palau de la Música Catalana – this concert hall was built in the Catalan Modernisme style between 1905 and 1908 and is now a UNESCO World Heritage Site.
Picasso Museum
La Sagrada Família - Gaudi worked on this incredible, unfinished Roman Catholic Basilica for 40 years, famously joking "my client is not in a hurry!"
**YOU SHOULD KNOW:**
Las Ramblas comes alive in the evenings with street performances.

*The two cathedrals dominate the skyline.*

# Salamanca

Close to Portugal, Salamanca is built in glowing local Villamayor stone, earning the nickname of 'The Golden City'. It has the distinction of being a UNESCO World Heritage Site and was a European Capital of Culture in 2002. As with so many well-preserved Spanish cities, Salamanca is notable for the number of splendid early churches.

But the city's special claim to fame is the university, founded in 1218, contributing to the city's reputation as the place where the purest Spanish is spoken. It continues to play an important part in city life, economically and socially, with some 40,000 students ensuring that there are plenty of lively cafés, bars and affordable restaurants. As they come from many countries to learn that 'pure' Spanish, Salamanca is a cosmopolitan place, reinforced by the fact that tourism is its major industry.

The Plaza Mayor is the place to see and be seen at one of the pavement café tables – it was built in the 18th century and was once used for bullfighting; it is one of the finest squares in Spain, situated in the centre of the compact old town. It is also serves as an excellent base for exploration. Many of the city's best monuments may be found in the surrounding streets.

Look in particular for the Iglesia de la Purisma, the Monastery of St Ursula, the Capucin Church, the College of the Archbishop of Fonseca and – last but not least – the outstanding 16th century Monasterio de los Irlandeses, with its magnificent Renaissance court. Other notable monasteries and convents may be found in the Cathedral area. The Old Romanesque Cathedral was founded in the 12th century and has an amazing dome. The adjoining New Cathedral in Gothic style was begun in 1549 but not finally completed until the 18th century.

**POPULATION:**
160,000 (2005)
**WHEN TO GO:**
Spring or autumn – winters are sharp, summers scorching.
**DON'T MISS:**
The House of Shells, a 15th century mansion studded with the shells that represented the Order of St James, a fusion of Gothic and Moorish architecture.
One of the best-preserved Roman bridges in Spain, El Puente Romano over the River Tormes.
A stroll around the university quarter, for some wonderful facades in the ornate Spanish plateresque architectural style of the 15th and 16th centuries.
The museo Casa Lis, an outstanding example of early 20th century modernist architecture, now a much-visited tourist attraction.
St Esteban's Church, with a highly decorated façade and 17th century gilded high altar.
The Central Market, next to the Plaza Mayor, for bustling insight into all that's best in local life.
**YOU SHOULD KNOW:**
Salamanca is old – Hannibal (with or without his elephants) besieged the place in the third century BC.

# Málaga

It sometimes seems that everyone who's off to sunny Spain finishes up in Málaga, if only because they arrive at its busy international airport, entry point to the Costa del Sol – one of the planet's most popular tourist destinations. With an excellent climate, beautiful Mediterranean beaches and pulsing nightlife, that's perfectly understandable. But for those interested in such things, a closer look reveals that there was life before high-rise tourism.

Málaga has a long history of occupation and conquest – by Phoenicians, Romans, Visigoths, Moors and finally Christian Spain, also suffering damage in the Spanish Civil War. Its modern face is that of an intensely developed port city very much geared to commerce and servicing the needs of fun-loving tourists – a hub that has become a serious rival to Andalucia's official capital, Seville.

Yet there are plenty of reminders of Malaga's past. The old town behind the harbour has atmospheric little streets, squares and monuments, with a lively café culture and excellent boutique shopping. The main square (Plaza de la Constitución) is a focal point, as is the wonderful tree-lined Avenida and pedestrianized main street, Calle Marqués de Larios. Cheek by jowl is the imposing 11th century Moorish Alcazaba Fortress (now an archaeological museum), standing above a largely complete Roman amphitheatre. On an adjoining hill the Moorish Gibralfaro Castle has sweeping city views. The imposing Baroque Cathedral is missing a bell tower, earning the nickname La Manquita (one-armed woman). In honour of this and more, Málaga has bid to become a European Capital of Culture in 2016 – Viva Málaga!

Pablo Picasso (full name Pablo Diego José Francisco de Paula Juan Nepomuceno Maria de los Remedios Cipriano de la Santisima Trinidad Clito Ruiz y Picasso) was born here in 1881, and his birthplace is now a museum.

*Sunset over Málaga*

**POPULATION:**
558,000 (2006)
**WHEN TO GO:**
Summer for tourist action, spring and autumn for a less frenetic experience.
**DON'T MISS:**
The atmospheric crypt and fine tombs at the Baroque Santuario de la Virgen de la Victoria church.
A trip into the interior to explore some of the unspoiled villages that provide an authentic taste of traditional Andalucia, like Ojén (car hire is cheap).
The Official Málaga Bus Tour, a trip lasting one and a half hours that takes in all the best local sights.
The wonderful botanical gardens (Jardines de la Conception) on the outskirts of the city.
The Colosseum-like circular bullring, incongruously surrounded by modern high-rise blocks.
**YOU SHOULD KNOW:**
Film star Antonio Banderas often turns up for the Semana Santa, the colourful Holy Week Festival that he has been attending since childhood.

# Segovia

*El Alcázar*

The historic heart of Segovia is a UNESCO World Heritage Site, and it is easy to see why. This compact hill-top city is old Spain and Castille at its very best, with narrow pedestrian streets, intriguing alleys rich with the aromas of regional cooking and Europe's highest concentration of Romanesque churches. Around it all is a city wall with towers and gates, bordered by two rivers and a girdle of trees offering peaceful, shaded walks. And that's before mentioning the impressive Alcázar castle and famous aqueduct.

This is a place to soak up the atmosphere of historic Spain. The elongated Alcázar, rising from its rocky crag above the city and looking almost like a giant stone ship, sits on Roman and Moorish foundations. It was built, extended, altered and restored over many centuries of use successively as royal residence, prison and artillery school. Today, it is one of the most popular historical sights in Spain.

Another is the astonishing double-arched Roman aqueduct, rising to a height of 28.5 m (93.5 ft) in the pedestrianised Azoguejo Square, where it is at its most impressive – though this is but the climax to an ingenious irrigation system stretching into the mountains that still carries water today.

Segovia has wonderful churches. The late Gothic Cathedral with its dominant tower stands at the city's highest point, and has a richly decorated interior. The Church of St Martin is surrounded by a beautiful atrium and has a 12th century marble relief of its saint. San Juan de los Caballeros with its striking interior carving was the church of choice for Segovia's noble families.

Luckily, there are dozens of pavement cafés, restaurants and interesting shops for those who need a break from sightseeing, which can be quite exhausting in this most enchanting of cities.

# Cádiz

**POPULATION:**
131,000 (2007)
**WHEN TO GO:**
Summer, for the beautiful beaches and relaxed atmosphere that characterizes open-air Cádiz.
**DON'T MISS:**
The spectacular late 17th century Admiral's House, built from the considerable profits of the lucrative trade Cádiz enjoyed with the Americas.
An almost complete Roman theatre in the El Pópulo barrio, discovered by chance after a warehouse fire and said to be the second-largest known after that at Pompeii.
Candelaria Fortress, constructed in the 17th century to command the seaward approach to the city, now a convention centre.
A pair of extraordinary electricity pylons on either side of the bay, looking for all the world like modern sculptures.
The 1812 Monument in Plaza de España, a new square created between 1912 and 1929 to celebrate the liberal constitution proclaimed in Cádiz in 1812.
**YOU SHOULD KNOW:**
La Playa de la Caleta, the Old Town's popular beach, stood in for Cuba in the James Bond movie *Die Another Day* (but then Cádiz is twinned with Havana!).

A major port in south-western Spain, Cádiz is said to be the second-oldest continuously inhabited city in western Europe, since settlement by Phoenicians around the 10th century BC. The city has an unusual location – on a narrow island jutting out into the Bay of Cádiz, beyond another island that connects to the mainland. When approached from the sea, the ancient city presents a dramatic picture that Sir Francis Drake would still recognize from his hostile visit in 1587, when he torched part of the Spanish fleet in the harbour (though failing to take the fortified town).

The oldest part, within the remains of medieval walls, is called Casco Antiguo (Old City) – a warren of ancient quarters (barrios), including La Viña, Santa Maria and El Pópulo. Here, winding alleys connect with compact squares. Newer parts of the city have wide avenues and grander buildings, though further development is constrained by its physical location. Cádiz is gradually losing population and seems somewhat careworn.

Notable buildings include the landmark cathedral with its golden cupola, that took more than a century to build, starting in 1776, and this delay resulted in a mixture of architectural styles. The late Victorian Grand Theatre is built in a Moorish revival style that seems appropriate – Cádiz as a whole has a slightly Moorish feel. The old Town Hall is a fine neo-classical structure started in the early 19th century. The Tavira Tower is a reminder of the time when hundreds like it existed, from which merchants watched the sea for the return of their richly laden ships.

Cádiz Carnival, centred around Shrove Tuesday, is the people's fiesta, when everyone dons masks and fancy dress and has a riotous time. This is definitely the most dazzling carnival in mainland Spain, famous for amusing figures, satirical songs and general mayhem.

*The view from the beach in Cádiz*

# San Sebastián

Also known by its Basque name of Donostia, San Sebastián is on the southern coast of the Bay of Biscay. With a picturesque location and excellent town beaches, it is Spain's most fashionable seaside resort.

Most of the city dates from the 19th century and it is an elegant place without garish trimmings, curled around a horseshoe bay that contains the rocky isle of Santa Clara with its lighthouse and quay, a popular summer playground. In the bustling Parte Vieja (Old Town), tamarisk-shaded Almeda de Calvo Sotelo is at the heart of city life, with its cafés, shops and restaurants. At one end is the quaint fishing harbour and town hall (formerly a casino), from whence the green Parque-Alderti-Eder leads to the curving beachfront. The more energetic can continue past the royal bathing pavilion and take the funicular up Mount Igueldo, with its slightly down-market attractions.

The dominant Cathedral spire is a pointer to the New Town. The Cathedral itself is an imposing late Victorian edifice. Another noteworthy building is the Palacio de la Diputación, with an array of busts on the façade and pictures by local artist Ignacio Zuloaga within. Back in the Old Town, the fish market and arcaded plaza that was once used as a bullring are worth a visit, as is the early 16th century St Vincent's Church, the oldest in town.

The Kursaal Bridge over the Urumea River leads to another wonderful beach, recently artificially extended, and a seaside promenade that runs to Mount Ulia, almost 8 km (5 mi) away. The city has at least one fiesta in each month of the year, and there are half a dozen museums for the culturally inclined. But in truth, San Sebastián is a place for those who wish to enjoy the most refined of seaside holidays.

*The famous horseshoe bay at twilight*

**POPULATION:**
183,000 (2005)
**WHEN TO GO:**
The Spanish establishment heads for San Sebastián en masse in high summer, so for breathing space visit in late spring or early autumn.
**DON'T MISS:**
Magnificent views of city, sea and Basque uplands from the observation tower on Mount Igueldo.
The 18th century Baroque St Mary's Church, with a richly decorated exterior and wonderful, painted altarpiece.
From St Mary's, the stepped path up Mount Urgill, atop which is the Castillo de la Motta, with a chapel crowned by a large statue of Christ.
The city museum and library in the 16th century former convent of San Telmo.
A wallet-busting stroll round Paseo de Muelle, the best shopping area in the city.
**YOU SHOULD KNOW:**
In 1813 British and Portuguese troops expelled the occupying French, lost control and burned the unfortunate anti-French, pro-British city to the ground.

*The Alhambra Palace*

# Granada

**POPULATION:**
237,000 (2005)
**WHEN TO GO:**
Spring and autumn when the days
are warm and sunny, and the
temperature is perfect.
**DON'T MISS:**
Sacromonte, a hill overlooking the
city from the north, where Granada's
large gypsy community once
inhabited cave dwellings and now a
centre for traditional flamenco
dancing.
The Bib-Rambla quarter for an open-
air meal, before exploring the narrow
street of the Arab bazaar that runs to
the Cathedral.
Granada Cathedral itself, Spain's
finest Renaissance-style church –
started in 1529, continued for nearly
200 years and never completed (no
spires!).
The Charterhouse, a Carthusian
monastery founded in 1506 – a fine
example of Spanish Baroque
architecture, with an extensive
picture collection on view.
The 8th/9th century Bermejas Towers
– strong points on the walls
surrounding the Alhambra.
The Archaeological Museum of
Granada in Castril Palace, in the old
Arab area of Ajsaris favoured by the
city's Renaissance grandees.
**YOU SHOULD KNOW:**
The city's first bishop and patron
saint, Cecilio, is said to have been
martyred in the ancient catacombs
under Sacromonte Abbey.

This distinctive city at the foot of the Sierra Nevada Mountains has
been a settlement since the dawn of time, but is forever associated
with the period when it was under Moorish rule (8th to 15th
centuries, in 1492 it became the last enclave to be retaken by the
Catholic Spanish monarchy). The reason may be summarized in two
words – the Alhambra. This amazing hilltop palace and fortress
complex above the city, begun in the 13th century, tells the story of
Moorish presence in southern Spain – arriving as warlike conquerers
and departing as sophisticated aesthetes. The Alhambra is stunning
– though constantly altered and abused in subsequent centuries, it
remains an awe-inspiring monument to the distinctive local brand of
Islamic culture and craftsmanship that reached incomparable
heights in Granada.

The Alhambra shares the distinction of being a UNESCO World
Heritage Site with two more wonderful legacies of the long-lasting
Moorish presence – the nearby Palace of Generalife (summer
residence of the Moorish rulers) and the old casbah of Albaicín, a
maze of narrow streets with whitewashed houses and a wonderful
view of the Alhambra on the facing hill from St Salvador's Church
which – like so many in the city – is built on the site of an earlier
mosque. Granada has the largest extant collection of Moorish
buildings in Europe, and parts of those that have gone were
frequently incorporated into structures that replaced them and are
still obvious today. Even the *acequias* that feed the Arab fountains,
wells and baths are original.

A large student population ensures that Granada is a lively place
by day and night, with plenty of cafés, bars and clubs – but
paradoxically the Moorish capital of southern Spain is quieter in the
holidays when they all go home.

# Toledo

Declared a UNESCO World Heritage Site in 1986, Toledo is in central Spain, south of Madrid. Under the Moorish Caliphate of Cordoba, from the 8th century, Toledo experienced La Convivencia, an extended period when Jews, Christians and Muslims lived together in harmony. Today, it attracts an equally cosmopolitan crowd, being one of Spain's most attractive tourist destinations, with its magnificent setting, picturesque old town and a wealth of architecture and art treasures to be found.

The city is on a hill, surrounded on three sides by the deep gorge of the River Tagus. With its ring of ancient walls, great Cathedral and towering Alcázar, it presents a magnificent sight from afar, twice painted by resident El Greco around 1600 (see one in his museum). The town retains its original Moorish layout of irregular narrow streets and blind alleys with grated windows and courtyard houses. As was so often the case after the Christians returned, they made their mark with fine churches, often built on the sites of the mosques they replaced.

It is literally impossible to describe all there is to see in this magical city. Starting from the busy Plaza de Zocodover, go north to the Miradero, south to the Alcázar or east to the Hospital of Santa Cruz. Do all three and you will understand why Toledo stands as a living monument to the history of Spain . . . and appreciate that a month here would not be enough.

But if you see nothing else, at least be sure not to miss two of Toledo's most iconic buildings – Spain's principal Cathedral, the country's finest Gothic cathedral after Burgos, and the impressive Alcázar, which saw the last of many actions in the Spanish Civil War, holding out against republican forces for 68 days.

**POPULATION**:
76,000 (2005)
**WHEN TO GO**:
Spring or autumn – the midsummer heat (and tourist pressure) can be intense.
**DON'T MISS**:
The Synagogue of St Mary the White, a synagogue built by Moors under Christian rule for Jews around 1180, before finally becoming a church in the late 15th century.
El Greco's painting *The Burial of the Count of Orgaz*, in the Church of Santo Tomé.
The incongruously named Mosque of Cristo de la Luz (Christ of the Light), said to be where the first mass was said when King Alfonso VI conquered the city in 1085.
The amphitheatre and aqueducts, remaining from the time when there was a Roman fortified settlement.
The Arco de la Sangre, which will be recognized by fans of the quixotic Cervantes character Don Quixote.
A walk around the city walls – started by Visigoths, continued by Moors, completed by Christians.
**YOU SHOULD KNOW**:
Since ancient times, swordsmen and quill-cutters have recognized Toledo as the place where the very finest steel blades were made.

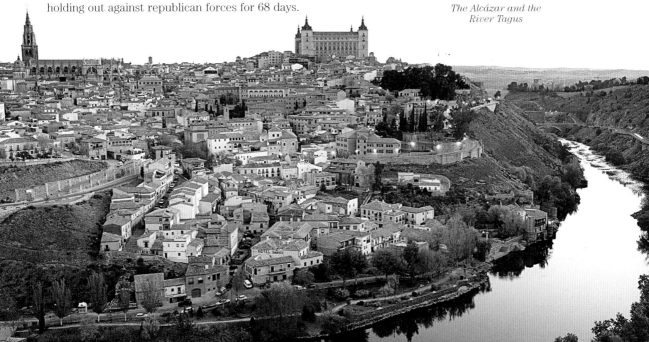

*The Alcázar and the River Tagus*

*Plaza del Ayuntamiento*

# Valencia

Spain's third-largest city is an industrialized conurbation on the east coast. After being conquered by the Moors (who seized it back from Spanish national hero El Cid), Valencia was finally retaken by James I of Aragon in 1238. Thereafter it became one of the Mediterranean's major cities, with considerable influence over the development of Spain – for example, it was Valencian merchants who funded Queen Isabella's sponsorship of the historic voyage undertaken by Christopher Columbus in 1492.

The city's busy port of El Grao and holiday beaches are away from the city centre, which is surrounded by extensive suburbs. But the heart of the old city still beats within its bustling modern counterpart, offering plenty of original character centred on Plaza de la Reina, which used to be the town square. The fine Cathedral (completed in the 15th century) is mainly Gothic. The octagonal bell tower is a city landmark, offering the best view of Valencia for those who brave its 207 steps. There are numerous splendid churches and the Lonja de la Seda (silk exchange) of 1498 is a UNESCO World Heritage Site. It, too, boasts a good viewing tower (only 144 steps!). The winding streets of the Barrio del Carmen contain many ancient buildings, and it remains a lively centre of everyday Valencian life.

There is also much to like about the Valencia that grew up outside the old city walls (now demolished), with its broad avenues and striking modern architecture, notably the amazing City of Arts and Sciences by celebrated local architect Santiago Calatrava that attracts four million visitors annually. But before leaving this thoroughly modern place, spare a thought for local teacher Cayetano Ripoll. He was the infamous Spanish Inquisition's last victim, executed here in 1826 for . . . being a freemason.

**POPULATION:**
807,000 (2006)
**WHEN TO GO:**
Any time – but Valencia has a mild maritime climate, so it's possible to visit in summer without getting fried.
**DON'T MISS:**
The Torres de Serranos, the old town's north gate built on Roman foundations in 1398 – with excellent views from its massive towers.
The splendid old medieval bridges over the green open space where the river (now diverted) used to run.
St Nicholas' Church, built on the site of an earlier mosque, noted for fine frescoes and pictures.
The modernist central covered market off busy Plaza del Mercado.
The local paella – Spain's national dish originated from Valencia.
An extraordinary musical fountain in the elongated Plaza del Cordillo, a hub of city life.
**YOU SHOULD KNOW:**
In 2007, the coveted Americas Cup sailing trophy was successfully defended here against the New Zealand challengers . . . by the landlocked Swiss holders.

# Madrid

Located on the river Manzanares, between the Sierra de Guadarrama mountains and the fluvial river basins, Spain's capital city is considered to be the main financial, cultural and political centre of the Iberian Peninsula. Growing quickly, on the orders of Philip II, from a little known 16th century backwater, the city's grand architecture is surprisingly coherent. The walls of the easily accessible, compact old town only fell in 1860.

Renowned for its golden triangle of art, located along the Paseo del Prado, Madrid is one of Europe's art-lovers' top destinations. The triangle comprises three museums: the Prado Museum, which houses works by both Velazquez and Goya; the Thyssen Bornemisza Museum, holding a largely private collection and the Reina Sofia, which famously won back Picasso's masterpiece, *Guernica,* from New York.

Aside from its abundant cultural and historical wealth, the city also possesses a very modern infrastructure and is equally famous for its youthful, heady atmosphere. Bustling cafés overflow into market places and squares, tapas bars spattered around every street corner entice hungry visitors, and the vibrant nightlife can see traffic jams well into the early morning.

Wander through the Puerta del Sol square and see the famous clock whose bells bring in the New Year, or have a pre-dinner drink in the neighbouring Plaza Mayor whilst imagining both the Spanish Inquisition and the bullfighting that once took place within its walls.

Madrid's festivities on patron saint days are a particular experience not to be missed, but be sure to book a bed in advance as the city hotels can fill up months beforehand.

*Plaza Mayor*

**POPULATION:**
2, 905,000 (2007)
**WHEN TO GO:**
May to October, though the city's charms are worth a trip any time.
**DON'T MISS:**
The Teatro Real with its restored 1850 Opera House.
The Royal Palace of Madrid
The Buen Retiro Park
The National Library
The Museum of Archaeology
The Lazaro Galdiano Museum
**YOU SHOULD KNOW:**
Madrid towers as Europe's highest city at 640 m (2,100 ft).

# Córdoba

In the 10th century, this Andalucian gem was the largest city in Western Europe and, perhaps, in the world, as well as a great cultural, political and economic centre. The city came to prominence when the Moors entered Spain in 711. By the middle of the century, Córdoba was ruled by Abd Ar-Rahman, a charismatic leader who introduced an ambitious building programme which was to elevate Córdoba to the world stage.

Abd Ar-Rahman's greatest legacy was the Mezquita mosque, one of the most breathtaking examples of Muslim architecture in Spain. The building evolved over the following centuries and, after Cordoba was retaken by the Christians, a cathedral was built inside. The Mezquita has many beautiful features including hundreds of marble and stone columns, forming  ranks of terracotta-and-white striped arches. There is also a lavishly decorated mihrab, or sacred prayer niche, with its amazing mosaic arch and stone cupola. The Chapel de Villaviciosa, the first Christian chapel to be built after the recapture in 1371 in the Mudejar style, blends in harmoniously with the mosque. The chapel's bell tower is on the site of the former minaret.

Surrounding the Mezquita is the medieval Jewish quarter, a labyrinth of narrow cobbled streets, little whitewashed houses and workshops with beautiful wrought-ironwork and tiny fountains with water splashing into basins of glazed tiles. The synagogue was built in the early 14th century in the Mudejar style, and is one of the very few remaining intact in Spain from that era. Inside are Mudejar stucco plant and star motifs and Hebrew inscriptions.

Other sights in Córdoba include the Alcázar de los Reyes Cristianos, the fortified palace built for Alfonso XI in the early 14th century. It was enlarged for Fernando II, and the Catholic monarchs held court here during the campaign to recapture Granada from the Moors. The building was also used during the Inquisition and has served as a prison. Features of note include a royal bathhouse, Roman mosaics and a sarcophagus. The pretty terraced gardens contain numerous pools and fountains.

The Palacio de Viani is a Renaissance palace, the 17th-century home of the Viana family. Outside the formal gardens make a nice place to stroll, while inside are grand galleries, impressive staircases, rich furnishings, porcelain and silver to admire.

*Mezquita, Córdoba*

# Santiago de Compostela

Santiago de Compostela is the jewel in Galicia's crown. It is north-west Spain's most famous city and has World Heritage status, receiving hundreds of thousands of visitors every year. In the ninth century, a tomb thought to be that of the apostle St James was discovered there, and by the Middle Ages the city had become the third most important place in Christiandom. During the Middle Ages, as many as two million visitors made their way here on foot each year, and in the twelfth century a monk named Aymery Picaud wrote the first guide book in the world in order to help them, describing in detail the best routes through France and Spain and the best places to stay. Today, both pilgrims and tourists still follow the ancient pilgrimage route across northern Spain to the towering cathedral, one of the most spectacular in the world.

Santiago Cathedral, with its distinctive twin spires, was built between the eleventh and thirteenth centuries on the site of a ninth-century basilica. Although there have been more recent additions, including the amazing Baroque façade, the interior remains as it was almost 800 years ago. Among its most notable features is the twelfth-century Portico de la Gloria with its three decorated arches. Christ, flanked by four apostles and eight angels, dominates the central arch, and St James stands directly below him on a column carved with the Tree of Jesse. The extremely ornate gilt and silver altar is also worth a look, and contrasts strongly with the dark simplicity of the rest of the interior.

The cathedral is not Santiago de Compostela's only outstanding architectural gem. The old town has many Gothic, Neo-classical, Romanesque and Baroque buildings and nearly all are on a grand scale. The Rajoy Palace, for example, was built in the eighteenth century to house visiting dignitaries and pilgrims. Today it is the town hall and the parliament building for Galicia's regional government. The Hostal de los Reyes Catolicos, next to the main façade of the cathedral, was commissioned by the Spanish king in the fifteenth century as a hostel and hospital for Santiago's visiting pilgrims. It is now one of Spain's state-run hotels.

**POPULATION:**
93,000 (2006)
**WHEN TO GO:**
March to September
**DON'T MISS:**
Santiago Cathedral – the two slender towers of this monumental building, reputedly built on the site of St James' original burial, dominate the city skyline from all directions.
Hostal de los Reyes Catolicos – dating from the 1600s and sitting adjacent to the cathedral's main facade, it is now used as a luxury hotel for passing dignitaries.
Rajoy Palace – this distinctive neo-classical palace, designed by Frenchman Charles Lemaur, is today the site of Galicia's Regional Government.
**YOU SHOULD KNOW:**
There is an entrance fee for the museum and cathedral cloisters.

*The twin spires of the Cathedral de Santiago de Compostela*

*The Plaza de Espana*

# Seville

Despite a challenge from thrustful Málaga, Seville remains the political, business and cultural capital of southern Spain. It bestrides the busy Guadalquivir River, which is navigable to the Atlantic coast. In common with much of Spain, Seville's recent economic growth has been rapid and it now sits at the centre of a major commercial and industrial conurbation.

For all that, evidence of its long history is everywhere, and despite the hustle and bustle of a modern city there are powerful reminders of traditionally flamboyant Spanish life to be found in the many barrios (old quarters) with their narrow streets and charming balconied houses. There are enough sights in Seville to satisfy even the most compulsive heritage addict, and it's possible to spend days wandering about soaking up the atmosphere.

The Roman period is represented by various ruins, including an aqueduct. Well-preserved remains of Itálica, 8 km (5 mi) out of the city, give a wonderful impression of what Roman Seville (then called Hispalis) must have been like. Moorish influence is also evident, with the Giralda minaret tower being a fine example. Built with sloping ramps to allow the muezzin to ride a horse to the top before calling the faithful to prayer, it was converted to a bell tower for the Cathedral after the Moors were expelled. The 15th century Seville Cathedral itself is a vast medieval Gothic triumph with a stunning, richly gilded interior.

Across from the Cathedral is the Alcázar with its beautiful gardens, developed over the centuries from a Moorish palace. Other special monuments include the 16th century Town Hall and ancient Torre del Oro, a watchtower on the river. The city also has many fine parks and gardens, notably the Maria Luisa Park built for the 1929 Spanish-American World's Fair.

**POPULATION:**
704,000 (2005)
**WHEN TO GO:**
Mid-summer heat in the city can be oppressive, so avoid July and August.
**DON'T MISS:**
A stroll along the river for some rare peace and quiet and a relaxed view of the city – there are several inviting parks along the way.
The Tapas Tour – invent your own, as nearly every bar offers a selection of these tempting snacks.
A leisurely trot around town in a traditional horse-drawn carriage.
Seville's Holy Week (Semana Santa en Seville) just before Easter, a traditional Spanish festival that is at once both seriously solemn and wonderfully light-hearted.
The Fine Arts Museum in an old friary, home to Spain's second-most-important picture collection (after that in Madrid's Prado).
One of the best of Seville's many churches – the 13th century Santa Ana in the Triana district, with its outstanding reredos.
**YOU SHOULD KNOW:**
Many a fine opera has been set in the city, including Bizet's *Carmen*, Beethoven's *Fidelio*, Mozart's *Don Giovanni* and *Marriage of Figaro* . . . and of course Rossini's *Barber of Seville*.

# Palma de Mallorca

Located on the south coast of the island of Mallorca, Palma is the capital of Spain's Balearic Islands. After the usual European experience of strife (occupied over the centuries by Phoenicians, Romans, Vandals, Byzantines and Spaniards, among others), the port was the base of corsair pirates in the 17th century, then flourished in the 1800s. But everything changed with the growth of tourism from the 1950s, completely altering the traditional culture of Palma. Over 10 million visitors arrive each year, so this isn't a place for quiet relaxation.

Yet plenty of fine old buildings remain from the pre-tourist era. Those approaching by boat see the famed Gothic Cathedral above the ancient Almudaina Palace, once the residence of Moorish kings. To the left – an elegant seaside promenade with its grand hotels and yacht harbour. To the right – glimpses of Palma's famous white beaches. Above it all – the white circular battlements of the imposing 14th century Bellver Castle.

This historical framework is surrounded by a cosmopolitan modern city. At its heart is the elongated tree-shaded central plaza (Es Born), an ideal place to sit with a coffee at the hub of the city's bustling social life, close to the exclusive shops on Avenida Rey Jaime III.

For all that tourism is king, Palma retains a real sense of history. Apart from many major historic buildings, there is plenty of vernacular architecture for those who appreciate original character. For example, the barrios (distinctive quarters) should definitely be explored – one of the most interesting being Portella, behind the Cathedral. Here you will find narrow streets, 15th century mansions and Arab monuments such as the old baths. And it may even double the pleasure to know that tourists only here for sun, sea and nightlife will be oblivious to it all.

**POPULATION:**
375,000 (2005)
**WHEN TO GO:**
Off season for the sights, summer for the beaches.
**DON'T MISS:**
The Drach Cave, an extraordinary complex of four caverns with thousands of stalactites.
The 15th century La Lonja, once the city's mercantile exchange and now a museum.
The flamboyant Palacio Vivot, a national monument, and the nearby 14th century Convent of St Francis.
An outing to the central market at Plaza Olivar, and bargain hunting at the Saturday flea market on Avenida Gabriel Alomar i Villalonga (which is nearly as long as its name).
The Cathedral treasure, including illuminated manuscripts, jewelled artefacts and relics of the saints, on show in the sacristy.
**YOU SHOULD KNOW:**
More than half Mallorca's total population lives in the city of Palma.

*The Cathedral of Palma de Mallorca*

# Ibiza

The city of Ibiza (also known by its Catalan name of Eivissa) is the capital city of the Spanish Mediterranean island of the same name. Although the resident population is small, numbers are hugely swelled by the influx of visitors and casual workers during the tourist season. For tourism – especially the wild nightlife enjoyed by the young – underpins this Balearic island's economy.

Ibiza town, above the harbour that has served as an entry point to the island for centuries, has not suffered the same intensive development apparent everywhere else. Approached from the sea, it would still be recognised by a traveller from times past. The cathedral sits proudly on its rocky promontory above a maze of narrow streets, alleys and jumbled white buildings, whilst the massive 16th century walls that protected the city over the ages still stand.

That doesn't mean Ibiza town is dull. It tends to be less busy in the mornings, as there isn't much accommodation and the previous night's revellers retreat to their out-of-town beds to sleep it off. This is a good time to check out the many and varied stalls and shops, or take a leisurely meal near the harbour, overlooking the bay. As evening approaches, the bars fill and the night's action begins to pulse.

The old town (D'Alt Vila, literally 'high town') must be explored on foot. Its dramatic main entrance is across a drawbridge and through the arched Tablas Gate, flanked by stone statues, from whence a cobbled courtyard leads to the main square. Climb towards the cathedral, enjoying wonderful views from spacious terraces and breaks in the ramparts at every level. Here, it is almost possible to believe that you've travelled back in time, to an historic oasis amidst the bustle of modern life.

**POPULATION**:
38,000 (2002)
**WHEN TO GO**:
Ibiza is one long rave from April to October, though summers are scorching. Winters are temperate and much quieter.
**DON'T MISS**:
The new museum in D'Alt Vila, illustrating the long history of this UNESCO World Heritage Site.
An envious wander around the marina to see the sort of yacht you could afford if you won the lottery jackpot . . . twice.
The small but rewarding Museum of Contemporary Art in the Plaça de la Catedral.
Ibiza town's nearest beaches, the family-friendly Talamanca and Figueretes.
The Puig des Molins Necropolis for relics left by the island's previous inhabitants, from the Carthaginians onwards.
The harbour-side monument to the many pirates who once frequented Ibizan waters.
**YOU SHOULD KNOW**:
The Gothic-Baroque cathedral is rather surprisingly dedicated to Holy Mary of the Snows.

147

*Waterfront at Oporto*

# Oporto

Built on granite cliffs overlooking the River Douro in northern Portugal, Oporto is a tangle of pretty lanes and crumbling buildings running steeply down to a medieval waterfront. It is hard not to be enchanted by Oporto's atmospheric riverside, dotted with old port-wine boats, narrow alleyways and pretty archways. Oporto, known to the Portuguese as simply 'Porto', is the second largest city in the country and one of the major financial and economic centres of the north-western Iberian Peninsula.

Portugal's best-known product, Port wine, was named after the city because it was originally shipped from Vila Nova de Gaia, just across the river. Since the 1850s producers have matured and stored their wine in warehouses there, and about 60 establishments scramble up the hill from the waterfront. Some offer tours and tastings.

Among the architectural highlights of the city, the twelfth-century Cathedral of Se, with its Romanesque rose window and Gothic cloister, is the oldest surviving structure. Among the other very old buildings are the small Romanesque Church of Cedofeita and the Gothic Igreja de São Francisco (Church of St. Francis) with its Baroque interior decoration and carved Tree of Jesse. The Baroque style is well represented in the city in the unbelievably elaborate interiors of the churches of St Francis and St Claire (Santa Clara), the churches of Mercy (Misericórida) and of the Clerics (Igreja dos Clérigos).

Beside the huge two-storey bridge of Dom Luis I which spans the Douro river, is the austere sixteenth-century Augustinian monastery of Serra do Pilar with its intricate wood carvings and gold-leaf altars. Also well worth a visit is the Neoclassical Palacio da Bolsa with its magnificent Arabic ballroom.

The people of Oporto have long been known as *Tripeiros* ('tripe eaters'), supposedly because the city went without meat in order to provide for the fleet which left the city to conquer Ceuta in North Africa in 1415. They had to subsist on tripe soup, even today a specialty of the city.

# Coimbra

After Lisbon and Porto, Coimbra is one of the most important cities in Portugal, playing a vital role as the chief city of central Portugal. Coimbra has a few interesting archaeological remains dating from the time it was a Roman town called Aeminium, but it was later on that the city grew in stature. It was the capital of Portugal from 1139 to 1260, and soon developed into an important cultural centre. This was due to the University of Coimbra, founded in 1290, one of the oldest universities in Europe. The city boasts many notable monuments from that era and beyond, and its monumental buildings and history attracts tourists from around the world.

The university was originally founded in Lisbon but moved to Coimbra in 1537 to a site on a hill by the River Mondego. The university is built around a large square, beneath which is the entrance to a Baroque chapel. The university library (Biblioteca Joanina) is perhaps the main tourist attraction – three beautiful rooms with painted ceilings holding more than 300,000 books on shelves made of fine woods.

The University's eighteenth-century botanic garden is another highlight. Founded in 1772, it occupies thirteen hectares (32 acres) and is considered to be one of the most beautiful in Europe. The Machado de Castro Museum, one of Portugal's most important art museums housed in the former bishops' palace is also worth a visit, as is Portugal dos Pequeninos Park, a collection of child-sized scale models of important Portuguese buildings.

The Roman ruins of nearby Conimbriga, 16 km (10 mi) from the city, make a fascinating excursion. They were first settled in the first century AD, but abandoned some 300 years later as the inhabitants fled to Coimbra to escape invasion. The walls of the city are well preserved, and the wonderful mosaic floors of many houses and public buildings remain. In the Roman baths, you can see the underground stone heating ducts beneath the now-missing floors.

**POPULATION:**
148,500 (2001)
**WHEN TO GO:**
Early July for the city's festival celebrations.
**DON'T MISS:**
Museo Nacional Machado de Castro – housed in the former Palace of the Bishops, this is one of Portugal's most important art museums, named after the renowned Portuguese sculptor, Joaquim Machado de Castro.
The university's botanic garden.
The monastery church of Santa Cruz – this is the most important monastic house of the Portuguese monarchy. Nothing remains of the early Romanesque monastery due to its complete restoration by respected architects and sculptors in the 16th century.
The city museum in the Edificio Chiado.
The *azulejos* (glazed tiles) of Coimbra.
**YOU SHOULD KNOW:**
Coimbra is still considered to be the main seat of learning in the country.

*Coimbra University*

# Lisbon

On the Atlantic coast where the River Tagus flows into the ocean, lies Portugal's capital city of Lisbon (Lisboa), nestled between seven hills. Lisbon is a beautiful, relaxed city full of contrasts, from modern high rises to Art Nouveau buildings, wonderful mosaic pavements, brightly tiled buildings and medieval Moorish architecture.

Its port has been in constant use for the last three thousand years by a number of different rulers, but it was most prominent and powerful between the fifteenth and seventeenth centuries, when Portugal was a wealthy nation. Much of this wealth was due to the explorer Vasco da Gama, who discovered the sea route to India in 1498. This led to a lively trade in spices and gem stones, bringing great wealth to Lisbon. In the seventeenth century, gold was discovered in Brazil, bringing in more money. However, in 1755 the city was severely damaged by an earthquake and the tsunami that followed. It was never to regain its former prominence.

Close to the harbour is the Praça do Comercio, one of the most elegant city squares in Europe. The surrounding buildings have attractive arcades along their facades. The city centre of Lisbon, Baixa, is organized in a grid pattern and was largely built after the earthquake. The oldest district is Alfama, close to the Tagus, which survived almost intact and retains many medieval buildings. For a view over the city, visit the Castello de São Jorge, a medieval castle built on a hill in the fortified citadel. The castle was the last stronghold of resistance if attackers managed to enter the citadel. It is a handsome rectangular building with ten towers.

Don't miss the façade of the church of Nossa Senhora da Conceição Velha. The church was rebuilt after the earthquake using rescued elements of the old building, mainly decorative pieces of the façade which date back to the sixteenth century. This façade is a great example of the Manueline style, or Portuguese Late Gothic, a sumptuous architectural style incorporating maritime elements and inspired by the discoveries of Vasco da Gama. This style marks the transition from Late Gothic to Renaissance.

Probably the most prominent monument of Lisbon and certainly the most successful achievement of the Manueline style is the magnificent Jerónimos Monastery, with its delightful cloister. Close by is the Belem Tower, built in the early sixteenth century to commemorate Vasco da Gama. This defensive, yet elegant construction is one of the symbols of the city, a memorial to Portugal's power during the Age of the Great Discoveries.

*A view of the Monastery of Sao Vicente de Fora and the Church of Santa Engracia*

# Évora

The Alentejo Province is a region of wide plains to the south of the Tagus River in Portugal. In the heart of this region, on a gentle hill surrounded by vineyards and beautiful rural scenery, lies the city of Évora, a UNESCO World Heritage Site. Its historic centre has been preserved in its original state and is surrounded by fortified walls and dominated by an imposing, fortress cathedral. The city contains monuments dating from many different historical periods: there are some 4,000 buildings of interest within the walls, including churches, palaces, gates and squares, yet Évora is a vibrant, forward-thinking university town.

Évora's history starts 2,000 years ago. It was known by the Romans as Liberalitas Julia, and remains from this period (including walls and rooms) and the monumental imperial temple of Diana, can still be seen. With its 14 Corinthian columns and part of the entablature, this is the best-preserved Roman monument in Portugal. During the barbarian invasions, Évora was under Visigoth rule, and in 715 the city was conquered by the Moors.

Évora was taken from the Moors by the Christian knight Geraldo Sempavor in the 12th century and became one of the most vibrant cities in Portugal during the Middle Ages. The court was often in residence here and Évora saw many royal weddings. Gothic in style, the cathedral dates back to the thirteenth century, but the cloisters and the doorway are fourteenth-century additions. The dome above the transept is unusual in Portuguese churches and the Baroque altar is a later reconstruction. Nearby is the Gothic church of São João Evangelista, a wonderful building founded in 1485. The nave is lined with stunning hand-painted tiles.

The university was founded by the Company of Jesus in 1551. Here great European Masters such as Clenardo and Molina passed on their knowledge to the students. In the 18th century, the Jesuits were expelled, the university was closed and Évora went into decline. Évora's lively cultural, artistic and historical past is well documented in the many surviving monuments from each historic period, all part of the rich heritage of this museum-like city.

**POPULATION:**
50,000 (2006)
**WHEN TO GO:**
Spring or autumn.
**DON'T MISS:**
Palace of Vasco da Gama – notable for its Manueline cloister and preserved Renaissance murals.
St. Francisco Church – the skulls and bones of 5,000 monks line the walls. There are even two desiccated corpses hanging from the wall. An inscription reads 'we bones that are here await yours'.
University of Évora.
Roman temple of Diana.
Évora Cathedral – the best-preserved Roman monument in Portugal.
Aqueduct of Agua de Prata – built in 1531 to 1537 to supply the city with water, its huge arches stretch for 9km (6 mi). Remarkably, houses, shops and cafés occupy one end of the aqueduct.
**YOU SHOULD KNOW:**
This is the best remaining example of Portugal's 'Golden Age'.

*The ruins of the Roman Temple of Diana dominate the centre of Évora.*

# Beja

**POPULATION:**
22,000 (2004)
**WHEN TO GO:**
May to June, before the summer invasion of their 'secret gem' by Portuguese visitors.
**DON'T MISS:**
The wonderful 7th century column carved with birds attacking a snake in St Amaro's Church.
A slice (or two) of the city's tasty speciality – Pão de Rala, a cake-bread made with pumpkin.
St Andrew's Chapel, whose main walls are entirely decorated with 16th century tiles.
The *Árvore de Jessé*, a wonderfully elaborate wooden carved work in the 13th century St Mary of the Market Church.
Pizões, an excavated Roman villa outside the city that was part of an important farming estate.
**YOU SHOULD KNOW:**
Never say 'Vive l'empereur' – in 1808 Napoleon's troops sacked the city and massacred the inhabitants.

Once named Pax-Julia by Julius Caesar, the hill city of Beja is the traditional capital of the Baixo Alentejo agricultural region in Portugal's deep south. The place was fought over and occupied frequently. It fell under Muslim rule in the 8th century and was not finally regained by the Christians until the 13th century, by which time it had been virtually destroyed by constant conflict. Further strife followed in the 17th century and in the early 1800s during the Peninsular War.

All this considered, it's not surprising that Beja is dominated by an impressive 13th century castle that replaced fortifications previously erected by the Moors and Romans. The central keep is the highest in Portugal, at 40 m (130 ft). Climb the 197 spiral steps for a sensational view of the town and rolling tree-dotted plains beyond. One of Portugal's few remaining pre-Romanesque churches – the whitewashed St Amaro's – stands next to the castle.

The beauty of Beja is in its undoubted sense of history, reinforced by the fact that it hasn't spread unchecked but remains an unspoiled and original place. Moorish architecture is visible everywhere in the cobbled streets. The city's cultural gem is the regional Museum da Rainha D Leonor. This is a national monument full of treasures, located in a former convent dating back to the 15th century, an impressive building topped with intricate Gothic lattice-work. A bell tower and spire complete the romantic picture. This was the home of Mariana Alcoforado, a 17th century nun who fell in love with a dashing French officer and wrote him five passionate love letters that were later published in France to wide acclaim. Some say they were lovers, others that she saw him but once from a window.

*The castle and surrounding city*

# Venice

Once the wealthiest city in Europe, Venice is arguably also the most beautiful. Built on wooden piles in the middle of a lagoon on Italy's Adriatic coast, Venice wears its riches with pride. In its heyday, this city state had strong trade links with the Byzantine Empire and the Muslim world. During the late thirteenth century, over 3,300 Venetian trade ships dominated Mediterranean commerce. Throughout this prosperous time, the city's most prominent families competed with each other to build the grandest palaces and support the most talented artists.

The main artery of the city, the Grand Canal, sweeps in an elegant curve through its centre. A vaporetto (water-bus) trip down the Grand Canal will reveal the faded elegance of more than 300 palaces, revealing the city's beautiful blend of Europe and Byzantium. And it is these private palaces and houses, rather than the public monuments, which make Venice so appealing. Explored by gondola or on foot, the narrow alleys and backwaters of the city reveal all its decorative detail which reflects its past wealth and importance.

Venice was governed by the Great Council, made up of members of the most influential families. The Great Council appointed public officials and elected a Senate of 2–300 men. The Senate chose the Council of Ten, an elect group which handled the administration of the city. One member was elected' Doge', the ceremonial head of the city.

The Doge's Palace, the ducal home and seat of power for 700 years, was largely constructed from 1309 to 1424 and is a stunning Gothic creation with the canal on one side and St Mark's Square on the other. Next to the palace on St Mark's Square is St Mark's Basilica, is the most famous of the city's churches and one of the best-known examples of Byzantine architecture. The cathedral has been the seat of the Patriarch of Venice, archbishop of the Roman Catholic Archdiocese of Venice, since 1807. It is famous for its sheer opulence, and its wonderful gilded Byzantine mosaics. Venice boasts some great works of Renaissance art. The best galleries are the Accademia, the Galleria Giorgio Franchetti in the Gothic Ca' d'Oro and the Peggy Guggenheim Collection.

Venice may be one of the biggest tourist attractions in the world, but however busy it is, few visitors are not overawed by its beauty, elegance and grandeur.

**POPULATION:**
271,000 (2006)
**WHEN TO GO:**
The two weeks before Lent for the Carnevale.
**DON'T MISS:**
Murano – this island just north of Venice is famous for its glasswork.
A gondola ride.
Torcello – the most intriguing and atmospheric of the islands in the Venetian lagoon. Don't miss the stunning Basilica di Santa Maria Assunta on the dusty piazza.
The Lido – Venice's seaside.
La Fenice opera house, one of the most beautiful in the world.
**YOU SHOULD KNOW:**
The city is a UNESCO World Heritage Site.

*The Grand Canal*

# Ravenna

This major city in north-eastern Italy was once a seaport, but is now connected to the Adriatic by canal. Its origins are lost in the mists of time, but it was an important Roman settlement – Julius Caesar gathered his forces here before fatefully crossing the Rubicon. In common with many Italian city states, Ravenna experienced frequent changes of leadership over the centuries, but its most enduring contribution to Italy's heritage was made in the 5th and 6th centuries. Eight early Christian monuments remain from that period, collectively a UNESCO World Heritage Site.

The octagonal Baptistry of Neon is the oldest, once part of the Great Basilica built around 400 AD and destroyed in 1734. The Byzantine Mausoleum of Galla Placidia has a cupola entirely covered in mosaics. The small Arian Baptistry was converted to a Catholic oratory when the Arian brand of Christianity was discredited. The tiny cruciform Archiepiscopal Chapel may be found in the Ravenna Bishops' Palace. The much larger Basilica of Sant'Apollinaire Nuovo was once the palace chapel of the Arian King Theodoric. Theodoric's Mausoleum is a decagonal stone structure in Gothic style. The Basilica of San Vitale is the most famous, and one of the most important Byzantine structures in Western Europe. The Basilica of Sant'Apollinare in Classe is another splendid Byzantine church, dedicated to the city's patron saint. These extraordinary places with their brilliant mosaic decoration must be seen to be believed.

There are many more fine old buildings to be found along the old canals and in the old city centre, which is largely pedestrianized with cafés and small shops tucked away in narrow streets and side alleys. To enjoy the vivacious atmosphere of a lively Italian city at its very best, sit out in the elegant Piazza del Popolo on a summer evening.

*The splendid Byzantine Basilica of Sant'Appollinare Nuovo*

# Bologna

Despite suffering considerable bomb damage in 1944, Bologna's historic centre, the second largest in Europe (after Venice), contains a wealth of important Medieval, Renaissance and Baroque monuments which offer countless attractions for the visitor.

The capital city of the Emilia-Romagna area of northern Italy, Bologna boasts Europe's oldest university, which was founded in 1088 when Bologna was a wealthy, independent commune. The historic centre of the city is beautiful and among its highlights is the Church of San Domenico, which features some early sculptures by Michelangelo and a shrine made by Nicola Pisano.

Bologna first developed along the Via Emilia as an Etruscan and later a Roman colony. Because of its Roman heritage, the central streets follow the grid pattern of the Roman settlement. The original Roman ramparts were replaced by medieval fortifications which can still be seen today, and finally by a third set of ramparts built in the 13th century. The city is famous for its medieval defensive towers, some twenty of which are still standing. There were originally over 200 towers in Bologna, built by wealthy families partly in an effort to outdo each other and partly for defensive purposes.

The two towers that survive in the city centre, leaning precariously above the Piazza di Porta Ravegnana, are well-known landmarks today. The Garisenda tower is 49 m (160 ft) tall and leans 3.2 m (10 ft) from the vertical. It was originally considerably taller: in 1360 the top half was taken down as it was considered dangerous. It is still closed to the public to this day. The tower built by the neighbouring Asinelli family in 1119 is an astonishing 97 m (318 ft) high. Climb the 498 steps for a breathtaking view of the red-tiled roofs of the city and beautiful countryside beyond.

Since ancient times, Emilia-Romagna has been Italy's most fertile wheat and dairy region, and it is famous for its food and wine. Bologna is renowned for its culinary tradition and some regard it as the food capital of Italy. It has given its name to Bolognese sauce, a meat-based pasta sauce known locally simply as *ragù*.

*An aerial view of Bologna*

**POPULATION:**
400,000 (2006)
**WHEN TO GO:**
Spring or autumn.
**DON'T MISS:**
Piazza Maggiore – the heart of Bologna and its Roman core, this is one of the finest squares in the whole of Italy.
Palazzo Comunale – houses typical Bolognese paintings and furnishings from the 14th to the 19th centuries.
Basilica of San Petronio – dominating the Piazza Maggiore, this is considered to be the fifth greatest church in the world. It contains one of the world's largest sundials, a 66m (216 ft) astronomical clock designed by the astronomer Cassini in 1655. The Asinelli tower for a spectacular view of the city.
Basilica of Santo Stefano – this complex of religious edifices, known locally as 'Sette Chiese' (Seven Churches), is home to the fifth largest church in the world.
**YOU SHOULD KNOW:**
The Museo Civico Archaeologico has one of the best Etruscan collections in Italy.

# Milan

How can the self-appointed world style capital be covered in anything less than a book? Especially when it is a major industrial, financial and commercial centre which has become one of Europe's richest cities. And that's without even mentioning its outstanding heritage and vibrant culture. The answer is to see Milan for yourself, and make of it what you will.

In contrast to the somewhat laid-back reputation of southern Italy, the Milanese take pride in working – and playing – hard. The city has sprawled outwards and the centre is now dedicated to offices, quality shops, restaurants and bars. Milan is a rail hub, with five stations. It's easy to get around, with a Metro and an extensive tram network.

Amidst the frenetic energy of Milan, there are a few quiet places and many sights worth seeing. The Sempione Park is one of the city's few green spaces. The astonishing wedding-cake Duomo Cathedral in its fabulous square is the second-largest church in Italy, after St Peter's in Rome. It was begun in the late 14th century, occupying the site of the central Roman forum, and eventually completed in the 19th. It has literally thousands of marble statues. The grand 18th century La Scala is the home of opera in Italy. The 15th century Sforza Castle is now an art gallery that has Michelangelo's last sculpture. The St Ambrose Basilica is one of Italy's most ancient churches (built 379-386, with later bell towers).

These are merely the tip of a monumental iceberg, but this is a city that moves with the times – or even tries to get ahead. A number of old industrial zones are being redeveloped with typical Milanese flair, ensuring that this go-ahead city retains its rightful place at the forefront of Italian life.

*Milan's Duomo, the second largest church in Italy*

# Syracuse

First settled by Greeks in the 8th century BC, this ancient city on an island off Sicily was once described by Roman philosopher-statesman Cicero as "the greatest Greek city and the most beautiful of them all". Two millennia later, UNESCO agrees – the historic centre of Syracuse is a World Heritage Site. For all that, parts of the modern city are undoubtedly seedy and run-down, in typically Sicilian fashion.

After the tempestuous political upheavals endemic to the region, Syracuse suffered a real earthquake, in 1693 – a catastrophe that changed the city's face. It was extensively rebuilt in Sicilian Baroque style, now considered to be the classic architecture of southern Italy.

Syracuse was originally confined to the fortified island of Ortygia, which still seems to be the heart of a city that has spread extensively to the mainland. Here, it is possible to explore three thousand years of history in a small area that is medieval in character. The harbour front provides access to the web of ancient streets within, through the 15th century Porta Marina. The elongated Piazza del Duomo is impressive, surrounded by imposing buildings. The Cathedral itself incorporates the Temple of Athens (5th century BC). The Regional Art Museum, with an extraordinary collection of medieval art, is housed in the 13th century Bellomo Palace.

Four quarters existed on the mainland in Greek times: Achradina (nowadays the modern area around the station); Tyche (see extensive catacombs and the archaeological museum); Neapolis (now a fascinating park with extensive Greek and Roman remains); Epipolae (stretching to the outer defensive walls).

This is a city where the enduring stamp of history – Greek, Roman and Baroque – has created a remarkable and very special place to explore. See for yourself!

*Fishing boats along the waterfront*

**POPULATION:**
123,000 (2004)
**WHEN TO GO:**
Try to avoid high summer, when the Sicilian sun can be (and usually is) merciless.
**DON'T MISS:**
The pretty Arethusa Fountain on Ortygia, in Greek legend where the nymph Arethusa, hotly pursued by river god Alpheus, was changed into a freshwater spring by the goddess Artemis.
The Olympian Temple of Zeus, just outside the city, built in the 6th century BC.
A stroll along the Alfeo Promenade on Ortygia, to the 13th century Castello Maniace with wonderful sea views.
The Ear of Dionysius, a man-made cavern in the extraordinary stone quarries to be found alongside well-preserved Greek and Roman remains in the Archaeological Park.
The Basilica of St Lucia, a Byzantine church built where the saint was martyred in 303 AD, with atmospheric catacombs.
One of the most completely preserved Ancient Greek defensive complexes in Western Europe – the Castle of Euryalos, 8 km (5 mi) outside the city.
**YOU SHOULD KNOW:**
The northern part of the city was badly damaged by Allied bombing in World War II, and hastily redeveloped without too much thought.

# Palermo

**POPULATION:**
676,000 (2006)
**WHEN TO GO:**
June, July and August are the dry, very hot summer months – the other seasons are cooler.
**DON'T MISS:**
Palermo's Regional Art Gallery in the Palazzo Abbatellis near Piazza Marina, for a huge art collection in a medieval palace.
The Puppet Museum (Museo delle Marionette) to learn about this local tradition – and hopefully see a performance.
The macabre catacombs lined with the long dead at the Convento dei Cappuccini.
The amazing Baroque interior of the Church of Jesus (Chiesa del Gesù), built by Jesuits in the 16th century.
The Regional Archaeological Museum (Museo Archaeologico Regionale), with national status and an extraordinary collection of artefacts illustrating Sicily's long history.
Palermo's Botanical Garden, founded in 1785 and the largest in Italy – allow plenty of time.
**YOU SHOULD KNOW:**
Palermo's patron saint is St Rosalita, credited with the miracle that saved the city from the dreaded Black Death in 1624.

The main city and capital of Sicily was settled in the 8th century BC by Phoenicians attracted by the natural harbour beneath the looming bulk of Mount Pellegrino. Palermo fell successively under Roman, Byzantine and Saracen rule. The Muslims were ejected by an 11th century Norman crusade, before Sicily fell in turn to the Holy Roman Empire, the Angevins, Aragon, Spain and Naples. This long and troubled history was not ended by incorporation into modern Italy (in 1860), for Palermo was badly damaged in World War II and remains a blighted city with serious social and economic problems – mainly associated with the Mafia, which has a stranglehold on every aspect of island life.

Despite that, Palermo has distinctive character, fine monuments and a colourful way of life. The city is hectic, intimidating and fascinating by turns. There are interesting buildings aplenty to be admired, plus good museums, markets and restaurants. The Normans left their mark – the Palazzo dei Normani (a former royal palace) should not be missed, with its mix of Arab-Norman-Byzantine style unique to 12th century Sicily. Within is the outstanding Palatina Chapel. The former Norman Royal Park in the western part of the city contains two impressive castles – Zisa (summer residence) and Cuba (hunting lodge).

There are too many superb churches to list, but worthy of special mention are the Cathedral (a former mosque), San Giovanni degli Eremiti (1132), the Norman St Cataldo's with its distinctive domes and the 17th century Baroque San Giuseppe dei Teatini. In truth, there are a dozen others that deserve equal mention.

Anyone who is put off by Palermo's slightly dubious reputation will be missing a worthwhile experience. After all, the cruise ships stop here, so it must be worth seeing!

*Mount Pellegrino looms over Palermo.*

# Turin

Approaching this major industrial city on the River Po through endless dreary suburbs, it's hard to imagine what lies ahead – a pleasing if slightly grubby centre with gracious Baroque streets, wonderful churches, opulent palaces and extraordinary collections of antiquities and art. Many of the finest buildings date from the 15th century, when Turin belonged to the Duchy of Savoy, becoming its capital in 1563 and, briefly, the capital of unified Italy in 1861.

When the Italian capital moved on, Turin industrialized, rapidly becoming the country's major manufacturing centre. The hectic energy that swirls around is expressed in suicidal traffic – much of it consisting of Turin-made Fiats. Efforts are being made to smarten up the city and improve traffic flow, with infrastructure and redevelopment projects everywhere.

The city centre is laid out in an easy-to-follow grid plan. The Via Roma is the grand main street, lined with expensive shops and cafés. It gives access to some of the best squares, like the splendid oval Piazza San Carlo and Piazza Castello, with its imposing royal palaces. The only early monuments to have survived are palaces and churches, as Turin was extensively rebuilt in the early 1700s.

The Residences of the Royal House of Savoy (here and in nearby towns) are collectively a UNESCO World Heritage Site. Turin's include the 17th century Palazzo Reale and castle-like Palazzo Madama. Other noteworthy monuments include the Renaissance Cathedral (Duomo), still impressive despite ongoing restoration following a fire, and Turin's most elaborate church, Santuario della Consolata, with an ancient statue of the Madonna to be seen in the crypt. And no visit to Turin would be complete without a visit to the National Museum in Palazzo Carignano, if only for mementoes of local boy Garibaldi, the long-haired revolutionary who unified Italy.

**POPULATION:**
908,000 (2004)
**WHEN TO GO:**
Summer – winters are cold, spring and autumn can be damp and foggy.
**DON'T MISS:**
The eccentric Mole Antonelliana, actually built in the 19th century but looking older, that today houses the National Cinema Museum.
The bustling Sunday-morning Balôn flea market, not far from the Cathedral.
The Palatine Towers (Porte Palatine) – an old city gate of part-Roman origin.
The Agnelli artistic legacy – the newly opened Pinacoteca Giovanni e Marella Agnelli, containing the fabulous art collection of Fiat mogul Gianni Agnelli.
The Agnelli industrial legacy – the Museo dell'Automobile, Italy's only motor museum of note.
The 18th century Basilica di Superga, atop a hill outside the city (ride up on the Rack Railway), for a superb view of Turin with the Alps in the distance.
Egizio Museum, for the world's second-most-important collection of Ancient Egyptian treasures (saves a trip to Cairo to see the most important).
**YOU SHOULD KNOW:**
Tests have shown that the famous Turin Shroud, once believed to be the cloth that covered Jesus in his tomb, only dates from the Middle Ages.

*Mole Antonelliana, the 'Eiffel Tower of Torino'*

# Florence

Florence is the cultural centre of Italy, and perhaps of the Western world. Crammed with galleries, wonderful buildings and world-class art treasures, this unspoilt late-medieval city clearly demonstrates its importance in the cultural and political development of Europe. The architectural jewel of Florence has to be the Cathedral of Santa Maria del Fiore, known as the Duomo, a Gothic masterpiece. Its magnificent dome was built by Filippo Brunelleschi, and inside there are beautiful frescoes by some of Italy's greatest artists. The Campanile tower (partly designed by Giotto) and the Baptistery buildings are also well worth a visit. The Baptistery started out as a Roman temple; its bronze doors were among the earliest large bronze castings in the Renaissance period. Both the dome and the tower are open to tourists and provide excellent views over the city rooftops.

At the heart of the city in Piazza della Signoria is the awe-inspiring Fountain of Neptune created by Bartolomeo Ammanati. This famous marble sculpture lies at the end of a Roman aqueduct, still in working order. A stroll around the city streets will reveal many Renaissance architectural masterpieces, including Brunelleschi's Ospedale degli Innocenti (foundling hospice), the Pazzi chapel in the Church of Santa Croce, Michelangelo's work at San Lorenzo, and the Laurentian Library.

Renaissance Florence was dominated by the Medici, the most powerful family in the city from the 15th to the 18th century. They patronized many artists, and the city's two major art galleries, the Uffizi and the Pitti Palace, were created for their art collections. The Uffizi was first opened to visitors in 1591, which makes it one of Europe's first museums. Today it houses the greatest collection of Italian and Florentine art in the world. On the other side of the river is the Pitti Palace, which contains some of the Medici family's private works, as well as a large number of Renaissance masterpieces, including several by Raphael and Titian, and a large collection of modern art. Next to the Palace are the lovely Boboli Gardens, displaying a whole host of interesting sculptures.

The Arno river passes through the centre of Florence, and by wandering along its banks, you can enjoy the unspoiled skyline of domes and towers. Be sure to see the Ponte Vecchio, with its built-in houses and shops. Built in 1345, this is the only bridge in the city to survive World War II.

**POPULATION:**
370,000 (2005)
**WHEN TO GO:**
Spring or autumn
**DON'T MISS:**
The Duomo – this cathedral plays a large part in making Florence's skyline one of the most picturesque in the world. Completed in 1466 after 170 years of work, it holds up to 30,000 people. Its domed roof is symbolic of the meeting of Renaissance craft and culture and stands at a height of 114.5m (375 ft).
The Uffizi – one of the most famous galleries in the world, the collection of universally acclaimed masterpieces on display here, including works by da Vinci, Michelangelo and Rembrandt, is simply overwhelming.
The Palazzo Pitti.
The loggia dei Lanzi's open-air sculptures.
A picnic in the Boboli Gardens – from here enjoy the expansive city views as well as the distinguished collection of sculptures on display.
The churches of San Miniato al Monte, Santa Maria Novella, Santo Spirito and Orsanmichele.
**YOU SHOULD KNOW:**
You can book ahead for the Uffizi to avoid long queues.

*Santa Maria del Fiore*

# Siena

**POPULATION:**
56,000 (2006)
**WHEN TO GO:**
July or August for the Palio.
**DON'T MISS:**
The Palazzo Pubblico and the Torre del Mangia – the palace was built in the 13th century to house the republican government.
The duomo – this medieval cathedral takes the form of a Latin cross. Both the exterior and interior contain examples of striped black and white marble, the symbolic colours of Siena due to the black and white horses of the city's legendary founders Senius and Aschius.
The Museo dell'Opera del Duomo – houses the best of Siena's paintings and sculptures, including some of the best Italian Gothic and Renaissance art in the country.

Surrounded by vineyards and olive groves, Siena sits on the northern edge of the Crete Senese, a landscape of soft, rounded hills bathed in warm, golden light. One of the most beautiful cities of Tuscany, it is set on three hills linked by a maze of winding alleys and steep steps. The Piazza del Campo, a stunning paved square, stands at the heart of the city, overlooked by the magnificent Duomo. Siena is home to one of the oldest universities in Europe, which lends a bustling, vibrant atmosphere to this historic place.

The city started out as an Etruscan hilltop town, but by 30AD the Romans had established a military outpost here. The Lombards arrived in 6th century, followed by the Franks. Between the 9th and 11th centuries, the church played an active role in governing the city, but the inhabitants soon claimed their right to govern and administer their town.

The city's wealth and military power grew quickly and friction developed between Siena and Florence, as both cities tried to enlarge their territory. There were many battles between the two cities, but

eventually Siena was incorporated into Florentine territory. Despite these turbulent times, in the years 1150–1300 the city flourished and beautiful monuments such as the Duomo, the Palazzo Pubblico and the Torre del Mangia were built. However, a devastating plague hit Siena in 1348 and killed three-fifths of the population, after which the city was slow to recover.

In the centre of the city is the enormous, scallop-shaped Piazza del Campo. One of the greatest squares in the world, it is overlooked by the Palazzo Pubblico and the soaring Torre del Mangia. Collectively, they are a UNESCO World Heritage Site and represent a millennium of Siena's cherished aspiration of independence and (not always successful) democracy.

On the 2 July and the 16 August every year, the Piazza del Campo hosts the Palio, a world-famous bareback horse race round the cobbled streets of the city. Rival processions fill the town, each in their own colourful medieval dress, with screeching bands and flying flags. These races have been run continuously for at least 500 years and are a part of Siena's living history.

The Pinacoteca Nazionale – a wonderful art gallery displaying local art dating from 1200-1300.
The Piazza del Campo – this shell-shaped piazza lies at the heart of Siena and has served as a focus for life in the city for centuries. It is regarded as one of the most beautiful civic spaces in Europe and is the venue for a medieval horse race that takes place each year in July or August.
The church of San Domenico.
**YOU SHOULD KNOW:**
There are entrance charges for most historic sites.

*The Torre del Mangia towers above the Piazza del Campo and Siena.*

# Naples

**POPULATION:**
984,000 (2005)
**WHEN TO GO:**
Mild winters, hot summers, so take
your pick (Roman emperors always
chose the summer).
**DON'T MISS:**
The mysterious Church of San
Lorenzo, with an original Roman
street beneath.
More underground Naples – the
catacombs of San Gennaro in the
north, and the old Greco-Roman
reservoir system reached from Via
del Tribunali.
A trip out to the famous ruined
Roman towns of Pompeii and
Herculaneum, overwhelmed by the
eruption of Vesuvius in 79 AD.
The Umberto Gallery, a classic
Victorian glass-roofed shopping
arcade with tempting shops, cafés
and bars.
Fascinating workshops of traditional
artisans in the old city's San Gregorio
Armeno.
The nearby Church of St Gregory, a
wonderful example of Neapolitan
Baroque architecture with frescoes,
early cloisters and a fountain.
**YOU SHOULD KNOW:**
Naples has made a massive and
fattening contribution to world
cuisine – the ubiquitous pizza was
invented here.

*A view across the city*

"See Naples and die" goes the old phrase – but things aren't quite as bad as that, even though Italy's third-largest city has plenty of rough areas and is home to the powerful Camorra (local Mafia). It is the largest and most prosperous city in southern Italy, overlooking the Bay of Naples and overlooked in turn by the brooding volcanic presence of Mount Vesuvius, mainland Europe's only active volcano. The historic centre became a UNESCO World Heritage Site in 1995.

Perhaps the city's slightly dubious reputation explains why it gets fewer visitors than its undoubted attractions merit – it is a beautiful place with a long history attested to by many fine monuments. Or maybe it's the manic traffic! The vibrant old city is chaotically Italian – narrow medieval (and earlier) streets, no pavements, no street signs, no traffic lights, no parking restrictions, street markets and eager hawkers, washing hanging everywhere . . . yet somehow it all seems to function perfectly.

There are heritage sights a-plenty, including half-a-dozen castles. The Bourbon palace of Reggia di Capodimonte (now a museum) dominates the city, and has a superb view of the bay. Down on the water, the 12th century Castel dell'Ovo is a stern presence. Fine churches abound – the Cathedral, Santa Chiara, San Lorenzo Maggiore, Gesù Nuovo. Museums include the important National Archaeological Museum and the San Martino Museum in a wonderful old monastery. From the old town, the pedestrianized Via Toledo with its smart shops leads to the new centre though – despite an energetic restoration programme – the city's slightly seedy underbelly is never far away.

Actually, despite all the contrasts and contradictions, it is easy to sum up this extraordinary city – visitors either love Naples to bits . . . or hate it on sight!

# Verona

Strategically located where the River Adage emerges from the Alps onto the Northern Italian plain, Verona is near Lake Garda on a loop of the fast-flowing river. It is a city of bridges (ten of them) and was once the most important town owned by Venice on the mainland (terra firma). Richly endowed with picturesque streets and squares, art and architecture, it is hardly possible to imagine a city that has a more appealing character. It is, quite rightly, a UNESCO World Heritage Site.

The city's history is well illustrated by famous monuments and buildings. The amphitheatre built around 30 AD is the third largest in Italy and there are other Roman remains, such as a theatre and the rebuilt Gavi Arch. The 4th century shrine of Verona's patron saint, St Zeno, lies beneath the stunning Basilica of San Zeno Maggiore, a triumph of Romanesque architecture built in the 12th century. Other Romanesque masterpieces include the small Basilica of San Lorenzo, the large Church of Santa Maria Antica and the striking Cathedral, with its fine Gothic interior. Indeed, there are so many fascinating churches in Verona that a month could be spent viewing them.

The old town's central feature is the elongated Piazza del Erbe, once the Roman forum and now the scene of a lively market. This must surely be one of the most delightful old squares in all Italy. Nearby Piazza dei Signori is surrounded by palaces, including one now serving as the Town Hall. The Loggia del Consiglio is one of the finest early Renaissance buildings in the country, crowned by statues of famous Veronans. The city walls are a 15th century architectural statement, that were built to serve both a defensive and aesthetic function – marvel at the Porta del Palio.

*The view from the top of the Torre del Commune*

**POPULATION:**
260,000 (2006)
**WHEN TO GO:**
Verona gets crowded in midsummer, so June and September are good for those who like breathing space.
**DON'T MISS:**
The Natural History Museum, with an exceptional collection of fossils and archaeological remains.
Castelvecchio Museum in a 14th century castle, with superb sculptures, statues and paintings . . . plus a great view of the city's terracotta roofscape from the platform on the keep.
The imposing Gothic tombs of the ruling Scaglier family adjoining the Church of Santa Maria Antica.
Sweeping views from the top of the Torre del Commune (lift, not stairs!).
The Dominican Church of Sant'Anastasia by the river (built in Gothic style (1290-1323) for the wonderfully decorated interior.
Scaligero Bridge, a fine 14th century structure restored after damage in World War II.
**YOU SHOULD KNOW:**
Verona is the home of ill-starred Romeo and Juliet, and an old stone balcony falsely claiming association with the fictional lovers is a popular attraction.

*The Colosseum*

# Rome

In central Italy where the River Aniene joins the Tiber lies Rome, a powerful political and economic centre for 2,500 years. No only does the city ooze history, both ancient and more modern, it is also the capital of a thoroughly sophisticated and forward-thinking nation. Most visitors are awestruck by the sheer pace of life here, mainly fuelled by espresso coffee, but there are also moments of tranquil reflection. Whether shopping on the Via Veneto, visiting ancient ruins or admiring the work of Leonardo Da Vinci, visitors rarely go away disappointed.

Rome is one of the few major European cities that escaped World War II relatively intact, so central Rome remains essentially Renaissance and Baroque in character. With more than 900 churches and basilicas, it has been for centuries the centre of the Christian world. Among the most important of the churches are San Giovanni in Laterano, Santa Maria Maggiore and San Lorenzo Fuori le Mura.

In the middle of Rome is Vatican City, a separate sovereign state and the enclave of the Holy See. Here is Saint Peter's Basilica and its huge forecourt designed under the direction of Pope Alexander VII so that the greatest number of people could see the Pope give his blessing from the façade of the church. In Vatican City there are also the prestigious Vatican Library, the Raphael Rooms and other important works by Leonardo Da Vinci, Raphael, Giotto and Botticelli. The Vatican Museums, founded by Pope Julius II in the sixteenth century, display works from the fabulous and extensive collection of the Roman Catholic Church, including the world-famous Sistine Chapel.

Rome boasts a wealth of important art treasures to tempt the visitor. The best an be found in the Galleria Borghese, the Palazzo Doria Pamphili, the Capitoline museums, the Museo Nazionale delle Terme, the Galleria Colonna, and the Palazzo Barberini with its National Gallery of Antique Art.

The ancient Roman ruins are, of course, among the best in the world. The highlights include the sumptuous imperial palaces on the Palatine Hill, the temples in the forum, Augustus' *Ara Pacis* (altar of peace), the huge Baths of Diocletian, the exquisite Pantheon, the eerie catacombs and the chill of the Colosseum where, like the Circus Maximus, a discontented population was kept in check by often bloodthirsty public spectacles.

**POPULATION:**
2,600,000 (2005)
**WHEN TO GO:**
Any time of year.
**DON'T MISS:**
The Palatine Hill – an open-air museum with wonderful views of the Forum.
The Forum – this huge site (a good map is advisable!) is where public meetings would have been held and famous orators would have spoken. This is where Mark Anthony delivered his speech following the assassination of Caesar.
The Castel Sant'Angelo – originally commissioned by Roman Emperor Hadrian as a mausoleum for himself and his family and located on the banks of the Tiber, this is one of Rome's finest sights.
The Spanish Steps – these 138 steps join the Piazza di Spanga and the Trinita dei Monti church and were designed in 1723. The house at the base of the steps is where the poet John Keats lived and died.
The Borghese Gardens – this is the largest and most elegant park in Rome. It houses a lake, temples, fountains and several museums.
**YOU SHOULD KNOW:**
Most tourist attractions have entrance fees.

# Reggio di Calabria

Visit Milan to see a modern, stylish and energetic Italy. Visit Reggio di Calabria on the toe of Italy's 'boot', just across from Sicily, to experience something very different. Here the pace of life is slow and this city, dating back to the 8th century BC, with its palm trees and sparkling sea seems to inhabit a different country. The surrounding terrain is a marvel of mountains, rugged coastline and ancient villages where time seems to have stood still, as old-fashioned locals practise their traditional way of life.

This is not a great place to shop – there are up-market shops on streets like Corso Garibaldi, but choice is limited and prices are steep. Nor is it a destination for those interested in heritage, though good architecture and art are to be found. The city walls, now in four divided sections, were built by Greek settlers before the time of Christ. The National Museum of Greater Greece houses the two famous Riace Bronzes, life-sized nude male statues from the fifth century BC. There are remains of Roman baths. The impressive Cathedral is the largest church in Calabria, and the Aragonese Castle dates back to the 6th century. But Reggio di Calabria simply isn't organized to cash in on its history as northern cities do, so you have to work at it.

Instead, it is a place to laze around along the waterfront Lungomare Botanical Garden, eat well-cooked local produce or buy local speciality *briosca con gelato* at a traditional ice cream parlour before taking the few steps from city to beach. Or hire a car and explore Calabria, for a true picture of Old Italy before mass tourism arrives to change it for ever. The Calabrese say it all – Buon Divertimento (Enjoy!).

**POPULATION:**
186,000 (2006)
**WHEN TO GO:**
Summer, when laid-back life beside the impossibly blue water is irresistible.
**DON'T MISS:**
The chance of a miracle – visit the glass tomb of St Gaetano, a parish priest who died in 1963 and was canonized in 2005, to be found in the church that bears his name.
Calabrian siestas (take three hours in the middle of the day, every day) – there's not much point in seeking any action when half the city's asleep.
The Town Art Gallery, with a good selection of works by Italian artists including the Sicilian Antonello da Messina (1430-1479).
Villa Zerbi, where the Venice Biennale stages its southern exhibition.
Nearby Scilla, where the *fata morgana* optical illusion makes Messina across the water in Sicily seem to glitter above the sea.
**YOU SHOULD KNOW:**
Some 80 per cent of Reggio di Calabria was destroyed by the earthquake of 1907 – the worst modern quake recorded in Western Europe.

*The Cathedral*

# Genoa

**POPULATION:**
620,000 (2006)
**WHEN TO GO:**
Summer, for all the open-air attractions round the harbour and in the old town.
**DON'T MISS:**
Genoa's signature building – the world's oldest working (and tallest brick) lighthouse, La Lanterna.
The Palace of San Giorgio above the old harbour, where Venetian explorer Marco Polo was imprisoned in the late 13th century, using the time to write an account of his travels.
Stone-built twin towers of the medieval city gate that is one of Genoa's famous landmarks.
The grand monument in Acquaverde Square to favourite son Christopher Columbus (he donated some of his Americas prize money to alleviating poverty in Genoa).
The renowned monuments and statues in the Staglieno Cemetery.
A stroll around the Boccadasse, the atmospheric old mariners' quarter on the city's eastern waterfront.
**YOU SHOULD KNOW:**
Genoa's flag is the red cross on a white ground of St George, identical to the national flag of England.

A major city and seaport in northern Italy, Genoa was the birthplace of Christopher Columbus. There has been a settlement here since the dawn of time, that already had a long and troubled history before Christ was born. During the Dark Ages it remained obscure, but then emerged as an independent city-state with a large merchant fleet, protected by one of the most powerful navies in the Mediterranean. The hustling atmosphere of the large, workaday modern city has prejudiced Genoa in tourist terms, which is unfair – the medieval old town is the equal of any in Europe.

Genoa's busy port is still vital to the local economy, and was smartened up for the city's recent term as a European Capital City of Culture. The old harbour is a 'must see', if only to ascend the bizarre Il Bigo monument (erected to celebrate the Columbus quincentennial in 1992) for incomparable views of city and sea (as far as Corsica on a clear day). The harbour has a maritime museum and aquarium.

From there, it is a steep climb up narrow medieval streets full of tempting little shops and punctuated with magnificent churches to three main squares at the heart of the old city – Banchi Square, once the grain market and now home to flower sellers, Ferrari Square and Matteotti Square. Be sure to find the imposing Ducal Palace. Close by is the wonderful Baroque Gesù Church, containing two Rubens paintings.

The old city's contrarily named Strada Nuovo (now Via Garibaldi) was made a UNESCO World Heritage Site in 2006. This mid-16th century district contains the palaces of Genoa's most eminent families. For a lesson in Genoese architecture over the centuries, see the Cathedral of St Lawrence, consecrated in 1113 and added to until the late 1600s.

*A view of the city's eclectic architecture*

# Vicenza

Straddling the River Bacchiglione, Vicenza lies on the edge of the fertile Po plain, between Alpine foothills and the volcanic Bérici Mountains. The city came under Venetian rule in the 15th century, sharing its fortunes with those of the great city state until seized by Napoleon in 1797. An exploration of the cobbled streets and town walls of this compact medieval city centre is hugely rewarding.

The influential 16th century architect Andrea Palladio (of 'Palladian style' fame) was apprenticed and worked here, leaving many examples of his work in the city, including the Palazzo Chiericati, now the City Art Gallery. Another Palladio masterpiece is the Basilica Palladiana with its open colonnades. This stands in the heart of the old town, at the Piazza dei Signori, a square surrounded by early buildings that include the Town Hall (Palazzo della Ragione). Vincenza, together with Palladian villas in the surrounding area, is a UNESCO World Heritage Site.

Another fine square is the Piazza del Duomo, which contains the splendid 15th century Cathedral (built on the foundations of three earlier churches), faced in red and white marble with a decorative interior. The Bishops' Palace is a 15th and 16th century structure behind a 19th century façade.

Vicenza's main street (inevitably Corso Andrea Palladio) is lined with palaces, surprisingly not all by the master! These include the Palazzo dei Commune and the Gothic Palazzo Da Schio (known as The Golden House). The Church of Santo Stefano has a Madonna Enthroned by Palma Vecchio and the 13th century Church of Santa Corona a Baptism of Christ by Giovanni Bellini. At the end of the street is the Teatro Olimpico, designed by . . . take a wild guess. In fact Vicenza is not so much about Location, Location, Location as Palladio, Palladio, Palladio.

*Piazza dei Signori*

**POPULATION:**
119,000 (2007)
**WHEN TO GO:**
Summer – all those Palladio buildings positively shimmer in bright sunlight.
**DON'T MISS:**
Palladio's La Rotonda Villa on the outskirts of town – in addition to monumental buildings in the city, he is famous for elegant villas built for wealthy Venetians.
The magnificent views of city and mountains from the Basilica di Monte Berico pilgrimage church, reached by climbing the Portici di Monte, series of arcades just south of town.
The notable pictures in the Churches of Ara Coeli, Carmine and St Catherine.
A gold trinket to remember Vicenza by – there are still many goldsmiths plying their traditional trade here (it's sometimes called The City of Gold).
The tombs of many illustrious Vicentines in the 13th century Church of St Lorenzo of the Friars Minor.
A walk along the river, to find the four bridges and see a side of the old city that is very different from the Palladian splendour of the shop window.
**YOU SHOULD KNOW:**
Whisper it if you dare, but the great Palladio was actually born Andrea di Pietro della Gondola . . . in Padua.

*The recently stabilized Leaning Tower*

# Pisa

There's a lot more to Pisa than the famous Leaning Tower, though that's an impressive start. The origins of this Tuscan city on the River Arno are lost in the mists of time, but as the main port between Genoa and Ostia it was an important Roman settlement. Pisa reached its zenith as a maritime power in the 11th century.

Indeed, it was loot from supporting the Norman crusade to evict Saracens from Sicily that provided funds to begin construction of what must surely be one of Italy's finest monuments – the walled Campo dei Miracoli (Field of Miracles) to the north of the old town centre. Miraculous indeed – the Leaning Tower (the Cathedral's bell tower) is but one element of this superb early complex, the others being the Cathedral of St Zeno itself, the circular Baptistry of St John and the massive Camposanto (the Holy Field, a monumental cemetery). This is, inevitably, a UNESCO World Heritage Site – one of the best!

After being conquered by Naples, Pisa went into decline – the population today is much the same as it was in the Middle Ages, helping to preserve Pisa's romantic medieval character. The ancient university (founded in 1343) has become one of Italy's top universities, and tourism now makes a huge contribution to the city's economy.

After enjoying the miracles, it's well worth escaping the crowd by wandering around the old town's peaceful streets, admiring medieval palaces and university buildings. There are also fine bridges and churches to enjoy, including the Gothic masterpiece Santa Maria della Spina on the river bank and the octagonal Sant'Agata. The city is also a place to shop, with up-market areas like elegantly arcaded Borgo Stretto and a host of tempting little shops in the back streets.

**POPULATION:**
90,000 (2005)
**WHEN TO GO:**
The Field of Miracles gets very crowded in the summer holidays, so try June or September.
**DON'T MISS:**
One of Pisa's major landmarks – the Knights' Square (Piazza dei Cavalieri) on the site of the Roman forum.
The Museo dell'Opera del Duomo, with Cathedral treasures and sculpture by the 13th century father-and-son sculptors Nicola and Giovanni Pisano.
Historic Palazzo Reale, the palace where Galileo Galilei showed the Grand Duke of Tuscany the planets he had discovered with his telescope.
Two more Leaning Towers of Pisa – one at the end of Via Santa Maria and the other on the Piagge riverside walk.
Works of art in the churches – many of them have works by Italian masters.
**YOU SHOULD KNOW:**
If you want to climb the 294 steps of the recently stabilized Torre Pendente (Leaning Tower of Pisa) you must buy a ticket and wait for up to two hours.

# Sorrento

This small city has a superb location on its own peninsula jutting out into the Bay of Naples, with wonderful views across the water to Mount Vesuvius and Naples itself. This, coupled with proximity to the historic remains of Pompeii and Herculaneum, makes Sorrento a popular tourist base. There are ferries from the harbour to Amalfi, Capri, Ischia, Naples and Positano, whilst the famous Amalfi Drive connects Sorrento and Amalfi via a spectacular cliff-top road.

Sorrento was settled long before Roman times, and the modern town largely follows the layout of the old. There are many ruins and traces of former occupation in surrounding areas, including old tunnels down to the sea and the reservoir that served the underground aqueduct network. Some of the more interesting sites cannot be visited, but only seen from above.

A strong defensive location made the city hard to capture, but it still underwent various ups and downs – including a sacking by Muslim pirates in 1558 and an outbreak of the Black Death in 1656. But it remained an important centre of the southern Campania region, based on trade and agriculture, developing rapidly in the 19th century with the advent of genteel tourism, an activity that has since become the mainstay of the city's economy.

In that context, the city's strengths are twofold. It is well organized to serve the needs of visitors who merely wish to relax, with a charming harbour area (no beach!), pedestrianized streets, tempting shops, numerous cafés and a variety of restaurants. Sorrento also serves as an ideal base for exploration of the surrounding area with its wonderful coastal scenery and historic attractions. There are many organized tours on offer, some rather expensive, but for those who like to set their own agenda public transport is excellent . . . and affordable.

**POPULATION:**
17,000 (2004)
**WHEN TO GO:**
The summer is best – the place is rather quiet outside the tourist season.
**DON'T MISS:**
The Museo Correale di Terranova, with an eclectic family collection that includes much of the traditional local Sorrento woodwork alongside antiquities, paintings and porcelain.
A walk along cliff-top paths, to enjoy the orange and lemon groves and intriguing glimpses of old ruins, plus precipitous views down to the sea.
The Sedile Dominova, a 15th century arcaded loggia where the town's nobility used to hold council.
A visit to the Art Nouveau Grand Hotel Victoria – not necessarily to stay, but to inspect the remains of the villa of Roman Emperor Augustus in the gardens.
Supreme self-indulgence at Davide's – boldly but accurately described as *Il Gelato* (the Ice Cream), with over 60 flavours to choose from.
A stroll through medieval Via Pietà in the old town centre, past the 13th century Venerio Palace and 15th century Correale Palace, now part of the Baroque Santa Maria della Pietà.
**YOU SHOULD KNOW:**
Sorrento is renowned throughout Italy for production of Limoncello, an alcoholic digestif flavoured with lemon rind.

# San Marino

**POPULATION:**
4,000 (2005)
**WHEN TO GO:**
April to June for temperate weather
without Italian high summer
tourist pressure.
**DON'T MISS:**
The now-disused station and tunnels
of the railway built by Italian dictator
Benito Mussolini to connect San
Marino and Rimini.
San Marino's small state museum,
with a number of interesting exhibits
– a joint ticket to see the Palazzo
Pubblico is available.
A generous slice of the national
chocolate layer cake – the
patriotically named Torta De Tre
Monti (Cake of the Three Peaks).
The Church of St Francis, which also
contains an art gallery and museum.
A cable car ride from the city down
to Borgo Maggiore.
**YOU SHOULD KNOW:**
Napoleon refused to seize San
Marino, commenting 'Why, it's a
model republic!'. And Abraham
Lincoln was made an
honorary citizen.

This is the capital city of The Most Serene Republic of San Marino, a landlocked mini-state in Italy's Apennine Mountains not far from the Adriatic Sea. It has an area of just 61 sq km (23.5 sq mi) and was founded in 301 by a Christian stonemason fleeing the religious persecution of Roman Emperor Diocletian. It has a constitution written in 1600 and is the world's oldest extant democracy. Clinging to the upper slopes of Mount Titano, San Marino City is no longer the republic's largest town. But for centuries it was the only town, until the tiny country expanded beyond its lofty city limits by purchasing small amounts of additional territory over time.

In the past, echoing its roots, the principal industry of San Marino was stone quarrying and carving, but the city has become a popular tourist destination visited by over three million people a year. In addition to enjoying far-reaching views and exploring the charming old town, they are very well catered for by a large number of shops, bars, cafés and restaurants.

The fortified city is largely pedestrianised, with long cobbled streets that wind up the mountain (fitness required!), lined with medieval houses and churches. Above are the city's most famous landmarks – the three defensive towers located on Mount Titano's three peaks. The oldest is the 11th century Guaita, the highest is Cesta (13th century) and the third is Montale (14th century). The first two are open to the public, with Cesta having a museum dedicated to St Marinus. The Pallazzo Pubblico (Public Palace) is worth seeing. It is both town hall and the republic's centre of government, and is not as old as it appears, being a 19th century construction on the site of a much older building serving the same purpose.

*The historic Rocca Guaita fortress*

# Valletta

Benjamin Disraeli visited Valletta, Malta's capital city, in August 1830, on the recommendation of Lord Byron. He described it as 'a city of palaces built by gentlemen for gentlemen' which 'equals in its noble architecture, if it does not excel, any capital in Europe'. The fortified city is built on a rocky peninsula on the island's north-east coast, surrounded on three sides by two beautiful harbours: the Grand Harbour and Marsamxett harbour.

The foundation stone of Valletta was laid in 1566 by Jean Parisot de la Valette, the Grandmaster of the Order of Saint John. The Knights chose this site for its strategic importance after the Siege of Malta in 1565. The new city was to strengthen the Order's position in Malta, effectively binding the Knights to the island. The city was designed by an Italian military engineer, Francesco Laparelli, who provided a sewage system and piped fresh water in case the fortress was ever besieged. Many of the most important buildings were built by a Maltese architect, Gerolamo Cassar. Ancient fortifications surround this lovely Baroque city, characterized by narrow streets, fountains and parapets supporting coats of arms.

The Grandmaster's Palace, built by Cassar for the Knights, currently houses the House of Representatives of Malta. It features an armoury, housing one of the finest collections of weapons of the period of the Knights of Malta in all of Europe. The magnificent St John's Co-Cathedral is also well worth a visit. Its austere façade hides an ornate Baroque interior, with painted ceilings and superb carved stone work. It houses many works of art, including Caravaggio's *The Beheading of John the Baptist*, the only painting he signed. The Manoel Theatre has a stunning oval auditorium decorated with gold leaf. Built in 1731, it is the third oldest theatre in Europe still in use, and can be seen on a guided tour.

*A view of Valletta from the sea*

**POPULATION:**
6,000 (2005)
**WHEN TO GO:**
Spring or autumn
**DON'T MISS:**
The former Grand Master's Palace – this almost square building occupies an entire block and is the house of the government in Malta.
The National Museum of Fine Arts – this occupies one of the city's finest Baroque palaces, built by the Knights of St John.
The panoramic views of the harbour from the Upper Barracca Gardens.
The Cathedral of St Paul – situated in Independence Square, it is built in neo-classical style with a spire that is a famous Valletta landmark.
**YOU SHOULD KNOW:**
The whole city is a UNESCO World Heritage Site.

*The view north from the Ledra Museum and Observatory*

# Nicosia

This troubled place remains the world's only divided capital city, serving as capital of the official Republic of Cyprus and of the unrecognized Turkish Republic of North Cyprus. The 1974 Turkish invasion cut Nicosia – and the country – in half, a painful situation (for the majority Greek Cypriot population) that remains to this day. The northern (Turkish) and southern (Greek) parts of the city are divided by the 'Green Line', strictly policed by the United Nations. The shock and disruption caused by the invasion took a long time to overcome, but 'official' Nicosia is fast becoming a dynamic and interesting city.

To experience the atmosphere of times past, head for the old city, encircled by thick Venetian walls built in the 16th century. Here, narrow streets run between old sandstone houses with ornate balconies and there are plenty of small shops, tavernas and cafés. Explore the medieval buildings, old churches and fascinating museums that bring the long history of this ancient settlement to life. Find the central Eleftheria Square, then follow the pedestrian-only Ledra Street in to the liveliest part of the old town. Of especial interest is Laiki Yitonia, a renovated 18th century enclave where local craftsmen and artisans display their wares along winding cobbled lanes awash with bourgainvillea. A colourful open-air market takes place in Eleftherios Venizelos Square every Wednesday.

Outside the old walls, a modern metropolis has sprung up, against the backdrop of the Kyrenia Mountains with the distinctive Pentadaktylos (Five-Finger Mountain). This contemporary commercial and cultural centre has become the island's main shopping centre, with some of the best shops concentrated in Archbishop Makarios Street and parallel Stasikratous Street. The inhabitants of southern Nicosia devoutly hope they are creating a city that will one day become the capital of a reunited island.

**POPULATION:**
270,000 (Greek section, 2004)
**WHEN TO GO:**
Hot in summer, perfect in spring and autumn, cool in winter.
**DON'T MISS:**
The Cyprus Museum in City Gardens – a highly recommended display with artefacts going back to the 11th century BC.
Famugusta Gate, one of only three in the old Venetian city walls.
Liberty Monument at the corner of Koraes and Nikoforus Phokas Streets, celebrating the island's successful fight for independence that ended in 1959.
Impressive interiors at Agios Ionnis Greek Orthodox Cathedral, built in 1662 on earlier foundations.
The excellent city views from the Ledra Museum and Observatory on the 11th floor of the Shacolas Tower.
**YOU SHOULD KNOW:**
In 1191, Richard the Lionheart conquered Cyprus on the way to his first crusade . . . and promptly sold it to the Knights Templars.

# Heraklion (Iráklion)

As long ago as 2000 BC, Heraklion was the port of Knossos, the capital of the Minoan civilization in northern Crete. The ruins of this ancient city, where the mythological Minotaur had his lair, survive remarkably intact, 5 km (3 mi) inland.

The site of Heraklion was settled by Saracen pirates in 824 AD. They built a huge moat around it and used it as a stronghold from where they marauded the Mediterranean coast and islands, successfully fighting off the forces of the Byzantine Empire for nearly 140 years before they were finally defeated. Eventually Heraklion was acquired by Venice and for four hundred years it was the most important commercial and cultural centre in the Eastern Mediterranean. At the end of the 17th century, after a 22-year siege, the Ottoman Turks gained control. Finally, in 1897, the Cretan resistance movement succeeded in gaining independence. The islanders chose to become part of Greece a few years later.

Today, Heraklion is a thriving modern capital city, the commercial hub of Crete. But, wandering through the old town, you are forcefully reminded of its magnificent, if bloody, past – the incredible medieval city walls and massive prison-fortress, built by the Venetians using forced Cretan labour; the fascinating mix of architecture, going back 800 years, with beautiful Venetian and Ottoman buildings.

An ornate 17th century fountain, Liondaria, dominates the Plateia Venizelou, a delightful central square lined with cafes and shops. At the food market your senses are assailed by the brilliant coloured fruit and vegetables, local honeys, olive oils and wines, the scent of charcoal mingled with oregano wafting from tavernas, the hubbub of Heraklion street life. Bars and music venues are open at all hours, and the city, the fourth largest in Greece, exudes an atmosphere of cosmopolitan exuberance, buzzing with energy.

**POPULATION:**
138,000 (2001)
**WHEN TO GO:**
Crete is at its most beautiful in the spring. July and August can be very hot.
**DON'T MISS:**
Archaeological Museum – magnificent collection of Minoan art and culture, one of the finest museums in the world.
Historical Museum – Medieval, Renaissance and folk art, icon and fresco collections and memorabilia from the Cretan struggle for independence.
The Loggia – magnificent 17th century Venetian building, now used as the Town Hall.
A plate of *bougatsa* – a local cream cheese pastry.
Korai – narrow lanes full of tavernas and restaurants where the locals hang out.
The local shops of Leoforos Kalokerinou.
Arhanes – a beautiful historic town in spectacular surroundings 15 km (9 mi) from Heraklion.
**YOU SHOULD KNOW:**
Heraklion was the home town of the artist El Greco (Domenicos Theotokopoulos); the airport is named after Nicos Kazantzakis, a famous Cretan philosopher and writer, author of *Zorba the Greek*.

*Koules fortress built in Venetian times.*

# Patras (Patra)

The port of Patras, situated near the Gulf of Corinth in the northern Pelopennese is known as the 'Gate to the West', linking mainland Greece to the Ionian islands, Italy and Western Europe. It is the third largest city in Greece, the second largest port after Piraeus, and a major commercial, scientific and technical centre. In 2006, the city was the European Capital of Culture.

The city centre has two separate parts. The largely 19th century design of the lower town, adjacent to the port, has small parks and distinctive squares where there are innumerable little cafes and tavernas. The awesome Agios Andreas, a Cathedral of monumental proportions, towers over you from its position on the seafront. You go up a series of steps to reach the older, upper part of town, which has a picturesque air about it. There is a wonderful ruined Venetian castle and gardens at the highest point of the city, from where there is a staggering view of the coast.

Apart from the city centre, Patras cannot be described as beautiful. Like so much modern Greek urban development, lax planning laws have enabled a concrete jungle of shoddy design to sprawl out from the city centre. However, there are some truly magnificent sights and the city has a thriving, forward-looking buzz about it, with a flourishing indie music, arts and theatre scene. The futuristic Charilaos Trikoupis cable-stayed bridge has become a symbol of the city – an engineering triumph, built in 2004, that crosses the Gulf of Corinth to link the Pelopennese peninsula with the rest of mainland Greece. It is an awe-inspiring masterpiece of modern design, especially at night, when it is illuminated.

*Agios Andreas Cathedral*

# Thessaloniki

*The town and harbour*

'The mother of Macedonia' takes time to reveal itself from beneath layers of modernity. The second largest city in Greece, Thessaloniki is not only stuffed with early Christian, Byzantine and Jewish monuments but also has some beautiful vernacular architecture, wonderful food, a vibrant nightlife and flourishing international arts scene.

The city was founded on the coast of Northern Greece in 315 BC by the King of Macedon in honour of his wife, Thessalonika, the sister of Alexander The Great. Under the Roman Empire it was a thriving port and important Jewish colony, becoming an early centre for Christianity after St Paul preached in the synagogue here. Later, as part of the Byzantine Empire, Thessaloniki was second in importance only to Constantinople itself. It has a fascinating multi-cultural past, with Greek Orthodox, Ottoman Muslim and Sephardic Jewish communities all rubbing along together. In the 17th and 18th centuries, under the Ottoman Empire, it was the largest Jewish city in the world. It has always been a major commercial and cultural centre, the hub of South East Europe, and today has the largest student population in Greece.

Thessaloniki is a city of many parts. The flashy shops, hotels and restaurants on the elegant waterfront Nikis avenue and Plateia Aristotelous exude an atmosphere of unadulterated luxury. In striking contrast, on the way up to Eptapyrgio, the topmost point of the city, there are the higgledy-piggledy lanes of Ano Poli, where charming wooden houses are built overhanging the street, and small churches and tavernas are secreted down alleyways. The city's monuments – the Rotunda and Karnara, and churches of Agios Demetrios and Agia Sofia – are all magnificent. There are countless bars, restaurants and clubs and at night the city comes alive. Amazingly, although Thessaloniki is such a lovely city, it has escaped the notice of the tourist trade so is pleasurably hassle-free.

**POPULATION:**
977,000 (2001)
**WHEN TO GO:**
September to December for the Dimitria arts festival. November for the International Film Festival – the most important cultural event of South Eastern Europe.
**DON'T MISS:**
Museum of Byzantine Culture.
Jewish History Museum.
Agios Nikolaos Orfanos – a plain-looking church on the outside with amazing 14th century interior frescoes.
Modiano Market – wonderful food market with Roma street musicians.
The Bezesteni – 15th century covered market specializing in textiles and jewellery. One of the best preserved Turkish monuments in the city.
Osios David (Latomou Monastery) – charming, hidden away 6th century church with shady courtyard and incredible interior mosaic.
**YOU SHOULD KNOW:**
The emblem of the city is Lefkos Pyrgos (The White Tower) a 15th century round fort on the waterfront. It became a symbol of repression and terror under the Ottoman Empire when it was used as a prison and execution ground. When the city was liberated from Ottoman rule, the citizens whitewashed it in a ritualistic act of purification. Lefkos Pyrgos is no longer white but it remains a symbol of freedom for all Thessalonians.

# Athens

This legendary city – named after Athena, the goddess of wisdom – is over 3,000 years old. Athens was the world's first democratic state. Known as the 'Cradle of Western Civilization', its culture spawned the great philosophers and writers – Socrates, Plato and Aristotle among them.

Do not let your initial impression of Athens close your mind to this wonderful city. The eighth largest metropolis in Europe, it appears, through the heat haze and traffic fug, a distinctly uninspiring concrete mass sprawling across the plain of Attica on the coast of south-eastern Greece. But give yourself time to explore central Athens, a relatively small area, and a different picture emerges. Starting from Syntagma, the central square, you will discover far more than a pile of ancient monuments; although, of course, there are plenty of those too.

The world's greatest cultural monument, the Parthenon, towers over the city from the top of the Acropolis. As you climb up to it through the narrow winding streets of Plaka, accompanied by live music drifting out from bar doorways, you begin to savour the influences that have shaped the history of this remarkable city. The atmosphere is pervaded with an almost oriental charm – a hotchpotch of Byzantine churches, neo-classical architecture, old mosques, tavernas and simple whitewashed houses. Just to the north, Monastiraki is a bazaar area even more redolent of the east, where you will find one of the best flea markets in Europe. In glaring contrast, Ermou, round the corner, is one of the chicest shopping streets in Europe.

Athens is a wonderfully animated outdoor city. The inhabitants are relaxed, confident and courteous, and there is a vibrant street life day and night. The obligatory fleeting visit to the Parthenon that most tourists make on their way to the islands is simply not enough to appreciate the charm of 'the largest village in Greece'.

Taking the metro – an impressive experience in itself – from Omonia to Piraeus, the largest port in Europe. Watch the boats come in while eating take-away souvlaki, and explore the famous Kaminia area.
Cape Soúnio and The Temple of Poseidon (70 km [44 mi] from the city centre).
**YOU SHOULD KNOW:**
Athens has more theatrical stages than any other city – 148 in all. The ancient Herodes Atticus Theatre on the slopes of the Acropolis is the venue for the summer Athens Festival of music and theatre which takes place every year.

*The Acropolis towers over the city below.*

# Corfu (Kérkyra)

*The rooftops of Corfu*

Corfu is the largest and northernmost of the beautiful, lush Ionian Islands. It lies off the Albanian coast at the entrance to the Adriatic Sea. Corfu Town, its elegant capital city, built on a peninsula on the east coast of the island, is a UNESCO World Heritage Site – an authentic, fortified Mediterranean port, enclosed by two magnificent Venetian citadels.

Throughout its history, going back to the 9th century, Corfu has always been a renowned cultural centre for the arts, literature and music – a heritage that still thrives today. For hundreds of years it was a major trading centre under the rule of Venice, then briefly, France, before becoming British territory for most of the 19th century, finally being annexed to modern Greece in 1864. The city is renowned for its wonderful Venetian and British neo-classical architecture.

The Spianáda is a huge central square, which has at its northern end the fine 19th century British Residency, used later as a palace by the Greek royal family. Along one side, there is the Listón, a lovely French-built arcaded street lined with cafes. But the real character of this historic city is to be found while losing yourself in the kantounia – a labyrinth of narrow cobble-stoned lanes – where you will find the city's best architecture and where there is an almost magical surprise round every corner. Do not miss what remains of the old Jewish quarter, the ancient Campiello district, and Kofineta, the area behind the Spianáda.

Corfu exudes an air of Italian rather than Greek culture and has a unique atmosphere. It is one of the most charming island cities to be found anywhere, with a character and history that cannot fail to seduce you.

**POPULATION:**
37,000 (2003)
**WHEN TO GO:**
Easter, to experience Ta Karnivalia when the whole city goes wild the last Sunday of Lent. September for the Corfu Festival – a music and arts festival.
**DON'T MISS:**
The Forts Paleó Froúrio and Néo Froúrio.
The 16th century Agios Spyrídon – Corfu's most important church, named after the island's patron saint.
The Archaeological Museum.
The secluded café and gardens behind the palace (which houses the Museum of Asian Art and Modern Art gallery).
The British cemetery.
Paleokastritsa – a lovely town 26 km (16 mi) away.
**YOU SHOULD KNOW:**
Corfu has a cricket pitch, a legacy of British rule, which is still in use today.

# Rhodes

This ancient city, founded in 408 BC, is situated on the north-eastern tip of Rhodes, the largest of the Dodecanese islands, in the Aegean Sea off the coast of western Turkey. Its citadel, a World Heritage Site, was built by the Knights Hospitalier in the Middle Ages and is one of the best-preserved medieval gated cities in Europe.

In ancient times, the city flourished as the capital of a province in the Roman Empire. Its strategic position at the crossroads of Europe, the Middle East and North Africa ensured its prosperity as a major trading post and it acquired a many-layered, multi-cultural identity. Later, the island came under Turkish governance until the Italians invaded in 1912. They demolished all traces of Ottoman buildings in the city while ruining the original 13th century Hospitalier Palace by renovating it in an extravagant fake medieval style to be the dictator Mussolini's holiday home. Only in 1948 was Rhodes united with the rest of Greece.

The delightful Old Town, built by the harbour, is an intriguing warren of over 200 narrow lanes, criss-crossing at crazy angles, many without names. The only way to get your bearings is to take yourself back to Sokratous, the main street, and start again. At the Plateia Simi you will see the ruins of the Temple of Venus, dating from the 3rd century BC. And on Ippoton (Street of the Knights) you will stumble across a fascinating slice of medieval history.

Today, Rhodes retains its position as the cultural and commercial capital of the eastern Aegean at the same time as being a major international tourist destination. It succeeds in remaining a lovely old port city, providing a superb tourist infrastructure and lively modern ambience without in any way compromising the richness of its past.

**POPULATION:**
80,000 (2004)
**WHEN TO GO:**
April to October
**DON'T MISS:**
Mosque of Suleiman – built in honour of Suleiman the Magnificent, it continues to function as a mosque in spite of the precarious angle of its minaret.
Archaeological Museum – offers a collection of Classical, Hellenistic and Roman sculpture.
Municipal gallery – an impressive collection of Modern Greek art.
The subterranean grave complexes at Korakonero – these ancient cemeteries date back to Roman and Hellenistic times.
Valley of the Butterflies – a unique biotope. Here you can see thousands of brightly coloured butterflies in a beautiful shady valley.
The nightlife of the New Town.
**YOU SHOULD KNOW:**
The massive medieval city walls of the Old City are 4 km (2.5 mi) in perimeter and in places nearly 12 m (40 ft) thick.

*The city walls and Palace of the Grand Masters*

# Antalya

In only 25 years what was once the rundown fishing town of Antalya has transformed itself into the capital of Turkey's Mediterranean coast. This attractive seaside city is the cultural and tourist centre of southern Turkey. In the summer it accommodates as many as 2 million people, attracting them with a vibrant nightlife, superb shopping and miles of beaches as well as a picturesque old quarter and plenty of cultural sites and events in and around the city.

A major part of the charm of Antalya is its spectacular setting. It is built on travertine cliff terraces overlooking the sea, with the snow-capped Taurus Mountains as a backdrop. The symbol of the city, the Yivli Minare – a 38-m (125-ft) high, 13th century tiled minaret – reaches up into the sky from the picturesque lanes of the historic Kaleiçi district, full of old Greek, Italian and Turkish buildings. The cobbled streets wind down the cliff to the city's ancient Roman harbour, where there is the 19th century Iskele Mosque, built over a natural spring, and an award-winning marina.

Despite the inevitable concrete blocks, the modern part of the city has pleasant boulevards fringed with palm trees, expensive shopping streets Isiklar, Ataturk and Cumhuriyet, and the amazing Konyaalti pebbled beach that extends miles to the west, backed by an attractive cliff top promenade of hotels, shops and restaurants with all sorts of entertainment and activities. A short way off to the east is the Lara beach – miles of sand, becoming progressively more deserted the further you walk.

There are wonderful views of the mountains in the distance, while, close by, there are beautiful landscapes and fascinating archaeological sites. Antalya is an almost perfect resort, combining the cultural and entertainment attractions of a city with the pleasures of a beach holiday.

*A view towards the harbour*

# Erzurum

Erzurum is built on a 1,950-m (6,400-ft) high plateau, surrounded by the Eastern Anatolian Mountains. It is the junction of the old Central Asian trade routes, and was the base for the Turkish War of Independence – the Erzurum Congress of 1919 effectively ended Ottoman rule in Turkey. The house in which the revolutionaries stayed is now the Ataturk Museum in a side street off Çaykara Caddesi.

Even though Erzurum has suffered some horrendous earthquakes in its time, a considerable number of remarkable old buildings still survive to attest to its past. It was the eastern bastion of the Byzantine Empire before being overrun by Mongols, Arabs and Central Asian Turks. The Sunni Seljuks left their mark in the form of the multi-columned Ulu Cami (Grand Mosque) built in 1179, and the magnificent 13th century Çifte Minareli Medresi (theological seminary) with twin tiled minarets and superb stone carvings depicting a dragon, the tree of life, and a twin-headed eagle – the symbol of the city. The Yakutiye Medresi is another splendid seminary, with a beautiful portal and tiled minaret.

Erzurum was absorbed into the Ottoman Empire in 1514, resulting in the lovely Lalapasa Mosque, and the Rüstem pasa caravanserai, built under Suleiman the Magnificent. Today, this latter building is a bazaar.

Erzurum is renowned for its exceptionally cold weather and there is excellent skiing at Palandöken Mountain, only 10 km (6 mi) away. It is the cultural centre of eastern Turkey – Ataturk University is one of the best higher education institutions in the country. In many ways, it is a western city and there is a surprising amount of nightlife. However, for the traveller, it still has the thrill of the frontier about it – a corner of civilization in a remote region that has always been in political turmoil.

*The towers of the Çifte Minareli Medresi*

**POPULATION:**
361,000 (2000)
**WHEN TO GO:**
Erzurum has an extreme climate – very hot in summer and snowy winters.
**DON'T MISS:**
The Three Tombs, Üç Kümbetler.
Çobadede Bridge.
Citadel and Clock tower.
Eating Cag kebab – a local speciality.
**YOU SHOULD KNOW:**
There is a local, semi-precious, black jet stone – oltu tasi – unique to Erzurum. It has been used to make jewellery, prayer beads, boxes and ornaments since the 18th century and you can watch craftsmen at work in the bazaar.

*Corinthian columns in what was the Agora (city market) during Roman times.*

# Izmir

Overlooked by Mount Pagos on the west coast of Turkey, Izmir is the third largest city and second port after Istanbul. The ancient city, originally called Smyrna, was destroyed by the Persians in 545 BC. It was re-founded by Alexander the Great and was an important city in both the Roman and Ottoman Empires. From the end of the 15th century, Sephardic Jews settled here, as well as Armenians, Greeks and Levantines, each contributing to its culture.

In 1922, there was a huge fire – a disaster from which Izmir took many years to recover. It finally re-emerged, transformed into an attractive, prosperous city living up to its cosmopolitan heritage, and surrounded by reminders of its ancient roots in the form of Kadifekale – the remains of Alexander the Great's fortress on the top of Mount Pagos, and the Roman Agora on the slopes below.

The liveliest area in Izmir is Kemeralti, a central bazaar district starting at Anafartalar Caddesi (Street of the Whirling Dervishes) stretching to Konak Meydani, a large waterfront square with a fabulously ornate 25-m (80-ft) tall clock tower, Saat Kulesi – the city's symbol. Along the shoreline, Karsiyaka is a lush, leafy district with superb Ottoman mansions as well as some very pretty traditional *sakiz* – small, typically Mediterranean houses.

In the Jewish quarter, the Asansör, an outdoor elevator built in 1907, is an important landmark, and Havra Sokagi is a bustling fruit and vegetable market street with nine synagogues in it.

Izmir has a relaxed lifestyle and western attitude to gender rare in Turkey. Its superb position on the Aegean Sea has ensured that it has always been open to a wide variety of cultural influences and is quick to welcome change. The modern city of Izmir deserves far more international recognition than it has received.

**POPULATION:**
3,097,000 (2007)
**WHEN TO GO:**
Any time. The hot summer months are made bearable by a refreshing north-west wind.
**DON'T MISS:**
The superb 16th century Hisar mosque.
The 18th century caravanserai, Kislaragasi Han, with its bazaar.
Ethnography Museum – a beautiful building with a reconstruction of a circumcision room and wonderful folk art collection.
St. Polycarp Church – the oldest Christian church, built in 1625.
The city's largest synagogue, Beth Israel.
The attractive port district of Alsancak (Punta), and the Kordonboyu – a delightful 3-km (2-mi) long seafront promenade.
**YOU SHOULD KNOW:**
The ancient ruins of Ephesus are only a 50-minute drive from Izmir.

# Trabzon

Founded by Greek colonists, with a history going back to 1000 BC, Trabzon is an important port on the Black Sea coast of north-eastern Turkey. The city was at one time the western terminus of the Silk Road.

Trabzon has always been a major trading centre with boats plying the Black Sea and a land route to Central Asia across the Zigana Pass – famously crossed by Xenophon and his Ten Thousand. The city retained its independence under the Roman and Byzantine Empires and was even the centre of its own empire, but eventually came under Ottoman control. In World War I, Trabzon was captured by the Russians for a time and the city's inhabitants include a sizeable (and much despised) Russian minority, which has increased since the collapse of the Soviet Union.

Trabzon is magnificently situated, squeezed between the sea and the Pontic Mountains, whose rugged, forested slopes descend directly to the coast. The city consists of three main districts, built along the ridges that slope down to the waterfront. The commercial quarter is nearest the harbour, with the university buildings to the south. To the west, there is a historic district with some lovely houses and old churches around Ortahisar Mosque. Then there is Kunduracilar, an intriguing bazaar area of ramshackle wooden houses and narrow streets. On a hill, just beyond the far western limits of the city, there is the beautifully situated, spectacular Byzantine church, Ayasofya Müzesi.

The location of Trabzon, with a mountain barrier between it and the rest of Turkey, has set the city somewhat apart and given it a strong sense of its own cultural identity. Even today, many of the inhabitants, although Muslim, speak their own Greek dialect.

**POPULATION:**
275, 000 (2006)
**WHEN TO GO:**
Spring and autumn. Typical Black Sea climate with some rain all year round; can be oppressively hot in summer; cool, wet winter with snow on the mountains.
**DON'T MISS:**
Ataturk Köskü – beautiful late 19th century villa built for Ataturk.
Trabzon Museum – impressive Byzantine collection.
Boztebe – a small park with panoramic views over the city.
Kaymakly Monastery – 3 km (2 mi) from the city centre.
The 14th century Sümela Monastery – built into the rock 50 km (30 mi) south of Trabzon.
Uzungöl Lake – a superb natural setting and views 70 km (44 mi) south of Trabzon.
**YOU SHOULD KNOW:**
This is a deeply conservative part of Turkey where people uphold traditional values, respect for authority, and gender roles.

*The Sümela Monastery near Trabzon*

# Istanbul

Istanbul is an utterly bewitching city – a mesmerising, schizoid medley of sumptuous palaces, domes and minarets, cobble-stoned streets, decrepit old wooden houses, squalid concrete tower blocks, graceful art nouveau apartments, international fashion shops, bazaars and beggars, street vendors and stray dogs and, above all, the boats of the Bosphorus and the promise of the Orient.

A city has been here since the year dot, bridging the gap between Europe and Asia. Over the centuries, it has been the capital of the Roman, Byzantine and Ottoman Empires and undergone three name changes – Byzantium, Constantinople, Istanbul. After the Republic of Turkey was founded in 1923, it was replaced by Ankara as the capital, but, with its awe-inspiring heritage, Istanbul remains Turkey's cultural and economic centre.

Istanbul straddles the Bosphorus Strait, looking towards Europe but with its soul firmly rooted in Asia. On the European side, the city is divided once more, north and south of the Golden Horn inlet. In the south are the superb World Heritage sites of the Blue Mosque, the magnificent 15th century Topkapi Palace, and Ayasofya – the "mother of churches", a masterpiece of Byzantine architecture. Here too is the Grand Bazaar, Kapali Çarsi, a vast labyrinth of narrow covered passageways selling everything from cheap tat to carpets worth thousands. Only a few minutes walk is Suleymaniye Caami, a spectacular Ottoman Mosque, and, further west, the old city walls and the beautiful Kariye Camii.

North of the Galata Bridge, there is a magnificent 14th century Genoese landmark, Galata Kulesi, with a fantastic view. From here, the city takes on a distinctly European guise. The main boulevard, Istiklal Caddesi – lined with superb fin-de-siècle architecture – leads up to Taksim and the impressive Monument of the Republic.

Everywhere you turn in this compelling city, you stumble over the melancholic remains of a magnificent imperial past – neglected, ignored bits of history. Istanbul enchants the traveller with haunting memories – the breathtaking interior of the Blue Mosque, the smells and clatter of the fish market, the tiny boats vying with huge tankers in the Bosphorus – apparently fleeting impressions that remain forever.

**POPULATION:**
10,291,000 (2007)
**WHEN TO GO:**
Spring or autumn. The summer months are very hot and it often snows in the winter.
**DON'T MISS:**
Taking a cruise up the Bosphorus and admire the *yali* lining the shore – old wooden mansions, once the summerhouses of wealthy Istanbullus.
The experience of a genuine Turkish bath in the Çemberlitas or the Cagaloglu hamams.
A tour of the Dolmabahçe Sarayi – a sumptuous palace with the largest chandelier in Europe.
The atmosphere of the Egyptian Spice Market and surrounding streets.
The buzzing port area of Karaköy, with the Balik Pazari fish and vegetable market, cheap local restaurants and street food.
The Ortakoy Mosque and area.
**YOU SHOULD KNOW:**
Some of Istanbul is extremely poor. Like all major cities, it attracts immigrants in search of work, many of whom are living in *gecekondus* – illegally built squatters' dwellings on the outskirts of the city. Do not let western prejudices and annoyance at street hustlers get in the way of your appreciation of the city.

# Shkodra

**POPULATION:**
81,000 (2004)
**WHEN TO GO:**
Spring or early autumn: mid-summer is
when the whole of the eastern Balkans
decamps to the nearby Adriatic.
**DON'T MISS:**
The 18th century Bazaar, with the 19th
century ambience and 21st century
secrets.
Ura e Mesit (Mesi Bridge), 13 stone arcs
soaring high over the Kiri River, with a
central span 22 m (67 ft) wide and 12 m
(37 ft) high. A mid-18th century
masterpiece.
The panoramic view from the Rozafa
Castle complex – with the city and Lake
on one side, and the confluence of the
Rivers Drin and Buna, across their
floodplains to the sea, on the other.
Zogaj, a nearby fishing village of *kulla*
houses (like upturned round stone pots,
each with its own internal well) and no
modern building whatsoever on Lake
Shkroda. Neither the place, nor its mode
of life, has changed in 2,000 years.
Shkodra's 'city songs' – highly lyrical
(and nowadays often naughty)
appreciations of their city and its'
flowers', in a form unique to Shkodra
and very different musically from any
other folkloric Albanian style.
The pelicans and other incredible birdlife
around the Lake.
**YOU SHOULD KNOW:**
Shkodra has a wonderful old hamam.

Shkodra's location is magnificent. Its diamond shape is bounded by two rivers, a lake and Rozafa Castle, a fortified complex towering 132 m (402 ft) above its western edge; and the horizon on all sides is bounded by the blue haze of forested mountains. Most visitors can't wait to reach these local amenities, but the city itself deserves closer scrutiny.

Shkodra was the capital of the Illyrian Kingdom up to 168 BC, when the Romans realised its importance as an economic and cultural centre on the Balkan trade routes. Ever since, and for the same reasons, the city has been occupied by Slavs, Byzantines, Serbs, Venetians and Ottomans. Shkodra fiercely resisted all its invaders, but several centuries of assimilation bred a local tradition of multi-ethnic and religious tolerance that, along with a jaunty good humour, characterises the modern city.

The oldest part of town (the Serresh and Gijadol quarters) is a warren of alleys shaded by tall walls, set with high gates and awnings over shop windows recessed into the stone. Beyond what was a walled city, wider streets lit by what look like quadruple gas lamps from the Paris Metro, and lined by comfortable, confident houses in pastel colours, show what 19th century prosperity could do for a chap. Recent years have brought an explosion of building along avenues set in grids of white houses, a response to the rampant capitalism of post-communist Albania.

Shkodra's minarets and church towers are its best metaphor for tolerance and welcome; but although basic infrastructures are in place, the city needs to balance the scars of its industrial potency to make the most of its tourist potential. Come anyway, before everyone catches on about this alternative Mediterranean time warp.

# Tirana

Albania's capital is a work in progress. Effectively, Tirana begins in 1990, with only the architectural history of Italian fascism to build on. Mussolini's favourite architects demolished the two oldest districts, Mujos and Pazari, in the 1920s, and imposed their grand plan of monumental government buildings along the broad sweep of Deshmoret e Kombit (Boulevard of the Martyrs).

With the vast empty acres of Skanderbeg Square at one end, and the University at the other, they created the perfect arena for King Zog to review goose-stepping troops; and Enver Hoxha needed only to adapt it to serve his dictatorship. Determinedly isolationist,

Hoxha let the dust and mud of what had for several centuries been little more than a large feudal village, settle on everything except the Blloku quarter. Here, for 35 years, lived the communist elite in villas that would impress anyone, but which astounded Tirana's deprived citizens when the heavily policed cordon was lifted in 1990, and they saw it for the first time.

Tirana woke up, and it's been manic ever since. Where just 700 vehicles were permitted under Hoxha, 300,000 now jam the streets. The drab fortresses of public buildings have been repainted in bright colours. Thousands of illegal, ramshackle buildings have been bulldozed to reveal the River Lana, and whole parks cleared to allow people some respite from a city buzzing with energy and new building. So new, and built so quickly, that many new streets still don't have names. Blloku is full of cafés, bars and shopping malls that westerners would kill for. The price, of course is pollution. Tirana is one of the dirtiest cities in Europe, choked with the diesel fumes of traffic and new industries. Water, gas and electricity are still sporadic – but Tirana is a Mediterranean city, and despite its grinding poverty, it is finally finding its way towards prosperity. Meanwhile, it's a glorious place to visit, because Tirana's citizens have recovered their humour.

*Many of the drab public buildings have been repainted in bright colours.*

**POPULATION:**
586,000 (officially 2005; but estimates of the real influx say 1 million)
**WHEN TO GO:**
Any time except high summer when the pollution really hurts.
**DON'T MISS:**
The mosaic on the façade of the National Historical Museum, called 'The Albanians'.
The Et'hem Bey Mosque, built 1789-1821, the only survivor along Deshmoret.
The mass *xhiro* (promenade) of young and old every evening on Deshmoret.
The elegant stone arches of Tanner's Bridge, the Ottoman footbridge over the Lana.
The new (2005) cable car from the Institute of Physics to near the top of Mt Dajti, where people go to enjoy a picnic away from the traffic.
The International Centre of Culture, known as 'the Pyramid' and place to meet.
**YOU SHOULD KNOW:**
Go while Tirana is still in its energized state of flux. For all its problems, it is a really exciting city.

# Gjirokastra

**POPULATION:**
30,000 (2006)
**WHEN TO GO:**
Any time of year, but go soon before it really does become a museum. The National Folk Festival of music takes place here every four years (2008-12-16…)
**DON'T MISS:**
The 17th century Turkish baths, where you're sure to make local friends.
The carcass of an American jet fighter plane in the courtyard of the Citadel, along with abandoned cannon from previous eras. It's a local joke, of course, but it sets off the grim realities of the castle's historical functions very well.
The 18th century Ottoman Mosque; and other denominational churches of similar vintage.
The possibility of taking a boat trip from the nearby coast to Corfu (Kérkyra).
The chance of talking to Gjirokastra's residents in one of the cafés or little squares.

Designated by UNESCO as a 'museum-city', Gjirokastra is a rare example of a well-preserved Ottoman town. Its name translates as 'silver fortress', and it is completely dominated by the huge citadel at its heart, on a steep hill overlooking the lush valley of the River Drin. The fortress has existed since at least the 1st century, but the present medieval castle belongs to the 13th century, after which the town expanded down and around the citadel hill.

Its narrow, cobbled streets twist through a series of outstanding examples of *kulle*, the characteristic tower houses of the region, always of stone, and always with slate roofs. The style reached its purest form in the 17th century, but in Gjirokastra, the prosperity of local farmers and merchants encouraged them to create ever more elaborate versions. Looking down from the castle, you can see the individual slate roofs getting bigger and bigger. Unfortunately, you can also see the 'new' town: acres of ugly, haphazard, pre-fabricated slums, their wiring askew, and full of rubbish, spreading into what is otherwise a beautiful river valley whose fields and meadows are backed by elegant mountains.

Beat depression by taking tea or plum liqueur in the 17th century Old Town bazaar, or just roaming the streets and their timewarp. It may be called a 'museum', but Gjirokastra is very much a living, working town, and it owes its immaculate preservation as much to local pride as to Enver Hoxha, the dictator who held Albania in isolated stasis for 40 years, and pumped money into this, his home town. For the moment, that isolation works in visitors' favour, because nowhere else can you step into the east Mediterranean world of yesteryear, where the cultural currency is still an authentic combination of Albanian, Greek, Macedonian, Vlach and Ottoman influences. Practically speaking, that means friendly and hospitable.

*The characteristic tower houses*
(kulle) *of Gjirokastra*

# Mostar

Rebuilt, restored and repaired, Mostar is back in business as a beautiful, 500 year-old, working town, gloriously set in the lower Neretva valley. It gazes over the figs, grapes, pomegranates, rose hips and lemons that fill the valley floor, greened by the river whose thick waters power and swirl just below its windows. Mostar's Ottoman Old Town straddles both banks, and is known for its riverside restaurants and cafés, hanging at often crazy angles over the unruly grasses and chaotic wild-flowers of the riverbank – and the water, wild enough to attract rafters. The river's Old Bridge (Stari Most), a 28-m (90-ft) arched parabola built in 1566, and as much a symbol of Mostar's entrenched philosophy as of its Ottoman architectural integrity, frames the ancient stone buildings, clambering on each other's roofs up the rocky banks. Weathering will obliterate any sign that the bridge, now rebuilt, was destroyed by artillery fire in 1993.

The Old Town is compact enough to walk around. Among its minarets, hamams and café culture stands the Muslibegovica House, one of Mostar's greatest treasures, and a National Monument of Bosnia. At 300 years old, it's considered the most beautiful Ottoman house in the Balkans. Most guidebooks correctly tell you it's a museum, preserving the architecture, furniture, fittings and domestic trivia of an aristocratic Ottoman family, and you can even stay there overnight. It's much more. It's a private guest-house, not a state hotel, and it's run, in person, by the same family who have owned it for 150 years. Returned from their wartime exile, they restored their house over seven years, then opened the museum as a gift to Mostar and their shared roots with both Muslim and Croat. More than the bridge, the attitude demonstrates why Mostar is not a mosaic of cultures and traditions, but a melting pot of them. An inspirationally beautiful city.

**POPULATION:**
127,000 (2005)
**WHEN TO GO:**
April to October
**DON'T MISS:**
The almost medieval view of cobbled walkways, stone-arched barns, minarets and wood-framed buildings, from the 16th century 'Crooked Bridge' over a tributary of the Neretva.
Sipping a smoothie with the well-dressed patrons of the cafés surrounding the shopping mall in more modern Mostar, to the west of the Old Town, on the Croat (west) bank.
Bulevar Revolucije – the former Front Line between Croats (west) and Muslims (east), where bombed-out buildings and bullet pockmarks keep stark vigil.
The Austro-Hungarian public baths.
Diving off the Old Bridge – for a small fee, members of the Mostar Diving Club will dive 23 m (75 ft) into the emerald waters; or you can do it yourself and get a certificate to prove it.
**YOU SHOULD KNOW:**
In an Ottoman house, the women's courtyard is called 'haremluk', and the men's courtyard is 'selamluk'.

*Houses and shops along the banks of the Neretva River*

# Banja Luka

**POPULATION:**
245,000 (est. 2007); nearer 300,000 during summer when many former residents re-visit property.
**WHEN TO GO:**
April to September, when a chain of music and theatre festivals make the most of the parks and riverside.
**DON'T MISS:**
The golden domes and Classicist grandeur of the Orthodox Church of Christ the Saviour.
The Museum of Republika Srpska (aka the Museum of Bosanska Krajina, the region's former name).
Watersports on the Vrbas River – the site of the 2005 European Rafting Championships.
Banj Hill and waterfall, on the Vrbas near Krupa on the edge of the city.
**YOU SHOULD KNOW:**
There is a significant community of émigré Banjalukans in the city of Hamtramck, Michigan – 8 km (5 mi) from downtown Detroit.

The gentle hills that slope down to the Banja Luka valley bring a patchwork of thick woods and fields reaching into the heart of Banja Luka city itself. Famous since Roman times for its natural beauty, Banja Luka is still full of tree-lined avenues, gardens and parks, fanning out either side of the swift Vrbas River. In fact, the Romans were the first to fortify the riverside bluff now occupied by the ivy-clad, medieval fortress brooding quietly in its surrounding meadow. It's a serene venue for concerts and summer picnics – and an extraordinary asset to the busy capital (officially, only since 2003), of Republika Srpska, the autonomous entity established within Bosnia-Herzegovina after the ethnic cleansing of 1992-5.

The ramshackle ancient shops and houses, and labyrinth of cobbled lanes that characterized Banja Luka's Austo-Hungarian and Ottoman old city centre were razed by an earthquake in 1969. The wonderful 15th and 16th century mosques survived, only for all 16 of them to be totally destroyed in the 1990s, allegedly by Serbian extreme nationalists. Among them was the Ferhadija mosque, a national monument. Now, most of the others are under construction, but attempts in 2001 and 2006 to rebuild the Ferhadija have proved that political passions still simmer close to the surface: progress is slow.

Even so, Banja Luka's new role as a seat of government has revived some of the prosperity of its 'golden age' after World War I, and brought new life as much to its grand buildings of the era, as it has to the charming cafés and terraces around Veselina Maslese and Gosposka Streets. The Banski Dvor ('Halls of the Ban', or neo-feudal lord, a title used by the 20th century Yugoslav Kingdom) now unites the city's history with its culture and politics. The palatial former residence houses the National Assembly, a concert hall, restaurant and art gallery – in a very democratic elegance.

*One of the many golden domes of the Orthodox Church of Christ the Saviour*

# Sarajevo

Sarajevo is a cosmopolitan dynamo of a city. It has renewed itself on the principle of 'what doesn't kill you makes you stronger', taken to its literal maximum. Morally and physically brought to its knees in the conflict of the 1990s, the city now represents the essence of the Balkans in a clever new way. Instead of synthesizing the Oriental and European cultures at the heart of the entire region, it encourages the distinctness of both, making a physical reality of the ethics of harmony and co-existence.

*A view over Sarajevo*

Ferhadija is Sarajevo's main artery. At one end it's an Ottoman-style street of small shops, balconies, awnings and arches, rich in the scented exotica of produce and goods; gradually it broadens into a leafy shopping avenue of grandiose Austrian buildings. Along the way, or close on one of the intriguing sidestreets, you pass the city's – and the Balkans' – denominational history, including the Gazi-Husrev Bey Mosque, the Roman Catholic Cathedral, the old and new Serbian Orthodox churches, and the Old Jewish Temple. All of them are places of active ministry rather than tourist attractions, and a reminder not only that Sarajevo has recovered the tradition of tolerance it so nearly lost, but that Sarajevo is where one Empire split itself between Rome and Byzantium, and where the people of the eastern Orthodox, the Ottoman south, and Roman Catholic west met and clashed.

Go to Sebilj, axis of Bascarsija, the city's most historic district. The general clamour of trading, the muezzin's wail confounding the snatches of over-luscious mid-eastern music, and mingled smells of livestock and cooking, combine to befuddle any sense of being still in Europe. A tram-ride away you feel you might be in Vienna. It's such a good trick, and it gets even better when crowds promenade before thronging the cafés and bars of Strosmajerova and Bazardzani in the Old Town. You'll make friends for life.

**POPULATION:**
400,000 (2007)
**WHEN TO GO:**
December to March for winter sports in the vicinity (Sarajevo hosted the 1984 Winter Olympics); August for the Film Festival; year-round for pure pleasure.
**DON'T MISS:**
The Sarajevo Tunnel Museum – explore and marvel at the hole in a suburban garden near the airport, used to ferry supplies into the besieged city.
The amazing views over the city from the steep hills on both sides.
Markale market place – where the August 1995 bombing prompted the NATO military intervention, which eventually halted the war.
The Latin Bridge, where Gavrilo Princip shot the Arch-Duke Franz-Ferdinand in August 1914, and World War I began.
Admiring Sarajevo's beauty and grace from a tram – the system was the first in the Austro-Hungarian Empire, and opened in the mid-1870s.
**YOU SHOULD KNOW:**
A 'Sarajevo Rose' is a distinctive scar in the road made by the impact crater of a shell and its shrapnel spatter. There are many such gruesome landmarks.

*St Mark's Church in Markov Square*

# Zagreb

On the Sava River near the southern slopes of Mount Medvednica lies the Croatian capital of Zagreb, a glorious Austro-Hungarian city full of lovely churches, museums and art galleries. Once two towns, the city is divided into upper and lower areas, each with its own distinctive character. The vast main square, Trg Bana Jelacica, separates the two halves.

With its winding cobbled streets, Gornji Grad, the upper town, is clearly the oldest part of the city. It is set on two hills and boasts a wide array of lovely buildings, as well as the city's main market. Built in 1217 but remodelled over the years, the Cathedral has a stately neo-Gothic façade and twin steeples which were added in the 1880s. Inside it is breathtaking. The north wall features the Ten Commandments written in a twelfth-century script.

St Mark's Church, dating from the 13th century but rebuilt in Gothic style in the 14th, is famous for the red, white and blue tiles on its roof arranged in the coats of arms of Zagreb and the kingdoms of Croatia, Dalmatia and Slavonia. Its south portal is thought to be the work of sculptors of the Parler family from Prague, and is celebrated for its artistic composition and the number of statues. The Lotrscak Tower, built in the 13th-century to protect the city gates, affords spectacular views over the city. For over 100 years, a cannon has been fired from the top of the tower at noon.

Zagreb's lower town, Donji Grad, is revered for its elegant squares, gardens, wide boulevards and parks. It can be reached by funicular railway from the upper town. Donji Grad was built to a grid design in the late nineteenth century and is now home to most of Zagreb's numerous museums. These reflect the history, art and culture not only of Zagreb and Croatia, but also the rest of the world. The Archaeological Museum's most famous exhibits are the Egyptian collection, the Zagreb mummy and the oldest Etruscan inscription in the world. The Croatian Natural History Museum holds an extensive collection of Neanderthal remains, while the Museum of the City of Zagreb deals with the cultural, artistic, economic and political history from Roman times to the present day. Also well worth a look are the Arts and Crafts Museum, the Ethnographic Museum, the Croatian Naive Art Museum, and the Mimara Museum, comprising 3,750 works of art from different cultures and civilizations.

**POPULATION:**
780,000 (2001)
**WHEN TO GO:**
March to October.
**DON'T MISS:**
St Catherine's Church – one of the finest churches in Zagreb dating from the 17th century.
Mirogoj Cemetery – the most peaceful place in town, this beautiful cemetery is surrounded by parkland.
Medvednica Nature Park – over 60 per cent of this 23,000-hectare (56,800-acre) park is covered with forest, some of the trees reaching a height of 150 m (492 ft).
Maksimir Park – designed in 1784, this is the biggest park in south east Europe. It is home to an old oak forest, sunny open spaces and romantic lakes.
**YOU SHOULD KNOW:**
The city was once two towns.

# Trogir

This historical gem along the Adriatic coast of Croatia, is such a treasure that the whole city is a UNESCO Heritage Site. The name has evolved from the original given by the Greeks, Tragurion, or Goat Island. Now nicknamed 'The Stone Beauty', it is an island city teaming with palaces, fortresses and churches dating back to the Hellenistic period. It has a rich tapestry of history, having been settled by the Greeks and Croats, attacked and occupied by Venetians and Austrians. The architecture of the city is special for this reason as each era of occupation or settlement has left its mark.

The medieval centre of Trogir is home to a castle and tower and many other buildings from the Romanesque, Gothic, Renaissance and Baroque periods. Built at the east end of the island, looking out over the sea, the most famous monument in Trogir is the Cathedral of St Lawrence. Home to Radovan's Portal, one of the most valuable monuments of Dalmatian stonemasonry by the great Croatian artist, the Cathedral was rebuilt in 1213 after the sack by the Saracens. Staying on the eastern side of the island, the St Barbara Church is the oldest and one of the best preserved chapels on the island. Hidden under an arch at the end of the main street, this fine example of pre-Romanesque art dates back to the 9th century. The Benedictine Monastery of St Nicholas houses the Greek relief of Kairos (the God of a happy moment) which dates back to the 3rd century BC.

By far the best way to experience the city is to wander and get lost in the rabbit warren of streets as you go. The many coffee shops that line the city streets are perfect for relaxing and people watching. There are often difference types of music and folklore events happening each night, so look out for posters advertising events.

The island has something for everyone, with rich architecture and meandering streets at its heart, and palm lined beaches stretching out to the crystal blue waters of the Adriatic Sea. The most popular beach is Okrug Beach, a bustling place with restaurants and bars that keep going late into the night. Quieter beaches can be found on the neighbouring island of Ciovo which is a 12km (7.5mi) drive off the island over a small stone bridge. For water sports, including diving and fishing, head to Medena Beach.

**POPULATION:**
13,000 (2001)
**WHEN TO GO:**
June or September guarantee you good weather and the city will be much less crowded.
**DON'T MISS:**
Do some island hopping on the nearby Ciovo, Solta or Drvenik. Ciovo is regarded as Trogir's beach and enjoys a family atmosphere. Its highest peak is Vela Straza which offers magnificent views across the island.
Cathedral of St Lawrence – built between the 13th and 17th centuries, this is the most imposing monument in the city.
The Greek relief of Kairos – Kairos is the Greek God of 'a happy moment'. The relief, dating back to 1064, is kept in the city's Benedictine nunnery.
**YOU SHOULD KNOW:**
Bird flu was found in the region in 2006, and while the risk of infection is very low, avoid visiting poultry farms or places you may come into contact with caged or wild birds.

*A view across the city to the waterfront*

# Zadar

**POPULATION:**
72,000 (2006)

**WHEN TO GO:**
Although very busy, the summer months of June to September are best to make the most of the warm sea.

**DON'T MISS:**
Take a trip 15km (9mi) north to the ancient island town of Nin to see the Roman theatre and the Church of the Holy Cross, the smallest cathedral in the world.

**YOU SHOULD KNOW:**
Be careful not to wander into sensitive regions north of Zadar as there are still landmines left over from the war. Look out for the skull-and-crossbones symbols and yellow tape.

Zadar, 115km (70mi) northwest of Split, is a microcosm of history and events that have shaped Croatia and the Dalmatian coast. Inhabited since Neolithic times, Zadar has seen hundreds of years of change, becoming a Roman colony and later the administrative centre of Dalmatia during the Byzantine era and fought over by Venice, Austria, Hungary, France, Italy, Germany then under siege during the most recent war of 1991-1995. The 9th century saw years of attacks from the Venetians, and while violence took place outside the city walls, within them, the culture and art which characterizes the city today was developing.

The location of Zadar, most probably the reason for its role in so many conflicts, makes it popular with tourists today. To the west is the beautiful Adriatic Sea, and to the north, hundreds of islands. Tourism in the area goes back to the nineteenth century and it is easy to see why as the city is easy to get round on foot and there is a lot to see. The history of Zadar is fascinating and a trip to the church of St Donat, the pre-Romanesque symbol of the city, is an essential. Zadar has four patron saints: St Simon, St Krsevan, St Anastasia, St Zoilo, (perhaps a product of so many years of conflict) and each has a church and other monuments commemorating them scattered around the city. The daily fish and vegetable market, one of the largest in Croatia, is a lovely insight into the areas surrounding Zadar as people come from Lake Vrana, Ugljan and Pasman to sell their wares.

The city is surrounded by walls on three sides, and a Venetian lion still guards the city at Port Gate and Town Gate after all this time. Spend an evening enjoying a glass or two of Maraskino, a liqueur made popular during the 19th century which has been produced in Zadar since 1821 then head out to the tree-lined waterfront. Its newest attraction is a Sea Organ, a series of 35 pipes facing the sea which contain whistles. As the sea air blows through the whistles, chords ring out along the waterfront.

*The tower of St Stosija*

# Split

Under a dramatic mountain backdrop on a beautiful stretch of Adriatic coastline is Split, Croatia's second-largest city. Home to Roman Emperor Diocletian's monumental palace, Split offers a wealth of Roman ruins, Gothic and Baroque architecture and fascinating museums.

In 295 AD Diocletian ordered a magnificent palace to be built here. For ten years he oversaw the quarrying of stone and the construction of his palace, the walls of which are 26m (85ft) high. It has a classic symmetrical layout with two intersecting streets. Built partly as a private villa and partly as a fortified camp, the palace has some noteworthy features, including the Temple of Jupiter and circular temples to Cybele and Venus. The Roman Empire of the time took inspiration from foreign influences, hence the Egyptian sphinxes outside the Temple of Jupiter and outside Diocletian's mausoleum.

In the 7th century nearby residents fled into the now-disused palace to escape invading barbarians, and so the palace became the commercial and residential area it still is today. Many new buildings were erected inside the walls, incorporating parts of the Roman palace and obscuring its layout. From 1420 until the early 19th century, Split was ruled by the Venetians and became a wealthy trading port. Gorgeous Venetian-Gothic palaces were built and the resulting mixture of architecture is unique.

Diocletian's mausoleum now houses one of the oldest Catholic cathedrals in the world, dedicated to St Domnius. The domed interior has eight columns and a thirteenth-century pulpit of superbly worked stone. The bell tower offers amazing views of the whole area, but the climb up is tiring.

Within the palace is Split's Town Museum, a marvellous piece of Venetian-Gothic architecture, built as a palace for the Papalic family in the fifteenth century. It recounts the history of Split in a series of drawings, coats of arms, weapons, furniture, coins and documents. In the Archaeological Museum there are fascinating artefacts from the Roman and early Christian period, including reliefs based on Illyrian mythical figures. Founded in 1820, this is the oldest museum in Croatia and most of its monuments originate from Central Dalmatia. Here you will see Greek pottery, Roman glass and an extensive collection of ancient coins.

Diocletian's Palace was designated a UNESCO World Heritage Site in 1979, as much for its medieval Gothic and Baroque buildings as for its Roman remains.

*The very pretty waterfront*

**POPULATION:**
221,000 (2007)
**WHEN TO GO:**
In the summer for the music and theatre festivals.
**DON'T MISS:**
The Bronze Gate – this is the main entrance to Diocletian's Mausoleum.
Jupiter's Temple.
Marjan Hill – enjoy spectacular views of the city from here.
Diocletian's Mausoleum – one of the most impressive Roman ruins in existence and built of Brac, a white stone native to Split.
Mestrovic Gallery – contains many of the works of Ivan Mestrovic, widely considered to be one of the most important sculptors of the 20th century.
The Archaeological Museum – houses fascinating relics from Roman and early-Christian periods.
**YOU SHOULD KNOW:**
The Palace and the buildings within it are a UNESCO World Heritage Site.

# Varazdin

**POPULATION:**
49,000 (2005)
**WHEN TO GO:**
The best weather is between April and September.
**DON'T MISS:**
Hire a car and take a trip to the nearby town of Varazdinske Toplice and visit the thermal springs.
**YOU SHOULD KNOW:**
If you're driving in the area you should be aware that it is illegal to have any alcohol at all, and you must have your headlights on and dipped at all times.

Tucked away in the most northern part of Croatia on the banks of the Drava River 79km (49mi) north-west of Zagreb, is Varazdin, known as the 'Baroque Capital of Croatia' or 'Croatia's Vienna'. The 800 year-old city is also famous for its textile and food industry and more recently has been known as the 'City of Flowers' in honour of the colourful blooms that line the city streets and squares.

The historic centre of Varazdin has a great number of palaces built mostly in the 18th century. These were responsible for changing the city into a place for artisans and wealthy landowners, and it was the capital of Croatia until it was mostly destroyed by fire in 1776. By the 19th century it was rebuilt and expanded, becoming the industrial centre of north-western Croatia. The city also has many churches and religious buildings, with six churches, two chapels and one monastery.

The town centres around a medieval fortress, the product of Turkish raids during the 12th century, which has been modified over time and has since been radically transformed into a Gothic-Renaissance building. The Church of Saints Fabian and Sebastian is one of the most beautiful in the city. Originally built as a wooden church in the 17th century, it was rebuilt in stone with the addition of a steeple in the 18th century, adding to the skyline of a city already peppered with steeples and spires. As well as preserving architecture, the city is concerned with preserving its traditions, and you can see the changing of the old guard, the 'Purgari', outside city hall each week.

*Varazdin Castle*

The famous Varazdin Evenings of Baroque is the main festival in north-western Croatia. The festival which has been running since 1971 is spread over eighteen days from the end of September to the beginning of October, celebrates the heritage of Croatian Baroque and other types of music. The city buzzes with a proud atmosphere during this period as performers of live music and visual artists line the streets. For something a bit different, head to the Herzer Palace with its bizarre collection of more than ten thousand preserved insects, collected by Franjo Koscec.

# Dubrovnik

Dubrovnik lies in the extreme south of Croatia on the Dalmatian coast. Its beautiful setting on a peninsula jutting out into the clear waters of the Adriatic is further enhanced by the limestone peaks that form a backdrop to this handsome city and the border with Bosnia-Herzegovina. The ancient city walls protect a well preserved historic city centre, designated a UNESCO World Heritage Site in 1979.

From when it was founded in the 7th century, the town was under the protection of the Byzantine Empire. After the Crusades it came under the sovereignty of Venice (1205–1358), and later became part of the Kingdom of Hungary after the Peace Treaty of Zara in 1358. Between the 14th century and 1808 the town ruled itself as a free state named Repubblica di Ragusa. Its success was based on maritime trade, with its huge fleet of merchant ships carrying goods to western Europe. In the Middle Ages, it was the only city-state in the region to rival Venice and achieved a remarkable level of development. It became an important centre for the development of the Croatian language and literature, and home to many notable poets, playwrights, painters, mathematicians, physicists and other scholars.

However, its decline began after a forceful earthquake in 1667, which destroyed many of the Gothic buildings. New Baroque buildings were erected, and ever since the fortified medieval walls have largely protected the city from the wars raging around it. In the early 1990s the Yugoslav People's Army besieged Dubrovnik and ruined many of its buildings. However, painstaking restoration has now returned the city to its former glory.

The best way to explore the city is by walking along its enormous outer walls, built between the 12th and 17th centuries. The walls, up to 25 m (82 ft) high and 6 m (20 ft) thick, punctuated by 16 towers, offer lovely views of the sea and the tiled roofs of the city. The city itself is also a joy to stroll around. Explore the main street, Placa, with its white limestone paving dating from the 1460s, and the Sponza Palace, one of the few buildings not damaged by the earthquake. Other notable sights include the Rector's Palace, the Cathedral, the Franciscan Monastery and the Dominican Monastery with its lovely 15th-century cloister built in Gothic-Renaissance style.

The Dubrovnik Summer Festival is the most significant cultural event in Croatia and includes theatre and classical music performances as well as folk music events.

**POPULATION:**
50,000 (2001)
**WHEN TO GO:**
In summer for the festival.
**DON'T MISS:**
The city walls.
The Orthodox Church.
The Dominican Monastery.
Elafiti Islands.
Sponza Palace.
**YOU SHOULD KNOW:**
Dubrovnik is also famous for its lovely sandy beaches.

*Dobrovnik was founded in the middle ages.*

# Prizren

**POPULATION:**
221,000 (2006)
**WHEN TO GO:**
May to September – when there's
more of everything going on.
**DON'T MISS:**
The 1615 design and internal artistry
of the Sinan Pasha Mosque.
The small but hugely appropriate
ethnological museum in the Prizren
League building.
The lone minaret of the Arasta
Mosque, otherwise destroyed in 1963.
Wednesday Market day, when the
local villages come to set up their
stalls with crafts, wood-carvings, and
all manner of curios.
The ornate filigree work traditional to
Prizren itself.
The Serbian Orthodox Episcopal
Residence, now restored.
**YOU SHOULD KNOW:**
Leon Trotsky came to Prizren as a
journalist, to report the massacre of
the first Balkan War.

Heading south through the patchwork fields and dusty vineyards of south-western Kosovo, Prizren solidifies in the haze as a series of domes, minarets and stone steeple-belltowers pushing up above the red roofs crowded at odd angles to each other. The cluster thins to either side, where the green foothills of two converging ranges meet, forming a V-shape that contains the city. Closer, you see that a river busies its way out of the hills, twisting round a rocky promontory topped by a watching castle, and disappears among the houses below. The momentary stillness is shattered by the real heirloom of Prizren's antiquity, the flood of noise from people, traffic, animals and machines, passionately involved in keeping their ancient city alive.

Prizren has been busy and prosperous since the 11th century, threatened only by its sacrifices to its perennial involvement in the conflicts between Serb and Byzantine/Ottoman/Albanian that continue to this day. The evidence of its past and present importance is everywhere. Follow the cleverly-patterned cobbled streets, lined with dozens of 18th and 19th century Ottoman houses that don't exist anywhere else on the same scale, to the stone piazza of Shadervan Square, where young and old gather every day to walk, chatter or sit at the numerous cafés and bars. Take the steep road behind the mosque to the small perfection of 14th century St Saviour Church and the 11th century Kaljaja Fortress with its upper and lower 'towns'. Cross the Ottoman bridge, past its contemporary 15th century, fabulous Gazi Mehmed Pasha Hamam – dual baths for men and women, capped with multiple little domes pierced for air-vents – to gaze on the restored medieval frescoes of the 12th century Orthodox Cathedral of the Virgin of Ljeviska, itself a casualty of the achingly old politics, as recently as 2004, and nearing re-completion. Prizren is too wonderful for the politics of antagonism.

*The Sinan Pasha Mosque which dates from the early 17th century*

# Ohrid

On the shores of Lake Ohrid in south-west Macedonia lies the town of Ohrid, probably the most beautiful in the country, with its steep, cobbled streets and lovely chapels. Archaeological finds indicate that this is one of the oldest human settlements in Europe. It is first mentioned in Greek documents from 353 BC, when it was known as Lychnidos (city of light). Only much later, in 879 AD, was it renamed Ohrid, probably deriving from the Macedonian *Vo Hrid*, 'the town on the hill'.

*The beautiful Sveti Naum Monastery*

The town became Christian early on – its first known bishop was Zosimus, in about 344 AD. Many fine churches and monasteries were built: most are Byzantine, and some are from the late Middle Ages, when the town was known as the 'Slavic Jerusalem'.

Ohrid as it is today was built mainly between the 7th and 19th centuries. During the Byzantine period, it became a significant cultural and economic hub, serving as the episcopal centre of the Orthodox Church. Besides being a holy city, it was also a centre for learning and pan-Slavic literacy. The restored church at Plaoshnik, destroyed by the Ottoman army, was one of the oldest universities in the West, dating back to the 10th century. At the beginning of the 11th century, Ohrid briefly became the capital of Macedonia's greatest medieval ruler, Tsar Samuil, whose fortress still presides over the city today. This fortress may lie on the site of an earlier one built by Alexander the Great's father, Philip II of Macedon.

During Ottoman times, Ohrid remained the seat of the Ohrid archiepiscopacy, which once had jurisdiction over the regions of the Danube, Thessalonica and Albania. Evlia Celebia, an Ottoman traveller from the fifteenth century, observed that Ohrid had a chapel for every day of the year. Those that have survived stand as a testament to the superb artists who have been drawn here. There is a huge body of exquisite religious artwork – fabulous icons, frescoes and mosaics created in different eras. The thirteenth-century church of St Clement has beautiful frescoes, while the monastery of St Panteleimon has more than 800 icons from the 11th to 14th centuries.

The National Museum of Ohrid is testament to some of the earlier inhabitants of the area. There are some stunning grave goods found in the ancient Greek cemetery in nearby Trebenishta, and more recent discoveries from Gorna Porta including a 5th-century BC golden death mask and glove, and the Roman theatre.

**POPULATION:**
56,000 (2002)
**WHEN TO GO:**
July or August for the
Ohrid summer festival which offers a
fine selection of theatre and music.
**DON'T MISS:**
Church of St Sophia – houses art and
architecture from the Middle Ages.
Church of St Clement – home to a
world-famous collection of
Medieval relics.
The Roman theatre – built some
2,000 years ago. One of the most
fascinating discoveries has been that
of the names of the audience
members engraved on their seats.
**YOU SHOULD KNOW:**
This is a UNESCO World Heritage Site.

# Skopje

**POPULATION:**
507,000 (2002)
**WHEN TO GO:**
September to November
**DON'T MISS:**
The Old Bazaar – this is the largest
Bazaar in the Balkans and the most
pleasant part of the city to wander
around. Tiny, pastel-coloured shops
line the cobbled streets.
The Church of Sveti Spas – houses a
magnificent carved altar screen. The
courtyard contains the tomb of
Macedonia's national hero,
Goce Delcev.
Views from the Kale Fortress.
Mustapha Pasha's Mosque – built in
1492 by Grand Vizier Pasha, this is a
beautiful example of Islamic
architecture and is visible from most
places in the Old Bazaar.
**YOU SHOULD KNOW:**
An earthquake in 1963 nearly
flattened the town, but most of the
ancient churches survived.

Skopje, the capital city of Macedonia, lies on the upper course of the Vardar River. It has been inhabited since at least 3,500 BC but at first glance it looks like a modern city constructed largely from concrete. This is because a huge earthquake destroyed 80 per cent of the city in 1963, killing over a thousand inhabitants. Numerous cultural monuments were seriously damaged, but happily the Old Bazaar and the ancient churches and mosques of the Old Town were spared.

In 148 BC, Skopje came under Roman rule, then subsequently passed into the hands of the Byzantine Empire. In 1392 it was conquered by the Turks and remained part of the Ottoman Empire until 1912. The city's character changed markedly during this period. The Ottomans imported Islam and built many mosques, hamans and caravanserai. The Turkish writer Dulgar Dede visited the city at this time and wrote: 'I travelled for many years across that country of Rumelia and I saw many beautiful cities and I was amazed at Allah's blessings, but not one impressed and delighted as much as the heavenly city of Skopje across which passes the Vardar River.'

Among the city's sights are the fifteenth-century stone bridge, with 11 arches, which leads over the Vardar River to the Old City. Here you will find the Daut Pasha hamam, an extensive public bath complex that now houses the National Art Gallery's special collection. Here too is Mustapha Pasha's Mosque, undoubtedly one of the most beautiful buildings in Skopje. It is an endowment of Mustapha Pasha, an eminent figure in the Turkish state during the rule of Sultan Baiazid II and Sultan Selim I. The year of Mustapha Pasha's death (1519) is engraved on the entrance of his mausoleum.

On a high cliff overlooking the River Vardar are the ruins of the 5th-century Kale fortress, offering wonderful views over the city. The

*A view across the city*

present fortress was built by the Byzantines in the 6th century, but the earliest traces of life here date back to the Neolithic period and early Bronze Age.

The little church of Sveti Spas (the Holy Saviour), was built in the 17th century, and boasts a wonderful iconostasis carved from walnut wood. In the courtyard stands the sarcophagus of Goce Delcev, a leader of the national liberation movement who was killed in 1903.

Skopje is a welcoming city with a great deal of interesting historical monuments. It also boasts a fascinating Old Bazaar, one of the largest and most colourful of its kind in Europe.

# Gostivar

Gostivar spreads itself wide in the clear, clean air of the flatlands at the immediate foot of the Sar Planina, Macedonia's most important mountain region. It sits astride the rushing headwaters of the Vardar River, Macedonia's biggest, which rises close to the city but reveals nothing of the mighty stream it becomes 388 km (243 mi) later at Thessaloniki. The river has contributed a lot to Gostivar's importance as the trade centre of the upper Polog region: the Roman historian Livy records the settlement (then called Drau-Dak) being attacked by a force of 10,000 during the third Macedonian War, so it was obviously worth the effort. Today you can still see why.

Though Gostivar shares with other Macedonian cities a long chronology of conquest and re-conquest by Serbs, Bulgarians, Ottoman Turks, Italians and Albanians, it has followed each cycle of destruction not by replacement, but by modernization. Full Macedonian independence has given the city new impetus – the dusty main square is a green and pleasant park where people sit and chat or drink coffee in the cafés. Down-at-heel 18th and 19th century buildings have recovered their upper-storey charm, and steel and plate-glass windows at street level showcase Gostivar's success in marrying history to its trading future.

It's still a southern European market town, with the sounds, smells, flavours and sights of its multi-ethnic cultural and religious history. On Tuesday market days, the whole city fills with the villagers and produce of the local hills and valleys. The flashing colours, music and dancing that follow are evidence of Gostivar's leading role in keeping folkloric traditions alive, while still providing the modern infrastructures that enable visitors to see its regional treasures. Within Gostivar itself, the minarets and Orthodox church towers, wonderful 19th century Ottoman mansions and old streets, sit in harmony with the city's new sense of modern scale, space and materials.

**POPULATION:**
81,000 (2002)
**WHEN TO GO:**
May to September for regional summer delights; December to March for the local skiing and the winter mountain wonderland.
**DON'T MISS:**
The 1566 Ottoman, octagonal, stone Clock Tower commanding the heart of the city.
The 1688 Beg Mahala Mosque.
The dramatic Vrutok Gorge just outside the city, source of the Vardar River.
The herbs and feta cheese from the Sar Planina, the summer 'ocean of grass' which forms the largest, compact mountain pasture in Europe. You have to try the cheese.
The Monastery of Lesok near Brezno village towards Tetovo – including the 1326 Church of the Holy Virgin, an excellent example of the best of Byzantine architecture.
**YOU SHOULD KNOW:**
The Sarplaninec, one of the world's great sheepdog breeds, originated in the Gostivar region.

# Podgorica

**POPULATION:**
137,000 (2003)
**WHEN TO GO:**
September to June. Mid-summer
temperatures reach 40 ℃ (104 ℉).
**DON'T MISS:**
The Millennium Bridge.
Supporting Podgorica's major
industries – wine, brandy, and
tobacco.
The Natural History Museum.
The extraordinary richness of the
small artefacts recovered from 5,000
years of local history in the
Podgorica City Museum.
The Montenegrin National Theatre,
Children's Theatre and Puppet
Theatre, pinnacles of a tradition you
may easily see in some of the
enthusiastic street theatre troupes.
Dvorac Petrovica (Petrovic's Castle)
and Perjanicki dom (House of the
Honour Guard) – two of the best art
galleries.
**YOU SHOULD KNOW:**
From 1946-92, Podgorica had to live
with the name of Titograd.

Clever Montenegro, for getting its new capital so right, so quickly. The Mediterranean's newest republic only won its international spurs in 2006, and although it had been anticipated for some time, the dream's realization sent Podgorica into overdrive. The city had the glories of its own history to live up to, and a nation for whose future it needed to lead by example. With great charm, it is doing both. Less predictably, it's doing it with verve, imagination and, frankly, unexpected sophistication.

Location helps. Montenegro is a country of really beautiful mountains, but Podgorica is the only one of its cities built on the flat; in fact, on the confluence of the Ribnica and Moraca Rivers, where the fertile Zeta plain meets the rich loam of the Bjelopavlici Valley, and anything grows. It's been a major trade centre in its Illyrian, Roman, imperial Slav, Turkish and communist phases, but its significance as a modern crossroads is far greater. The highest mountains and best skiing lie just to the north; fabulous beaches and gems of historic towns are under 30 minutes away via the new Sozina tunnel to Bar, Montenegro's principal port; and in every other direction the latest technology is beginning to catapult both capital and country from Europe's most backward to most advanced.

Podgorica is demonstrating how to seize the best of the new while magnifying the riches of the past. Stara Varos and Drac, the oldest quarters, are largely Ottoman. Their narrow curves thread between ancient houses, revealing little market places, the two surviving mosques and the Turkish Clock Tower. Un-ostentatious restoration makes them glow, and the familiar thump of dominoes in the cafés is an invitation. Across the river, glass and steel temples proclaim the new investment, the outstanding success of the two stock markets and service-industries – gleaming evidence of the taste that governs Podgorica's crazy ride into the unknown. Go quickly, if not sooner.

# Belgrade

Unusually for a city of such antiquity, size and influence, Belgrade has made little effort to advertise its distinctive attractions beyond its immediate community. Its ethnological culture has always been rich; and its 2,000-year history on the tectonic borders of east and west has infused its people and traditions with a habit of friendly courtesy. So you get a terrific welcome, but you have to work a bit to tease the best from the city.

Belgrade is a constant surprise. It sprawls across the confluence of the Danube and the Sava Rivers without especially exploiting either; Ada Ciganlija, one of 16 river islands, has 7 km (4.5 mi) of very popular, Hawaiian-style beaches, but the huge waterscapes are given over to wildlife and some truly wild night-life, conducted on *splavovi* (barges) and in café-bars in secluded inlets. From their vantage, you can see the skyline of Blokovi (Blocks), the notorious three sets of 42, 80 and 50 identical skyscrapers, which share the Novi Beograd quarter with heavy industry, but which also conceal Chinatown and large artistic communities. Zemun, another district, looks more central European than Balkan – its spires and handsome facades stalled in the Habsburg era of 1720 (and yet it's olde-worlde Zemun that is reputed to be Mafia-run, not the grey Blocks).

In central Belgrade, nothing predates the destruction of 19th century wars, but the quality and grandeur of its architecture is stunning. The oriental city is transformed by Serbian neo-Classicism, Art Nouveau and neo-Byzantine masterpieces of civic and sacred art, both in the cobbled bohemian quarter of Skadarlija, an intimate jumble of cafés, exhibitions and the best *kafanas* (traditional Serbian restaurants), and Prince Michael Street, pedestrian heart of smart shopping and über-cool. Lack of restrictions give Belgrade a classy edge on all forms of entertainment – but you'll have to find out exactly what's going on at the SKC (Student Cultural Centre), across from the high rise landmark called the Beogradanka.

**POPULATION:**
1,575,000 (2006)
**WHEN TO GO:**
April to October, when the river-bank café culture offers greatest choice.
**DON'T MISS:**
The medieval (1190) Cyrillic manuscript Miroslav's Gospel at the National Museum.
The Temple of Saint Sava, the largest Orthodox Church in the world.
Bulevar Revolucije – the 12-km (7.5-mi) central thoroughfare lined with palaces, museums and a host of public buildings including many of Belgrade's best.
The Kalemegdan Fortress.
The enormous flea market at Novi Beograd.
The 1820 Turkish *turbe* (inn), opposite Holy Archangel Michael Cathedral.
**YOU SHOULD KNOW:**
The office of the University Rector is in the palatial 1863 mansion donated to Belgrade by a Danube riverboat captain, Serbia's richest man.

*A view of the Zemun district*

# Novi Sad

**POPULATION:**
217,000 (2002)
**WHEN TO GO:**
April to October, for the festival
season, and the best of the Danube.
**DON'T MISS:**
The 'Athenian' grace of the 19th
century classical Library of Matica
Srpska – the oldest and most
important cultural institution in Novi
Sad or Serbia.
The neo-Gothic Cathedral in Freedom
Square.
The museums inside Petrovaradin
Fortress, with antiquities showing its
continuous occupation since
Paleolithic times, and fortification
since 3000 BC.
Talking to locals at the next café table
– they really will tell you what's new.
Taking a boat trip on the Danube from
the quay by the Varadin Bridge.
The little mountain of Fruska Gora, a
national park of woods and 16
Serbian Orthodox monasteries, within
the city limits 10 km (6 mi) from the
Old Town on the Danube's far bank.
**YOU SHOULD KNOW:**
Apply early for your tickets for the
next EXIT Festival.

All Europe knows the EXIT summer rock music festival, held since 2000 in a 17th century fortress on a large island in the middle of the Danube. The 200,000-strong crowd that actually gets there rapidly realizes that the throbbing atmosphere of Petrovaradin Castle and its rip-roaring bohemian community extends to the city on either side of the river, and lasts all year. Novi Sad may be Serbia's second city, but it's first in civic pride and dynamic attitude.

Novi Sad has a very strong sense of identity, developed in the teeth of Ottoman, Austro-Hungarian or any other kind of historic rule. As capital of the Vojvodina region since 1694, it is resolutely Serbian; and since Serbia's full independence in 2006, it has consolidated its status as patron of Serbian culture and tradition. The city is typical of central Europe, full of grand squares and magnificent 19th century architecture that gained it the nickname of 'Serbia's Athens', and replaced the city destroyed in the revolution of 1848. The Danube quays, busy day and night, make an elegant promenade past Novi Sad's most elite districts of cafés and river terraces, punctuated by stunning architecture of the same inspiring modernism as Liberty Bridge, rebuilt in 2005. A less obvious, but equally popular city symbol is the huge, glass, steel and concrete NIS (Serbian Petroleum Industry) HQ on Liberation Boulevard. Novi Sad's bouncy, youthful citizens lack pomposity, and welcome the evidence of 21st century industrial expansion that is restoring prosperity. In any case, you'll find that all recent building is softened by the sudden appearance nearby of more cafés and bars.

Novi Sad's playground is Petrovaradin. Besides the castle and laid-back hoopla of what's effectively another old town, the island's woods and meadows are the perfect antidote to the city's pacy, urban ethic.

*The clock tower*

# Ljubljana

If your perceptions prickle with déja-vu, and a quick check of all five senses registers total satisfaction, and on top of that an adrenalin surge warns you that something utterly surprising and wonderful is going to happen – you're almost certainly in Ljubljana. It is a successful blend of the best of old and new; of small-town friendly with imposingly formal; of architectural beauty and ruthlessly modern function.

Small for a city, it punches well above its weight in ambience, looks, things to do, and treasures to behold.

The city owes its architectural beauty to two earthquakes. The first, in 1511, destroyed most of medieval Laibach, its name as the capital of the Austrian Habsburg Duchy of Carniola. Rebuilt as the late Renaissance became Baroque, the city handpicked the finest Italian architects to create the facades, arched courtyards and ornate staircases for the magnificent churches, palaces and public and private buildings you see today. One of many masterpieces is Venetian sculptor Francesco Robba's *Fountain of Carniolan Rivers* (1751) in front of the Renaissance Town Hall. The Napoleonic wars brought a stylistic interregnum, but a second earthquake in 1895 created a golden opportunity for the city to employ its native son, Joze Plecnik – the man who had just restyled chunks of Prague and Vienna as bywords for modern grace. From 1921, Plecnik composed the new Ljubljana in Neo-Classicist and Secessionist (Austrian Art Nouveau) styles. Whole sections of the city, churches, markets, and even bridges, are testament to his presiding inventive genius.

Ljubljana's other secret is its youth and energy, shared by every age group, and every sector. Summer is a non-stop festival of music and theatre of every kind; and the thronged streets of the Old Town, where willows droop over the riverside café terraces, bubble with the happy, cosmopolitan buzz of Europe's most elegant and exciting new party firing up.

*The beautiful architecture of Ljubljana*

**POPULATION:**
280,000 (2007), (not counting the extra student population of 50,000)

**WHEN TO GO:**
June to September for festivals of music, theatre and art.

**DON'T MISS:**
Ljubljana Castle – the city's most spectacular sight, and repository of every stage of its history in the different buildings within the complex.
The Krizanke Summer Theatre, sited in the 13th century and Baroque monastery complex of the Teutonic Knights, and redesigned by Plecnik on Renaissance principles.
Strolling and chilling among the cafés and oddity shops on Trubarjeva cesta, Mestni trg and Stari trg, parallel to the river walks.
The 'Summer in Old Town' Festival of (mostly) free classical music concerts, in the loveliest churches, inner courtyards and squares, and the best way to discover them.
Tromostovje – Plecnik's 'triple bridge' over the Ljubljanica River.

**YOU SHOULD KNOW:**
Ljubljana looks even better from a hot air balloon.

# Yerevan

**POPULATION:**
1,000,000 (2002)
**WHEN TO GO:**
Spring or autumn
**DON'T MISS:**
The enormous Vernisaj art and flea market in the central city, every weekend. Brilliant.
The Matenadaran Institute – illuminated manuscripts and ancient books. Yerevan's world-class treasure.
The Tsitsernakaberd (Genocide Memorial) to the 1.5 million Armenians massacred by the Turks in 1915.
The ruins of Erebuni Fortress, the original capital founded in 782 BC, in the city centre.
The spectacular 4th-13th century cave monastery system at Geghard (35 km [22 mi] away), rival to Petra in Jordan, where the Cathedral and two churches are built deep inside the rock.
Armenian cognac – you can visit the distillery.
**YOU SHOULD KNOW:**
Christmas Day in Yerevan is on 6th January, every year.

As the capital of a country that wears its history on its sleeve, Yerevan has comparatively little to show. It sprawls in the fertile valley below Mount Ararat (looming snow-capped across the Turkish border), and looks reasonably enticing when it catches the evening sun. The reality is haphazard and ramshackle.

Yerevan has existed since the Urartian heyday of 780 BC as a strategically important crossroads on the caravan routes between Europe and India. Rich in resources and culturally sophisticated, it has been a target for Roman, Persian, Arab, Mongolian and Turkish invaders. Their legendary contributions to the city were systematically torn down under Russian Tsarist rule, but the real changes came under the USSR. After 1921, Yerevan was transformed into an industrial metropolis, and 're-designed' according to an arrangement that ignored almost everything of historic or aesthetic importance. Churches, mosques, the Persian Fortress, the 16th century baths, the bazaars and caravanserais were demolished in favour of concrete blocks of various dimensions, draped with tangled telephone and other wires.

Since real independence in 1991, the pace of change in Yerevan has increased, and now it's a much more comfortable place to visit. Incredibly, though, there's a lot of opposition to the move to demolish the Soviet-era monstrosities (led by Jermaine Jackson, among others!) – a view of preserving the past which misses the whole point of Yerevan, which is that its residents keep their city in their hearts, and share it with you in their hospitality, in their optimism, their ready-reference to everything that has happened to their city as though it were both yesterday and tomorrow. This is not fanciful: what Yerevan has ever had, has been taken from them. Nearly all their remaining artefacts (manuscripts, sculptures, porcelain, etc) are portable, and have survived. Re-building, happily, goes on.

*The Saint Krikor Lusavorich Cathedral*

# Echmiadzin

Nowhere demonstrates better than Echmiadzin Armenia's ability to retain and foster its distinct cultural identity, no matter what the assaults or upheavals history hits it with. Echmiadzin is Armenia's holiest place, the seat of the Catholicos (Spiritual Leader) of the Armenian Church, and tabernacle of the soul of Armenia's self-belief.

The Cathedral complex, churches, public offices and houses from top to bottom of the social scale, would elsewhere be souvenirs of history; here they are testament to the longevity of a continuous commitment, to both a religious philosophy, and the Armenian culture of which it is the core. Echmiadzin has an extraordinary atmosphere. Just walking the streets, sharing daily routines with the residents, it feels like a communications centre, sending and receiving spiritual signals round the world. You stroll in and out of, between and round buildings and shops whose fabric could be anything from 3rd to 21st century, increasingly aware that they represent a living continuum of dedication to a culture that was ancient when the Cathedral was founded in 303 AD. You can even visit the remains of the pagan, fire-worshipping society that preceded it.

Echmiadzin is absorbing and often beautiful. It provokes awe and wonder. Everywhere it shows how Persian, Byzantine, Latin, Greek, Azerbaijani, Syrian and many other influences have been transmuted into a single Armenian entity. Church and State house amazing artefacts whose exquisite intricacies will make you objectively breathless; until at some point, like the Catholicos' Throne Room in the Cathedral complex, the dazzle of wrought gold is almost overwhelming. That's when you should head for Echmiadzin's Zbosaigee (strollers') park, outside the meticulously groomed complex. Lively and unkempt beneath the shade of tall trees, the park is where people hang out to talk or play or eat. Being friendly, they'll be happy for you to join in, which you might feel is a sort of twinning of souls.

*Home of the Catholicos, the Spiritual Leader of the Armenian Church*

**POPULATION:**
64,000 (2007)

**WHEN TO GO:**
April to November. On Sundays, the churches are full of people, incense and music.

**DON'T MISS:**
The 'peasant' church of Astvatsatsin (1767) where the majority of common folk worshipped, being denied entry to the grand churches and monasteries.
The Khachkars, stone relief tablets, many of brilliant quality, found in the Cathedral complex and most of the other churches. Collectively, they form a resumé of Armenian folkloric philosophy – each one is a story symbolizing a belief or moral.
The Manougian Museum in the complex, for its illuminated manuscripts. It is often closed, but insist, if necessary offering a small donation to the museum's upkeep.
Hovhannes Hovhanessian's elegant house and gardens, typical of Old Echmiadzin, now a museum to the liberal intellectual circle that challenged entrenched 19th century feudal attitudes, and was purged by Stalin after 1936.
The music: Komitas Square, the heart of the city, is named after Armenia's musical hero, who brought its sacred music to the world, and preserved its now flourishing folkloric culture. You'll find it everywhere.

**YOU SHOULD KNOW:**
A *b'rdooch* is Armenian for a sandwich.

# Baku

Even its residents refer to the three cities of Baku. The Icheri Shekher (old town) is the magnificent walled fortress set on the Apsheron Peninsula of the Caspian Sea. The Russians restored its towers in 1806, so the 12th century medieval city is still very much a living entity of narrow streets, mosques, palaces, caravanserais and ancient buildings. To the south is the area known as Boomtown, built on the profits of the first wave of oil exploitation after 1872. Broad avenues of beaux-arts architecture look out across fine beaches, and the museums of Fine Arts, History and Literature have appropriate homes in the huge mansions of pre-Revolutionary millionaires. The third city lies behind, backed up into the hills that line Baku Bay, and is an altogether grimmer urban assemblage of monolithic, Soviet drabness. Since 1990, that Soviet skyline is changing as 21st century skyscrapers bite into it with spendthrift speed but variable taste and quality. The phenomenal recent expansion now extends to townships on islands in the bay, including one, 'Oil Rocks', built on stilts 100 km (63 mi) offshore in the Caspian.

If you've got money, Baku can be a fabulous, high-stakes playground. Money buys a cleaned beach, air-conditioning, shelter from freezing polar winds, and gardens in an otherwise semi-arid salt marsh. But ethnographically, Baku's cosmopolitanism is confined to the upper echelons of business and politics. Despite being endowed with a treasure-trove of historic cultures, since 1990 the Azeri government has deported much of Baku's significant Armenian community, which had prospered there since the 15th century. Even the restoration of Jewish property and synagogues appropriated by the Soviet Union could be seen as a cynical exercise in international placation. Outside the elite, you can't avoid politics in Baku, and commenting on them can easily reveal the city's least attractive, official character. Stick with uncomplicated tourism.

**POPULATION:**
2,040,000 (2005)
**WHEN TO GO:**
February to May and October to December.
**DON'T MISS:**
Climbing the Old City walls.
The breathtaking splendour of the 15th-16th century Shirvan-Shah Palace complex.
The view from the Maiden's Tower.
Taking tea in the medieval caravanserais.
The mock Italian Gothic Academy of Sciences, recently built by a local millionaire in imitation of the Contarini Palace in Venice.
Fountain Square.
The chess tables and cafés along The Boulevard, where everyone strolls.
**YOU SHOULD KNOW:**
The Battle of Stalingrad was fought over control of Baku's oilfields.
Baku was originally settled by Zoroastrians, who thought the spontaneous flames from natural oil and gas leaks were religious omens.

*A Turkish mosque*

# Nakhchivan

A narrow strip of Armenia separates the Nakhchivan Autonomous Republic from its national and political parent, Azerbaijan, which makes life very difficult for Nakhchivan City. Its illustrious history as an important crossroad on one of the great trade routes between Europe, India and China justifies its status as capital of a geographically independent state, but the running sore of violence that has embroiled the entire Caucasus since the collapse of the Soviet Union has left it isolated and completely dependent on the political mood in Baku. Nakhchivan is in fact Azerbaijan's second city, yet the colossal effort it makes to play the part only emphasizes the dust of unemployment, crippled industry and infrastructure, and endemic violence, settling thick on the dream.

It could be, as it was, beautiful. It's spread across the foothills of the Zanzegur chain of the Lesser Caucasus Mountains, next to a river, its ancient heart marked by narrow streets and a cluster of historic monuments. Ptolemy wrote of its bustling charm, lush gardens and prosperity in the 2nd century BC, when it was already more than a thousand years old and, according to legend, the place where Noah docked the Ark. Now, anonymous blocks of both Soviet and more recent vintage shut out many of the best views of anything interesting, and you're lucky to get water out of the tap twice a day. Nakhchivan City has survived Alexander, Tamurlaine and Stalin; and it will survive its role as hostage, with Nagorno-Karabakh, in the Armenian-Azerbaijani dispute.

Visitors have the option of enjoying the city's many interesting historical sites or taking a trip to the surrounding countryside to explore this wonderfully atmospheric semi-desert region.

*The Mausoleum of Momine Khatan*

**POPULATION:**
360,000 (2007)
**WHEN TO GO:**
Avoid the extremes of midwinter
(-30 °C [-22 °F]) and midsummer
(42 °C [108 °F]).
**DON'T MISS:**
The turquoise glazed decahedron of the
12th century Momine Khatan
Mausoleum.
The stunning intricacies of regional
patterns at the State Carpet Museum,
newly housed in the 200 year-old palace
of the ruling Khans.
The 12th century octagonal tomb of Yusuf
Ibn Kuseir.
Playing chess as a means of returning the
universal offers of hospitality.
**YOU SHOULD KNOW:**
The city hospital famously – and
successfully – treats lung diseases by
leaving patients overnight down a local
salt mine.

# Hrodna

Often called by its Polish name, Grodno, Hrodna bears similar hallmarks of 800 years of shifting central European power to other regional capitals in Belarus. Officially, it has been Lithuanian, Polish and Russian, with a happily multi-ethnic culture including significant Ruthenian and Jewish contributions; but its soul has always belonged to Belarus. Hrodna's most ancient – and prized – structure is the Kolozha (Russian: Kolozhskaya), the 12th century Church of Saints Boris & Gleb, and the only surviving monument of Black Ruthenian medieval architecture. The old city developed round this hub, its castle, churches, palaces and grand houses assuming a grandeur that reflected its rising political importance, which can be measured by the presence in 1705, at the consecration of the confidently high Baroque Cathedral on Batory Square (now Soviet Square), of both Peter the Great and Augustus the Strong.

Hrodna still retains more of its original streets and historic buildings than anywhere else in Belarus. Only 50 per cent was destroyed by Germany in World War II; it was the Jewish 39 per cent of its residents that disappeared. Since then, much has been restored – which makes it even more incredible that in 2007, Hrodna is facing a greater threat than the Nazis to

*An Orthodox church*

**POPULATION:**
317,000 (2005)
**WHEN TO GO:**
April to October
**DON'T MISS:**
Vulitsa Sovetskaja, Hrodna's favourite cobbled promenade, lined with quirky shops and cafés, and with a tree-filled park at its southern end.
The Bernardine Monastery, completed in 1618 and renovated in 1680 and 1738, covering every style from Gothic to Baroque; and its beautiful grounds.
The church of the Bridgettine Convent, and its wooden two-storey dormitory of 1642.
The polychrome Russian Revival extravaganza of the Orthodox Cathedral (1904).
Stanislawow, a summer residence of the last Polish king.
The 254-m (833-ft) high TV tower, built in 1984 and already quaint.

its fabric. City officials want to demolish an entire quarter built in the 1920s and 30s. Called the New World, the area is a unique stylistic example of European constructivism en masse, and people are proud of it. Nevertheless, it remains at risk of being flattened in favour of new roads, offices, and a sports centre with parking.

It seems a pity that such a pleasant place, unmarred by the light manufacturing industries by which it lives, and with a history as glamorous as anyone else's, might wilfully erase a whole chapter of its past. Its present deserves better, especially now that it has regained control of its own destiny.

# Brest

If you want to go from Berlin to Moscow by car or train, you go through Brest (formerly Brest-Litovsk). In 800 years it has belonged to Lithuania, Russia and Belarus; but it has always been the border town with Poland. The city's strategic importance derives from its command of a promontory on the western branch of the Bug River, the site of the original fort and of the present citadel of Brest Fortress. During the 14th-16th centuries, the city achieved international political and cultural significance. Under Russian rule, it became a dull, provincial place, until the railway arrived in 1870-85, and nondescript manufacturing boomed. Industrial revolution and the railway raised Brest to the highest magnitude of importance as a military and civil transport hub – a role which brought the city its finest hour.

In 1941, Germany attacked the USSR, and Brest Fortress was among the first to face the invaders. The defence of Brest is a bright flame in the annals of hopeless courage, and is commemorated by the shattered, concrete ruins left by the epic battle. In 1971, these were topped by a gigantic Red Star hollowed out of ferro-concrete, and the complex renamed the 'Brest Hero-Fortress'. It's a classic Soviet-era grandiosity, but you can't fault the sentiment and the citizens of Brest draw strength and character from it.

It's not a lovely city, though there are some beautiful buildings reflecting its history. These days it's ruggedly devoted to the bureaucracy of trade and travel. There are huge marshalling yards for the trans-continental trains; complicated customs sheds engulfing the Berlin-Warsaw-Moscow autoroute; parks and weighbridges for thousands of cars and trucks; and a whole system of piers and docks for the river traffic using the Dnieper-Bug Canal to reach the Black Sea. Unlovely – but transience on this scale creates an exciting and edgy atmosphere that feeds the city's mysterious and constant buzz.

**POPULATION:**
305,000 (2006)
**WHEN TO GO:**
April to October.
**DON'T MISS:**
The Resurrection Church of Brest, seat both of a Greek Catholic bishop, and of the Armenian bishop-primate of Belarus.
The outdoor Railway Museum.
Central Square, of a slab-sided characterless monotony to send you running to the nearest bar.
Belovezhskaya Puscha National Park (70 km [44 mi] N), a biosphere reserve of world distinction, where a medieval forest is home to the rare wisent (European bison).
**YOU SHOULD KNOW:**
Brest has been sacked four times: by Mongols (1241); by the Teutonic Knights (1379); by the Khan of Krim (Crimea) (c.1490); and by the Nazis.

*City Hall*

# Minsk

The famous invitation to 'relive the ghosts of Communism's past with a warm cappuccino' was originally issued on behalf of Minsk. It's a perfect summary. Minsk is still new to its role as capital of a fully independent nation, still struggling with youthful optimism towards a neo-socialist ideal, but with only the failed model of Soviet-style communism for inspiration. Its long-term history as Ruthenian, Lithuanian, Rus Khanate, and Polish regional centre means little for the moment. Go to any bar, café, or student or factory canteen, and you'll find a lively discussion (all right – heated argument) about how to get the best of the west without embracing the injustice inherent in unchecked capitalism. Hopefully, and probably, the dialogue will continue all the way to the newest nightclub or sushi bar (which may have run out of sushi – that's not the point!).

Physically, Minsk remains Stalinist, the totality of its city centre architecture a stark reminder that Minsk and its citizens went to Hell in 1941-44. The Soviet Union took charge of a region of which 80 per cent was rubble, whose population was reduced to 50,000, and whose culture (Orthodox, Catholic, Yiddish and Tatar in its pre-Russian roots) had been simply wiped out. The Soviets chose to rebuild, but not to re-construct; and their very first project was the spanking new, mammoth KGB building (1947). Railway Station Square is also typical of the grandiose bulk preferred for state utilities and offices, set on broad avenues and squares wide enough for' the people' to express their scripted gratitude and choreographed happiness.

The need finally to set its trauma to rest means the pace of change in Minsk is now frenetic. The buzz of activity is exciting (if slightly bewildering) for visitors from western Europe, who take the process of self-government so much for granted they ignore it most of the time. Choose Minsk for a refresher course in daily realities.

**POPULATION:**
1,780,000 (2006)

**WHEN TO GO:**
May to October and any time you feel strong enough to talk politics, religion, music, theatre, and the future in general.

**DON'T MISS:**
The open-air markets, where migrants (Georgia, Armenia, Azerbaijan, Syria, Lebanon, Algeria, etc) and the Belarus Roma community wield an unexpected influence.
The massive tractor factory, symbol of Minsk's resolute, but still largely unmodernized, heavy manufacturing industries.
The Great Patriotic War Museum, to understand exactly why the citizens of Minsk remain obsessed by World War II.
The colonnaded 18th century City Hall (rebuilt 2003), overlooked by the Cathedral of the Virgin (1700-10, rebuilt 1997), for a flavour of Minsk's former magnificence.
The very moving Island of Tears and its recently built memorial church.

**YOU SHOULD KNOW:**
Minsk was honoured as a Hero-City in 1974, none too soon.

# Telavi

There are two excellent reasons to visit Telavi: red and white. Telavi is the capital of Kakheti, Georgia's principal wine making region, and it is the area's proudest boast that no visitor can stay sober for long. In fact, visitors don't really stand a chance, because Kakhetians epitomize the national characteristics of conviviality, hospitality, and a general desire to hug you in an orgy of tearful emotion. And then a few more unmissable toasts…

Telavi's traditions have been honed down thousands of years, and the small town wears its history lightly. At its heart lie the honey-coloured, crenellated walls of the ancient town. Now they enclose the 18th century Palace of Herekle, the royal church, a history museum, art gallery and the remains of the basilica; while round it, the town is spread organically, linked by gentle gardens, courtyards, and tree-filled squares to the fertile vineyards and pleasant countryside from which it makes its living. Outside the town, history continues to be a living presence. Set among the fields and woods are countless churches dating from the 6th to the 17th centuries, their icons, gold utensils and vivid frescoes bearing testament to the permanence of local faith in their land and culture.

Telavi is not a romantic town, for all its beauty and tranquil rural charm. Unless you talk to people, it's difficult to enter the spirit of the place. There are few cafés or restaurants, but a simple greeting will usually lead to delighted introductions, a beaming joke or two, and in all probability, chairs being dragged up round a bottle of wine, or, if you get lucky, of *chacha*, privately distilled wine vodka that tastes better than it might sound. Make your excuses when the conversation starts getting sentimental, and retire to bed.

**POPULATION:**
28,000 (2006)
**WHEN TO GO:**
Late summer to autumn, around the grape harvest.
**DON'T MISS:**
The cathedral of Alaverdi and its beautiful walled compound.
Gremi Castle – a fantasy fortress complex set on a huge rockface, crowned by a church.
The Ikalto Monastery.
Tasting the wine along the Kakhetian Wine Route near Telavi.
The Davit Gareja Monastery, a 6th century cave complex on a wild and remote desert mountain overlooking the Azerbaijani border, with extraordinary 9th century frescoes.
**YOU SHOULD KNOW:**
In Telavi, never refuse to join in a toast; but never, ever toast someone with beer – it means you wish them bad luck.

# Tbilisi

It's a pity that Georgia is fringed by regional disputes (Chechnya, Ossetia and Abkhazia) that have made travel difficult for visitors, because Tbilisi is the kind of place you might want to stay forever. It's built along the hills of the twisting Mtkvari river valley, a lively, energetic capital city of entrenched charm and sophistication.

One of the great trading cities along the Silk Road, it has been effortlessly multi-cultural for over 5,000 years; confident in its unique traditions that were ancient before any of the great empires (Roman, Byzantine, Mongol, Persian, Ottoman, Russian) tried and failed to absorb it. It has a ramshackle but debonair elegance. Leafy avenues of 19th century houses wind away from the old town of narrow streets where carved wooden balconies lean crazily over the hillside courtyards and gardens; and exotic cooking smells and buzz of street-chatter share life secrets with the solemn beauty of ancient buildings.

It gets better. To visit Tbilisi is to be an honoured guest. Learn to say 'gamarjabat' ('hello'), as locals do to each other in residential districts, and you may all too easily end up having the time of your life. Georgians are incredibly hospitable, and want you to love their city; and to this end are totally capable of embracing you into their house, their friends and family, and their toasting rituals. Not to join in is rude, but who could refuse when the sentiments are so genuine?

Of course, since the 'Rose Revolution', Tbilisi is still struggling to adjust to the harsh economic reality of Russian sanctions: the usual infrastructures of a modern industrial and political capital are now timed to the power-cuts. The city deals with these things with its habitual panache, which means being as serious about work as it is about play. The combination fuels Tbilisi's genetic vitality. Be there to enjoy it.

**POPULATION:**
1,350,000 (2004)
**WHEN TO GO:**
When its trees and flowers are in bloom; especially Easter Monday when every churchyard is filled with tables of families feasting and toasting their forebears and each other, and, eventually, you.
**DON'T MISS:**
Singing and dancing – Tbilisi's folk choirs are famous, and music is part of every celebration. Rustaveli, heart of Tbilisi's shopping district, has lots of music stores.
The enormous market (open-air and covered) near Vakzal metro station.
The Sulphur Baths in the Old Town, a staggering confection of blue and pink mosaic tracery, its high arches like a temple.
6th century Siony Cathedral and 7th century Anchiskati Basilica.
The gold treasury and icons at the History Museum.
Narikala Fortress, on a hill with a panorama of Tbilisi.
Shardeni Avenue in the Old Town, in fact a narrow alley filled with cafés and laughter.
**YOU SHOULD KNOW:**
Traffic in Tbilisi is lethal. Norms like headlights, seatbelts, or giving way to cars or pedestrians simply do not apply.

*The Narikala Fortress overlooks the city*

# Kutaisi

**POPULATION:**
250,000 (2007)
**WHEN TO GO:**
Between spring and autumn.
**DON'T MISS:**
The Gelati Monastery complex (9 km
[5 mi] away), founded in 1106 by
Georgian national hero King Davit
Agmashenebeli (the Builder) on a
beautiful, forested hill site.
The Museum of History and
Ethnography, housing icons and
other artefacts saved from the
pillage of Kutaisi's most historic sites.
The opportunity to talk to local
people, and perhaps share their
legendary hospitality.
Eating the extra-delicious Kutaisi
version of *khachapuri* (Georgian
cheese bread).
**YOU SHOULD KNOW:**
With so much hardship in the city,
there are many pickpockets: be alert
but be gentle, because most are
bumbling amateurs in need of food.

Kutaisi is Georgia's second city, so its collapse, since 1992, as the economic and industrial centre of the west has not been compensated by the kind of international institutions and grants that have benefited the capital, Tbilisi. It has also suffered badly from armed conflict in nearby Abkhazia, which has swollen its population with refugees, drained its few resources, and inevitably raised the crime rate. Worst of all, it has inhibited tourism, which is the obvious economic panacea for a beautiful city with an amazing history, and a host of great and small treasures to show off.

Kutaisi used to be the capital of the ancient kingdom of Colchis (6th-1st century BC). According to legend, it is where Jason came to steal the Golden Fleece. Even now, its setting on green hills astride the picturesque Rioni River retains many features of its medieval form; and with the snow-capped Caucasus peaks on one side, and the beaches of the Black Sea a few kilometres away on the other, the city exerts a magnetic charm on its few visitors.

Kutaisi's totem is the 11th-century Bagrati Cathedral, on a hill overlooking the river. It's a masterpiece of medieval Georgian art and architecture, whose bulk and splendour dominates the cobbled streets of wooden houses leading to it, and of the entire city beyond – a panorama of warm roofs, domes, mosques and church spires nestled among green trees and the spikes of hundreds of cypresses. Neither the Ottomans, who bombed the Cathedral in 1692, nor the Russians, who completed the job in 1770, could detract from its magnificence. Currently there are plans to restore it. Kutaisi folk are like that – optimistic, rugged, and determined to enjoy their future.

*Bagrati Cathedral*

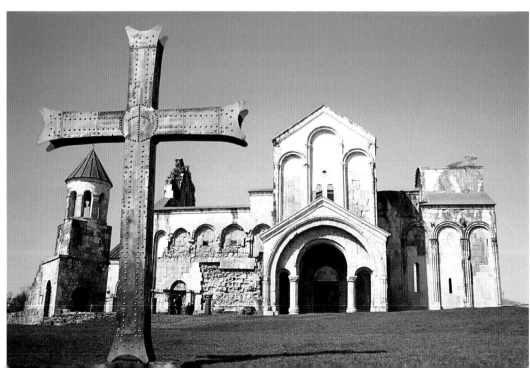

# Yalta

Blessed with a microclimate caused by its superb location on a shallow bay, facing south, with the Crimean Mountains rising sharply behind, Yalta feels more Mediterranean than it has any right to. In most other ways, it's no different from its less lucky, neighbouring seaside resorts, but to the Imperial Russian aristocracy who discovered it and made it famous, its facilities meant little. They could afford to build palatial homes away from the town and still call them 'dachas' – to share not just the extra summer warmth and milder winters, but the notion of holidaying on the same terms as the people who flocked to it.

From 1860, the south coast of the Crimea was considered to be a vast health resort. When Yalta became first choice of royalty, it attracted more money, better architecture and maintenance, and more and better facilities of every kind. It couldn't lose. Soviet leaders moved in where Tsars and Princes had bailed out, and the proletariat followed, panting. Only since 1991, when its necessarily wealthy clientele discovered the freedom to travel, has Yalta been exposed to the economic realities of having pretension thrust upon it.

It's perfectly pleasant. Everyone strolls down the palm-lined Promenade with its bars, cafés, rides, hawkers, buskers, circus acts and sandy beaches. But the rich have gone to the real Mediterranean or wherever, and only very recently has Yalta woken up to the legacy it has been left by its 19th and 20th century success. And it's just fabulous. The whole world knows it because of the Yalta Conference of 1945. Three world leaders stayed in three Royal Palaces in the immediate vicinity, just three of lots of spectacular buildings that constitute a veritable tourist magnet, a unique asset worth seeing even if you hate the seaside and the very idea of 'resort'. Come to Yalta before its custodians embalm its Imperial and Soviet history in revisionist sterility.

*The fairy tale Swallow's Nest Castle*

**POPULATION:**
81,000 (2005)
**WHEN TO GO:**
Any time of year – but only the foolhardy swim in winter.
**DON'T MISS:**
Tsar Alexander III's 1889 Massandra Palace, subsequently Stalin's personal 'dacha'.
Tsar Nicholas II's creamy, classical Livadia Palace, venue for the 1945 Conference.
The fairy tale neo-Gothic, turreted Swallow's Nest Castle, on a bluff overhanging the sea.
Chekhov's house, and Tolstoy's too.
The Palace of Yemir Bukhara.
The lovely woods and vineyards flourishing in the hills around Yalta.
**YOU SHOULD KNOW:**
Yalta is linked to Simferopol by the longest (79 km [49 mi]) trolley-bus route in the world.

# Lviv

*The Art Noveau Main Railway Terminal*

With so many five-star historical attractions grabbing your attention in and around Lviv, it's all too easy to be distracted from appreciating the effort residents have to make to keep their city, and themselves, going.

Looking down from 13th century Vysoki Zamok (High Castle) on the domes and spires of the old walled city, and beyond, to Hapsburg-era boulevards full of stunning examples of Baroque, Gothic and Renaissance architecture, Lviv's role as gateway city between east and west Europe seems romantic rather than grafting. Of course, the (three) cathedrals, churches, palaces and institutions packed around 16th century Ploshcha Rynok (Market Square) are in fact emblems of Lviv's success in playing the diplomatic game of several centuries, and surviving the bloody conflicts between Poles, Lithuanians, Russians, and Germans with less damage than most other cities in the region. Unfortunately, up close, the cobbled streets are patched, and multicoloured facades literally crumbling. There's no money.

Knowing this, visitors are amazed by the energy buzzing through the civic corpse, and by the resolute good humour – only slightly cynical – that the locals bring to the lack of facilities and services, and to their daily dealings with bureaucracy and petty political corruption.

Along Prospect Svobody (Freedom Avenue), Lviv's main thoroughfare (actually built on top of the heavily-polluted river which ran beside the city walls), there are, certainly, lots of smart international shops. But the pavements, here and everywhere throughout Lviv's squares, alleys and Soviet-era high-rise districts, are lined with people hawking fruit and vegetables, pastries, books, clothes, sticks of furniture, bric-à-brac, and anything which might be a 'soviet' souvenir. It's the pragmatism of survival: where a medieval building can also be both café and mobile phone repair shop, you feel Lviv is flexing itself to be reborn into its new, glorious future – and that really is a romantic thought. Go soon.

# Kiev

Kiev was settled more than 10,000 years ago, and the city established in 482 AD was already famous when the Vikings brought their name of Kiev-Rus to the region on their way to Constantinople. Stand before the city's immense Golden Gate, dating back to 1037 (you'll find it, prosaically, next to the Zoloti Vorota metro station), and it's easy to understand why Kiev's medieval authority was absolute. Only its eventual subjugation by the united Mongol hordes in 1399 reduced its status, and ceded Russian unification to the newcomer Moscow. But Kiev had already played the cultural trump by bringing Byzantium to Russia, with its religion, alphabet and stress on autocracy, and the city is still proud that its Ukrainian culture underwrites the whole of Russia. Neither the catastrophic destruction of its fabric and annihilation of half its population by the Germans, nor Stalin's savage attempts to atomize its independent spirit, brought it to its knees. Ironically, post 1990 Ukrainian freedom nearly did so, but Kiev survived that shaky start, too, and is now succeeding in regenerating its glory.

Its woods, parks and gardens have always made Kiev a beautiful city, and underneath the bustle of its extremely lively street life, you're still aware that the city is made up of three distinct settlements – Starokievsky, Pechersk and Podol. The main thoroughfare, Kreshchatik, brightly lit by shops, cafés and public buildings, runs where a small stream with woods on either side divided them. Modern Kiev now straddles the Dnieper, an appropriately major European waterway. Hundreds of gold, green, blue and red domes march from the high bluff of the ancient Upper Town down its steep west bank, each of them a marker of Kiev's rough and turbulent past. On the broad floodplain to the east lies the monotonous jumble of predominantly Soviet, post-War expansion. The frantic energy you feel on both sides is that of Kiev in the overdrive of renewal.

*The gilded domes and spires of St Sophia Cathedral*

**POPULATION:**
2,660,000 (2004)
**WHEN TO GO:**
In spring or summer when all the botanical gardens and parks are blooming; or in winter when the lake freezes and all Kiev goes ice-skating.
**DON'T MISS:**
11th century Cathedral of St Sophia, the most beautiful example of Russo-Byzantine architecture, now a state museum; it is one of Ukraine's greatest treasures.
The five domes of 19th century Desyatynna Church, with what remains of the 10th century church built by St Vladimir inside it.
The Cave Monastery of Kievo-Pecherska, already famous in 1051. The complex contains catacombs, several churches and countless treasures – but you have to buy your own candle to see them.
The Sunday concerts of Ukrainian choral and folk music at the Museum of Rural Life.
The Jewish Quarter of Podil and its old river port.
**YOU SHOULD KNOW:**
The hardy locals who swim daily during the winter months in the freezing water of the Dnieper River are known as 'walruses'.

*The Opera House*

# Odessa

The 'Pearl of the Black Sea' and Ukraine's third largest city, Odessa preens itself on its balmy climate, seaside vistas and miles of white beaches. Its two bustling ports, oil terminal and industrial hub facilities are sited where they can't threaten the city's considerable allure as a holiday destination. Best of all, it has the excited and exciting self-awareness of (very slightly wasted) youth, as confident of its contribution to national prosperity as it is of its elegance and the glamour it represents to visitors. Its ambience is palpably more Mediterranean than Slavic.

Odessa was designed from scratch as recently as 1792, when Russian Imperial expansion annexed the region. French was the Court language of the era – and Odessa's architects and first few Governors were French. The new city was so successful that numerous landowners, magnates, merchants and factory owners built their own compounds to fit the overall plan. Odessa's leafy boulevards are lined with Russian-flavoured masterpieces of Classicism and Art Nouveau reminiscent of the Right Bank in Paris; and their names (Frantcuzky, etc.) acknowledge Italian, Greek, Jewish, Albanian and other communities contributing to Odessa's growth. The first Governor, the Duc de Richelieu, and his successors all got name-checked streets, and Odessa's cosmopolitanism was confirmed for all time by Pushkin, who wrote 'you can smell Europe' there.

Much of Odessa's darker history is equally glamorous. Richelieu's statue commands the top of the 142-m (466-ft) long Potemkin Stairs down to the Port, immortalized by Eisenstein as the scene of the workers' massacre during the 1905 uprising.

If you like the idea of 'extreme tourism' (modeled on extreme sports), try negotiating 'the catacombs' – the huge labyrinth of tunnels underneath Odessa which began as limestone quarries for the new houses, and were completed by smugglers after being officially abandoned. They are neither mapped nor safe, but they are fun, Odessa-style.

**POPULATION:**
1,200,000 (2004)
**WHEN TO GO:**
In spring for the Festival of Laughter on April 1st, a public holiday in honour of Odessa's irrepressible sense of humour.
**DON'T MISS:**
The buildings along Primorsky Boulevard, typical of Odessa's 'Golden Age'.
The Krasnaya Hotel of 1899, formerly called the Bristol.
The Fine Arts Museum in the former Pototsky Palace.
The Italian Baroque façade of the Opera and Ballet Theatre.
Commemorating the Russian Imperial pogroms as well as the Nazi atrocities of World War II, at the Jewish Heritage Museum.
The vast, open-air Seventh-Kilometer Market, biggest of its kind in Europe.
**YOU SHOULD KNOW:**
Odessa is ultra-proud to have been awarded the title of 'Hero-City' in 1945.

# Cesky Krumlov

In a country packed with historical marvels, Cesky Krumlov is utterly outstanding. The little town is tucked into a horseshoe bend of the Vltava River, sited in the 13th century to take advantage of the ford across such an important trade route. The town is beyond picturesque: its steep grey roofs are a jumble of odd angles above the half-timbered houses painted ochre, blue, yellow, cream and rose pink. Alleys twist round each other, so that there's always a surprise – a balcony, a courtyard, an arch with some new vista – to pull you forward even as you want to spend all day examining the exquisite detail of this living, breathing, slice of history. Don't let the throng of other tourists stop you. Like you, they can't help being agog with excitement: this beguiling fairytale town just keeps making you smile.

It developed, perhaps inevitably, in symbiosis with the huge and equally magnificent castle on the rocky bluff across the river. The complex of Krumlov Castle is second only to Hradcany in Prague, in size and dynastic significance. It was developed as a stronghold of the Rosenberg family from 1302. They gave the old Gothic structure a dramatic Renaissance extension, guided by the finest Italian architects, to match the family's rising political star. Three centuries later, it belonged to the Eggenburg line, who began a major reconstruction in the new Baroque style. The Schwarzenberg dynasty followed, and for a century added more and more exotic halls, staircases, gardens, theatres, pavilions and even a riding school – in increasingly High Baroque taste. And what happened in this vast, fortified cornucopia of art, elegance and beauty was reflected in the town below. Their fates were always entwined, and their mutual survival is one of those miracles for which we should all be eternally grateful. Go.

**POPULATION:**
14,000 (2005)
**WHEN TO GO:**
Year-round. It is quieter in winter, but never empty. The Five-Petalled Rose Festival celebrates the Summer Solstice, when the whole town goes medieval and there is jousting, folk theatre on the river bank, and brilliant, interactive fun and games.
**DON'T MISS:**
Entering the town through the Bjdegovice Gate, the 400 year-old start of your adventure.
Allowing time to enjoy the Castle – the Hall of Masques; the Golden Coach that carried a Holy Roman Emperor to his Vatican coronation; the Baroque Theatre with its original props; the medieval fortress at its core; and so on. Endlessly fascinating.
The Cathedral of St Vitus, a rare example of Czech Gothic medieval style.
Enjoying one of the many concerts – of all kinds – in some unexpected corner.
The Egon Schiele Museum – he lived here for some time.
**YOU SHOULD KNOW:**
The film of *Pinocchio* was shot here.

*A view across the rooftops to the castle*

# Pilsen

**POPULATION:**
163,000 (2005)
**WHEN TO GO:**
Year-round. The Cultural Festival is in
spring, the Jazz Festival in summer, and
the Film Festival in autumn. Winter is
for looking beautiful in the snow.
**DON'T MISS:**
The mid-16th century Renaissance
Town Hall.
The West Bohemian (Art) Gallery, in the
converted Gothic building of Masne
Kramy (the Butchers' Shop).
The Brewery Museum – followed by the
Brewery tour.
The Franciscan monastery.
The Great Synagogue – built in 1892 and
incorporating every style from Moorish
to Art Nouveau. The world's third
biggest, after Budapest and Jerusalem.
**YOU SHOULD KNOW:**
Despite attempts by the then
Czechoslovakian governments of the
communist era to suppress the fact,
Pilsen was liberated from the Nazis by
General George S Patton and the US 3rd
Army on May 6 1945.

Your first sight of Pilsen is of ultra-modern industrial superstructure, which is a perfect expression of its economic significance to the Czech Republic, and of its own prosperity. It's home to a colossal brewery, to whose particular style of beer the city has given its name, and to the Skoda company, which since 1859 has been a stalwart of international engineering. The surprise is that Pilsen was equally successful four centuries before the industrial revolution.

The evidence is the city's historical centre. Founded in 1295 by Wenceslaus II as Plzen, Pilsen rapidly became one of Bohemia's most important trade centres, closely associated with its German neighbours, Nuremberg and Regensburg. Culturally, it oversaw the printing of the first Czech book, the *Trojanys Chronicle* in 1468; and it was the centre of Catholic resistance during the Hussite Wars. Briefly (1599-1600) the Royal capital of Emperor Rudolf II, the city waned after the end of the Thirty Years War – but it had already acquired the architectural treasures that still characterize its heart. Wenceslaus always intended the city to be big, and the historical centre still is. Dominated by the Gothic, late 13th century St Bartholomew's Cathedral, and its 102-m (335-ft) steeple, Pilsen's great square is a dictionary of medieval, Renaissance and early Baroque vernacular architecture, Czech with a German accent. Their functions vary, but each building is among the finest stylistic demonstrations of its era. The magnificence extends to the surrounding streets, built on a grid system and (as Wenceslaus decreed) unusually wide to enhance their elegance and nobility.

Pilsen's historic integrity also runs underground. From the 13th to the 19th centuries, the city developed a huge complex of cellars and tunnels two and three levels deep, beneath the centre. Through wars, pestilence and strife, they helped preserve the city above. Every visitor will be grateful.

*The Great Synagogue*

# Ceske Budejovice

Even the locals refer to it simply by its English name, Budweis – and Ceske Budejovice is indeed where the beer originated. Since the 13th century, its prosperity has depended on brewing, salt and silver, which was once mined and minted for the treasury of Bohemian Kings. Industrialization in the 1890s galvanized the beautiful, former royal city, and brought it its present status as political, economic, and cultural capital of South Bohemia. It also recharged Budejovice's historic centre, initially with a riot of Belle Epoque buildings, and more recently, with the wealth to restore the extraordinarily rich examples of late medieval, Renaissance, and early and High Baroque architectural styles for which it is renowned.

*A decorated façade*

It was founded in 1265 on the confluence of the Vltava and Malse rivers, by charter of King Premysl Ottokar II. By emphasizing the city's royal and ecclesiastical status, he successfully established it as a counterbalance to the powerful House of Rosenberg, and after 1611, to the Hapsburgs. It remained a German-speaking enclave until 1890. The city benefited in the shape of the biggest town square in the Czech Republic, laid out like a giant chessboard, and generations of wealth and reflected grandeur. From the looming 72 m (236 ft) height of the Black Tower (1550), you can see the blend of details, picked out against pale blues, yellows, pinks and ochres, that somehow harmonizes the profusion of styles in Budejovice's maze of ancient streets. You can also see how the 'new' Budejovice has been integrated with the historic centre by the clever use of the river banks and thickly-wooded parks. In the arcades running round the square, or in the Vcela (Bee) Palace, a lavish, golden-coloured Belle Epoque extravaganza whose first floor bay windows and fan-shaped skylights conceal a bank, tell-tale steel and glass projecting slightly above the cornice shows how Budejovice can seamlessly graft new onto old. It's a typically Czech, and lovely, city to visit.

**POPULATION:**
100,000 (2007)

**WHEN TO GO:**
April to October, the best time for strolling in pedestrianized Lannova trida, for exploring, and for a beer in a river bank café.

**DON'T MISS:**
The important medieval frescoes in the 13th century Dominican Monastery, used as the Royal Mint for 200 years to 1785, before reverting to the monks.
The church-like bulk of Rennaissance Masne Kramy (the Butchers' Shop), established in 1365 by King Charles IV to sell bread and meat, and continuously in use since.
The Budvar brewery tour.
The charmingly elegant Baroque Town Hall (1727-30), with its murals and bronze gargoyles; and its exuberant contemporary Samson's Fountain, in the middle of the square.
The Belle Epoque Austro-Hungarian train station in the 'new' town.
Discovering the details of Europe's first horse-drawn railway, which ran between Budejovice and Linz from 1825-32, at the South Bohemian Museum.

**YOU SHOULD KNOW:**
Ceske Budejovice was, for a while, the Royal brewery for the Emperor of the Holy Roman Empire.

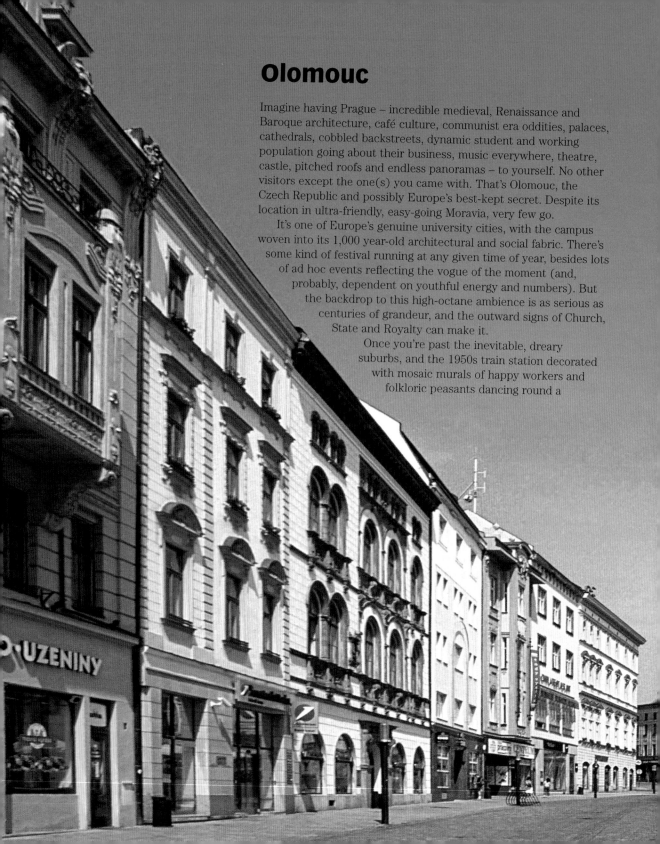

# Olomouc

Imagine having Prague – incredible medieval, Renaissance and Baroque architecture, café culture, communist era oddities, palaces, cathedrals, cobbled backstreets, dynamic student and working population going about their business, music everywhere, theatre, castle, pitched roofs and endless panoramas – to yourself. No other visitors except the one(s) you came with. That's Olomouc, the Czech Republic and possibly Europe's best-kept secret. Despite its location in ultra-friendly, easy-going Moravia, very few go.

It's one of Europe's genuine university cities, with the campus woven into its 1,000 year-old architectural and social fabric. There's some kind of festival running at any given time of year, besides lots of ad hoc events reflecting the vogue of the moment (and, probably, dependent on youthful energy and numbers). But the backdrop to this high-octane ambience is as serious as centuries of grandeur, and the outward signs of Church, State and Royalty can make it.

Once you're past the inevitable, dreary suburbs, and the 1950s train station decorated with mosaic murals of happy workers and folkloric peasants dancing round a

hammer-and-sickle, you enter a showcase of Baroque city planning. In fact, the city is much older. It ruled Moravia from the 11th century to 1642, and a great deal from that era survives. Apart from several palaces, the Renaissance is represented by a complex of merchants' houses called' Pod bohatymi kramy' ('Under the rich shops'); before that, the last Premyslid-dynasty King, Wenceslaus III was murdered in 1306, in the Chapter house of the 11th century Cathedral.

Olomouc's Baroque status rests on the extensive rebuilding following the Thirty Years War. The Upper and Lower Squares of the west city centre are simply stunning – and crowned by the Holy Trinity Column, Olomouc's thank-offering following the Plague. Hapsburg Empress Maria Theresa consecrated it in 1754, reportedly furious that, at 35 m (115 ft), the column was taller than Prague's!

**POPULATION:**
102,000 (2007), boosted by 18,000 students.
**WHEN TO GO:**
Year-round. Of the many wonderful festivals, May's Song Festival is an international choral competition, when choirs spontaneously burst into song while sightseeing, or sitting in a café. The Olomouc City Festival in June is ten days of concerts, theatre, art, processions and a whipped-cream battle.
**DON'T MISS:**
The halls, chapel and tower of the Renaissance Town Hall (1444) – its huge medieval astronomical clock was destroyed in World War II, and replaced in 1953 by a Social Realist-style version, with a mechanical conga line of Happy Workers and Lenin's birthday.
The café terraces between 11th century St Wenceslas Cathedral and the Squares – for the panorama of the old city walls and the gamut of history below.
Hradisko Monastery – the oldest in Moravia.
The severe Gothic face of St Moricz Church – with a glorious Baroque interior.
The Hauenschild Palace, where Mozart wrote his 6th Symphony.
**YOU SHOULD KNOW:**
The 'Guttery Breath of the Knight of Lostice' is Olomouc's infamous stinky cheese, and is sold with a lid, mints and the offer of a toothbrush.

*Statues along the Charles Bridge*

# Prague

Prague has been the political, cultural, and economic centre of the Czech state for over 1000 years. Lying on a bend in the River Vltava, half-way between Berlin and Vienna, it is set on seven hills topped by lovely castles and churches. Prague is widely considered to be one of the most beautiful cities in Europe. In 1993, after the split of Czechoslovakia, Prague became the capital city of the new Czech Republic. Since the end of Communism, Prague has become one of the most visited cities in Europe, famous for its café culture and vibrant nightlife in the most beautiful surroundings.

The city's heyday was during the fourteenth century and the reign of Charles IV. Charles founded the first university in central, northern and eastern Europe, today known as the Charles University. He also founded New Town, adjacent to the Old Town, rebuilt Prague Castle and Vysehrad, and erected Charles Bridge. Under his reign, many new churches were built, including St. Vitus' Cathedral, and Charles was crowned Emperor of the Holy Roman Empire. He wanted Prague to be one of the most beautiful cities in the world, dominating the whole empire, with Prague Castle dominating the city and the Gothic Cathedral dominating the castle. To this end, he created many beautiful buildings which are still with us today.

The castle was founded in the 9th century, and has since remained the seat of power. It is one of the largest castles in the world, and houses the crown jewels of the Bohemian Kingdom. Just outside is the eighteenth-century Sternberg Palace (Sternberský palác, home to the National Gallery with its superb collection of Old Masters. The complex also contains the wonderful Royal Gardens and the stately Gothic St Vitus' Cathedral, begun in 1344. The walls of the chapel that houses the tomb of St Wenceslas are lined with precious stones and beautiful paintings.

Prague's old town (Staré Město) is an atmospheric area of cobbled streets, alleyways, superb churches and palaces. The Little Quarter (Malá Strana) lies below the castle walls. This district features many notable historic buildings, among them St Nicholas Cathedral. The Charles Bridge is another must-see. Built in 1357 with a tower at either end, it offers spectacular views of the city to those who cross it.

# Kutna Hora

Kutna Hora feels spooky and surreal. It's as though the town went into a coma several centuries ago, cut adrift like some magnificent architectural *Marie Celeste*.

Around 700 years ago, Kutna Hora was renowned throughout Europe as the source of the wealth of the Kings of Bohemia, and the seat of royal power. In 1300 Wenceslaus II created the impetus that gave it status to rival Prague. He codified the legal and technical terms by which an existing silver mine could be ruthlessly exploited, and tapped into a seemingly endless stream of silver. Thereafter, with a short break in which the new town was burned to prevent it falling into enemy hands, his successors stood – as you can today – on the terrace of the Italian Court, the royal palace and Mint, gazing across the fabulously rich valley community at the twin Gothic spires of the Cathedral of St Barbora, patron saint of the miners who built it. In 1541, the mine flooded, and a further 200 years of war, plague and famine left the town all but abandoned. In 1770, the mine finally closed. As you wander the town's narrow lanes, glimpsing the surrounding forests from every corner, it's hard to shake off a powerful feeling of hubris at the degree of suffering in such a lovely and apparently fortunate place.

Kutna Hora's other treasure is an overtly surreal memento mori. It is the Sedlec Ossuary, where the bones of over 40,000 plague victims of the 14th and 15th centuries were kept in vast heaps until 1870, when a woodcarver employed by the local landowners took up the macabre hobby of using the bones to decorate the church above. Four bone pyramids greet you in the chapel, and a gigantic bone chandelier hangs in the centre of the nave. Garlands of skulls drape the vaults, and bone monstrances flank an altar crammed with other bone creations.

**POPULATION:**
21,000 (2006)
**WHEN TO GO:**
April to September, when concerts are held in the wooded amphitheatre in the valley, and music festivals brighten the town itself.
**DON'T MISS:**
Palazkeho Namesti, the main square, and a delightful place of reflection.
The 12th century Cathedral of the Assumption of the Virgin Mary, built by the Cistercians.
The mining museum housed in the Hradek Chapel, next to St Barbara's Cathedral.
The 16th century mines, reaching depths of 500 m (1,640 ft) – so deep that miners wore a leather apron which they could sit on to slide quickly down to work.
The private rooms and Royal Audience Hall of Wenceslaus IV.
The Gothic St James's Church, with its 83 m (272 ft) steeple.
**YOU SHOULD KNOW:**
The US dollar is named after Kutna Hora's silver 'tolar'.

*Human bones are on show in Sedlec Ossuary Chapel of All Saints.*

# Karlovy Vary

*The town has a wonderful
fin-de-siécle elegance.*

Karlovy Vary, also known by its German name of Karlsbad, is one of the world's most famous spa towns, synonymous with fin-de-siècle, jaded elegance, and just a soupçon of disreputability. It lies along the river valley of the Tepla in Bohemia, its tree-lined avenues of neo-classical and Art Nouveau mansions stretching either side of the water, vying with the grand hotels for proximity to the twelve principal hot springs, and 300 smaller ones whose mineral-rich properties are the source of the town's reputation.

At least the cycles of Karlovy Vary's fame have been consistent. Its name derives from its founder, Czech King and Holy Roman Emperor Charles IV. He praised the beneficial effects of the local springs by granting privileges in 1374 to the existing settlement, which in turn benefited from the royal endorsement. By the time Queen Victoria came to the British throne in 1837, the crowned heads of Europe were all related, and Karlovy Vary hit the international big time. Entrepreneurs and hoteliers vied for the aristocracy's custom not just with ornate colossi to house and entertain them, but by naming each spring, and building neo-classical colonnades in wood and stone where the 7 per cent of people who owned 84 per cent of Europe might nurse their fragile digestive tracts, and discuss war and the weather. In fact, until Kaiser Wilhelm declared war on his first cousin in 1914 and brought the whole social system of four centuries to a juddering collapse, Karlovy Vary was privy to more political action than all Europe's parliaments and palaces combined.

Reborn in a more democratic spirit, the town is now restoring its tarnished elegance, and reclaiming its position as one of the best and most accessible of the Czech Republic's spa resorts. It has poise and grace to match its newly-painted beauty, but carries its effortless aristocratic hauteur with a reassuring wink. We are all welcome now.

# Brno

The capital of Moravia and the Czech Republic's second city, Brno is proud of its history, but prouder still of its future. Culture vultures looking for a historical fix will get it in spades from this former stronghold of the medieval Prmyslid dynasty, which subsequently twice saw off besieging Hussites, in 1428 and 1430; the Swedes, during the Thirty Years War, in 1643 and 1645; and finally, after rebuilding itself as a Baroque fortress, the Prussians in 1742. With nothing left to prove, but a superb collection of churches, monasteries, palaces, squares, markets and monuments still magnificently extant to prove it with, Brno returned to what it did and does best – industry and commerce. Culture was to be pursued only in tandem with progress.

As a civic philosophy it's hugely successful, and Brno is wide-awake to the notion of modernity that makes other cities shudder. It established its Exhibition Centre as long ago as 1928, and nurtured its growth (retarded by Nazis and Communists) to its current annual statistics of 40 trade fairs and 1 million visitors. The city appreciates motor racing, so after years gauging what it can do and what people enjoy, hosts regular car and motorcycle events at the highest international levels. On top of that, just for fun, every June it hosts Ignis Brunensis - not a show, but an international fireworks competition which attracts 200,000 people. It makes September's wine festival look positively traditional, except that the city is surrounded by vineyards and nobody is likely to leave empty-handed.

You have to love a city that thinks so positively and comes up with the active and/or interactive goods. Brno's unofficial symbol is the former Bauhaus Director Mies van der Rohe's Tugendhat Villa in the town, listed recently by UNESCO as a masterpiece of functionalism. It's perfect – visitors know that Brno will do anything possible to help them enjoy themselves.

**POPULATION:**
399,000 (2007)
**WHEN TO GO:**
Year-round – there is always a fair, festival, or major event going on.
**DON'T MISS:**
The view from the 63-m (207-ft) high tower (built 1240) of the Old Town Hall (from 1373 -1935).
The torture chamber of Spilberk Castle, on the hill overlooking Brno.
Svobody Namesti (Freedom Square), Brno's medieval heart, with its Plague Column and intriguing buildings, like the Renaissance House of the Lords of Jupa (1589-96).
The twin spires and original 12th century crypt of the neo-Gothic Cathedral of St Peter and St Paul (aka the Petrov) – its current form is the latest of several over nine centuries.
The Museum in former Dietrichstein Palace (1614-20), on Zelny Trh, (Cabbage Market), used by Russian General Kutuzov in 1805 when meeting Napoleon.
Menin Gate (c. 1500) the only remaining piece of Brno's fortifications.
**YOU SHOULD KNOW:**
The Petrov Cathedral bells ring noon at 11.00 am, a tradition since the Swedish siege of 1645.

*Pruchodni Street*

# Kosice

Like so many central European cities buffeted by the political vagaries of history, since the' velvet divorce' of 1993, Kosice has struggled with an identity crisis. It lies close to the border with Hungary, Poland and Ukraine, and though it has always been an important regional centre, with a familiar huddle of church spires, fortified towers, and rows of ornate public and private buildings grouped in its historic heart, it has only been Slovakia's second city since the 1950s, when the communist government built a gigantic steel works on the edge of a hitherto nondescript, small town. Its population boomed, magnifying its existing ethnographic uneasiness. Hungarians (who call it Kassa) flocked to seize new opportunities in what for them had been a Hungarian city for longer than it had been anything else. Slovaks vied with them; and both groups tried to keep out the historically ostracized and underemployed Roma who acknowledge no national boundaries. The ever-decreasing local community of Ruthenians (Rusyns) felt culturally excluded, and they were.

Regeneration in the new Slovak Republic, and restoration of the city's historic fabric and treasures, have turned those negatives into positives: Kosice's residents now celebrate their multiethnic urban society with its plethora of dialects and customs. It makes their city different, more fundamentally cosmopolitan, by resolving age-old cultural antagonisms with an appreciation of mutual, future development. Kosice feels and behaves independently from the rest of Slovakia, and most people are proud of that. You can't help noticing the city's positive atmosphere, the one essential characteristic Kosice needed to begin to transform its industrial legacy as thoroughly as it has done its historic centre. Cosmopolitan it may be, but Kosice is not sophisticated.

**POPULATION:**
240,000 (2003)
**WHEN TO GO:**
Any weekend, for the markets.
**DON'T MISS:**
The 14th century Urbanova veza (tower) above its own arcade.
The magnificence of the Gothic Cathedral of St Elizabeth, Slovakia's biggest.
The all-singing, all-dancing fountains in pedestrianized Hlavna ulica (main square).
The 15th-17th century gold coins in the East Slovak Museum. Stashed long ago, they were discovered by accident in 1935.
Meeting people on the 5 km (3 mi) Children's Railway up the 14 km (9 mi) Cermel Valley, where all Kosice goes for its picnics and fresh air.
**YOU SHOULD KNOW:**
The 1723 Immaculata statue, on its column in the square, commemorates the plague years of 1710-11 on the site of the former public gallows.

*Cathedral of St Elizabeth*

# Bratislava

*The castle (Bratislavsky Hrad) overlooks the town.*

Throughout the Soviet era, Bratislava was often dismissed as the drab, industrialized second city of Czechoslovakia, hardly worth a glance. Even its historic Old Town was deemed of little interest, as tatty as the pollution-stained suburbs spreading in every direction. Well – Surprise! Since 1990, few places can have done more, or more successfully, to reclaim and scrub-up their past; and nowhere else has official bureaucracy combined determined regeneration with irrepressible glee and a genuinely amusing sense of humour. Bratislava, restored as capital of an independent Slovakia, is bursting with life.

Once the frontier of the Roman Empire, it was called Pressburg when its strategic importance, straddling the Danube, was recognized with heavy fortifications in the 12th century. By 1536, with the Turks in Budapest, it was confirmed in authority as the Hungarian capital, and hosted nineteen imperial coronations in the next 300 years. By then the Old Town and environs were packed with castles, palaces, spires and churches, and it was in the Mirror Hall of the Primate's Palace, in 1805, that Napoleon signed the Peace of Bratislava after Austerlitz.

This is the kind of history that Bratislava is revitalizing, with pedestrian precincts and a policy of encouraging street cafés and bars, so that the city's historic heart, deserted after 6.00 pm as recently as 1995, is now ablaze with light, music, street theatre and strolling couples. And statues – like the Napoleonic soldier leaning over your shoulder as you sit on a bench; or the grinning, helmeted man emerging from a manhole (Why? There are some wonderful answers…); or 'Schöne Nazi', an old gentleman doffing his top hat to the sky (commemorating a man who lost his mind after the deportation of his Jewish fiancée).

History in Bratislava has human empathy, and a human scale. The city doesn't tout itself in competition with other European capitals. It is far too busy and entertaining being itself.

**POPULATION:**
450,000 (2006)
**WHEN TO GO:**
Any time of year but be prepared for rain.
**DON'T MISS:**
Hviezdoslavovo Square.
The 11th century Cathedral of St Martin (try to ignore the traffic noise along the Danube).
The giant box of the 15th century Hrad (Castle), and its view across the riverplain to the huge Communist-era blocks of the Petrzalka housing estate, home to a third of the city.
Michalska and Venturska Streets, lined with some of Bratislava's finest Baroque palaces.
The exhibition of medieval torture in the dungeons of Stara Radnica (Old Town Hall).
The Jewish Museum, lest we forget.

*The historic centre has recently been given a face-lift.*

# Presov

Presov, set in the High Tatra Mountains where eastern Slovakia bumps into Ukraine and Poland, has a cultural significance far beyond its compact size. On the surface, it has the bumptious exuberance of a typical university town, always keen to burn the candle at both ends. It is also a regional centre for Slovakia's best skiing, and fantastic, scenic hiking, so throughout the year its numbers are further swollen by visitors looking for a good time. Luckily, Presov was spared from total destruction in World War II, and not only preserved its lozenge-shaped historic centre, but has recently given it a thorough face-lift; which means that citizens and students alike have a wonderful, historic theatre in which to dramatize themselves.

In fact, Presov's history is concentrated around one main square, which reveals the ethnographical confrontations of both past and present. At its widest point the 14th century Catholic Cathedral (with marvelous, modern Moravian stained glass and a sumptuous Baroque altarpiece) challenges its Protestant counterpart opposite; and both are shown to be architectural floosies by the stark simplicity of the mid-17th century Lutheran church next door. All are in daily, local use, evidence of the strength of both historic religious reformism in outer Hungary when everyone else was suffering the Counter-Reformation, and of continuing tensions in the present community. These are intensified by Presov's less obvious role as the only cultural centre of Slovakia's ancient Ruthenian minority, and of Roma from all over the countryside. After rubbing together so long, Presov has developed an air of relaxed warmth among its still provincial, distinct communities. Student high-fives and laughter provide the perfect lubricant.

**POPULATION:**
94,000 (2004)
**WHEN TO GO:**
Winter sports, or summer hikes?
**DON'T MISS:**
The creamy pastel 18th century facades around Hlavná Ulica (main square).
The unfeasibly massive iconostasis of the Rococo Greek-Orthodox Cathedral.
The Town Hall, where Béla Kun's Hungarian Red Army declared the short-lived Slovak Socialist Republic in 1919.
The early medieval castles of Saris and Kapusiansky, 15 km north of Presov.
The Jewish Synagogue.
**YOU SHOULD KNOW:**
The Irish Pub closes at 7.00 am, when the bar next door opens.

# Nitra

Nitra takes Slovakia back to its very beginnings, and remains the guardian of its spiritual and cultural soul. The first Slavs displaced the Celts and settled here in the 5th century. By 828, Slovakia's founding national hero (often compared to England's Alfred the Great) Prince Pribina welcomed Christianity to a united Slovak territory of trans-European influence. Despite annexation by the Moravian Empire in 833, Christianity flourished, especially after SS Cyril and Methodius arrived from Byzantium. Cyril translated the sacred texts into the vernacular, and Methodius was consecrated by Pope Hadrian II as Nitra's first Bishop in 870.

What followed is freely visible on Zobor Hill, the steep hill in the middle of Nitra with its huge medieval Castle ruins and Cathedral complex, which includes the first Benedictine monastery. With the river Nitra curling round its base, and the pedestrianised squares and streets of 1,000 years of development, the city might seem like many other Slovakian regional centres. Unlike any of them, Nitra, old and new, has the stamp of modern prosperity. Thanks to the city's setting in beautiful, hilly countryside, famous for its vineyards and agriculture, it got a head start on the post - 1993 Slovakian economy, by already being, since 1974, the site of a colossal agricultural exhibition centre, and an agricultural university. The people who flock to its historical centre were coming anyway, to the annual Trade Fairs, festivals, symposia, and exhibitions that bring more than 1.5 million people to town every year.

It's almost unfair that Nitra should have the most interesting local history, the least industry and for some years much more money for better infrastructures (hotels, etc); plus a crackling ambience created by reveling students and off-duty business-folk. You suspect that it's all a reward for the city's early Faith.

**POPULATION:**
87,000 (2002), but frequently swelled to bursting.
**WHEN TO GO:**
During spring, summer or autumn, avoiding all the trade fairs except the festival of the Classical Guitar.
**DON'T MISS:**
The Saturday market in pedestrianized Stefanikova Sreet; with Mostna and Sturova Streets, the focal point of shopping generally, and of café life.
The 14th century frescoes and ornate choir loft of the Gothic Upper Cathedral.
The medieval apse of St Emmeram Cathedral, linked to the Baroque (1622-42) Lower Cathedral extension.
The incomparable view from Vazel's Tower (ask in the Cathedral for the key).
The liquid gold of the local wine.
**YOU SHOULD KNOW:**
Eat early – like most of Slovakia, Nitra lunches from 11.00 to 13.00, and dines from 17.00 to 20.00.

*St Emmeram Cathedral*

# Pecs

**POPULATION:**
157,000 (2005)
**WHEN TO GO:**
March to September, when the Theatre Festival is the annual highlight of a regular chain of festivals and events.
**DON'T MISS:**
The 4th century Cella Septichora, discovered in 1900; a labyrinth recently set with walkways to give visitors the best view of its magnificent treasures.
The neo-Romanesque Cathedral.
The restored exoticism of the Mosque of Pasha Yakovali Hassan.
The Zsolnay Museum, dedicated to the marque's fabulous Art Nouveau ceramics, tiles and porcelain, and renovated in 2007. The Zsolnay factory is still producing in Pecs.
The Vasarely Museum, celebrating one of the founders of Op-Art.
Some of Hungary's most interesting 20th century art, in various museums.
**YOU SHOULD KNOW:**
The wine, especially the champagne varietal, is delicious.

Pecs is a tranquil, university town, relatively unscathed by the ravages of war or the excesses of communist-era industry and architecture. Its rambling centre is human-scale and walkable; 2,000 years of history washed by the sub-Mediterranean climate of southern Hungary. Look up from any street, in any direction, and beyond you see the wooded foothills and vineyards of the Mecsek Mountains. Visitors have always appreciated the beauty of Pecs – but it took a happy accident in 1975 to transform the cognoscenti's secret into a world-class destination of choice. Pecs had a fountain. In 1975, reluctantly, everyone agreed that its mechanism was so cranky that it had to be replaced. Digging deep, workmen discovered a unique Early Christian necropolis of outstanding artistic and architectural merit and extent. In conjunction with the city's existing Roman, medieval Hungarian, Ottoman and Austrian treasures, the product of 200 years of excavation and revelation during which the necropolis lay hidden, the warren of chambers filled with richly symbolic frescoes and artifacts confirmed Pecs as a natural choice for European Capital of Culture (2010).

It's one of history's great conundrums that, apart from some spontaneous ravaging and laying waste, nobody ever wanted to destroy Pecs. Even the Ottomans spent their 140 years lovingly remodeling it as an R & R centre for their armies marauding elsewhere. In fact, the Inner City Parish Church standing at the modern city's heart is the 11th century Gothic St. Batholomew's, converted into the mosque of Pasha Gazi Kassim by making a minaret out of the steeple, and re-converted in 1686 to its current state, complete with original Arabic inscriptions behind the crucifix (the steeple disappeared in 1753 – now a metallic tower rises mechanically to a height of 15 m (50 ft) each time the bells are rung). You'll never see a more beautiful model for ecumenism. Here, and throughout Pecs, you're looking at peace and beauty written dramatically in the city's fabric.

*The Town Hall*

# Szeged

When you first gaze on Szeged's exemplary layout of boulevards and avenues, even if you know its long history, it's incongruous to picture the city as the 5th century capital of Attila the Hun. This glorious claim to fame gains weight from Szeged's prime location, straddling the arterial River Tisza just below its confluence with the River Maros. For the earlier Romans, the existing Jazig tribal settlement provided an important bridge to the province of Dacia; and for a further 700 years of the Great Migration, it prospered from the gold and salt trade that prompted its takeover and formal founding by nomadic Hungarian tribes in about 1138. History records a typical pattern of pillage, wholesale destruction and rebuilding; culminating in 200 years of Ottoman rule, which ended in 1686, when Szeged's Habsburg liberators promptly took over the city for themselves. After its bid for independence failed in 1849, the city threw its efforts into trade and industrial expansion.

Present-day Szeged's defining moment came during the Great Flood of 1879. The dykes burst, and the entire city, including its majestic castle, was washed away. Just 265 of 5500 buildings survived. It was a blessing in horrific disguise. All Europe chipped in for a new city, with Haussman's Paris, and ideas from Brussels, Rome, Berlin and London as models. Szeged's present homogenous architecture preserves the eclecticism and Art Nouveau of the late 19th century, arranged on a network of three rings, crossed by broad, central avenues. Organised, modern, the expanding city boomed as the cultural and economic centre of south-eastern Hungary. It almost succumbed to the wholesale theft of its assets by the Nazis and collaborating quislings, and by the slugfest ransacking of the Soviet era. Now it's a lively university city of rare elegance and charm – and those 265 surviving buildings include some gems from each era of its turbulent past.

*City Hall*

**POPULATION:**
177,000 (2007)
**WHEN TO GO:**
From June to August, for the annual Szeged Open-Air Festival, Hungary's biggest – a varied programme of all kinds of theatre and music, performed in the square in front of the dramatic twin spires of the Votive Church.
**DON'T MISS:**
The medieval Tower of St Demetrius.
The spectacular Votive Church of 1910, celebrating Szeged's revival after the flood.
The Ottoman Baths.
The Ferenc Bridge, modeled on the Venetian 'Bridge of Sighs'.
The huge and ornate Great Synagogue, completed in 1903, one of Europe's biggest.
The distinctly southern ambience of Roma music around the cafés and terraces among the arcades and quaint streets of the surviving old town.
**YOU SHOULD KNOW:**
The Albert Szent-Györgyi Medical School is named after the faculty member who won the Nobel Prize for being the first to isolate vitamin C – which he extracted from a genuinely local, Szeged paprika. Not a lot of people know this.

# Budapest

**POPULATION:**
1,600,000 (2007)
**WHEN TO GO:**
August for the Sziget Festival of music and culture.
**DON'T MISS:**
The Great Synagogue and the Jewish Museum.
Gellert Hill for its wonderful views.
Heroes' Square – this is one of the city's major squares. In the centre stands the Millennium Memorial with statues of the seven tribe leaders who founded Hungary in the 9th century.
Views from the Tower of St Stephen's Basilica.
**YOU SHOULD KNOW:**
Originally Budapest was three towns that merged in 1873.

Known as 'the Pearl of the Danube', Budapest is made up of three distinct towns: Óbuda and Buda (the historic medieval city on Castle Hill) are on the west bank of the River Danube, and Pest (the administrative and commercial city) is on the east. In 1873, the three towns merged, and today large areas of architectural, archaeological and cultural importance are listed as a UNESCO World Heritage Site.

The heart of Budapest, around the Castle Hill area, is a beautiful part of the city, despite suffering many times from invasions by Celts, Romans, Huns, Ottomans and Austrians. In World War II, the city was partly destroyed by Allied air raids, then besieged during the Battle of Budapest when the attacking Russians and defending German and Hungarian troops caused major damage. The Hungarians, however, have always rebuilt their city and today it is as lovely as ever.

Buda Castle, on the southern tip of Castle Hill next to the old Castle District, is the historical seat of the Hungarian kings in Budapest and today houses the Historical Museum of Budapest. It displays marvellous

paintings, including those of Eastern European and Hungarian artists as well as modern artists such as Picasso and Lichtenstein. Nearby, the neo-Gothic Mathias Church has a colourful roof, and a wonderful interior which was renovated in the 19th century back to its 13th-century splendour. The gallery contains sacred relics and medieval stone carvings, along with replicas of the Hungarian coronation jewels.

In Pest, be sure to visit the National Museum dedicated to the history and natural history of the country. St Stephen's Basilica, with its neo-Renaissance dome, offers 360-degree views of the city for those with a head for heights. The National Opera House is spectacularly ornate, built during the glory days of the Austro-Hungarian Empire, while the Parliament building is well worth seeing, as are the Hungarian crown jewels on display there.

If you tire of cultural sightseeing, visit Margit-sziget, one of the islands in the Danube which is a popular recreational area for tourists and locals alike, with its park, Japanese garden, small zoo and musical fountain. Another island in the Danube, Óbudai-sziget, hosts the Sziget Festival every year in August, one of Europe's largest music and cultural events.

*The view of Parliament across the Danube from Fisherman's Bastion*

*The domes of the Cathedral founded by King Stephen I.*

# Esztergom

Church and State combine in Esztergom in miniature grandeur. The setting is incomparable – commanding the great Danube Bend, where the river makes a right-angled turn south towards Budapest, and forms the current border with Slovakia. In physical size, it has never been bigger than its present small-town size. In stature, where Esztergom once commanded, central Europe trembled. Its heyday began in 960, when Hungary's ruling Arpad princes chose the already important Moravian fortress as their royal seat and capital. King Stephen I was crowned in 1000 and set up the Archdiocese of Esztergom which is still the seat of the Roman Catholic Primates of Hungary. The first Cathedral was built between 1001 and 1010. For 300 years, Esztergom controlled not only the bodies and souls of Hungary, but also the vital pan-European trade flowing up and down the Danube.

Incomparably rich and splendid, once Esztergom's political power was broken by the 13th century Mongol invasion, the city's history wove a dramatic pattern of bloody massacre, devastation and reconstruction on the same sites. What you see now includes evidence of Celtic, Roman, Moravian, medieval Hungarian, Tatar, and Turkish occupations – whole fragments of which are incorporated into the dazzling buildings that survive; and they include everything from Gothic, Romanesque and Renaissance, to Ottoman, Baroque, Rococo, and Hungarian Classicist styles. Even after the city's mutilation during the Nazi retreat of 1944, meticulous restoration has preserved every layer, and archaeology is still recovering more. Better still, many original artefacts squirreled away at the start of each fresh catastrophe, have returned to Esztergom's breathtaking museums. Jewels, chalices, fabrics, paintings, tapestries, and a thousand other small *objets* show the exquisite workmanship available only to the highest Royal, Civil and Ecclesiastical Powers. Like a Russian egg, Esztergom reveals itself gradually, down to its finest detail. You can stroll round it, or choose to stop for an awe-struck month.

**POPULATION:**
30,000 (2007)
**WHEN TO GO:**
Come between June and August for the annual Esztergom Castle Theatre Festival. May and September are less crowded, and beauty may be quietly beheld.
**DON'T MISS:**
The sublime Hungarian classicism of the enormous 19th century Cathedral, incorporating elements of its Baroque predecessor (1774), and the early 16th century Bakocz Chapel.
The Cathedral Treasury (entrance inside the Cathedral), housing one of the world's richest collections of sacral art from the 9th-19th centuries, including the finest masterpiece of all European goldsmiths' art, the medieval Matthias-Calvary Cross.
The 10th, 11th and 12th century remnants of the Hungarian Royal Palace, with Renaissance renovations and Turkish additions; especially the beautiful Romanesque Castle Chapel.
The restrained beauty of Baroque domestic architecture in the streets of Vizivaros (Watertown), from c.1730, especially around the market in Szechenyi Square.
**YOU SHOULD KNOW:**
If you can, and it's easy, arrive by boat on the Danube.

# Lublin

Always a crossroad between east and west Europe, Lublin has had to struggle harder than most places to restore its civic health following the GBH of the 20th century. The physical devastation it suffered may have been common to many historic cities in central Europe, but as the ancient capital of eastern Poland, Lublin was a forum for Polish, Jewish, Lithuanian and Belarusian cultures interacting on each other. Since the 13th century, it had developed international respect for its centres of law and of learning, including one of Europe's greatest Yeshivot, the Jewish centres for rabbinical training. The city was 40 per cent Jewish. When that community was massacred by 1945, Lublin's tradition of instinctive ecumenism seemed to die with it.

There's a happy ending. Although Lublin hasn't done nearly as well economically as other Polish cities from EC membership, it has re-established itself on the model of the typical, historic, university city where higher learning and cultural exchange is as important a currency as manufacturing. Seven centuries of architecture speak its proud past in the rebuilt and beautiful Stare Miasto (Old Town) with its castle, cathedral, courts, and ancient streets where sudden arches broach dark alleys. Beyond the Brama Krakowska (Kraków Gate) in the 14th century city walls, modern Lublin isn't big enough for low-budget, 20th century concrete to matter very much before you reach the tranquil countryside surrounding the place.

Nowadays, Lublin is a lively university city where 80,000 students come to learn, drink and play. The Old Town is a hive of cafés and bars, activity and discussion. Recently (2007), among non-Jewish Lubliners, there's even been a revival of interest in Hassidic dancing. Call it a straw in a brisk breeze – but it looks like Lublin is succeeding in reclaiming the cultural synthesis of its past.

**POPULATION:**
360,000 (2006)
**WHEN TO GO:**
For students, any time. Otherwise, June, when students have exams, school is still in, and Lublin is at its picturesque best.
**DON'T MISS:**
The medieval layout of Stare Miasto, with its churches, burgher houses and gates. Whispering in the Acoustic Sacristy of the Baroque Cathedral: no secrets here. The Holy Trinity Chapel in Lublin Castle – a world-class monument combining western, Gothic architecture with exceptional early 15th century Byzantine-Ruthenian paintings. Pausing for a moment at Zamek Lubelski, the majestic empty vista in front of the castle: it used to be the Jewish quarter until it was razed by the Nazis. Just one (out of 100) *shtibl* (prayer house) remains. Majdanek Concentration Camp, just outside the city. The barracks and crematorium are preserved in all their horrific detail as a historical site, not a museum.
**YOU SHOULD KNOW:**
The countryside around Lublin is empty of mass tourism and really lovely; but you should take an insect repellant when you visit.

*The Great Market Square has some fantastic architecture.*

241

# Kraków

**POPULATION:**
760,000 (2006)
**WHEN TO GO:**
Between April and October.
**DON'T MISS:**
The Barbican.
Czartoryski Museum – houses works
by great artists such as Da Vinci
and Rembrandt.
The church of St Peter and Paul.
The Old Synagogue.
The Gallery of 19th-century
Polish Painting.
**YOU SHOULD KNOW:**
The Jewish quarter houses no Jewish
residents. They were all exterminated
in the Holocaust.

*St Mary's Church*

On the Vistula River in a valley at the foot of the Carpathian Plateau in southern Poland lies the charming and historic city of Kraków. Its Old City (Stare Miasto) is home to about six thousand Renaissance, Baroque and Gothic buildings and more than two million works of art. Kraków is the only large city in Poland that remained intact during World War II and today it is a well-preserved medieval city, with picturesque cobbled streets, numerous churches, museums, cafés, restaurants and bars.

The Old City is surrounded by a ring of lightly-forested parkland, known as the Planty, the site of the old city walls and moat. It is overshadowed by the Wawel, the long-fortified hill at its southern end. This is a symbolic place of great significance for Polish people as it is crowned by the Royal Castle and the Cathedral. The tenth-century castle, considered by many to be the most beautiful in Central Europe, was extended and restored in the sixteenth century and contains the royal apartments and magnificent contemporary tapestries. The cathedral saw the coronation and burial of Polish royalty for 400 years, and its golden domed chapel is considered to be the finest Renaissance example in the country.

Kraków's Old City also boasts an impressive central market square with the Gothic St Mary's Basilica. Built in the fourteenth century, it features the famous wooden altar carved by Veit Stoss. Every hour, a trumpet call sounds from the tower. The tune was first played during a Tatars' invasion in the thirteenth century by a guard who wanted to warn the citizens against the attack. He was shot while playing, and still today the melody breaks off at the moment he died.

In the centre of the market square is the impressive sixteenth-century Renaissance cloth hall, and the rest of the square is filled with countless stalls, selling numerous products from local artisans. The Town Hall Tower is all that remains of the Gothic-Renaissance Town Hall; the rest was destroyed by the Austrians in the nineteenth century. Today it houses a museum and offers wonderful views over the city.

Kazimierz, the perfectly restored Jewish quarter, offers a poignant excursion. This is a Jewish neighbourhood without Jews. The 65,000 Jewish inhabitants who lived here at the start of World War II were first forced to live in appalling conditions in the Jewish Ghetto across the river in Podgorze, before eventually being exterminated in the nearby Plaszów Concentration Camp.

# Warsaw

Poland's capital is everything you expect from a European city revelling in its rediscovery of the freedom to express itself. Warsaw has reclaimed every aspect of its history, from its Catholicism and proud monarchism to the trauma of its suffering during World War II and the lean years of the Soviet era. Its new skyline of soaring towers is a metaphor of the city's fundamental energy, good sense and wry humour: instead of tearing down the monumental Palace of Culture and Science (Stalin's compulsory gift, and a triumph of socialist realism in granite and grossness) dominating its ancient heart, the city turned it into a throbbing centre for entertainment and incorporated it into its future.

Warsaw is in any case a miracle. 86 per cent of its buildings were destroyed in World War II, and rebuilt exactly as they were, restoring both the city's history and its soul. The inner city (Srodmiescie) contains both the beautiful Old Town (Stare Miasto) of ancient palaces, squares and cobbled streets of 17th and 18th century houses, and the clunky blocks of Stalinist mauso-architecture round Constitution Square. Deprived of the threat they once implied, people have begun to enjoy them as time capsules. This casual cosmopolitanism is typical.

Ready humour and bossy charm, driven by the youthful energy of a city in which a fifth of its residents are under twenty years old, make Warsaw a lot of restless fun. It has already shaken off the drab of its former reputation, along with the edgy and, frankly, dangerous outlaw years that briefly replaced it. The pace of change is getting faster. The city is claiming its rightful place among the great capitals, and doing so with intelligence, style and considerable grace.

*The Old Town*

**POPULATION:**
1,900,000 (2006)
**WHEN TO GO:**
The city's excellent street-life and cafés make the most of spring and summer; or come for the 'Warsaw Autumn', which starts in September with the International Festival of Contemporary Music, followed in early October by the Warsaw Film Festival, Jazz Jamboree and the Chopin Piano Competition.
**DON'T MISS:**
The Stadion Dziesieciolecia (10th Anniversary Stadium) in Praga Poludnie district – perpetually due for redevelopment, but still one of Europe's biggest flea markets. Umschlagplatz in Muranow district, a monument in memory of Warsaw's Jewish Ghetto, at the place where Jews were gathered for transportation. Harrowing.
**YOU SHOULD KNOW:**
In Warsaw, Mardi Gras (Fat Tuesday or Tlusty Cwartak) is Pazcki Day (Doughnut Day) – but the doughnuts are legendary!

243

# Poznan

**POPULATION:**
580,000 (2005)
**WHEN TO GO:**
Summer – close to the city, there are
lots of beautiful parks with lakes,
palaces and castles.
**DON'T MISS:**
The Poznan Nightingales, a boys'
choir that gives concerts throughout
the year.
Organ concerts in the Fara Church
from July to September at 12.15 pm
every day.
The Bazaar building next to Plac
Wolnosci (Liberty Square), where,
following an address by the pianist
and patriot Paderewski, the shot was
fired that sparked the Wielkopolska
Uprising of 1918 that took Poznan
out of Prussia and back into Poland.
The Museum of Musical Instruments
in Stare Rynek.
The palace of Rogalin, surrounded by
its park, south of the city.
**YOU SHOULD KNOW:**
Under Prussian rule, Poznan became
a military centre known as Festung
Posen (Fortress Poznan).

Over 1,000 years old, Poznan is known as the Cradle of Poland. It lies on the Warta River, and its most ancient and sacred site is Ostrów Tumski, the island where, in 966, Prince Mieszko I accepted Christianity in symbolic baptism of the Polish nation; and where his son, Boleslaw the Brave, became Poland's first crowned king. The Gothic cathedral that replaced Mieszko's castle in 968 is still standing – and it's typical of Poznan's revised modern priorities that the best view of it is from the 85-m (260-ft) high Economics Academy on the west bank, because since 1925 the city has been famous for its vast, annual trade fairs.

The combination of heavy, agro-industrial mindset and pride in its royal and religious ancestry makes Poznan surprisingly fascinating. The legacy of successive Swedish, Prussian and Russian occupations (not to mention the brief but marked depredations both of Napoleon and Nazi Germany) is marked by its expansion rippling out from the Stare Rynek (Old Market Square) at its heart. The renaissance Town Hall is flanked by equally magnificent Baroque facades, and the nearby Fara Church is as lovely as anything in Europe. A little further, the 'new' town centre of the 19th century includes Kaiser Wilhelm II's Imperial Palace, a grim, neo-Romanesque, white elephant which he never used; his Throne Room is now a cinema. Incongruously close, and overlooking the classical façade of the

*The Renaissance Town Hall*

Opera, stands the Okraglak, a Soviet-era circular department store so hideous it's brilliant.

Of course Poznan has the scars of industry, like anywhere – but some of the factories and long tenements for workers are art-deco marvels. The point is, that whatever history has thrown at it, Poznan has made it its own, and given it a Polish soul.

# Gdańsk

**POPULATION:**
459,000 (2006)
**WHEN TO GO:**
May to October.
**DON'T MISS:**
The National Museum.
St Mary's Church – located in the Old Town, this is believed to be the largest brick church in the world.
The Town Hall – a stunning building that now houses a museum charting the formation and history of the city.
The adjoining seaside town of Sopot – a 25 minute train journey from the city, this is Poland's premier beach resort, an affluent destination with luxury shops, cafés and casinos.
Oliwa Cathedral and Monastery.
**YOU SHOULD KNOW:**
World War II started here.

Situated on the Baltic Sea in the north of Poland, Gdańsk is a beautiful port city with a long history. The fort was built in the 980s by Mieszko I of Poland, as defence against the pagans. By the beginning of the fourteenth century, the city had became a busy trade centre with around 10,000 inhabitants, but in 1308 it was seized and demolished by the Teutonic Knights. The city again prospered under the control of the Knights, and in 1361 it became a full member of the Hanseatic League, a trading monopoly which operated in the Baltic at the time. By the middle of the sixteenth century it was the most important Baltic port, and Poland's largest city.

This former power and wealth is obvious to visitors – the buildings are bigger and the streets broader than in other medieval cities. The city has many fine buildings from the time of the Hanseatic League. Most attractions are located near Long Street and Long Market, a pedestrian area known as Royal Road as the former path of processions for visiting kings. The Golden Gate is one of the most notable attractions. It was designed by architect Abraham van den Blocke in 1612–14 in place of the 13th century Gothic gate and forms a part of the old city fortifications. Next to it is the late-Gothic building of the Brotherhood of St George.

St Mary's Church is possibly the largest brick church in the world. Started in 1379, it is over 100 m (328 ft) long, and the nave is 66 m (217 ft) wide. It is an aisled hall church with a transept, and can accommodate 25,000 worshippers.

*A row of colourful houses*

Dlugi Targ is the beautiful main square, and nearby is the fourteenth-century town hall and many other architectural gems, including the unique seventeenth-century houses of St. Mary's Street. Take time to stroll through the old streets and along the river banks of the ancient port which has been so significant in European history. It was here that World War II started in 1939, when the German battleship *Schleswig-Holstein* attacked the naval fort at Westerplatte. Much of the city was devastated during the war, but almost all of its historic centre has been painstakingly restored.

# Veliko Tarnovo

The three hills of Veliko Tarnovo are a physical narrative of Bulgaria's most dramatic historical moments. It is one of the country's oldest and most picturesque cities, and though its power has long since waned, it remains Bulgaria's most significant political, cultural and religious symbol. The title 'Veliko' ('Great') was added to its name in 1965 in recognition of its importance.

Tarnovo is visible for miles. The massive medieval gates of what was between 1185 and 1393 the primary fortress of the second Bulgarian Empire lead to Tsarevets, the hilltop compound of the Royal and Patriarchal Palaces. Trapezitsa Hill, opposite and on the right bank of the Yantra River, held the inner city fort where Church met State. Among the ruins of 17 churches is Assenova Makhala, 'Assen's Place' where medieval Bulgarian heroes Assen and Peter proclaimed the end of Byzantine rule. The forty Holy Martyrs Church now stands there – this is where Tsar Ferdinand Saxe-Coburg Gotha declared Bulgaria's complete independence in 1908. Sveta Gora (holy mountain) lies to the south, with the old town and most of the present city spread around it. The Church of St Kiril ans St Methodius was one of many where medieval monks fostered spiritual and cultural growth: today the University of the same name, and dozens of educational institutes, provide enlightenment for a new generation.

The students bring a sense of upbeat liveliness to an historic city. Veliko Tarnovo is one of the architectural gems of the Bulgarian National Revival, the period from the mid-18th century to 1878 when by its attractive vernacular – so very different from anything Ottoman – architecture itself was used to subvert Turkish rule. Samovodska Charshiya (Wood-Nymphs Market) is one typically charming street of dozens. Filled with buzzing student life, and with quite a few more recent, knockabout cafés and bars, Veliko Tarnovo is one of the loveliest places in Bulgaria.

*Houses in the Old Town*

**POPULATION:**
73,000 (2005)
**WHEN TO GO:**
Year-round – Veliko Tarnovo is beautiful in snow or sunshine.
**DON'T MISS:**
The Church of St. Dmitri of Thessaloniki.
The Museum of National Revival in the former Turkish Konak (Town Hall), where the 1879 first National Assembly drafted the 'Tarnovska Constitution'.
The Ethnographic Museum.
Baldwin's Tower – a reconstruction on an authentic medieval site.
Walking the castle walls.
The miniatures and illuminated manuscripts of the Tarnovo Schools of Literature and Arts, and other 13th-19th century antiquities in the museums and institutions.
**YOU SHOULD KNOW:**
In the 14th century, Tarnovo's cultural pre-eminence in the Slavic Orthodox world earned it the title of the 'Third Rome'.

# Sofia

**POPULATION:**
1,220,000 (2007)
**WHEN TO GO:**
April to October - but with no summer festivals, the city is 'officially' quiet during July and August. Unofficially, you won't notice.
**DON'T MISS:**
The former Royal Palace at Battenberg Square, now the National Art Gallery.
The open-air cafés and bars filling the forecourt of the Ivan Vazov National Theatre – the plum-coloured, gold-frescoed, modern (c.1900) classicist, ideal of a public arts building.
The coral reef of golden domes that make the Alexander Nevsky Cathedral one of the biggest Eastern Orthodox churches in the world.
The Bulgarian Academy of Science – a cream dream of an 18th century palace.
**YOU SHOULD KNOW:**
Spartacus, gladiator extraordinaire, was born in Sandansky, an ancient spa town on the edge of the city limits.

*Alexander Nevsky
Cathedral*

The second oldest city in Europe, Sofia is absolutely stuffed with 7,000 years worth of eye-watering treasures. Only recently has it acquired the laissez-faire informality to make that glory attractive to visitors. Fired by the unrestrained energy of its post-1989 generation, Sofia's new ambience is its guarantee of pole position as hot new capital – especially for anyone with an interest in Byzantine art and architecture.

Start drooling. Boyana, a 10th and 13th century church on the edge of the city is covered from top to bottom in vivid frescoes credited by international specialists as 'the best examples of eastern medieval art during its twelve centuries of history'. It was opened to the public only in 2006. The Church of St Sophia was built by the Byzantine Emperor Justinian in the 6th century. Fifth-century St George's has stunning 14th century frescoes. The endless list isn't at all confined to a single era.

Sofia belonged to Alexander the Great 800 years before the Emperor Constantine called it 'my Rome', and fashioned it into the walled fortress still visible, woven into the modern fabric of tree-lined avenues and great squares. It acquired Oriental trappings of fountains, hamams, minarets and mosques with huge domes to match the bulbous extravaganzas of the Orthodox Rite, during 400

years of Ottoman subjugation. The synagogue has existed since 967. Royal and aristocratic palaces, and elegant avenues of modern classicism mark the monarchy that followed liberation in 1878. And since 1989, the whole, quirky, amazing, grand, extraordinary hotchpotch has been infused with a café and club culture as sophisticated as anywhere, but cheaper and more accessible. Street-life is booming in 300 parks, the flea markets and the open-air book emporium of Slaveykok Square and Vitosha Boulevard, heartland of an intellectual culture that Paris's Left Bank lost years ago. Sofia's a big city. There's nothing you can't do – except that you will never have done it this way.

# Bourgas

The fourth biggest city in Bulgaria, Bourgas takes quiet pride in its traditional virtue of solidity. People who live there are aware that the city has a reputation as an industrial heavyweight, which it is, and therefore to be given a wide berth, which it is not. Like a scarred boxer, Bourgas wants you to like it for its success in performing unglamorous work very well, and not for its superficial looks.

Bourgas is certainly more highly industrialized than any of its Black Sea neighbours. Its oil refinery has a number of associated chemical plants, but they are all contained on or near the coastal lakes behind the city. Iron ore is also locally mined, and exported via the deep-water harbour, which is home to Bulgaria's ocean fishing fleet. As if those activities weren't dowdy enough, Bourgas is the centre of a major salt extraction plant – but disused salt pans have the unexpected benefit of producing a gloopy black mud said to be highly beneficial as a skin treatment.

If its industrial suburbs are seedy, the city centre is anything but: Bourgas welcomes visitors who are looking to avoid the crowds and noise associated with some Black Sea resorts, and presents itself with a well-bred air of comfort and family values. Since 1903, when its development got a major boost from the arrival of the railway, the late 19th and early 20th century cityscape has never been corroded by the concrete of lumpen communism in its heart. Its streets of pastel-coloured buildings take in parks and squares that guarantee the kind of tranquil lifestyle attractive to tourists who want the beach without the non-stop frenzy popular elsewhere. Its 6,000 university students are lively enough. Bourgas is an alternative Black Sea, where you can hear yourself think, and enjoy a healthy rest.

**POPULATION:**
206,000 (2006)
**WHEN TO GO:**
May to September – but the city's International Folklore Festival happens only once every four years.
**DON'T MISS:**
The Museum of Nature and Science. The Ethnographic Museum. The wonderfully odd Gramophone Sculpture at one end of Bogoridi Boulevard. The Sea Garden beach with the open-air summer theatre. The Cathedral of SS Kiril & Metod. The 1980s 'social-realism' of the Court at Troikata Square – formerly the Communist Party HQ.
**YOU SHOULD KNOW:**
With curious historical symmetry, Bourgas originated as a colony for military veterans set up by Vespasian. The Roman Emperor asked them to keep watch on ship movements while resting.

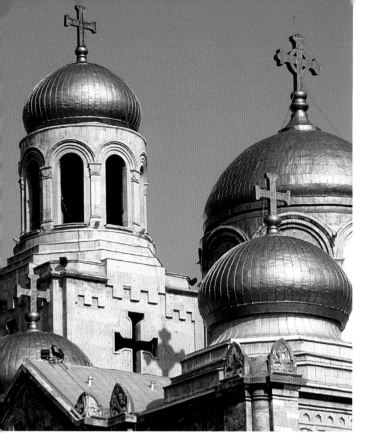

*Cathedral of the Assumption*

# Varna

The memorial to the Battle of Varna in 1444 looks like a single-storey outhouse with a classical façade. Set into an ancient Thracian burial-mound on the edge of a Black Sea beach, it hardly does justice to the last major battle of the Crusades, the subsequently inevitable fall of Constantinople in 1453, and the subjugation by the Ottoman Turks of half Europe, for four centuries. Varna does not have a sense of proportion.

It does have space. The many civilizations that have passed its way have left a cultural kaleidoscope of colour and fine workmanship. All of them wanted a place in the sun, and on a grand scale with garden attached. Varna's centre is full of huge, glorious architecture like the Dormition of the Theotokos Cathedral, the Roman baths (originally 100 m [328 ft] wide, with a furnace room like a football pitch) and the Euxinograd Palace. The Ottoman city of wooden houses and narrow alleys hardly survives: after 1878 the emerging Bulgarian middle class built comfortable neo-Classical, Art Deco and Art Nouveau homes in their place. The medieval city walls went into the neo-Byzantine Cathedral, new boulevards, and elegant new mansions. Even so, Varna is crammed with places to ogle and admire, and still with gardens in-between.

Varna's carefree sense of taking pleasure where you can has always included rich and poor. It still does, but the facilities are getting better for everyone. The space still exists for opulent villas and exclusive enclaves, and the skyline both in the centre and on the beach shows how fast new money is arriving. Only the roads pose a threat to the city's traditional greenery. Varna is on the cusp of yet another re-invention as a tourist attraction, and the signs are excellent that the city will continue to grow without losing its long tradition of wine and laughter to either regulation or resort snobbism.

**POPULATION:**
358,000 (2007), swollen by over 4 million annual visitors.
**WHEN TO GO:**
April to October for the best weather though October to March is quieter.
**DON'T MISS:**
The medieval cave monastery, Aladzha.
Bungee-jumping from the 50-m (164-ft) high Asparuhov Bridge.
The oldest (c. 500 BC) gold treasure hoard in the world at the Archaeological Museum in an ornate 19th century former girls' school.
The Museum of Ethnography.
The 17th century Cathedral of the Holy Mother, just one of a dozen breathtaking churches.
The Sea Garden – a complex of attractions including Cosmonauts'Alley, the 1912 Aquarium, the Museum of Natural History, an alpineum and Children's Corner.
**YOU SHOULD KNOW:**
Varna was the point of origin for the ship Demeter in Bram Stoker's *Dracula*.

# Nessebar

Known as the 'Pearl of the Black Sea', Nessebar is a staggering testament to the cultural sophistication of ancient civilizations – and to the amazing insouciance with which modern society treats such riches. It perches on a small peninsula near Bulgaria's border with Romania, reached only by a narrow, 400 m (1,312 ft), man-made isthmus. With water on three sides, it's just the right size and location for an exclusive holiday resort; and most of the people who live there would be delighted if it becomes one.

Space is an issue, because nearly half the ancient city is now underwater (remember to bring your wetsuit). What's left is still huge, and every inch a visual and historical feast. The beautiful 'modern' city would be an attraction on its own – a complete 18th and 19th century town in the Bulgarian National Revival style. Its narrow lanes are cool and dark where the overhanging upper floors almost touch across the cobbles. The stone facades are often brightly decorated, and wooden panelling lines the ceilings and walls of the airy, first-floor living rooms. Blasts of music and flapping clothes lines add to the bustle of people, markets and thronged cafés, all washed by the sound and smell of the sea.

Already delightful, every corner of Nessebar offers an extra miracle. Woven into its fabric are the fortifications, churches, paintings and artefacts of its 12th-6th centuries BC existence as the Thracian trade centre of Mesembria; of its importance as an Hellenic community; of its growth under Rome and Byzantium; and of its zenith during the medieval Bulgarian Empire (from which era alone, eight out of forty 11-14th century major churches survive). You could spend a lifetime exhilarating over the wealth of cultural and artistic detail Nessebar takes for granted; or think about them in the beach-side cafés and bars. Or both. Good idea.

**POPULATION:**
10,000 (2005) – plus some 10,000 visitors on any summer day.

**WHEN TO GO:**
May to September, to combine history with Beach Fun; October to March for a more tranquil look.

**DON'T MISS:**
The early Byzantine (c.700) Basilica of St Sophia (aka Old Metropolitan), built on an ancient agora.

The 11th century St Stefan (aka New Metropolitan), one of the last medieval Bulgarian basilicas, with perfectly preserved, Italianate murals painted 1593-9.

The 10-11th century Church of St John the Baptist, a very rare survival showing the transition from a formal basilica to a cross-domed church.

The 12-6th century BC ruins of fortress walls, carved towers, Hellenic agora, acropolis and dwellings. Many remains are substantial – and continue underwater.

The colourful ceramics of Christ Pantocrator – one of Bulgaria's best-preserved medieval churches.

The extravagantly-decorated façades and interiors of the 19th century Lambrinov and Muskoyannis houses, typical of the Black Sea style of Revival architecture.

**YOU SHOULD KNOW:**
There are no Roman remains in Nessebar because, according to Roman documents elsewhere, the town considered itself too ancient to acknowledge Roman rule.

*Basilica of St Sophia*

# Bucharest

Bucharest has always worried about its place in the club of European capitals. It still relishes its nickname of 'Little Paris', earned between the two World Wars when its elegant avenues were thronged by the sophisticated elite of Vienna, Prague and Berlin, and French was virtually the language of government. Hitler and Ceausescu dumped on that aspiration, but having seen off both, and survived a distinctly wobbly decade of rudderless hardship in the1990s, Bucharest is finally growing into its new shoes. The city is enjoying being Romanian for the first time. It has discovered the advantages of belonging to both west and east, and that it doesn't need to imitate any other culture.

The results are spectacular. Twenty-first century architecture is everywhere piercing the concrete excesses of communism and Ceausescu with steel and glass. Simultaneously, the city has embraced its history, from the Curtea Veche – the remains of Bucharest's medieval royal court – to Lipscani, the recently pedestrianized district which best displays the 19th and early 20th century elegance it once coveted. Along the revitalized Calea Victoriei, Bucharest's attempt at a Champs Élyssées, beautiful monuments like the imitation Arc de Triomphe, 18th century churches, and glass-roofed arcades like the Macca-Vilacrosse have been brought back to life. The chain of lakes that crosses the city has the Cismigiu Gardens, built to a German design in 1847, as its recreational centerpiece of waterside cafés and botanical delights. Palatial 19th century buildings like the CEC Palace hold banks and other institutions. Ceausescu destroyed the greater part of Bucharest's historic centre to build the Centrul Civic, the world's second or third biggest building. The city can't change it back – but it has learned both to mock its hubris, and to put it to good use.

Re-defined, Bucharest is a terrific demonstration of Romanian potential, and an original new European capital for visitors to enjoy.

*Centrul Civic – the House of the People*

# Sibiu

Before it was Sibiu, it was Hermannstadt, the biggest and richest of the 'Siebenburgen', the seven, 12th century walled citadels built by German settlers known as Transylvanian Saxons. By the 14th century, it was already an important trade centre, and its nineteen governing guilds could afford the lavish fortifications needed to protect their impressive homes and continuing prosperity. And prosper the city did, by retaining its ethnic and cultural roots as it gradually melded with Transylvanian Romania. By the time the Austro-Hungarian Empire was dissolved in 1918, the newly Romanian Sibiu's carefully-nurtured trading tradition had laid the foundations for its present status as one of Romania's most successful industrial cities, and – because by example it inspires others to respect its history – the beneficiary of most international investment.

The first time you see it is a staggering experience. Sibiu's original Old Town is still there, complete and working. Unlike Carcassonne or nearly any other medieval walled city, the fairy-tale beauty of the ensemble of gables, towers, crenellations, grand squares, archways, palaces and courtyards is the product of continuous occupancy and hard work. It's a world-class tourist attraction by accident, not restoration.

Sibiu's original town plan is delightfully feudal. The Great Square of the Upper Town is still the commercial outlet and symbol of its wealth; as the Lower Town of colourful, half-timbered houses and cobbled streets is the manufacturing area, crammed against the imposing walls and fortified towers overlooking the river. Between the two, a catacomb of stairways, ramps and arched tunnels connects the three rings of fortification. Inside and out, it's all authentic. The only oddity is that the whole place still feels, as well as looks, so Germanic, since between 1950-90 the majority of the ethnic German and Hungarian communities emigrated back to Germany. If they'd stayed, they could have shared the city's pride in being designated European City of Culture for 2007.

*Architectural detail of Palace Luxembourg. Sibiu was first mentioned in records in 1191 and has many well-preserved medieval buildings.*

**POPULATION:**
155,000 (2002)

**WHEN TO GO:**
Year-round. Any place so picturesque looks just as good in snow or rain.

**DON'T MISS:**
The best towers – the 15th century Arquebussiers', Carpenters' and Potters'; and the 16th century Great Tower, site of Sibiu's first theatrical performance, in 1778.
The UNESCO-listed and totally stunning Great Square, first mentioned in 1411 – a selection of the best and rarest of 13th century Gothic to 18th century Baroque buildings.
The 16th-18th century icons and library of the Brukenthal Palace, a museum since 1790, three years before the opening of The Louvre.
The 13th century Passage of Steps, a masterpiece of twin staircases and archways connecting the Upper and Lower Towns.
The medieval turrets and doorways of the charming little houses in Goldsmiths' Square.

**YOU SHOULD KNOW:**
In the 17th century, Sibiu was the eastern terminus of the postal service.

# Constanta

**POPULATION:**
345,000 (2007)
**WHEN TO GO:**
April to October.
**DON'T MISS:**
Casa cu Lei ('House with Lions'), a
late-19th century blend of pre-
Romantic and Genoese styles.
The Great Mahmudiye Mosque
the biggest wooden mosque
in Romania.
Mamaia – 5 km (3 mi) north of the old
centre, with some of the best
beaches and friendliest people.
The panorama of the harbour from
the Romanian Navy Museum, with
exhibits like Greek triremes and a
17th century Venetian, celestial globe.
**YOU SHOULD KNOW:**
The Constanta Aquarium holds 60
species of fish from the Black Sea
and the Danube Delta. Local
restaurants will serve you most of
them, including sturgeon.

*Orthodox Church*

Originally a Greek colony, 6th century BC Tomis, it was renamed after his half-sister Constantiana by the Roman Emperor Constantine the Great 850 years later. Ottomans shortened that to Constanta during its most prosperous era between the 13th-15th centuries but eventually it declined under Turkish rule. The city was revived as a port and resort by King Carol I of Romania, and during the 19th century it gained the elegant mansions and hotels which first made it internationally famous. It grew exponentially to its present ranking as fourth biggest port in Europe without threatening the miles of white, sandy beaches on which its tourism depends, and leads a successful double life as industrial leader and tourist magnet.

Constanta's old centre and original harbour reveal the durability of its success. Piata Ovidiu, dedicated in 1887 to the poet Ovid, exiled here by the Emperor Augustus in the year 8, is built round the remains of a colossal complex on three levels that once linked the upper town to the harbour. Developed continuously from the 4th- 7th centuries, you can still see how the workshops, warehouses and shops inter-related, and the nearby Roman baths and aqueduct. The greatest treasure of all is the 850 sq m (9,150 sq ft) of intricate, colourful mosaics, which comprise one of the world's longest mosaic pavements.

You'll see ruins everywhere, with the rest of Constanta's history arranged around them. Besides encouraging the boulevards and avenues, King Carol built mosques and churches as practical gifts to beautify the resort. The Art Nouveau Casino's sumptuous architecture came later in the early 1920s; and the pedestrian area surrounding it, with its bars and cafés, is still Constanta's favourite evening promenade, with the best view. Constanta may not be electric with action, but it's beautiful, civilized, and absorbing. It takes a long history to create that.

# Brasov

With an excellent eye for strategic geography, a group of German craftsmen invited by the 12th century Hungarian King Geza II to settle and develop Transylvania chose the crossroads of the trade routes between Western Europe and the Ottoman Empire as their home. They called their city Kronstadt, and with the wealth that poured in over two centuries, created a fortress and fortified walls to protect its riches from the constant attacks of the Khanate hordes to the south and east. The Saxons gradually excluded Romanians from a share of the ever-increasing trade booty, but enough Romanians remained to get rich on smuggling instead, and to endow their own Orthodox church – the first in Transylvania – and library, besides establishing Romania's first printing press in 1558. It set a pattern. Saxon Brasov expanded steadily beyond its typically German Old Town, adapting to wars, disasters and politics to achieve its present industrial importance; while its Romanian community laid the foundations for the whole country's cultural development, including the first Romanian-language newspaper in 1838.

In the Great Fire of 1689, Habsburg invaders destroyed most of Brasov's earliest structures. Repair and renewal took 100 years, but today you can see Brasov's twin histories recorded in the dazzling artefacts and architectural variants from the 12th-19th centuries. Brasov is more complete than most of the seven Saxon Transylvanian towns founded in the 12th century, but the expulsion of its ethnic Saxon population as recently as 1945-7 left the old city feeling like a film set, stripped of its continuous working link to its trade and prosperity. Fortunately, it bounces back into life with the ancient Junii Feast, a celebration of spring accompanied by dramatically caparisoned squadrons of local horsemen performing arcane rituals in this most exotic setting. As pagan as it is Christian, Junii reminds you of the enormity of Brasov's significance to Romanian culture in all its phases.

**POPULATION:**
285,000 (2002)
**WHEN TO GO:**
April to October; January if you value incredibly romantic snowscapes.
**DON'T MISS:**
Marienkirche, the 'Black Church', built 1385-1477, and restored after the 1689 fire.
Plata Sfatului, the glorious medieval Germanic heart of the old city; with the 1420 Council House (and much older Trumpet Tower) on its own in the middle, and the Renaissance Hirscher House is outstanding among its cafés and buskers.
The stone Citadel of 1553, part of the outer fortifications.
Dracula's Castle – the local name for Bran Castle (1377), built by the Brasov Guilds as the actual frontier post in the mountain pass from Wallachia.
**YOU SHOULD KNOW:**
Before World War II, one of Brasov's largest factories produced Romania's first fighter planes.

*Dracula's Castle*

# Yakutsk

*Interior of the cathedral*

It's 450 km (281 mi) below the Arctic Circle, a major port and
trading centre on the River Lena, and it's built on continuous
permafrost. Temperatures range from regular lows of -51 °C (-60 °F)
to regular July highs of 32 °C (90 °F). It was founded in 1632 as a
Cossack fort, but only developed in the 1880s and 90s when gold
and other minerals were discovered in the area. Stalin industrialized
the recovery of these reserves using forced labour from the gulags.
The Kolyma Highway, linking Yakutsk to Magadan, was also built
then: it became known as the Road of Bones. As you stand in this
busy city, dodging the latest 4-wheel drives, limousines and trucks,
and struggling against snow-blindness, you wonder how that history
combines with the presence of so many magnificent churches in
such a wilderness, and question the obvious frenzy of so much
simultaneous new building.

Yakutsk is rich beyond any imaginable dream. As the capital of
the Sakha Republic, it is the funnel for around 30 tons of gold, a fifth
of the world's rough diamonds, huge quantities of oil and gas, and a
catalogue of other precious stones and minerals, that reach

competing world markets every year. But wealth alone doesn't explain the extraordinary, frontier-deluxe atmosphere in the city. It's cultural alienation. You're just as likely to hear Yakut spoken in the street as Russian. Russia is no longer the dominant cultural force, and the only Russians admitted to the sanctums of the city's power elite are those directly involved in selling its commodities. Tribal bonds in Yakutsk are ancient and strong. Occasionally, Evenks (over 10,000 years in the region) dismiss even Yakuts as newcomers because they only moved in with Genghis Khan. Yakutsk is an exotic city made fabulous by valuable tangibles, as well as mere banknotes. Its charm and fascination is that the city offers visitors lots of clues to its secret identity. You just have to come and decipher them.

# Derbent

For at least 5,000 years, succeeding civilizations and empires have known that the route from central Europe to the Middle and Far East, including the Silk Route, must squeeze between the sheer slopes of the Caucasus Mountains and the western shore of the Caspian Sea. Derbent, the most southern city in Russia, guards the narrowest strip. It is the city built around the legendary Gates of Alexander, where, at the end of the 5th century AD, the Persian Sassanid dynasty built two parallel stone walls from the mountains to the sea, blocking the entire 3 km (2 mi) gap. Until recently, the whole of the city of Derbent was built between these walls, and it still retains the majority of its medieval fabric.

You enter a cultural and time warp when you enter the 6th century Caspian Gates at the seaward end. The walls are 3 m (10 ft) thick, and the tower still rises its original 9 m (30 ft). The city within is medieval and eastern, and its heart is a huge citadel, where the baths, mosques, caravanserai and even cemeteries are still in use. The 6th century Juma Mosque is built over a Christian basilica, and it has a 15th century madrassa, evidence that the city thrived for as long as its location retained its strategic significance, which it did for 1500 years until the 19th century. The original Sassanian fortifications were used continuously by Persian, Arabic, Mongol, and Timurid armies. When you look down from the stone walkways behind the crenellations, the biggest surprise is that the walls were not impregnable. However, the modern Azeri city has absorbed so much from ruling alien cultures that visitors can rejoice in the quality and variety of Derbent's extensive attractions. For its part, Derbent can rejoice because diminishing regional instability means more visitors will be able to come.

**POPULATION:**
101,000 (2002)
**WHEN TO GO:**
Year-round.
**DON'T MISS:**
Walking the walls, especially where they rise to meet the mountains.
The markets, and tea stalls within the walls, virtually unchanged since the 6th century.
The 18th century Khan's mausoleum.
The 17th century Kyrhlar and Bala mosques.
The 18th century Cheterbe mosque.
The architectural hallmarks of the various gates and gateway arches.
**YOU SHOULD KNOW:**
The Russo-Persian War ended when Peter the Great ceded Derbent back to the Nadir Shah by the terms of the 1735 Ganja Treaty.

# St Petersburg

Described by Dostoevsky as' the most artificial city in the world', St Petersburg was founded by Tsar Peter the Great in 1703 as the capital of the Russian Empire, which it remained for more than two hundred years until the government moved to Moscow after the revolution of 1917. This is a beautiful city with a rich history, and offers many treats for lovers of art and architecture.

Tsar Peter built the city after reconquering the Ingrian land from Sweden at the beginning of the Great Northern War. He named it after his patron saint, the apostle Saint Peter, and envisaged it as a great city dedicated to art and culture. He chose a site on what was then a large swamp, the delta of the Neva River, on the edge of the Baltic Sea's Gulf of Finland. Due to the adverse weather and geographical conditions, there was a high mortality rate among workers on his new city, so Peter levied a yearly conscription of 40,000 peasants from all parts of the country. Half of them died or escaped on the long trek there.

The Neva River, with its many canals and their granite embankments and bridges, sets St Petersburg apart from other Russian cities. Dominated by the Baroque Winter Palace, stretching 200 m (660 ft) along the river front, it is imbued with Russian imperial history. Commissioned by Tsarina Elizabeth, the lavish interior of the palace

*The Winter Palace*

reflects the opulent lives of the tsars. Catherine the Great added the Hermitage in 1764 to house her private art collection, now one of the largest in the world.

The main street in the city is Nevsky Prospekt, along which there are many rewarding sights. These include the Rastrelliesque Stroganov Palace, a monument to Catherine the Great, the Art Nouveau Bookhouse, the Anichkov Bridge with its remarkable horse statues, several eighteenth-century churches, an enormous eighteenth-century shopping centre, a nineteenth-century department store and the Russian National Library.

There are dozens of Baroque and Neoclassical palaces in the city, and an amazing array of churches. The astonishing St Isaac's Cathedral has an enormous dome covered with gold, and the Cathedral of Peter and Paul in Palace Square contains the tombs of Peter the Great and his successors. The huge neoclassical Kazan Cathedral on Nevsky Prospekt is modelled on St Peter's in Rome and well worth a visit. The Alexander Nevsky Monastery comprises two cathedrals and five churches in various styles. It is also known for its cemetery, with the graves of many well-known figures, such as Dostoyevsky, Krylov, Ilyich, Tchaikovsky and Mussorgsky.

# Nizhny Novgorod

Nizhny Novgorod came to prominence as Muscovy's frontier defence against the Kazan Tatars. Using the confluence of the Volga and Oka Rivers as a natural moat, the huge red brick Kremlin (1508-11), with 11 of its 13 original towers, still dominates the city skyline. Bolshevik devastation left only the Archangel Cathedral, a 13th century building restored between 1624-31, inside its walls, along with the remains of local merchant Kuzma Minin, who by expelling the Polish Army from Moscow brought Russia's 'Time of Troubles' to a close, and ushered in the 300-year Romanov dynasty. Nizhny prospered, becoming the Russian Empire's trade capital in the mid-19th century. The gigantic Russian Revival palace that was built in 1896 for the Russian Trade Fair remains a centrepiece of the style that characterizes much of the modern city centre; and the Fair itself persuaded Henry Ford to open a huge truck and tractor plant in the 1920s.

Meanwhile the writer Maxim Gorky, born in Nizhny in 1868, had become famous by writing about the ghastly life of the city's proletariat, and in 1932 Stalin changed the city's name in his honour. Stalin also closed 'Gorky' to foreign visitors, who were only allowed back in 1991, when Nizhny got its name back. Now the city holds an annual Festival of Music to honour Andrei Sakharov, exiled there during the closure to prevent him speaking freely to fellow scientists. Turning on the lights has brought Nizhny full historical circle. With visitors arriving in thousands, Bolshaia Pokrovskaia is again packed with life, as it was when the handsome rows of Revivalist houses and institutions lining it were first built. The 18th century wooden buildings and arcades of Varvarskaia reverberate with buzzing cafés and terrace bars. With IT industries transforming some of Nizhny's sprawling suburbs, the city is uplifted and uplifting. It's an elegant return to business.

**POPULATION:**
1,500,000 (2007)
**WHEN TO GO:**
April to September, with the Sakharov Music Festival as season finale.
**DON'T MISS:**
The austere, 5-domed Cathedral (1632) inside the medieval precincts of the Monastery of the Caves.
The early Baroque originality of the Church of the Virgin's Nativity.
The huge dome of the 1822 Empire-style Saviour Cathedral.
The Revivalist, 1856-80 'New Fair' Aleksandr Nevsky Cathedral on the river confluence.
The 5 green-tiled domes of the Assumption Church on St Elijah's Hill (1672).
The only surviving mid-17th century private merchant's house, Pushnikov.
**YOU SHOULD KNOW:**
The earliest extant manuscript of the Russian Primary Chronicle, the Laurentian Codex, was written for the Grand Duke Dimitri Konstantinovich in 1377, by a local monk called Laurence.

*The Church of the Virgin's Nativity*

*The Botanical Gardens*

# Sochi

The city of Sochi is technically 147 km (92 mi) long, but the port, best beaches and grooviest facilities are contained within the 12 km (7.5 mi) of Sochi proper. The city, at the heart of the 'Russian Riviera', is an oddity in many different ways. Oddest of all is that a city famous as a summer playground for the Russian elite should be hosting the Winter Olympics of 2014. Politics aside, there are good geographical and historical reasons why Sochi has reached this pinnacle of resort aspiration. Because it faces south, with the Caucasus Mountains rising immediately behind, it benefits from a microclimate that, in turn, has for a hundred years attracted interest from the most powerful people in Russia.

Russia's leaders, before and since the Revolution, invested heavily in the area, building homes for themselves, and ensuring that public funds maintained the quality of the city's facilities for all comers. Simultaneously, heavy industry was not allowed to infect the region, and even the international freight terminals are segregated. Visitors arriving by cruise liner are brought ashore at a quay full of sleek, ocean-going private yachts, moored in front of a series of cafés and restaurants whose colourful umbrellas and toned clientele have more in common with St Tropez than Stalin might have wished. The terminal building itself looks like a classical church, complete with steeple and spire – a very Russian touch.

Aside from the winter sports available an hour away, Sochi's tree-lined avenues are full of wooded parks, good museums and galleries, and a non-stop, ubiquitous, café and club-culture to amuse visitors drawn to a year-round sequence of festivals – of fashion, music, art, and anything quirky that might come along. There are 250 spas in the area, 30 botanical gardens of real interest, and the Russian National Wildlife Sanctuary and Caucasian Biosphere Reserve up the road are within the (technical) city limits. Sochi boasts that it can keep anyone amused, anytime, and it's true.

**POPULATION:**
400,000 (2007) – with full provision for 4 million visitors each year.
**WHEN TO GO:**
Year-round – the 'Velvet Seasons' Fashion Festival is in October; the Kentavr International Film Festival in November.
**DON'T MISS:**
The 14.7 ha (36.3 acres) of Riviera Park, crammed with palms, banana trees, facilities and fun.
The elegant, neo-classical Art Museum – Ivan Zholtovsky's 1939 masterpiece.
The bluntly Stalinist architecture of the Railway Terminal (1952).
The diminutive 1873 Cathedral of Archangel Michael.
Vera Mukhina's statues of the Muses at the Winter Theatre (1934).
**YOU SHOULD KNOW:**
You can swim in the Black Sea from April to October.

# Omsk

Imperial expansion created Omsk in 1716, when a wooden fortress was raised at the strategic river junction of the Om and the Irtysh to protect travelers and trade from marauding Kyrgyz nomads from the Steppes. You can still see the splendid Tobolsk and Tara Gates, and some of the other original, stone fortifications that replaced it by the end of the century. As frontier violence receded, Omsk became the administrative centre of Western Siberia and the Steppes of what is now Kazakhstan. Bureaucracy and religion flourished: the joke of the era was that you could buy ink by the bucket. But Omsk acquired cathedrals, churches, mosques and synagogues, plus a military academy to match the governor-general's mansion.

Trade boomed with the completion of the Trans-Siberian railway, and the lavish Siberian Exposition of 1910 showed the city centre much as it is today – handsome neo-classical terraces and mansions with an architectural Siberian twist. Briefly, after the Revolution, Omsk was proclaimed as capital of Russia (1918), and briefly held the imperial gold reserves. But Omsk's glory days were over. The Soviets moved the regional capital, and though it benefited from the influx of industry during World War II, the city remained an enclave of military manufacture and training, closed to visitors, until the military imploded in 1990.

While entrenched interests have been squabbling over the great city, Omsk's citizens have quietly set about reviving the very considerable historic remains, renewing their cultural affinities as Cossacks and Siberians, and setting a good example to visitors by letting their own hair down in situ. The annual Siberian Marathon, new leisure parks, and novel 24-hour sophistications of the Mayakovsky entertainment complex are all invitations to join an urban party that is only going to get better.

**POPULATION:**
1,134,000 (2002)
**WHEN TO GO:**
April to October.
**DON'T MISS:**
The five domes of the Russian Revivalist Dormition Cathedral, built in 1896, blown up by the Soviets, and carefully restored 2001-4.
The Siberian Cossack relics in the neo-classical Cathedral of St Nicholas (1840).
The late 18th century military jail where Dostoyevsky performed during his exile in Omsk.
The row of beautiful wooden merchant houses in Nikolsky Prospekt.
The Krestovozdvizhensky Orthodox Cathedral.
The ensemble of 1890-1900 buildings along and around Lyubinsky Prospekt, including two matched chapels, a terrace of town houses, and the splendid Omsk Theatre.
The Historical Museum in the former Governor-General's Mansion with its 'lighthouse' tower.
**YOU SHOULD KNOW:**
134 citizens of Omsk were awarded the title of 'Hero of the Soviet Union'.

*A perfect example of a wooden merchant house*

# Kaliningrad

**POPULATION:**
430,000 (2002)
**WHEN TO GO:**
April to October.
**DON'T MISS:**
The Kaliningrad Brandenburg Gate.
The early 14th century, brick, Gothic
Königsberg Cathedral on Kneiphof
Island, with 14th and 15th century
murals and wood carvings.
Ploshchad Pobedy (the city centre).
The Amber Museum, unique in
Russia, containing among 6,000
extraordinary exhibits of jewellery
and boxes once belonging to
Catherine the Great.
The austerity of the residential and
institutional quarters of the
Soviet city.
**YOU SHOULD KNOW:**
Königsberg Cathedral is the resting
place of locally born philosopher,
Immanuel Kant.

Kaliningrad is one of Europe's biggest political and cultural quirks. It is the capital of the eponymous exclave of Russia, on the Baltic coast between Poland and Lithuania, important to the motherland because it is Russia's only ice-free western port, but inaccessible directly from it except by air or boat. It has developed in isolation since 1945, when it was called Königsberg, and an exclave of Prussia since the Polish Corridor of Danzig had carved it away from the rest of Germany after World War I. Before that, Königsberg had had an illustrious history as a fief of the Teutonic Knights in the 13th century; as a member of the Hanseatic League; as capital of Ducal Prussia in fief to the early 17th century Polish Crown; and as capital of East Prussia under the Prussian Kingdom, and part of the German Empire from 1871.

Here's the curious part. Königsberg/Kaliningrad was bombed to bits by both the Nazis and the Allies in World War II, and was rebuilt in the most severe Soviet style. The reforms of glasnost and perestroika barely touched it. When communism collapsed, its immediate neighbours embraced the new political ground of consumer goods, EU membership, and visiting stag weekends. Kaliningrad didn't stir even when Russia finally did, and despite having the geographical autonomy and close access to do so better than anywhere else. This is a city that likes being Stalinist; and perversely now that the system's broken, it has inadvertently created a niche tourist market for the many people who would like to visit an authentic, Stalinist city. Kaliningrad has just enough older historical attractions to point the contrast, and the terrific potential of some of the Baltic's best beaches to develop. There is nowhere like it, much less so readily accessible. Go before the penny drops.

*Königsberg Cathedral*

# Vladivostok

Everything about Vladivostok sets it apart from the rest of Russia. Open to visitors only since 1991, it's revealed as a major seaport and naval base in a landlocked country, developed in geographical and political isolation as an extrovert, and now rejoicing in the opportunity to join the great cities of the Pacific Rim. It evokes San Francisco. Steep hills covered in high-rise blocks drop down to the inlets that comprise the great bay. A forest of masts and derricks to the left mark the naval docks and the quays and wharves of a major seaborne trade centre. On the right, dozens of cranes march uphill where new businesses and homes are replacing lumpen concrete with soaring steel and glass. Down by the waterside fish market on Ulitsa Admirala Fokina, bikini-clad local girls pack the boardwalk, watching boys from the yacht club; and in ramshackle back lots, teenagers ignore the patches of cement and chain-link fences to play volleyball. Bathers lounge next to cafés, bars and restaurants, or get a picnic of shrimp and sweet crab from the beer shacks. Better yet, unlike other Russian cities, Vladivostok does not close at night.

It's Russia's most exciting place to be. It may not be pretty, and it suffers from horrific air pollution in districts like the Pervaya and Vtoraya Rechka, where it is trapped in the hollows. It has few sights or great museums – but for visitors the action is in the living history on the streets and in the docks. You can walk freely among – and even photograph – the navy yards and the freight terminals, encouraged by enterprising beer and crab shacks. Away from the water, the evidence of sex and gambling tourism aimed at Chinese (who can't do it at home) isn't pleasant, but even that is characteristic of Vladivostok's freewheeling dynamism. San Francisco and Hong Kong must have felt the same long ago. Well, now it's Vladivostok's turn, so enjoy it while you can.

*The ornate façade of*
*Vladivostok railway station*

**POPULATION:**
595,000 (2002)
**WHEN TO GO:**
April to October.
**DON'T MISS:**
The Submarine Museum – inside a
World War II sub.
The 1912 Railway Station, eastern
terminal of the Trans-Siberian.
A guided tour through the recently
Top Secret catacomb defense network
and artillery emplacements.
The 'Statue to the fighters for Soviet
power in the Far East' overlooking the
harbour – the only statue in this naval
city never to have been vandalized.
A trip to the virgin forests, mountains
and beaches of the Primorye region
surrounding Vladivostok.
**YOU SHOULD KNOW:**
Vladivostok was the childhood home
of Hollywood film actor Yul Brynner.

# Irkutsk

**POPULATION:**
594,000 (2002)
**WHEN TO GO:**
Year-round – brutal winters are part
of the Siberia Experience.
**DON'T MISS:**
The Cathedral of the Epiphany, built
between 1718-46.
The neo-Gothic Polish Cathedral.
The ornate fretwork and bold colours
of many of the Decembrist
wooden houses.
The railway station.
The Kazansky Church.
The miniature 'Sydney Opera House'
on the 'island' park in the
Angara River.
**YOU SHOULD KNOW:**
The Regional Museum (housed in a
beautiful old mansion by the river) is
devoted to the nomadic culture of
the indigenous Siberians, the Buryats.

To travellers on the Trans-Siberian, it is simply 'the Stopover', because it's half-way. Irkutsk deserves much more respect. It lies on the broad (579 m [1,900 ft]) Angara River at its junction with the much smaller Irkut, where rolling hills mark the transition from flat west, to the thick, heavily wooded taiga of eastern Siberia. The rivers provide Irkutsk with plenty of waterfront, but some of its more important landmarks, like the monastery, the old fort, and the river port, are detached from the city centre by yet another tributary, the Ida. Irkutsk was founded on gold and fur in 1686, but gained its reputation as an intellectual and cultural centre from the early 19th century, when large numbers of artists, army officers, and aristocrats were exiled there after the Decembrist revolt against Tsar Nicholas I. Their beautifully decorated wooden houses are still among the city's greatest attractions.

The old, mainly wooden city burned down in 1879. By then, it was valued so highly for its unusually handsome avenues and amenities that it was immediately rebuilt, bigger and better. By 1900, it was called 'the Paris of Siberia'. During the Revolution it seethed with bloody encounters between Reds and Whites, but physically continued to look good, until industrialization under Stalin and Kruschchev created a different urban scale, which still tends to dwarf the city's surviving treasures.

With post-1990 Russia getting into its stride, the best of Irkutsk is re-emerging, and its new urban architecture is scaled to reflect its lofty but perfectly genuine traditions of taste. For this to work, the new money needs to work in symbiosis with Irkutsk's intellectual traditions as well. The Russian Academy of Sciences has nine major research institutes in the suburb of Academgorodok, so prospects look encouraging. Best of all, the academicians are now allowed to talk to visitors. Take advantage: Irkutsk is a great way to shrug off Siberia's negative history.

*Ornate shutters on a
wooden house*

# Yaroslavl

Yaroslavl is the most beautiful of the 'Golden Ring' of ancient Russian cities to the north and east of Moscow. Its heart is tucked into the angle of the junction between the Volga and the smaller Kotorosl, where Prince Yaroslav of the Kievan Rus fortified an existing Viking trading post in 1010. It reached the zenith of its political and economic power in the 16th century, and by 1612, during the Polish occupation of Moscow, it was Russia's second-largest city and briefly, the capital. During the 17th century, Yaroslavl's trade barons competed with each other to build ever more glitzy churches, and brought the finest craftsmen and artists from all over Europe to the city. Catherine the Great set her beady eye on its astonishing agglomeration of treasures, and had the medieval city re-cast on neo-classical principles. The radial plan of the modern centre is hers. You can still see more than 20 churches dating back as far as the 12th century, and Catherine's excellent artistic taste incorporated the porticos, parks, squares and monuments of the 16th and 17th into her master plan.

These days Yaroslavl rests sleepily on its historic laurels. It is still a major industrial centre of petrochemicals, tyres and diesel engines; and the Perekop district across the Kotorosl boasts some of the city's best parks and churches, including 17th century St John the Baptist on the riverbank slap bang next to the paint factory. It's unfortunate that Perekop is a seedy, run-down place of pre-Soviet *izbas* and factories, but the combination of sublime art and 21st century urban reality is typical. Fortunately, the huge residential areas ringing the centre have enough parks and, in Zavolzhsky across the Volga, birch and evergreen forests, for Yaroslavl's central masterpieces to retain the verdant riverside settings for which they were created. Try to arrive by riverboat.

**POPULATION:**
613,000 (2002)
**WHEN TO GO:**
April to October.
**DON'T MISS:**
The incomparable icons, illuminated inscriptions, and frescoes of the Church of St Elijah the Prophet, which also has some of the loveliest onion domes anywhere.
The Spassky Monastery, built in the 12th century on the site of a pagan temple, but with later additions.
The 18th century neo-classical City Hall.
The red brick and bright, tiled exterior of the Church of St Nicholas Nadein – an exemplar of the Yaroslavl Type, and with first-rank frescoes.
The Saviour Monastery of 1505-15.
Walking the river bank in the shadow of ancient lindens, in the city centre.
**YOU SHOULD KNOW:**
Yaroslavl lost its pre-eminence as 'mother of all crossroads' when St Petersburg was built.

*The Monastery of the Transfiguration of the Saviour*

# Moscow

Moscow is one of a handful of world cities that might be called irreducible. The harder you try to aim at it, the more it eludes you. You can't really separate its rich history from its daily role in writing the future: as the capital and barometer of the world's biggest country, Moscow is both dictator and victim of events, and this contradiction at the heart of its character is what provokes such strong responses in its visitors. You only have to stand in Red Square to feel the shocking difference between the familiar images and the actuality. The Kremlin and St. Basil's Cathedral radiate an aura of power that you feel physically, but with alternating exhilaration and discomfort. Even their beauty is manipulative. In this single place, Moscow draws together all the threads of Church and State in a demonstration of raw energy aimed at citizen and visitor alike.

Moscow hasn't always felt like this. It wasn't mentioned anywhere until 1147, though it rapidly assumed a central role in Russian affairs. The city was for a long time part of the northern Khanate, and paid homage to Batu, Genghis Khan's grandson and leader of the Golden Horde. The early Tsars had to co-exist with unruly Boyars until Ivan IV (The Terrible) finally made Moscow the seat of all real power in his expanding Russian state.

Though St Petersburg, a classical European city, remained Russia's capital from 1712 until the Revolution, it was

Moscow, a cultural amalgam of Asian steppe, Cossack marsh, and tribal Rus, that was targeted by both Napoleon and Hitler. Muscovites rebuilt it quickly whenever it burned, because then as now, it inspired passion. You can see the scars, and you can feel the city's Russian soul.

Now Moscow is on the cusp of another era, of unfettered capitalism *à la Russe*. The city seethes. In all its history, there's never been a better time to go.

*The colourful domes of St Basil*

# Jerusalem

In the Judean mountains, between the Mediterranean and the Dead Sea, Jerusalem, the capital city of modern Israel, has experienced an epic history going back to its foundation 5,000 years ago. Jerusalem has been the spiritual centre of the Jewish people since the tenth century, but it also contains a number of significant ancient Christian sites and is considered the third-holiest city in Islam. Over the centuries many different powers have fought for, ruled over and lost Jerusalem, including the Egyptians, Assyrians, Babylonians, Persians, Greeks, Romans, Byzantines, Arabs, Crusaders, Mamaluks, Ottomans and the British.

Jerusalem boasts relics dating back as far as 3,000 BC. The walled Old City lies at its centre, with Jewish West Jerusalem on one side and Arab East Jerusalem on the other. It has been traditionally divided into four quarters: the Armenian, Christian, Jewish, and Muslim Quarters. It is home to several sites of key religious importance: the Temple Mount and its Wailing Wall of significance for Jews, the Church of the Holy Sepulchre of significance for Christians, and the Dome of the Rock and Al-Aqsa Mosque for Muslims. There are so many attractions and sites here that it is impossible to list them all.

It was on the highly contested Temple Mount that Abraham is said to have prepared his son for sacrifice. The First and Second Temples were built on the site to be the repository of the Ark of the Covenant. The only remaining wall of the Second Holy Temple, known as the Western Wall, or Wailing Wall, marks the border between the Temple Mount and the Jewish quarter. Here Jews pray out loud, or push written prayers into the cracks between the ancient stones. The Jewish quarter contains numerous religious institutions, museums and archaeological sites, including the main Roman thoroughfare through the city, the Cardo.

Temple Mount is also of great importance to Muslims, as it is from here that Muhammad is said to have ascended to heaven. The gilded Dome of the Rock stands in the temple compound with the Al-Aqsa Mosque. It is believed to be the oldest extant Islamic building in the world. Bordering the same side of the Temple Mount is the Muslim quarter, entered through the main Damascus Gate. Rich in architecture from the Mamaluk period (1250–1516), the Muslim souk, with its winding alleyways, is a great place to explore.

Jaffa Gate is the entrance to the Armenian and Christian quarters. More than 1,000 Armenians live here, with much of their daily life taking place behind the high walls of the Armenian compound. In the Christian quarter is the Church of the Holy Sepulchre. Another site of huge religious significance, this is where Christ is supposed to have been crucified.

**POPULATION:**
732,000 (2007)
**WHEN TO GO:**
March to April; or September to November.
**DON'T MISS:**
Temple Mount – the most important religious site in the city. According to a commonly held belief in Judaism, it is to be the site of the final 'Third Temple' to be rebuilt with the coming of the Jewish Messiah. It is also the site of two major Muslim shrines, the Dome of the Rock and Al-Asque Mosque, whilst the Church of the Holy Sepulchre is of particular significance to Christians. This is one of the most heavily contested religious sites in the world.
The Wailing Wall – this western wall of the Temple Mount site is the holiest site in Judaism. It is all that remains of the Second Temple of Jerusalem and is regarded as being the main channel between Man and God.
Church of the Holy Sepulchre – venerated by most Christians as the place where Jesus was crucified.
**YOU SHOULD KNOW:**
Because of security measures, crossing between areas of the city takes time and can be a hassle.

*Dome of the Rock, Temple Mount*

# Akko (Acre)

**POPULATION:**
46,000 (2005)
**WHEN TO GO:**
All year.
**DON'T MISS:**
Museum of Heroism in the Citadel.
The Khan el Umdan – one of several
travellers' inns and camel stables.
Persian gardens of Bahji 3 km (2 mi)
north of Akko.
Ohr Torah Tunisian synagogue.
St George's Church.
Historical museum of Lohamei
Hageta'ot kibbutz, just north of Akko
– both fascinating and moving.
**YOU SHOULD KNOW:**
The population of Akko has the
greatest ethnic mix of all Israel's
cities, with Christian, Muslim, Druze
and Baha'i minorities.

The stunning UNESCO World Heritage Site of Akko, built on the northern tip of the Bay of Haifa, is one of the oldest settlements in the world, dating back to 1500 BC. The old part of the city, with its incredible collection of buildings, is enclosed by massive, remarkably intact city walls from which there are superb views of the bay.

Akko has a turbulent history. It was conquered by Alexander the Great, seized by the Egyptians, changed hands between Muslims and Crusaders, then sank into oblivion for nearly 500 years under the chaotic governance of slave-soldier Mamluks before eventually being absorbed by the Ottoman Empire. In 1918, the British captured it, using the 18th Century Citadel as a high security prison where they later held (and executed) Jewish political activists. In 1947 the Irgun (Zionist fighters) organised the 'greatest jail break in history' when 255 prisoners escaped. Finally, in 1948, Akko became part of Israel.

The city has beautiful mosques, churches and historic buildings going back to the 12th century. The Ahmed el-Jazzar, the largest mosque in Israel outside Jerusalem, dominates the skyline – a stunning 18th century Rococo design with a tall sliver of a minaret. Opposite is the partially excavated Crusader City, buried under a mound of earth during the building of the Citadel. An underground passage has been discovered, which gave the Crusaders a secret route to the harbour.

The markets of Akko are a delight: the 18th century Turkish bazaar, full of small artisan shops where you can haggle for souvenirs; the Shuq al-Abiad arcade with narrow passageways full of grocery stalls; and the vibrant street market along the main road, which sells everything from fresh fish and baked pastries to spices and perfumes – a glorious profusion of colours and smells.

*The old city harbour*

*Yafo Harbour*

# Tel Aviv-Yafo

Tel Aviv is less than a century old. It was founded in 1909 by Jewish immigrants, built from scratch along a beautiful strip of empty beach, just to the north of the ancient port of Yafo (Jaffa). The central area has been acclaimed for its many light-coloured stone buildings – designed by German refugees, trained in the Bauhaus School of Architecture, during the 1920s-30s – which have earned Tel Aviv UNESCO World Heritage status and the nickname 'the White City' (or, alternatively, 'Big Orange').

Waves of post-war immigration and 1950s austerity necessitated the erection of drab, cheaply built housing at the same time as the initial sheen of the city began to wear off, and Tel Aviv was in danger of becoming a characterless mass of concrete, while the beachfront piled up with detritus.

However, in the last 25 years, an influx of wealth has seen Tel Aviv acquire the trappings of a major 21st century world city with a liberal, animated and youthful outlook. The city has spread to incorporate Yafo, giving it some instant ancient heritage, and previously run-down historic districts like Neve Tzedek are becoming desirably hip places to live. An opera house has been built and new performing arts centres are springing up everywhere. A derelict port area in the north has been revitalized and the beach has been transformed into the cleanest urban beach in the world. Pedestrians and cyclists cruise down the Tayelet promenade in central Tel Aviv, between the Hayarkon (Herbert Samuel Boulevard) coast road, lined with luxury hotels and restaurants, and the people lolling on the beach.

Despite living under the cloud of terrorist violence, the inhabitants of Tel Aviv have not only maintained their equanimity but enjoy the success of their flourishing, multi-cultural, ultra-modern city with a spirit that is catching.

**POPULATION:**
384,000 (2007)
**WHEN TO GO:**
Spring and autumn. Very hot summers and surprisingly cold winters.
**DON'T MISS:**
Beit Ha-t'futsot Diaspora Museum and University campus.
Museum of Art.
Eretz Israel Museum Complex.
Yafo Flea Market.
Yafo Harbour.
The Carmel and Nahalat Binyamin markets, and bars round Allenby Street.
**YOU SHOULD KNOW:**
The greater Tel Aviv area is home to a third of the country's inhabitants. Tel Aviv is considered the most expensive city in the Middle East.

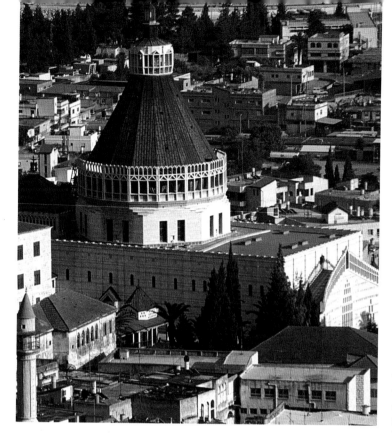

*The Basilica of the Annunciation*

# Nazareth

Although the name of Nazareth is practically synonymous with Christianity, the city is in fact more than 60 per cent Muslim and is the largest Arab settlement in Israel. It is the cultural and political capital for Israel's Arab community as well as a city of Christian religious sites.

The old city is 25 km (16 mi) from the Sea of Galilee, built in an enormous hollow. It is surrounded by 500-m (1600-ft) high hills, from the top of which are some wonderful views – especially from the Mount of Precipice, the city's highest point.

**POPULATION:**
65,000 (2006)
**WHEN TO GO:**
Very pleasant in spring and autumn. Extremely hot summers and rainy winters.
**DON'T MISS:**
The Saraya (Governor's House) – an elegant Levantine building to the east of the bazaar.
Church of St Gabriel.
Khan el Basha – beautiful caravanserai (inn) on Casa Nova Street.
The catacombs of Beit She'arim – burial caves, on main road to Haifa.
Nazareth Village – a lovely reconstruction, based on archaeological knowledge, of Nazareth in Jesus's time.
Basilica of the Transfiguration and Church of Elias, on Mount Tabor, 9.5 km (6 mi) from Nazareth.
**YOU SHOULD KNOW:**
Although the inhabitants for the most part co-exist harmoniously, Nazareth is in an area of tension and politics is a subject best avoided.

The central landmark, near the entrance to the bazaar, is the beautiful Basilica of the Annunciation – the largest church in the Middle East. Narrow stepped streets wind down towards it from the edge of town, where there are some lovely Levantine mansions perched on the upper rim. The bazaar area is the heart of the city. It is one of the largest markets in Israel – a maze of picturesque lanes becoming increasingly narrow the deeper you go. In the bazaar's main street is the Greek Catholic 'Synagogue' Church, supposedly the site of the synagogue Jesus attended, and the Franciscan Mensa Christi. And, in the bowels of the marketplace, there is the oldest mosque in the city, the early 19th century Al Abaid (White Mosque).

In a city packed with important churches, monasteries and convents, one of the loveliest is the Gothic Basilica of Jesus the Adolescent. There are also several Muslim shrines and numerous historical and archaeological sites.

Nazareth is not just a city for religious pilgrimage. Its Eastern ambience gives it a charm that makes you want to spend time dawdling in side street cafés, eating mouth-watering pastries and watching the old men smoking their nargileh.

# Jericho

The 'City of Palms', 40 km (25 mi) east of Jerusalem in the Jordan valley, claims to be the oldest city in the world. Jericho has a past stretching back some 10,000 years. It is a desert oasis, a beautifully green town that is the breadbasket of the West Bank. At 258 m (848 ft) below sea level, Jericho is the lowest city on earth.

The city's main water source is Ain al Sultan (Elisha's well), which rises near the Tel es-Sultan, the remains of the ancient city. The tel stands 21-m (69-ft) high, covering an area of 40,000 sq m (44,000 sq yd). Here you can see the archaeology of Jericho's inhabitation – 23 separate levels, including parts of the Neolithic town. City walls were built as early as 7000 BC, famously broken down by the blast from the trumpets of Joshua's Israelite army.

The splendid 8th century Hisham's Palace, 3 km (2 mi) from the town centre, is a wonderful example of Islamic architecture with beautifully preserved mosaics. It was built as a winter residence for the decadent poet-prince Caliph al Walid ibn Yazid. You can see what the royal priorities were from the numerous water tanks, bath houses and pools – said to have been filled with wine rather than water.

North of Ain al Sultan, there is an avenue of cypress trees leading to what was once a Byzantine synagogue. The beautifully intact mosaic floor has a central medallion inscribed Shalom al Yisrael (Peace for Israel). And in the wilderness just outside the city, there is the Maqam al Nabi Musa – an Islamic shrine to Moses.

Jericho is a popular tourist destination despite the political tensions. The city centre is spacious, with a friendly atmosphere and an attractive main street lined with garden restaurants.

*Diwan mosiac at Hisham's Palace*

**POPULATION:**
25,000 (2006)
**WHEN TO GO:**
Winter.
**DON'T MISS:**
Tulul Abu al Alaieq – King Herod's winter palace 2.5 km (1.5 mi) to the west of Jericho.
Greek Orthodox Monastery of St George – carved out of the rock face in a desert canyon, surrounded by a lush garden.
Greek Monastery of Temptation and views from top of Jabel Quruntal, where Jesus fasted and saw the devil.
Mosaics of the 4th Century Na'aran Synagogue.
Monastery of the Essenes, 20 km (12 mi) south of Jericho – site of the discovery of the Dead Sea Scrolls.
**YOU SHOULD KNOW:**
The West Bank of the River Jordan 8 km (5 mi) east of Jericho is a closed military zone. Do not be surprised to find that, as a result of the intifada, Jericho has a faintly forlorn air about it.

# Beirut

**POPULATION:**
1,500,000 (2005)
**WHEN TO GO:**
Best weather is in May/June and November/December; February can be particularly sunny so is a good time for winter skiing.
**DON'T MISS:**
Central market Souk el Barghout daily in El Bourj.
New urbanist architecture and Souk el Tayeb in Le Quartier des Arts.
The Sursock Museum – for the building alone, quite apart from its superb art collections.
René Moawad Garden in the Sanayeh district – one of oldest open spaces in the city used by children to play, old people to relax and artists to exhibit their work, and which, in 2006, was turned into an emergency open air refugee centre.
The Grand Serail – Ottoman mansion, the Prime Minister's Residence.
Gibran Khalil Gibran Parc – a garden in honour of the renowned Lebanese-American poet and philosopher.
**YOU SHOULD KNOW:**
Beirut has been chosen as UNESCO World Book Capital for 2009.

Beirut is beautifully situated on a promontory halfway along the Lebanese coast, overlooked by the Mountains of Lebanon. Its position on the eastern Mediterranean seaboard has ensured that, throughout its long history, Beirut has always been a melting pot – one of the most culturally and religiously diverse cities in the Middle East, with at least ten distinct Muslim and Christian sects. By the mid 20th century, it was known as the 'Paris of the Middle East' – the intellectual and commercial capital of the Arab world.

In 1975, sectarian tensions erupted into a brutal 15-year long civil war which led to the city's collapse into a no-man's land. Beirut had just regained its status as a cultural centre of some importance when the Israeli bombing raids of 2006 wreaked mayhem – causing immeasurable loss both in terms of human lives and to the city's brand new infrastructure.

Beirut, 'the City that will not die', has already risen from its latest ashes with a spirit that is awe-inspiring; but perhaps not altogether surprising – for at its heart is the central monument of Place des Martyrs (El Bourj), the site where six Lebanese nationalists were publicly executed by the Ottomans during a bid for independence in 1916.

Wherever you are in Beirut, the atmosphere is charged with a sybaritic spirit of enterprise in the pursuit of music, art, cuisine and intellectual stimulation; whether you are downtown in the central Achrafieh district, wandering around the bookshops of Hamra, or having a drink in the bohemian Gemmayze quarter, you can't help admiring the incorrigible hedonism of this city by the sea. From the cliff at Raouché, at the northern end of the Corniche there is a view of Pigeon Rocks, two huge monoliths that stand in the sea – a timeless testament to the resilience of this remarkable city's soul.

*The Grand Serail*

# Byblos

Byblos is one of several cities in the Middle East that claims to be the oldest continuously inhabited city in the world, with a history traceable to 7000 BC. Archaeological remains from the third millennium BC show signs of deliberate town planning with uniform, well-built houses. It has been given UNESCO World Heritage status as one of the richest archaeological sites in Lebanon.

For thousands of years, Byblos appears to have been a flourishing independent coastal city-state in the ancient land of Canaan, before becoming first an Egyptian and then a Phoenician trading colony. It played an important part in the paper trade, exporting cedar wood in exchange for papyrus and ivory. The western phonetic alphabet originated here, transforming human communication forever. The city fell to the armies of Alexander the Great, and by 800 BC the Greeks were using this new form of writing to spread their ideas.

Today, Byblos is a lively modern seaside town with traces of history everywhere you turn. Near the restored Roman-medieval harbour there are excavations revealing the remains of the various ancient settlements. The old part of town, a picturesque market district with cobble-stoned alleys, is overlooked by the well-preserved 12th century castle, built by the Crusaders as a military base from which to attack the armies of Saladin. Here too are the remains of the Roman amphitheatre and the Phoenician Royal Necropolis – in which the first papyrus with alphabetic writing was discovered. There are also three Egyptian temples, dating from 2700 BC – The Great Temple, Baalat Gebal (The Lady of Byblos – patroness of shipmasters), and the Temple of the Obelisks.

There are wonderful beaches along the shore and, even in winter, you can enjoy Lebanese cuisine in one of the excellent restaurants overlooking the Mediterranean.

**POPULATION:**
11,000 (2005)
**WHEN TO GO:**
May and June are the best months of the year.
**DON'T MISS:**
Medieval city walls – these encompass the old part of the city and date back to the Bronze Age.
Arts and Crafts Centre at the entrance to the Old Town – workshops for young artists and craftsmen in wrought iron, ceramics, weaving, etc.
Byblos Wax Museum – wax figures illustrate scenes from the history of Lebanon.
The beautiful, wild valley of Nahr Ibrahim, 6 km (4 mi) south of Byblos, leading to the Temple of Venus.
**YOU SHOULD KNOW:**
The word 'Bible' is derived from the city's name. (Ancient Greek: byblos = paper).

*The restored Roman-medieval harbour*

*The view from the Citadel*

# Aleppo

The northernmost of Syria's ancient cities, at the junction of trade routes linking Mesopotamia, the Fertile Crescent and Egypt, Aleppo was, for hundreds of years, one of the most important commercial centres in the Middle East. It was also hotly disputed territory, changing hands many times before eventually becoming part of the Ottoman Empire in the sixteenth century. With the collapse of the Ottoman Sultanate in 1922, it came under French mandate until Syria achieved independence in 1944.

The World Heritage listed Citadel of Aleppo is perhaps the most spectacular medieval fortress in the Middle East – an incredible monument built on a mound 50 m (165 ft) above the city, on top of remains going back to 1000 BC. Abraham is said to have milked his cow here. It is surrounded by a 22-m (75-ft) wide moat, with a single entrance through an outer tower on its south side. Inside, there is a 12th century palace built by Saladin's son, and two mosques. The Great Mosque, in particular, is outstandingly beautiful with a separate 11th century laced-stonework minaret.

The old city, encircling the Citadel, is a fascinating maze of narrow twisting streets and secret courtyards. The bazaar is an Aladdin's cave – the largest covered market in the Middle East. Its stone archways run for miles, with souks selling everything under the sun. The prosperity of Ottoman Aleppo is attested to by the sumptuousness of its *khans* (trading-centre inns where travelling merchants stay with their goods and camels) with their magnificent gateways, and the striking architecture of the medrassahs (religious seminaries), hamams (baths) and merchants' mansions.

Aleppo has the best examples of Islamic architecture in Syria and is known as the country's second capital. It is one of the most interesting cities in the whole of the Middle East.

**POPULATION:**
1,900,000 (2006)
**WHEN TO GO:**
March to May or September to October.
**DON'T MISS:**
Aleppo Archaeological Museum.
Bab Antakya – the old western gateway to the bazaar.
The Maronite Cathedral.
Armenian Church.
Church of St Simeon – 60 km (40 mi) from Aleppo, built in 473 AD in honour of Simeon who spent 37 years living on top of a column in order to get closer to God. It is one of the oldest churches in the world.
**YOU SHOULD KNOW:**
Although the population of Aleppo is 70 per cent Arab and Kurdish Sunni Muslim, it also has the largest Christian community in the Middle East, apart from Beirut. After the creation of Israel, an 'ethnic cleansing' social and political atmosphere led to the 10,000 strong Jewish community being forced to emigrate, mainly to the United States and Israel.

# Damascus

First settled in the third millennium BC, the Syrian capital of Damascus is thought to be one of the oldest continuously inhabited cities in the world, and has seen many invaders come and go. The streets of the old city, with the exception of the 'street called Straight' mentioned in the Bible, on which Saint Paul is supposed to have lived, are crooked and narrow. Encircled by a magnificent Roman wall with seven gates, the old city is divided into the market area, Muslim area, Christian area and the Jewish area.

Damascus has more than 200 mosques, 70 of which are still in use. The Umayyad Mosque was at one time the centre of Islam, and still the Muslim world's third most important site after Mecca and Medina. Starting out as a heathen temple, it was converted into a Christian church at the end of the 4th century when it was believed to contain the head of Saint John the Baptist. The mosque dates from the beginning of the 8th century, and is the best known of the old city's architectural treasures, with its splendid minarets and courtyard adorned with golden mosaics. Other mosques of interest to the visitor are the Sinani-yah, with its vibrant green-tiled tower, and the Tekkeyah, founded in 1516 on the riverbank west of the city as a refuge for poor pilgrims.

Another of the most famous buildings of Old Damascus is the Azem Palace, built by As'ad Pasha al-Azem, governor of Damascus in 1749. In 1954, the palace was turned into a museum of Syrian traditions. The building is a good example of traditional Syrian architecture.

The National Museum of Damascus is also worthwhile. The west wing contains pre-classical and Arab Islamic collections, while the east wing contains Classical and Byzantine collections.

Damascus has long been an important commercial centre, and offers great shopping opportunities today, particularly in the Souq al-Hamidiyah. In former times the city was famous for dried fruit, wine, wool, linens and silks, including Damask, named for the city. Today, handicrafts include silk and leather goods, filigreed gold and silver objects, inlaid wood, copper, and brass articles.

**POPULATION:**
4,500,000 (2005)
**WHEN TO GO:**
April to October
**DON'T MISS:**
Azem Palace – displays domestic artefacts from Syria's past, including clothing and household goods. It also houses the Museum of Popular Arts & Tradition. It's a great place to get a taste of Damascene culture.
Chapel of Ananias.
Al Nouri, Damascus's most famous hamam (Turkish baths).
**YOU SHOULD KNOW:**
Damascus is said to be the oldest continuously inhabited city in the world.

*The Umayyad Mosque and souk*

# Qom

*Fatima's Shrine*

Qom is the world centre for the theological study of the Shi'a Islam faith – the equivalent of the Vatican for Catholic Christians. It was the birthplace of last century's Islamic Revolution of Iran, masterminded by Ayatollah Khomeini, and is the most important place of pilgrimage after Mecca and Mashhad – the site of the shrine to Hazrat-e Masumeh, sister of the 9th century saint, Imam Reza, whose own shrine is in Mashhad.

Qom is a desert city 156 km (97 mi) south of Tehran. Any preconceptions about what a holy city should look like are immediately dispelled by the long, dusty route into town – uninspiring roadside shacks and petrol stations giving way to bland, featureless houses. Apart from a cupola gleaming in the distance, the place looks entirely characterless. But the shrine itself, in the centre of the city, is such a stupendous edifice – a massive golden dome, incredible mosaicwork, tiled and curlicued minarets soaring into the sky – that any sneaking flutter of disappointment gives way to wonderment.

The town itself remains frustratingly hidden – endless bare streets with high walls, reminiscent of Arab austerity rather than a Persian garden of delight. However, behind those blank walls, there is a hotbed of learning, ideas and political intrigue. The people of Qom are hospitable, and interested in showing strangers their city; it's just that they are as bemused by you as you are by them.

To the western tourist, this city of mullahs (priests) and medrassahs (theological schools) is a very peculiar place indeed, but none the less fascinating for that. There is a spirit of fervour among the pilgrims – whether they are a respectable cleric, a prosperous shopkeeper, or a woman wrapped head to toe in black – that is awe-inspiring. A visit to Qom certainly gets you thinking.

# Shiraz

The former, 18th century capital of Persia is one of the most romantic cities in the world, known as the city of 'Poetry, wine and roses. Two of Persia's greatest poets, Hafez and Sa'di, have their mausoleums here. Sa'di's is inscribed with the words 'From the tomb of a son of Shiraz, the perfume of love escapes – to be smelt still one thousand years after his death', while the poem engraved on Hafez's memorial starts: 'Sit near my tomb, and bring wine and music....'

The city is situated at an altitude of 1,600 m (5,260 ft) in the foothills of the Zagros Mountains, a fruit-growing region famous for its grapes. The first wine in the world was discovered here in its original clay jars – around 7,000 years old! Shiraz is a city of parks and trees, beautiful buildings and wide shady avenues. The road from the airport into town is lined with rose beds, a foretaste of what is to come – the city is renowned for its Persian gardens. The Bagh-e Khalili and the Bagh-e Eram are two that are especially outstanding.

The unique brickwork of the superbly built courtyards of the central Bazar-e Vakil is unlike any elsewhere. At the far end of the bazaar is the Saray-e Moshir – a magnificent 19th century pavilion where merchants used to conduct their business transactions. The Masjid-e Vakil (Regent Mosque), by the bazaar entrance, has finely decorated walls and ceilings, and beautiful stained glass work; and the bazaar itself is a gleaming treasure house of silversmiths, enamellists and jewellers as well as shops selling carpets, textiles, spices and copper.

In spring, when the unmistakeable, heady scent of orange blossom wafts through the air, there is no more romantic place in the world than Shiraz, the City of Love.

**POPULATION:**
1,256,000 (2005)
**WHEN TO GO:**
Pleasant temperate climate all year.
Best in late spring/early summer when the city's flowers are blossoming.
**DON'T MISS:**
Qor'an Gate – a modern, award-winning architectural wonder that replaced a 1,000-year-old gate, the entrance to the city.
Government Palace Museum.
Nasir-al-Mulk Mosque.
Naranjestan Qavam Museum – traditional 19th century merchant's house, with beautifully painted ceilings and façade, and exquisite mirrored porch.
Takieh Haft Tanan – a beautifully decorated pavilion in a lovely garden.
Shah-e Cheragh shrine.
**YOU SHOULD KNOW:**
There are more than 200 sites of historical significance in the immediate vicinity of Shiraz, including the World Heritage Site of the ancient city of Persepolis.

*The exterior of Bazar-e Vakil*

# Yazd

**POPULATION:**
434,000 (2005)
**WHEN TO GO:**
Desert climate - very hot during the
day and extremely cold at night.
Trees blossom in spring.
**DON'T MISS:**
Yazd Museum.
Tomb of the Twelve Imams – 12th
century.
Mausoleum of Sayed Rokn od-Din.
Bagh-e-Dhowlat – beautiful house
with stained glass windows and
garden.
Alexander's Prison (Zendan-e-
Iskander).
Chak Chak – important Zoroastrian
temple 52 km (32 mi) from Yazd.
**YOU SHOULD KNOW:**
Yazd is famous for its silk weaving,
ceramics and sweet shops. The
bazaars of Yazd are probably the
best place in Iran to buy silks,
cashmere and brocades.

Situated in a valley 1,215 m (3,990 ft) high, in the mountains of central Iran, the strange city of Yazd is not only one of the finest examples of desert architecture in the world but also a non-Muslim religious cult centre. The recorded history of the city goes back 3,000 years. Because of its remote desert location, it has been largely untouched by the ravages and upheavals of war, instead being a safe haven to which people migrated in times of trouble.

The city was once an esoteric cult centre, a refuge for mystics and Gnostics, and 5-10 per cent of the population are still Zoroastrian – an ancient Iranian religion, the forerunner of all the great monotheistic creeds. When Islam became the state religion of Persia, the Zoroastrians of Yazd avoided forcible conversion by paying a levy. Their Atashkadeh (Fire Temple) has a flame that has been kept alight continuously since 470 AD – for over 1,530 years! – and there is a Tower of Silence, where the dead are left, on the outskirts of the city.

Yazd has the largest network of *qanats* in the world – an ancient shaft-well conduit technology invented in Iran, which eventually caught on in desert cultures everywhere and is still in use today. Many of the houses have *badgirs* (windcatchers) to keep them cool and ventilated, and *yakhchals* – a sort of primitive refrigerator. Almost all the houses are built out of adobe – unbaked bricks made of sand, clay, straw and dung.

There are some exceptionally fine Islamic buildings and medieval city walls. The Amir Chakhmaq Mosque, next to the bazaar, has beautiful calligraphy on the portal and mehrab (niche showing the direction of Mecca) and the 14th century Jameh Mosque has an exquisite mosaic dome, but is best known for its towering gateway, soaring into the sky – the tallest entrance portal in Iran.

*The exquisite mosaic dome of the Jameh Mosque*

# Mashhad

In the 9th century, a holy Muslim cleric called Imam Reza was murdered in the nondescript desert watering hole of Sanabad, on the caravan route to Turkmenistan. The town immediately became known as 'place of Martyrdom' – Mashhad, and a shrine was erected, which, after Mecca, grew to be the most important Shia Muslim religious site in the world. The city attracts more than 20 million pilgrims and tourists a year and is known as the 'Mecca of the Poor'.

*The Imam Reza Mausoleum*

Mashhad is 800 km (500 mi) east of Tehran, in a fertile valley in the desert mountain region of Khorazan, renowned for the quality of its turquoise and marble. The city is a cultural centre of enormous significance – of secular as well as religious learning. It has one of the oldest libraries of the Middle East, the Astan-e Quds Razavi, which, among many rare and valuable manuscripts, contains the oldest known manuscript of the Qur'an. The holy shrine and museum hold an extensive collection of cultural treasures, paintings and manuscripts.

The Holy Precinct is a vast walled area in the centre of Mashhad. Over the past 1000 years, the shrine and surrounding buildings have been destroyed, ransacked, rebuilt and enlarged to create the marvel of inspired architectural genius that stands today. The magnificent golden dome over the shrine, the intricacy of the inlaid walls, the 15th century Gowhrzhad Mosque, with its 50-m (165-ft) blue dome and asymmetric minarets, is simply breathtaking. The sheer scale of its beauty is quite unlike anything else in the world.

Mashhad is a pleasant city with lovely parks and gardens. It is completely geared up for tourists with plenty of hotels and excellent restaurants, and is the second largest commercial centre in the country which is reflected in the busy atmosphere of purposeful enterprise.

**POPULATION:**
2,388,000 (2006)
**WHEN TO GO:**
September and October are the most beautiful months but Mashhad is also very pleasant in the spring.
**DON'T MISS:**
Astan-e Quds Museum.
Tomb of Nadir Shah Afshar – 18th century founder of the Assayid dynasty, a bandit leader who created a Persian Empire stretching to North India.
Gombad-e Sabz – beautiful green domed building.
Saraye Bazaar e-Reza – fabric and textile bazaar.
Torghabeh – lovely small town outside Mashhad. Very good shopping.
Tomb of Ferdowsi – Iran's famous poet, greatly revered – in Tus 24 km (15 mi) away.
**YOU SHOULD KNOW:**
Mashhad is renowned for its high quality wool; some of the best knotted carpets and rugs in Iran are produced here. They are easily recognizable from the complex curvilinear floral designs in dark blues and reds around a central medallion.

# Isfahan

**POPULATION:**
1,600,000 (2007)
**WHEN TO GO:**
Spring or Autumn
**DON'T MISS:**
Shah Mosque.
Imam Mosque – one of the most stunning buildings in Iran and celebrated for its tilework. There are an estimated 472,500 tiles used in the mosque.
The Royal Palace.
The Grand Bazaar.

Located in the lush Zayandeh River plain with the Zagros mountains providing a handsome backdrop, Isfahan is Iran's third-largest city. The city grew up in an oasis, allowing its inhabitants to grow fruits and cereal crops, as well as raising livestock, something which is impossible in the surrounding arid desert. Designated a UNESCO World Heritage Site, Isfahan contains examples of Islamic architecture from the 11th to the 19th centuries.

Isfahan's heyday was in the 16th century when Shah Abbas the Great, who unified Persia, made it the new capital of the Safavid dynasty. Under his rule, the Golden Age came to the city, and Isfahan

Sheikh Lotfallah Mosque – an architectural masterpiece built by Sheikh Lotfallah. A place of exceptional beauty intended to impress the listeners and the followers of the Shia religion.
**YOU SHOULD KNOW:**
Isfahan is famous for its glorious carpets.

became known as Nesf-e-Jahan, or 'Half of the World'. This was because the city held so many riches in wealth, geography, architecture and religion, and referred to the fact that so many cultures and nationalities met and mingled there. At the time it was one of the most prominent cities in the world, with over half a million inhabitants, and impressive parks, libraries, religious schools, shops, public baths and mosques. In 1722, Isfahan was raided by the Afghans which left much of it in ruins and marked the start of its decline.

One of the main reasons to visit the city is its monumental architecture, featuring all the traditional elements: gardens, platforms, porches, gateways, domes, arched chambers and minarets. Many of the sights are arranged around Imam Square, one of the biggest squares in the world and an outstanding example of Islamic architecture. The square features many buildings from the Safavid era. The Shah Mosque was built in 1611, and features beautiful mosaic tiles and valuable inscriptions. The splendid portal is crowned with two beautiful minarets, 42 metres high. Sheikh Lotfallah Mosque, on the eastern side of the square, is best known for the peacock at the centre of its dome which can be appreciated from the entrance gate of the inner hall. The fabulous Imam Mosque is a masterpiece of Chahar-iwan style and is known for its arabesque tiles, its dome and its Safavid decoration. To the west of the Imam

*The Masjed-e-Sheikh Lotfallah Mosque*

Square is the entrance to the Royal Palace (Ali Qapu), rich
in naturalistic wall paintings of flowers, animals and birds
by Reza Abbasi, the court painter of Shah Abbas the
Great. Isfahan's Grand Bazaar is one of the oldest
and largest bazaars in the Middle East and
dates back to the seventeenth century.
It offers an opportunity to shop for
Isfahan's famous Persian rugs,
among the most sought-after
in the West.

# Mecca

**POPULATION:**
1,294,000 (2004)
**WHEN TO GO:**
Inaccessible to non-Muslims.
November to February is the
pleasantest time of year in Saudi
Arabia, for Muslims to make Umrah;
or go on Hajj.
**YOU SHOULD KNOW:**
Any non-Muslim thinking of travelling
anywhere in Saudi Arabia should first
find out whether it is currently safe
and take note of official advice.

The sacred city of Mecca, in Saudi Arabia, is the geographical and spiritual focal point for all Muslims. It is incumbent on practising Muslims to make the Hajj (mass pilgrimage) journey, which takes place each year in the Islamic month of Dhu'Hijja, to the Ka'ba – the holiest place on earth – at least once in their lives.

The city is centred round Masjid al-Haram, the largest mosque in the world, first built in the 7th century but many times modified, demolished, rebuilt and extended so that it now accommodates up to 820,000 worshippers. It houses the Ka'ba, a huge, sacred granite box, said to have been built by Ibrahim (Abraham), and the holy Black Stone – believed to have fallen from heaven at the time of Adam and Eve.

The area of the old city immediately around the mosque has been razed in order to widen the streets after several tragic incidents of pilgrims being crushed to death during the Hajj stampede. The houses that remain are mostly closely built two- or three-storeyed dwellings built of local stone, with a few slums where pilgrims too poor to return home have settled. The city is economically dependent on the pilgrim trade. In recent years, it has expanded to accommodate the ever-growing number of visitors (up to 4 million at Hajj) and is now ringed by a freeway with high rise buildings and shopping malls.

There are only two ways to get to see Mecca – be a Muslim or risk death. In the 19th century, Sir Richard Burton, the renowned

*Muslim pilgrims pray in the holy city of Mecca.*

Victorian orientalist, let his curiosity get the better of him and famously slipped into the city disguised as an Afghani. It is not sensible to emulate this feat, unless you can recite the salah (prayers) – road checks ensure that any visitors are legitimate pilgrims.

# Medina

**POPULATION:**
1,300,000 (2006)
**WHEN TO GO:**
The most comfortable weather is November to February. The city is most crowded during Hajj (annual mass pilgrimage), when many pilgrims include a visit to Medina on their journey to Mecca.
**YOU SHOULD KNOW:**
Saudi Arabia is considered an unsafe country for non-Muslims, especially westerners. It is up to individuals to inform themselves of the current situation before they travel here and to keep up to date with official information and advice.

In 622 AD the prophet Muhammad left Mecca and was given sanctuary in the city of Yathrib, in the volcanic hills 320 km (200 mi) to the north. The city became known as Madinat al-Nabi – 'City of the Prophet of Allah', shortened to al-Madina, or Medina – 'The City'.

For the next 40 years, Medina was the capital of the Muslim world and, although the city gradually declined in political importance, as Islam spread across the Middle East to cities like Jerusalem and Damascus, it retained its spiritual significance – for it was here that Muhammad laid the foundation stone of the first mosque in the world, the Masjid al-Quba. When he died in 632, the Masjid al-Nabawi (Prophet's Mosque) was built on the site of his house. The al-Nabawi contains his tomb and is second in importance only to the al-Haram in Mecca.

The original Masjid al-Nabawi was 30 x 35 m (100 x 115 ft) built of palm trunks and mud, with three entrances. Its basic plan was the one adopted by mosques everywhere. Over the centuries, al-Nabawi has been rebuilt, embellished and enlarged many times; although smaller than the al-Haram, it is still a magnificent building, ten times its original size, with room for half a million worshippers.

Medina is enclosed by a huge 12th century wall, flanked by towers and a castle. Of the four entrance gates, the Bar al-Salaam, in particular, is renowned for its beauty. Outside the city walls there are suburbs of low houses, courtyards and gardens. The city is packed with religious monuments, shrines, and shops selling artefacts and holy trinkets.

Like Mecca, the holy part of Medina behind the city wall is *haram* (forbidden) to non-Muslims. However, many of the sights and facilities of the city are accessible to non-believers.

*Sunlight on Masjid al-Nabawi*

# Sana'a

Situated on a flat plain surrounded by dark basalt mountains, the Yemen capital of Sana'a has one of the best preserved and biggest medinas in the Arab world, boasting its own unique style of architecture. According to legend, the city was founded by Shem, one of the three sons of Noah, and has been throughout history one of the most important cities in Yemen.

The ancient clay walls of the city stand 6–9 metres (20–30ft) high, and surround over 100 mosques, 12 hammams (bath houses) and around 6,500 houses, many of which are 400 years old. The world's first tower blocks were built here – six- and seven-storey houses made from dark basalt stone and sun-dried mud-bricks. Their window surrounds are pale in colour and intricately decorated with elaborate friezes. Together with their panes, which were until recently made of thin slices of alabaster, they represent a unique architectural heritage.

The old, walled city, a UNESCO World Heritage Site, contains a wealth of architectural gems, including the majestic seventh-century Great Mosque, which was built at the time of the Prophet Muhammed and is one of the oldest in the Muslim world. Also worth a visit is the 1000-year-old Bab Al-Yemen (the Gate of Yemen). Richly decorated, this is an iconized entry point through the city walls.

One of the most popular attractions is Suq al-Milh (Salt Market), a vast maze of narrow alleys and winding streets, and one of the oldest souqs in Arabia. As well as salt, it has an astonishing and colourful variety of goods on sale from spices and every kind of foodstuff to pottery, silverware, antiques, copper, woodwork and clothing. Early morning or early evening are the best times to visit.

The National Museum is well worth a look. It is housed in the House of Good Luck (Dar as-Sa'd), once a royal palace dating from the 1930s. The museum contains a range of fascinating artefacts from the ancient kingdoms of Saba, Ma'rib and Ma'in.

**POPULATION:**
1,747,000 (2004)
**WHEN TO GO:**
October to March.
**DON'T MISS:**
The Great Mosque.
Bab al-Yemen.
The Salt Market.
The National Museum.
**YOU SHOULD KNOW:**
Although Yemen is a wonderful country, with much of old Arabia about it, there is ongoing trouble here; travellers should exercise caution, keep abreast of the news and heed local warnings.

*The unique architectural heritage of Sana'a*

*A city made of mud.*

# Shibam

**POPULATION:**
7,000 (2006)
**WHEN TO GO:**
April, May, September and October
are the best months. Very dry and
dusty from October to February.
**DON'T MISS:**
Al-Murshed Tourist House – seeing
the inside of a house adds a new
dimension to your understanding and
appreciation of the architecture.
Walking up the cliff path in the late
afternoon light to see the white roofs
of the town from above.
10th century Jami Mosque.
Man-made caves in the
mountainside – once used as
burial places.
The town gate and 13th century fort.
Watching the skill of the
metalworkers in the Souk.
**YOU SHOULD KNOW:**
Although Yemen is a wonderful
country, with much of old Arabia
about it, there is ongoing trouble
here; travellers should exercise
caution, keep abreast of the news
and heed local warnings.

There is something utterly surreal about Shibam's mud skyscrapers – a cubist sculpture sprouting out of the desert. This 2000-year old city on the southern edge of the Rub'al Khali (the Empty Quarter) is one of the most extraordinary and impressive architectural sights in the world, earning it the sobriquet 'Manhattan of the Middle East' or 'Chicago of the Desert'.

Shibam is built on a rock outcrop at the confluence of several wadis (riverbeds), surrounded on three sides by date-palm groves. Its design is a fascinating example of human ingenuity – constraints on space led to the city growing upwards rather than outwards. There are about 500 adobe (mud brick) tower houses, mostly dating from the 16th century, five to eight storeys high and up to 30 m (100 ft) tall, squeezed into an almost perfect quadrangle, only 1 km (0.5 mi) long, surrounded by a huge fortified mud wall.

The buildings themselves are a feat of mud construction, with walls up to 1 m (3 ft) thick at the base, tapering to as little as 30 cm (1 ft) at the top. Exquisite mashrabiyah (wooden fretwork window screens) and carved doors decorate the narrow plain facades. The ground floors are windowless storerooms; the flat, walled roofs are sealed with white limewash to make them watertight.

Shibam was once an important caravan stop and major trade centre for dates, textiles and frankincense. Today, although solely reliant on tourism and UNESCO World Heritage funding for economic survival, Shibam has so far avoided turning into just a 'show town'. The dusty streets, too narrow for traffic, have a relaxed, lived-in atmosphere; in the main square old men sit in the teashop smoking their *sheesh* (waterpipe) while children play. You get the feeling you are in a truly remarkable place – a step back in time to another world.

# Dubai City

Dubai, in the Arabian Peninsula, is the second largest developing city in the world after Shanghai, with 800 new residents a day – a cultural melting pot of over 70 nationalities. Dubai was a pearl trading centre until the 1930s, when it went into decline until the discovery of oil in the 1960s led to a sudden resurgence. Today, less than 3 per cent of Dubai's revenue comes from oil; most of it derives from the fact that it is a tax haven. The city has become a byword for luxury living – a base for international businesses, and a hide-away for celebrities, rock stars, and shadowy millionaires, who come for an epicurean lifestyle in a wonderful setting of sandy beaches and desert landscapes.

Dubai City is a delightful playground for the western tourist, providing every conceivable form of leisure activity. Palm Islands is the latest city project, an ambitious development expected to be completed in 2007 – three man-made islands, each in the shape of a palm tree with a trunk, crown and fronds, all enclosed by a crescent breakwater, with luxury hotels, private mansions, restaurants, entertainments and diving sites. This massive undertaking can be seen from space.

There is an attractive 'Old Quarter', Bastakia, reached by *abra* (water taxi) – an area of narrow lanes with a distinctly Arabian Nights charm. The late 19th century ornate, court-yarded houses were originally the homes of Persian pearl and textile dealers. In contrast, the Burj Dubai on Sheikh Zayed Road, due for completion in 2008, is a gleaming post-modern tower set in an artificial lake. It will be the tallest building in the world.

Dubai has breathtaking modern architecture, beautiful beaches, and a sophisticated entertainment industry. The city revels unashamedly in an air of conspicuous consumption – a triumph for consumer capitalism.

**POPULATION:**
1,492,000 (2006)
**WHEN TO GO:**
For the annual Shopping Festival, mid-January to mid-February, when 3 million people come to take advantage of discounts.
**DON'T MISS:**
The Burj-al Arab – an architectural masterpiece, particularly stunning when lit up at night, containing a luxury hotel and restaurants.
Jumeirah Mosque.
The Courtyard – a unique glass and steel building, combining building styles from all over the world, which houses art galleries and studios.
Deira Souks – Spice and gold markets.
Majlis Ghorfat Um-al Sheef – magnificent, restored sheik's residence.
Wild Wadi Water Park – for fantastic family entertainment.
**YOU SHOULD KNOW:**
Dubai has a hot and sometimes humid climate with many months recording temperatures of over 40°C (104°F).

*The Al Jahiliya district*

# ASIA

# Almaty

Almaty's rather rural-sounding name means 'apple rich' – after the renowned quality and variety of the region's apples. The reality, however, is rather different. Almaty is the commercial and cultural hotspot of Central Asia, ready to make its mark on the tourist map.

In 1911, a catastrophic earthquake flattened the city. Only the Svyato Voznesenskiy (Zenkov) Cathedral stayed standing. This 54 m (180ft) high edifice is one of the most extraordinary wooden buildings in the world – it was made entirely without nails! It stands, gaudily painted like a giant dolls' house and surrounded by roses, in the 28 Panfilov Heroes Memorial Park in the city centre.

The main Zelyoni Bazaar is more than just a market; it is a cultural hotchpotch of produce and people from all over Central Asia. Artists display their work in Zhybek Zholy (Silk Road), known locally as Arbat. For a superb view of the city and mountains, take the cable car up to Kok-tobe (Blue Hill), or walk up past the marijuana fields. Look out for Hotel Kazakhstan, a 102 m (335 ft) high modernist tower, the tallest building in the city, and the Central Mosque, built in 1999, a wonderfully elegant marble building with a huge blue dome.

The traffic is terrible – ageing cars rattle past in a cloud of exhaust fumes. But change is happening fast and things are improving all the time. Almaty is a city of pride, ingenuity and ambition, with a vibrant Asian arts and fusion music scene and a cosmopolitan population, poised to play its part on the international stage.

*Zenkov Cathedral is built entirely of wood and without any nails or screws.*

# Osh

The Fergana valley in the Tien Shan Mountains is the most fertile and densely populated region of Central Asia. Here, close to the Uzbek border, is the city of Osh – a modern town with a history going back at least 2,500 years. For hundreds of years it was a major intersection on the ancient trade route between China and the West, and a flourishing silk production centre.

The city centre is dominated by a 200 m (660 ft) hillock, the Takht-i-Suleyman, a 10th century Muslim shrine. At the top is a small 15th century mosque built by Babur – the founder of India's Mughul Dynasty. The shrine is especially revered by childless women, who come here to pray for fertility, and the mountain is dotted with colourful prayer rags, tied to trees and bushes – a practice common all over the East. For the people of this region, the Takht-i-Suleyman is the holiest Muslim place after Mecca and Medina.

Next to the bazaar is the Shahid Tepa – the largest mosque in Kyrgyzstan, originally built of wood in 1908. It has recently been renovated, with Saudi Arabian backing, to hold a congregation of 5,000.

And then there is the bazaar itself – the heart of Osh. The Jayma Bazaar is renowned as the largest, liveliest and most colourful open-air market in the whole of Central Asia. It sells everything under the sun from spices and honey to bicycle parts and cloth. The sight of Uzbek dealers – recognizable by their tyubeteykas (traditional skullcaps) – waving wads of notes, peasant women in bold floral-print dresses picking over the vegetables, street vendors frenetically haggling and shouting, makes you forget for a moment that you are in one of the poorest places in Central Asia. This is, after all, still a city of traders.

**POPULATION:**
235,000 (2003)
**WHEN TO GO:**
April to early June, or October – when the harvest is gathered and the mountains look particularly beautiful.
**DON'T MISS:**
The Great Silk Road Museum.
Statue of Kurmanjan Datka, 'Queen of the South' – an incredible Kyrgyz woman who led the opposition to Russian expansion in the 19th century.
Statue of Lenin – one of the few remaining in Central Asia.
The 16th century Rabat Abdul Khan Mosque.
**YOU SHOULD KNOW:**
Kyrgyzstan is generally a safe and hospitable country but it is extremely poor and there are ethnic tensions between the Kyrgyz and Uzbek communities which can erupt into violence; the border with Uzbekistan is in dispute and is very close by.

*Takht-i-Suleyman*

# Bishkek

Originally, Bishkek was a minor caravan stop on the Silk Road. By the end of the 19th century, the Russians had established a garrison here and dispatched peasants to settle the land. Kyrgyzstan was fully integrated into the USSR in 1926, and the name of Bishkek was changed to Frunze. On gaining independence in 1991, the city reverted to its old Kyrgyz name.

It is unlikely that the capital of Kyrgyzstan will be your top priority when travelling in this heartbreakingly beautiful country but inevitably it will be on your itinerary – Bishkek is unavoidable if you want to get anywhere else. If you bear in mind that you are in a country whose heritage lies in its pastoral nomadic culture and do not make unrealistic comparisons to western cities, you will be pleasantly rewarded, and even surprised by how much you enjoy it.

Do not expect to be inspired by the city's architecture. It is typically Soviet – from the imposing, marble faced, public buildings to the utilitarian apartment blocks surrounding interior courtyards, and rows of small houses all laid out on a rigid grid system. However, there are other attractions: Bishkek is very green (over 40 per cent of its area, with more trees than any other Central Asian city); two rivers run through it; all around you there are spectacular views of the snow-capped Tien Shan Mountains – a constant reminder that you are in no ordinary place.

In the summer, especially, strolling under the shady trees, Bishkek has an allure about it, a youthful, optimistic atmosphere, with its parks and markets, small teashops and welcoming restaurants. The people are friendly, if frankly curious, with a hospitable charm that derives from the Kyrgyz nomadic tradition.

**POPULATION:**
900,000 (2005)
**WHEN TO GO:**
The surrounding region is at its most beautiful in the autumn but good climate at any time of year.
**DON'T MISS:**
State Historical Museum – on Ala-too Square.
Museum of Fine Arts – good place to learn more about Kyrgyz folk art, and nomadic life.
The Statue of Manas, an epic folk hero.
Ala Archa National Park – breathtaking mountain scenery, glaciers and wildlife, a stone's throw from the city (half hour drive).
Burana Tower and Balbals – open air Museum of History and ancient stone sculptures, 80 km (50 mi) from Bishkek.
Lake Issyk-kul – 3 to 4 hours drive largest mountain lake in Asia and second largest in the world.
**YOU SHOULD KNOW:**
Kyrgyzstan is a poor country and Bishkek is not a particularly safe city at night, especially in the side streets around Ala-too – as a westerner you stand out a mile and are rich pickings.

*Burana Tower – an 11th century minaret*

# Samarkand

Capturing the town on his way to India, Alexander the Great described Samarkand as 'more beautiful than he had imagined'. In the fourteenth century, Timur Gurkani made the city the capital of his empire which stretched from India to Turkey. He turned the city into a magnificent centre of mosques and mausoleums, which was spoken of as 'the precious pearl of the world'. Today Samarkand is the third largest city in Uzbekistan, and is home to a dazzling array of architecture and culture representing its long and sometimes violent history.

Samarkand lies in a strategic position in the Zarafshan Valley on the ancient Silk Road, which helps to explain its turbulent past and mixture of cultures. The city has been won and lost by a great number of different powers over the centuries, including the Persians, Alexander the Great, the Arabs, Genghis Khan, Timur Gurkani (Tamerlane the Great), the Turks and the Russians. This led to a unique culture with Persian, Indian and Mongolian influences, a little of the West and the East.

Built after the death of Timur's grandson Muhammad-Sultan in 1403, the Gur-e Amir became the family mausoleum of the Timurid Dynasty. The fantastic blue ribbed dome dominates the skyline of central Samarkand. Inside, the broken, gigantic slab of jade commemorating the mighty Timur is said to be the largest jade stone in the world. One of the most beautiful of Samarkand's sights, Shah-i-Zinda (the tomb of the living king) houses the shrine of Prophet Muhammad's cousin, Qusam ibn Abbas, who brought Islam to the region. This is one of the oldest structures in Samarkand and a popular pilgrimage site.

Other notable sights include the Registan, a huge square in the centre of the city, surrounded on three sides by three universities: the medieval Ulugh Beg, the Sherdar and the Tilla Kari Madrasahs. Decorated inside and out with glazed bricks, intricate blue and turquoise mosaics and carved marble, these are perhaps the finest Islamic monuments in the world.

The Bibi Khanum Mosque is another architectural gem. It is one of the largest and most grandiose buildings in Samarkand, and its dome is the largest in the Muslim world. Most of the building collapsed in an earthquake in 1897 but it has now been restored by the Russian Government.

**POPULATION**:
412,000 (2005)
**WHEN TO GO**:
April to June, or September to October.
**DON'T MISS**:
The Gur-e Amir.
Shah-i-Zinda.
The madrasahs of Ulugh Beg, Sherdar and Tilla Kari.
The Bibi Khanum Mosque.
**YOU SHOULD KNOW**:
This is one of the oldest and most important cities of Asia.

*The Tilla Kari Madrasah in Registan Square*

# Bukhara

**POPULATION:**
268,000 (2002)
**WHEN TO GO:**
March to April and September to October.
**DON'T MISS:**
Climbing up the Kalyan Minaret or 'Tower of Death'.
Puppet Show at the Lyabi-Hauz.
The Four Minarets 'Char Minar'.
Mausoleum of Ismail Samani – a masterpiece of 9th century architecture.
Registan Square and Bolo-Khauz madrassah.
The 18th century Djami Mosque.
Taq-i-Sarrafan bazaar.
**YOU SHOULD KNOW:**
The most famous Persian carpet design – known as 'Bukhara' – did not originate here. Travellers first came across these carpets in the market place and mistakenly thought they were made locally.

Historically the holiest city of Central Asia, Bukhara is the fifth largest city in Uzbekistan, populated mainly by Tajiks. If you only go to one place on the Silk Road, it has to be the top of the Kalyan Minaret (Tower of Death) to gaze down on this mesmerizing city of subdued desert hues and sublime blue domes.

Bukhara has perhaps the most romantic past of any city of Central Asia. Originally founded in 500 BC, conquered by Alexander the Great, destroyed by Ghengis Khan, rebuilt by Tamerlane, and admired by Marco Polo, it became the intellectual and cultural heart of the Silk Road. Bukhara produced many of the world's greatest historians, scientists, writers and thinkers, including the great mystic Bahautdin Nakshbandi – the founder of the esoteric Sufi philosophy. The city also has a history of violence – during the 19th century 'Great Game' between Russia and Britain, Colonel Stoddart and Captain Conolly were forced to dig their own graves at the foot of the massive walls of the Ark Citadel before being executed as spies of the British Empire in 1842.

The winding mud streets of Bukhara were built around open pools which provided the water supply for both drinking and public washing. These were a terrible health hazard and most of them were filled in during the Soviet era. But Lyab-i Hauz has survived, a wonderfully romantic spot surrounded by mulberry trees, with a *khanaka* (Sufi lodging house), and madrassahs (schools) at either end. Nearby is the 14th century Kukeldash madrassah – the largest Islamic centre of learning in Central Asia.

This city of browns and blues, with its dazzling markets and mosaics, has an unhurried, dreamy atmosphere about it; the new has been assimilated into the old with the relaxed ease of a city confident of its place in history.

*The Kalyan Mosque*

# Khiva

Khiva is a perfectly preserved historic oasis city near the Karakum desert in the region of Khorezm. It was an important desert junction on the Silk Road, and became infamous in the 19th century as a den of iniquity – a city of slave traders, thieves and scoundrels. However, its history and influence go back to an era long before the Silk Road was established. Legend has it that it was the birthplace of Zarathustra (Zoroaster) the founder of the Zoroastrian religion. Whether true or not, Zoroastrianism certainly flourished here for almost thirteen hundred years from the 4th century BC, profoundly influencing the development of Judaism, Christianity, and Islam, and even Buddhism.

The artists and architects of Khiva were renowned for their skill and aesthetic sense; the composition of the buildings as well as the delicate woodcarving and ornamentation is stunning. The historic heart of the city, Ichan-Qala, is surrounded by the 10 m (30 ft) wall of the Kunya-Ark Citadel, enclosing narrow streets of flat-roofed clay houses with mosques, palaces, and more minarets than anywhere else in Central Asia, all complementing each other to make a harmonious whole.

The symbol of Khiva is the amazing 44-m (145-ft) high Islam Khodja Minaret, ringed with exquisitely traced white, turquoise and blue bands alternating with clay. The Djuma Mosque has beautiful realist artwork and 218 ornately carved wooden columns of different periods dating back to the 10th century. But perhaps the most remarkable edifice in a city full of incredible architecture is the Kalta-minor – an incomplete ceramic tower of intricately decorated glazed turquoise, blue and white that is truly sublime

Khiva is a unique example of a pre-Soviet Central Asian city in its entirety – an open-air museum.

**POPULATION:**
52,000 (2004)
**WHEN TO GO:**
Continental climate with hot summers and cold winters. Spring or autumn are probably the pleasantest.
**DON'T MISS:**
Piurulla-bai Palace.
Tosh-Kohvli Palace – preserved intact and complete with gates and harem.
Dishan-Kala hospital – an eclectic piece of early 20th century architecture, combining European and local styles.
Roghbonli Mosque – a beautifully decorated neighbourhood mosque.
Pahlavon Mahmud Mausoleum.
Amin Khan Madrassah – the largest educational institution in Khiva.
**YOU SHOULD KNOW:**
Khiva was the first site in Uzbekistan to be designated a UNESCO World Heritage Site, in 1990. Even though it is an amazing place, it has a strangely un-lived in atmosphere that is mildly disconcerting.

*Kalta-minor tower*

# Tashkent

At first, you may be disappointed that Tashkent is not the Arabian Nights fantasia that its name suggests. But once you have got over the initial shock of the Soviet architecture, you realize that there is much more to this city than meets the eye, with plenty of its heritage still intact at the same time as being the cosmopolitan capital of 21st century Uzbekistan.

Tashkent, like all the Silk Road cities, has a romantic and turbulent history. From the time of the 8th century Arab occupation, it grew to be an important trade and cultural centre. The city was flattened by Ghengis Khan and his Mongol hordes but its fortunes revived under Tamerlane (Timur) and it went on to become the richest city in Central Asia. In the 19th century, it fell into the hands of Tsarist Russia, and a European quarter was built to the east of the old city. However, almost the whole city was destroyed either in the 1917 Russian Revolution or in the devastating earthquake that shook the entire region in 1966.

Today the remnants of the eski shakhar (old town) in the west of the city are well worth seeing – a maze of mud brick houses with mosques and madrassahs (schools) that have been spared by Soviet planners. Khasret Imam is a 16th century square with the Bharak khan madrassah, the Kaffal Shashi mausoleum and two mosques. The Eski Juva bazaar at the 9th century Chorsu (crossroads) is a huge, colourful market that has been operating from the same site for 2,000 years. The 15th century Djammi Mosque and 16th century Kukeldash madrassah are nearby.

The government has poured money into Tashkent's infrastructure and it is an impressive place to visit, with tree-lined streets, pleasant parks and fountains, and excellent public transport.

*The Friday Mosque in Chorsu Square*

# Shakhrisyabz

On 9 April 1336, Timur (Tamerlane) – one of the world's greatest warlords – was born near the town of Kesh, 100 km (60 mi) from Samarkand. He progressed from sheep rustling to founding an empire that survived for 500 years and which, at its height, stretched from southwest Turkey through the whole of Central Asia into India and China. He made Samarkand his capital, but did not forget Kesh. He commissioned the building of the vast white palace Ak-Saray – a masterpiece of design that took 25 years to build – and renamed the town 'Shakhrisyabz' or 'Green City'.

Much of the town was destroyed by Abdullah Khan, Emir of Bukhara, in the 17th century, but many historic sites remain, including the dazzling blue, white and gold mosaic portal of the Ak-Saray Palace. Over the entrance are the words: 'If you doubt our power, look at our buildings'.

The mausoleum that Timur erected for two of his sons who pre-deceased him is an exquisite example of 14th century architecture. And there is the mausoleum he prepared for himself, although he ended up buried in Samarkand.

Shakrisyabz is off the beaten track, and the locals get on with their day-to-day lives unassumingly amid their legendary history. One can only hope that its recently acquired World Heritage status will help the people of Shakrisyabz economically without destroying the town's character.

# Kabul

**POPULATION:**
2,994,000 (2005)
**WHEN TO GO:**
Avoid the boiling summer or freezing winter.
**DON'T MISS:**
Id Gah Mosque.
Pul-e Khishti Mosque.
Shah-do-Shamshira Mosque.
Kabul Museum – much of its collection has been lost or looted but it is gradually being restored and the building itself is worth seeing.
The magnificent view from TV Tower Hill.
Darul-Aman Palace.
The tomb of Nadir Shah.
**YOU SHOULD KNOW:**
Kabul is desperately poor and there are an estimated 60,000 street children living in terrible conditions.

Kabul is recovering from a tragedy – a decade of civil war and such extreme violence that the city's whole infrastructure was destroyed, 50,000 people died and thousands more fled for their lives.

This great city is over 3,000 years old. It was once the capital of Babur's Mughal Empire, and became the capital of modern Afghanistan in 1776. Kabul lies in the centre of Afghanistan, high on the Afghan plain at 1,800m (5,900 ft) – one of the highest capital cities in the world – with incredible views of the ever-changing colours of the mountains.

In the 1970s, Kabul was one of the most romantic destinations in the world. Western travellers made a beeline for the cheap hotels, teashops and bazaars of Chicken Street to revel in the exotic sights, sounds and smells of the east. The city was renowned for its hedonism, cheap living and bazaars as well as its welcoming hospitality and the kindness of Afghans to strangers.

Afghanis have a long tradition as a nation of bird fanciers. The Ka-Farushi bird market, in a narrow dusty lane near the Kabul River, is humming with activity. The ramshackle row of shops is stuffed with cages of fighting birds, canaries, songbirds and pigeons; money is changing hands, wagers are being laid, the city is returning to normality.

Another sign of hope lies in the restoration of the Bagh-e Babur (Babur's Garden). The walls around Babur's grave have been rebuilt, the terraces restored and hundreds of apricot, fig, mulberry and nut trees have been planted. The miniature white marble mosque built by Shah Jahan may be small but is as beautiful a piece of architecture as the Taj Mahal. The garden has come to symbolize the aspirations and pride of the Afghani people and is a monument to the future as much as it is a memorial to the past.

*The white marble mosque in Babur's Garden, built by Shah Jahan*

# Herat

Described by Herodotus as 'the breadbasket of Central Asia', Herat lies in the heart of a grape growing region in western Afghanistan. It is renowned for its architecture, bazaars, and gardens as well as its intellectual and artistic culture and Persian Sufi (Islamic mystical) religious tradition.

During its long history as a major city on the Silk Road, Herat changed hands as often as Central Asian Empires rose and fell but invariably retained its influential position as the centre of learning, culture and trade. It is miraculous that so much of the city's heritage is intact after the recent devastation inflicted on it – a horrendous six-year Taliban orgy of violence and destruction, which only ended in 2001, when the central government re-established control.

The massive battlements of the 13th century Arg (citadel) and the 800-year-old Masjid-i-Jamei (Friday Mosque) dominate the Old City. The Mosque is one of Afghanistan's most cherished architectural treasures, renowned for the colours and patterns of its intricate mosaic work. Master craftsmen have been engaged in a continual process of restoration since 1943 when the old tile workshop was re-opened specifically for the purpose.

Another incredible monument is the 15th century Gazargah, on a hill 5 km (3 mi) outside the city – a memorial to the 11th century Sufi master, Abdullah Ansari, whose blue marble tomb is inscribed with his verses. The shrine is maintained by the Sufi dervishes (holy men) who live there.

Four roads, each lined with bazaar shops, meet at Chahr Suq, the central square. The bazaars are humming, the traditional Herati glassblowers are plying their trade, and the brightly coloured and tasselled *gharries* (horse-drawn taxis) are out on the streets. The Heratis, renowned for their indomitable spirit, are on their way back to prosperity.

**POPULATION**:
349,000 (2006)
**WHEN TO GO:**
At its most beautiful in the early spring.
**DON'T MISS:**
The 15th century Gohar Shad Musalla (prayer ground of mosque, madrassa and mausoleum) – only tantalizing fragments survive but 9,000 trees have been planted round it and repairs are being carried out to restore at least some of it to its former glory.
Namakdan Pavilion – 17th century twelve-sided pavilion with views over Herat.
Windmill by the tomb of Jami. The windmills here are of a 7th century design, pre-dating windmills of Europe and China.
The remains of the Yu Aw Synagogue in the Momanda district, which used to be the Jewish quarter.
Kherqa Mubarak Mosque.
**YOU SHOULD KNOW:**
During the Taliban rule 1995-2001, an underground network of artists and writers set up the 'Golden Needle Ladies Sewing Classes' where, under the guise of giving needlework lessons, they taught literature to young Herati women. Some 29,000 girls received a secret education, with both teachers and students risking death. Today Herat is considered safe but you should obtain up-to-date information before travelling.

*The Masjid-i-Jame (Friday Mosque)*

*The Mausoleum of Ahmad Shah*

# Kandahar

**POPULATION:**
450,000 (2006)
**WHEN TO GO:**
Avoid July and August, when even the locals find it unbearably hot.
**DON'T MISS:**
Mosque of the Hair of Muhammad – early 19th century.
Da Shahidan Chowk, off the Shah bazaar – a busy square, colourful part of Kandahari street life.
Sher Surkh – a charming village 5 km (3 mi) to the south
The Chilzina – a chamber cut out of rock in the cliff, ascended in 40 steps, that forms the westernmost defence of the city.
Shrine of Mir Wais Khan, the chieftain who declared Kandahar independent from the Persians in 1709.
Shrine of Baba Wali – terraces shaded by pomegranate trees overlooking the valley.
**YOU SHOULD KNOW:**
At the time of writing, travel in the south of Afghanistan is fraught with danger and Kandahar is occupied by Canadian peacekeeping forces.

Archaeological evidence suggests that Kandahar is among the earliest human settlements in the world, with remains 10,000 years old. Its recorded history goes back to 330 BC when Alexander the Great founded a city called Alexandria in this strategic location that links India with the Middle East. It became the home city of the Durrani Pashtuns, one of whose leaders, Ahmad Shah Durrani, founded Afghanistan, making Kandahar his capital in 1748.

Today Kandahar is still a tribal city in the heart of warlord territory, a thrilling but dangerous place. It is a major trading centre for wool, textiles, grapes and pomegranates – and opium. It is renowned for its glittering bazaars, piled high with the silks, mirror work, ornamented birdcages, and silver-wired and beaded chillim pipe stems for which the city is famous.

The old part of the city is laid out much as it was when Ahmad Shah Durrani drew up his original plan, probably modelled on Herat – a rectangle with four main bazaar streets meeting at a central square, Chahr Suq – although little remains of the city wall or the Arg (citadel). Unsurprisingly, the most important monument is the Mausoleum of Ahmad Shah, a graceful octagonal building of plain brick decorated with blue green and yellow tiled niches, topped by tall minarets connected by a floral balustrade. The relatively spare exterior contrasts with the sumptuously rich tiled, painted and gilded colours inside. Next to the mausoleum is Da Kherqa Sherif Ziarat – 'the Shrine of the Cloak of the Prophet Muhammad' – one of the holiest places in Afghanistan. It has exquisite tile work and an incredible door inlaid with lapis lazuli, silver and travertine.

Kandahar was the birthplace of the Taliban movement and the last city to fall in 2001.

# Jalalabad

The site of Jalalabad in eastern Afghanistan has been occupied since the 2nd century BC. It lies in an oasis on the south side of the Kabul River in a region of overwhelming stark beauty – the savage mountain badlands of the tribal area where Osama bin Laden is thought to have been based. Jalalabad is the final city on the road from Central Asia before it crosses the drug-smugglers territory of the Khyber Pass into the Indian subcontinent. In AD 630 Xuan Zang, a famous Chinese Buddhist monk, arrived here thinking he had reached India.

The present city was built in 1570 by Jalal-uddin Muhammad Akbar, the third ruler of the Mughal Empire. The city has a long history as a royal winter retreat where the wealthy built their two- or three-storeyed residences along broad avenues lined with peepul trees. In the 1970s it became a popular tourist resort among western travellers making their way to India, well known for its relaxed atmosphere and traditional hospitality.

The centre of the city is small – a main bazaar road with narrow lanes leading off it. Here carpets are strewn all over the street and gaudily painted buses, garlanded with tassels and baubles, full of heavily burqaed women, turbaned Pushtu tribesmen, sacks, bags, boxes and birdcages drop off their passengers among the donkey carts and motor-rickshaws in a melée of dust and noise.

In the 1990s Jalalabad became a Taliban stronghold. Tragically they destroyed or desecrated most of the 23,000 Greco-Buddhist sculptures for which Jalalabad was renowned. Fortunately the ancient manuscripts discovered here in a clay pot – the oldest surviving Indian manuscripts of any kind – were safely ensconced in the British Museum.

Jalalabad is a city on the mend, in the process of restoring itself to the atmospheric frontier town it was before the Taliban.

**POPULATION**:
96,000 (2002)
**WHEN TO GO**:
April, when the scent of orange blossom fills the air and writers gather to hold the Mushaira annual poetry reading festival.
**DON'T MISS**:
The Seraj-ul-Emorat – a beautiful palace and gardens in the centre of the city.
Mausoleum of Amir Habibullah – set in a grove of orange trees.
Hadda 11 km (7 mi) – archaeological site reduced to ruins by the Taliban but still a historical curiosity, where Osama bin Laden housed his wives and children in tents.
**YOU SHOULD KNOW**:
At the time of writing this part of Afghanistan was extremely dangerous. Check the security situation before travelling.

*The Great Blue Mosque*

# Mazar-i-Sharif

The 'Tomb of the Exalted One', Mazar-i-Sharif, came into being in the 12th century when an influential local mullah declared that he had received a divine revelation that Ali, the fourth Caliph of Islam, was buried here, 20 km (12 mi) away from the important ancient city of Balkh. The Sultan immediately ordered a shrine to be built despite the fact that Ali was already buried the other side of Persia, in Najaf, Iraq.

In the 1870s, Balkh was stricken with malaria and the city was abandoned. People flocked to nearby Mazar and a city began to grow around the shrine. Today it is Afghanistan's fourth largest city, renowned for the historical and archaeological sites in nearby Balkh. It is a bustling Central Asian town with wide straight roads and busy markets where modernity and tradition collide and you are just as likely to be run over by a camel or donkey cart as a truck. The city is the centre of Afghanistan's carpet weaving industry and a trading centre for lambskins, cottons and silks and as well as more nefarious products – the *charas* (hashish) of the region is renowned for its exceptional quality.

The shrine of Hazrat Ali, the monumental Great Blue Mosque, dominates the centre of the city. It is the holiest place in Afghanistan – a beautifully preserved, exquisite mosaic edifice of predominately lapis blues and golds in Herati tiling. Thousands of white pigeons inhabit the courtyard. Tradition has it that one in seven is a spirit and that any grey pigeons will turn white in 40 days because of the sanctity of the surroundings.

Mazar-i-Sharif was one of the last holdouts against the Taliban. There was bitter fighting and both sides committed terrible atrocities. The city finally fell into Taliban hands in 1998 and was liberated in 2001.

# Lahore

This one-time capital of the Mughal and later the Sikh Empire is a city steeped in culture, learning and the arts. Lahore was already renowned as a cultural centre by the 12th century, but really came to prominence in the 16th, when it came to be regarded as the quintessential Mughal city. When the British gained control in 1849, they restored much that had been damaged during Sikh rule and added some fine colonial Gothic architecture including the High Court and University buildings.

Some of the finest surviving Mughal architecture in the world is to be found here, including the World Heritage Site of Lahore Fort, a masterpiece containing mosques and palaces in marbles and mosaics, and the Shalimar Gardens, a classic example of a Mughal terraced garden with channels, waterfalls, and lodges in which to sit and admire the view.

The national monument of Pakistan, Minar-e Pakistan stands in the middle of Iqbal Park – a 60-m (197-ft) tall minaret built on the spot where the Muslim League passed the Lahore Resolution demanding a homeland for the Muslims of India in 1940. Nearby is the magnificent 17th century Badshahi Mosque, a striking building of red stone and white marble, one of the largest mosques in the Indian sub-continent.

Much of the old city wall remains intact and the narrow lanes of the bazaars are a lively scrum of rickshaws, donkey carts and street hawkers. Anarkali is one of the oldest markets in South Asia, and Ichhra Bazaar is in a district of beautiful old *havelis* (Mughal houses).

Lahore lives up to its sobriquets of 'Garden of the Mughals' and the 'heart of Pakistan'. It is one of the most beautiful, atmospheric, and cultured cities of South Asia as well as being a shoppers' paradise.

**POPULATION:**
8,896,000 (2006)
**WHEN TO GO:**
December to February are cold months. From May onwards the city gradually gets hotter until the monsoon breaks, usually at the end of July.
**DON'T MISS:**
Data Durbar – site where Sufi Saint Al Hajweri is buried with a pre-Mughal mosque.
Chauburji – once an extensive garden, now a bustling market.
Lahore Museum – some of the finest Mughal artefacts in the world.
Kim's Gun.
Mausoleums of Jehangir and Noor Jehan.
Hiran Minar – hunting grounds of the Mughal emperors.
**YOU SHOULD KNOW:**
Lahore is the fifth largest city in South Asia with the largest and most prestigious university.

*The striking 17th century Badshahi Mosque*

# Peshawar

**POPULATION:**
3,242,000 (2006)
**WHEN TO GO:**
Peshawar enjoys a benign climate from mid-September to mid-May. The heat in the summer months is unbearable. The fasting month of Ramadan is strictly observed here, so is best avoided.
**DON'T MISS:**
Kotla Mohsin Khan – 16th and 17th century domes and magnificent gateway.
The Sethi houses near Chowk Yagar – wooden-framed, unbaked brick houses several storeys high, with carved heavy wooden doors and ornamental balconies.
Khyber Bazaar – lively market.
Ghor Khuttree – a museum that was once a Buddhist site, then a Mughal caravanserai, a Sikh temple, and a fire station.
Drinking mango milkshakes in Gora Bazaar, Saddar Street.
**YOU SHOULD KNOW:**
Shopkeepers in the bazaars will often invite you to join them for *kawa* (green tea). However hot and thirsty you are it is impolite to accept. It means little more than 'hello'. Only if they ask three times should you say yes (because then it is rude to refuse).

*Ablutions at Mahabat Khan Mosque*

The ancient city of Peshawar stands on a plain at the entrance to the Indian sub-continent below the wild mountains of the Khyber Pass. It was the last bastion of the British Raj before the badlands of Afghanistan, a frontier town with a history that is Buddhist, Mughal, Sikh, British, and above all Pathan (Pashtun). For the surrounding region is entirely Pathan tribal territory. The capital of Pakistan's North West Frontier Province, Peshawar is one of the most beguiling cities in the world – a place of poetry, intrigue, romance and adventure.

The British cantonment is a gracefully faded colonial district of broad streets and bungalows around Saddar Road and the legendary Green's Hotel. The main road leads past the railway station to Bal Hisar Fort, a forbidding Mughal edifice still very much in use, that glowers down over the Old City – a labyrinth of bustling bazaars, where motor-rickshaws plough mercilessly through the motley throng of turbaned tribesmen, veiled women, beggars, street hawkers, students, spies and sweepers. Inscrutable moneychangers sit cross-legged at their stalls along the edge of Chowk Yadgar (Square of Remembrance). To the west is the jewellery bazaar and the Mughal Mohabbat Khan Mosque; to the east, Ghanta Ghar (Cunningham Clock Tower); and to the south, the renowned Qissa Khawanni bazaar (Market of Story Tellers). Here in the maze of narrow streets are scenes of frenetic activity – of copper-beaters and leather-workers, cloth merchants, perfumers, sweetmeat sellers – a glorious confusion of sights and sounds and smells that can fill you with wonder one minute and revulsion the next.

Peshawar is a city of haunting nuances, that has grasped the imagination of writers and poets since time immemorial, and that immerses the traveller in a mystifying and intriguing alien culture.

# Islamabad

In the early days of independence it quickly became clear that Pakistan needed a capital that would reflect the culture, traditions, and aspirations of the whole country. So a site was chosen in the heart of Pakistan, easily accessible from even the remotest areas, in a region with thousands of years of history where there are still plentiful traces of the ancient Indus Valley Civilisation.

Islamabad was designed by Greek architects, planned on a triangular grid in a beautiful natural setting, its apex pointing to the lovely Margalla Hills. It was built only 13 km (8 mi) away from the historic city of Rawalpindi, the national Army Headquarters, and it was envisioned that the cities should run into each other, providing a contrast between ancient and modern.

*The Shah Faisal Mosque*

Islamabad is the greenest city in South Asia with broad tree-lined streets, elegant public buildings and well-organised bazaars. The pavements are shaded by flame trees, jacarandas and hibiscus and there are lovely parks and gardens like the Chattar Bargh, the Rose and Jasmine Garden, and Shakar Parian Hills – a terraced garden with waterfalls and woods from where there are panoramic views. Nearby is the Lok Virsa Museum – a superb collection of folk art and embroideries.

The huge white marble Shah Faisal Mosque, renowned for its architecture and immense size, is the city's major landmark, closely followed by the Saudi-Pak Tower – noted for its almost solid exterior and blue tiling. The National Monument is a striking sculpture made of red granite and marble in the form of an opening flower, each petal representing the provinces of Pakistan.

Originally an administrative city, Islamabad has changed its character in recent years and has become an important financial and business centre with a much livelier atmosphere. It is an outstanding example of a planned city.

**POPULATION:**
1,018,000 (1999)
**WHEN TO GO:**
From October to March when it gradually gets hotter until the monsoon breaks in July or August.
**DON'T MISS:**
Taxila – Buddhist archaeological World Heritage Site 30 km (20 mi) away.
Lal Masjid – the Red Mosque stormed by government troops in July 2007.
Daman-e Koh Park – beautiful views.
Nurpur Village – 4 km (2.5 mi) away has a shrine to a 17th century saint, the Barri Imam (Holy man of the Woods) who lived here for 12 years in a cave.
**YOU SHOULD KNOW:**
Although Islamabad is superficially far more western than anywhere else in Pakistan, it is still important to remember that you are in a Muslim country and should respect the traditions and manners of the inhabitants if you do not want to cause offence.

*The bustling city of Quetta is known for its hospitality and hotch-potch of cultures.*

# Quetta

The 'fruit basket of Pakistan', Quetta is a fascinating tribal city at the meeting point of Pushtu and Baluchi lands. At the time of the Afghan War in 1839, a captain in the British Army described the orchards here as: 'a wild luxuriance of growth such as I have never dreamt of seeing in fruit trees...covered with blossoms which perfume the air'.

The British gained control of Baluchistan in 1876 and established Quetta as an elegant colonial garrison town – popularly known as Little London. A devastating earthquake in 1935 cost 90,000 lives and flattened the city. So this is not a place of historic architecture and ancient heritage; it is famous for the authentic colour of its street life, its atmosphere of adventure, and the warm hospitality of its people.

The city derives its name from *kwata* – the Pushtu word for 'fort'; and Quetta is indeed a natural fort. It sits 1,675 m (5,500 ft) high at the head of the Shal Valley, barricaded on three sides by awe-inspiring mountains of barren copper-red rock. Strategically placed in the borderland by the Bolan Pass – the only way through the impenetrable Toba Kakar Mountains into Afghanistan – and also lying on the overland southern route that connects Iran to the Indian sub-continent, Quetta is a haven for smugglers and tribal fighters. It became a favourite haunt of overland travellers in the 1960s and 70s, known for its hospitality and hotch-potch of cultures – Baluchis in embroidered hats, Pathans striding around under huge turbans, Hazari gypsy women in long floral skirts milling around the colourful bazaars that sell everything from fine Baluchi mirror work to 'diverted' western aid cooking oil.

Quetta is a truly intriguing place – a hotbed of political and criminal activity that welcomes strangers in a surprisingly genuine spirit of openhearted human warmth.

**POPULATION:**
756,000 (2004 estimate)
**WHEN TO GO:**
Extreme winter and summer temperatures. Valley is most beautiful in spring when wild tulips start to flower and fruit trees blossom.
**DON'T MISS:**
Archaeological Museum.
Hanna Lake 10 km (6 mi) – a beautiful mountain lake.
Hazarganji Chiltan National Park – 20 km (12 mi) – dramatic scenery and wildlife.
Sampling the Baluchi cuisine especially *sajji* (spiced leg of lamb roasted on charcoal).
Urak Valley – beautiful spot with fruit trees 21 km (13 mi) from Quetta.
**YOU SHOULD KNOW:**
The railway station at Quetta is the highest in Asia. At the time of writing Quetta is thought to be a hotspot for Taliban activity.

# Karachi

It is hard to believe that less than 200 years ago this sprawling megacity was an inconsequential fishing village known as Kolachi. The British saw its potential as an international port and from first acquiring it in 1843 they rapidly built it up so that by 1876 it had become the thriving city of Karachi with paved streets, municipal buildings, mosques and a magnificent dockside, which today are beautiful examples of period colonial architecture. With the end of the Raj and Partition in 1947, Karachi was made the capital of Pakistan. It was replaced by Rawalpindi in 1958, when it went into a period of decline.

However, in the 21st century Karachi has come into its own again as the commercial and technological hub of Pakistan with its share of multi-millionaires and a burgeoning arts scene with the National Academy of Performing Arts, the annual Music Festival and the Kara Film Festival.

When you are fed up with shopping in Saddar, or the Empress Market, or the innumerable bazaars that line the streets, and have admired the Quaid-e Azam Mausoleum and the Masjid-e Tooba – the largest single-domed mosque in the world – and had your fill of colonial architecture, within minutes you can be riding a camel on the beach at Clifton, admiring the world's second largest fountain at Seaview, enjoying a meal in one of the hip restaurants at Boat Basin, or just sitting on the scarily high cliff tops gazing out over the sparkling Arabian Sea.

Karachi is a multicultural city with a unique character; a mixture of Western, South Asian and Middle Eastern influences give it an extraordinarily vibrant ambience. It is known locally as 'City of Lights' because of its liveliness. Its very vastness is a thrill in itself, and it is potentially a wonderful tourist destination.

*The Chaukundi Tombs*

**POPULATION:**
18 million (2007 estimate)
**WHEN TO GO:**
November to February are the pleasantest months but even in high summer the sea breezes help to relieve the worst of the heat.
**DON'T MISS:**
Mohatta Palace – a museum that was originally a magnificent private summer residence.
Frere Hall – a lovely example of British colonial architecture.
Moenjodaro and the Chaukundi Tombs – amazing ancient remains from the Indus Valley Civilization.
Holy Trinity Cathedral and St Andrew's Church.
Towers of Silence.
Zainab Market – for embroideries and carpets.
**YOU SHOULD KNOW:**
Although it has a larger middle class than any other city in Pakistan, there is still a distressing disparity between rich and poor here which inevitably causes tensions.

# Mumbai

*Taxi cabs outside Victoria Station*

This megalopolitan monster – India's largest city – was originally an island archipelago, inhabited by fishermen and Buddhist monks. The islands were acquired by the Portuguese who gave them to Charles II as a dowry for marrying Catherine de Braganza. In 1668, the Crown offered the lease to the British East India Company for a mere $10 per annum. They rapidly established their west coast headquarters here, carried out massive land reclamation and building projects, and transformed seven muddy islands into the colonial city of Bombay, the most important port on the Arabian Sea. Since then the city (which changed its name to Mumbai in 1995) has never stopped growing.

Traditionally, the first thing a visitor to Mumbai is shown is the Gateway of India, an Indo-Saracenic monument on the waterfront. The last British troops left India via this gateway in 1948 in a symbolic gesture of renunciation of this great city that had been the trading hub of their Empire. Overlooking it is another of the city's most famous icons, the magnificent Taj Mahal Palace Hotel, built in

1903 by the 'father of Indian industry', Jamsetji Tata, after he had been refused entry to a hotel because he was a 'native'.

Mumbai is the most westernised, cosmopolitan and frenetic city in India. Day and night, its streets teem with people of all complexions, cultures and creeds. It is a city of contradictions and extremes, where phenomenal wealth rubs shoulders with heart-wrenching poverty. Migrants come from all over Asia, lured by dreams of Bollywood – the largest film industry in the world – and the promise of material success. People continue to flock to this 'city of gold', because whatever else about Mumbai, one thing is certain – it is a city of chance, where both dreams and nightmares are spun into reality.

# Ayodhya

Ayodhya is a city of pilgrimage on the banks of the River Sarayu, the supposed birthplace of three religious figures – Sri Rama, Rishabhadeva (the founding father of the Jain religion) and, according to some believers, Buddha himself. In classical times it was one of the largest and most venerated places in India, 'a city built by gods and as prosperous as paradise itself'. Under the Mughal Empire it lost its commercial influence to Lucknow, and has never regained it.

However, Ayodhya has never lost its place in the Indian national psyche. It is one of the seven holiest cities – of enormous historic and religious significance to Hindus, Jains, Buddhists and Muslims alike. This small rustic city, full of ancient temples, attracts hordes of pilgrims throughout the year.

There are said to be 7,000 temples here, at least 100 of which are of outstanding importance. The main place of worship is the ancient citadel of Ramkot, an incredibly impressive building overlooking the city. It is visited all year round but especially at the festival of Ram Navami in March or April. The Hanuman Garhi in the town centre is as famous for its architecture as its religious significance – a massive fort-like structure with circular towers, approached by 76 steps. Legend has it that Hanuman the monkey god lived here in a cave. The Nageshwarnath Temple, said to have been established by Kush, the son of Rama, is an ornate white building that stands tall among the other temples. Among several lovely temples at the Gupta Ghat is the Chakra Harji Vishnu, where there is an imprint of Sri Rama's feet.

There are also ancient Buddhist sites and Jain temples and shrines scattered throughout the city. The latter are instantly recognizable by their wonderful beehive domes.

**POPULATION:**
75,000 (2001)
**WHEN TO GO:**
October to March.
**DON'T MISS:**
Swarg Dwar – where Lord Rama is said to have been cremated.
The Kanak Bhawan or Sone-ke-Ghar – images of Sri Rama and Sita wearing gold crowns.
Treta-ke-Thakur – 18th century temple built at the same time as the adjoining ghats (steps to the river).
Rishabhadeo Jain temple.
Lakshman Ghat.
Kala Ram temple.
**YOU SHOULD KNOW:**
There used to be a 15th century mosque, the Babhri Majid, torn down by Hindu religious zealots in 1992 and replaced with the Rama Janmabhumi on the grounds that the mosque had been built over a shrine marking Rama's birthplace. The destruction instigated some of India's worst religious riots, with 2,000 deaths, and was considered the most serious threat to India's identity as a secular nation since independence in 1947. There are plans to build a large temple, which is causing continuing religious clashes. The matter is now in the hands of the courts.

*Pomegranates on sale near the Charminar*

# Hyderabad

This cosmopolitan city, the capital of the state of Andhra Pradesh, is renowned for its rich history and superb architecture as well as its unique quality of life. Hyderabad is dotted with mosques, forts, palaces, tombs and temples, and on every street corner there are *irani chai* houses, where people sit for hours watching the world go by.

A Muslim ruler, Muhammad Quli Qutb Shah founded Hyderabad on the southern side of the River Musi in 1586. He employed Persian architects to build him a city that would be a recreation of Paradise. The central monument is the Charminar, a triumphal arch that Muhammad Quli had built in honour of his adored Hindu wife. It is a subtle mix of Islamic and South Indian architecture that embodies the culture of the city and stands as its icon. Nearby is the Makkah Masjid – the second largest mosque in India, which took 78 years to build. Its huge pink granite colonnades are each carved from single blocks of stone. On a hilltop overlooking the city is the beautiful Birla Mandir – a marble Hindu temple.

A new Dynasty was started by Asaf Jah in 1724. He entitled himself "Nizam" (hereditary governor) and the city expanded to become capital of the largest princely state in India. To the south of the city is the 19th century Italianate Falaknuma Palace, a stunning memorial to the Nizams' power. Their princely era finally ended in 1948 when Hyderabad was incorporated into the rest of India.

Better known as "Cyberabad" for its thriving information technology industry, Hyderabad today is one of the most developed as well one of the most interesting cities in India. It is a 21st century city with its own unique heritage – a fascinating fusion of Islamic and ancient Southern Indian cultures.

**POPULATION:**
6,112,000 (2006)
**WHEN TO GO:**
November to February.
**DON'T MISS:**
Chowmahalla Palace – seat of the Nizam, with a beautiful garden.
Saalar Jung Museum – with a huge collection of artefacts; the largest one-man collection of antiques in the world.
The world's longest wardrobe, built on two levels, in the Purana Haveli – official residence of the Nizam.
The sound and light show at Golconda Fort – one of the most magnificent fortress complexes in India, with a 10-km (6-mi) long outer wall and 87 bastions 11 km (7 mi) away.
**YOU SHOULD KNOW:**
The Koh-I-Noor Diamond comes from the diamond mines around Hyderabad that made the city rich. Hyderabad is also known as the 'city of pearls'; the famous pearl market in Patthargatti is a road lined with shops selling every conceivable variety.

# Udaipur

Rajasthan is renowned for its beautiful cities, but Udaipur, the 'City of Lakes', must be the most romantic of them all – a gleaming fantasy of 17th and 18th century palaces, temples, gardens, havelis (courtyard houses), bazaars and museums, all in the most wonderful waterside setting.

According to legend, the Rajput Maharana of Mewar, Udai Singh, was out hunting one day when he met a holy man meditating on a hill who told him it was a favourable spot. So in 1559 he decided to build a palace here and in 1568 made Udaipur the capital of his kingdom.

A boat ride on Lake Pichola in the setting sun is enough to quicken the senses of even the most jaded tourist. There are two islands, on which stand gleaming white magical palaces – the Jag Niwas and the Jag Mandir. The lake is enclosed by hills, and the City Palace runs along the eastern bank. This magnificent building is one of the largest marble palaces in the world – a maze of courtyards, terraces, hanging gardens, cupolas and luxurious apartments.

To the north, the manmade Fateh Sagar lake has a beautiful island – the Nehru Garden, a huge fountain, and the Udaipur Solar Observatory. Perched on the hillside overlooking the city, is the Monsoon Palace, the royal summer residence. And from the Sajjan Niwas garden, a short climb takes you up to the ridge of the old city wall from where you can gaze down over the plains.

In the old city, the curlicued stucco work and colourful painting round the doorways of the whitewashed *havelis* is straight out of a picture book. Cows and elephants wander around the narrow cobblestoned lanes of the bazaars where artisans ply their trade. Udaipur really is a fairytale city, 'like no other place on earth'.

**POPULATION:**
559,000 (2001)
**WHEN TO GO:**
September to March.
**DON'T MISS:**
City Museum.
Jagdish Mandir – largest temple in Udaipur, with music and chanting throughout the day.
Bharatiya Lok Kala Mandal – excellent folk art museum.
Bagore-ki Haveli – a lovely 18th century residence on the waterfront where you can see displays of Rajasthani dancing and music.
Fateh Prakash – palace with crystal collection and jewel-studded carpet.
Eklingji – 8th century temple complex with 108 sandstone and marble temples 22 km (14 mi) from Udaipur.
**YOU SHOULD KNOW:**
Udaipur was the birthplace of Bagheera, the black panther, in Kipling's *The Jungle Book*. Udaipur was ranked 7th top city in the world 2007 by *Travel & Leisure* magazine.

*The City Palace dominates the town.*

# Darjeeling

This 'Queen of the Hills' sits on the border between Sikkim and Nepal, high up in the Himalayas at 2,134 m (7,000 ft). It is one of India's best-loved hill stations, set in some of the most spectacular scenery in the world. During the Raj, the British came here in droves to escape from the sweltering heat of the plains and it is still an incredibly popular tourist resort.

In the early 19th century, a delegation from the British East India Company on their way to Sikkim stopped in a village here and decided that it was a good place to build a sanatorium for their sick soldiers. They negotiated a lease with the ruler of Sikkim and started to clear the densely forested hills and build a town. In 1841, they set up an experimental tea plantation which was so successful that soon tea estates were established on all the surrounding hills. Within a decade, the population had grown from 100 to 10,000 and, when the Himalayan Railway opened in 1881, Darjeeling became even more popular. After the Chinese annexed Tibet in 1950, thousands of Tibetans fled across the border and settled in Darjeeling, both in the town and in their own colony just outside. The majority of the town are ethnically Nepali but, as well as the large Tibetan community, there are Sherpas, Biharis, Bengalis and Anglo-Indians.

Darjeeling today has the picturesque façade of a colonial town, with mock Tudor houses and Gothic churches. In Chowrasta, the main square, there are ponies for hire, and from the Hindu Mahakala Temple on Observatory Hill there is a fantastic view of Kanchenjunga, the third highest mountain in the world. For trekkers and mountain lovers, this is paradise.

**POPULATION:**
108,000 (2001)
**WHEN TO GO:**
Avoid the monsoon season June to September when it rains a lot.
**DON'T MISS:**
Tibetan monasteries – Ghoom, Bhutia Busti, and Mag-dogh Yolmowa, where the monks will show you ancient manuscripts and sell you beautifully painted *thankas*.
Tibetan Refugee Self-help Centre – displays and sales of arts and crafts.
The view from Tiger Hill as the sun rises – 11 km (7 mi) from Darjeeling.
Taking a ride on the Darjeeling Himalayan Railway – a World Heritage Site.
Lloyd Botanical Gardens – includes rare orchids.
Padmadja Naidu Himalayan Zoo – conserves and breeds rare Himalayan species.
**YOU SHOULD KNOW:**
The temple monkeys look charming but can be presumptuous. If you are carrying any food, it is likely to be cheekily snatched from you.

*Tea gardens on the slopes with the Himalayas in the background*

# Lucknow

For many hundreds of years the ancient city of Lucknow was at the heart of Northern Indian culture. The city was the capital of the Awadh region, the 'granary of India', so was always of great strategic importance to whatever imperial power was ruling at the time. Under the Mughal Empire, the Nawabs (local rulers) gave Lucknow a unique and enduring legacy – 'wisdom, women and wine'. They were great philanthropists who encouraged learning, music, poetry, fine food, good manners and gracious living; their tolerant rule resulted in a symbiosis of all that was best in Hindu, Islamic and Sikh cultures. Their heritage can be seen in the architecture of the city's magnificent buildings – the Bara Imambara, Chhota Imambara and Rumi Darwaza are notable examples

The British displayed a lamentable ignorance about the culture of this sophisticated society and they made themselves hated for their high-handedness. They were eventually forced to abandon their Residency in the Siege of Lucknow, during the Indian Mutiny of 1857. In the early 20th century, the people of Lucknow were a major force in the Indian Independence Movement. After independence, the city retained its economic and intellectual status as one of the most important cities in North India.

Today, after a period of decline, this vibrant city is making an economic comeback. Regarded as one of the finest cities in India, it combines sophistication with old world charm. There are still traditional districts like Aminabad bazaar – a chaotic market where you can buy just about anything – and even in the slick shopping district of Hazratganj you will stumble upon family owned shops dating back to the Raj, still making and selling the incredible chikan embroidery work for which Lucknow is so famous.

**POPULATION:**
2,541,000 (2006)
**WHEN TO GO:**
October to February.
**DON'T MISS:**
Chhattar Manzil – an imposing edifice, built by the nawabs.
The Residency – remains of the building, bombed out in the Mutiny – and museum set in lovely gardens.
Clock Tower.
Shaheed Smarak – a tower to commemorate the Indian Mutiny.
Asafi Masjid – Mosque in the Bara Imambara.
La Martiniere College.
**YOU SHOULD KNOW:**
Lucknow is the centre for Kathak Indian classical dance.

*Chota Imambara*

# Jodhpur

**POPULATION:**
846,000 (2001)
**WHEN TO GO:**
October for the Marwar song and dance festival.
**DON'T MISS:**
Government Museum.
Jaswant Thada – Royal cremation ground with a memorial made from thin sheets of white marble.
Mahar Mandir – temple with 84 pillars dedicated to Shiva.
Osiyan – Jain temple, 60 km (38 mi) away.
Mandore – The ancient capital before Jodhpur, with lovely gardens, stupas and tombs, 9 km (6 mi) away.
**YOU SHOULD KNOW:**
The riding trousers known as 'jodhpurs' are named after the tight/baggy trousers worn by the men of Jodhpur.

The empty hills of the Thar Desert are a spectacular setting for the Rajput fortress city of Jodhpur. The forbidding 15th century Mehrangarh Fort, perhaps the most majestic fort in the whole of India, looms over the city from the top of a hill. Its walls, up to 36 m (120 ft) high and 21 m (70 ft) wide, seem to sprout out of the hilltop – an extension of the rock on which they are built. The Mehrangarh is a massive edifice containing palaces, courtyards and gardens with fabulous views from its ramparts.

Jodhpur is called the 'Blue City' because many of the houses are painted with a blue tint that reflects the sunlight, keeping the interiors cool. The city was founded in 1459 by Rao Jodha, chief of the Rathore clan of Rajput warriors, who claimed to be directly descended from Rama. The city grew into a major trading centre, maintaining a semi-autonomous status under both the Mughal Empire and the British Raj. Today Jodhpur is the second largest city in Rajasthan.

In this washed-out desert land, it is the people and markets that provide the colour; the women's embroidered jackets and long skirts stand out like bright jewels in the narrow lanes of Girdikot and Sardar, bustling bazaars where the rows of tiny shops sell everything from textiles and silver to spices and sweets.

The Umaid Bhawan Palace is one of the largest as well as most recent palaces in India. It began as a social project to provide employment for the townspeople in a time of famine in the 1920s. The building employed more than 5,000 men for 16 years and is an outstanding example of Art Deco Indo-Colonial design. Today, it is a five star hotel, museum, and home of Gaj Singh, Majarajah of Jodhpur.

*Mehrangarh Fort and Jodhpur*

# Margao

Ever since the first hippies descended onto the beaches of Goa in the early 1960s, travellers have tended to rush through Margao – the gateway to southern Goa – in an urgent desire to broaden their minds with a cocktail of music and marijuana by the sea. This is a pity; Goa has a culture that goes back thousands of years, to be discovered in the hinterland rather than on the beaches. It is the smallest state in India and was the last to achieve independence from colonial rule, in 1961. There are still many traces of its 400 years as a Portuguese colony, immediately apparent in its wonderful hybrid architecture.

Margao is one of the oldest recorded cities in Goa. It was an important Brahmin settlement, famous for its temples and university. In 1543, the Portuguese invaded and demolished many of the Hindu temples, erecting churches in their place. The ancient Damodar Temple to the north of the city was replaced by the Largo de Igreja (Holy Spirit) – a fantastic Indian-Baroque edifice with an interior dripping in gilt, crystal and stucco. Opposite is a row of palatial colonial mansions in a square lined with mango trees.

From Largo de Igreja, the road splits – one way leads toward the city proper, the other to a small chapel on Monte Hill. It is worth making this climb for the sake of the fantastic view from the top. In the city centre, there is a lively, chaotic atmosphere in the old fish market and bazaars around Praca Jorge Barreto, the main square. Margao has an old world charm about it that is well worth tearing yourself away from the beach to absorb properly, so that when you get home you will have acquired more than a suntan.

*The Church of the Holy Spirit,*
*Largo de Igreja*

**POPULATION:**
78,000 (2001)
**WHEN TO GO:**
October to March.
**DON'T MISS:**
House of Seven Gables (Sat Banzam Ghor) – a landmark mansion.
Chapel of St Sebastian and Pandava caves.
Grace Church.
Sri Damodar Temple.
Menezes Braganza – grandest colonial mansion of Goa, in Chandor, a small village 13 km (8 mi) from Margao. Inside you can see the diamond encrusted toenail of St. Francis Xavier.
Cabo de Rama – crumbling fort, named after Rama. Beautiful views from its ramparts, which are lined with cannons, and a small church which is still in use, 25 km (16 mi) south of Margao.
Rachol Seminary.
**YOU SHOULD KNOW:**
Margao has the best covered market in Goa – a labyrinth of stalls where it is still possible to get a bargain.

*Humayun's Tomb*

# Delhi

The capital of the largest democracy in the world is also one of the oldest cities in the world. There is evidence of continuous human habitation from at least 2000 BC, and the remains of seven major cities have been unearthed. Delhi has not only seen empires rise and fall but has been the capital of several of them.

Delhi is two entirely separate cities: the city of the Mughals – Old Delhi; and New Delhi – an inspired grand design by the great British architect, Lutyens. Two broad central boulevards bisect each other. The Rajpath runs from the magnificent presidential palace, Rashtrapati Bhavan, to India Gate, a spectacular 42 m (140 ft) arch commemorating the 90,000 or more Indian soldiers who died fighting British wars. The Janpath leads to the main shopping district, Connaught Place, a series of elegant colonnaded terraces in concentric circles, modelled on Royal Crescent in Bath. It is all splendid and indeed familiar, with the road congestion typical of all major cities.

Old Delhi is altogether another world. Chandni Chowk, the main thoroughfare, leads you into a compelling web of mysterious dark lanes and teeming bazaars, a maelstrom of traffic and people, and pariah dogs and flies, and everywhere the smell of dust and incense, spices and sewage. After weaving your way through the street hawkers, mendicants, naked vagrants, wandering cows, bullock carts, snake charmers, cycle rickshaws, bedraggled women, waif-like children, the Red Fort is a soothing place to recover from sensory overload – a magnificent 17th century Mughal seat of power, with walls 2 km (1.25 mi) long, acres of garden and Chatta Chowk covered bazaar. Nearby is Jama Masjid – India's largest mosque with two 40 m (130 ft) tall minarets. The 13th century Qutab Minar is even taller at 72.5 m (238 ft).

Delhi is a complex, challenging city – infuriating, fascinating, baffling, loathsome and wonderful in equal measure. It has to be seen to be believed. And having been once, you want to go back for more.

**POPULATION:**
13,783,000 (2001)
**WHEN TO GO:**
February to April or October to November to avoid extremes of temperature and the monsoon. Delhi is one of the last places you want to be in the summer.
**DON'T MISS:**
Jantar Mantar – astronomical observatory near Connaught Place.
Purana Qila – the Old Fort, one of the most famous monuments in Delhi.
Humayn's Tomb – World Heritage 16th century tomb surrounded by garden.
Swaminarayan Akshardham Temple – huge elaborate temple of red sandstone built by controversial Hindu cult organization BAPS in 2005; a major tourist attraction.
Meena bazaar – antiques flea market.
Karol Bagh – said to be the largest shopping area in Asia.
**YOU SHOULD KNOW:**
Getting around in Delhi is a bit of a mission. Always agree the price with the rickshaw-wallah (driver) before you start and, if tempers flare, remember that the money means an awful lot more to him than it does to you. It's all too easy to find yourself getting in a stew over what turns out to be pennies.

# Srinagar

Surrounded by snow-capped peaks and beautiful lakes, the lovely city of Srinagar in the valley of Kashmir has one of the most pleasant climates in India. This is why it has been a popular summer retreat for centuries, attracting the wealthy from the plains of India travelling to avoid the oppressive heat. This was a popular getaway for the Mughal emperors who left their mark in the form of beautiful mosques and stunning gardens.

Srinagar lies on the banks of the Jhelum River, a tributary of the Indus. A lively, vibrant place with a number of stunning parks, it is well known for the nine ancient bridges that connect the two parts of the city on opposite banks of the river. The city is famous for its lovely lakes, particularly Dal Lake, and the pretty houseboats floating on them. Be sure to take a boat tour of the lake inlets to get a glimpse of the life and wildlife along its banks.

The Mughal Gardens are among the highlights of a visit to Srinagar. They include Chasma Shahi, the royal fountains; Pari Mahal, the palace of the fairies; Nishat Bagh, the garden of spring; Sahlimar Bagh on the banks of Dal Lake, built by Emperor Jahangir; and the Nashim Bagh.

The city of Srinagar reflects the cultural heritage and religious diversity of the surrounding state of Jammu and Kashmir. This can be seen in the holy sites in and around the city. On a hill to the south-east of the city is the Hindu Shankaracharya Temple, dedicated to Shiva. It was constructed in 371 BC by Gopadatya, and offers great views of the city. The Hazrathbal shrine is one of the most revered pilgrimage sites in Islam as it houses the sacred hair of Muhammad (Moi-e-Muqqadas). Sadiq Khan laid out a garden here in 1623 on the left bank of Dal Lake and constructed a Pleasure House. Situated in the old city and large enough to accommodate 30,000 worshippers, the Jama Masjid Mosque was built in 1398 by Mughal Sultan Sikandar and is also worth a look.

**POPULATION:**
895,000 (2001)
**WHEN TO GO:**
June to September.
**DON'T MISS:**
A Shikara ride on Dal Lake.
Mughal Gardens.
Khanqah of Shah Hamadan, the first mosque built in Srinagar.
**YOU SHOULD KNOW:**
Srinagar is known as 'the Venice of the North'.

*Houseboats on Dal lake*

# Amritsar

**POPULATION:**
1,004,000 (2001)
**WHEN TO GO:**
Most temperate between October and March. The Divali festival is particularly lively here.
**DON'T MISS:**
Akhal Takht – directly in front of the temple, the second most sacred site where spiritual leaders discuss matters of concern to the community. The exquisite floral decoration and stone inlay work was done in the early 19th century by Muslim craftsmen hired specifically for the purpose.
Ram bagh and palace of Maharaja Ranjit Singh.
Serai Amanat Khan – a beautiful Mughal tomb and gate in a small village nearby.
Mosque at Fatehabad – 40 km (25 mi) away. Walls are decorated with beautiful floral motifs.
Durgiana (Lakshmi Narayan) Temple.
Changing of the Guard at Wagha border crossing – 25 km (15 mi) away. A charming, old-fashioned ritual display in which Indian and Pakistani soldiers in full military dress come to within a foot of each other.
**YOU SHOULD KNOW:**
The name 'Amritsar' is derived from *amrit sarovar*, meaning 'holy pool of nectar'. According to popular belief, there was a pool deep in the forest, known to wandering mystics since antiquity, where Buddha is said to have spent time meditating, and Valmiki wrote his celebrated epic the *Ramayana*. The tank of water that surrounds the Golden Temple is that same pond. It is fed by an underground spring, which supplies it with *amrit* (holy water or nectar).

Amritsar is one of the most awe-inspiring places in South Asia. You are flung back in time into a whirling maze of noise and heat, elbowing and dodging your way through narrow 17th and 18th century lanes packed with people and handcarts. This is one of the busiest markets in India and you have no choice but to be swept along by the crowd, eventually finding yourself at the Golden Temple in the heart of the city.

The Golden Temple is the cultural and spiritual centre of the Sikh religion. In the 16th century, Guru Ram Das (the fourth of the ten gurus of Sikhism) bought some land, built a holy tank and founded a city. The tank is a small square lake, in the middle of which sits the temple itself, reached by a walkway. All around the courtyard of the tank, people are praying, preparing food, resting, or bathing to the constant rhythmic sound of drums, flutes and chanting. However sceptical one may be, it is impossible not be affected by the spirituality of the atmosphere here. It is a truly extraordinary place.

Under the Raj, Amritsar was the site of a terrible atrocity. On April 13 1919, General Dyer ordered his troops to open fire without warning on a protest meeting of unarmed civilians, including women and children, leaving 379 dead and 1,200 wounded. A famous memorial to the victims stands at the east end of the Jallianwala Bagh (Park).This outrageous massacre helped turn millions of moderate Indians into bitter opponents of the British.

The 'gateway to the Punjab', Amritsar is a thrilling introduction to India; it is finally getting long-needed improvements to its infrastructure so that it can become the world-class tourist destination it deserves to be.

*The Golden Temple*

# Varanasi

On the banks of the River Ganges in northern India, the colourful holy city of Varanasi (Benares), has been an important cultural, historic and religious centre for more than 5,000 years. Presided over by Shiva, Varanasi is the most important Hindu pilgrimage site in the world. Described by Mark Twain as 'older than history, older than tradition, older even than legend, and looks twice as old as all of them put together!', this city offers a spectacle visitors never forget.

*The ghats (stone steps) viewed from the Ganges*

The ghats (stone steps) along the river banks are the main focus of religious activity. Here the pilgrims have a ritual bath in the water and perform *puja* to the rising sun, in accordance with centuries of tradition. It is believed that bathing in the sacred waters results in the remission of sins and that dying here circumvents rebirth. This is why many old and sick Hindus come to the city to die, surviving their last days on alms given to them by the faithful. Their funerals take place on the river banks; their bodies are burnt on funeral pyres and the remains are tossed into the water.

One of the largest, the Dasashvamedh Ghat offers good views of the river and all the hustle and bustle along its banks. This is believed to be where Brahma sacrificed ten horses to pave the way for Shiva's return to Varanasi after a period of banishment. Other special ghats are the Asi, Barnasangam, Panchganga and Manikarnika.

The Kashi Vishwanath Temple, on the banks of the sacred river, was built in 1780 by Maharani Ahilyabai Holkar of Indore. Home to the shrine of Lord Kashi Vishwanath, it is one of the twelve revered Jyotirlingas of Shiva, the shrines where he is worshiped in the form of a phallus of light. This temple is the place of pilgrimage for millions of Hindus every year, and is the most sacred shrine in Varanasi. Its original structure was destroyed by the Mughal Emperor, Aurangzeb. The gold plating of the dome was done during the nineteenth century by Maharaja Ranjit Singh of Punjab.

Close by this important Hindu pilgrimage site is Sarnath, a place of great meaning to Buddhists. Lying 12 km (7 mi) from Varanasi, Sarnath is where Buddha preached his first sermon and revealed the eight-fold path that leads to the attainment of inner peace, enlightenment and the ultimate, nirvana. Ashoka, the great Mauryan emperor, erected magnificent stupas here, including Dharmarajika Stupa at a staggering 33.5 m (109 ft) high, to honour Buddha's presence. Today, the Archeological Museum at Sarnath displays many ancient relics, among them countless images of Buddha and Bodhisatva.

**POPULATION:**
3,150,000 (2001)
**WHEN TO GO:**
November to March.
**DON'T MISS:**
Dasashvamedh Ghat – known as 'the ghat of ten sacrificed horses'. From here, there is a great view of the riverfront.
The Kashi Vishwanath Temple, also called the 'Golden Temple'. It is of huge religious importance to Hindus as Lord Shiva is enshrined here.
A boat trip on the Ganges at dawn.
Hindu pilgrimage site, Sarnath – this is where Buddha is believed to have delivered his first sermon. The ancient ruins here date from between the 3rd and 11th centuries AD.
**YOU SHOULD KNOW:**
Countless touts and beggars will vie for your attention.

*Tibetan Buddhist Monastery*

# Gangtok

This centre of Tibetan Buddhist culture is everything it is cracked up to be – brightly painted pagoda-roofed houses, monasteries, stupas, parks and, all around, prayer flags fluttering in the breeze.

The city is in the beautiful setting of the misty, rhododendron-covered slopes of the lower Himalayas. It is built along the side of a hill, 1,780 m (5,480 ft) high, and was a tiny hamlet until 1840 when the Enchey Monastery was founded. The village soon became a pilgrimage site, growing to be the capital of Sikkim.

There are panoramic views of the Himalayas from The Ridge, a beautiful flower-lined roadway that runs above the city, with the Governor's Residence and the White Lodge at one end and the Palace Gate at the other. A bit further out of town is the tiny Hindu temple Ganesh Tok, from where there is an even more breathtaking view.

The huge white Do-Drul Chorten, surrounded by 108 prayer wheels, is a major landmark and one of the largest and most important stupas in Sikkim. The Namgyal Research Institute of Tibetology is a wonderful example of Tibetan architecture, with ornate woodcarvings and murals. It is a renowned centre of Buddhist learning with a vast collection of rare Buddhist books, icons, thangkas and manuscripts.

Gangtok is a fascinating mix of tradition and modernity, and of three cultures – Indian, Nepali and Tibetan – living in harmony. Even though there are minority Hindu, Christian and Muslim communities, there has never been any inter-religious strife and the atmosphere is suffused with serenity. Lamas in red and gold robes wander amongst the bustle of the Lal Bazaar, spinning their prayer wheels and chanting invocations, while the sound of the trumpets from the Rumtek Dharma Chakra Monastery drifts across the valley as a reminder that you are in Buddha's lap.

**POPULATION:**
90,000 (2005 estimate)
**WHEN TO GO:**
Avoid the rains from June to September. Go in January for Chaam – religious, masked dancing festivities, March to May for the rhododendrons in flower or October for wonderfully clear skies.
**DON'T MISS:**
Deer Park – with statue of Buddha and fabulous views.
Government Institute of Cottage Industry – the place to buy *thangkas*, hand-made paper, carpets and other arts and crafts.
Tsomgo/Changu Lakes – two beautiful holy lakes 35-40 km (22-25 mi) from Gangtok.
Jawarharlal Nehru Botanical Garden.
Views from Tashi and Hanuman Temple.
**YOU SHOULD KNOW:**
The site of the Enchey Monastery is on the spot where the tantric master Lama Druptob Karpo (renowned for his power of flight) is said to have landed after flying off the top of Maenam Hill in South Sikkim.

# Chennai

Chennai, on the Coromandel Coast of the Bay of Bengal, is the capital of the state of Tamil Nadu. It is India's fourth largest city and is renowned as a centre of south Indian music and dance as well as for its architecture, cultural heritage, and wonderful sandy beaches.

The city's origins go back to the 17th century. In 1639 the British East India Company struck a deal with the local nayak (ruler) to build a warehouse. In 1640 they built Fort St George, one of the first British bastions in India, which became the hub around which the city grew. Gradually they gained control of the region, although there was a lot of wrangling with the French and wheeling and dealing with local rulers until the late 18th century. During the Raj, the city grew into a major commercial centre.

Chennai has a fascinating range of buildings. Much of the city has a colonial feel, with long avenues of tall trees and fine Indo-Saracenic architecture (a style of building mixing Mughal with Gothic). There is also the Portuguese 16th century San Thome Basilica, and the Kapaleeshwar Temple – a fantastic example of Dravidian (Tamil) architecture with intricate carvings. In the sprawling estate garden of the World Headquarters of the Theosophical Society (established here in 1886) there are shrines to all the major world faiths.

Chennai is a historic south Indian city with a leisurely pace of life and an entirely different, less frenetic atmosphere than the cities of the north. It is the base for the Tamil movie industry (dubbed Kollywood) which churns out 300 films a year, and the centre for Bharatanatyam classical dance. It also has one of the longest beaches in the world, Marina Beach – 13 km (8 mi) of golden sand to relax on.

**POPULATION:**
4,350,000 (2006)
**WHEN TO GO:**
Chennai is said to have three seasons: hot, hotter, and hottest. Go for Pongal (harvest festival) celebrated in January and lasting for five days.
**DON'T MISS:**
Connemara Library.
Sri Parthasarathy Temple – an 8th century shrine.
Guindy National Park – the only National Park in a city.
Chennai Museum – fabulous building stuffed with chaotic collections.
Mahabalipuram – ancient temples and rock carvings 50 km (30 mi) along the coast from Chennai.
**YOU SHOULD KNOW:**
Emulating Mumbai (Bombay) and Kolkata (Calcutta), the city changed its name to Chennai in 1996 because Madras was perceived to be of Portuguese origin, although this is by no means certain, and the origins of the name Chennai are equally suspect.

*The intricate carvings on the Kapaleeshwar Temple*

# Puri

**POPULATION:**
158,000 (2001)
**WHEN TO GO:**
October to March, or June/July to
witness the Rath Yatra Festival.
**DON'T MISS:**
Narasimha Mandir – temple where
anger, frustration and anxiety are
vanquished.
Haridasa Thakura Samadhi.
Tota Gopinath – temple.
The Five Holy Takhats.
The famous Sun Temple with its
Kama Sutra sculptures at Konark
40 km (25 mi) to the north of Puri.
Raghurajpur – an artisans' village
specializing in pattchitra paintings
12 km (7.5 mi) from Puri.
**YOU SHOULD KNOW:**
The word 'Juggernaut' is a corruption
of Jagannath and comes from the
Rath Yatra Festival.

Puri is a wonderful beach resort on the coast of the Bay of Bengal. It is one of the oldest cities in eastern India and one of the four holiest points of pilgrimage for Hindus, traditionally seen as a holy place to die.

The city is dominated by the 12th century Jagannath 'Lord of the Universe' Temple. It is an incredible 65 m (214 ft) high sculpted stone edifice, one of the tallest temples in India. The temple complex, which contains more than 120 shrines, occupies an area of 4.3 ha (10.7 acres) enclosed by two 15th century walls.

Walking through the narrow lanes of the city, you become aware that everything here is centred on the temple's existence. Everywhere the air is filled with the scent of incense and each house has its own temple or shrine, varying in size and splendour according to the wealth of the occupants.

Every summer, at the festival of Rath Yatra, images of the Hindu trinity of gods are taken out from the inner sanctum of the Jagannath Temple on gigantic, lavishly decorated cars (chariots). These are dragged 3 km (2 mi) along Bada Danda (Grand Road) to Gundicha Temple to the accompaniment of mantras and music, where they rest for nine days before being pulled back again.

Despite its religious significance, Puri has an incredibly relaxed, hedonistic atmosphere. There are miles of golden-sand beaches and you can go out with the local fishermen to cast their nets; some of them act as *nuliahs* (lifeguards) and for a small fee will take you out to brave the huge waves. There is even a point on the beach where, by some quirk of the coastline, you can watch the sun both rise and set. This is the place to feel at one with the universe.

*A Brahma Bull outside the Jagannath Temple*

*The Palace of the Winds*

# Jaipur

Jaipur is one of the most important heritage cities in India and a major tourist attraction. It is the capital of Rajasthan, the ancient desert state of the Rajputs – a Hindu caste of warriors greatly respected by both the Mughals and the British. Jaipur is called the 'Pink City' after its ornately decorated stucco buildings, painted to replicate the red sandstone of Mughal architecture.

The founder of Jaipur was a far-sighted astronomer king, Maharajah Sawai Jai Singh. Realizing that there would soon be a water shortage due to a growing population, he relocated his people in 1727. He designed his new city according to the principles of Shilpa-Shastra, an ancient Hindu architectural theory based on auspicious geometric and astrological lines. The old walled city is laid out as a mandala in nine parts, one for each astrological sign, with broad streets and gardens.

The Chokri Sarhad is a huge palace complex, a fascinating blend of Mughal and Rajput design. The Maharajah's family still live here in the Chandra Mahal. Opposite it is the Jantar Mantar astronomical observatory, and, abutting the palace wall, the Hawa Mahal (Palace of the Winds) – an archetypal example of Rajput architecture – built for the royal women to see into the street without being seen themselves.

There are three stupendous forts on the edge of the city – the Amer, Jaigarh and Nahargarh – each in its own way attesting to the greatness of Rajput culture. The maharajahs of Jaipur were benevolent rulers, tolerant of other religions. Jainism flourished here and Jaipur is still one of the most important Jain centres in India.

Jaipur is heaven for shopping. Jauhari Bazaar and Badi Chaupar are full of traditional Rajput ornaments, paintings and block-printed textiles, carved wood, leather, precious and semi-precious stones, pottery and the famous Jaipur quilts.

**POPULATION:**
2,324,000 (2005)
**WHEN TO GO:**
March, for Holi (the festival of colours) and the Elephant Festival.
**DON'T MISS:**
Jal Mahal – a palace sitting in the middle of a lake filled with water hyacynths.
Ram Niwas Garden with the Albert Hall museum.
Vidyadhar Gardens, 8 km (5 mi) away.
Sisodia Rani Ka Bagh – lovely gardens, 10 km (6 mi) away.
Kanak Vrindavan – garden with temple of Govind Deo Ji adjoining Amber Fort.
Chokhi Dhani – a funfair 18 km (11 mi) from the city centre where you can watch folk dancing, listen to traditional music, have elephant and camel rides, and eat your fill.
**YOU SHOULD KNOW:**
This is a city that relies heavily on the tourist trade; if you want to photograph snake charmers, camel drivers, holy men, etc. you are expected to pay, and it would be churlish not to.

*The Victoria Memorial*

# Kolkata

The history of Kolkata is bound up with the British East India Company. The Company built the outpost of Fort William at the end of the 17th century as their main base in India. The city grew around it, and from 1772 until 1911, Kolkata (or Calcutta as it was then known) was the capital of British India. There was constant tension with the Nawab of Bengal, the local ruler, which led to the legendary incident of the 'Black Hole of Calcutta' in 1756, when British prisoners, held in one of the Nawab's dungeons, were suffocated from heat and overcrowding.

Kolkata is the cultural heart of modern India and has a long tradition of producing great writers, artists, musicians and political thinkers. In the 19th century it became the centre for the Indian Nationalist Movement seeking independence from colonial rule. Today it is still renowned for its artistic and intellectual life as well as being the centre of the Bengali film industry.

A traveller's first impressions of Kolkata are ones of utter confusion. The familiarity of English street names and Victorian architecture is immediately reassuring but the noise, traffic and squalor swamp you with sensory overload – roads packed with cars, cows, handcarts, rickshaws, pariah dogs and people all competing for space. By the time you catch your first glimpse of a corpse floating down the River Hooghly, you are too numb to absorb it as anything abnormal – and so you adjust to this compelling place, called the 'City of Joy'. Give yourself time – explore the tall, narrow side streets, where the canopies of the trees meet to cast dappled pools of shade, and begin to feel something of the animated soul of this enigmatic, ramshackle city – the city of the great Bengali poet, Rabindranath Tagore: 'I shall be born in India again and again. With all her poverty, misery and wretchedness, I love India best'.

# Mysore

Mysore is a city so steeped in mythology and romantic history that it cannot fail to capture the imagination. It has long been renowned for its yoga, reiki and ayurvedic schools and as a perfect tourist city with its tall trees, tongas and oxcarts, palaces, temples, gardens and lakes, pleasant people and unhurried atmosphere. Recently the city has had a major economic shot in the arm from the information technology industry and is undergoing rapid expansion and modernization, creating new opportunities for its population. Although this might make it seem less immediately attractive to the tourist, in the long term it is likely to turn it into one of the most vibrant and attractive cities in India.

According to Hindu mythology, the region around Mysore was controlled by the destructive demon king Mahishasura until he was vanquished by the goddess Chamundeshwari. There is a 12th century temple dedicated to her on top of Chamundi Hills, reached either by road or by climbing 1,000 steps through wooded slopes where monkeys chatter in the trees. Halfway up the steps is an awesome black granite statue of Nandi, Lord Shiva's Bull. The view from the top is a spectacular panorama of the city's palaces and miles of the surrounding southern Indian countryside.

Mysore was ruled by the Wodeyar Dynasty from 1399 until 1947 and, together with the renowned Tipu Sultan, they have left an incredible heritage of beautiful buildings. The Amba Vilas (Mysore Palace) in the city centre is an awe-inspiring Indo-Saracenic edifice. Another magnificent Indo-Saracenic monument is Rajendra Vilas, a summer palace in Chamundi Hills. The Jayalakshmi Vilas, on the campus of Mysore University, is a museum housing a priceless collection of artefacts. And there are many more. Not for nothing is Mysore known as the 'City of Palaces'.

**POPULATION:**
1,038,000 (2001)
**WHEN TO GO:**
For the Dasara Festival in September/October when the whole city celebrates for 10 days and all the palaces are lit up.
**DON'T MISS:**
Jaganmohan Art Gallery – a fine collection of 19th-21st century paintings.
St Philomena's Church – a Gothic cathedral, one of the largest in India.
Devaraja market – a colourful fruit and vegetable market with a sumptuous array of flowers and spices.
Melkote – 12th century temple town 60 km (38 mi) from Mysore.
Sri Ramakrishna Ashram.
Daria Daulat Bagh museum.
Tipu Sultan's summer palace with beautiful frescoes.
**YOU SHOULD KNOW:**
Mysore's sandalwood and silks have the reputation of being the best in the world.

*Maharajah's Palace illuminated at night*

# Haridwar

**POPULATION:**
221,000 (2003)
**WHEN TO GO:**
March to April or October to November.
**DON'T MISS:**
Shanti Kunj – famous ashram where people come to learn yoga and meditation.
Bharat Mata Mandir – multi storey temple, the only one of its kind; each floor represents an era of Indian history.
Mansa Devi Temple – lovely view from the top.
Rishikesh – a lovely hill town, 24 km (15 mi) to the north, where the Beatles studied Transcendental Meditation under Maharishi Mahesh Yogi.
Chanda Devi – temple 6 km (4 mi) away on the other side of the river.
**YOU SHOULD KNOW:**
Haridwar is a completely vegetarian and alcohol-free city.

Haridwar, the 'Gateway to God', is a lovely old Hindu city in the foothills of the Himalayas. It lies at the point where the River Ganges flows out from the mountains into the plains of India and is one of the seven holy cities, where moksha (spiritual liberation) can be obtained.

All sorts of swamis and gurus have their headquarters here, in streets of beautiful old havelis (mansions) with exquisite murals and stonework. The city is a famous centre for ayurvedic medicine and traditional learning, and the riverside is lined with ancient temples, ashrams, and dharamsalas (pilgrim rest houses). Through the din of the city, Haridwar exudes a wonderful atmosphere – holy cows roam around the narrow streets of Jwalapur bazaar, where stalls are piled high with heaps of brilliant red holi powder, bottles of holy Ganges water and garlands of marigolds; and wild-haired, orange-robed saddhus squat in the shade of the peepul trees, meditating or sharing a *chillum* (pipe).

Haridwar is one of the four holy cities that holds the Khumb Mela every twelve years – humanity's largest festival, when 7 million people gather to purify themselves – next celebrated here in 2010. Every April there is a pilgrim festival and huge numbers of people visit throughout the year to pray and bathe from the holy ghats (bathing steps).

The Har-ki-pauri is one of the most sacred ghats in India. Here, every night at dusk, there is the magical Aarti ceremony: prayers to the goddess Ganga are chanted to the accompaniment of conch shells and bells, then everyone releases a *diya* (candle in a little clay dish of flowers and incense) to float in the Ganges; hundreds of flickering lights disappear into the distance downriver, carrying away all evil.

*The daily wash in the Ganges*

# Kochi

Flanked by the Arabian Sea and the western ghats on the south-western coast of India, Kochi is a lovely seaside city and the ideal starting point for a tour of Kerala. The culture and architecture of this Indian gem has been shaped by those who have occupied the city in its turbulent past, including the Arabs, British, Chinese, Dutch and Portuguese.

At the beginning of the 12th century, Kochi was the seat of the Kingdom of Cochin, a princely state which traces its lineage to the Kulasekhara empire. It became an important spice-trading centre in the 14th century, dealing in pepper, cardamom, cinnamon, cloves and other products native to the area's lush soils. Occupied by the Portuguese in 1503, Kochi was the first European settlement in India and remained the capital of Portuguese India until 1530. The city was later occupied by the Dutch, the Mysore and the British. It was the first princely state to willingly join the Indian Union after independence in 1947.

Kochi boasts many cultural treasures and historical buildings, including St Francis' Church, the oldest European church in India and burial place of Vasco da Gama, the Portuguese explorer who died in 1524. Vasco House, on Rose Street, is thought to have been his former home. With its glass-paned windows and sweeping verandahs, it is one of the oldest Portuguese homes in the country. Santa Cruz Cathedral was built by the Portuguese in 1505, but destroyed by British invaders in 1795. It was rebuilt in 1905 and is famous for its painted ceilings.

Built by the Portuguese in 1555, Mattancherry Palace was gifted to the Raja of Cochin, Veera Kerala Varma, partly as compensation for a temple they had demolished, and partly as a bribe to gain favours. The Dutch took over the palace in 1663 when they took Cochin from the hands of the Portuguese, and made it in to what it is today. Its simple exterior belies its very decorative interior. The central hall on the first floor was the Coronation Hall of the Rajas, and their dresses, turbans and palanquins are on display.

The Raja gave the area known as 'Jew Town' to the Jewish community to protect them from persecution. The Paradesi Synagogue, built in 1568, is magnificently decorated with Chinese tiles and Belgian chandeliers. Another noteworthy sight is Kalady, on the banks of the River Periyar, the birthplace of Sri Adi Sankaracharya the Hindu philosopher. The Adi Sankara shrine and eight-storey painted Adi Sankara Keerthi Sthambam are a must-see for any visitor.

*Fishing nets hang out to dry*

**POPULATION:**
596,000 (2001)
**WHEN TO GO:**
March to October.
**DON'T MISS:**
Mattancherry Palace – houses Kerala murals depicting Hindu temple art and exhibits from the Rajas of Kochi.
St Francis' Church – the first European church to be built in India, in 1516. It was the original burial place of Vasco da Gama, before his body was returned to Portugal.
Paradisi Synagogue – built in 1568, this beautiful building was named after the 'foreigners' or 'white Jews'. Hundreds of hand-painted tiles decorate the floor.
The Adi Sankara shrine – this is an 8 storey high, brilliantly painted memorial, guarded by 2 elephant statues and dedicated to one of India's foremost philosophers.
**YOU SHOULD KNOW:**
Kochi is also known as Cochin.

*Ferry boats on the Buriganga River*

# Dhaka

**POPULATION:**
6,725,000 (2006)
**WHEN TO GO:**
Avoid monsoon season (May to September) when the city can be flooded – and often is.
**DON'T MISS:**
The National Museum, containing a large collection spanning the Hindu, Buddhist and Muslim periods.
Sadarghat, the main waterfront area on the river in the Old Dhaka area for some energetic local colour.
Ahsan Manzil Museum, the beautiful former home of the Nawab of Dhaka.
The wonderful Baldha Garden, created in 1904
**YOU SHOULD KNOW:**
Under 17th century Mughal rule, Dhaka was at the centre of the world-wide muslin trade.

Formerly Dacca, Bangladesh's capital is the country's largest city — indeed, one of the largest in the world. From afar the high-rise skyline could be mistaken for a typical American city, but close up Dhaka and its sprawling metropolitan area on the banks of the Buriganga River could only be in the Third World.

The city has a long and turbulent past. Most recently, there was serious violence following Indian independence and partition in 1947, when Dhaka became the capital of East Pakistan – conflict that didn't really cease until Bangladesh became independent in 1971 after a bloody struggle with West Pakistan.

Since then, the city has battled with endemic poverty, crime, pollution and congestion. But it remains the political, cultural and commercial centre of Bangladesh, and as the young country has started to find its feet Dhaka has tackled problems with gusto, though the process is not helped by the city's phenomenal growth rate.

This frenetic place is choked with traffic, notably rickshaws (some

400,000 of them), with increasing prosperity adding thousands of scooters, taxis and cars. The place is also thronged with bustling bazaars, roadside stalls, peddlers, street vendors and beggars, making Dhaka seem daunting. However, the city does have a growing middle class that demands – and is starting to get – more sophisticated facilities (hotels, shops and restaurants) of the sort that appeal to visitors.

Once the initial shock subsides, the city offers plenty of interesting sights to go along with the hectic pace of life. There are mosques, Hindu temples, Christian churches and Buddhist temples. There is some wonderful modern architecture like the Parliament Building. The 17th century Lalbagh Fort that featured in the Indian Mutiny of 1857 overlooks the old city and is well worth exploring.

# Bagerhat

Modern Bagerhat would not normally attract the interest of a discerning traveller. This cotton textile centre in the south west of Bangladesh has a couple of university colleges but is unexceptional . . . or would be, were it not home to the historic mosque city of Bagerhat, revered by Bangladeshis as the cradle of Islam in their country.

This UNESCO World Heritage Site is situated outside modern Bagerhat where the Rivers Ganges and Brahmaputra merge. Formerly known as Khalifatabad, the city was founded by the Turkish general Ulugh Khan Jahan (also known as Khan Jahan Ali) in the 15th century, and some 50 major monuments remain. For all that, visitors who expect a compact collection of buildings will be disappointed.

In fact, this is a lost city, because much of the original infrastructure has gone – there were once roads, bridges, palaces and reservoirs linking the many mosques that have survived. These are scattered across a wide area and time is required to explore thoroughly, even by car. Indeed, part of the charm of the place is that it hasn't become a well-organized tourist attraction. Lesser mosques can be discovered by following footpaths that wend through fields and beside ponds. At the end, you may well find a wonderful 15th century building . . . without another person in sight.

Top of the 'must-see' list is the Shatgumbad Sixty-Pillar Mosque, which is one of the most spectacular (and one of the oldest) in Bangladesh. It has 60 pillars and 81 *gambuj* (domes). Khan Jahan Ali's Tomb is also impressive, and should be visited. It stands on a high artificial mound surrounded by a wall. A number of smaller mosques will be obvious, but the whole 50 take some finding.

**POPULATION:**
52,000 (2005)
**WHEN TO GO:**
Winter (November to March), to enjoy the lost city without needing waterproof clothing.
**DON'T MISS:**
The Singar Mosque — a square, single-dome mosque near the Shatgumbad Mosque, typical of the smaller mosques to be found scattered around the countryside.
The Thakur Dighi reservoir near Khan Jahan Ali's tomb complex, containing marsh crocodiles said to grant wishes to those who feed them.
The Nine-Dome Mosque on the western embankment of the Thakur Dighi.
An excursion to the nearby Sundarbans UNESCO World Heritage Site, the magnificent mangrove forests in the delta of the Ganges, Brahmaputra and Meghna rivers.
**YOU SHOULD KNOW:**
Women are not allowed inside Khan Jahan Ali's tomb, which is still a place of active worship.

# Chittagong

**POPULATION:**
3,920,000 (2007)
**WHEN TO GO:**
November to March is best for cool, dry weather, but in any event avoid monsoon season (June-October).
**DON'T MISS:**
The Tomb of 9th century Sultan Bayazid Bostami, close to the city at Nasirabad – see the turtles said to be the descendants of evil spirits cast out by the great holy man.
British and Commonwealth war graves, and those of soldiers of other nationalities, who died fighting on the Burma (now Myanmar) Front in World War II.
The Shrine of Shah Amanat in the city centre, visited by hundreds of people every day who seek to pay homage to the Islamic saint.
An outing to Sitakunda, some 37 km (22 mi) from Chittagong, for some wonderful temples including one with a footprint of Lord Buddha.
Foy's Lake, an attractive reservoir just outside town with surrounding parkland providing an ideal spot to relax.
**YOU SHOULD KNOW:**
In the 16th and 17th centuries Portuguese pirates controlled Chittagong, which they called Porto Grande.

Bangladesh's second-largest city, Chittagong, is also its principal seaport — with almost all the country's imports and exports passing through its busy harbour. The city is also a major commercial and manufacturing centre that generates vast revenues for a generally poor country that only came into existence in 1971 (the independence of former East Pakistan being declared in Chittagong).

It is perhaps unfortunate that one of those industries – the extraordinary ship-breaking operations that take place on the shores of the Bay of Bengal rather than in a proper shipyard – have given Chittagong something of a negative image, for this dangerous business is definitely not on the agenda for visitors, who are not welcome in the vicinity of this polluting activity.

Actually, Chittagong itself is relatively clean, with plenty of green hills within its boundaries to offer relief from the bustle of city life. The highest point within city limits is the Batali Hill, with panoramic views of sea, port and city.

There are a number of interesting old buildings, such as the East India Company's massive 18th century Court Building standing on Fairy Hill with a commanding bird's-eye view of the city. Chittagong College is one of the oldest and most prestigious academies in Bangladesh. Chandanpura Mosque in the old city is a multi-domed architectural wonder. Baitul Falah is the largest *masjid* (mosque) in Chittagong.

But for all its visible history, this is a boom city, with rapid development completely transforming its traditional face as endless new buildings shoot up to join those but recently completed. The streets are clogged with traffic – buses, cars, scooters and rickshaws – and the inevitable beggars and hawkers swarm everywhere. Many visitors are almost relieved to leave the city for nearby beaches, or to journey into the unspoiled hinterland.

# Thimphu

Prayer flags flutter in the wind as you reach Thimpu, the capital of a country with a style all of its own. At a height of 2,320 m (7,656 ft) Shangri-la, as it is sometimes known, is set in a long, wooded valley in the heart of the Himalayas, scrambling up the hillside from the Wang Chhu River.

A Tibetan monk made this country a Buddhist sanctuary in 1616, when the valley had already been settled for centuries. However, it was not until 1961, when the much-revered king named Thimpu as his new capital, that the city began to develop. Until the late 1950s there were no roads, electricity, paper currency, or schools – indeed Bhutan was completely closed to outsiders until 1974, when the first Western visitors were invited to the coronation of the present Dragon King.

The city consists of low-rise structures with large flat roofs, highly decorated wooden shutters and balconies, and paintings or Buddhist motifs on the white walls. All new buildings must follow this traditional Bhutanese style. Lanes twist and twirl their way up the hill, all leading to the central Clock Tower Square, with its fountains and prayer wheels, restaurants and little shops. A large memorial shrine, containing religious paintings and tantric statues, dominates the town, busy with colourfully dressed people circling it, chanting mantras. The most impressive building, the Trashicchoe Dzong, stands on the hill above – housing the throne room and the King's offices, it is also the summer residence of the Chief Abbott and his monks.

It's expensive to visit Bhutan, and expensive to stay here – a deliberate policy to keep tourism at a low level. Bhutan is poor in material goods, but boundlessly rich in other qualities – contentment, inner peace and dignity. Children are taught in English, and many go on to foreign universities, bringing their learning back home. This is still a world informed by Buddhist principles, and long may it last.

*Buddhist prayer flags*

**POPULATION:**
50,000 (2003)
**WHEN TO GO:**
September and October, March to May.
**DON'T MISS:**
The National Library, with its amazing, historical Bhutanese texts.
The Folk Heritage Museum, displaying the traditional culture in a traditional house.
Changangha Temple – the oldest in the valley and Tangu Cherry, a beautiful monastery.
The Textile Museum, displaying textiles from the 1600s to today.
Thimpu's weekend market, full of gorgeous local produce, textiles, masks, jewellery, and handmade knives.
The many colourful Buddhist festivals.
**YOU SHOULD KNOW:**
Bhutan was the world's last country to receive television (2002).
There are no traffic lights in the city – a set was installed but they were considered too impersonal and replaced with two traffic policemen.
2007 marked the centenary of Bhutan's monarchy, but as it was an inauspicious year in the Bhutanese calendar, celebrations take place in 2008 instead.

# Patan

Patan, now often known by its original Sanscrit name of Lalitpur, is one of the major cities of Nepal and is generally considered to be the oldest and most beautiful of the three royal cities in the Kathmandu Valley (the others being Bhaktapur and Kathmandu itself). Lying on high ground on the south side of the Bagmati River, it was originally built on a layer of deposited clay in the centre of an ancient dried lake called Nagdaha in the 3rd century BC by Emperor Ashoka of the Kirat Dynasty.

The city was first formed in the shape of the Buddhist Dharma-Chakra (Wheel of Righteousness) and legend has it that Emperor Ashoka erected four *thurs* (mounds) or stupas on the perimeter and one in the centre: their size and shape giving the city a true sense and feeling of antiquity, enhanced by the more than 1,200 Buddhist monuments of different types that are scattered throughout the city.

Durbar Square, a UNESCO World Heritage Site in the heart of the city, contains the Royal Palace which consists of three main *chowks* (places where paths intersect), the Central Mul Chowk, Keshav Narayan Chowk and Sundaru Chowk, holding in its centre a masterpiece of stone architecture, the Royal Bath called Tushahity.

The fountain in the north of the square, Mani Dhari, is its oldest structure probably dating from the 10th century, being vast and sunken with its first gallery still 2 m (6.5 ft) below street level and descending a further 2 m (6.5 ft) to where water springs from three makara-(half animal, half fish) shaped spouts, all presided over by the goddess Lakshmi and two mythical beings, called barumes.

There are many festivals in Patan – and throughout Nepal – during July and August, including Janai Purnima, a time of ritual bathing and changing of the sacred Janai threads, and Gaijatra, the Festival of the Holy Cows, when people parade wearing many kinds of hats, all with a picture of a cow pinned on them.

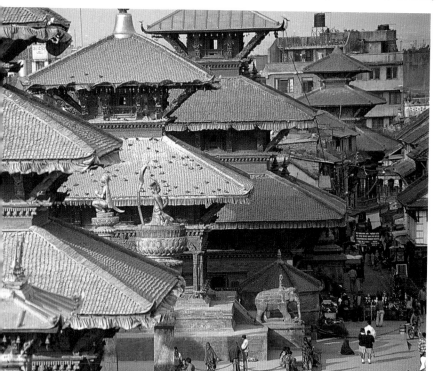

*The Royal Palace*

*Durbar Square*

# Kathmandu

Kathmandu, the gateway to the Himalayas, is set high up in an emerald green valley, surrounded by terraced hills. The beating heart of Nepal and totally cosmopolitan, it was the home town of the Newars, the country's master craftsmen and super tradesmen. Trade created Kathmandu – for a thousand years the city controlled the most important caravan route between Tibet and India, so not surprisingly it has easily embraced the tourist business.

In many ways the city is seemingly unchanged since the Middle Ages and indeed it contains no less than four UNESCO World Heritage Sites (Durbar Square, the Swayambhu and Bauddhanath Buddhist stupas and the Hindu temple of Pashupati). Yet in some parts of the city it appears to be just another polluted concrete jungle. Kathmandu has one of the highest rates of inflation in Asia and although there is more money around than before, most of it remains with the upper class.

Popular with westerners since the 1960s as a key stop on the hippie trail, Kathmandu has an enchanting old town, the area between Kantipath (the main north/south road), west to the Vishnumati River – a visual feast of rose brick and ancient wood-carved temples and palaces. Durbar Square is a non-stop carnival, with temples and monuments as well as the former Royal Palace, home of the ancient Malla kings.

**POPULATION:**
729,000 (2006)
**WHEN TO GO:**
October/November for balmy air, good visibility and lush green after the monsoon.
**DON'T MISS:**
Pashupatinath Temple, a Hindu funeral site on the banks of the Bagmati River.
Seeing Mount Everest and the Himalayas on a one-hour mountain flight.
Buying clothes, cushions and bags from Maheela, a women's foundation.
Exploring the complex of royal palaces in Hanuman Dhoka (Durbar Square).
Guheswari Temple – a historic holy shrine to the goddess Guheswari.
The Shiva Temple of Jaishi Dewal, famous for its erotic carvings.
**YOU SHOULD KNOW:**
Nepal has its very own living breathing goddess – the Kumari Devi – a young girl aged between four and puberty, chosen very carefully to meet thirty-two physical requirements, ranging from the shape of her teeth to the length of her toes. She lives in the Kumari Bahal beside Durbar Square.

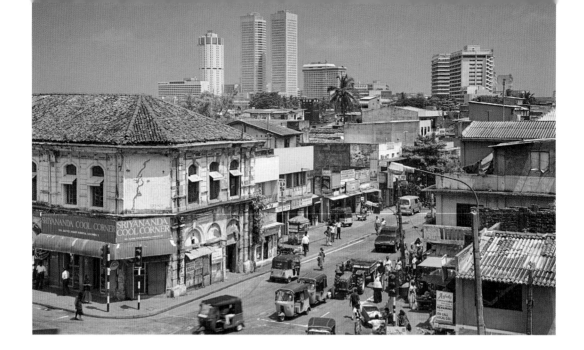

*The Slave Island area of Colombo with the twin towers of the World Trade Centre in the background*

# Colombo

**POPULATION:**
642,000 (2001)
**WHEN TO GO:**
February to April. Daily temperatures of 28 °C (82 °F) can be expected all year round. The only major change in the Colombo weather occurs during the monsoon seasons from May to August and October to January.
**DON'T MISS:**
Dehiwala Zoo – the highlight here is an afternoon elephant show.
The National Museum – with a fine collection of historical works.
The Art Gallery – a mixture of classical and local art.
The Jami Ul Alfar Mosque in the Pettah area – one of the oldest mosques in Colombo.
The Murugan Hindu temple in Slave Island district – a spectacular building.
The view from Gallery Island – a good place to soak up the city.
**YOU SHOULD KNOW:**
In the dry months night temperatures rarely drop below 20 °C (68 °F), so check out the air-conditioning in your hotel room upon arrival.

Because of its strategic location in the Indian Ocean, Colombo has since Roman times been a major trading post for east-west trade. The name Colombo, first used by the Portuguese in the early 16th century, is a possible corruption of the old Sinhalese name Kolon thota, meaning 'Port on the river Kelani'. By way of various treaties and alliances possession of the port passed from the Portuguese to the Dutch and then to the last colonizers, the British. This cultural diversity is reflected in the variety of names, faces, architecture and cuisine that is evident throughout the city.

The 35-km (22-mi) taxi ride from the airport gives you an idea of the urban sprawl that is Colombo. Though the 15 districts of the city itself are officially home to around 650,000 people, the Greater Colombo area houses around 1.5 million more.

Colombo's setting is a mixture of hills, marshes and flatlands. There is an extensive canal network and Beira Lake in the city centre can temper the heat of the tropical sun. The northern town border is formed by the Kelani River, which meets the ocean at the district of Modera.

To the north of Colombo is the Fort district, the city's business heart, full of bookshops, cafés and department stores as well as the modern high-rise World Trade Centre and the Bank of Ceylon. If you journey south you will enter Galle Face Green, Colombo's seaside. Travel south again and you will reach Cinnamon Gardens, the city's most elegant district with its tree-lined streets and fashion-conscious residents – great for people watching.

# Kandy

In the Kandy Valley, nestling among the tea plantations clothing the surrounding hills in central Sri Lanka, lies the sacred city of Kandy. Although the capital, Colombo, remains the prime commercial centre, Kandy is the cultural capital of Sri Lanka with a rich heritage of living monuments. This quiet and homely city is a stunning location to learn about the history and culture of Sri Lanka.

Originally called Senkadagala after the hermit Senkada, this city is a sacred Buddhist site. The Royal Palace was the capital from 1592 until 1815 when it came under British rule. Built by King Vikramabahu III of Gampola, it lies in the centre of the island, surrounded by a large lake and the Mahaweli, the longest river in Sri Lanka. The last King, who transformed Kandy into a celestial city, designed the white stone parapet that runs along the lakeside. Seen in the lake's reflection, the cloud-like drift on the walls and wave-like swells make the city look as if it is floating in the sky.

The best-known monument in Kandy is the sacred pilgrimage site of the Temple of the Tooth, said to house one of Buddha's teeth. Legend has it that the tooth was smuggled here in the hair of a princess after being taken from the flames of his funeral pyre. The relic of the tooth of the Buddha symbolizes a fourth-century tradition that used to be linked to royalty, since the protector of the relic was seen to be fit enough to rule the land. Thus, the Royal Palace and the Temple of the Tooth were associated with the administrative and religious functions of the capital city.

During July or August every year, Sri Lanka's grandest celebration takes place, the Kandy Esala Perahera. The ten-day festival ends on the night of the full Moon, its highlight is a procession of drummers, dancers and decorated elephants carrying a duplicate of the Buddha's sacred tooth. Even after British rule, Kandy has preserved its function as the religious capital of the Sinhalese and a place of pilgrimage for Buddhists.

Surrounded by a loop of the beautiful Mahaweli River, Peradeniya Botanical Gardens are well worth a visit. Dating from the 14th century and the reign of King Vikramabahu III, the garden is known for its orchid house, spice garden and magnificent tropical trees.

**POPULATION:**
110,000 (2001)
**WHEN TO GO:**
During the annual Esala Perahera Festival in July or August.
**DON'T MISS:**
The Royal Palace – consists of many buildings, including the quarters of the royal concubines, the queen's chambers and the armoury. The council chambers, built in 1784, are a unique example of Kandyan architecture.
The Temple of the Tooth – this is where Buddha's tooth is kept and a parade is held in July and August each year to celebrate this.
A walk along the River Mahaweli.
Peradeniya Botanical Garden – a beautiful park filled with tropical foliage. Earl Mountbatten had his headquarters here during World War II.
**YOU SHOULD KNOW:**
This is the largest city in Sri Lanka's hill country.

*The Temple of the Tooth*

# Hong Kong

**POPULATION:**
6,980,000 (2007)
**WHEN TO GO:**
Autumn or spring.
**DON'T MISS:**
The Spring Lantern Festival.
A trip across the harbour, either by day or by night on the famous Star Ferry.
The bus ride over the 'top' to Stanley.
**YOU SHOULD KNOW:**
Many of the shops shut for days during the Chinese New Year.

Hong Kong seems like a contradiction in terms: a modern city where traditional values of hospitality are held dear, English pubs next to dim sum restaurants and double-decker buses passing hawkers selling chicken feet. This fusion of East and West is the legacy of a century and more of British rule before the colony was returned to China in 1997.

The main entertainment and commercial areas are in the north of Hong Kong Island, while the east is residential and the south is green with pretty bays; Kowloon Peninsula is built up, while the New Territories and the Outlying Islands are more peaceful.

Famed for its 24-hour lifestyle, shopping, street vendors and food stalls, bright lights, skyline, skyscrapers, and beautiful harbour, Hong Kong is one of the world's premier destinations. Less well known are

*Victoria Harbour at night*

the beaches of Repulse Bay and the Outlying Islands and the hiking trails of the New Territories.

The view from Victoria Peak across the skyline is stunning and Ocean Park is beautiful and the shopping and nightlife in the upmarket areas such as Central and Causeway Bay are among the best in the world. Mong Kok is the site of amazing Chinese markets, where vendors sell food, medicines, clothing and fabrics, knick-knacks and just about anything else you could ever want or need.

The food in Hong Kong is first class, from international restaurants serving every type of food you can imagine to the street food that is sold on every corner.

Hong Kong is a place that you will fall in love with.

# Jinan

Jinan, the 'city of springs' is the capital of Shandong Province. It is also the cradle of one of China's early civilizations, the Longshan Relics Culture, known for its exquisite fine black pottery, which at its best is as thin as eggshells.

It is also the site of one of the earliest phases of the Great Wall, begun in 685 BC.

The springs and lakes that abound in the city are its chief draw: the '72 famous springs' emerge from underground and flow towards Daming Lake. Among the most famous is the Baotu Spring, where the water foams out from the ground. The Lake of Five Dragons is beautiful at any time of year, but especially when the cherry blossom is out. The Lantern Festival takes place each year in Baotu Spring Park, while the Lotus Festival is in the Daming Lake Park.

Licheng County is one of the important sites for the development of Buddhism and monuments that stand here include the Four-door Pagoda, the ruins of the Shentong Temple, a variety of monks' tombs and the Thousand-Buddha Mountain, where the Double-Nine Festival takes place each year. Within the Lingyan Temple there are beautiful coloured clay statues of the Buddha.

The Shandong Provinccial Museum and the Jinan Municipal Museum are both worth spending time in.

Quancheng Square lies next to the city moat and has a musical fountain. It is the site of most of the city's public entertainments, and is always buzzing.

**POPULATION:**
5,900,000 (2004)
**WHEN TO GO:**
Spring or autumn.
**DON'T MISS:**
Daming Lake Park – contains exquisite pavilions and gardens. The lake is also known as 'Great Brightness Lake' and is fed by 72 famous springs.
The walk up Hero Mountain.
English Corner on Sundays, when people will come and practise their English on you.
People watching in Quancheng Square in the evenings.
**YOU SHOULD KNOW:**
The city's main shopping mall is underground next to Quencheng Square.

*Da Xiangguo Si, Temple of the Chief Minister*

# Kaifeng

**POPULATION:**
801,000 (2004)
**WHEN TO GO:**
Spring or autumn.
**DON'T MISS:**
The Iron Pagoda – which is in fact made out of bricks. Built in 1049 and still standing strong!
Kaifeng Museum – houses some 20,000 artefacts, many dating back to the Ming Dynasty.
Buying silk and embroidery – Kaifeng is renowned for its fine silks and embroidery so be sure to purchase some in one of the city's many enchanting markets.
**YOU SHOULD KNOW:**
Kaifeng is destined to join the tourist trail. Get there before everyone else does.

One of the ancient capitals of China, Kaifeng sits south of the Huang He (Yellow River), to which it is linked by the Grand Canal. Its most famous monument is the Iron Pagoda (Tie Ta), which is in fact built of bricks and covered with glazed brown tiles. It was built in 1049 and has survived remarkably well. Po Ta is a six-sided pagoda, covered in tiles with images of the Buddha. It dates back to the Ming Dynasty. The Shanshangan Huiguan is an ornately decorated guildhall, built in the 18th century with stone carvings, brickwork and woodwork.

The Da Xiangguo Si is among China's most famous Buddhist shrines and is best known for its statue of Avalokitesvara.

Longting Gongyuan (Dragon Pavilion Park) sits on the site of the former Imperial palaces. It has two beautiful lakes and a pavilion which dates back to the late 17th century.

The attraction destined to put Kaifeng on the tourist map is the Qingming Shanghe Yuan. It is based on a scroll in the Forbidden City in Beijing that depicts Kaifeng in the 12th century and is full of reconstructions of bridges, shops, restaurants and other buildings. Dancers and musicians perform rituals of that era and there are also embroidery demonstrations.

# Kashgar

At the foot of the Tian Shan mountains, and with the Karakorams to the south, on the site of an oasis and at the junction of two branches of the ancient Silk Route between East and West, Kashgar (in modern Chinese, Kashi) has long been an important commercial and political centre. In an area that has been fought over for centuries, it has passed between different nations again and again. In a region that receives only a few millimetres of rain a year, the oasis made this area worth fighting over.

At the city's heart lies the Id Kah Mosque, the largest in China, with yellow walls and an architectural style all its own. The tomb of Abakh Khoja is the holiest Islamic site in the region and is a pilgrimage destination. It is a beautiful 17th-century building covered in coloured tiles.

Tourist shops tend to be a rip-off so avoid those and head for the local craft workshops or the market. Local specialities include colourful hats and kilims. Don't start haggling unless you intend to buy.

On Sundays the locals converge on the markets: the Mal Bazaar is the livestock market, while the Yengi Bazaar is where you will find almost anything else (this is also open during the week).

**POPULATION:**
205,000 (1999)
**WHEN TO GO:**
Spring or autumn: summers can be boiling hot and winters absolutely freezing.
**DON'T MISS:**
The Sunday market.
The locals' folk dancing, which blends traditional Chinese dance with Islamic influences.
**YOU SHOULD KNOW:**
Being this far west, the area's main religion is Islam.

*The tomb of Abakh Khoja*

*Largo do Senado – the main square*

# Macao

**POPULATION:**
520,000 (2007)
**WHEN TO GO:**
Any time of year, although it tends to be hot and humid in summer.
**DON'T MISS:**
The Formula One Museum, where the winning cars of both Ayrton Senna and Michael Schumacher are on display and driving simulators allow you to experience racing around the high speed tracks.
The casinos – have a flutter on the Cotai Strip where Macao's best casinos are located.
Watching the Dragon Boat races, held in honour of the poet Wat Yuen who drowned himself as a protest against corruption.
**YOU SHOULD KNOW:**
Macao's autonomous region status is guaranteed until 2049.

A former Portuguese colony, back in Chinese hands since 1999, Macao's culture is a fusion of the two, as is its food. The Historic Centre of Macao World Heritage Site includes 28 monuments and eight public squares.

The Portuguese had been here since the mid-16th century and their buildings dominate parts of the old town, epitomized in the main square, Largo do Senado. To the north are the ruins of St Paul's Cathedral, above it stands the Monte Fort, with a small history museum. Between the square and the Cathedral there is a splendid little church called St Dominic's. Both the Old Protestant Cemetery and the Cemeterio de São Miguel Arcanjo are worth a visit.

The A-Ma Temple is one of the most important in the city, built in the mid-15th century and dedicated to the goddess Matsu. Her festival is in April. Other festivals include the Feast of the Drunken Dragon and the Feast of Bathing of Lord Buddha in May, the Dragon Boat festival in June and the Hungry Ghosts Festival in late August or early September.

The Macao Tower provides views across the city from the revolving restaurant at the top, as well as some of the best food in the city, which is saying a great deal. The food here is varied: Cantonese cuisine and ingredients mingle with Portuguese, Brazilian, Goan and Angolan dishes. This is fusion food at its best!

However, most people come to Macao for the gambling: the recently opened Venetian, a huge casino resort on the Cotai strip, is drawing more visitors to the island than ever before. Modelled on its sister resort in Vegas, it boasts 3,400 slot machines, 800 gambling tables, 3,000 suites, huge retail and convention areas and a 15,000 seat arena for high-profile entertainment and sports events. It houses the biggest casino floor in the world at 51,000 sq m (550,000 sq ft) and is the largest single structure hotel building in Asia and the second-largest in the world.

# Luoyang

To put it simply, Luoyang is one of the most influential cities on the planet. It can lay claim to the inventions of paper, printing, the armillary sphere (which was extremely important for the development of astronomy and navigation), the seismogram and the compass. The first officially sanctioned Buddhist temple in China was built here and both Taoism and Zen have their roots here. The city seems to have originated in the 21st century BC, and for centuries this was the most important place in China.

During the time when the Eastern Han Dynasty held sway (from AD 25), they built their tombs here and the Luoyang Ancient Tombs Museum is one of the highlights of any visit. The first Baima Si (White Horse Temple) was built in AD 68, although the current building is much later. The Shaolin Temple is one of the first important Zen buildings.

Another Buddhist site here is on the World Heritage List – the Longmen Shiku (Dragon Gate Caves or Longmen Grottoes). From AD 493 onwards, more than 30,000 Buddhist statues were carved here.

Other important buildings include the Guanlin Temple – built to commemorate the warrior Guan Yu, who was a hero during the Wu Kingdom.

The limestone landscapes around the city are beautiful and include White Cloud Mountain, the Long Yu Wan National Forest Park, the Ji Guan limestone cave and the Yellow River Xiaolangdi scenic area.

**POPULATION:**
6,384,000 (2004)
**WHEN TO GO:**
Spring or autumn.
**DON'T MISS:**
The Luoyang Museum.
The Wancheng Gongyuan (Peony Festival) in April.
Buying some of the bronzework or glazed pottery.
Longmen Grottoes, in the south of Luoyang city – an area of 2,000 grottoes, 40 pagodas and around 100,000 statues!
**YOU SHOULD KNOW:**
Many of the local food specialities feature Yellow River carp.

# Qufu

**POPULATION:**
650,000 (2004)
**WHEN TO GO:**
Spring, summer or autumn.
**DON'T MISS:**
The Confucius Culture Festival, held to celebrate the birthplace of China's greatest thinker. It includes a sacrifice ceremony and academic seminars.
The Temple of Yan Hui (Yan Hui was Confucius' most prominent disciple).
The Kong Family Mansion – Kong is the family name of Confucius and his descendants. This huge complex consists of 463 buildings, all luxuriously furnished.
**YOU SHOULD KNOW:**
The yellow roofs of the temple are unusual: the colour was otherwise reserved for the Emperor.

Known chiefly for three major monuments, Qufu is a beautiful city. It was the birthplace of the philosopher Confucius, and his presence still infuses the city.

Kong Miao, the Temple of Confucius, is a large complex, which together with the cemetery and the Kong family mansion, makes up a World Heritage Site. Among its most important monuments and buildings are the Star of Literature Pavilion, the Hall of Great Perfection (Dacheng Hall), the Stela Pavilions, the Apricot Platform (Xing Tan Pavilion), the Gate of Great Perfection and the Hall of Confucius' Wife. The complex is second in size in China only to the Forbidden City in Beijing. Its red walls are designed to complement the green of the surrounding trees. There are beautiful symbolic carved dragons guarding parts of the temple.

The cemetery where Confucius' grave lies is a little north of the town. More than 100,000 of his descendants are buried here. It has been planted with thousands of trees to give the appearance of a forest and late in the afternoon when the crowds have gone, it is a peaceful place to stroll or cycle.

The Kong family mansion was inhabited until 1937 by descendants of the philosopher who tended the cemetery and temple and conducted services there. The buildings here now date to the late 1880s: there are nearly 500 rooms. Look out for the Five Strange Objects.

Qufu's central importance in the culture of China makes it a must-visit city.

*An archway leads to Confucius Forest.*

# Nanjing

Nanjing (Nanking, Nankeen) was founded in the 8th century BC and has been China's capital at various times in the past. The treaty signed here in 1842, at the end of the first Opium War, opened up the five Treaty Ports to British trade and granted Hong Kong to Britain.

Nanjing is rich in architecture from many periods of its long history, from the massive city wall to the buildings erected when the Nationalist government designated the city as the national capital, including several foreign embassies, the Presidential Palace and the former central government buildings.

The city is renowned for its green spaces and open areas, including Purple Mountain Scenic Area, Ulong Tan Park (Black Dragon Pond), Zhenzu Spring Park (Pearl Spring Park) and Yue Ya Lake (Crescent Lake).

Purple Mountain contains some of the city's most famous historic relics, the World-Heritage listed Ming Dynasty tombs, as well as Sun Yat-Sen's mausoleum.

One of the most popular destinations for locals and tourists alike is the beautiful Confucius Temple, with a beautiful bridge and several nearby floating tea houses with gold roofs.

An interesting monument is the Nanjing Yangtze River Bridge, built in the 1960s. The statues of workers, farmers and soldiers are masterpieces of 'Socialist Art', each carrying the tools of his trade and Mao's Little Red Book.

Nanjing is a lovely city, with beautiful buildings and parks, stunning modern architecture, world class shopping and a charm all its own.

*Traditional buildings along the Huai River*

**POPULATION:**
6,070,000 (2006)
**WHEN TO GO:**
Spring, autumn or winter.
**DON'T MISS:**
The Ming Dynasty tombs.
A performance by one of the many traditional opera companies.
The International Plum Blossom Festival on Plum Hill.
The Nanjing Massacre monument.
The nightlife in the Nanjing 1912 area.
Tangshan Hot Spring.
**YOU SHOULD KNOW:**
It pays to buy a pass that allows you entry to many of the main parks.

# Qingdao

**POPULATION:**
2,584,000 (2004)
**WHEN TO GO:**
Any time of year.
**DON'T MISS:**
Laoshan National Park, home to the
famous Mount Lao.
The Wind of May sculpture in May,
a burning torch symbolizing
Qingdao's development.
The mermaid shows at
Underwater World.
The Qingdao Beer Museum and the
Qingdao International Beer Festival
held every year in August.
**YOU SHOULD KNOW:**
The name Qingdao means
'Green Island'.

Qingdao owes its existence to its strategic location on China's east coast. The former site of a German colony and naval base, it is probably best known for the Qingdao Brewery, founded in 1903, which produces China's favourite beer.

A favourite holiday destination for Chinese people because of its beaches and good weather, it lines the southern tip of the Shandong Peninsula. There are kilometres of bays and beaches that are always crowded during Chinese holidays.

Because of its role as a major trading port on the Yellow Sea, Qingdao has a high standard of living and has a reputation as one of the best places to live in China.

Although some of its German-era architecture has been lost because of redevelopment, there are several well preserved and protected buildings in Ba Da Guan, the old area of town towards the west of the city, together with some Japanese architecture. The most obvious German building is St Michael's Cathedral, a Romanesque/Gothic mixture, which was completed in 1934 while the Governor's residence is a Bavarian-style castle. In places, the city resembles a Bavarian town. The only remaining Buddhist shrine is the Zhanshan Temple, at the foot of the hill of the same name. It was built in 1945 and has five halls and large numbers of statues of the Buddha.

As a holiday destination, Qingdao has the usual assortment of fast-food restaurants and there is not really a local cuisine. However, good Chinese food can be found on Hong Kong road and downtown in the main nightlife spots. Qingdao has a large Korean ex-pat community and so Korean food is also popular here.

# Pingyao

**POPULATION:**
490,000 (2002)
**WHEN TO GO:**
Spring or autumn.
**DON'T MISS:**
The Wang and Qiao mansions. Wang
is the largest residence in China, a
huge compound of 123 networked
courtyards and 1,118 rooms.
Zhenguo Temple – don't miss the
'Hall of Ten Thousand Buddhas'.
Shuanglin Temple – contains over
1,500 scultures dating from the Yuan
Dynasty. It is often called the
'Oriental Treasure House of
Painted Sculptures'.
**YOU SHOULD KNOW:**
Pingyao is famed for its tasty beef.

Ancient Pingyao, listed as a UNESCO World Heritage Site in 1997, is a small city with broad streets, best known for its Ming Dyasty buildings and its near-intact city wall. There are more than 4000 old structures within the city, including temples, open-fronted shops and family compounds. Wandering around the old city allows you to see the different types of housing that different classes of people inhabited, from imposing mansions to the homes of the poor. The typical style of homes in the city is a courtyard surrounded by buildings on all four sides. Some are simple, single buildings while others hae parallel courtyards or a string of connected spaces. The buildings are timber, painted grey, and tiled and the grander ones have intricately carved woodwork on the doors and windows, with symbolic sculptures. A speciality of the city is the animal-shaped tiles on the roofs and pediments on the richer houses.

The imposing city walls are said to be shaped like a turtle, with the head and eyes represented by the north and south gates and the paired east and west gates standing for the feet. There are two wells just outside the south gate, which presumably represent the eyes. There are four corner towers and 72 watch towers and the whole is surrounded by a deep moat.

The tower that stands at the centre of the city is known as market tower because traditionally the market was held around its foundations. Other beautiful buildings here include the Confucius Temple, the Military God Temple, the Wealth God Temple and the Lucky Fortune Temple. As might be expected in this highly planned city, they are arranged symmetrically.

This is a beautiful city, and is well worth visiting to get an idea of how many Chinese cities would have looked in the past.

*The ancient city of Pingyao*

# Suzhou

**POPULATION:**
6,073,000 (2006)
**WHEN TO GO:**
Spring or autumn.
**DON'T MISS:**
The Classical Gardens.
Pin Jiang Road – take a stroll along this beautiful ancient road paved with hand-cut stones over 1,000 years old.
The Silk Museum.
Huangcangyu Nature Reserve – the most attractive sight in Suzhou with forests, caves, springs, pools and temples.
Wuliu Scenic Area – visitors can taste the high quality mineral water here.
Baita East Road – this street remains undeveloped so maintains many Ming era store fronts.
**YOU SHOULD KNOW:**
I M Pei, the internationally renowned architect, was born here.

*The city is known for its traditional waterside architecture and beautiful gardens.*

Perhaps now best known for its traditional waterside architecture and beautiful gardens, Suzhou was the capital of the Wu kingdom for more than eight centuries and a centre of the silk industry. It is often referred to as the Venice of the East.

At almost every turn, you come across a pagoda or a beautiful garden. The gardens were listed as a UNESCO World Heritage Site in 1997. Among the best are the Humble Administrator's Garden (Zhou Zheng Yuan), the Garden of the Master of the Nets (Wang Shi Yuan), the Mountain Villa with Embracing Beauty (Huanxiu Shanzhuang) which is one of the most important water and rock gardens and the Surging Wave Pavilion (Canglangting). There are smaller gardens dotted throughout the city and these are usually more peaceful places to relax. Among the best of these is the Wufeng Xianguan and Yi Yuan.

The traditional buildings of the city include the Beisi, North and Yunyan pagodas, the Cold Mountain Temple, the Pan Gate and the Baodai Bridge.

Suzhou is also renowned for its arts and crafts. The Kunqu form of Chinese opera originates here, and Suzhou Pingtan is a local storytelling tradition that involves singing. Silk and embroidery are important crafts, as is jade carving.

For a taste of old China, with all its culture and traditions set in a beautiful landscape, this is the place to be.

# Shanghai

The largest industrial city in China, Shanghai sits on the estuary of the Yangtze River. It is a fascinating, frenetic city in which the best of traditional and modern China combine. The iconic modern skyline of Pudong, the world-class shopping and food, the culture and traditional buildings are among the finest in the country.

For sightseeing and shopping, the areas around People's Square and along the Huangpu River have much to offer. Nanjing Road and Huaihai Road are where the best fashion shops are to be found and the latter is also known for its antique shops, cafés and the charming French Concession area. Wander along The Bund to admire the historical buildings and for great views across the river to Pudong.

For weary tourists wanting a break from the frantic pace of the city (and the constant soundtrack of car horns!), the Yuyuan Garden offers welcome respite. This is a beautiful and tranquil area, with bamboos, stone bridges over waterways, ponds with koi and rock gardens all combining to create a serene, calming atmosphere.

Among the old buildings in the city are the Longhua Pagoda, the Jade Buddha Temple and the Tomb of Lu Xun. Chongming Island, Zhujiajiao Water Town and Qibao Ancient Town are also worth visiting. Cultural highlights include the Shanghai Museum and performances in the Shanghai Grand Theatre, both of which are amazing modern buildings.

But take the time to step away from the usual tourist haunts, the fashionable shops and alluring glare of the neon lights, wander down the plethora of side streets and you will discover a world away from the polished, modernized China this country wants the world to see. Here you will gain the best insights into Chinese culture and traditions as inhabitants go about their daily lives seemingly oblivious to your presence amongst them.

**POPULATION:**
18,700,000 (2006)
**WHEN TO GO:**
Spring, summer or autumn, though air pollution can be a problem in summer.
**DON'T MISS:**
The residences of Sun Yat-Sen and Chiang Kai-Shek.
The People's Square.
The world-renowned Shanghai Museum.
The Art Deco Sassoon House.
Shopping on the Nanjing Road – a toy train transports foot-weary shoppers from one end to the other!
The vast and fascinating antiques market in the French Concession.
The historical buildings along the Bund, and the glittering view of Pudong at night.
Steaming hot Shanghai dumplings.
**YOU SHOULD KNOW:**
The number of road fatalities in Shanghai is incredibly high and the driving is often hair-raising! Take care when crossing roads and look out for the motorbikes mounting the pavements, as they frequently do.

*The old and new Shanghai*

351

*The view from Gulangyu Island across to Xiamen*

# Xiamen

One of the five Treaty Ports opened up to the British in the 1840s, Xiamen is a tourist-friendly city with both ancient and modern interest.

Gulangyu Island is where many of the foreign residents made their homes. It is a car-free haven with interesting buildings and is a popular weekend getaway destination.

Although development is rapid here because of the city's special economic zone status, there are many beautiful open spaces and parks that are protected, including Yuandang Lake, which is renowned for its flocks of wild egrets and the beauty of the scene after dark when the sculptures are illuminated. Bai lu Zhou Park is where the locals go in the evening to enjoy themselves. The Botanical Garden is a wonderful place to wander around and look at the plants.

Among the older buildings is the Tang Dynasty Nanputuo Temple, which is counted among China's national treasures. Its green-roofed pavilions are beautiful. Within its precincts are the Hall of Great Mercy, the Precious Hall of the Great Hero, the Hall of Heavenly Kings, and a variety of pagodas.

The Hulishan Fortress, which dates from the late 19th century is unusual in that its foundations are made of a mixture of camphor, glutinous rice, brown sugar, tree sap, sand and clay. The granite fortress has a fine collection of Ming Dynasty cannons. It looks out towards islands that are still under the control of Taiwan.

# Wuhan

One of the seven ancient cities of China, Wuhan is now a thriving modern metropolis and one of the largest hub cities in the country. It is made up of Wuchang, Hankou and Hanyang and so is sometimes called the 'Three Cities of Wuhan'.

One of its most iconic buildings, the Yellow Crane Tower, was originally built in AD 223, but it has been damaged by fire many times and the current version dates from 1981 although you would not know it from the outside. The lift inside is a giveaway!

The Hubei Provincial Museum is well worth spending a day in, as it has rich collections of ancient tombs, including a set of bronze *bianzhong* (concert bells), fossils and musical instruments. Make sure that there will be a show on when you are there: traditional music is played on replicas of ancient instruments and there is an accompanying dance show. The Rock and Bonsai Museum is also a good place to while away an hour so so.

At night, head for Ji Qing Jie, where you can eat street food to the accompaniment of traditional folk music (or sometimes rock or pop music). In the morning, many locals head for Hu Bu Xiang to catch breakfast on the go.

Mao Zedong had a villa overlooking West Lake, and the views from here are beautiful, as are those from Mo Hill.

**POPULATION:**
9,700,000 (2007)
**WHEN TO GO:**
Spring or autumn.
**DON'T MISS:**
Shopping on Jianghan Road.
Snake Hill Park, where Mao's villa and Yellow Crane Pagoda are situated.
**YOU SHOULD KNOW:**
Sun Yat-Sen's 1911 uprising which led to the overthrow of the last Imperial Dynasty started here.

*The Yellow Crane Pagoda*

# Yinchuan

**POPULATION:**
736,000 (2005)
**WHEN TO GO:**
Spring or autumn.
**DON'T MISS:**
The Jade Emperor Pavilion.
Shengtiansi Pagoda.
Helan Shan Scenic Area for the
Suyukou Forest Park and Helan Shan
cliff paintings.
Shapotou resort – here you will
discover a landscape of marvellous
contrasts, an unusual combination of
desert and rivers.
**YOU SHOULD KNOW:**
Yinchuan gets very cold in autumn
and winter.

Yinchuan boasts more than 60 historic monuments, including pavilions, pagodas, mosques, temples and Imperial tombs, and is set among the spectacular scenery of the Ningxia Plain, with the Helan Shan to the west and the Lüliang Shan range to the east.

At the foot of Helan Shan – in the XiXia Wanglin National Park – lie nine Imperial tombs of the Western Xia kings, together with almost 150 aristocrats' graves. Each Imperial tomb was surrounded by an outer wall and they were embellished with turrets, archways, pavilions with stelae, inner sanctums, halls of remembrance and altars. The remoteness of the site means that they are some of the best preserved tombs in China.

There is a mixture of traditional and modern buildings here and the city's beauty means that despite its remoteness it is a popular destination. Among its attractions is the nearby Sha Hu (Sand Lake Scenic Resort).

Islam is an important force here, and there are hundreds of mosques in the region. Among the most beautiful is the Nanguan Mosque, which is a modern rebuilding of a Ming Dynasty original.

The Haibao Pagoda, is a pavilion-style building of nine tiers, counted as one of the most important in all China. Locals say the top of it resembles a peach. The windchimes that hang from the corners make it a special place on windy days.

The Jade Emperor Pavilion is one of the very few old all-wood buildings left in the city, dedicated to the chief god, whose bronze statue stands in the pavilion. It has exquisite curved roofs, red-laquered balustrades and eaves. Its bell tower stands to the east and its drum tower to the west.

*The city is home to many beautiful pagodas*

# Dunhuang

Sitting near an oasis, close to the junction of the northern and southern Silk Routes, Dunhuang has long been an important city both militarily and culturally. One of its ancient names is 'Sha Zhou' (beautiful desert oasis). Its chief claim to fame is the nearby Mogao Caves, a group of nearly 500 cells and cave sanctuaries with wall paintings and statues that were carved out and decorated over a millennium. As well as carving and decorating the caves, the Buddhist monks collected manuscripts and scrolls and other artefacts from traders and travellers who passed through. This was once both the most westerly garrison on the frontier and the only way to get farther west, through either the Yangguan Pass or the Yumenguan Pass.

The Crescent Moon Spring sits within the giant Mingsha Shan which overlooks the city. Its name means humming-sand mountain, and it is called after the noise the sand makes as it moves in the wind. Next to the lake is a traditional Han-style pagoda. Sledding down the dunes is a popular activity.

Another very special feature of the area is the surviving sections of the Han Dynasty Great Wall, which were built in concrete-like slabs. There are also remnants of about 80 beacon towers. If danger threatened, large bundles of reeds were burned to create smoke signals.

**POPULATION:**
100,000 (2004)
**WHEN TO GO:**
May to September.
**DON'T MISS:**
The Mogao Caves.
A camel ride to Mingsha.
Shan–Yueyaquan National Park.
The Great Wall.
**YOU SHOULD KNOW:**
The area is prone to sudden dust storms, so bring glasses, hat and something to protect your face.

*Mogao Caves temple complex
on the Silk Road*

# Chongqing

Sitting at the head of the lake created by the Three Gorges Dam, Chongqing is an inland port city set in an amazing landscape and with a rich culture and history. It was the temporary site of Chiang Kai-Shek's Nationalist government in the 1940s. It is one of the main starting points for tours of the Three Gorges.

West of the main city are the Dazu Rock Carvings; carved during the Tang Dynasty, they are mainly on Buddhist themes and are a World Heritage Site.

In the city, the Great Hall of the People is a modern building, but looks spectacular as it was built in traditional style.

There are several sites associated with World War II in the city, including the former residence of Joseph (Vinegar Joe) Stilwell, head of American operations here. Another site of interest is Song Qing Ling's Residence. She was the wife of Sun Yat Sen, while her younger sister married Chiang Kai-Shek.

Red Crag Village (Hong Yan Cun) is where Mao Zedong and Zhou Enlai stayed for their negotiations with Chiang Kai-Shek Nationalists, which led to the latter leaving for Taiwan and to the Communists gaining control over China.

The Old Town, in Sha Ping Ba is a small group of streets with shops catering mainly for tourists.

*The Dazu Rock Carvings*

安阳市佛教用品 工艺礼品展销

# Anyang

*The ancient pagoda complex of Wenfeng Ta*

Anyang City is one of the 'Seven Ancient Capitals of China' and one of the key sites in the development of Chinese culture. In the west of the city, archaeologists have found evidence that people were living here in caves more than 25,000 years ago, as well as of early Chinese cultures. Some of the earliest writings known – oracle inscriptions on bone and tortoiseshell – were found here.

The Tianning Temple compound has been here for well over 2,000 years, while its Wenfeng Pagoda is thought to date from AD 925, although the current version was built during the Ming Period (1368–1644). This five-storey, octagonal, red-brick tower is unique, topped with a dagoba steeple, and is the city's symbol. Other traditional architecture can be seen in the Xiuding Temple Pagoda and the Mingfu Temple Pagoda.

Yin Xu, an archaeological site first discovered in 1899, is the ancient capital of the late Shang Dynasty (1300–1046 BC), an extremely prosperous period in the Bronze Age. The foundations of more than 80 houses have been unearthed, together with the royal tomb of Fu Hao and several royal buildings. The grave goods from Fu Hao's tomb are superb and a testament to the sophistication of Chinese culture at this time.

**POPULATION:**
5,250,000 (2002)
**WHEN TO GO:**
Late spring to early autumn.
**DON'T MISS:**
The Tianning Temple – one of the largest zen buddhist temples in China. Also home to the Wenfeng Pagoda.
The 10,000 Buddha Ravine.
Yue Fei Memorial Temple.
The Soul Spring Temple.
The Taihand Linlu Hill Scenic Area.
**YOU SHOULD KNOW:**
The tomb of Fu Hao is in the Yin Xu Museum.

**357**

*Liurong Pagoda situated in the Liurong Temple complex*

# Guangzhou

Guangzhou, set on the Pearl River, is the capital of Guangdong Province, the largest city in China and the birthplace of the Chinese revolutionary Sun Yat-Sen, the first president of the Republic of China. In English it is better known as Canton. It has been continuously occupied since the third century BC. The old centre of the city is Liwan and many of the top tourist destinations are here or in Fangcun, including Shamian Island and the Xiguan residential area, which has old houses that used to be occupied by upper class families .

One of the city's best-loved attractions is the Temple of the Six Banyan Trees (the Liurong Temple), named after a famous poem written here by Su Shi. The temple is 6th-century, while the octagonal Flower Pagoda (Hua Ta) is 17 storeys high and dates back to the third century.

Shamian Island is the site of many colonial era buildings, including the Cathedral of Our Lady of Lourdes. Another church is the Shishi Sacred Heart Church.

The Sun Yat-Sen Memorial Hall on Yuexiu Hill is dedicated to this local hero and is set within a pretty park. The ancestral Chen Clan Temple dates from the 19th century and is filled with statues and ivory carvings commemorating members of this wealthy family.

The city has a large number of good museums, including the City Art Museum (calligraphy, Tibetan Buddhist art, traditional Chinese painting and sculpture), Ghangzhou Sculpture Park, Nanyue Royal Tomb Museum, Guangdong Museum of Art (contemporary, particularly local works), Guangzhou Uprising Museum, Guangdong Revolutions History Museum, President Sun Yat-Sen Museum and the Peasant Movement Institute.

There are several lovely parks, and the walk along the riverside is also a must.

**POPULATION:**
12,600,000 (2000)
**WHEN TO GO:**
October to November or April to May.
**DON'T MISS:**
Haggling in one of the many markets.
Zhenhai Tower.
White Cloud Mountain.
**YOU SHOULD KNOW:**
Guangzhou was for many years the only place in China that Westerners could visit.

# Guilin

Guilin is known chiefly for its spectacular setting on the the Lijiang River and its beautiful historic buildings.

Guilin's scenic splendour is difficult to comprehend. Large emerald-green limestone karsts seemingly float on the Li River, whose natural beauty and historic treasures combine to create a magical landscape.

Its symbol is Elephant Trunk Hill (Xiangbi), which really does look like a giant elephant dipping its trunk in the water to drink. It was a sacred place and there are ancient inscriptions carved in and around the moon-shaped cave under the elephant's 'throat'. The Puxian Pagoda stands on top of the hill. It too has many inscriptions from the Tang and Song Dynasties. Another highlight created by the action of water on the limestone of the area is the Reed Flute Cave (Lu Di Yan), with impressive stalagmites and stalactites. Solitary Beauty Peak (Wangfu) is also worth a visit, while Seven Star Park has a decent geological museum.

Near the centre of the city lies the Tomb of Prince Jingjiang, which epitomizes the wealth enjoyed by the area during the Ming Dynasty. The best place to head to get a flavour of the culture that many different people have brought to the region is the Li River Folk Customs Centre.

**POPULATION**:
670,000 (2003)
**WHEN TO GO**:
April to October outside Chinese national holidays.
**DON'T MISS**:
A river cruise from Guilin to Yangshuo – one of the most scenic routes in China. This 83 km (52 mi) trip will take around 4 nights.
Daxu Ancient Town – be sure to visit the Longevity Bridge, Seven Star Tombs and Gaozu Temple.
Yangdi Village, with its elegant waterfalls, winding waterways and beautiful beaches.

*Duxiu Hill lies in the centre of Guilin*

# Beijing

**POPULATION:**
17,200,000 (2007)
**WHEN TO GO:**
Any time, but autumn is best.
**DON'T MISS:**
The Forbidden City.
Tiananmen Gate and Square – at 44
hectares (109 acres), this is the
largest open urban square in the
world. See where the protests of
1989 unfolded.
The Great Hall of the People – built
to commemorate the 10th
anniversary of the People's Republic.
Today it is where parliament meets.
Beijing Ancient Observatory.
The nearby section of the Great Wall,
located 55 km (34 mi) from the city.
The Badaling Pass is a great place to
view one of the world's most
incredible sights. Saviour the
magnificent views from the cable car
that takes you to the top of the wall,
or walk it if you're feeling energetic.
Shopping in Wangfujing or Xidan.
**YOU SHOULD KNOW:**
If you want to see Beijing Opera at
the Laoshe Tea House, you will need
to book in advance.

The capital of the People's Republic of China, Beijing has been inhabited for well over 3,000 years, and has a rich history, culture and architecture. After the years of the cultural revolution, economic activity in China is increasing hand over fist and nowhere more so than in Beijing.

The main tourist attraction is, naturally, the Imperial Palaces of the Forbidden City – now known as the Palace Museum – the private Inner Court and the administrative areas of the Outer Court. Its entrance, the Tiananmen Gate – the Gate of Heavenly Peace – is the epitome of imperial architecture. It is a UNESCO World Heritage Site, as is the Summer Palace, a vast royal park whose landscape, lakes and buildings are designed to ensure that the viewer gets the most out of every viewpoint. There are more than 3,000 structures within the park. The third part of the trio of extensive Imperial sites on the World Heritage List is the Temple of Heaven, a huge temple complex with breathtaking buildings, while the Ming Dynasty Tombs (also on the list) are not only beautiful but important because of what they reveal about early medieval beliefs. There are more than 20 other important temples in the city, all of them worth a visit.

Even older remnants of human occupation were found within the municipality at Zhoukoudian, where archaeologists discovered the remains of Peking Man and an early modern human. The ongoing excavations are also a World Heritage Site.

Fantastic as Beijing's cultural heritage is, it is also a modern, thriving city, full of enterprising, energetic people. It would be a pity to deny yourself the pleasure of haggling for a bargain in one of the markets, such as the Pan Jia Yuan flea market or Hon Qiao where you can buy silk, pearls, turquoise and coral.

*The Forbidden City*

# Hangzhou

One of the most important cultural centres of China, Hangzhou is also particularly known for its spectacular scenery, which has been described in poetry and painting for centuries. It lies within the Yangtze Delta, on the banks of the Quitang River and at the end of the Grand Canal, so water features large.

West Lake (Xi Hu) is the area's greatest attraction and it is famed for its Ten Prospects and Ten New Prospects, which are said to be the most beautiful, but to be frank it is spectacular from just about every direction. Many of the islands, all but one of which are artificial, have temples, palaces, pavilions and pagodas. The most visited attractions here include the Ling Yin Temple, Solitary Hill, the Six Harmonies Pagoda and the Mausoleum of General Yue Fei. Baochu Pagoda is at the top of the hill to the north of the lake, but is worth the walk. Huanglong Cave is another popular destination in this area.

Several of the museums in the district are devoted to the region's products including the National Silk Museum and the Tea Museum.

The villages of Longjin, Manjuelong and Meijiawu are good places to go to see tea being picked.

Guo's Villa (Guo Zhuang) is a beautiful traditional private garden, one of the best in the region, using the traditions of Taoism to create a harmonious mix of water, open and enclosed spaces, light and shade which eventually opens out to overlook the lake.

Hangzhou is one of the most beautiful places in the world.

*Bridge over West Lake in Hangzhou*

**POPULATION:**
3,932,000 (2003)
**WHEN TO GO:**
Any time of year.
**DON'T MISS:**
A trip out to the West Lake's islands (also called Xizi Lake).
The silk market on Tiyuchang Road.
Spending an afternoon in a traditional tea house.
The ferry ride down the Grand Canal. This is the longest man-made waterway in China, at 1,764 km (1,200 mi), and taking a ferry ride down it is a great way to take in the traditional river towns and experience local culture.
The Buddhist carvings in the Feilai Feng Caves – the 300 stone carvings here in Hangzhou's most famous site date from 907 to 1368.
**YOU SHOULD KNOW:**
Marco Polo claims to have come here and described the city as 'beyond dispute the finest and noblest in the world'.

# Fuzhou

**POPULATION:**
6,600,000 (2003)
**WHEN TO GO:**
Any time of year.
**DON'T MISS:**
The hot springs.
Buying the local alabaster carvings.
A Min Opera performance.
**YOU SHOULD KNOW:**
One of the city's nicknames is
Banyan City, after all the banyan
trees planted here.

Fuzhou prides itself on its ancient cultural, historical and literary associations. Not only did the philosopher Zhu Xi live here, but this is one of the places that Marco Polo visited. It was also one of the five Treaty Ports set up by the Nanjing.

While the monuments here are not spectacular, they are extremely good. Hualin Temple is known to date back to at least 964 AD, but may be a lot older, and is, perhaps, the oldest wooden building in China. The black and white pagodas (Wu Ta and Ba Ta) and the Dizang, Xichan and Yongquan temples are all well worth a visit. Sanfang Qixiang is a rare survivor of the ancient houses. A tomb that is worth a detour is that of Lin Zexu, who led an attempt to defeat the British during the 19th century.

The landscape here is also beautiful: the West Lake is an artificial lake set in gardens and created in AD 262, while Gu Shan (Drum Mountain) is spectacular, with a Taoist temple. Its archives are supposed to have been written in the monks' blood. The cablecar to the temple is an easier option than the steep climb. Bai Yn Shan is worth an even stiffer climb for the views and the experience of drinking tea in a cave. The forest park on Qu Shan has spectacular views, stunning waterfalls and a monkey sanctuary.

The area is also known for its three craft specialities, carvings made from the unique local form of alabaster, lacquer work and cork carving.

*Xichan Temple*

# Chengdu

The site of a thriving Bronze Age culture more than 4,000 years ago, Chengdu has a character all its own. It was for hundreds of years the official site for the production of silk brocade for the Imperial family and still prides itself on the quality of the silks and satins sold here.

Like many cities in China, old and modern jostle for room. Areas of pretty streets of traditional houses butt up to vibrant shopping streets – like Chunxi Road – which are bedecked with neon signs. Jin Li is one of the lovely old-fashioned parts of the city.

Sichuan is renowned for its cuisine and the food in Chengdu is reputed to the the best. It is also known for its high number of both tea houses and bars.

The city regained its former importance during World War II when the Nationalist government of Chiang-Kei Shek moved year when the Japanese threatened to overrun the country, and it was among the last cities to fall to the Communists.

Chengdu boasts two of the most popular attractions in this part of China: Chengdu Zoo and the Panda Research Base.

There are several very good museums in the city, including the Sichuan science and Technology Museum (with the famous robot orchestra) and the Sichuan University Museum.

One of the most popular local cultural activities is the Sichuan Opera show, with a variety of acts including musicians, magicians, dancers and fire-eaters.

Chengdu is a magical mix of traditional and modern China.

**POPULATION:**
10,597,000 (2005)
**WHEN TO GO:**
Spring or autumn, although the former is less likely to be grey and wet.
**DON'T MISS:**
The Jin Sha Excavation site.
The Tang Dynasty Wenshu Temple.
The World Heritage Site of Mount Qingcheng.
**YOU SHOULD KNOW:**
Some Sichuan food can be quite spicy. The recommended way to cool down is a glass of peanut milk (ground peanuts, water and sugar).

*Wenshu Monastery, the largest and best-preserved monastery in Chengdu*

# Harbin

**POPULATION:**
9,462,000 (2005)
**WHEN TO GO:**
Any time of year, although it is
extremely cold in winter.
**DON'T MISS:**
A trip to the Siberian Tiger Park.
Unit 731 Museum – this is where
thousands of Chinese civilians were
tortured by Japanese experimenters.
Victims were exposed to various
diseases, poisonous gases, and other
dreadful tortures. An emotive yet
harrowing place.
The Harbin Beer Festival.
Watching the locals dancing the
*niu yang ge.*
The two-yearly Harbin Summer
Music Festival.
**YOU SHOULD KNOW:**
The average temperature in winter is
-17°C (1.4°F).

*Ice sculptures in
Taiyangdao Park*

Unique in China, Harbin is the capital of Heilongjiang Province and bears the marks of its closeness to Russia in both its architecture and its food. Because of its position on a branch of the Trans-Siberian Railway, its role as a place of refuge for exiled Russian aristocrats after the Russian Revolution and a period of Soviet rule.

St Sophia's Cathedral in the Butou district is the most obvious Russian building, built of red brick with a green onion dome, but there are also entire streets of old Russian-style terraced housing, untouched since the Russians left. The cathedral is now the Harbin Museum of Architecture. Several other Russian churches escaped destruction during the Cultural Revolution, but they are mostly not in use.

The Harbin International Ice and Snow Sculpture Festival runs from January until the ice melts. The Snow and Ice Festival features giant carvings in snow, while the Ice Lantern Festival has large statues and buildings carved in ice with lanterns softly glowing inside.

Just outside the city is the Siberian Tiger Park, dedicated to preserving these beautiful but endangered big cats. The squeamish should avoid the feeding sessions.

*The Potala Palace and Stupa*

# Lhasa

The holiest centre of Tibetan Buddhism, Lhasa is the traditional seat of the Dalai Lama. One of the highest cities in the world, it sits at the foot of Mount Gephel. The name means Land of the Gods. At the east of the city you will find the Barkhor Street Market and the Jokhang Temple (Tsuglagkhang), while the western part is where all the hotels, restaurants and other tourist infrastructure lies.

The Potala Palace (Podrang Potala) perches on Mount Marpo Ri. There has been a stronghold here for at least 1400 years, but the current version is chiefly the work of the Fifth Dalai Lama in the 17th century and the Thirteenth Dalai Lama in the 20th century. It is a steep climb up to the palace and it spreads over several floors, so visiting the museum here is not to be advised before you acclimatize to the altitude. The Dalai Lama's main residence until 1755, and then the winter residence until the mid-20th century, the palace is now a museum with shrines, antiques and scriptures. The inner, Red Palace contains the tombs and shrines of the Lamas, while the outer, white palace contained residential areas and the administrative offices. The Norbulingka, a short distance to the south, was the summer residence and has been undergoing restoration.

The Jokhang Temple was first built in the 7th century to shelter statues of the Buddha, most importantly the Jowo Sakyamuni Buddha. It is traditional for pilgrims to perform the *koras* by walking around the three concentric paths that encircle the temple.

Although the city is at risk of becoming a theme park if care is not taken by the authorities, it still has the atmosphere of one of the holiest sites on Earth.

**POPULATION:**
257,000 (2004)
**WHEN TO GO:**
March to October.
**DON'T MISS:**
The Sera Monastery – covers an area of 12 hectares (28 acres). Its name means 'rose', after the roses that adorn the surrounding hills in the summer months.
The Tibet Museum.
Buying Tibetan rugs.
Drinking *pöcha* (Tibetan butter tea) or Chang beer.
**YOU SHOULD KNOW:**
Non-Chinese nationals require a permit to visit Tibet.

*Taipei 101 towers above a busy street.*

# Taipei

Originally a small village, Taipei became an important centre for the export of tea in the 19th century. After the Japanese acquired the island in 1885, the city expanded rapidly, and it became the seat of Chiang-Kai Shek's government in 1949.

The city has a wealth of architecture from throughout its history, from the 17th-century Kuantu Temple to the modern Taipei 101. One of the most popular temples in the city is the Lungshan Temple, originally built in 1738–1740, although the current structure dates from 1945. Chingshui Temple has some of the best Ching-Dynasty architecture and decorations, while the Confucian Temple is the opposite, being almost totally plain except for inscriptions. The Chihnan Temple is not for the faint-hearted; it is at the top of a flight of stairs reputed to have 1200 steps. There are dozens of other temples in the city that are also worth visiting.

The most popular tourist attraction is the National Palace Museum, which is full of Chinese and Japanese works of art, and is a must-visit. The Chiang Kai-Shek Memorial Hall, recently and controversially renamed the National Taiwan Democracy Memorial Hall, is a monument to the former leader that houses a museum dedicated to him. The surrounding gardens are a favourite place for locals to practise Tai chi in the early morning. The ornate National Theatre Hall and National Concert Hall can also be found in the grounds.

The smaller Sun Yat-sen Memorial Hall is set in a large park and houses a library and exhibition halls and concerts are often held here. The architecture is magnificent.

Taipei is also renowned for its wide range of food from all over the Far East and its shopping. The Weekend Jade Market near Renai Road is a must, as is the Chinese Handicraft Mart on Xuzhou Road. International designer brands can be found on Zhongshan North Road, while Tihua Street – the best preserved old street in the city – is where many of the locals head for fabrics, traditional medicines and dry goods and there are dozens of local shopping areas both in the centre and in East Taipei.

This beautiful city is a mixture of traditional and modern, global and local and is a true must-see.

**POPULATION:**
9,560,000 (2007)
**WHEN TO GO:**
Any time of year.
**DON'T MISS:**
Shopping, shopping and more shopping.
The Taipei Lantern Festival.
Eating stinky tofu!
The views from the observation platforms of Taipei 101.
Shilin Night Market.
Yanmingshan National Park.
**YOU SHOULD KNOW:**
It's best to buy an *Easycard* for use on public transport.

# Tainan City

A former capital of the island in Imperial times, Tainan is full of historic buildings, including beautiful temples and parts of the successive sets of fortifications, including Chikan Tower (Providentia Fort) and Anping Fort (originally called Orange Fort and then Fort Zeelandia), both built by the Dutch in the 17th century. The former has interesting stone carvings of animals while the latter has wide views over the ocean and coastline. The Anping district is also well known for its pretty little streets with traditional small houses with symbols to ward off evil, and shrines.

The most famous of Tainan's multitude of temples is the First Confucian School/Temple, which was built in 1665. Although it has been enlarged and reconstructed several times over the last 350 years, the compound contains the most complete set of temple buildings and altars and associated buildings. Tseng Chen-Yang Mu is worth a visit for its Ming Dynasty tombs.

Tainan Fu Cheng-Huang Miao, Hsien Cheng-Huang Miao and Anping Chen Cheng-Huang Miao are temples to the city god Chen-Huang, who meted out justice. All three temples are stunning. Other temples and shrines include Koxinga's Temple.

Tainan is also renowned for its snack food and its night markets, and is sometimes known as the city of snacks, which are available both at the markets and from street vendors. Specialities include pearl milk tea, shrimp rolls, Dan Dan Noodles and coffin toast.

**POPULATION:**
758,000 (2006)
**WHEN TO GO:**
Any time of year.
**DON'T MISS:**
An organized trip to the mangrove reserves, the migrating ground of the rare black-faced spoonbill.
The 19th century Eternal Fortress situated on the coast.
The night markets – there are around a dozen of these dotted all over the city. Wares on offer include clothes, toys, food and souvenirs. Some also offer live entertainment.
**YOU SHOULD KNOW:**
A free tri-lingual map (English, Chinese and Japanese) is available at most railway stations.

*Tainan City is home to many beautiful temples*

# Kaohsiung

**POPULATION:**
1,511,000 (2006)
**WHEN TO GO:**
Any time of year.
**DON'T MISS:**
Tuntex Sky Tower – get a spectacular view over the city from the 75th floor. The elevators are among the fastest in the world, travelling at speeds of 750 m (2,460 ft) per minute.
A boat trip on the Ai River – visit the surrounding rainforest and encounter many species of wildlife, flowers and trees. It has become known as the 'Love River' due to its romantic scenery.
The Sizihwan Scenic Area.
**YOU SHOULD KNOW:**
The best ways to get to the island of Chijin are through an underwater tunnel or ferry.

Kaohsiung is on the south-west coast of Taiwan, lying on the Ai River and facing the Taiwan Strait across the Island of Chijin. It is the second largest city in Taiwan and its busiest port, founded under the Ming Dynasty as a fishing port. It is still famous today for its wealth of seafood restaurants, especially on Chijin. At night, Liouho Night Market is one of the most popular tourist destinations, where you can barter for crafts, clothes, seafood, small electronics, pets and, especially, food.

Scenic areas of the city that can be thronged with tourists include the Fisherman's Wharf and the Urban Spotlight Arcade, which is well known for its illuminations. The Tuntex Sky Tower is an 85-storey building with an observation deck that offers panoramas over the city, the harbour and the mountains behind.

Religious buildings in and around the city include the Holy Rosary Cathedral, originally designed in the 19th century and rebuilt in the 1920s in a mixture of Gothic and Romanesque styles. It is particularly renowned for its Christmas Eve celebrations.

The Fo Guang Shan Monastery is now only partly open to the public, in order to protect the monks' need for peace and quiet, but it is still well worth a visit.

The city's long history and its current status as a centre for industry are represented in its museums, including the Museum of Fine Arts, the National Science and Technology Museum, the Kaohsiung Astronomical Museum and the Kaohsiung Hakka Cultural Museum.

Kaohsiung is a spectacular place, with soaring modern architecture, stunning scenery and a vibrant culture.

*Wuli Pagoda on Lotus Lake*

# Osaka

Osaka is not only a vibrant modern city, but is the site of one of the most ancient large settlements in Japan, which has been important as a sea and river port on and off for centuries. Burials have been found that date back to thousands of years BC, while there are oyster-shell mounds that date from the 5th and 6th centuries AD, commemorating the funerals of important rulers.

Today, Osaka is one of Japan's major commercial and shipping hubs and is internationally famous for its gourmet food and shopping, in Minimi's Namba, Dotonbori, Amerikamura and Shinsaibashi areas, as well as Den Den Town for electricals and the longest shopping arcade in Japan, Tenjinbashi-suji.

Like most old cities, Osaka has a wealth of temples and shrines, including Shitenno-ji, reputed to be the first Buddhist temple in Japan, and Sumiyoshi Taisha, one of the earliest Shinto shrines, thought by some to date back to the early 3rd century.

Osaka's long history and culture are celebrated in many museums and galleries, including the Osaka Museum of History; the Museum of Oriental Ceramics; Osaka Prefectural Museum of Kamigata Comedy and Performing Arts and the Osaka Municipal Museum of Art. There are also science, natural history and childrens' museums. The National Museum of Art is underground, and its collections concentrate on modern art. The city is also known for its traditional kabuki and *bunraku* (puppet) theatres.

Other attractions include Osaka Aquarium Kaiyukan, the second largest in the world, and Shin-Umeda City, with its floating garden observatory 170 m (560 ft) above ground, an underground shopping centre and a Zen garden.

Osaka Castle Garden is a favourite place for both locals and tourists, especially when the cherry trees are in blossom: the castle itself is a reproduction. Other open spaces include Nakanoshima Park, Sumiyoshi Park and Tennoji Park, designed by one of the country's best gardeners, Jihei Ogawa.

*The 16th-century Osaka Castle*

*Statue of the Amida Buddha*

# Kamakura

Set on the southern coast of Honshu, about 50 km (30 mi) south-west of Tokyo, Kamakura overlooks Sagami Bay and is backed by mountains, which made it an ideal site for a shogun fortress. However, its chief claim to fame now is its multitude of shrines and temples. It is a popular destination for day trips from the capital.

Among the city's most famous monuments is the statue of the Amida Buddha. He has sat here, exposed to the elements since the 15th century after a tsunami caused by an offshore earthquake washed away the temple that once housed him. There has been a bronze statue of the Buddha here since the middle of the 13th century, but it is not known whether this is that original. It is more than 13 m (43 ft) high and weighs more than 90,000 kg (90 tons).

To detail all the shrines and temples in the city would fill a book, but among the best known are the Tokei-ji (a refuge, or nunnery, for women who would stay there for three years in order to obtain a divorce); the Engaku-ji; the ten remaining sub-temples of Kencho-ji; and the ancient Kannon Temple of Hase-dera, which houses a huge wooden statue of Kannon. The most important shrine in the city is the Tsurugaoka Hachiman Shrine. It was built near Yuigahama in the mid 11th century, but brought here in 1191 by the founder of the Kamakura shogunate, who wanted its protection. It is dedicated to the Emperor Ojin and his wife and mother.

**POPULATION:**
171,000 (2005)
**WHEN TO GO:**
Spring or autumn.
**DON'T MISS:**
A trip on the Enoshima Electric Railway along the coast.
The delicious local senbei rice cakes.
The Tsurugaoka Hachiman Shrine.
**YOU SHOULD KNOW:**
Kamakura was Japan's capital between 1192 and 1333.

# Tokyo

Tokyo is one of the busiest cities on the planet: the pace of life here never seems to slow down. From sightseeing outside the Imperial Palace to shopping in 'Little Hong Kong' in the new area of Odaiba everything carries on at breakneck pace. A thriving town called Edo since the early 17th century, it became the new capital of Japan when Emperor Meiji moved the imperial court here in 1869. As well as some of the best shopping in the world, in places such as Ginza, Shibuya, Ikebukero and Shinjuku, Tokyo is home to a rich variety of cultural attractions. In Ueno Park, the Tokyo National Museum has twenty galleries filled with artefacts from 1,500 years of Japanese history. The National Museum of Western Art nearby has a large collection of Impressionist works, and other institutions here include the Municipal Art Gallery, the National History Museum, the National Science Museum and the Gallery of Far

**POPULATION:**
12,570,000 (2006)
**WHEN TO GO:**
Any time of year.
**DON'T MISS:**
The bullet train.
Taking a traditional bath in the hot springs in Azabu-Juban.
Shomben Yokocho.
The trip to Mt Fuji.
The Meiji Shrine.
Tokyo Tower.
**YOU SHOULD KNOW:**
Greater Tokyo has over 30,000 residents making it the largest metropolitan area in the world.

Eastern Art.

Shinjuku is also home to the Shinjuku Gyoen National Garden, which has both Japanese and European style gardens, and a tea-house where visitors can take part in the traditional tea ceremony. The area is also a very popular centre for nightlife, as is the Roppongi quarter. Ginza is home to the Kabuki-za Theatre.

In Asakusa, you will find the Sensoji Temple, the Five Storied Pagoda and Nakamise, a traditional shopping arcade, as well as the Hanayashiki Amusement Park. Harajuku is where the young hang out, while Azabu-Juban is upmarket and Akihabara is the place to head to buy electronics.

Whatever you look for in a city, Tokyo has it in spades, from beautiful gardens to theme parks, and fine art galleries to the biggest fish markets in the world.

*The Shinjuku district*

# Fukuoka

Fukuoka is claimed by many to be the oldest city in Japan, and there is archaeological evidence that the area was important in the very early history of the country. Dazaifu, 15 km (10 mi) to the south, was an important administrative centre by the mid 7th century and there is speculation that the capital was here.

Kublai Khan tried to invade this area repeatedly in the late 13th century, and one of the city's best museums is the Genko Historical Museum in Higashi Koen, which has exhibits of Japanese and Mongolian arms and armour of the time. Other museums include the Fukuoka Art Museum in the lovely Ohori Park (where the much-restored Fukuoka Castle can also be found), the Fukuoka Asian Art Museum, the Fukuoka City Museum, which has items from the city and surrounding region, and the Hakata Machiya Folk Museum, which is dedicated to the traditional culture of the area.

Culture here also extends to popular festivals. Hakata Dontaku is an 800-year-old festival held in early May, when traditional plays are staged all over town. Hakata Gion Yamakasa is a men-only affair in July when teams of loincloth-clad men, representing their own districts, race around the city carrying extremely heavy floats.

But Fukuoka is not just a city with a long history: it is one of the fastest growing and most dynamic cities in the world. There are few really old buildings (and many traditional houses had to be demolished after the earthquake in March 2005). However, important monuments include the Gokuku, Kashii and Hakozaki shrines and the Tenmangu Shrine in Dazaifu. The Shofuku-ji Temple is reputed to be the first Zen temple in Japan, the Sumiyoshi Shrine is one of the oldest in Kyushu and the So family tombs are spectacular.

Tenjin is the place to go for shopping, and Nakasu and Nagahama-Dori are the best places for food. Street food here includes a local style of ramen, made with pork broth called *tonkotsu*, widely available from the stalls known as *yatai*.

*Fukuoka is one of the fastest growing cities in the world.*

# Matsuyama

One of Matsuyama's most popular attractions is the Dogo Onsen, reputed to be the oldest hot spring bath house in Japan, fed by hot waters leaking up through an underground fault. There is a variety of bath houses here, including the late 19th-century Yushinden, built for the imperial family.

Matsuyama Castle (Matsuyama-jo) was built perched on Katsuyama Hill in the early 17th century, in a position that reminds everyone of the importance of the town's rulers. Its ruins have been designated a national treasure.

Matsuyama prides itself on being the centre of the art of haiku: the great 19th-century haiku master Masaoka Shiki lived here and his house and museum are always busy. Gudabutsuan, on Ichibancho, is another house where he lived for a while, and is a beautiful example of traditional housing of the area.

Other famous natives of Matsuyama were Yoshifuru and Saneyuki Akiyama: their birthplace is now a museum dedicated to the memory of these two great military strategists.

The art gallery in Shiroyama Park is excellent, and its annexe is the pretty French-style building, Bansuiso, on Ichibacho.

More restored castle buildings are to be found in Dogo Park, where the Yuzuki-jo (Yuzuki Castle), together with its gardens and surrounding buildings, show how the inhabitants would have lived from the 13th to 16th centuries.

Matsuyama is an important site on the Shikoku Pilgrimage and among its most important monuments are the Joruri, Yasaka, Jodo and Ishite temples. The last is one of the most important. An important Buddist monument is the Isaniwa Shrine on Dogo Hill, one of the best examples of the Hachiman-zukuri (war god) style of architecture.

Life in Matsuyama rarely reaches the hectic pace of some of Japan's larger cities. It is a quiet, yet welcoming place, renowned for its literary and historic connections.

*Matsuyama Castle overlooks the city.*

**POPULATION:**
513,000 (2004)
**WHEN TO GO:**
Any time of year.
**DON'T MISS:**
A ride on one of the Iyo Railway's street cars, especially the Botchan Densha.
Eating one of the famous tarts made in the area.
The Botchan Gizmo Clock – chimes on the hour (between 8 am and 9 pm) when figures depicting scenes from the novel *Botchan* (widely thought of as Japan's most popular novel) emerge.
New Year at Ishiteji Temple.
Saka no Ue no Kumo Museum – documents how the Japanese people rebuilt their country after the Meiji Revolution and Russian Conflict.
**YOU SHOULD KNOW:**
Shikoku means 'pine tree mountain'.

*Tahoto Pagoda and the
Five-Storied Pagoda,
Miyajima Island*

# Hiroshima

Destined to be known forever as the first city to be attacked with an atomic bomb, Hiroshima has rebuilt itself as a modern, vibrant city: within ten years of the end of World War II, the population had reached pre-war levels again.

The city had been important during the Shogun, Edo and Meiji periods, and the rebuilt castle has a museum dedicated to life during the Edo period, while the Hiroshima Museum of Art has one of the best collections of French Renaissance art in Asia.

The beautiful gardens of Shukkei-en are not far from Ground Zero, and highlights include the Rainbow Bridge and the tranquil pond. Mitaki-dera is a beautiful shrine set within grounds that include three waterfalls whose waters are used during the annual Hiroshima Peace Memorial Ceremony. The Tahoto Pagoda was brought from Hirogawa in 1951 as a memorial to the victims of the bombing.

The contents of the Peace Memorial Museum are harrowing, as is the Peace Memorial (also known as the A-Bomb Dome), the remains of the former Prefectural Industrial Promotional Hall which is thought to have been directly under the blast. The park also has a memorial dedicated to the children who died, the Cenotaph for the A-bomb Victims and the Hiroshima National Peace Memorial Hall.

Elsewhere, Hijiyama-koen is a large park with both manicured gardens as well as some forest areas. The Manga Museum and the Museum of Contemporary Art are within its boundaries.

While it is impossible to forget the tragic events of 1945, Hiroshima's people have rebuilt their city and their lives and created a welcoming, modern city unique in Japan, famed for the quality of its restaurants, offering a wide variety of cuisines.

**POPULATION:**
1,160,000 (2004)
**WHEN TO GO:**
Any time of year.
**DON'T MISS:**
Miyajima Island – a strikingly beautiful island, home to the Tahoto Pagoda.
Peace Memorial Park and Hiroshima Peace Memorial Museum – dedicated to the citizens killed by the bomb. The park is home to many monuments paying tribute to the victims and the museum documents details of the tragedy.
The tram system.
**YOU SHOULD KNOW:**
Don't bring up the subject of the bombing with the locals unless they mention it first.

# Nikko

Just two hours' journey west of Tokyo lies the pilgrimage town of Nikko. It is set within stunning mountain scenery, but its importance lies in its Buddhist and Shinto temples and shrines, which were declared a UNESCO World Heritage Site in 1999. Three of the most important of these are the Futarasan Jinja, Rinnoji and Nikko Toshogu. The first two belong to the second part of the 8th century, when the Buddhist monk, Shodo, built several shrines, temples and other buildings here, but perhaps the most famous of the three is the Toshogu, a shrine built in honour of the powerful Shogun, Tokugawa Ieyasu after his death in 1616. The first shrine in his honour was relatively simple, but his grandson, Tokugawa Iemitsu, later erected the much more elaborate shrine we see today, covered in carvings and paintings, as well as a highly ornate one for himself. Their grandeur emphasizes the power the Tokugawa Dynasty once held.

The area is also full of other monument, including Torii, beautiful bridges, ornamental bell towers, gateways, pagodas, statues, hallways and other temples and shrines. The Nikko Toshogu Shrine Museum of Art is also here. The Tosho-gu complex lies within a beautiful landscape, with views of the surrounding countryside, which is among the most spectacular in Japan.

**POPULATION:**
94,000 (2006)
**WHEN TO GO:**
April to October.
**DON'T MISS:**
The three wise monkeys carving on the Nikko Toshogo.
Nikko National Park, west of the city, an area of outstanding beauty.
The region's hot springs.
The annual recreation of Ieyasu's funeral rites in May.
**YOU SHOULD KNOW:**
It can get very cold here in winter.

*Niten-mon gate*

# Kobe

**POPULATION:**
1,530,000 (2007)
**WHEN TO GO:**
Any time of year.
**DON'T MISS:**
A taste of Kobe beef.
The 19th-century foreign homes in Kitano.
A harbour boat cruise.
The Onsen resort town of Arima Harbourland and its great ferris wheel.
**YOU SHOULD KNOW:**
The Kobe earthquake – or Great Hanshin earthquake – of 1995 was one of the most costly disasters in Japan's history, and its economic effects are still felt today.

One of the earliest cities in Japan to become open for trade with other countries – after the prolonged isolation of the late Edo period – in 1868, Kobe is a cosmopolitan, welcoming place.

The beautiful Ikuta Shrine is the most important monument, and might be described as the city's raison-d'être. According to literature, it was founded in the early 3rd century as part of military rites and the forest behind it is dotted with markers commemorating battles. Other important shrines include Nagata-ku, which was founded at the same time.

Kobe is renowned as a centre of the fashion industry and its chief shopping areas are Motomachi and Sannomiya, which are also the hubs for its nightlife. Next to Motomachi lies the city's Chinatown - Nankinmachi - a thriving, bustling area.

One of the most iconic structures of Kobe is Kobe Port Tower, a strangely shaped metal structure (technically known as a hyperboloid) 108 m (over 350 ft) high, with an observation deck near the top which allows views over the port. The views across the Akashi Strait from the Akashi-Kaikyo suspension bridge are also stunning, as are those from the Venus Bridge.

Kobe sits at the foot of the symbolic Rokko mountain range with popular walking, kiking and sightseeing areas, which is easy to access from the city by cable-car. It is home to Japan's first golf course. The range is famous for its colours in autumn. The hot springs of the Arima onsen lie the other side of the range.

Kobe is also the site of the oldest mosque in Japan, built in Kitano in the 1930s in a traditional Turkish style.

*The port and the Maritime Museum*

# Takayama

Takayama, often called Hida Takayama to distinguish it from the other towns and cities of the same name, is a beautiful place, with old streets and buildings, and a distinctive atmosphere born of its relative isolation on the banks of the Miyagawa River. The old part of the city is widely regarded as the epitome of what Japan used to be and the historic centre – Sanmachi – manages to retain this impression without becoming either twee or over-commercialized.

Traditional crafts are among the area's specialities, and the city is particularly known for its lacquerware, carpentry and pottery, which can be seen in the Takayam-shi Kyodo-kan, the local history museum.

The skill at carpentry is particularly evident in the many monuments that still dot Takayama, including the Hida-Kokubun-ji temple's three-storey pagoda and the Ankoku-ji Temple and Storehouse, which dates back to 1408 and is a recognized national treasure.

The best ways to see the area are from the top of the nearby Mount Norikura – a dormant volcano to the east, or the 3.2 km (2-mi) Shin-Hotaka Ropeway.

The Hida Cultural Village is an open-air museum, in which traditional houses of the last two centuries have been collected. They are beautiful in their simplicity and perfectly designed to cope with the heavy snowfall that affects this area in winter, sometimes for months on end. The gassho-zukuri farmhouses are named after their roofs, which are shaped like praying hands.

**POPULATION:**
97,000 (2007)
**WHEN TO GO:**
Spring, summer and autumn.
**DON'T MISS:**
The spring and autumn festivals.
Mount Norikura, part of the
Northern Alps.
The Shin-Hotaka Ropeway – this
cable car ride provides spectacular
and far-reaching views of the
Northern Alps.
The Oku-Hida Onsen Villages.
The Hida-no-Sato folk village.
**YOU SHOULD KNOW:**
Takayama is at high altitude and can
get very cold in winter.

*Bridge across the
Miyagawa River*

*The cherry trees in bloom at Kanazawa Castle*

# Kanazawa

**POPULATION:**
455,000 (2006)
**WHEN TO GO:**
Spring, summer or autumn.
**DON'T MISS:**
The Noto Peninsula National Park.
Kenrokuen Garden – one of the castle's outer gardens. It is beautifully landscaped, contains lovely water features, and is home to many species of trees and plants.
The local sake, which is reputed to be among the best in Japan.
Kanazawa Yasue Gold Leaf Museum – Yasue Takaaki was an artist who devoted his life to working with gold leaf. In 1974 he spent his fortune on a place to display his work. Today it is a museum.
**YOU SHOULD KNOW:**
Kanazawa means 'Marsh of Gold'.

Kanazawa, on the north coast of Honshu, has a long and complicated history, much of which can be read in its surviving historic buildings and monuments. It has been the centre of power of 'The Peasant's Kingdom' of the Ikko Buddhist sect; one of the largest cities during the Edo period, of which several streets remain, centred round its castle with samurai mansions and complexes, temple areas and merchants' houses; and an army stronghold during the Meiji period.

Little of the original Kanazawa Castle survives: it was badly damaged by fire in the 17th and 19th centuries. What remains is being restored. Ishikawa-mon is its old back gate. Its outer garden, Kenrokuen is widely considered to be among the top three in Japan. In the corner is the mid-19th-century Seisonkaku Villa, an elegant building with bright interior decoration. Less elegant, but equally popular with visitors, are the one-time geisha houses in Higashi.

Samurai were given estates according to their status and wealth, and a few of their houses remain in the city, as do some merchants' houses, which are very long and narrow because they were taxed on their width, not their floor area.

Important monuments in the city include the Oyama Shrine, built in 1875. Its triple-storey Shinmon Gate is a harmonious mixture of Japanese and Dutch styles. Even the railway station has an amazing gateway. Teramachi and Utatsuyama are the temple districts. Myoryuji Temple, also known as the ninja dera, even though it is nothing to do with ninjas, has an astonishing number of hidden doors and secret passageways.

Kanazawa is a centre for the production of gold leaf, and the Kanazawa Yasue Gold Leaf Museum is a must.

# Kyoto

If you conjure up a mental image of traditional Japanese architecture and gardens, it's likely that it's a fairly close match to the historic areas of Kyoto. It was the capital of Japan from 794 until the 1860s, when Emperor Meiji relocated to Edo. It is one of the few cities in Japan to retain large numbers of older buildings, and 17 properties here, consisting of 198 monuments, make up the UNESCO World Heritage Site of the Historic Monuments of Kyoto, which was declared in 1994. Among the best known of these are Kinkaku-ji (the Golden Pavilion) and Gingaku-ji (the Silver Pavilion). The latter is a beautiful, two-storey wooden pavilion set among traditional Japanese gardens. Kinkaku-ji is, if it is possible, even more elegant and striking. It was built in the late 14th century as a country villa but was converted to a temple after the owner's death. In the same district, Higashiyama, the Kiyomizu-dera is an amazing structure, built on the side of a steep hill – it's wooden platform gives spectacular views over the valley in which the city sits.

The monuments of the World Heritage Site were chosen because they each represented a particular style of architecture and an era in the city's development, but Kyoto has so much more to see: there are some 1,700 Zen Buddist temples, 300 Shinto shrines and assorted villas associated with the imperial family. Kyoto's historic buildings and gardens were once the source of inspiration and aspiration for the rest of Japan. Their beauty is still a source of inspiration for many people today.

**POPULATION:**
1,474,000 (2006)
**WHEN TO GO:**
Spring, summer or autumn.
**DON'T MISS:**
The Imperial Palace.
The traditional townhouses and cobbled lanes of Sannenzaka and Ninenzaka.
Toji and Sanjusangendo Buddhist temples.
Shgakuin imperial villa.
**YOU SHOULD KNOW:**
The Kyoto Protocol was signed here in 2002, with objectives set out to reduce greenhouse gases and prevent climate change.

*The Golden Pavilion*

# Seoul

**POPULATION:**
10,400,000 (2006).
**WHEN TO GO:**
September to November and
March to May.
**DON'T MISS:**
Gyeongbokgung Palace and
its museums.
Changdeokgung Palace and its
Secret Garden.
Mount Namsan Park.
Yeouido Park.
Mount Inwang, its temple and
famous Shamanist shrine.
Seoul Tower, offering the best
panoramic view of the city.
**YOU SHOULD KNOW:**
A quarter of South Korea's
population lives in the greater
metropolitan area of Seoul. There are
40 universities here.

Seoul is a city rushing headlong into the 21st century. Established as the capital of the Korean peninsula in 1394, it has a turbulent and bloody history. Colonized by Japan in the early 1900s, it gained independence in 1945. The Korean War (1950-1953) fought between the north and south and backed by communist China and the western allies respectively, left Seoul in tatters. It has since totally reinvented itself, thanks to an aggressive economic policy.

Set amongst eight mountains, and divided by the Han River, Seoul is now one of the most populous and successful cities on earth. The speed with which it has been transformed has produced a fascinating combination of ultra-modernity and ancient tradition. Seoul has the most skyscrapers of any Asian city. You can 'shop 'til you drop' in designer stores, one of which has seventeen floors above ground and seven beneath, or buy electronic items in a market comprising twenty buildings containing 5,000 shops.

If tradition is more your thing, the old Joseon Dynasty city, now the downtown area, contains many historic buildings. There are five major palaces to see, including the fabulous Changdeokgung, beautifully restored and listed by UNESCO. Visit wonderful Buddhist temples and take part in a tea ceremony with the monks, and don't miss Namdaemun, the Great South Gate and Korea's national symbol. For those with an interest in modern history, guided tours of Seodaemun Prison, notorious during the Japanese occupation, are available.

The city is safe and easy to get around, and its inhabitants are friendly and helpful. To improve the environment, millions of trees have been planted, and the city is full of splendid parks. Koreans love to socialize over food, and Seoul is packed with restaurants, grillhouses, bars and clubs. Seoul is the country's economic powerhouse, as well as its cultural and political centre, and it shows.

*The skyline at dusk*

# Gyeongju

Gyeongju, one of South Korea's best-loved destinations, lies in the south-eastern corner of the country. Set over a number of small hills, the city has expanded and modernized during the last sixty years, and manufacturing is more important to the economy than tourism. For almost 1,000 years the Korean Peninsula was ruled by the Shilla Dynasty, which reached its zenith between the 7th and 10th centuries, and Gyeongju was its capital.

*The Pulguksa Temple*

The historic centre lies on the banks of the Hyeongsan River, an area that has suffered regular flooding since the city's inception, often due to typhoons. Modern flood controls have helped enormously however, and the last major flood was in 1991. Gyeongju is often described as one of the world's largest open-air museums and its four historic areas were designated World Heritage Sites by UNESCO in 2000. An important centre for Korean Buddhism, Mount Namsan is, incredibly, home to 122 ruined temples, 64 stone pagodas, 53 stone statues and 16 stone lanterns. It also has a fortress, a pavilion and a quantity of Buddhist images carved into the rock face. A number of hiking trails wind around Namsan, and this is a fantastic way of seeing some of the sights.

The Hwangnyongsa area boasts the ruins of two amazing temples; the eponymous site was once the largest temple ever built on the peninsula. There are also areas containing ruined fortresses and royal tombs, from which thousands of treasures have been excavated. Many of these can be seen in the excellent National Museum.

This is a pleasant city to visit, with many traditional houses remaining. If you tire of historic sites you can try watching Ssireum, traditional Korean wrestling, or yutnori, a fascinating but incomprehensible board game played with wooden sticks. There are plenty of places to stay downtown, or enjoy the pleasures of the resorts at the nearby Bomun Lake.

**POPULATION:**
280,000 (2004)
**WHEN TO GO:**
April, May, September and October.
**DON'T MISS:**
Cheomseongdae Observatory, one of the best examples of an ancient observatory in Asia.
The Heavenly Horse Tomb.
The fortresses of Wolseong and Myeonghwal.
The Temple of Bulguksa and the Grotto of Seokguram.
The annual Silla Cultural Festival, held in October.
The cherry blossom in April.
**YOU SHOULD KNOW:**
Formal education has a longer history here than in any other part of Korea – the first National Academy was established in the 7th century. Of the three universities here, two are Buddhist institutions and the third specializes in tourism related studies.

# Luang Prabang

On a strip of land where the mighty Mekong and Khan rivers meet, lies the Loatian city of Luang Prabang, with its atmospheric backdrop of misty lush hills. This fascinating city was the royal capital from the fourteenth century until the Lao monarchy was overthrown by the communists in 1975. Luang Prabang is one of the most beautiful cities in the world; in 1995 it was designated a UNESCO World Heritage Site as the best-preserved city in south-east Asia.

Luang Prabang is celebrated for its temples and monasteries. Distinctive golden temple roofs dominate the old city, prayer flags flutter in the breeze and evocative gongs echo around the town. This city is also known for its Royal Palace (Haw Kham). It was built near the river in 1904 for King Sisavang Vong and his family, so official visitors could disembark from their boats directly below the palace and be received there. The Crown Prince Savang Vatthana and his family were the last to occupy the palace as the monarchy was overthrown in 1975 and the Royal Family were taken to re-education camps. The palace is now a museum, and makes a fascinating visit.

Xiang Thong is the main street of the city, lined with traditional Lao wooden houses mixed with European architecture, reminders of the French Colonial era. Gilded-roofed temples, decorated with mosaics and murals of the Buddha, sit beside nineteenth-century shuttered windows and decorative balconies.

Strolling around this atmospheric city is a peaceful and uplifting experience, with its

*Novice monks in front of Wat Saen Temple*

pretty streets shaded with palms and flowering trees. When you tire of temples and palaces, climb up Phou Si Hill to watch the sunset or enjoy a cool drink on the banks of the river. Shop in the bustling markets or visit one of the many monasteries. Wat Xiang Thong is the oldest monastery in town and one of the most beautiful, the perfect place to soak up the serene and spiritual atmosphere that still pervades here.

# Vientiane

On a sweeping curve in the Mekong river, right on the Thai border, lies the Laotian capital of Vientiane. This sleepy city is a charming collection of lovely temples, French colonial buildings, ramshackle riverbank homes and pretty yellow Indochinese shop houses. In the centre of Vientiane is Nam Phou Place with its fountain, and most of the city's important sights are located within walking distance from here.

Patuxai (Victory Gate) was built in the 1960s to commemorate those who fought in the struggle for independence from France. It rather resembles the Arc de Triomphe, but the style is definitely Laotian, with its numerous kinnari figures (half woman, half bird).

The Great Stupa (Pha That Luang) is an important Buddhist temple built in the sixteenth century by King Setthathirat. It is believed to be sited on the ruins of a thirteenth-century Khmer temple, which in turn was built on a third-century Buddhist temple. Relics of the Buddha are said to be contained here. The stupa was destroyed by the Thai invasion in the nineteenth century, but later rebuilt to its original design. The Black Stupa (That Dam) is also worthy of a visit. Laotians believe it is inhabited by a seven-headed dragon which tried to protect them from the Siamese army which invaded in 1827.

The city's oldest temple, Wat Si Saket was built in 1818 under King Anouvong. It displays the Siamese rather than Lao style of Buddhist architecture, with a surrounding terrace and ornate five-tiered roof, which kept it safe during the Siamese invasion. Its cloister wall has more than 2,000 ceramic and silver representations of Buddha. The wat also houses a museum.

Vientiane is a joy to explore, simply for its pace of life. Buddhist monks in orange robes stroll along the shady, tree-lined streets and invite you to visit their temples so they can practise their English on you. On the banks of the Mekong, you can watch water buffalo as they graze peacefully, barely looking up as you pass.

**POPULATION:**
200,000 (2006)
**WHEN TO GO:**
November to March, or August.
**DON'T MISS:**
The Mekong River.
Wat Si Saket.
That Luang.
The colourful market (talat sao).
**YOU SHOULD KNOW:**
'Vientiane' is the French version of the Lao Viangchan.

*The Great Golden Stupa*

# Hanoi

The area around Hanoi, on the lush banks of the Red River, has been settled for at least five millennia. Vietnam was invaded by the Chinese in the 15th century and the French in the 19th, and both have left their mark. Hanoi became the capital of North Vietnam after the French were evicted in the 1950s and of the whole country after the Americans were ejected from South Vietnam in the 1970s, both following violent insurgencies.

As the country's most influential city for the past thousand years, Hanoi is Vietnam's cultural centre, and every Dynasty has left its mark, with a host of interesting monuments and cultural sites, including over 600 temples and pagodas.

The French in particular influenced the character of modern Hanoi, with their colonial style of architecture to be seen everywhere. Note in particular the grand colonnaded opera house, the Vietnam State Bank building, St Joseph's Cathedral, the Presidential Palace, Hanoi University, the Hotel Sofitel Metropole and elegant boulevards like Phan Dinh Phung Street.

There is, of course, a huge amount of recent development and associated economic activity. In a hundred years, Hanoi has grown from a town with a few dozen streets to a vibrant metropolis that attracts large numbers of country people and houses millions. But the old centre has survived and is largely unchanged. The old quarter was – and is – the haunt of merchants and craft workers specializing in traditional trades and skills, such as silk trading and jewellery manufacture. Hoan Kiem Lake, a city landmark, is close by and there are regular day and night markets.

This cultured place has a number of interesting museums, including the National History Museum, National Museum of Fine Arts and the Revolution Museum.

*The Tortoise Pagoda on Hoan Kiem Lake*

# Dalat

Don't think that a trip to the self-proclaimed 'Valley of Love' in Vietnam's temperate Central Highlands will be a romantic journey . . . though that does not stop the mass invasion of hopeful honeymooners. Nearby Dalat is in the running to become the world capital of kitsch, and the whole city seems like a giant theme park-cum-zoo, complete with a mini-Eiffel Tower, strolling elephants, stuffed animals and prowling locals dressed as giant rabbits or gun-toting cowboys. But despite all those Vietnamese honeymooners, the city isn't overcrowded with Western tourists.

*Chua Linh Phoc Buddhist Temple*

Dalat retains a picturesque flavour of its colonial origins. It was established as a cool mountain resort by the French in the early 20th century, and many of their stylish villas and boulevards remain, though wholesale modern development is fast diluting the original charm. A central feature of the city is the large man-made Xuan Hong Lake, best enjoyed in the early morning mist before the tourist hustlers arrive, or from the relative safety of a boat.

There is a bustling central market which still manages to offer a wide selection of the colourful produce, orchids and flowers for which this fertile area is renowned, amongst all those incredibly reasonable Rolex watches and designer fashions (not!).

An excellent way to see the beautiful countryside around the city – and places that could be found no other way – is to take a trip (or two!) with the famed Easy Riders, locals with motorbikes who usually speak English and offer personal tours into the hills. For those not interested in Dalat's overblown tourist attractions, the stunning mountain scenery and relief from the sticky heat of the lowlands make the long road trip from Ho Chi Minh City worthwhile.

**POPULATION:**
120,000 (1999)
**WHEN TO GO:**
The temperature hardly varies all year round, but winter (November-April) has much less rainfall.
**DON'T MISS:**
A pedal-powered tour for two of town and surrounds on a hired 'Love Machine' (tandem to you!).
Bao Dai's Palace – actually a stylish 1930s villa where Vietnam's last Emperor enjoyed a playboy lifestyle after World War II.
A bottle of local wine – Dalat's newest commercial enterprise has got off to a surprisingly drinkable start.
An excursion to two famous waterfalls outside town – Pongour Falls and Prenn Falls.
The beautiful Tuyen Lam Lake, 5 km (3 mi) south of town, where rivers, springs and forest meet.
**YOU SHOULD KNOW:**
Silk embroidery pictures, for which Dalat is famous, are best bought at the market rather than expensive galleries.

# Hue

*Hien Nhon Gate is one of the gates of the Forbidden City.*

With its beautiful setting on the banks of the Perfume River in central Vietnam, its lovely gardens and parks, and its royal monuments, Hue is a city with a long and distinguished history. Despite the bitter battles that took place here during the Tet Offensive in 1968, its air of romance, refinement, scholarship and spirituality has continued. Many of its priceless monuments were destroyed in the fighting, but many others still remain. It is not, however, simply the wonderful historic relics which make this city so attractive to visitors, it is also a lively, thriving place, home to five universities but with a more leisurely pace of life than Hanoi or Ho Chi Minh City. In 1995 it was given independent city status by the government to mark its growing economic importance.

The first nobleman to reach Hue was Nguyen Hoang in 1601, who built his capital here. He was followed by a succession of nine further feudal lords. The tenth Nguyen lord proclaimed himself Emperor Gia Long in 1802, and founded the Nguyen Dynasty. Hue soon became known for its cultural activity, and the Emperor built a huge citadel with a Forbidden City at its heart, reserved for the sovereign's use. The Imperial City, enclosed by a wall 7 m (23 ft) high and 20 m (66 ft) thick, was constructed using 80,000 artisans from all corners of the country.

Despite a devastating fire in 1947 and heavy shelling during the Vietnam War, the Imperial City is still awe-inspiring. Renovations have been continuous since 1975 and received a boost when Hue became a UNESCO World Heritage Site in 1993. Don't miss the Ngo Mon Gates, an elaborate granite structures built during the reign of Emperor Minh Mang where he used to preside over formal ceremonies. The Thai Hoa Palace, where the emperor received high dignitaries and foreign diplomats, is also a must. There are countless other ancestral altars, Chinese assembly halls, pagodas, temples and fascinating museums to be explored, too.

Hue is also famous for its royal mausolea, dotted around the city in the valley of the Perfume River. Seven of the Nguyen kings built their own tombs and these make pleasant excursions. They feature elegant architecture and offer a pleasant and atmospheric reminder of the past importance and wealth of the city. Many are located in beautiful settings, particularly the tomb of Tu Duc. The mausoleum is like a royal palace in miniature, located by a tranquil lake in a lush pine forest.

# Hoh Chi Minh City

The largest city in Vietnam is located on the banks of the Saigon River near the delta of the Mekong River. Until 1976, this was Saigon – capital of South Vietnam. Following its conquest by the Vietnam People's Army, large parts of the surrounding area were incorporated into Hoh Chi Minh City, named in honour of North Vietnam's revolutionary leader who died in 1969.

Visitors and locals alike tend to abbreviate the name to HCMC or continue to use Saigon, especially in relation to the original urban centre. This great city is the fast-beating heart of Vietnam. It is dynamic and industrious, serving as the country's economic and cultural focus. Those who know say it is hardly changed from pre-Communist days, though there has been a great deal of modern development since 1975.

There are plenty of interesting old buildings, museums and galleries to be found in HCMC, as would be expected in a former French colonial capital, plus some striking modern architecture. But the real joy of this vibrant place is the city life of South East Asia as it really is. The traffic – largely consisting of overloaded motorbikes and scooters – is ferocious, with little respect for small details like pavements and pedestrians, though there are miraculously few accidents. There are endless bars, restaurants, markets, street vendors and the old-fashioned cafés famous for strong coffee brewed in the cup.

This is a city of contrasts, with traditional ways of doing things rubbing shoulders with rapid modern developments and the increasingly international character of a 21st century city. This juxtaposition of old and new is never more striking than at the Phung Son Tu Pagoda, a small and dusty oasis of peace surrounded by the high rises of modern Ho Chi Minh City.

**POPULATION:**
6,240,000 (2005)
**WHEN TO GO:**
During the tropical dry season (December to April).
**DON'T MISS:**
The General Library, if only to see one of the finest buildings in the whole of Vietnam.
Reunification Palace — formerly South Vietnam's Presidential Palace, and left 'as was' . . . complete with a replica of the original tank that crashed through the gates, symbolically ending the war.
The extremely emotive War Remnants Museum (once provocatively called 'The Exhibition of American War Crimes') with various displays and hardware from the Vietnam War.
French-built Notre Dame Catholic Cathedral in the city centre.
The Dam Sen Water Park, to cool down by riding the spectacular water slides.
Ben Thanh Market, offering a huge selection of goods and produce, plus an authentic slice of Vietnamese city life.
**YOU SHOULD KNOW:**
Saigon was known as 'The Pearl of the Far East' for the number of fine colonial buildings in the city.

*The City Hall is a wonderful example of an old French colonial building*

# Phnom Penh

**POPULATION:**
2,000,000 (2006)
**WHEN TO GO:**
Phnom Penh has two distinct seasons. The rainy season, from May to October, can see temperatures as high as 40 °C (104 °F) and is generally accompanied by high humidity. The dry season lasts from November to April when temperatures can fall to 22 °C (72 °F). The best months to visit the city are from November to January when temperatures and humidity are lower.
**DON'T MISS:**
The Royal Palace – a citadel built in 1813.
Cheeng Ek Killing Field – a harrowing memorial to the 1970s Khmer Rouge Genocide.
The Central Market – to buy food, jewellery, clothes and shoes.
Wat Pnomh – the city's spiritual centre.
The National Museum – a graceful terracotta building worth viewing in its own right.
**YOU SHOULD KNOW:**
At weekends locals and tourists alike converge on the east bank of the Tonle Sap River to enjoy food and street entertainment – a riot of colour and definitely not to be missed.

The capital of the Kingdom of Cambodia, Phnom Penh is located at the confluence of three rivers - the Mekong, the Bassac and Tonle Sap. The city is divided into three sections – the north, an attractive residential area, the south or the French part of the city with its ministries, banks and colonial houses, and the centre with narrow lanes, markets, foods stalls and shops.

Although it is 290 km (180 mi) from the sea, Phnom Penh is a major port on the Mekong River, and is linked to the South China Sea via a channel of the Mekong delta in Vietnam. The city takes its name from the Wat Phnom Daun Penh (Temple Hill) built in 1373 to house five statues of Buddha on a man made mound some 27 m (89 ft) high.

It is difficult to think of Phnom Penh without conjuring up images of the Vietnam War and the subsequent madness of the Pol Pot regime and the city has many memorials dedicated to this period. The Khmer Rouge were driven out of Phnom Penh by the Vietnamese in 1979, when people began to return to the city.

Recently Pnomh Penh has undergone tremendous changes; tourism is once again booming and it is easy to see why, with broad boulevards, old colonial buildings, parks and green spaces that remind one of the country's French heritage.

For a city of its size Phnom Penh has as yet very few high-rise buildings and so few cars that traffic jams are rare. The best and cheapest way to explore the area is by cyclo (a pedal bike taxi service).

*Royal Palace*

# Chiang Mai

Thailand's great northern capital of Chiang Mai has a long and distinguished history. The earliest trace of this can be seen in the remnants of the original city walls, built in 1296, though the walls of the inner, moated, squared inner city that we see today were erected in about 1800. Chiang Mai is very approachable: though expanding fast, it feels small and the centre is well defined. Above it all, the mountain of Doi Suthep rises to 1,676 m (5,530 ft), forming a perfect backdrop.

Chiang Mai's climate is easier to cope with than that of Bangkok, and the city is a magnet for foreigners, tourists and residents alike. It has a laid-back, friendly atmosphere, and despite being a starting point for trekking and exploring the far north, many people succumb to its charms and look no further.

With well over 100 Buddhist temples, some of Burmese or Shan origin, there are also mosques, Hindu temples, one Sikh temple and Christian churches, reflecting the cosmopolitan nature of the inhabitants. Chiang Mai is also known for its shopping. As the largest trading centre for the hill tribe groups in the north, its shops and markets are a repository of wonderful handicrafts, from carved wooden furniture and large, hand-painted umbrellas, to fabrics, silk and cotton clothing and jewellery.

Recreation in the city caters for all tastes – restaurants featuring many different cuisines abound, and there are bookshops, cinemas, sports, clubs, bars, art galleries and exhibitions, and the excellent National Museum. Here you can learn Thai massage, or take Thai cookery classes. Stroll down to one of the live music venues on the banks of the Ping River, or enjoy the spectacle of one of Chiang Mai's several annual festivals. This is a place in which to relax and have fun.

**POPULATION:**
700,000 (2005)
**WHEN TO GO:**
November to March.
**DON'T MISS:**
Wat Phra That, one of northern Thailand's most sacred temples near the summit of Doi Suthep.
The Night Bazaar.
The Winter Fair, Songkran Water Festival, Umbrella Festival and Flower Carnival.
Wat Chiang Man, founded in 1296, the oldest temple in the city.
Cruising on the Ping River.
**YOU SHOULD KNOW:**
The most commonly found hill tribes (mountain inhabiting ethnic minorities) are: Akha, Lahu, Lisu, Mien, Hmong and Karen. It is possible to stay in their villages during trekking trips.

*Wat Phra That Doi Suthep Temple*

# Bangkok

**POPULATION:**
9,000,000 (2005)
**WHEN TO GO:**
November to March.
**DON'T MISS:**
Wat Arun, the Temple of the Dawn.
Lumphini Park.
Chatuchak Market, open Saturdays
and Sundays.
Chinatown and Pahurat, the
Indian district.
A traditional Thai massage at Wat Po.
The National Museum.
**YOU SHOULD KNOW:**
Bangkok's Thai name is Krungthep,
meaning 'City of Angels'. Its full Thai
name is Krungthep mahanakhon
bowon rattanakosin mahintara
ayuthaya mahadilok popnopparat
ratchatani burirom udonratchaniwet
mahasatham amonpiman
avatansathir sakkathatitya
visnukamprasit.

Bangkok can at first seem rather overwhelming. The city teems with people, the roads are jammed with traffic, and motorbikes carry entire families, none of whom wear helmets. The humidity and noise is exhausting, and the smell is a potent combination of drains, exhaust fumes and fabulous food. Thailand's capital is both excitingly ultra-modern and absolutely traditional. Beneath the soaring skyscrapers, glitzy shopping malls, and beautiful temples lies a living, working city, bursting with people from all over the country intent on making a better life for themselves.

Flowing from north to south is the Chao Praya River, and taking an express boat trip is an excellent way of seeing the place – stopping off perhaps to see the Grand Palace and the Temple of the Emerald Buddha, Wat Po, containing the largest reclining Buddha in Thailand, or to enjoy a cool drink on the terrace of the famous Oriental Hotel. Away from the centre, you can still see rickety wooden stilt houses on the water's edge, children swimming in the water beneath. Back on land, use the quick and clean Skytrain or Metro to get you from A to B – Bangkok is not a city to walk about in much, it's too hot and too busy.

The more time you spend in Bangkok the more you will enjoy yourself. It's impossible to get bored: there are so many monuments, museums, exhibitions, restaurants, clubs, bars, shops and markets that there's always somewhere new to go, something else to try. Taxis are cheap and air conditioned, street food ubiquitous and delicious. If you want some peace go to the Suan Phakkard Palace and admire the five traditional wooden houses, filled with wonderful antiques and artworks, from the tranquil garden.

Bangkok is a great city that keeps going 24 hours a day. Don't be put off by its immensity, just go with the flow and you will find innumerable treasures and pleasures here.

*The Grand Palace*

# Lampang

A stop on the Bangkok to Chiang Mai railway line, Lampang attracts more Thai tourists than foreigners, and as a result is charmingly low-key. Founded in the 7th century, beside the Wang River, Lampang was always a success. By the late 1800s, it had carved itself an important place in the teak trade, inspiring a British-owned company to bring in loggers from Burma, then part of the Empire, to harvest the surrounding teak forests. Wealthy Burmese teak and opium merchants built gorgeous teak houses here and sponsored new temples, which can still be seen.

*Wat Phra Kaew Don Tao Temple*

The first thing to strike the visitor arriving in town is the number of horse-drawn carriages, a delightful form of public transport. What better way could there be to go sightseeing than to be clip-clopping along, a Thai in a cowboy hat in the driver's seat, acknowledging his colleagues with cheery waves of his whip. Wat Phra Kaew Don Tao is an impressive Burmese style temple on the north side of the river where, from 1436 to 1468 the Emerald Buddha, Thailand's talisman, resided. Today the most sympathetic structure in the complex is a crumbling old brick temple, set between trees covered with Buddhist maxims.

Have a look at Many Pillars House. Built in 1896, this wonderful example of a wealthy Lanna-style home is full of enough Burmese and Thai antiques to make your mouth water. Walk through streets of lovely wooden shop houses, wander along the river and stop for a sunset drink or dinner at one of the old wooden bars at the water's edge. It's a delight to be in a city not particularly geared to foreigners, where the iced coffee is good and scrumptious food can be eaten in the company of Thais rather than westerners.

**POPULATION:**
43,000 (1997)
**WHEN TO GO:**
November to March.
**DON'T MISS:**
Wat Prathat Lampang Luang –
Northern Thailand's most magnificent Lanna-style temple complex.
Wat Chedi Sao, with its 20 chedis and 15th century, solid gold seated Buddha.
The Young Elephant Training Centre – you'll want to take one home…
Ceramics and cotton weaving – Lampang is famous for both these crafts.
**YOU SHOULD KNOW:**
Lampang's official symbol is a white rooster.

*Kuching State Mosque*

# Kuching

**POPULATION:**
500,000 (2006)
**WHEN TO GO:**
Gawai is a Dayak festival that takes place on the 1st June, so see the city then, all lit up.
**DON'T MISS:**
The Sarawak Museum, showcasing the culture of Sarawak, is one of the best in the region.
The waterfront – recently transformed into a landscaped promenade called 'The People Place'. Enjoy a drink here at sunset.
Main Bazaar – made up of a row of two storey shophouses situated on Kuching's oldest street. Good for local handicrafts and antiques.
**YOU SHOULD KNOW:**
English is not spoken here as widely as on Peninsular Malaysia.

The capital city of Sarawak is the fourth largest city in Malaysia. Often referred to as Asia's best kept secret, this is an exotic city and melting pot of several cultures, including Dayak, Iban, Muslim and Chinese. There has been much speculation surrounding the origin of the name, with some believing it comes from the Indian name for port, and others the Malay word for cat. There is a Cat Museum and several fantastically tacky cat statues dotted around the city which are often dressed in traditional costume during major festivals.

The city has been developing since 1841 when a British advisor to the Sultan of Brunei was made Raja of the region. Then, Kuching was unreachable by any other route except the River Sarawak around which city life now centres. The Astana, the residence of the bygone white raja, is now the Governor's home, and can be viewed from across the river. The recently landscaped riverfront is a must for exploring historical buildings where old colonial meets colourful Malay and Chinese shop fronts, and it comes alive at night with people jogging and meeting for an evening stroll or meal. The musical fountain is a draw every evening with families and tourists enjoying themselves, and the observatory tower is worth the climb for the view over the city and across the river.

This is a really busy, buzzing city but it hasn't lost any of its old world charm with the modernization that has gone on recently. The Main Bazaar, Kuching's oldest street, is ideal for shopping for souvenirs, and you can find wooden carvings and other artefacts from Iban longhouses. The food and market stalls make this area a browsers paradise and is ideal for whiling away an afternoon.

The architecture of the city is as diverse as its people. Buildings range from the modern high rise hotels to colonial buildings and Chinese influences. The Chinese Museum provides an insight into the establishment and growth of the Chinese community which now comprises a third of Kuching's population.

# George Town

The capital of the island state of Penang has a wonderful feeling of a bygone age having been colonized in 1786 by a trader of the British East India Company. Now ranked as the tenth most liveable city in Asia, it is rich in colonial-era architecture, but this is now dwindling as modern buildings spring up while heritage controls are still to be developed.

Walking aimlessly around George Town is the best way to see it, as crumbling shop fronts from colonial days pepper the streets and transport you back to another era. Many buildings combine colonial and Chinese styles, testimony to the blend of cultures in the city, and George Town has one of the largest collections of nineteenth and early twentieth century buildings in South East Asia. Cheong Fatt Tze Mansion, winner of UNESCO's Asia-Pacific Heritage 2000 Award for Conservation, is a fantastic example of the melting pot of cultures. Head to the Colonial Quarter to see the best architecture and Fort Cornwallis is a must-see for an insight into the founding of George Town, and marks the spot of the first landing on Penang.

George Town is comprised mostly of Chinese and Muslim dwellers, and that is reflected in the religious sites around the city. Things are much older here, though, and the temples and mosques date back to the nineteenth century.

Eating is huge in George Town, and almost all social interaction focuses around a meal. Penang is famous for its food, namely the street hawkers and the seafood caught from its shores. Choose from Nyonya, Chinese, vegetarian, Indian, Malay, Hakka, seafood and desserts.

For a different temple experience head to Snake Temple, dedicated to a Buddhist priest and healer, and inhabited by green tree snakes and venomous vipers. Watch out for the snake handlers who will pester you to hold a snake so they can take your photo.

If you arrive in May or June the Penang International Dragon Festival takes place in a flourish of activity and colour on the Teluk Bahang Dam. Drums beat to keep the rowers in time and crowds roar from the shore, cheering their team on. This is a two day festival, during which teams from across the world descend on a George Town at its best.

*The Thousand Buddhas Pagoda*

**POPULATION**:
1,310,000 (2006)
**WHEN TO GO:**
Try to plan your trip around a festival to see a different side to the city. There are many to choose from – Hindu, Muslim or Buddhist.
**DON'T MISS:**
A trip above George Town to Penang Hill for a stunning view of the city and some respite from the humidity below.
**YOU SHOULD KNOW:**
The island is 2km (1.25mi) from the mainland at the narrowest point, and 13km (8mi) at the widest. It is linked to the mainland via the Penang Bridge or the ferry.

# Kuala Lumpur

Kuala Lumpur, or KL to those familiar with it, is the economic and cultural centre of Peninsular Malaysia, sprawling over 243 sq km (95 sq mi). Despite the gleaming modern glass and metal buildings that dominate the skyline, the gems of KL are hidden amongst the older parts of the city. It is a place of cultural diversity as Malays, Indians and Chinese mix easily throughout the city that so represents their individual cultures, whether in architecture, lifestyle, festivals or religious beliefs.

To get an insight into Malaysia's folk art and for a bit of haggling, head to Central Market where you'll find pottery and wood carvings and might even be lucky enough to see a demonstration of glass blowing or batik painting. At night there are performances of Malay dancing and shadow puppets amongst the bustle of the market traders. Chinatown is a wonderful mix of heady smells and noise with colourful stalls and market hawkers shouting as you pass. Little India is a riot of colour and aromas in the older section of the city, with people bustling by at all times of the day. You might want to choose to shop at one or the other, as you'll find lots of the same items for sale in all the markets.

The Petronas Twin Towers, the second tallest in the world at 451.9m (1482ft) and 88 storeys, are Kuala Lumpur's most famous landmark, and can be seen from every angle of the city. Take the lift to the 41st floor for spectacular views across the city. This towering victory for engineering and architecture stands out in sharp contrast to the small shops of bustling Chinatown and Indo-Moorish architecture of much of KL, as the old and new rub shoulders in this most eclectic of cities.

There is much to do here, and for an easy way to peek at the animals that inhabit Malaysia, head to the National Zoo where 400 species of mammals, birds and reptiles await you. For an insight into the three main cultures of KL, visit their religious sites. The beautiful Sri Mahamariamman Temple is KL's most important Hindu temple and its ornate vibrancy dates back to 1873. Thean Hou Temple is KL's most famous, and one of the most impressive in Malaysia. It is an amalgam of Taoist and Buddhist shrines, each as striking as the next. The Masjid Jamek, or Sunset Mosque, is a wonderful sight at sunset as the pinks and creams of the building glow luminescent against the twilight sky. The Lake Gardens are a great day out for the family, boasting a butterfly park, planetarium, orchid garden, walk-in aviary and insect museum. The Islamic Arts Museum is a collection of Muslim treasures not to be missed for an insight into Muslim life. The building itself is stunning, and comprises many elements of traditional Muslim architecture.

*The Petronas Twin Towers*

**POPULATION:**
1,800,000 (2004)
**WHEN TO GO:**
KL is hot and humid all year, but the wetter season from March to April and September to November, while unpredictable, can often be more bearable to tourists.
**DON'T MISS:**
Having a meal in the revolving restaurant in the KL Tower for fantastic views across the city while you eat.
**YOU SHOULD KNOW:**
You will need to dress appropriately when visiting mosques and temples. Ensure you are suitably covered.

# Cebu City

Inhabited for at least 3,000 years, Cebu was one of the earliest points of contact with Spain: Ferdinand Magellan arrived here in 1521 and the city was breifly capital of the Spanish colony in the third quarter of the 16th century. It has long been an important trading centre and is now a rapidly expanding and developing city and the Philippines' top tourist destination. As the site of the first conversions to Christianity, it is an important cultural centre. The oldest church in the Philippines is the Basilica Minore del Santo Niño, on Magellans Street, which houses an image of the Holy Child left here by Magellan and is an important pilgrimage centre. Other churches include the Chapel of the Last Supper in Mandaue and the Naga and Argao churches, while the Phu-Sian Temple can be found in Beverly Hills. Other colonial buildings include the Fort San Pedro and the Liloan Lighthouse.

Colon Street is the oldest street in the Philippines and a major entertainment hub with theatres, monuments and museums as well as shopping arcades. For a more relaxing break, head for the beaches of Mactan, Argao or Carmen or try Central Cebu National Park, the Bolok-Bolok Mineral Springs, Sudlon National Park or the Cawasan Falls. There is excellent diving at Badian, Mactan, Moalboal and Olango and lagoons and caves to explore at Calanggaman and Gato.

Art lovers can take in the University of San Carlos Museum or the Casa Gorordo Museum, housed in the former residence of the Filipino Bishop of Cebu, while bargain-hunters shoud aim for Carbon Market.

Cebu is a modern city still completely at home with its rich cultural past.

**POPULATION:**
719,000 (2000)
**WHEN TO GO:**
Any time of year: the peak seasons are December to January and Holy Week.
**DON'T MISS:**
Magellan's Cross.
The Sinulog Festival in late January.
Colon Street, the oldest street in the Philippines.
**YOU SHOULD KNOW:**
Cebu City is known as 'Queen City of the South'.

*Fort San Pedro*

# Manila

**POPULATION:**
1,582,000 (2000)
**WHEN TO GO:**
Any time.
**DON'T MISS:**
The Baywalk – this is the city's main promenade. The chief attraction is the Baroque church of Malate. Chinatown – the world's oldest Chinatown! Enjoy the Chinese architecture, food, gifts and jewellery. The Chinese Cemetery.
**YOU SHOULD KNOW:**
Malacanang Palace is not open at the weekend.

Capital of the Philippines since Spanish colonial times, and an important trading centre since the late 16th century, Manila is one of the most cosmopolitan cities in the world. Originally inhabited by the Tagalogs, there have been successive waves of migration and invasion from tribes from elsewhere in the region to the Spaniards in the 1570s, the Chinese, the Americans in the 1890s and the Japanese in the 1940s. The historic city – Intramuros – is surrounded by the olds walls the Spanish erected soon after their arrival and many of the city's highlights are contained within this area, with old colonial buildings and churches, including Manila Cathedral and the San Agustin Church and Museum complex. The Bahay Tsinoy Museum is also here. Other important museums include the Intromuros Light and Sound Museum, the Museo ng Maynila (Museum of Manila) and the Children's Museum (Museo Pambata). Pre-conquest culture can be explored in the Museum of the Parish of Our Lady of the Abandoned (Santa Ana).

Chinatown is a must for most visitors, with bustling restaurants and shops, food markets and, paradoxically one of the best Baroque cathedrals in the western hemisphere. In the Old Palace neighbourhood you will find not only the Malacanang Palace itself (now a museum), but the Church of San Sebastian, constructed entirely in steel and some of the best-preserved colonial architecture in the city.

Fans of Art Deco architecture should head to the campus of the Far Eastern University, a complex of 'modern' architecture with stunning murals and sculptures.

Manila's cultural diversity is represented in its wide variety of religious sites, from synagogues to Spanish-style churches, Chinese and Hindu temples and mosques. Visitors are drawn back again and again.

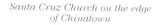

*Santa Cruz Church on the edge of Chinatown*

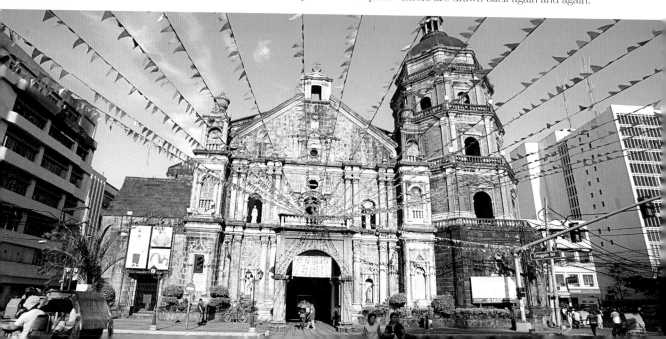

# Singapore

One of the few city-states in the world, Singapore is a nation of 63 islands, covering 705 sq km (272 sq mi), which lies at the southern tip of the Malay Peninsula. In 1819, when still a sparsely populated fishing village, it was colonized by the British East India Company in order to exploit its geographical position as a tactical outpost along the Spice Route.

Occupied by the Japanese during World War II, Singapore subsequently reverted to British rule, later becoming part of the merger that established Malaysia in 1963. Two years later it became an independent republic. Since that time the state has seen a dramatic economic boom, owing to both foreign investment and government-led industrialization, which has created a modern economy based on electronics and manufacturing. Today, Singapore is the fourth largest foreign exchange trading centre and the 18th wealthiest country in the world.

With its spotless streets, arrays of concrete and glass post-modern architecture and thousands of foreign expatriates, Singapore can at first feel strikingly modern and anonymous. However, beneath the glitzy surface of Orchard Road's designer complexes lies a wealth of multi-cultural diversity. This undeniably Asian city unites Malay, Chinese, Indian, Arabic and European traditions, from ancestor worship to horse racing, to create a colourfully contrasted landscape of vibrant diffusion.

Wander the streets of Chinatown, Little India and Geylang Serai to get a feel for the city's segregated past. Visit the colourful Sri Mariamman Temple, admire orchids in 67 hectares (166 acres) of botanical gardens and indulge in some of the world's most delicious and diverse cuisine in the abundant hawker markets and food stalls. And, if the humidity gets too much, you can recapture the colonial era whilst reclining with a cocktail beneath one of Raffles Hotel's lazy fans.

**POPULATION:**
4,550,000 (2007)
**WHEN TO GO:**
January to May (although the tropical climate means humidity and rainfall are consistently high).
**DON'T MISS:**
Marina Bay Floating Stadium.
The Esplanade Theatres on the Bay.
The stunning Singapore Art Museum.
Walking along the waterfront to Merlion Park.
The view over the harbour from Clifford Pier.
The Jurong Bird Park.
**YOU SHOULD KNOW:**
Singlish, the local colloquial dialect of English which has many Creole-like characteristics, and incorporates vocabulary and grammar from various Chinese dialects, Malay and Indian languages, is commonly spoken on the streets of Singapore.

*The Central Business District*

# Ubud

**POPULATION:**
8,000 (2002)
**WHEN TO GO:**
May to October.
**DON'T MISS:**
The museums.
The nightly dance and musical
performances.
The food, which is some of the best
in Indonesia.
**YOU SHOULD KNOW:**
Ubud is often called the cultural
heart of Bali.

Located in central Bali, Ubud has changed from an artists' colony and backpackers' hideaway in a sleepy backwater to a sophisticated town with fantastic museums, traditional mansions and stunning architecture and is Bali's centre for fine arts, crafts, dance and music, all set among beautiful landscapes.In the early part of the 20th century Westerners such as Walter Spies and Willem Hofker collected together the best Balinese artists in an informal training academy and thus created Ubud as an artistic centre. Their legacy lives on in the many museums here, including the Museum of Fine Arts, the Seniwati Gallery of Art by Women and the Museum Rudana, and in the thriving artistic tradition of the town and the surrounding area.

Many of the villages around Ubud are home to specialist art and craft communities, set among traditional rice terraces, ancient temples and idyllic landscapes. A particular feature of the area is the palaces – *puris* – which housed the local princes. One of the best is the Puri Saren Agung, once the home of Tjokorde Gede Agung Sukawati, the last King of Ubud: his family still live here and host dance performances.

Other buildings and monuments here include many beautiful temples including the Pura Taman Saraswati. At Pejeng, just outside the town, temples include the Goa Gaja, Pura Kebo Edan, Pura Pusering Jagat and Pura Agung Batan Bingin. The 14th-century reliefs of Yeh Pulu are among the vest to be found.

A very popular, if less highbrow, attraction is Monkey Forest Park where visitors can feed the 200 long-tailed macaques and visit the temple.

The many artistic activities here give the town and surrounding area a unique character and when combined with the vibrant colours of the surrounding landscape Ubud ticks all the boxes.

*Pura Dalem Agung Temple*

# Solo (Surakarta)

Known to the locals as Solo, but officially called Surakarta, Solo is the older of the two royal cities of Tengah (Central Java). It lies on a green plain ringed by the active volcanoes of Lawu, Merapi and Merbabu.

The city's royal connections can be seen in such buildings as the Mangkunegaran Palace, which is typical of the large complexes that they built for themselves. Colonial architecture is also in evidence, for instance in the Catholic church on Slamet Riyadi Street and the Mayor's House on the same street.

Traditional Javanese culture is more easily found in the Keraton complex or THR amusement centre, where gamelan performances are often staged. Another popular form of entertainment is the shadow puppets. Performances can last for up to eight hours.

*Taxi outside the Kraton*

The city is renowned for its two large markets, the rebuilt Pasar Gede and the Pasar Klewer, which specializes in batik. Further off the beaten track is Pasar Triwindu, an antique/junk market, where it is possible to find real bargains.

The Kraton, the main royal palace, is largely a reconstruction after a disastrous fire in 1985. It has lots of European-style detail, such as the statues, lamps and furniture. The meditation tower – the Panggung Songgo Buwono dates from 1782. There is an interesting small museum in the Kraton grounds.

**POPULATION:**
572,000 (2004)
**WHEN TO GO:**
May to November.
**DON'T MISS:**
Pasar Gede market.
The 8th-century Prambanan Temple nearby.
The cave of Java Man at Sangiran.
Buying streetfood from a *Kaki Lima*.
**YOU SHOULD KNOW:**
Gunung Merapi means 'Mountain of Fire'. It last erupted in 2006 and is Indonesia's most active volcano.

# Jakarta

**POPULATION:**
8,972,000 (2004)
**WHEN TO GO:**
Any time of year.
**DON'T MISS:**
A trip on the monorail.
A *gamelan* performance.
Buying some batik cloth.
The many specialist street markets.
A tour to one of the many 'Betawi
Cultural Institutions'.
**YOU SHOULD KNOW:**
It takes courage to drive in the city.

The capital of Indonesia and sitting on the far north-west coast of
Java, Jakarta has been settled since at least the fourth century. Its
location near the Sunda Strait made it an ideal location for a trading
port as the strait allowed passage between the Indian Ocean and the
Java Sea.

Sunda Kelapa is the site of the 16th-century Dutch trading post,
and there are still colonial buildings in the old part of the city.
Evidence of Jakarta's colonial past can also be seen in the Immanuel
Church (Gereja Immanuel). Like many other Indonesian cities,
Jakarta has a thriving Chinese population and Chinatown here is
popular with visitors, as is the open-air museum of Taman Mini
Indonesia Indah (Indonesia in Miniature) which has examples of
traditional architecture from all over Indonesia. Over recent
decades, the area known as Old Batavia (Batavia was the city's name
under Dutch rule) has undergone extensive restoration, and several

*The port of Old Batavia*

old buildings have been rescued. The Old Supreme Court houses a museum of fine arts and porcelain while the Old Town Hall is now the Jakarta Museum (Fatahillah Museum). Other museums include the Armed Forces Museum (Museum Satria Mandala); the Puppet Museum (Museum Wayang), which houses an extensive collection of the shadow puppets used to illustrate traditional stories; the Maritime Museum; the National Museum and the Textile Museum (Museum Tekstil), which explores the art of batik cloth. Another popular destination for tourists is the Pasar Ikan Fish Market, which is also a great area for dining in the evenings.

Jakarta is a rapidly growing city and its energy, combined with its diverse cultural influences, make it a fascinating place to explore.

# Bandung

Set on a large, flat plain within a wide river basin and straddling the River Cikapundung, Bandung's relatively cool climate, strategic defensive location and surrounding fertile area made it an ideal choice for the Dutch East India Company as an inland resort for tea-plantation owners, with boutiques, restaurants, hotels and cafés. Sitting on the site of a long-extinct volcano and surrounded by others in the Parahyungan Moutains, it is dominated by Tangkuban peak in the north. It is renowned for its Dutch colonial architecture, including the old 1920s barracks, now the Gedung Sate government building. Other renowned Dutch colonial buildings include the Art Deco Savoy Homann and Preanger Hotels and Gedung Merdeka. Many of the old colonial buildings here combine European style with traditional elements of local buildings making them a unique and harmonious mix.

Although Bandung grew rapidly after independence after World War II and most of the southern half of the city dates from after this period, remnants of the old colonial way of life are still evident in the cafés of Braga Street. Dago is one of the main business and entertainment districts and Dago Street is equally renowned for its café culture.

Linked directly to Jakarta by road and rail, Bandung is still a popular weekend destination for people from the capital, who come here to relax, enjoy the atmosphere and shop – the city is renowned for it's food and cheap shopping. There are many small outlets, called *distros*, that specialize in unbranded goods, the work of individual designers and entrepreneurs.

It may not be the quaint resort that it once was, but Bandung is still a great place to chill out.

**POPULATION:**
2,511,000 (2004)
**WHEN TO GO:**
May to October.
**DON'T MISS:**
Braga Street – the city's famous 1920s promenade street. Its chic cafés, boutiques and restaurants have earned it the nickname 'Paris van Java'.
Old Chinatown.
Shopping in the *distros* – Cihampelas and Cibaduyut Streets are good places to start.
**YOU SHOULD KNOW:**
The wet season runs from November to April.

AFRICA

# Alexandria

The bustling coastal city of Alexandria has a distinctly Mediterranean feel. Situated in the Nile delta, on the northern coast of Egypt, it lies along a sweep of bay, its backdrop the sparking Mediterranean Sea. The city is Egypt's main port, commercial and industrial centre, as well as being one of the most popular Middle Eastern holiday resorts. During the summer months visitors arrive from far and wide, enjoying the coffee shops and cafés, and relaxing on the beach under the shade of a parasol.

Alexandria was founded by Alexander the Great, c.331 BC, as a centre of culture and learning linking Greece to the riches of the Nile Valley. Within the century his city had grown to rival Rome, and was home to Greeks, the world's largest Jewish community and Egyptians. The Great Library of Alexandria, the largest in the world was established, and the Pharos Lighthouse, one of the Seven Wonders of the World, was built. During the following 1,700 years the city rose and fell during numerous invasions, and by 1810, when Mohammed Ali, the Ottoman governor of Egypt, decided to revive it, Alexandria was just a fishing village surrounded by the ruins of its past.

Today, Midan Saad Zaghlul, the large main square facing the waterfront, is the entertainment hub of the city. The Corniche is dotted with casinos and tall, colonial buildings and, in an effort to regain its cultural status, an amazing new complex has been built at its western end. The Biblioteca Alexandrina contains, amongst other things, a superb library.

A French underwater archaeology team have been working here for years and have so far discovered the remains of the Pharos Lighthouse and some astonishing antiquities from what was once the Royal Quarters. Alexandria may not have the Pharaonic treasures of Luxor or Cairo, but its cosmopolitan atmosphere and fascinating history make it well worth exploring.

*The bustling coastal city of
Alexandria at sunset*

# Aswan

Aswan is the ancient city of Swenet, which was in antiquity the frontier town of southern Egypt. It was located on the main trading route between Egypt and the southern lands, where gold, slaves and ivory passed into Egypt. It lies at the first of the seven Nile cataracts which are created by exposed granite. This makes the river impassable to boats above Aswan, and thus the town became a thriving trade centre. From this frontier town to Alexandria in the north, the Nile flows for more than 1200 km (750 mi) without obstruction.

*The Nubian village on Aswan's Elephantine Island is a popular tourist attraction.*

The quarries at Aswan were celebrated for their stone, especially for the granitie rock called Syenite. This rock was used to create the colossal statues, obelisks and temples found throughout Egypt.

Today Aswan is the third largest town in Egypt, and one of the largest in Upper Egypt. It has a bustling outdoor market, Sharia el-Souq, full of the bright colours and aromas of spices, jewellery, textiles and tourist souvenirs.

Aswan is one of the driest inhabited places in the world. Due to its laid-back atmosphere, the town became popular as a winter resort with Europeans attracted by its picturesque riverside setting and the rumours that the dry heat provided a cure for various ailments. A Nile-side Corniche was created for the visitors, providing moorings for steamers. This is the most attractive waterfront boulevard in Egypt and has been compared to the French Riviera. Hire a felucca and float on the river, admiring the gorgeous views of palm-covered islands and sandy white hills. At the southern end of the Corniche is the Old Cataract Hotel – built in 1899 and famous as one of the grand locations for the film *Death on the Nile*.

The ancient temple of Kom Ombo stands on the east bank of the Nile just outside Aswan. The temple was mainly dedicated to the god Sobek, the crocodile god, together with his wife. It is of Greco-Roman structure, dating back to the year 119 BC when Ptolemy VI built it out of limestone.

Philae Island was a rocky island in the middle of the Nile, just south of Aswan. The Ancient Egyptians built a magnificent temple on this island for the goddess Isis, but it was submerged after the first Aswan dam was built in 1906. The temple has, however, been moved to a new island and is well worth a visit.

**POPULATION:**
1,116,000 (2001)
**WHEN TO GO:**
Between October and April.
**DON'T MISS:**
A felucca trip on the Nile – these traditional sailing boats offer a great way to see the Nile. Be sure to check exactly what you're paying for before boarding.
Sharia el-Souq market.
Nubian dancers at the Cultural Centre.
The temple of Kom Ombo.
The Aswan Museum.
Elephantine Island – this beautiful island is the largest in the Aswan area and is full of fascinating ruins dating back to predynastic times..
**YOU SHOULD KNOW:**
Abu Simbel, the stunning temple of Ramses II, can be reached from Aswan.

# Luxor

If you want to see Pharaonic Egypt in all its glory, visit Luxor, a city unlike any other on earth. The extraordinary quality, quantity and scale of the monuments here, liberally scattered on both banks of the Nile, is impossible to truly appreciate without seeing them for yourself. Visitors have always come here, but despite today's tour buses and the phalanxes of Nile cruisers, you can still sometimes find yourself alone in front of a superb bas-relief, carved over 3,000 years ago.

Known as Thebes, the city's glory days were between 1540-1069 BC, following the reunification of the country by Montuhotep II and the removal of the capital to Thebes. The Temple of Karnak, dedicated to the god Amun, is gigantic – its Hypostyle Hall, just one part of the complex, could easily hold Notre Dame Cathedral. In the golden afternoon light the sight of 134 enormous columns soaring upwards, casting diagonal shadows, is utterly astounding.

Luxor Temple, started by Amenhotep III and added to by many, including Tutankhamun and Ramses II, stands overlooking the Nile. The avenue of Sphinxes, obelisks, papyrus columns, monumental gateways, huge statues and spectacular reliefs must be seen. Floodlit at night, it is magnificent.

*The destroyed Colossus
of Memnon*

Crossing to the west bank, you'll suddenly come upon the Colossi of Memnon, all that remains of Amenhotep III's funerary temple, once as large as Karnak. The great necropolis that is in the Valley of the Kings, contains 62 excavated tombs, the most beautifully decorated of which is probably that of Seti I. Hatshepsut's Temple and the Temple of Ramses III are both majestic sights.

Luxor town itself is full of hotels, restaurants and shops. Persistent hustlers suggest felucca trips, caleche tours, taxi hire, and much more. Hire a bicycle and set off early, rest up somewhere during the midday sun, and get going again later. By the evening, after a meal and a beer, you'll have just enough energy left to fall into bed.

# Cairo

Africa's largest city, Cairo is really a collection of different districts divided only by the Nile, which flows sedately through it. The amazing antiquities of the Egyptian, Coptic and Islamic civilizations that can be seen here add another dimension to the vibrant, chaotic, noisy, multitudinous, multi-racial feel of the place. This is the Arab world's most accessible political and cultural centre, a magnet for the agricultural poor, and the site of a population explosion bar none.

*The Citadel in Cairo*

Cairo is overwhelming – grab a taxi and visit the last of the Seven Wonders of the Ancient World: the Pyramids of Giza. Built over 4,600 years ago, and known throughout the world, your first sight of them rising from the desert is awe-inspiring. Nearby sits the Sphynx, equally unbelievable – try the son-et-lumière one night for a mind-blowing experience. The Museum of Egyptian Antiquities is another must, but unless you've got months a guided tour might be useful – the Museum holds infinitely more than the fantastic Tutankhamun exhibition.

Modern Cairo is based around Midan Tahrir (Liberation Square), on the east bank, not far from the Islamic, medieval city, its narrow streets home to hundreds of Islamic monuments, the chief of which is Ibn Tulun's austerely beautiful mosque. Coptic Cairo, probably the birthplace of the city, is a peaceful area of cobbled alleys, convents, churches and synagogues, and the Coptic Museum contains many treasures, including particularly fine textiles. The City of the Dead is also a city of the living – this huge area of domed, carved, palatial mausoleums had it own monasteries and schools, and is inhabited quite happily by many of the city's homeless.

Come early in the evening, make sure that you are ensconced near the Nile with a cold drink in your hand. As the call to prayer rings out and the buildings glow in the setting sun, time is suspended for a moment, allowing you to catch your breath before plunging into Cairo's hyperactive nightlife.

**POPULATION:**
18,000,000 (2006)
**WHEN TO GO:**
October to April.
**DON'T MISS:**
The Citadel.
The Hanging Church and Ben Ezra Synagogue in Coptic Cairo.
Heliopolis – a relaxed residential district with Art Deco 'Europe-meets-Arabia' architecture.
Khan al-Khalili bazaar.
The Northern walls and gates.
Sultan Hassan Mosque.
Bayt al-Suhaymi, the finest medieval house in the city.
**YOU SHOULD KNOW:**
The Roman name for Cairo was Babylon, and Egyptians call it Misr. 'Cairo' derives from *Al Qahira*, meaning 'the triumphant', after the word for the planet Mars.

*The former Catholic Cathedral on the waterfront*

# Benghazi

Libya's second city, Benghazi lies on the Gulf of Sidra, a large inlet of the Mediterranean Sea, just southwest of the ancient Greek city of Berenice. It is the main city of the Cyrenaica region, a major economic centre and a busy port. Heavily bombed during World War II, it was subsequently rebuilt and became one of North Africa's more attractive cities. There remains an old quarter within the town, as well as a large archaeological area. Demographically mixed, the city is home to many Egyptians and Cretans as well as more recent immigrants from other African countries, such as Sudan.

Founded by the Greeks in 347 BC, Benghazi came under both Roman and Byzantine rule before being taken by the Arabs in the 7th century. The Ottoman Turks took the city in the mid 16th century and held it until 1911, when it was captured by Italy. At this time its population was only about 20,000 people. The Italians created a modern city outside the old Arab quarter, and enlarged the port, making it an important Allied objective during World War II. With the help of the Libyans, who had been miserably treated by Mussolini, the Italians were defeated, and Benghazi became joint capital city, with Tripoli, of independent Libya. After the revolution in 1969, it took second city status, and the country's new-found oil wealth helped turn it into a modern Libyan showpiece.

Tourism in Libya is in the early stages of development, and most visitors use the city as a base from which to visit the ancient Greek ruins in Cyrene, or to make excursions into the desert. There are, however, interesting sights to see within Benghazi, good beaches nearby, and the Jabal al Akhdar, or Green Mountains, a lovely, mountainous region to explore.

# Ghadames

One of the oldest pre-Saharan cities, Ghadames stands in an oasis on the edge of the Sahara, close to the border with Algeria. A UNESCO World Heritage Site, it is a wonderful example of a traditional settlement, built specifically to minimize the extremes of the desert climate. In 1986 the population left the city for a newly built, modern town nearby. However, most families still own their houses in the old town, moving back during summer to escape the worst of the punishing heat.

First inhabited about 5,000 years ago, it became a Roman outpost and later an episcopate of the Byzantine Empire, the inhabitants having converted to Christianity. After the Arab invasion of 667 AD, the people reverted to Islam, and the city changed hands many times before Libya achieved independence. Ghadames was an important Saharan trading post, and by the early 19th century, 30,000 fully laden camels arrived here every year to sell both goods from all over Africa, and slaves. Today the economy has shrunk to camel breeding and a little agriculture, and the hope is that tourism may prove to be its saviour.

Enclosed by a wall, the white-painted houses, entirely built of mud, lime and palm trunks, have beautifully decorative front doors and interiors. Covered alleyways, with occasional openings to the sky, divide them, creating an almost underground feel to the place. Seven districts were built to house seven clans, each with its own public area in which festivities could be enjoyed. The ground floor of every house contained supplies, with the living quarters upstairs. The flat, rooftop terraces, each connected to the next house by a walkway, were strictly for women, who were not permitted to walk through town unless accompanied by a male relative. Though relatively small, this so-called 'Pearl of the Desert', is an absolute must for visitors to Libya.

**POPULATION:**
20,000 (2005)
**WHEN TO GO:**
October to May.
**DON'T MISS:**
The Cultural Museum.
The Main Square.
The Traditional House.
The Great Mosque.
Ain-al-Dibana Lake.
Sunset viewed from the top of one of the huge nearby dunes.
**YOU SHOULD KNOW:**
The city takes its name from Roman times, when it was known as Cydamus.

*The white painted houses of the old town*

# Tripoli

Tripoli is a delightful, lively Mediterranean city situated on a bay in western Libya, close to the Tunisian border. Tourists tend to come here en route to the magnificent Roman sites nearby, but it is well worth spending a few days exploring the sights and soaking up the ambience of Libya's largest city, main seaport and economic hub. Tripoli has a long and complicated history, as do all the other Libyan towns and cities.

Divided into two sections, the skyline is dominated by the Assaraya al-Hamra, or Red Castle, an enormous citadel built by the Spanish in the 16th century. Today this houses the fascinating national museum and overlooks the walled medina. Three gates lead into the medina, which was laid out and fortified by the Romans. It is a marvellous tangle of narrow streets and covered souks, where friendly traders ply customers with mint tea or coffee whilst selling everything from fine jewellery to Gaddafi souvenirs. Most of the historic buildings are within these Roman walls, and at the medina's northern end stands the triumphal arch of Marcus Aurelius, erected during the 2nd century AD, and the only surviving Roman monument in Tripoli.

The new town was built largely during the Italian occupation in the first half of the 20th century. Green Square, situated close to the Corniche, boasts one of two large fountains dating from this era and a large Italian-built cathedral was converted to a mosque after their departure. Oil money and the lifting of UN sanctions has helped open Tripoli to more foreign business and tourism, and the city has expanded to include residential suburbs, the university and the largest hospital in North Africa. Just in case you forget who's in charge, enormous billboards are dotted all over town, featuring 'Brother' Gaddafi's familiar face.

*The National Museum was once a fortress.*

# Kairouan

*The Great Mosque*

Known as the Mecca of North Africa, Kairouan in eastern Tunisia has been a religious pilgrimage site since 670, and Islam's fourth holiest centre after Mecca, Medina and Jerusalem. In the seventh century, Oqba Ibn Nafi chose the site to build a military post to control the Berber hordes. It was far enough from the sea to be safe from attack, but divine inspiration also played a part in his choice of site. Firstly, he found a golden cup there that he had last seen on a trip to Mecca long ago. Secondly, he found a spring connected to the holy well of Zem Zem in Mecca. Finally, 'noxious beasts and reptiles', which he had previously banished for eternity, appeared to him. A city soon grew up, with luxuriant gardens and olive groves. Ibn Nafi was killed by the Berbers 15 years later, but the city was soon recaptured and became a major holy site.

Kairouan's medina is a living museum of Islamic art and architecture. The Great Mosque lies at the far north-eastern end of the medina. It was first constructed by Oqba Ibn Nafi, but has been rebuilt several times since. Its minaret is thought to be the oldest in the world. The windows in the minaret increase in size as the structure reaches skyward, giving an interesting perspective. The prayer hall has a huge number of columns holding up the ceiling, all thought to date from Roman times. And in fact all of the materials used in the Mosque's present incarnation are thought to be the original materials used in its construction. Because of the Great Mosque's religious significance, it is believed that seven trips here by the faithful are equal to the one-time pilgrimage to Mecca.

There are plenty of other sights in Kairouan to tempt the visitor. The mausoleum of Abi Zamaa El Balaoui is a marvellous architectural complex with a fine courtyard and dome richly decorated with medieval tiles. It is the most visited tourist attraction in Tunisia. The Mosque of the Three Doors has wonderful decoration on its exterior which has remained beautifully preserved since the ninth century. The Reservoir of the Aghlabites is also worthwhile. Dating from the ninth century, it has an ingenious hydraulic system to move water from one pool to the other.

When you tire of the cultural sights, Kairouan's souk, situated in the medina, is world famous, offering a wide range of carpets, ceramics and leather goods.

**POPULATION:**
150,000 (2003)
**WHEN TO GO:**
Spring or autumn.
**DON'T MISS:**
The Great Mosque – considered to be the fourth holiest site in Islam (after Mecca, Medina and Jerusalem). Only Muslims are permitted to enter the mosque.
The Mausoleum of Abi Zamaa El Balaoui – this lavishly decorated mausoleum resonates with spiritual significance; it is the burial place of the companion of prophet Mohammad.
The Mosque of the Three Doors – only Muslims are permitted to enter the mosque, but its main feature is its elaborate façade with its strong Andalusian influence.
Carpet shopping in the souks.
**YOU SHOULD KNOW:**
The street names here change often, and usually have two names to begin with!

411

*A beautifully tiled terrace with the minaret of the Great Mosque in the background*

# Tunis

Situated close to the Mediterranean coast, Tunis is the capital city of Tunisia. It lies on a large Mediterranean gulf behind the Lake of Tunis, and the city extends along the coastal plain and surrounding hills. At the centre of the more modern areas of town, including those built in the colonial era, lies the old medina. Built in the seventh century, the medina remains the heart of this diverse port city.

Covered alleys, hidden passages and tunnelled bazaars make up the lively medina, which appears to have changed little since it was built. Traders and artisans hawk their wares and create an enticing energy filled with exotic scents and vivid colours. When you tire of shopping, there are around 700 historical monuments to see in the medina, including palaces, mosques, mausoleums, madrasas and fountains dating back to the Almohad and Hafsid periods. Of special note is the Great Mosque (Zitouna). Its name means 'olive tree', and comes from the founder of the mosque who taught the Koran under an olive tree. It was erected in the ninth century by the Aghlabid rulers, but its famous minaret is a nineteenth-century addition.

Also in the medina is the Dar-al-Bey (Bey's Palace) built by the Turks, which features architecture and decoration from many different styles and periods. The Bardo Museum, housed in the Hasfid Palace, has the most impressive collection of Roman antiquities and mosaics from Ancient Greece and the nearby ruins of Carthage.

Just through the Bab el Bahr (a gate through the medina walls) is the modern city, divided by the grand Avenue Bourguiba. Here the colonial-era buildings provide a clear contrast to the older structures in the medina. The Bab el Bahr is also known as the Sea Gate as at one time there was just open grounds here, leading down to the lake of Tunis. The French colonists called it the Porte de France, and it became a symbol as the gate between the Oriental and European parts of the city.

In Tunis' suburb of Carthage, are the ruins of the ancient city of Carthage, home to Hannibal and his elephants. It was destroyed in 146 BC, but rebuilt by Julius Caesar a century later as a symbol of the resurrection of Africa. It became the second city of the Empire after Rome, and enjoyed a period of decadence and prosperity. Arab invaders destroyed the city once again in the late 15th and early 16th centuries. Not much is known about the original city as it was so badly destroyed and later pillaged, but archaeological work continues to unlock its secrets.

**POPULATION**:
729,000 (2004)
**WHEN TO GO**:
Spring or autumn.
**DON'T MISS**:
The medina, or old quarter, dates from the 7th century AD. Often described as a living museum, it is a labyrinth of ancient mosques and palaces.
The Great Mosque – it was founded in 732 AD, but various extensions over the years have resulted in an eclectic mix of styles.
Bey's Palace – it is believed to stand on the remains of a Roman theatre and is a real architectural gem.
Bardo Museum – houses the finest collection of Roman mosaics in the world, as well as priceless artefacts from Tunisia's past.
The ruins of Carthage – these include dwellings, temples, shrines and baths.
**YOU SHOULD KNOW**:
The medina is a UNESCO World Heritage Site.

# Sousse

Lying on the Gulf of Hammamet, Sousse is a lovely, lively place to visit, combining the pleasures of a seaside resort and a beautiful, old medina, surrounded by crenellated walls. Some two hours from Tunis, Sousse has a long history – Phoenicians, Romans, Byzantines and Arabs all settled here and left their mark.

By the 9th century AD this was already an important trading and military port town. The medina here, listed by UNESCO in 1988, is not huge, but is certainly large enough to get lost in. Many of its twisting alleyways are covered by vaulted brickwork, and lovely tiles decorate the walls. Here you can spend hours haggling for carpets, leatherware, silver or pure woollen blankets and, if you're really smart, go home with a bargain. The Great Mosque was built at this time, a simple, austere building, its sole decoration are the arches within. Although most mosques have a minaret this has a cupola, which was added in the 11th century.

The city's Archaeological Museum can be found in the 9th century Khalef al Fata tower in the Kasbah, on the outskirts of the medina, and contains a collection of largely Roman mosaics, statues and tombs, including an amazing head of Medusa, second only to the Bardo Museum in Tunis. The view from the tower is splendid. The Ribat, a smaller, square fort with a tower, is within the medina, and was built in 820 AD by Islamic warrior monks to protect the population.

When you tire of sightseeing and shopping, head off to the long, sandy, northern beach, with its string of modern hotels. Sousse is the holiday venue of choice for many Tunisians, and the beach nearest the centre of town is often crowded with friendly families enjoying themselves in the sunshine.

**POPULATION:**
156,000 (2004)
**WHEN TO GO:**
April to November.
**DON'T MISS:**
The Traditional Tunisian House Museum.
The Catacombs.
Sousse International Festival (July to August).
The Roman Amphitheatre in El Jem.
Port El Kantaoui leisure complex and marina.
**YOU SHOULD KNOW:**
Sousse has a red light district in the north west of the medina, reached through two overlapping walls that screen the street. Women visitors may want to steer clear of this area.

*Port El Kantaoui*

# Tozeur

**POPULATION:**
40,000 (2005)
**WHEN TO GO:**
October to April.
**DON'T MISS:**
The Great Mosque.
Dar Cherait Museum.
The Festival of the Oases (November
to December).
Arabian Nights theme park.
The Berber villages of Midés, Chebika
and Tamerza.
**YOU SHOULD KNOW:**
Ong Jemel, located nearby, was used
as a location during the filming of
some of the *Star Wars* films as well
as *The English Patient*.

The city of Tozeur, in the west central part of the country, has long been well known, both inside and outside Tunisia. Situated on the edge of a vast palmerie, it produces high-quality dates named 'Deglet Nour', or Fingers of Light, which are exported all over the world. Apart from agriculture, this large oasis relies heavily on desert tourism.

Since time immemorial, Tozeur has been a trading post for caravans coming from the sub-Sahara to trade with the coastal cities. An important Roman outpost named Thusuros, it was taken by Arabs in the 7th century and by the 15th century Tozeur's population was three times what it is today, its economy based around trading black African slaves for dates. By the time the French arrived in 1881, the slave trade was over, the population decimated by cholera and Tozeur was in serious decline.

Today the 14th century medina has been restored to its former glory. Notable for its extraordinary yellow brickwork, the houses of both the old town, and those newly built, conform to the original style of elaborate geometric designs formed in relief. All the narrow streets, walls and facades are decorated in this distinctive way, to astonishing effect. Even the doors are highly decorative, often sporting two or three knockers, probably representing the man, woman and children of the household within.

Pottering around the medina you will find all sorts of local crafts to buy, and there are two intriguing museums to visit. Cycle around the peaceful, shady palmerie, with its complex irrigation system, and admire the strawberries, grapes and plums growing amongst the date palms. There's plenty to do here – take a trip into the Sahara, cross the causeway over the nearby salt lake, Chott el-Jerid, with its surreal, salt encrusted surface, or enjoy a flight in a hot air balloon for a bird's eye view.

*The elaborate geometric designs
of the brickwork in the medina*

# Oran

*Oran Bay seen from Santa Cruz Fort*

Algeria's second city, Oran lies on the Mediterranean and is one of the country's main ports as well as being a thriving commercial centre. It boasts two universities and numerous artistic institutes, all of which contribute to the easy-going atmosphere. This is the city which gave birth to Rai music, now known worldwide, which is a modern mix of Bedouin folk music and Arabic love poetry, with a little French, Spanish and Moroccan influence thrown in for good measure. The city divides naturally into the old quarter, with its Arab, Berber, Ottoman and Spanish architecture, and the new, which was built by the French from the 1830s onwards.

Founded by Moorish Andalucians in the 10th century, Oran facilitated trade between Spain and this part of North Africa. In 1509, the city was occupied by Spain, and up until 1831, when France captured Oran, it changed hands back and forth between Spain and the Ottoman Empire. Held by Vichy France during World War II, it was surrendered to the Allies in 1942, becoming an important strategic headquarters. Torn apart by a bloody civil war in the 1950s, Algeria finally achieved independence from France in 1962, and 200,000 French citizens departed en masse.

Aside from being close to some great beaches and lovely fertile countryside full of market gardens and vineyards, the city has many intriguing sights. The ancient Kasbah lies next to the Spanish town, which is dominated by the beautiful Cathedral of St. Louis, while the Great Mosque, built in 1796 to celebrate Oran's liberation from Spain, dominates the Ottoman area. After a hard day's sight-seeing, spend the evening people-watching in one of the many pleasant restaurants along the Front de Mer, take in a show at the Arts Centre or catch some Rai music in a club – whatever you do, you'll find the city both interesting and amusing.

**POPULATION:**
1,000,000 (2004)
**WHEN TO GO:**
April to October.
**DON'T MISS:**
Abdelkader Mountain.
Santa Cruz Fort.
Demaeght Museum.
Cathédral de Sacré Coeur.
Cap Blanc.
Madagh.
**YOU SHOULD KNOW:**
Oran's name originates from ancient Moorish words meaning 'Two Lions'. Legend tells of lions here c.900 BC, the last two of which were killed nearby. Famous names from Oran include Albert Camus, Yves Saint-Laurent, and Rai musicians Cheb Hasni, Cheb Khaled and Rachid Taha.

# Algiers

**POPULATION**:
3,500,000 (2004)
**WHEN TO GO**:
October to May to avoid the hottest summer sun.
**DON'T MISS**:
Villa Abd-el-Hair – one of Algiers oldest residences, located in the 'Garden of Test'.
Notre Dame d'Afrique – located on a cliff overlooking the Bay of Algiers, it is similar in style to its namesake in France.
Church of the Holy Trinity.
New Mosque – built in the shape of a Greek cross and surrounded by a huge white cupola.
Museum of Fine Arts.
History Museum.
**YOU SHOULD KNOW**:
Algeria's liberation struggle is brilliantly captured in the Oscar-winning film *The Battle of Algiers* (1965).

In 1881 the French writer, Guy de Maupassant wrote: 'It is so beautiful, this city of snow under dazzling light,' and indeed, approaching the city from the sea, one's first impression is of a mass of white-washed buildings spilling down the hills to the coast, with forested mountains rising behind them, and the immense, 90 m (297 ft) high, Martyr's Monument dominating the skyline.

Algiers has had a long and turbulent history. Originally a small, Phoenician trade port, in 950 AD the town was established under Berber rule, and named Al-Jazair – still its Arabic name. Changing hands many times, it fell to Barbarossa, the famous pirate, in 1529, becoming the capital of the so-called Barbary Coast. Piracy grew and became so prevalent that by the early 1800s the US navy, followed by the British and the Dutch, attempted to halt it. Finally, in 1830, France attacked Algiers, and began their 132 years of colonial rule. During World War II the city hosted the Allied forces headquarters, and those of the Free French government under Charles de Gaulle. It was the focal point of the liberation struggle in the 1950s and became the capital of independent Algeria in 1962. Its recent past is also troubled.

The upper part of the city is the old Kasbah, a tangled labyrinth of narrow alleys, steps and run-down houses leading up to the crowning citadel. This area is a UNESCO World Heritage Site, and plans are afoot to rescue and renovate it. The lower level looks utterly French, with wide boulevards, grand, arcaded Beaux-Arts buildings, gleaming white apartment blocks with blue shutters and wrought-iron balconies. There are fascinating mosques and churches, universities and colleges, imposing public buildings and, most of all, there are museums. Five mega-projects are planned to transform the city and attract tourism on the same scale as Marrakech and Tunis, and indeed Algiers has the potential to do just that.

*Djamaa el Djedid Mosque in the Grand Square*

# Ghardaia

*The simple, medieval architecture of Ghardaia blends into the hills.*

Ghardaia is an extraordinary collection of five stone settlements, carved into the hills around the M'Zab oasis, in the northern Sahara desert. In 1982 the entire valley was listed as a UNESCO World Heritage Site, as an example of traditional human habitation that is perfectly adapted to its natural environment. The houses, which are only two storeys high and painted white or blue, have their own terraces and courtyards and are built into the hillside in concentric circles, linked by narrow streets leading around and up to a single, crowning minaret.

Ghardaia is inhabited by Mozabites, a group of Algerian Berbers belonging to the conservative Ibadi Muslim sect. Banished in the 11th century, they elected to move to this remote and inhospitable place in the desert. Their life patterns formed a sensible, ecologically sound rule – when the population outgrew the prayer hall of the single, underground mosque, built against the heat, a new settlement was started on another hill, thus producing easily defended towns sited high above the palmerie, orchards and well-tended fields in the valley below.

The Mozabites organized their water resources, sinking wells and dams, and building sluices and channels that ensure the maximum benefit from the water that comes from the occasional flooding of the M'Zab Wadi – every drop is used, stored or recycled. This turned the brown, stony, barren valley into the green oasis that it is today, proving that even the Sahara can be made fruitful.

Today Ghardaia is a centre for date production and well known for its beautiful rugs and cloth. The simple, medieval architecture blends into the hills, and traditionally clothed men and women go about their business in much the same way as they have been doing for the past 1,000 years. The sense of harmony between man and nature is tangible.

**POPULATION:**
120,000 (2005)
**WHEN TO GO:**
October to April.
**DON'T MISS:**
The daily souk.
Beni Isguen.
Bou Noura.
El Atteuf.
Melika.
**YOU SHOULD KNOW:**
Ghardaia is under religious administration, and a guide is needed to visit Beni Isguen. Photography of women is prohibited, and permission must be granted for photography of men or children. Ghardaia was built around a cave inhabited by a revered holy woman named Daia, and she is still venerated by Mozabite women today.

417

# Fez

*The Karaouine Mosque*

Fez, situated in the heart of northern Morocco, was the imperial capital under the Merenid, Wattasid and Alaouite dynasties and has for centuries been the intellectual, historical and spiritual centre of the country. For many years it was one of the major cultural cites of the West, rivalling the great university towns of Europe. Today it retains the feel and look of a medieval Islamic city, and as you wander through the labyrinthine shady streets of the old town, exotic smells of mint and spices wafting through the air, you feel you have gone back in time.

The old town is one of the largest living medieval cities in the world, the souks stretching for over a mile. It has changed very little over the passing years, still featuring the 'traditional seven elements': mosques, medersas (Koranic schools), souks (markets), fondouks (lodging and trading houses), fountains, a hamam (steam bath) and a bakery. The narrow alleyways are filled with artisans creating and selling their wares using traditional techniques. You can see leathers being treated in the tanneries, copper pots being soldered, brass plates being engraved, and a whole host of colourful ceramics, embroidery, carpets and food stuffs being hawked in a constant round of buying and selling.

The gates and walls of the old town (Fez el-Bali) remain intact, adding to the mystery inside. The towering Medersa Bou Inania, a theological college built in 1350, dominates the city and is one of the most spectacular buildings in the whole of Morocco. With elaborate carving, tile work and decorative stucco, this was the last and grandest monument built in Fez by a Merenid Sultan, designed to rival the Karaouine mosque, the largest in North Africa.

The Boujeloud Gardens (Jardins de la Marché Verte) are a peaceful oasis of calm, offering a well-earned rest from the bustle of the old town. Sip a glass of mint tea at the pleasant open-air café, and nibble on some tooth-achingly sweet pastries to give you the strength to continue. Move on to the Dar Batha Palace, built at the end of the nineteenth century for the reception of foreign ambassadors. It houses the Museum of Moroccan Arts and Crafts, but is worth a visit just for its cool courtyards and tranquil gardens.

# Tangier

In northern Morocco at the western entrance to the Straits of Gibraltar, where the Mediterranean meets the Atlantic, lies the multicultural city of Tangier with the Rif Mountains rising majestically behind it. Founded by Carthaginian colonists in the early fifth century BC, the city has since come under the power of many different rulers, including the Romans, Vandals, Byzantines, Arabs, Portuguese, British, Spanish, all of whom left their indelible mark on the city before it passed into Moroccan hands. Tangier is best known for its medina, the old Arab town with two markets: the Grand Socco and the Petit Socco (the Spanish word for souk). Today these bustling markets offer great shopping opportunities, with everything from spices and nuts to pottery, carpets and leather goods.

Many great names from the world of the arts have been captivated by the sights and sounds of the city on the Straits. Many have spent long periods here, some have even made it their home. Past inhabitants and visitors include the likes of Paul Bowles, William S. Burroughs, Jack Kerouac, Tennessee Williams and the Rolling Stones. The status of international free zone which the city enjoyed for a number of years made it a popular place for international spying activities, especially during the Cold War. It was also a smuggling centre and attracted foreign capital due to political neutrality and commercial liberty. All this added to the city's celebrity and sense of mystery.

Other great places to visit in the city include the Mendoubia Gardens, with their eight-hundred-year-old trees, and the Sidi Bouabid Mosque, which dominates the medina with its beautiful minaret. The Kasbah Square, with its portico of white marble columns is also worth a look, as is the great Mechouar where the pashas used to give audience.

**POPULATION:**
670,000 (2004)
**WHEN TO GO:**
Any time of year.
**DON'T MISS:**
The Grand and Petit Soccos.
The Mendoubia Gardens.
Sidi Bouabid Mosque.
The Kasbah Square.
The Mechouar.
**YOU SHOULD KNOW:**
There are some good beaches nearby.

*The octagonal minaret on the Kasbah mosque*

*The Mausoleum of King Mohammed V*

# Rabat

Morocco's capital, Rabat, is a delightful surprise, its old quarter full of charm. Lying between the Atlantic coast and the estuary of the Bou Regreg River, it feels pleasantly provincial and is less of a tourist destination than Marrakech or Fez. Divided between the old city and the new, it is easy to walk around – the sometimes tedious hassle that occurs elsewhere is less prevalent here.

Some of Rabat's long and complex history is visible in its 12th century Almohad era walls and monuments, and its Kasbah and medina, which were both rebuilt by Andalucian pirates. Muslims of Moroccan extraction, these were refugees who were expelled from Christian Spain in 1610. Forming an anarchic republic here, their pirate fleet, the Sallée Rovers, captured merchant ships as far afield as the Caribbean during the next 200 years. In 1912, when the French formed a Protectorate here, they built the new town outside the walls, and re-established the city as their capital, which King Mohammed V elected to retain on gaining Moroccan independence in 1956.

The fortified Kasbah is like a Spanish village, light and airy, all the houses are sparkling white with blue paintwork. Enclosed by huge walls, one enters through the Oudaia Gate, one of the finest of Moorish gates, built in 1195. Visit the 17th century Royal Palace, with its Museum of Moroccan Arts and enjoy the beautiful Andalucian gardens. A viewing platform at the northern end of the Kasbah gives splendid views over the harbour and the ocean.

The medina, also walled, is more orderly than most. Wander through the clean, narrow, residential streets, stone houses with studded wooden doors rising on either side. Turn a corner and find a mass of busy little shops and stalls, working craftsmen and cafés. The new town, with its parks and tree-lined streets, is obviously French, and contains all the embassies and government buildings.

**POPULATION:**
1,700,000 (2007)
**WHEN TO GO:**
Best between March and November.
**DON'T MISS:**
The Royal Palace – this sumptuous building is the official residence of King Hassan II.
Mohammed V Mausoleum – an imposing structure of white marble dedicated to the sultan who lead Morocco to independence.
Hassan Tower, one of Morocco's national symbols.
Chellah Necropolis and gate – ruins meet nature in this 14th century necropolis. It is over-run by trees, plants and animals.
Ech-Chianha and Skhirat beaches.
**YOU SHOULD KNOW:**
The Royal Dar es Salaam Golf Club, just outside Rabat, is one of the top 50 golf clubs in the world.

420

# Essaouira

Essaouira is probably Morocco's best known and loved coastal city. In part, this is thanks to the influx of foreigners who, during the last 20 years, have fallen in love with the place, bought up crumbling old riads and beautifully restored them as homes or chic hotels. However, foreign influence is nothing new here, and the fusion of several different cultures is what gives Essaouira its open-minded, cosmopolitan atmosphere.

Essaouira has a long history – the off-shore islands were used by Phoenician sailors in the 7th century BC and for 1,000 years it was an important trading port. The Portuguese built a fort here in 1506, but Essaouira was created by Sultan Sidi Mohammed and his French architect, Théodore Cornut who, in 1760, designed much of the city and its fortifications. The Grand Place, surrounded by handsome white buildings, and grid pattern streets, owe more to France than Africa.

Walk the high, red ramparts of the Skala de la Ville, fortified with cannons facing the sea, for fabulous views, before visiting some of the many thuya wood artisans' workshops beneath. Visit the vibrant port to watch the fishing fleet come in, then eat freshly caught sardines grilled on makeshift BBQs and admire the colourful boats in every stage of construction. Wander through the medina and the mellah, (the old Jewish Quarter), stop for a fresh orange juice or a coffee and eat the delicious, still-warm croissant you just bought.

Essaouira is an enchanting place, full of art galleries and antique shops, musicians and craftsmen. Lying at the tip of a vast, sandy bay, it allows long, slow walks towards Diabat and its ruined Portuguese 'castle in the sand', made famous by Jimi Hendrix in the 1960s. Surfers have discovered the rolling waves of 'Windy City', and their activities just enliven the bustling, colourful spectacle.

**POPULATION:**
70,000 (2006)
**WHEN TO GO:**
All year round.
**DON'T MISS:**
The music festival in June – this 'International Festival of Sacred Music' lasts for 5 days and attracts thousands of visitors.
Sidi Mohammed Ben Abdellah Museum – an ethnographic museum.
The Isles of Mogador, breeding grounds of the rare Eleanor falcon.
**YOU SHOULD KNOW:**
Orson Welles chose Essaouira's fortifications as the backdrop to his film of *Othello*.

# Meknes

**POPULATION:**
536,322 (2004)
**WHEN TO GO:**
February to June, September to
November.
**DON'T MISS:**
Dar Jamai Museum.
Medersa Bou Inania.
Moulay Ismail's Mausoleum.
The monumental gates to the
Imperial City.
The Fantasia Festival in September.
Volubilis – a fantastic, ruined
Roman city.
**YOU SHOULD KNOW:**
Moulay Ishmael had 4 wives, 500
concubines and 800 children. He
once asked Louis XIV for the hand in
marriage of his illegitimate daughter,
Marie Anne de Bourbon, and
was refused.

Situated on a fertile plain, Meknes lies roughly halfway between Fez and Rabat. One of Morocco's four Imperial Cities, it is a prosperous place, its economy based on the fruit, vegetables and grain produced in the surrounding countryside. Less visited by tourists than most of the country's cities, it has a quiet, rather solemn atmosphere due, no doubt, to the enormous architectural monuments built by the utterly ferocious and megalomaniac Sultan Moulay Ismail.

The Meknes medina was designed by the first Almohad sultan, Abdel Moumen, during the 12th century. Several hundred years of political confusion followed until, in 1672, Moulay Ismail succeeded to the throne, and determined to make Meknes his new capital. His 50,000-strong army of slaves constructed a huge Imperial City, which included dozens of palaces, gardens, ponds, storehouses and stables, incompletely surrounded by 25 km (16 mi) of vast, looming walls. For 55 years Moulay Ismail ruled with a rod of iron, taking Tangier, Larache and Asilah from the Christians, building mosques and kasbahs throughout the country and slaughtering at least 30,000 people along the way.

Today, some of these creations are in ruins – the 1755 earthquake caused severe damage. However, the sheer scale of what remains is awesome. The Royal Stables were built to house 12,000 horses, the granaries look as though they could hold enough food to feed the whole country, and the massive walls are wide enough to be roads.

Exiting the Imperial City via the monumental Bab Mansour, you come into Place El Hedim, a huge square surrounded by shops and cafés, where storytellers and snake charmers entertain the locals. You'll need a rest and a drink before setting off to explore the medina and the mellah before finally crossing the bridge to the Ville Nouvelle and your hotel.

*One of many elaborate gates in Meknes*

# Marrakech

Marrakech, in southern Morocco, has for centuries been a meeting place for tourists, a social hub where people have got together to enjoy themselves. At one time it was the southern tribesmen and Berber nomads coming into town to sell their wares in the market, spend some of the proceeds on pleasurable pursuits and stock up on goods. Now they have been joined by tourists from all over the world, but this doesn't seem to have affected the way of life here. Standing in the old city's main square, the Djemaa el-Fna, as the sun goes down and watching the myriad entertainers work the crowds, you feel as though you have been transported back to the Middle Ages.

Here snake charmers, acrobats, monkey tamers, henna artists, jugglers and storytellers jostle for position with magicians, fire-eaters and fortune tellers. Boxers, astrologers and men with scorpions crawling on their faces all contribute to the melée which has remained basically unchanged for centuries. Yet the rest of Marrakech is changing rapidly and developing into a wealthy, hip and thoroughly modern city. To those who know it, these changes are even discernible in the Djemaa el-Fna, which has recently been smartened up and paved, and is now closed to traffic.

Along the side of the square are the glorious souks, a huge area of twisting covered alleyways which are fascinating to explore. There are metalworkers' souks, woodworkers' souks, dyer's souks, leatherworkers' souks and plenty of goods for sale, including beautiful carpets and colourful ceramics.

While the Djemaa el-Fna and the souks must be the highlights of a trip to Marrakech, there are plenty of other things to see and do. The old city is surrounded by nearly 10 km (6 mi) of unbroken mud brick walls, punctuated by towers and battlements, which cast shadows across the rich, red soil. At nearly 70 m (230 ft) high, the minaret of the Koutoubia mosque is the city's main landmark, and possibly the most perfect Islamic monument in North Africa.

Rebuilt by the Saadians in the sixteenth century, the Ben Youssef Medersa is the largest building in the medina. No surface has been left undecorated and there is clear inspiration from Andalusian art. Another legacy left by this dynasty is the Saadian Tombs, highly decorated and set in a beautiful garden.

*Evening at the foodstalls in the market place and public square – the Djemaa el-Fna*

**POPULATION:**
650,000 (2005)
**WHEN TO GO:**
April to November.
**DON'T MISS:**
Djemaa el-Fna – this square and market place in the city's old quarter is an unbelievable experience. The heady mix of market stalls, story tellers, acrobats and snake charmers is a sight to behold.
Saadian Tombs – beautiful tombs in the Beaux-art style.
The Koutoubia minaret.
El Badi Palace – now ruins as much of this huge palace was destroyed in the collapse of the Saadian dynasty but enough of it remains to give an idea of the sheer opulence they lived in.
A stroll through the souks.
**YOU SHOULD KNOW:**
Watch your bag or wallet in the crowds of the Djemaa el-Fna.

# Timbuktu

Timbuktu is a city with a magnificent past, situated close to the Niger River, on the edge of the Sahara. Inscribed by UNESCO in 1988, it was then listed as being endangered by desertification. A preservation programme ensued, and by 2005 it was removed from that list.

Established by nomadic Tuaregs in the 12th century, Timbuktu rapidly became one of the richest places in the world, thanks to its proximity to the Niger. Caravans brought slaves, ivory, gold and salt – at that time of equal worth by weight – all of which was taken further north or south. Timbuktu's fabulous wealth became world famous. By the 15th century the city had become an intellectual and spiritual centre. The Djinguereber Mosque, a mud brick building built in 1327 is the oldest in West Africa, and is said to have been the Spanish architect Gaudí's inspiration. In 1581, Sankore University was built, as well as several other madrassas (colleges). Scholars wrote books and a phenomenal collection of manuscripts was collected in 120 libraries.

In 1591 Moroccan mercenaries invaded, and tribesmen began making violent attacks on the town, beginning its long slide into oblivion. In 1898 the French occupied Mali, removing entire libraries to Europe. In response, the remaining manuscripts were hidden in the desert. Today, a new library is being built, and those manuscripts remaining are slowly being returned to it, providing an unprecedented wealth of written African history.

Timbuktu is dishevelled, dusty and poor, but history is redolent in the narrow, parched streets that remain much the same as they were centuries ago, minus many of the houses' huge, metal-studded, wooden doors that have been sold and replaced with corrugated iron. Camels stand and stare under the sparse shade of the acacia trees and airborne sand gets into everything, even the bread. Nevertheless, Timbuktu's legendary status brings thousands of visitors each year, and perhaps this will revive something of the city's former glory.

*The Sidi Yahia Mosque*

# Djenné

Situated on the Niger delta in central Mali, Djenné is the oldest-known city in sub-Saharan Africa which is still inhabited. Throughout history, it has been an important trade centre, as well as a centre of Islamic learning and pilgrimage. Today it is famous for its mud brick (adobe) architecture, particularly that of its Great Mosque which is the largest adobe building in the world.

The city was established around 800 AD as a meeting place between the Sudan and the tropical forests of Guinea. During the 16th century it became an important trading centre due to its location: it was on the river route through to Timbuktu, and on the route to gold and salt mines. The city was ruled by Moroccan kings, Tukulor emperors and the French at different times through its history, but commercial activity eventually moved to Mopti and Djenné declined in importance.

The original Great Mosque, built in 1240 by the sultan Koi Kunboro, was thought too extravagant by Sheikh Amadou, who replaced it with a smaller version in the 1830s. The current mosque, built around 1907, is one of the most stunning examples of Muslim architecture in Mali. The mosque has been designated a UNESCO World Heritage Site and features architectural elements found in mosques throughout the Islamic world.

Every spring, local masons repair the mud structure. This event has turned into an annual festival which includes the whole community. Small boys churn the mud before the event, women carry buckets of water perched on their heads while men bring the mud through the square. On the evening before of the event, drums and flutes are accompanied by chanting.

Other attractions include the Tomb of Tupama Djenepo, a young girl who was entombed here in the 12th century as a sacrifice to give prosperity to the people of Djenné. Legend has it that she went willingly and her family was honoured. Just outside Djenné are the remains of the ancient town of Djenne-Jeno. Although there is not much to see, the site is atmospheric. Visitors must be accompanied by a guide from the Mission Culturelle, who will offer insight into this ancient site which dates back to the 3rd century BC.

The weekly market around the mosque is one of West Africa's most colourful markets with thousands of traders coming here from all over the region.

**POPULATION:**
12,000 (2007)
**WHEN TO GO:**
In spring for the annual repairs to the mosque.
**DON'T MISS:**
The Great Mosque – built in 1907 out of sun-dried mud bricks, held together by mud and plastered over with mud.
Djenné weekly market – held every Monday. The square fills with colourful foods and fabrics, interesting smells and a great mix of people.
Tomb of Tupama Djenepo – legend has it that this young girl was sacrificed on the founding of the city to give prosperity to the people of Djenné.
The remains at Djenné-Jeno – the site of the oldest known settlement in Africa, dating from 3rd century BC.
**YOU SHOULD KNOW:**
Non-Muslims cannot enter the mosque.

*Traders flock to Djenné for the weekly market held around the Great Mosque.*

# Agadez

**POPULATION:**
89,000 (2005)
**WHEN TO GO:**
December to February.
**DON'T MISS:**
The Camel market.
Camel trekking in the Air Mountains.
4 wheel drive expeditions into the
Ténéré Desert.
The oasis towns of Timia and
Iferouane.
**YOU SHOULD KNOW:**
Tuaregs are the original Canaanites
of the Bible – Canaan means 'land of
the purple people'. Despite the
accord reached with the government
in 1995, rebel groups demanding
more autonomy, staged an attack on
Agadez airport in June 2007. No
casualties or serious damage
was done.

The mud-walled city of Agadez lies beneath the foothills of the stark and beautiful Air Mountains, just west of the classic sand-dune sea of the Ténéré Desert. An ancient trading town, it grew around the crossroads of the trans-Saharan caravan routes that linked Egypt and Libya to the Lake Chad area and Nigeria. The epitome of an exotic desert town, it is home to Fulani and Hausa tribesmen as well as nomadic Tuaregs, who walk the streets in their billowing blueish-purple robes, faces half covered by swathes of dark fabric.

Founded in the 11th century, Agadez was a major Tuareg city, becoming a Sultanate in the 14th century. At its zenith during the 16th century it had a population of 30,000. The city declined during the 17th century after the Moroccan invasion of Sudan, but continued as a centre of Islamic learning. It was taken over by the French, around 1900. Nowadays, still a Sultanate, Agadez is on the 'Uranium Highway' linking Air to Niamey. A French owned uranium mine lies 250 km (156 mi) to the north, its extractions fuelling France's nuclear power stations.

The main sight here is the Grand Mosque, built in 1515. Said to be the highest mud-brick minaret in Africa at 27 m (89 ft), it was re-built in 1844 to the original design, spiked with traditional wooden crossbars. Nearby stands the three storey Sultan's Palace – arrange a visit and, possibly, meet the Sultan.

The old town is a maze of narrow alleyways between single storey houses, some of which have beautifully decorated facades. At its heart is the Grand Marché where Tuareg people do business with southern Hausa traders. Here are desert handicrafts including Tuareg leather and silverwork. Agadez crosses, of unique geometric design, have protective symbolism, and are worn by almost all Tuaregs. Watch them being made in the Artisan Centre and take one home as a reminder of this remote and romantic place.

*The Grand Mosque dates from the 16th century.*

*Kano Mosque*

# Kano

Nigeria's second most populous city, Kano is the economic hub of northern Nigeria, and the main distribution centre for the cotton, cattle and peanuts produced in the surrounding agricultural region. Known for its leather goods since the 1400s, its tanned goatskins were sent to North Africa and thence to Europe, where they were called Morocco leather.

Founded about 1,000 years ago by a blacksmith in search of iron, stone tools discovered here are indicative of prehistoric settlement in the area. Kano quickly became one of the seven independent Hausa city-states, and a major centre for trans-Saharan trade. By the 15th century, Kano had embraced Islam and the first mosque and the Emir's Palace were erected. Early in the 19th century a Fulani Islamic leader ousted the Hausa Emir in a jihad, and Fulani Emirs have retained power here ever since. In 2000, Sharia law was introduced, and has now been controversially extended to the non-Muslim area of the city. Sadly, Christians are no longer able to visit the old Central Mosque.

The Old City was enclosed by huge mud-brick walls, most of which have been allowed to crumble, though some of the original gates remain. The Emir's Palace is a splendid example of Hausa architecture, and the Gidan Makam Museum is in a restored palace, and worth seeing. At the heart of the Old City lies Kurmi market, a vast, noisy, crowded, chaotic and colourful place, selling anything and everything. Hail one of the seemingly endless supply of moped taxis to take you to a further market in the Sabon Gari, or foreigners' quarter, which claims that 'If it can be found in Nigeria, it can be bought in Sabon Gari'.

**POPULATION:**
2,000,000 (2004)
**WHEN TO GO:**
November to March.
**DON'T MISS:**
The ancient dye pits, still in use.
The Sabuwar and Dan Agundi gates – these gates were used to control the movements of people in and out of the city.
Gidan Makama Museum – displays architectural pictures and relics detailing the history of Kano.
The Durbar Celebrations – these colourful events take place twice a year and are hosted by the Emir of Kano. Expect much music, dancing and elaborate costumes.
**YOU SHOULD KNOW:**
Nigeria's oil wealth has, if anything, destabilized the country, and tension exists between the Muslim and Christian populations.

# Saint-Louis

**POPULATION:**
176,000 (2005)
**WHEN TO GO:**
November to May.
**DON'T MISS:**
Saint-Louis Museum.
Langue de Barbarie National Park.
National Park of the Birds of Djoudj.
Saint-Louis Jazz Festival in May.
Blues Festival in January/February.
Guet N'Dar fishing community.
**YOU SHOULD KNOW:**
Despite being so close to the
Mauritanian border, you can't cross
the border here. The actual crossing
point is 100 km (62.5 mi) upstream.

The old, colonial city of Saint-Louis lies at the mouth of the Senegal River, a mere 10 km (6 mi) south of the border with Mauritania. Made up of three parts, the heart of Saint-Louis lies on a narrow island in the river. Separated from the Atlantic Ocean by a sand spit known as the Langue de Barbarie, also part of the city, it is connected by two bridges. The island is similarly joined to the mainland and third part of the city, by the Faidherbe Bridge, constructed by and named after Louis Faidherbe, the French colonial governor, in 1897.

A fortified trading post was established, on the then uninhabited island of N'dar, by French traders in 1659. The first permanent French settlement, it was named after Louis XIV and was the centre of trade along the river. Slaves, beeswax, hides and ambergris were all exported from here and the city rapidly became a major economic player. A Franco/African Creole community of merchants, the Métis, sprang up, producing a vibrant and distinctive urban culture.

*A Saint-Louis taxi*

During the late 1800s Louis Faidherbe was responsible for modernizing and developing Saint-Louis, but the city declined as Dakar gained in importance. Today, Saint-Louis is still a trading centre, but tourism has become important to its economy. Since being listed by UNESCO in 2000, Saint-Louis is beginning to be restored, restaurants and hotels are opening, and the future looks bright.

Most of the colonial architecture is on the island and consists of two storey buildings, the ground floors often shops, with red, tiled roofs, high wooden ceilings, wooden shutters and balconies with wrought iron balustrades. More imposing buildings include the old governor's palace. Saint-Louis is close to excellent national parks and long sandy beaches. It is renowned for its music festivals, and the annual, lantern-lit procession that takes place in December.

# Abomey

Abomey lies some 145 km (91 mi) north of Benin's 'Slave Coast', the Gulf of Guinea, and until the late 19th century, it was the capital of the mighty Fon kingdom. This kingdom lasted from 1625 to 1900 and was ruled by 12 successive kings. All but one had their own palace built within a huge, all-encompassing mud wall, protected by a deep ditch filled with thorny acacia.

By the 1800s the compound was huge, covering 44 hectares (108 acres). It enclosed villages and fields, a market place, barracks, the palaces with their ceremonial halls, and a harem for 800 women. The kings were regarded as sacred beings, with mystical, religious and worldly power. However, their wealth was largely amassed from the sale of thousands of prisoners of war to European slave traders. In 1892, when the French defeated the last independent king, he torched the place before escaping.

Today, the Historical Museum of Abomey contains the palaces of King Guezo and King Glele, and the many buildings, courtyards and pillars, made of mud, hardwood, bamboo and palm are incredibly impressive. Having no written history, earthen bas-reliefs depicting the major events, myths and customs of the Fon people decorated the palace facades. Those of Glele's palace show, amongst other things, that companies of ferocious female warriors fought alongside men. The Museum contains over 1,000 items, mainly of royal provenance and still used ceremonially today. These include weapons, jewellery, musical instruments, altars, royal emblems and thrones. Guezo's throne, placed on four human skulls, makes a powerful statement.

Abomey today is the centre of an agricultural region as well as a tourist attraction, and although no longer an official kingdom, many royal descendants live in the palaces you are visiting, and are still revered.

*A courtyard in the palace of King Guezo*

**POPULATION:**
121,000 (2004)
**WHEN TO GO:**
November to May.
**DON'T MISS:**
Dozoéme, the ancient blacksmith's village.
The Hall of Jewels.
The Ajalala.
The Voodoo Festival each January 10th.
**YOU SHOULD KNOW:**
65 per cent of Benin's people are advocates of voodoo. Thousands of slaves were transported from Benin to Brazil, Cuba and Haiti, and their religion lives on in those countries today.
Abomey's remarkable Royal Palaces were added simultaneously to UNESCO's World Heritage and World Heritage in Danger lists in 1985. Restoration work has since removed the site from the endangered list.

*The magnificent Cape Coast Castle*

# Cape Coast

Cape Coast is a place with a fascinating history. Set around the rocky promontory that protects the bay, the city climbs up the steep hills surrounding the centre, colonial architecture, from the early 1800s is evidence of the city's past. The magnificent Cape Coast Castle, a UNESCO World Heritage Site, looms over the crashing waves, from the battlements a row of black cannons point towards non-existent ship-borne enemies.

Known as Oguaa and already a settlement and market, the Portuguese bought the plot of land in the early 1600s and built a castle for their trading post. Changing hands between Sweden, Denmark and the Netherlands, the Castle changed and grew. In 1664 it fell to the English, and became the administrative centre of the Gold Coast. So it remained until 1877, when the capital was moved to Accra.

Cape Coast Castle, with its peeling, white painted exterior, was built to protect timber, ebony and gold, but it rapidly became the centre of the slave trade. This is a deeply impressive place. Thousands of slaves languished in dreadful conditions in the dungeons here, traded for guns, tobacco and beads, before being shipped to the New World. There is an excellent museum in the castle, and guided tours that are both illuminating and moving. From either end of the battlements two other historic forts can be seen: in all, some 60 forts and trading posts were built along this coast.

Cape Coast was the birthplace of the country's first newspapers, and of the nationalism that finally won its independence. Today it is Ghana's centre of excellence in education, and something of a resort town, with splendid beaches nearby.

**POPULATION:**
110,000 (2004)
**WHEN TO GO:**
June to September.
**DON'T MISS:**
Fort William and Fort Victoria. Elmina town, with its two castles. Kakum National Park, with its canopy walkway.
**YOU SHOULD KNOW:**
Vasco da Gama is thought to have come here on his voyage of discovery to India. Louis Armstrong believed that his ancestors were shipped to America from Cape Coast Castle.

# Accra

Accra, lying on the Gulf of Guinea, is Ghana's capital and everything you would expect of a large West African city with a colonial past. The country's administrative and economic centre, it is crowded, noisy, lively, colourful and full of friendly people. It has elegant colonial architecture, modern buildings made of steel and glass, and lively, shambolic shanty towns on the outskirts.

The site of Accra was first settled by the Ga people in the late 16th century, as a series of villages. The Portuguese, British, Danish and Dutch built fortified trading posts nearby, all of which have been subsumed into the inexorably spreading city. In 1877, having already bought up all the trading rights, the British made Accra the capital of their Gold Coast Colony, which lasted until Ghana gained independence in 1957 – the first African colony to do so.

The National Museum is a great place in which to refresh your knowledge of Ghana's history. Its spectacular display of ethnography and art is one of the best in West Africa. This may spur you on to buy a piece of contemporary art or jewellery, which you can find in the Centre for National Culture with its permanent national collection, artworks for sale and many craft stalls.

The 17th century Christiansborg Castle, built by the Danes, is the seat of government, close to the liveliest part of the city, Osu. The oldest neighbourhood, Jamestown, is still a large, active fishing harbour, where gaily-painted boats arrive with their catches of still-flapping fish, scales glinting silver, pink and yellow in the early morning sun. Climb up the lighthouse and admire the views. Accra is more of a 'now' city than a monument to the past. Its fantastic, jam-packed markets are a hive of activity, the nightlife, music, drumming and dancing is exciting, and if you need a break, you can always go to the beach.

**POPULATION:**
2,000,000 (2004)
**WHEN TO GO:**
June to September.
**DON'T MISS:**
Independence Square – built in 1961 in preparation for a visit from Queen Elizabeth II.
W.E.B. DuBois Memorial Centre – both DuBois and his wife are buried here. The centre is dedicated to his work and his fight for the emancipation of his people.
Aburi Botanic Gardens.
Kwame Nkrumah Mausoleum – this is the resting place of the Ghanaian president, a pioneer for African independence who lit the symbolic flame in Independence Square to highlight the fragility of freedom.
Labadi Beach.
**YOU SHOULD KNOW:**
The name Accra comes from the world *Nkran* meaning 'ants'. It refers to the numerous anthills in the surrounding countryside.

*The fishing harbour of Jamestown*

# Asmara

**POPULATION:**
500,000 (2004)
**WHEN TO GO:**
September to March.
**DON'T MISS:**
The neo-Classical Governor's Palace, now the National Museum.
The Impero cinema – a fabulous Art Deco construction.
The Opera House – a beautiful building decorated in a Romanesque style.
Medeber market – this busy market involves a huge number of Asmarinos recycling absolutely everything!
A trip on the Eritrean State Railway – recently restored, this enchanting railway line spirals down from Asmara to meet the Red Sea at Massawa. Not for the faint-hearted!
The Asmara Piscina.
**YOU SHOULD KNOW:**
Eritrea is Africa's youngest country, having become independent in 1993.

High on the edge of the Kelbessa Plateau lies a hidden jewel of a city. Asmara, Eritrea's capital, sees little tourism, yet it is a remarkable example of a well-planned, Modernist, Italian city. Instantly appealing, Asmara's broad streets are lined with palms, its clean pavements busy with cafés, pizzerias and ice cream parlours. Most foreigners here are either UN soldiers or NGOs, all of whom must be thrilled to have been posted to such an unexpectedly delightful place.

Founded in the 12th century, Asmara gained prominence in 1884, when it became the capital. In the late 1800s Italy began colonizing Eritrea and soon a narrow-gauge railway was built linking Asmara to the coast, underpinning the importance of the town. By the late 1930s, Mussolini decided to turn Asmara into a showcase city, the flagship of his projected African Empire. During the following six years he created 'Little Rome', a well-designed city full of Art Deco, Cubist and Futurist architecture, symbolic of the 'excellence of Fascism'.

The smallish, pastel-hued centre is easily explored: colonial houses and villas draped in bougainvillea are liberally scattered throughout, alongside some magnificent public buildings in several different architectural styles. The neo-Romanesque cathedral (1922), serves as a landmark – its belltower visible wherever you are. The Orthodox church, the synagogue and the Khalufa el Rashidin Mosque are all of interest, the latter, built using Carrara marble, fronts a dark stone, geometrically patterned square.

Despite Eritrea's political troubles, Asmara and its *dolce vita* atmosphere has remained relatively unscathed. Pretty girls sit gossiping over lattés and handsome young men show off their muscles at the swimming pools. At sunset the town takes to the streets for the *passegiatta*, exchanging greetings and glances as they go. Later, nightclubs and lively bars abound, and everyone has fun. This is a city with a difference – Neapolitan ice cream to an African tune.

*The neo-Romanesque cathedral serves as a landmark.*

# Khartoum

*The Presidential Palace on the banks of the Blue Nile. This building replaced the original that was razed by the Mahdi's forces after General Gordon was killed on its steps.*

Khartoum, the capital of Sudan, is beautifully situated at the convergence of the Blue Nile, which flows west from Ethiopia, and the White Nile, which flows north from Uganda. This is where the two rivers join forces and make their way up to the Mediterranean. The shape they form resembles an elephant's trunk – 'al-Khartum' in Arabic. Greater Khartoum includes the areas of North Khartoum across the Blue Nile and Omdurman across the White Nile.

Founded by Muhammad Ali of Egypt, as an army outpost in 1821, Khartoum developed as a regional trading centre, becoming prosperous through the slave trade. European explorers based themselves here while organizing expeditions into the interior. However, this era of peaceful expansion ended in1884 when the Mahdi's troops besieged the town for many months, a battle which ended in General Gordon's death and the massacre of the English and Egyptian forces. Re-taken by Lord Kitchener in 1898, the city was rebuilt to the design of the Union Jack flag, and the city centre retains a colonial aspect to this day.

In the recent past Khartoum has received an enormous number of refugees fleeing neighbouring nations during times of conflict, and the shanty towns of the outlying areas have grown exponentially. This slow-moving city is undergoing badly needed redevelopment and several huge projects are underway. Meanwhile, it's a pleasant place to explore – the National Museum contains wonderful antiquities from Nubian times as well as two reconstructed pharaonic temples, built by Queen Hatshepsut and Tuthmosis III. If you are interested in the present rather than the past, visit the largest market in the country at Omdurman, itself a traditional Muslim suburb founded by the Mahdi in the 1880s.

**POPULATION:**
1,000,000. Greater Khartoum: 4,000,000 (2005)
**WHEN TO GO:**
November to March.
**DON'T MISS:**
The Ethnographical Museum.
The People's Palace.
Whirling Dervishes at the Hamed el-Nil Mosque.
The weekly camel market.
The Mahdi's Tomb.
The Royal Cemetery of Meroe, containing the amazing narrow pyramids of the Meroitic pharaohs (592 BC – 350 AD).
**YOU SHOULD KNOW:**
Sudan is the largest country in Africa, and the site of the ancient Nubian civilization. Predominantly (and militantly) Muslim, Arabic is the common language, but over 100 other languages are spoken amongst the 500 plus ethnic groups living in the country.

433

# Antananarivo

**POPULATION:**
1,403,000 (2001)
**WHEN TO GO:**
May to October.
**DON'T MISS:**
The markets – or zomas – once the longest single market in the world, but now split into different areas.
Antaimoro paper, made from bark and flowers.
The Astronomical Observatory in Antananarivo University.
Tsimbazaza Zoological Park and the Malagasy Academy Museum – to see lemurs, aye-ayes and more.
Lake Anosy and its war memorial.
**YOU SHOULD KNOW:**
Due to its position 1400 m (4600 ft) above sea level, Antananarivo enjoys a Mediterranean climate and is home to animals and plants found nowhere else on earth.

Antananarivo is the capital of the world's fourth largest island, Madagascar. Most visitors come here to see some of the island's remarkable, endemic species of flora and fauna, and they almost all arrive at the international airport here. Built on the hillsides and summit of a long, narrow ridge, roughly in the centre of the island, and surrounded by vast rice-producing plains, Antananarivo has no major 'sights' to see, but is a very pleasant place to spend a few days.

Founded in about 1625 as the base of the Hova chiefs, the name Antananarivo, 'city of the thousand' derives from the 1,000 men set to guard it. Of the several kingdoms on the island, the Merina kingdom became prominent and by 1810, Radama I made Antananarivo capital of the island. In 1895 Madagascar came under French rule; the wooden city was rebuilt in stone and brick, and roads, steps and squares were added. Independent since 1960, Madagascar has struggled through various socialist dictatorships to the democracy it enjoys today.

The ruins of the Rova – the Queen's palace – visible from wherever you may be, crowns Antananarivo and offers wonderful views. Burnt down in 1995, it is still possible to visit, but thus far only the chapel has been rebuilt. Nearby stands the former prime minister's palace, storing an unusually personal collection of Royal belongings that were retrieved from the Rova.

The centre of town, Haute Ville, is small enough to explore by foot, but the whole city is a warren of steep streets, cobbled paths and flights of steps. Although the more important buildings are solid structures, there are still numerous picturesque wooden houses, with shutters attesting to their French heritage.

*The whole city is a warren of steep streets, cobbled paths and flights of steps.*

The spires of some fifty churches rise above the largely low-rise city, including both an Anglican and a Catholic cathedral. At sunset, when the surrounding hills turn blue and the buildings take on a golden glow, Antananarivo looks glorious.

# Gondar

In the north-west of Ethiopia, near the shores of Lake Tana, lies the fortress city of Gondar, the ancient capital of Ethiopia. Until the 16th century, the Ethiopian emperors led a nomadic lifestyle, living in temporary camps as they moved around their realms. Beginning with Emperor Minas in 1559, they began spending the rainy season near Lake Tana each year, often at the same site. The encampments they created flourished as cities for a short time, including Emfraz, Ayba, Gorgora and Dankaz.

*Fasilides' Palace*

Gondar was founded by Emperor Fasilides in about 1635. Legend has it that a buffalo led the Emperor to a pool where a hermit told him he would locate his capital. Fasilides had the pool filled in and built his castle there, the recently restored Fasilides' Palace. With its huge towers and looming battlement walls, it seems as if a piece of medieval Europe has been transported to Ethiopia. Subsequent emperors added to the site, building their various palaces nearby in the Royal Enclosure.

The Royal Enclosure is surrounded by a towering wall 900-m (2,953-ft) long, and is filled with juniper and wild olive trees. In addition to Fasilides' Palace, it contains the royal archive, Iyasu's Palace, Dawit's Hall, stables, a banqueting hall, Mentewab's Castle, the library, chancellery and many churches. The architecture of these buildings clearly shows Hindu and Arab influences, but was subsequently transformed by the Baroque style brought to Gondar by Jesuit missionaries.

By the Qaha River just beyond the city are Fasilides' Baths. Here there is a formal bathing pool and pavilion, standing above the ground on piers. The pavilion is reached by a stone bridge which could be raised in times of battle. Every year, a ceremony takes place in which the baths are blessed and opened for bathing.

**POPULATION:**
194,000 (2005)
**WHEN TO GO:**
September to November.
**DON'T MISS:**
The Royal Enclosure – an immaculate set of European castles dating back to the 1600s.
Fasilides' Baths – located in Gondar's fortress city of Fasil Ghebbi, Ethiopia's first capital city. The baths once belonged to the Emperor Fasilides and are still used for the annual religious festival of Timkat-Epiphany.
**YOU SHOULD KNOW:**
The Palace is a UNESCO World Heritage Site.

*Navigating Lake Tana on a papyrus reed raft.*

# Bahir Dar

The lovely, small city of Bahir Dar grew up around a Jesuit settlement on the southern shore of Lake Tana, Ethiopia's largest body of water. As the capital of the Christian Amhara region, the city is expanding rapidly, with government offices, factories and businesses all opening up here. It also has a university, and the number of music clubs and bars in the city reflect the large population of young people.

The backdrop of sparkling blue water with fishermen in papyrus boats, the streets lined with tall palms and jacaranda trees and the gardens rich with pointsettia and hibiscus all combine to give Bahir Dar the feeling of a resort. Indeed many people come here to explore the marvels of Lake Tana, the source of the Blue Nile.

Thirty seven islands dot the surface of the huge, 3,600 sq km (1,390 sq mi), lake, and on twenty nine of them are fantastic monasteries and churches, dating from between the 11th and 16th centuries. Hire a boat for a day's exploration, but beware – some sites are forbidden to women. The 14th century Ura Kidane Mehret, on the Zeghe peninsula is marvellous – decorated inside and out with frescoes of biblical scenes and containing a number of fabulous illuminated bibles, it is open to all.

Some 30 km (19 m) from Bahir Dar are the startling Blue Nile Falls – a magnificent 400 m (1,320 ft) wide cascade of water plunges over a 45 m (148 ft) drop into the chasm below, producing thunderous noise and, catching the sunshine, the spray reflects brilliant rainbows of colour. Approaching across a 17th century castellated Portuguese bridge and up a grassy slope, the Falls suddenly appear before you in all their glory.

**POPULATION:**
167,000 (2005)
**WHEN TO GO:**
September to May.
**DON'T MISS:**
Dek Stephanos, with its astonishing collection of icons.
Emperor Haile Selassi's Palace, with its great views.
The Saturday market, known for weaving and woodworking.
**YOU SHOULD KNOW:**
Over 80 ethnic groups live in Ethiopia, but despite the Amharas being only the third largest, Amharic is the country's official language.

# Addis Ababa

Addis Ababa lies sprawled across the foothills of Mount Entoto, in the centre of Ethiopia. This is the political, economic, and educational hub of the country, itself largely undiscovered by mass tourism. Ethiopia's distinguished cultural legacy has remained unaffected by outside influence – it is one of only two African countries that were not colonized by Europeans.

Ethiopia's history goes back for over 2,000 years – some of the earliest hominids (about 3 million years old) have been discovered here. Powerful kingdoms and different capitals came and went, until the country was finally re-united in 1855. In 1886 Taytu Betul, the wife of Emperor Menelik II, built a house near the Filwoha hot springs, which was transformed into the Imperial Palace and new capital. Meaning 'New Flower', Addis Ababa remains the seat of government, but the president lives in the National Palace, built for Emperor Haile Selassie in 1955.

Rising to a level of over 3,000 m (9, 900 ft), the city's oldest, upper section, is home to St George Cathedral (1896) and Addis Ababa University. Its narrow streets and market squares are 450 m (1,485ft) above the surrounding metropolis. Beneath it is the main commercial section, with tree-lined avenues, museums, restaurants and hotels as well as over 90 embassies and consulates. It is the headquarters of both the UN Economic Commission for Africa and the African Union, and home to a large foreign population.

Here modern office buildings rub shoulders with colonial villas. One of the world's largest pre-fabricated buildings, now a convention centre, lies close to Holy Trinity Cathedral, the site of Sylvia Pankhurst's tomb. Throughout the city, traditional wattle and daub huts can be found, goats and chickens patrol every small patch of land. Mules and donkeys mix with traffic, reminding the visitor that the city grew from a handful of villages settled by nobles who followed their emperor here less than 150 years ago.

**POPULATION:**
3,628,000 (2007)
**WHEN TO GO:**
October to March.
**DON'T MISS:**
The National Museum, containing Lucy, the oldest known hominid in the world.
The Ethnological Museum.
The Merkato – one of the most amazing and one of the largest open air markets in Africa.
The Menelik Mausoleum.
Walking on Mount Entoto, especially between the churches of St Mary and St Raguel.
**YOU SHOULD KNOW:**
Ethiopia's capital cities used to move when the surrounding wood, used for building and fuel, ran out. Menelik II organized the planting of hundreds of thousands of Eucalyptus trees, creating a permanent greenbelt around the city; hence Addis Ababa used sometimes to be referred to as Eucalyptopolis.

*A view of the sprawling city*

# Harar

**POPULATION:**
122,000 (2005)
**WHEN TO GO:**
November to May.
**DON'T MISS:**
Harar's famous Hyena men, who
feed hyenas by hand in a nightly
ritual.
The 16th century Jami Mosque with
twin towers and a slender minaret.
Medhane Alem Cathedral.
Ras Mekonin's house – where Haile
Selassi grew up.
The Harar Cultural Museum.
The Rimbaud House, where the
renowned French poet lived.
The Babile Elephant Sanctuary, east
of Harar; the sanctuary shelters a
rare, endemic elephant as well as
black-maned lions and other animals.
**YOU SHOULD KNOW:**
Surprisingly, despite its Islamic
credentials, Harar has a brewery that
produces pale lager, stout as well as
Harar Sofi, a non-alcoholic drink.

The extraordinary walled city of Harar is one of Ethiopia's treasures, a city of great historical and religious significance, and the capital of the Harari region. Situated on a hilltop at 1,885 m (6,220 ft), at the eastern end of the Ethiopian highlands, the city overlooks the Ogaden Plains to the south, and the Danakil Desert to the north, while the fertile Harer Mountains are on its western flank.

For centuries a major commercial centre thanks to its location, Harar, the world's fourth most holy Islamic city and already a centre of Muslim culture and learning, became the capital of the Adal Sultanate in 1520. From here a war was launched against the Ethiopian Christians that almost succeeded. Culturally, religiously and economically the town flourished, and by 1647 it was issuing its own currency. Briefly controlled by Egypt, Harar was incorporated into Ethiopia in 1887, and though it subsequently declined commercially, it remains as spiritually important as ever.

This is a city of shrines and mosques and minarets. In just 1 sq km (0.39 sq mi) the 90 mosques are thought to be the largest concentration of mosques in the world – prior to 1887 entry to the city was forbidden to non-Muslims. The city walls are 5 m (16 ft) high and built of locally quarried stone. Fascinating domestic architecture, unique in Ethiopia, stands along 368 narrow, cobbled alleys. Some have open plan ground floors dominated by a raised area upon which to socialize and chew the *qat* that grows in the nearby mountains.

Adares, as the inhabitants are known, have a language of their own, and the women still wear gorgeous, traditional clothing. The city is famous for its fine basketware, silver jewellery, textiles and bookbinding, and there are plenty of opportunities to acquire all of these. Harar has been extended beyond its encircling wall, but stroll through its lanes, or sip a cup of superb, locally grown coffee and you will feel as though you are in another world.

*The food market*

# Mombasa

*Fort Jesus, founded by the Portuguese in 1593, is now a national monument.*

Mombasa, Kenya's second city, is the largest port in East Africa. Separated from the mainland by two creeks, there is a bridge to the north, and a causeway and railway line to the west. It is only when travelling south, by ferry, that its island location is really noticeable.

Founded by Arab traders during the 8th century, Mombasa was already prosperous when Vasco da Gama visited in 1498. Two years later Portuguese forces arrived, heralding centuries of struggle between the Portuguese and the Shirazi Arabs. In 1840 the Sultan of Zanzibar, who later ceded its administration to Britain, took the town. In 1963, Mombasa became part of the newly independent Kenya.

This is a Swahili city, although it has had a culturally and racially mixed heritage for so long that it has blended seamlessly together. Its hot, steamy climate informs the pace of life here – slow and easy going. This is Kenya's base of coastal tourism – cruise ships and containers dock at Kilindini, the modern, deepwater harbour, but tourists arriving by train or plane generally head for beaches further north or south.

Mombasa's Old Town is a place of narrow, winding streets and charmingly dilapidated, Arab-influenced architecture, featuring carved doorways and long, fretworked balconies. Overlooking the sea stands Fort Jesus, built by the Portuguese in the 1590s and now an interesting museum. The city's atmosphere is friendly, the bars and restaurants are lively and stay open late.

Walking through the Old Town is a sensory pleasure – everything looks exotic and colourful, people dress in kangas and kikois – brightly coloured, printed cotton cloths - and the air reverberates with the scent of spice. Visit the Old Harbour, where each day beautiful, traditional dhows and other small boats deliver fresh fish and goods from along the coast. The faces you'll see, the colours, noise and laughter, make Mombasa a genuinely successful melting-pot of a place.

**POPULATION:**
700,000 (2004)
**WHEN TO GO:**
June to March to miss the rains.
**DON'T MISS:**
A dhow cruise around the harbour – no trip is complete without a magical cruise on a traditional Mombasan boat.
The overnight train to Nairobi.
A trip to one or more of the beaches to the north and south.
The famous elephant tusks on Moi Avenue – arches made out of intersecting tusks form a letter 'M' for Mombasa. They were built to commemorate the visit of Queen Elizabeth II in 1952.
Wandering around the labyrinth of narrow lanes and quaint shops in the Old Town.
**YOU SHOULD KNOW:**
North of the city centre, on the way to Nyali Beach, is East Africa's largest crocodile farm, Mamba Village, where interesting tours can be taken.

**439**

*The I&M Bank tower in the busy centre*

# Nairobi

Kenya's capital city, Nairobi is a relatively recent invention, and its success is largely due to its location. Situated at 1,661m (5,450 ft) above sea level, approximately halfway between Mombasa on the coast and Kampala, capital of Uganda, it enjoys one of the most benign climates in the world. With temperatures rarely rising above 25 °C (78 °F) and never below 10 °C (50 °F), the city is too cool for the malarial mosquito, and never unpleasantly hot.

In 1899 the building of the Uganda Railway line produced a need for a supply depot and camp. Nairobi was chosen because of its proximity to several rivers – indeed its name comes from the Maasai words for cool waters. After an outbreak of plague and the burning of the town, it was completely rebuilt, and in 1905 it replaced Mombasa as the capital of the British Protectorate. Growing rapidly as an administrative centre, British big game hunters began to visit Nairobi, prompting the building of several grand, colonial-style hotels. Ever more British ex-patriots decided to settle here and between 1920 and 1950 their numbers grew from 9,000 to 80,000, causing tension with the local tribes and sparking the Mau-Mau rebellion. Kenya finally gained independence from Britain in 1963.

Today Nairobi is a disjointed mix of first-world skyscrapers, big business, restaurants, glitzy malls, wealthy ex-pats in colonial villas or gated communities, and teeming slums such as notorious Kibera, full of those who have moved here from the interior, or refugees from Somalia or Sudan. There are also long-established communities from India and Pakistan.

Despite its problems, this is a vivid, lively, cosmopolitan city. People take their fun seriously and music and nightlife go on until daybreak. There is plenty to see, from museums and galleries to the wonderful Nairobi National Park on the outskirts of town. Also notable are the city's green spaces - Uhuru Park, in central Nairobi, is one of several excellent spots to visit if you need respite from big city life.

**POPULATION:**
2,800,000 (2005)
**WHEN TO GO:**
Any time, though the rainy season is March to June and November to December.
**DON'T MISS:**
The bar at the Norfolk Hotel, the oldest in town, for a glimpse of the old colonial highlife.
The National Museum.
The Giraffe Centre, established to protect the endangered Rothschild giraffe.
Karen Blixen Museum, the former home of Karen Blixen (Isak Dinesen), author of *Out of Africa*.
Westlands Market.
The twice-weekly Maasai Market.
**YOU SHOULD KNOW:**
On a clear day it is possible to see both Mount Kenya and Mount Kilimanjaro from Nairobi.
Nairobi has a reputation for crime and is often called Nairobbery by the locals – don't carry valuables about, especially at night.

# Kampala

Kampala, the capital city of Uganda, has risen like a phoenix from the war-torn ruin it was less than 30 years ago. Built across several hills and not far from Lake Victoria, this is a vigorous, spirited city with a strong sense of its own achievement and positive about its future possibilities. Reasonably safe to walk around, and bursting with sociable, enthusiastic and well-educated locals, this is a great place to meet people and talk the night away.

Milton Obote achieved independence from Britain in 1962, but in 1971 he was ousted by Idi Amin, a dictator whose excesses of violence and greed brought the country to its knees, before engineering the disastrous war with Tanzania that caused him to flee in 1979. Leaders then came and went, and in 1980 Yoweri Museveni, a guerrilla army leader, took the power which he retains today, despite some opposition in the north of the country.

Nakasero Hill is really the city centre, but Kasubi Hill is historically significant. Here are the Kasubi Tombs, sacred to the Buganda people as the resting place of several Kabakas, or kings. Surprisingly, the tombs are large traditional thatched buildings, made of bark cloth and reeds. A great, white mosque dominates Kibuli Hill, and the Protestant and Catholic cathedrals of Namirembe and Rubaga have hills of their own.

There are many NGOs in Kampala and a well-established ex-pat community. The markets are fun – Owino seems to sell just about everything, and looking at the crowds in their brightly coloured clothes, unrecognizable African foodstuffs piled high on rickety stalls, the general hustle and bustle is hugely atmospheric. There are smart Western style complexes too, but most of all there's a really buzzy nightlife here, a casino, bars and clubs, restaurants and music – at weekends the city never seems to go to sleep.

**POPULATION:**
1,209,000 (2002)
**WHEN TO GO:**
June to September and December to February.
**DON'T MISS:**
The Entebbe Botanic Gardens.
The Uganda Wildlife Education Centre – a rescue centre for some of Uganda's wildlife, much of which was decimated during the Uganda/Tanzania war.
Ngamba Island Chimpanzee Sanctuary, Lake Victoria.
The Parliament building and Independence monument.
Nommo Art Gallery.
**YOU SHOULD KNOW:**
The name Kampala translates as 'hill of antelopes'.

*A view of the sprawling city*

# Zanzibar

**POPULATION:**
206,000 (Zanzibar City in 2002)
**WHEN TO GO:**
September to March.
**DON'T MISS:**
The Slave Market and memorial – the slave trade continued in Stone Town for some 30 years after it was abolished in 1873.
The Peace Memorial Museum.
The Palace Museum – the Sultans' palace from the 1890s to 1964.
Dr. Livingstone's house, built for a sultan and inhabited by many Victorian explorers and missionaries.
The Nasur Nurmohamed Dispensary – a beautifully restored building and the Cultural Centre.
**YOU SHOULD KNOW:**
Freddie Mercury, singer with the band Queen, was born in Stone Town.

'Zanzibar' – the word immediately conjures up images of an exotic, distant island, ringed with sparkling, azure seas and impossibly white, empty beaches, the air heavy with the scent of cloves. Stone Town, the old centre of Zanzibar City, lives up to the dream. Set on a peninsula on the west coast, it is a wondrous blend of Arabic, Indian and African culture and style, with some European influence thrown in for good measure.

For centuries, ships carried spices and slaves between Africa and Asia, and until the late 1800s, Stone Town, the hub of Arabian interests in East Africa, was ruled by Omani Sultans. As Dar es Salaam and Mombasa gained importance, Stone Town declined. By 1964 the last Sultan had been removed and Zanzibar united with mainland Tanganyika to become part of Tanzania. Most of the foreigners left the island, their vacated buildings, confiscated by the government, gradually falling into shabby disrepair. Fortunately, the listing by UNESCO in 2000 has produced renewed interest in renovating and conserving this quintessentially Swahili heritage.

The Arab Fort, started by Portuguese and finished by Omanis in 1701, is the oldest building here, its high, castellated, chocolate-coloured walls hiding a green space, shops and a café. The town is littered with gorgeous buildings. Narrow, shadowy paths are lined with Arab houses, plain facades hiding splendid interior courtyards. Long windows are set within deep niches, and first floor walkways enabled Omani women to socialize without being seen in public.

You'll see massive hardwood doors, intricately carved by Indian craftsmen and decorated with Indian style brass spikes, and beautiful balconies, some original and some added later. Low stone benches in front provide seating for local men, who spend hours there, putting the world to rights. There are so many outstanding buildings to be seen, and such a lot of romantic history that you mustn't be tempted to skip the city in favour of the beach.

*The Nasur Nurmohamed Dispensary – a beautifully restored building and the Cultural Centre*

# Dar es Salaam

*The harbour of Dar es Salaam*

To most foreigners Dar, as it is affectionately known, is Tanzania's first city, and in many ways it is. The official capital however, is Dodoma, where the country's parliament is located. Dar es Salaam's success is centred upon its huge, natural, deep water harbour, and its position as the transport hub of the country has attracted many international companies.

In 1866 the Arabic Sultan of Zanzibar, spotting the potential of the bay, began to build a palace here, changing the existing name to Dar es Salaam, 'haven of peace'. Interest in Dar was revived when the German East Africa Company established itself in 1887, making it their colonial administrative and commercial base. In the early 1900s, the railway was built, and when the British captured the German colony in World War I, Dar was the natural capital and expansion continued apace. By the time Tanzania gained independence in 1961, it already had a multi-cultural feel, and Middle Eastern, Indian and European communities, as well as Tanzanians, were well settled in.

Don't just use Dar as a stepping-stone for Zanzibar or the white sand beaches to the north and south – stay a few days to enjoy it. The centre of town fans out from the harbour, itself endlessly fascinating, with graceful traditional dhows slipping between cruise ships and cargo boats towards the vibrant, noisy and colourful fish market on the northern side.

Various imposing German buildings around the harbour draw the eye, such as St. Joseph's Cathedral, but more interesting is to wander the streets of the Asian district, snacking on delicious South Indian titbits. Kariakoo Market is worth visiting, although it can be an intense experience – very hot and very crowded – and at the Mwenge craft market you can watch craftsmen at work. At night there's plenty going on: busy bars and lively clubs and lots of loud, live music.

**POPULATION:**
2,500,000 (2005)
**WHEN TO GO:**
September to March.
**DON'T MISS:**
The National Museum.
Nyerere Cultural Centre and Nyumba Ya Sanaa for local art and culture.
The Village Museum – displays many typical dwellings of different tribes from different parts of the country. Tribesmen came from all over Africa to ensure that they were represented in this museum.
The Botanical Gardens.
**YOU SHOULD KNOW:**
Beware of pickpockets and make sure you take taxis at night.

443

# Maputo

**POPULATION:**
967,000 (2004)
**WHEN TO GO:**
Any time of year, but it is at its prettiest in spring when the flowers are in bloom.
**DON'T MISS:**
The Associação Núcleo de Arte artists' collective.
The Museum of the Revolution.
**YOU SHOULD KNOW:**
Praça dos Trabalhadores railway station was designed by Gustav Eiffel.

The capital of Mozambique, Maputo lies on the Indian Ocean at the west side of Maputo Bay. It was founded in 1876 as Lourenço Marques, named in honour of the Portuguese merchant who first explored the area in the mid 16th century. Neglected after independence and during the civil war, the city is slowly recovering. There are wide, leafy avenues, charming old buildings and flower-filled gardens and the later 20th-century buildings are easy enough to ignore.

Maputo is home to an ever-more popular arts scene as the National Art Museum is a must. The Associação Núcleo de Arte artists' collective has gained international renown for its work, especially the works made out of decommissioned weapons, such as *The Tree of Life*.

The central market in the Baixa district is renowned for its seafood, which forms the basis of much of the local cuisine. Cooking here is a mixture of influences including Portuguese, Muslim and South African, making eating out here a unique experience. Different areas also specialize in South Asian, Portuguese, Middle Eastern and African food. A good place to head for is the upmarket Polana area, which is also where most of the curio sellers and tourist shops are. The Avenida de Guerra Popular is where the best African fabrics can be found and wooden carvings, such as small boxes and picture frames are a speciality.

*A view of the Maputo skyline*

# Moçambique town

**POPULATION:**
21,000 (2007)
**WHEN TO GO:**
Any time of year.
**DON'T MISS:**
The Church of Nossa Senhora Baluarte.
The museum in the old Palacio Govierno.
**YOU SHOULD KNOW:**
The island is joined to the mainland by a bridge.

The town on the Ilha de Moçambique (also spelled Mozambique) is a UNESCO World Heritage Site and was once the capital of Portuguese East Africa. It was an Arab port for centuries before the arrival of the Portuguese, who made it into a major stopping point on voyages to and from India and points east. The earliest building here is the Church of Nossa Senhora Baluarte, which dates to 1522 and is probably the oldest standing European building in the southern hemisphere. The Fort of São Sebastião was built at the north end of the island and the majority of the historic buildings are here, in what is known as Stone Town. Most of the locals live in Reed Town in the south. Other highlights include the churches of Santo Antonio and the Misericordia, the palace and chapel of São Paulo, which now houses a museum, the Holy House of Mercy's hospital, which is now the museum of sacred art. The ensemble was given World Heritage listing because of the way the same techniques, materials and decorative principles had been used since the 16th century. The loss of trade because of the opening of the Suez Canal and the inauguration of the port of Nacala to the north left Moçambique as a backwater, thus accidentally preserving its historic structures.

# Port Louis

On the north-west coast of Mauritius, Port Louis was founded in 1735 by the French. Originally a stopping point so ships bound for India could restock on necessities, it became part of the British colony after the island was seized in 1810. After slavery was abolished in 1834, the British brought in huge numbers of indentured labourers from China and, in particular, the Indian subcontinent, and their descendants make up a large part of the population, giving the island's culture and food a unique mix.

The landing-site for the labourers is now the UNESCO World Heritage Site of Aapravavasi Ghat. Another area by the port is the Caudan Waterfront, which is a popular meeting place for the young and has a huge food court. Chinatown is a great place to shop and eat, while the Port Louis Bazaar is renowned for its cheap goods and is well worth spending some time rummaging round in search of bargains. Kadafi Square is among the best places to seek out local delicacies.

Among the many other historical buildings are the Port Louis Theatre, the Casernes Police Barracks, St Louis Cathedral and Fort Adelaide, or La Citadelle, which was built by the British in the 1830s. It dominates the city and – like the Signaux Mountain – is a great place to go to get an overview of the city. Even older is the Champ de Mars race course.

There are three museums, the Natural History Museum, the Blue Penny Museum and the Mauritius Stamp Museum.

Outside the city are the beaches and resorts, where visitors can simply lounge in the sun or enjoy the water sports in the warm, clear waters of the Indian Ocean.

**POPULATION:**
148,000 (2003)
**WHEN TO GO:**
May to September is slightly cooler.
**DON'T MISS:**
The stamp museum, for Mauritius' famously beautiful stamps.
The walk up Signaux Mountain.
The Champ de Mars race course, the oldest (1812) in the Indian Ocean and the second oldest in the Southern Hemisphere.
Port Louis Bazaar.
Mauritian Chinatown.
**YOU SHOULD KNOW:**
Port Louis is the second most important financial centre in Africa (after Johannesburg).

*A view across Port Louis to the waterfront*

# Johannesburg

**POPULATION:**
3,226,000 (2001)
**WHEN TO GO:**
Any time of year, although winter can
be cold.
**DON'T MISS:**
The Hector Pieterson Museum.
The Rosebank Rooftop Flea Market.
The Sterkfontein Caves, where fossils
of early hominids have been found.
**YOU SHOULD KNOW:**
In spring, when the jacarandas
flower, the whole city seems to
turn mauve.

Established in 1886 as a gold-mining town, Johannesburg is the capital of Gauteng province, but is not, as is often thought, South Africa's capital. It has had a troubled past and the collapse of the apartheid regime meant that for several years large parts of the city were no-go areas, but this situation is now improving.

Among the most popular destinations in the city is the Mandela Family Museum in Soweto's Orlando West, while the Apartheid Museum is worth spending an entire day visiting. The art gallery is the biggest on the continent and has both European and African paintings, and the Museum of Africa concentrates more on the region's history and culture, including a large collection of ancient petroglyphs.

The more affluent areas of the city are in the north and north-west: Melvilla is particularly well known for its nightlife and bohemian living. Tours of the former townships such as Alexandra and Soweto are becoming increasingly popular.

Of course, the area is rich in wildlife and the Lion Park is where visitors can get up close to lion cubs and drive through an enclosure with prides of adults, as well as antelope, giraffe and zebra. Johannesburg Zoo is the largest in Africa. The Walter Sisulu Botanic Garden is one of the last large green spaces in the city and is home to a wide variety of plants and birds.

The Lesedi Cultural Village is home to traditional food and dances of the various cultures of the region, a reminder of the area past and its rich cultural heritage, which is now allowed to flourish once more.

*The Nelson Mandela Bridge*

# Cape Town

*The Victoria and Albert Waterfront development includes shops, restaurants and an aquarium.*

Also known as Kaapstad or iKapa, Cape Town lies at the foot of Table Mountain and is the capital of Western Cape Province and the site of South Africa's legislative capital. To the other side of the city lies the Cape Peninsula and the two geological features make up the UNESCO World Heritage Site of Table Mountain National Park.

One of the most popular areas within the city for tourists is the Victoria and Albert Waterfront, which has hundreds of shops and restaurants and the Two Oceans Aquarium. It is also the departure point for trips to the apartheid-era jail on Robben Island and to the seal colonies on Duiker and Seal Islands.

There are lots of pretty Cape Dutch buildings, especially in the old government buildings in the central business district, along Long Street and in Constantia. Long Street is also a good place to head for some of the best restaurants in the country and the city's most popular clubs and bars. The British colonial era is seen in the city hall and the Rhodes Memorial, while the iniquities of apartheid can be seen in the District Six Museum, which commemorates the area's residents who were forced to leave when it was declared a whites-only area.

Because slaves were brought from the Far East, there is a high proportion of people of south-east Asian heritage in the city and the Bo-Kaap (formerly known as the Maylay Quarter) is another popular destination. It has been refurbished and is full of quaint, brightly coloured buildings.

The cablecar up to the top of Table Mountain is a must, in good weather, and there are tracks leading to the end of the Cape Peninsula. Both areas have an abundance of wildlife.

There is so much to see and do in Cape Town, you'll need to come back again and again.

**POPULATION:**
2,950,000 (2001)
**WHEN TO GO:**
Spring, summer and autumn: winter is cold and wet.
**DON'T MISS:**
Robben Island.
The Cape Town Minstrel Carnival in early January.
The views from Table Mountain.
Tours of the Cape Flats and Khayelitsha townships.
A trip to the Cape Winelands.
The Castle.
Whale watching in Hermanus Bay.
**YOU SHOULD KNOW:**
The water is warmer on the False Bay side of the Cape.

# Pretoria

**POPULATION:**
1,884,000 (2005)
**WHEN TO GO:**
Spring, summer or autumn.
**DON'T MISS:**
Freedom Park.
The Fairy Glen Nature Reserve.
Tswaing Meteorite Crater.
Wonderboom Nature Reserve and its
1000-year-old fig tree.
**YOU SHOULD KNOW:**
The Cullinan Diamond was found at
the Premier Mine in Cullinan in 1905.
The Star of Africa, cut from the
diamond, dazzles in the royal sceptre
– part of the Crown Jewels on show
in the Tower of London.

One of South Africa's three capital cities, Pretoria is the administrative centre. It was named after Andries Pretorius, a Voortrekker hero, by his son Marthinus and was founded in 1855 to serve as the capital of the new Transvaal Republic. The area saw conflicts with local kingdoms and during the Anglo-Boer Wars because of both its strategic imporatnce and the rich mineral wealth being discovered in the area. The national government is housed in the Union Buildings at the top of the hill. The area had been home to several different nations for hundreds of years before the arrival of the Voortrekkers and their history can be traced in the National Cultural History Museum. Other museums cover the South African Air Force, the life of the Voortrekkers and local history, and include the ominous sounding Correctional Services Museum. Kruger House was the home of Paul Kruger, while Melrose House saw the signing of the treaty that ended the Anglo-Boer War in 1902. The giant Voortrekker Monument on Proclamation Hill south-west of the city centre, draws the eye from all around. It is now a museum.

The city is within easy reach of several important wildlife sanctuaries, including the Groenkloof Nature Reserve, while the National Zoological Gardens are near the city centre. Steam enthusiasts can take the circular tram ride round the city.

A unique attraction is Coin World, the shop of the South African Mint where Kruger Rands and jewellery are for sale.

*The Union Buildings*

*Durban's golden sands*

# Durban

South Africa's busiest port, Durban was also for many years its most popular tourist destination, although more international tourists now head for Cape Town. It has a subtropical climate and stunning beaches. Although Vasco da Gama had landed in the area in 1493 and named it Natal, Durban's foundations date back only to the 1820s. The Indian workers the British brought here mean that Durban has a large Asian population.

Among Durban's most popular tourist spots are the beaches, bars and restaurants of the Golden Mile, the Suncoast Casino, uShaka Marine World – one of the largest aquariums on earth – the African Art Centre, Waterworld, the Maritime Museum and the Botanical Gardens. For those who can face it, the Fitzsimons Snake Park on Lower Marine Parade makes an interesting excursion. Many of the beaches have shark protection nets – shark attacks are not as common as all that, but there are Great Whites in the region – and the Shark Institute runs trips to watch them.

The large Indian population means that curry is a speciality of the city, especially Bunny Chow – a hollowed out chunk of bread filled with your choice of curry. Wilson's Wharf, off Victoria Embankment, has a wide variety of cuisines, as does Florida Road, which is also great for little boutiques. At the opposite end of the scale, the Gateway Mall is the largest in the southern hemisphere. Tourist Junction is home to good craft shops that sell 'designer quality' Zulu beadwork and wirework.

**POPULATION:**
3,347,000 (2004)
**WHEN TO GO:**
Any time of year.
**DON'T MISS:**
Glenholme Nature Reserve.
The Shark Institute – runs boat trips to watch the Great Whites.
The Golden Mile – the popular stretch of beachfront in the city. The wide stretch of golden sands provides excellent opportunities for sun-worshippers and swimmers to enjoy the sunshine and warm waters of the ocean.
The Surfing Museum – catalogues some of Durban's surfing history.
The Mahatma Ghandi Settlement at Phoenix.
**YOU SHOULD KNOW:**
In Zulu Durban is known as 'e Thekwini' meaning 'lagoon'.

449

# AUSTRALIA & NEW ZEALAND

# Hobart

**POPULATION:**
200,000 (2006)
**WHEN TO GO:**
October to April
**DON'T MISS:**
The arrival of yachts at the end of the
Sydney-Hobart race.
The Ten Days on the Island festival.
The Six-day coastal walk to South
Western Tasmania.
The Tahune Forest tourist nature
skywalk in the Huon Valley.
Port Arthur.
The view from the lookout point on
Mt Wellington.
**YOU SHOULD KNOW:**
The Hollywood actor, Errol Flynn,
grew up here.

In the south-east of Tasmania near where the waters of the Tasman Sea meet the Southern Ocean but sheltered from the worst of the weather and nestling under Mt Wellington, the lower stretches of the Derwent River were an obvious place for a settlement, and Hobart Town was founded here in the first years of the 19th century. Its deep-water port made it an ideal location as the base of whaling and seal-hunting operations (now long gone), as well as ship-building and other allied trades. Now the city is a major tourist destination, for its beautiful historic buildings, the surrounding vineyards and scenery and the yachting.

The port covers the area originally called Sullivan's Cove on the west bank of the Derwent and is now called Macquarie Wharf. It holds the same place in the heart of Hobartians as Port Jackson does for Sydneysiders and is still the focus of activity with plans to redevelop it. One area of the port already redeveloped is Salamanca Place, around Salamanca Square, which is popular with families during the day and for its clubs and bars at night. It is also host to the popular Salamanca Market on Saturdays.

Despite its relative isolation, Hobart has a vibrant culture, ranging from the classical music on offer from the Tasmanian Symphony Orchestera, Australia's oldest theatre, the Theatre Royal, a thriving contemporary music scene and several annual festivals.

*Hobart is the largest city on the island of Tasmania.*

*The gum trees in Kings Park on Fraser Avenue mask the city towers.*

# Perth

One of the most remote cities on earth, Perth is a lively place, set on the Swan River, which was named after the black swans first seen here by Europeans in the 1690s. Colonists arrived here in June 1829, and the settlement became the capital of Western Australia in 1832. However, the city seems much younger than that: the remaining Victorian buildings are mainly away from the city centre. It is also a city of migrants: about a quarter of the population was born overseas, which gives it a young, fresh feel. The lifestyle is largely outdoors, there are hundreds of kilometres of sandy beaches, and people here are sports-crazy.

Inland lies the winemaking area of the beautiful Swan Valley: the first vines were planted here within a year or so of Perth's foundation, while in the city itself attractions include Perth Zoo, the Perth Mint (Perth is an important service centre for the mining areas inland like Calgoorlie), the Perth Institute of Contemporary Art and the Aquarium's 98-metre (321-foot) underwater tunnel. The Swan River itself has areas dedicated to watersports, as well as boat trips up to the winemaking region.

The nightlife in Perth ranges from the clubs, restaurants and bars of central Northridge, and those of the chic area of Subiaco, to the Perth Concert Hall and His Majesty's Theatre. Outdoor concerts are held in the Subiaco Oval and King's Park, from where the sunsets are spectacular.

This remote city is vibrant, confident and friendly.

**POPULATION:**
1,456,000 (2006)
**WHEN TO GO:**
Spring or autumn
**DON'T MISS:**
Surfing at Scarborough Beach.
Rottnest Island and the quokkas.
A trip to the colonial town
of Fremantle.
Whale-watching trips run by the
Aquarium.
The final leg of the annual Red Bull
Air Race.
**YOU SHOULD KNOW:**
The afternoon breeze that cools the
city is called the 'Fremantle Doctor'
for its relieving effects from the
midday sun.

# Melbourne

Set around the natural harbour of Port Philip and founded in 1835 as a farming community, Melbourne might have remained a peaceful backwater, but for the the Victorian gold rush of the 1850s, since which it has remained one of Australia's chief cities. It was the capital of Australia from when the states federated in 1901 until the national Parliament moved to Canberra in 1927.

Melbourne's history can be read in its buildings: the booms of the 1850s, 1880s and early 1970s, its time as national capital and its current period of prosperity have all left their mark, from the massive Victorian town halls to the Windsor Hotel and Flinders Street Station and the current high-rises of the CBD. Most typical of this mixture of new and old is the tram system on which both heritage and modern trams run.

Like most Australian cities, Melbourne is well provided with parks, and is sometimes referred to as Australia's garden city. Carlton Gardens surrounds the Royal Exhibition Buildings, built for the international exhibitions of 1880 and 1888, and declared a World Heritage Site in 2004. The Royal Park includes the Royal Melbourne Zoological Gardens, while Albert Park is home to the Australian Grand Prix.

*CBD – Central Business District*

The Formula One race is just one of Melbourne's many annual sporting attractions. The Melbourne Cricket Ground, within the Yarra Gardens, is home not only to the Boxing Day test match and one-day internationals in summer, but Australian Rules football matches in winter. Melbourne Park is host to the Australian Open Tennis tournament each January, while on the first Tuesday in November, the entire nation is reputed to stop to watch the Melbourne Cup, the highlight of the spring racing festival at Flemington Racecourse.

Melbourne prides itself as the cultural capital of Australia, and has the Melbourne Museum, the National Gallery of Victoria, which has the largest art collection in the country and is spread over several buildings, and the Victorian Arts Centre, which hosts Opera Australia's performances here, the Melbourne Theatre Company and the Melbourne Symphony Orchestra, as well as several theatres in and around the CBD.

Melbourne is probably the most cosmopolitan city in Australia, and is the site of the world's first Chinatown, which has a wide range of mainly Cantonese restaurants. The city is justifiably renowned for its different cuisines, from Italian or Greek to Malaysian, Japanese or Thai.

# Brisbane

*Brisbane and its river – a great way to get around the city.*

Brisbane was founded in 1824 and became the capital of Queensland in 1859 when it became a separate territory. It remained relatively small until after World War II but in the last few years has become a popular place for both newcomers to Australia and people from states to the south to move to, because of its laid-back lifestyle, climate and easy access to both the Gold and Sunshine Coasts, which are within an hour or so's drive, and the southern part of the Great Barrier Reef . Closer still are the 360-plus islands of Moreton Bay, with beautiful beaches, great surf and thriving yachting and fishing communities. North Stradbroke Island (Straddie) is a popular escape, while Moreton Island itself is particularly known for the dolphin feeding sessions at Tangalooma.

Central Brisbane is set on a curve in the river of the same name, and most of the high rises are concentrated here, although one of the city's highlights, the City Botanic Gardens, lies at its southern end. The city is rich in parks and gardens, and Mt Coot-tha Forest Park, west of the centre is another botanic garden, set at the foot of the mountain, which is a popular place to visit at weekends and has spectacular views over the city towards the Pacific Ocean. Within the park is the Sir Thomas Brisbane Planetarium. Other popular places for families with children include the Lone Pine Koala Sanctuary, the Butterfly and Insect House in the South Bank Parklands and the artifical lagoon in the same area.

The oldest buildings surviving in Brisbane are the Old Windmill and Observatory in Spring Hill and St Stephen's Church, and several Victorian government buildings survive, such as the old Customs House, which is now part of the University of Queensland, and houses a small art gallery. The Queensland Cultural Centre is across the Victoria Bridge from the city centre, while out in St Lucia, the University also has museums and galleries and other museums are scattered throughout the city.

Shoppers are well catered for in the centre of town, but the city is also known for its markets, including the craft and clothing market at the Stanley Street Plaza, the indoor market in McWhirter's Markets – one of Brisbane's most beautiful buildings – and the Sunday market at Eagle Street.

**POPULATION:**
1,763,000 (2006)
**WHEN TO GO:**
Spring or autumn: it can be very hot and humid in summer and surprisingly cool and damp in winter.
**DON'T MISS:**
Eating Moreton Bay bugs.
The night life in Fortitude Valley and New Farm or the restaurants in Paddington.
A cricket match or Aussie Rules football game at the Gabba.
Abseiling down the cliffs at Kangaroo Point.
The alfresco cinema and city beach in the South Bank Park in summer.
**YOU SHOULD KNOW:**
The best way to get around the city is by the extensive hop-on-hop-off ferry services, including the high-speed City Cats.

# Sydney

**POPULATION:**
4,285,000 (2006)
**WHEN TO GO:**
Any time of year.
**DON'T MISS:**
The New Year celebrations.
The surf at Bondi.
Sydney Opera House.
The nightlife of Kings Cross, Darling
Harbour and the Rocks.
A bridge climb on the famous
Harbour Bridge – just so long as you
have a head for heights!
The breathtaking ferry ride from
Circular Quay to Manly.
**YOU SHOULD KNOW:**
What most people call Sydney
Harbour is actually called
Port Jackson.

Mention of the word Sydney brings to mind views of the iconic Opera House and Harbour Bridge, perhaps especially when they are lit up by the spectacular fireworks displays with which the city greets every New Year.

The Rocks, the site of the original settlement, has picturesque old buildings and is stuffed with craft shops. Within easy walking distance are the Harbour Bridge, the old Observatory, the Garrison Church, the Colonial House Museum and Cadman's Cottage. For those with a head for heights, the Bridgeclimb starts from close by, while spectacular views over the city can also be obtained from Sydney Tower on Market Street in the central district.

Along Macquarie Street you will find Parliament House, and the Sydney Mint and Hyde Park Barracks museums. Beyond, you reach the Domain, home to the Art Gallery of New South Wales, while the Australian Museum is just to the south. North of here is the best of Sydney's central parks, the Royal Botanic Gardens. It's large enough to lose yourself in, although the flocks of cockatoos ensure

that it is never particularly quiet. At Benelong Point lies Jorn Utzon's Sydney Opera House, which was declared a UNESCO World Heritage Site in 2007. Mrs Macquarie's Point is a good place to get views of it from this side of the water, but the best photo-opportunities are from the many ferries that criss-cross the harbour.

The Darling Harbour area is home to the massive Sydney Aquarium and up-market eateries, as well as the Powerhouse and Australian National Maritime museums. Sydney has one of the most diverse populations anywhere, and nearby Chinatown is well worth a visit.

Sydney has some 70 beaches, of which the most famous is Bondi and Manly the most upmarket. The beaches within the harbour are sheltered, while those on the ocean have fantastic surf. With its stunning harbourside setting, cliffs overlooking the ocean and surrounding bushland, Sydney is one of the most beautiful, welcoming and energetic cities in the world.

*Adelaide is known as the 'city of churches'.*

# Adelaide

Founded in 1836 as capital of the province of South Australia, Adelaide was laid out on a grid pattern with open spaces and surrounded by parkland, a scheme that is still much in evidence today. Always intended to promote religious tolerance, civil liberties and progressive politics, it has long attracted people of different denominations and is known as the 'city of churches', although the city let its hair down some time before the rest of Australia, in the 1970s. Influxes of people from different parts of the world over the last 170 years have given Adelaide a unique personality – part conservative, part progressive with a decided flair for the artistic, and a wide range of foods.

Adeleide is renowned for its culture and has such diverse events as the Festival of Ideas, Festival of Arts, the Adelaide Film Festival and the Fringe Festival, which has events and performances ranging from the spectacular to the frankly weird. Every other year, the three-week Adelaide Festival of the Arts is held in early autumn. As you would expect from a city that prides itself on its culture, it is well stocked with museums, including the Art Gallery of South Australia, the Migration Museum, the landmark South Australian Museum and the Tandanya Indigenous Cultural Institute. For those who like their culture a little louder, the city centre, the East End and the area around Light Square have plenty of clubs and bars, which are popular with the student population.

Central Adelaide is ringed with parks and there are dozens more throughout the larger metropolitan area, which stretches for some 90 km (55 mi) down the eastern side of the Gulf St Vincent and is backed by the ironically named Mt Lofty Ranges. The Botanic Park is the scene for the annual WOMAdelaide festival, while the city's streets are the home of the Clipsal 500 V8 Supercar race.

Like all Australians, people in Adelaide like their sport and there are two Australian Rules football teams, a soccer team and two national-standard basketball teams. The Southern Redbacks play at the Adelaide Oval, one of the oldest cricket grounds, while a new event, which is becoming increasingly popular is the annual Tour Down Under cycle race.

Adelaide is a beautiful, understated city, which appears somewhat staid on the outside, but in fact is one of the liveliest places in the country.

**POPULATION:**
1,106,000 (2006)
**WHEN TO GO:**
October to April, but avoid December and January if you don't like the heat.
**DON'T MISS:**
The vineyards of the Barossa Valley – sample the delights of world-renowned vineyards such as Jacob's Creek and Penfolds.
Haigh's chocolates – the oldest family-owned chocolate manufacturing retailer in Australia.
An organized shark-diving trip.
Adelaide Central Market – featuring over 80 stores and traders offering everything from bakery goods to souvenirs.
**YOU SHOULD KNOW:**
While shark attacks are rare, if you see the spotter planes or hear the siren, get out of the water.

# Christchurch

As the name suggests, Christchurch was founded as a religious settlement, by Canterbury Pilgrims – who arrived here from the late 1840s, and the cathedral they built between 1864 and 1910 lies at the heart of the city to this day. It was designed by George Gilbert Scott and is a beautiful example of Victorian Gothic Revival architecture. The Roman Catholic Cathedral is a beautiful Renaissance style building.

Nestling between the Pacific Ocean, the Avon, Waimakariri and Heathcote rivers and the Port Hills, Christchurch is often called the Garden City, and among its best-loved open spaces are the Botanic Gardens in the city centre, and Victoria and Hagley parks.

New Zealand's iconic Kiwis may be encountered at the Southern Encounter Aquarium and Kiwi House, where they are housed as part of an active conservation plan, along with a wide range of marine life. Other wildlife parks include Orana Wildlife Park and Willowbank Wildlife Reserve. Cultural attractions include the Canterbury Museum, the Air Force Museum and the Christchurch Art Gallery.

Both Captain Scott and Ernest Shackleton set off for the Antarctic from here, and the International Antarctic Centre's Antarctic Attraction seeks to recreate the life of explorers to the southern continent.

Christchurch is set on a flat plain, and the best way to get good views across the city is to take the Summit Road, which has several stopping points.

**POPULATION:**
414,000 (2006)
**WHEN TO GO:**
Spring, summer or autumn.
**DON'T MISS:**
The views from Mount Pleasant Trig towards the Southern Alps.
The tram ride around the central area.
**YOU SHOULD KNOW:**
The Maori name for New Zealand is 'Aotearoa' meaning 'land of the long white cloud'.

*The City Loop tram in Cathedral Square*

# Auckland

**POPULATION:**
1,330,000 (2007)
**WHEN TO GO:**
Any time of year.
**DON'T MISS:**
Waiketere Ranges Regional Park.
The walk up to the crater of
Mount Eden.
The view from the top of the
Sky Tower.
**YOU SHOULD KNOW:**
Auckland sits in the middle of a
dormant volcanic plain.
Auckland's nickname is the City
of Sails.

Centred on a narrow isthmus between the Hauraki Gulf of the Pacific Ocean and the Tasman Sea, Auckland is dominated by water and mountains. To the north, Waitemata Harbour is guarded by Rangitoto Island, the youngest of fifty or so volcanoes and vents that created the land here.

With sheltered harbours, easy access to the sea, and a strategic location it is an obvious place for settlement and Maori had lived here for nearly 500 years – chiefly on the volcanic heights – before it was established as the capital of New Zealand in 1840, a title it kept for only 25 years.

The western beaches are great for surfers and there are good beaches for swimmers at Devonport, Long Bay and Mission Bay, and the harbours are filled with yachts – this is one of the most popular places in the world for sailors. For landlubbers, the nightlife is centred around Queen Street, Ponsonby Road and Karangahape Road. Several of the extinct volcanoes and islands, such as Mount Eden, Waiheke Island and North Head, are natural parks and have remnants of prehistoric settlements and later fortifications. Other popular areas for exploring include the Hunua Ranges and the Waiketere Ranges Regional Park. Indoors, Kelly Tarlton's Underwater World is popular, and the Auckland Art Gallery has an important collection of works by New Zealand artists.

Auckland is reckoned to be in the top ten cities in the world to live in: with its stunning location, it's not hard to see why.

*Auckland harbour and skyline at dusk*

# Wellington

The capital of New Zealand since 1865, Wellington is also its cultural hub, renowed for its café culture, nightlife and thriving arts scene. It sits at the south-western point of North Island, overlooking the Cook Strait, and is known for the pretty Wellington harbour, created by an active geological fault which is causing the land to the west of the harbour to rise up. At the top of the hill is the Botanic Garden, which can be reached on the funicular railway or the cable car from Lambton Quay.

The centre of the city is extremely compact, so everything is within easy reach. Te Papa Tongarewa (the Museum of New Zealand) is a must-see among the many museums.

There are all sorts of artistic activities with both professional and community theatres, performances by the New Zealand Symphony Orchestra, the National Opera Company and Royal New Zealand Ballet. There are festivals celebrating almost everything, from the biennial International Festival of the Arts and the annual International Jazz Festival to the New Zealand Affordable Art Show, the Cuba Street Carnival and the World of Wearable Art.

Wellington's café culture is outstanding: local roasteries produce some of the best coffee in the world and it also has some of the finest restaurants, serving everything from Malaysian to Lebanese food and all points in between. Courtney Place is the centre of the action at night.

This is a beautiful city, in a stunning location, and no visitor can ever be short of things to do.

*Wellington Harbour*

**POPULATION:**
431,000 (2006)
**WHEN TO GO:**
Any time of year.
**DON'T MISS:**
The Cuba Street Carnival in
late February.
Taking the cable car up to Wellington
Botanical Gardens.
The view from Mount Victoria.
The seal colony near Red Rocks
Karori Wildlife Sanctuary.
**YOU SHOULD KNOW:**
Landing at the airport can be fun
because of the strong cross winds.

# AMERICAS AND THE CARIBBEAN

# Montreal

Montreal, the third largest city in Canada and the largest in Quebec is centred on the island of the same name and named after the three-headed peak of Mont-Royal. Europeans first settled here in 1642, although they had first been here more than a century earlier when the St Lawrence Valley was claimed for France. This French heritage is still proudly exhibited today, even though the city has a very eclectic mix of cultures and peoples, it still has a distinctly French feel, even though the region became a British possession in 1760. The city's predominantly Roman Catholic heritage can be seen in the Basilica of Notre-Dame, St Joseph's Oratory and the Cathedrale Marie-Reine-du-Monde.

Montreal is justifiably famous for its award-winning modern architecture and was recognized as a UNESCO City of Design in 2006.

Whether sipping a cappuccino at an outdoor café in Little Italy, gambling at the massive Casino de Montreal complex or exploring historic Old Montreal, you will find the energy of this urban playground contagious. The international flavour of the city pervades all aspects of daily life, from the award-winning cuisine to the jazz festival and music scene, large gay community, fashionable shops and edgy arts scene.

Montreal is divided into neighbourhoods, each representing a unique and lively part of this fabulous, tourist-friendly city. There is a wide range of museums, including the fantastic Museum of Fine Arts in the downtown area. This area was formerly known as 'the Golden Square Mile', because of the large, luxurious houses built by the wealthy Scottish and English industrialists who helped to shape the city's political and social life. It is now also home to some spectacular modern architecture.

Cultural life is centred around the Place des Arts, which is home to the Montreal Symphony Orchestra, l'Orchestra Métropolitan, I Musici de Montreal, the Opera de Montreal and the Grands Ballets Canadiens, as well as several modern dance troupes and the internationally famous Cirque du Soleil. There is also a lively contemporary music scene. The Quartier Latin is the place for literature and theatre buffs. The city is host to a number of annual festivals including the International Jazz Festival, Francofolies, Just for Laughs, the Osheaga Festival, Pop Montreal and the massive Fireworks Festival.

The oldest part of the city is Vieux-Montreal and it is here that the feeling of being in old

*Montreal's skyline at dusk with the 'Old Port' area in the foreground*

Europe is strongest, especially in St Denis which feels like the Left Bank of Paris. Saint Laurent Boulevard, Saint-Catherine Street West and Crescent Street are the centres of the city's nightlife.

For those who want to get away from it all, the Parc du Mont-Royal is a beautiful landscaped park on the mountain of the same name, which offers a range of activities and amazing panoramas.

Shopping is centred around Saint-Catherine Street but in winter the locals head for the Ville Souterraine, an vast underground area with more than 1600 shops, 30 cinemas and some 200 restaurants, all sheltered from the harsh winter above.

Montreal truly is a city with something for everyone.

# Halifax

Founded by the British in 1749 and proclaimed a city in 1841, Halifax has a rich history and a wealth of sites to visit. Set along the edge of the world's second largest natural harbour (although there are other contenders), the area has evidence of a native American presence dating back thousands of years and was the foremost British stronghold on the eastern seaboard of North America during and after the American War of Independence and the Napoleonic Wars.

The glacial drumlin of Citadel Hill makes an ideal vantage point for a fort. The Halifax Citadel National Historic Site is the fourth incarnation of the fort here and there are demonstrations by period soldiers. Province House – the site of Canada's first legislature – is a beautiful Georgian building built in the local sandstone.

Another National Historic Site is Pier 21, where there are exhibitions about the harbour's history as a place of arrival and departure for troops, child refugees from Britain, war brides and immigrants.

Annual events here include the Nova Scotia Military Tattoo in the Metro Centre in early July and the Halifax International Busker Festival on the waterfront in August. This area is also home to the Maritime Museum of the Atlantic and is full of shops and restaurants. Spring Garden Road is another draw for shoppers.

The city's green spaces include Point Pleasant Park, on the tip of Halifax Peninsula, whose many buildings include the 1790s Prince of Wales Martello Tower. Performances of Shakespeare take place here. The Public Gardens are Victorian in style and a quiet refuge. Both parks were affected by Hurricane Juan in 2003.

The lighthouse at Peggy's Cove, a 2½ hour scenic boat ride from the city, is one of the most photographed monuments in Canada.

**POPULATION:**
359,000 (2006)
**WHEN TO GO:**
Spring to autumn
**DON'T MISS:**
The Discovery Centre.
The Art Gallery of Nova Scotia.
Alexander Keith's Brewery Tour.
Whale-watching tours.
The town clock playing the
Westminster Chimes.
**YOU SHOULD KNOW:**
The city claims to be the home of
'hurley on ice', the precursor of
ice hockey.

*The town clock*

*The Parliament buildings*

# Victoria

At the southern end of Vancouver Island, Victoria is an important port city, the capital of British Columbia and home to a large naval base. Although both the British and the Spanish had explored the area in the eighteenth century, the Hudson's Bay Company did not set up a trading post here until 1743 and it rapidly expanded after the discovery of gold on the mainland, until it lost out to Vancouver City after the Canadian Pacific Railway reached the west coast.

The city's character is defined by the large number of Edwardian homes, and public and residential buildings, as well as the abundance of greenery in the city's gardens and public parks. The world-renowned Butchart Gardens are on the Saanich Peninsula, along with the Dominion Astrophysical Observatory, the Victoria Butterfly Gardens and the planetarium.

Many of the tourist attractions are in the downtown area, including Christ Church Cathedral, and the Royal British Columbia Museum, the Victoria Bug Zoo and the Pacific Undersea Gardens, as well as the oldest Chinatown in Canada. The Rockland area is home to the Art Gallery of Greater Victoria, while the CFB Esquimalt Naval Base has a museum dedicated to naval and military history.

Thunderbird Park is one of the highlights of any visit to Victoria, for its totem poles, traditional first nation buildings and beautiful landscape.

Set on beautiful Vancouver Island, with a buzzing nightlife and cultural attractions, Victoria may not be the most modern of cities, but it is among the most attractive and welcoming you will ever visit.

# Quebec City

One of the oldest cities in North America, Quebec City is the capital of the province of the same name and in Vieux-Quebec has the only surviving walled city in the Americas north of Mexico. The historic district of Quebec was designated a UNESCO World Heritage Site in 1985 for its cultural and historical significance. Its twin areas – Basse-Ville and Haute-Ville – surround the Château Frontenac. In Haute-Ville, you will find narrow lanes running between grey, high-walled houses reminiscent of a medieval French city, while lower down Cap Diamant Basse-Ville – the site of the original settlement – is home to a lively café culture and boutique shops.

The Château Frontenac is one of the city's dominant landmarks: this large hotel on the Cap Diamant is a model Loire château. The Basilica of Notre-Dame is also very French in feel. Another building left from colonial times is the Haute-Ville's Citadelle, a star-shaped complex of military fortifications. In Basse-Ville you will find the church of Notre-Dame des Victoires. One of the areas best-known attractions is the Musée de la Civilisation.

There is a wide range of museums that cover the history and culture of the region, among them the Musée de Quebec in the Parc des Champs-de Bataille, which has a fanstastic art collection. The park is the site of the battle that ended the rule of the French in North America and holds free concerts in summer.

At the other end of the year the Quebecois cheer themselves up with the biggest winter carnival in the world, which features a talking snowman called Bonhomme, who inhabits the Snow Palace and presides over horse-drawn sleigh rides, the International Canoe Race across the part-frozen St Lawrence River, dogsled races, parades and the International Snow Sculpture Event. What better way could there be to chase the winter blues away?

**POPULATION:**
718,000 (2005)
**WHEN TO GO:**
Any time of year, depending on your interests, but it can be very cold in winter.
**DON'T MISS:**
The Quebec City Winter Carnival – the biggest winter carnival in the world. It starts on the last Friday in January and lasts for 17 days. Activities include ice sculpting and dog sled racing and you can even have a snow bath!
The Musée de la Civilisation – covers the history of Quebec, promoting its Canadian identity whilst embracing the shared past of this multi-cultural city.
Montmorency Falls – at 83 m (272 ft) these are the highest falls in the province.
**YOU SHOULD KNOW:**
Quebec comes from the Algonquin word meaning 'where the river narrows'.

*Château Frontenac (left) is a dominant landmark.*

# Toronto

**POPULATION:**
5,598,000 (2006)
**WHEN TO GO:**
Spring to autumn
**DON'T MISS:**
Canada's Walk of Fame.
St Michael's Cathedral.
Fort York – founded in 1793 to
ensure British control of Lake Ontario.
At this time Toronto was actually
called York.
Kensington Market.
The Toronto Islands – these used to
be joined to the mainland, but a
storm in 1858 washed away the
sandbar. Today the islands are a
favourite spot for relaxing
on beaches.
The view from the top of the CN
Tower – on a clear day!
**YOU SHOULD KNOW:**
In winter Toronto is prone to Lake
Effect Snow.

*The skyline from Lake Ontario*

Sitting on the shore of Lake Ontario, Toronto is the largest city in Canada and its economic capital. It consistently rates among the best places in the world to live and according to UNESCO is the world's most diverse city. The French built a fort here in 1750, then it was re-established as Fort York by the British in 1793 before reverting to its old native American name in 1834. As well as the long shorefront onto the lake and large harbour, the city is intersected by rivers that have created steep gullies that run down towards the shore. The area's geology can also be seen in the escarpments of the Iroquois Shoreline, marking the boundaries of the old glacial lake that occupied the site in the last Ice Age.

Toronto's modern expansion has led to the development of a high proportion of skyscrapers, including the CN Tower, which at a height of 553.33 m (815 ft) is the tallest free-standing structure in the world.

In the historic Distillery District many old Victorian industrial buildings are being redeveloped to create an area dedicated to culture, shopping, dining and drinking, the arts and entertainment and is now listed as a national heritage site, while several of the major museums, including the Art Gallery of Ontario and the Royal Ontario Museum have been brought up to date. Other museums include the Bata Shoe Museum, the Gardiner Museum of Ceramic Art and the Ontario Science Centre. The Don Valley Brick Works has been restored as a heritage centre and park.

Toronto is home to two symphony orchestras, more than 50 dance companies and a handful of opera companies, and has dozens of music venues and theatres. Annual cultural events include the Caribana festival and Pride Week, the Canadian National Exhibition and the Toronto International Film Festival.

Shoppers should head for Yorkville or the Eaton Centre, while for foodies Greektown is also a must.

Toronto is a multicultural, buzzing city, with pockets of old buildings among skyscrapers, wooded ravines where one can lose oneself for a couple of hours, sports facilities second to none and scenery to make your head whirl.

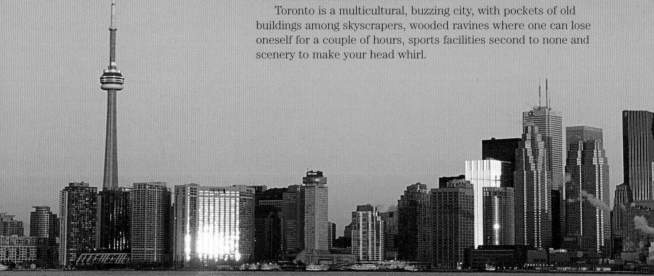

# Vancouver

Canada's fastest growing city, Vancouver is a magical place, full of contradictions. Named after the first European to discover the area, George Vancouver, it is the gateway to the Pacific, and its deep, sheltered harbour made it an ideal place for settlement, especially after the discovery of coal nearby led to the need for a port. Gastown harks back to those days, a quaint Victorian cobbled area now turned from a working port area to an upmarket area of art galleries, antique shops and boutiques. Right next to it is the Lookout Tower, an observation deck 33 floors above the Harbour Centre. A different range of views can be obtained from Stanley Park, a vast area of woodland, lakes and gardens, which also houses the city's aquarium.

*Vancouver harbour and skyline*

Vancouver is renowned for its easy-going, cosmopolitan lifestyle, with leisure activities including sailing and trips into the surrounding wilderness in summer and skiing in winter. With a long history as a port, it has communities from a wide range of backgrounds and its Chinatown is the second largest in North America, and is a must for its atmosphere, shops and restaurants. World cuisine is also a speciality of the city, including Indian, Italian, Greek, Japanese and Korean restaurants in their respective quarters, while Gastown is home to world-class international cuisine.

Culture is centred on Granville Island, which is home to both traditional arts centres and events and the city's sometimes wild nightlife. By day, it is the site of a vast public market. The city's museums include the Museum of Anthropology and the Vancouver Art Gallery, housed in a beautiful Edwardian building.

This vibrant city, set at the edge of the Pacific Ocean, with its mix of old and new, high culture and alternative bands, urban living and beautiful wilderness, has to be on anyone's list of places to visit.

**POPULATION:**
588,000 (2006)
**WHEN TO GO:**
Any time of year, as the climate is mild by Canadian standards.
**DON'T MISS:**
Gastown – the Old Quarter and original site of the famous saloon of 'Gassy' Jack Deighton. Expect cobbled streets, handsome buildings, quaint shops and plenty of bars and restaurants.
The beaches in summer.
Vancouver Island – a 45 minute ferry ride from the city, this is the best whale-watching site in the world.
Skiing in winter or sailing in summer.
Grouse Mountain – hike up or take the Skyride for a beautiful view of the city.
**YOU SHOULD KNOW:**
Vancouver is third only to Hollywood and New York as a North American film production centre.

*The Georgia State Capitol building*

# Atlanta

A city forever associated with the horrors of the American Civil War because of Margaret Mitchell's *Gone with the Wind*, Atlanta in fact has so much more to offer than memories of ancient conflicts. The capital of the south-eastern state of Georgia, and popularly known as The Big Peach, Hotlanta or A-town, Atlanta was a centre for the Civil Rights Movement in the 1960s.

Because General Sherman burned everything to the ground except the churches and hospitals, very little survives from before the Civil War, and most of the city's landmark buildings are from the 20th century, including the modernist High Museum and the many high-rise buildings downtown. One of the oldest buildings to survive is the Goodwin House, on Peachtree St, which dates back to the 1830s. Ashley Oaks Mansion on College Street, gives a real sense of what life here may have been like in the days before the Civil War.

Atlanta was the hometown of Martin Luther King, Jr and his childhood home on Auburn Avenue in the Sweet Auburn district is home to the Martin Luther King, Jr National Historic Site. The Presidential Library and Museum of another of Georgia's famous sons – Jimmy Carter – are on Freedom Parkway. The Margaret Mitchell House and Museum is on Peachtree Street, the main street of the city, which is now also home to many of the largest office buildings and shopping malls, as well as one of the best buildings in the city, the Fox Theatre.

Some of the earliest remnants of the population of the area can be seen in the ancient village site of the Etowah Indian Mounds and the Ocmulgee National Monument, while early colonial history can be explored at the Fort King George and Fort Morris State Historic Sites.

Atlanta has a reputation as being a green city because of its tree-lined streets, but there are also open green spaces such as the Stone Mountain State Park, Grant Park, Seminole Park and the Atlanta Botanical Gardens.

**POPULATION:**
5,138,000 (2006)
**WHEN TO GO:**
Spring or autumn: winters are usually mild but summers are hot and humid.
**DON'T MISS:**
Augusta National Golf Club – home to the Tour Championship.
Stovall Mill covered Bridge, the last covered bridge in Georgia.
Blue Ridge Scenic Railroad.
Etowah Indian Mounds – an archaeological site in Bartow County. The area was inhabited by Native Americans from as early as 1,000 AD.
Ocmulgee National Monument – this park is a memorial to the people of Atlanta, from Ice Age hunters to Creek Indians.
**YOU SHOULD KNOW:**
Atlanta is the birthplace of Coca-Cola.

# Chicago

Once synonymous with Prohibition-era gangsters, Chicago is now better known for its fantastic architecture, wonderful food and amazing shopping. At the far south-western tip of Lake Michigan, it has long been an important port city, and is now one of the United States' chief commercial centres. The birthplace of Frank Lloyd Wright, it has dozens of his early buildings, as well as some designed by his teacher, Louis Sullivan, and Mies van der Rohe, among others. Three of the tallest buildings in America are here: the iconic Sears Tower, the John Hancock Center and the Aon Center and the skyline as viewed across the river or from the lake is spectacular.

Chicago is a city of neighbourhoods, each with its own special character and charm: from the pretty Ukrainian village and its stunning traditional churches to the bustle of Chinatown and the villagy atmosphere of Greektown.

Shoppers have a wealth of choices, from Michigan Avenue and the Magnificent Mile to the Navy Pier – the latter is also a great place for foodies, as is Greektown. Culture-lovers are spoiled: the Art Institute of Chicago has one of the world's best collections, particularly of Impressionist paintings, while the Museum of Contemporary Art has more modern works. There are museums dedicated to history, natural history, Mexican fine art, science and industry and almost anything else you can think of. Music varies from the world-renowned Chicago Symphony Orchestra to the independent rock and rave scenes – Chicago also saw the birth of house and hip-hop, but is perhaps best known as the home of Chicago blues and soul, gospel and jazz.

For such a large city, Chicago has a wealth of open spaces, including many lakeside parks and beaches. Lake Michigan itself is a popular playground, especially with scuba divers who can explore the many wrecks that litter the lakefloor close to the shoreline.

Chicago is one of America's most popular tourist destinations, and if you visit, you'll understand just why.

**POPULATION:**
9,506,000 (2006)
**WHEN TO GO:**
Spring to autumn
**DON'T MISS:**
Chicago's famous pizza pie.
The Tiffany glass dome of Preston Bradley Hall in the Chicago Cultural Center.
The Cloud Gate sculpture in Millennium Park.
One of the walking tours or river cruises to see all the best architecture.
The view from the John Hancock Center.
A Chicago Bears or Chicago Bulls game.
**YOU SHOULD KNOW:**
The first skyscraper in the world was built in Chicago.

*The Wrigley building*

# Columbus

**POPULATION:**
1,726,000 (2006)
**WHEN TO GO:**
Spring to autumn
**DON'T MISS:**
Red, White, and Boom – the biggest
Independence Day firework display in
the Midwest.
Columbus Zoo and Aquarium.
Deer Creek State Park or the Wayne
National Forest, the only forest
in Ohio.
James Thurber House – home to
famous author and cartoonist for the
*New Yorker*, James Thurber and his
family, from 1913-1917. Visitors are
encouraged to sit on the chairs, play
a few notes on his piano and tap a
few keys on his typewriter.
**YOU SHOULD KNOW:**
The first kindergarten in the US was
built here.

The capital of Ohio, Columbus is known as a city that knows how to have fun and its large student population means that there is always lots going on. Among its best known events are the Oktoberfest in late September, ComFest, the Ohio State Fair, the Asian Festival in Franklin Park, the Columbus Arts Festival, the satirical Doo Dah Parade, the Festival Latino and the All American Quarter Horse Congress. It is also renowned for Red, White, and Boom, the largest Independence Day celebrations and fireworks display around. For those who come here at one of the rare times when there is not a festival going on, the city also has a wealth of other things to see and do, from the Victorian and German villages and the heritage districts of Old Oaks, Driving Park and Livingston Park, to the Columbus Museum of Art and the Ohio Craft Museum. Next door to the Ohio Historical Center is the Ohio village, a reconstruction of a 19th-century settlement. More modern are the Jack Nicklaus Museum (on the University campus, as is the Wexner Center for the Arts) and COSI, an interactive science and technology museum.

Short North is an area popular with both locals and visitors: it has an eclectic mixture of shops, restaurants and art galleries. Easton Town Center is definitely the upmarket area for shopping and eating, while the North West Market is ideal for people-watching. In the evenings, the riverfronts, and the Arena and Brewery districts are the places to go, while for those who need a break from the excitement, Franklin Park is among the best of Columbus' open spaces and is renowned for its conservatory's large collection of tropical plants.

The Ohio Statehouse is a beautiful pre-Civil War Greek revival building, while the explorer after whom the city is named is commemorated by the replica of the Santa Maria on the Scioto River.

*The Columbus skyline along the Scioto River*

# Honolulu

*Waikiki from the Diamond Head Overlook*

Perched near the southern tip of Oahu, in the middle of the Pacific Ocean, Honolulu is a thriving city full of bustling nightlife, while its beaches – including Waikiki – are among the most famous tourist playgrounds on the planet.

Like the other islands in the Hawaiian chain, Oahu is the top of a massive volcano, although it has been extinct for many tens of thousands of years and the rich volcanic soils give the island the lush green interior that acts as a backdrop to the city and beaches.

Settled by Polynesian migrants since at least the 12th century, in the 19th century Honolulu became an important stopping point for merchants sailing between Asia and North America and an important naval base for the US during World War II. Its maritime history can be seen in the Bishop Museum's Hawaii Maritime Center, located on the old royal pier near the Aloha Tower, the lighthouse whose distinctive Hawaiian gothic outline has greeted seaborne visitors to Honolulu since the 1920s. The main buildings of the Bishop Museum are home to a stunning array of Polynesian artefacts, millions of insects, the Hawaiian royal regalia and a planetarium. The Honolulu Academy of Arts has a world-class collection of works of art from all round the world, while the Hawaii State Art Museum concentrates on the work of local artists. Shangri La houses the art collection of the American heiress, Doris Duke.

The Hawaiian royal family was not overthrown until early in the 20th century, and their former home, the Iolani Palace, is a 19th-century spectacular, in a style variously known as Haiwaiian renaissance or American Florentine. Other buildings of the time that survive are St Andrew's Cathedral and Aliiolani Hale.

As is only to be expected, given its location on trade routes, Hawaii has a thriving Chinatown, which is also home to the Arts District.

With its lovely, laid-back attitude, and welcoming, friendly locals, Honolulu is truly a must-visit city.

**POPULATION:**
377,000 (2004)
**WHEN TO GO:**
Any time of year.
**DON'T MISS:**
The USS *Arizona* Memorial at Pearl Harbor.
People watching at Waikiki Beach.
A helicopter ride along the coastline.
The walk to the volcanic cone of Diamond Head.
Shopping for souvenirs at the Ala Moana Center.
**YOU SHOULD KNOW:**
Honolulu means sheltered bay.

*The Strip*

# Las Vegas

**POPULATION:**
1,778,000 (2006)
**WHEN TO GO:**
Any time, although summers are very hot and winters cool and windy.
**DON'T MISS:**
The Hoover Dam – located on the Black Canyon of the Colorado River and named after Herbert Hoover who played an instrumental role in its construction. The dam is key in producing the hydro-electric power (that powers Las Vegas) from the water of Lake Mead.
The Mojave Desert.
Taking in a show.
A day trip (or longer) to the Grand Canyon – carved away over millions of years and measuring 446 km (277 mi) in length, nothing prepares you for the vastness of the canyon. Take a helicopter ride to fully appreciate it.
**YOU SHOULD KNOW:**
Las Vegas sits in part of the Mojave Desert and is the fastest growing city in the US.

In its early history, Las Vegas was a stopping-off point for pioneer trails (the name means 'the meadows') and a staging post for the region's mines, and was at one point the site of a Mormon mission. Those days are long gone, and for the last 60 years and more the emphasis here has been on entertainment, gambling and other related activities. Its fortunes have waxed and waned over the years, but it is now the heart of the US gaming industry.

It is also known as the playground of the Brat Pack, where Dean Martin, Sammy Davis, Jnr and Frank Sinatra appeared to live hedonistic lifestyles that others could only dream of (or condemn). Now its casino hotels are still the venue for long-term residencies by such artists as Barry Manilow, Tom Jones, Elton John and Celine Dion.

Among the iconic buildings on the Strip – Las Vegas Boulevard South – are Caesar's Palace, the Mirage, the Excalibur – inspired by a medieval castle – the black glass pyramid of the Luxor, the MGM Grand, the Venetian and the Bellagio. In Las Vegas proper, the casinos include the Golden Nugget and the Golden Gate Hotel and Casino.

For those who don't want to spend their days in the casinos, the wealth here means that the shopping malls house almost every designer label on the planet and the food is of a quality to match.

While the opulence and decadence may not be to everyone's taste, Las Vegas is an experience not to be missed.

# Charlottesville

Founded in 1762 on the trade route known as the Three Notched Road and named after King George III's wife, Queen Charlotte, Charlottesville is best known as the seat of the University of Virginia, which was founded by Thomas Jefferson. The centre of the original town is in Court Square, and there are several buildings there that date back to the 1760s. A few blocks away, the downtown area is centre for both business and shopping. The Corner is usually teeming with students during university terms. The university is centred around The Lawn, with the iconic Rotunda, designed by Jefferson himself, and Stanford White's Old Cabell Hall.

Another building connected with Jefferson is Monticello, his old home. Perched on a muntain-top, it is where the city holds its annual Fourth of July celebrations and is visited by tens of thousands of people each year.

The Southwest Mountains, which run parallel to the Blue Ridge Mountains, form a backdrop to the city and like so many places in the region the area saw action during the American Civil War, although Charlottesville suffered little or no damage.

As well as being one of the longest outdoor shopping malls in America, Downtown Mall is also the place to head for something to eat and has one of the city's main attractions, the Virginia Discovery Museum.

Charlottesville is a beautiful city, with its original grid still clearly traceable in the historic centre.

**POPULATION:**
185,000 (2006)
**WHEN TO GO:**
Any time of year.
**DON'T MISS:**
Shenandoah National Park.
The Skyline Drive.
Monticello.
Ash Lawn-Highland – home of former president James Monroe between 1793-1826.
**YOU SHOULD KNOW:**
The city's motto is 'The best place to live in America'.

*The Rotunda Building at the University of Virginia*

# Austin

**POPULATION:**
1, 514,000 (2006)
**WHEN TO GO:**
Spring, autumn or winter.
**DON'T MISS:**
A trip into Texas Hill Country.
The view from Mount Bonnell.
Hippie Hollow.
Watching the bats emerge from the
Congress Avenue Bridge.
The artists selling their works in the
Renaissance Market.
**YOU SHOULD KNOW:**
The moonlight towers are used to
illuminate the centre of the city
at night.

Founded as the village of Waterloo in the 1830s and renamed in honour of Stephen F. Austin a few years later, Austin is the state capital of Texas. It is famous for its music scene, 'green' credentials and is reckoned by many people to be one of the top five cities to live in.

The downtown area is home to some medium-height buildings but views of the city's landmark State Capitol building, which is larger even than the national Capitol building in Washington, are protected from many locations and so true skyscrapers are a rarity, although taller buildings are increasing in number.

The main reason to visit Austin is for its cultural scene: the city calls itself the Live Music Capital of the World, and it is hard to believe otherwise. With a large student population, it has a correspondingly large number of nightclubs, especially around 6th Street, and live music venues. There are also growing theatre and arts scenes. Annual events include the Austin City Limits Music Festival, related to the long-running music programme of the same name, the Urban Music Festival, the Austin Reggae Festival, Eeyore's Birthday Party, the Pecan Street Festival, the Austin Film Festival and South by Southwest, a mixed music, film and multimedia festival.

There are also several good museums in the city, including the Texas Memorial Museum, the Harry Ransom Center, the Bob Bullock Texas State History Museum and the Blanton Museum of Art.

Austin prides itself on its lack of conservatism in comparison to some other cities: see if you can spot the car bumper stickers exhorting you to 'Keep Austin weird!'

*A view of Austin, the Live Music Capital of the World*

# Los Angeles

The 'City of Angels' is, of course, known for its links with the film industry. Almost everyone here appears to be an aspiring actor – it is definitely a city full of beautiful people. As much associated with the California beach 'n' surf lifestyle and music of the 1960s as it is with the urban rap and hard rock of the 1980s and 1990s, Los Angeles remains a hotbed of live music performances.

Over the years, Los Angeles has subsumed smaller neighbourhoods and many of these retain their own character, such as Chinatown and Little Tokyo, while farther out the wealthy areas of Venice Beach, Bel-Air, Beverley Hills and Pacific Pallisades are fun places to take a distant peek through the gates of the rich and famous.

Must-visit places for tourists to the area include Graumann's Chinese Theatre and the Hollywood Walk of Fame, the idiosyncratic Watts Towers – or any of the film studios when they are open for tours.

Sports fans should head for Dodger Stadium for a baseball game or to the Staples Center for a basketball match.

Naturally, shopping is a way of life for many here, and Beverley Hills' Rodeo Drive is a must, even if you are only window shopping.

For night life, where else is there to go but the now cleaned-up Sunset Strip or Hollywood Boulevard? In fact, there are plenty of other places to spend time, but it would be a shame to miss out on the glamour.

To escape the heat in summer, it's easy to head for the hills that surround the city, or the beaches or head for one of the many superb art galleries and museums.

**POPULATION:**
3,850,000 (2006)
**WHEN TO GO:**
Any time of year.
**DON'T MISS:**
Sunset Boulevard. Head to 'Sunset Strip' for shopping and nightlife.
Shopping on Rodeo Drive.
Taking in a studio tour – Paramount, Universal Studios and Warner Brothers all offer studio tours so you can check out where your favourite movies were made.
Star-spotting.
One of the summer concerts at the Hollywood Bowl.
**YOU SHOULD KNOW:**
Venice claims to be the home of skateboarding and rollerblading.

*The iconic 'Hollywood' sign lets you know where you are*

*Graceland – the home of Elvis*

# Memphis

On the east bank of the Mississippi, Memphis is famous for its musical connections. It is the home of its own brand of blues, gospel, jazz and soul, and through R&B, the wellspring of rock and roll. The list of people who grew up or became famous here reads like a who's who of the last 60 years of these types of music, from Muddy Waters, Sam Cooke, Tina Turner, Aretha Franklin and Al Green to John Lee Hooker, right through to Justin Timberlake. However, there is one person who will always be most closely associated with the city – Elvis Aaron Presley, and his former home Graceland attracts well over half a million visitors a year. The city's musical heritage is celebrated in the Stax Museum of American Soul Music, the Memphis Walk of Fame, the Gibson Guitar Factory and Showcase, the Center for Southern Folklore, the Memphis Rock 'n' Soul Museum and the Memphis Music and Heritage Festival. But it is not just about the past; Memphis' musical culture is still thriving, particularly in and around the Beale Street area.

A part of its history of which Memphis is not proud is the assassination of Martin Luther King, Jr, on 4 April 1968. The former motel where he was killed now houses the National Civil Rights Museum, which explores the history of the civil rights movement, important in an area that had previously been a centre for the cotton trade and relied on slavery for its wealth. The history of the cotton industry is examined in the Cotton Museum in the Memphis Cotton Exchange.

Other museums include the Memphis Books Museum of Art, the Peabody Place Museum, the Dixon Gallery and Gardens, the Children's Museum of Memphis, the National Ornamental Metal Museum, the Pink Palace Museum and Planetarium and Mud Island River Park's Mississippi River Museum.

More modern art is to be found in the eclectic galleries of area around South Main, the Cooper-Young neighbourhood, the Edge and the Power House, near Central Station.

**POPULATION:**
1,261,000 (2006)
**WHEN TO GO:**
Spring or autumn.
**DON'T MISS:**
Graceland – take a tour of Elvis Presley's estate.
A trip on the Memphis Queen – there is no better way to experience the Mississippi River than on a riverboat ride on one of these steamwheelers. The Memphis in May festival – music lovers from around the globe gather for this event. It consists of three days of music on four stages, featuring more than sixty nationally known and local artists. Past performers have included Bob Dylan, The Black Crowes and James Brown.
**YOU SHOULD KNOW:**
Graceland is set to undergo major redevelopment.

# Miami

Towards the south of Florida, and the gateway to both the Everglades and the Florida Keys, Miami is one of the most rapidly growing cities in America, with a skyline that is fast going to rival Chicago and New York.

With a large proportion of residents from Central and South America, as well as the Caribbean, Latin music rings through the air here, and the city is regarded as one of the club capitals of the world. There is also a rich bar culture, including the world famous Tobacco Road.

Miami's unique cultural mix means that it also has a unique food heritage and is home to 'Nuevo Latino', a mix of Caribbean, Latin American and European cooking styles using local produce. It is also known as Florribean.

A more poignant monument to people who have come here from farther south is the Freedom Tower; once newspaper offices, it later became a processing centre for refugees from Cuba and now holds a small museum about their life in America. It is also a beautiful building.

Contrary to popular report, it does rain here, and wet days are ideal to visit the Miami Museum of Science or the Miami Children's Museum, while other family attractions include Parrot Jungle Island, the Seaquarium and Miami MetroZoo.

Miami is not a place for those who want a quiet, relaxing break. Going to the beach is more about seeing and being seen than about sunbathing. There are almost as many aspiring models and actors here as in Los Angeles. However, its sheer vibrancy and joie de vivre make it a place not to be missed.

**POPULATION:**
4,920,000 (2006)
**WHEN TO GO:**
Spring, autumn or winter: summer is hot and humid.
**DON'T MISS:**
A Miami Dolphins game.
Palm Beach.
Supping a Cuba Libre or mojito.
The Ancient Spanish Monastery.
Biscayne National Park.
The Art Deco buildings of Miami Beach's South Beach.
**YOU SHOULD KNOW:**
No land here is more than 12 m (40 ft) above mean sea level.

*The Art Deco district of South Beach*

# Philadelphia

**POPULATION:**
5,823,000 (2006)
**WHEN TO GO:**
Spring, summer or autumn, although
it can be hot and humid in summer.
**DON'T MISS:**
The local culinary speciality: the
cheesesteak.
The Liberty Bell.
The Philadelphia Fringe Festival.
**YOU SHOULD KNOW:**
The Second Continental Congress, at
which the Declaration of
Independence was signed, was
convened here.

Philadelphia, or Philly as it is commonly called, was founded by William Penn as part of his colony of Pennsylvania, and became a city in 1701. The Quakers came here to obtain religious freedom not possible in post-Restoration Britain and the city has always attracted people escaping persecution. Several of the most important events in the history of the United States have happened here, including the signing of the Declaration of Independence in the building now known as Independence Hall. For a few years in the 1790s, Philadephia was the first national capital of the United States. It is also home to the Liberty Bell.

The city is known for its culture and is jam-packed with museums, including the Rodin Museum, the Philadelphia Museum of Art, the Benjamin Franklin National Memorial, the University of Pennsylvania Museum of Archaeology and Anthropology and the Academy of Natural Sciences. The Kimmel Center for the Performing Arts is the venue for concerts by the Philadelphia Orchestra, while the Philadelphia Opera resides at the Academy of Music. Literary Philadelphia can be studied at the Edgar Allan Poe National Historic Site.

There is a wide range of architectural styles on display, including Georgian, Queen Ann, Palladian, Gothic and Greek revival, from the early public buildings that survive to the Victorian 'row houses' that still make up many districts to modern skyscrapers. The oldest building in the city is the Old Swedes' (Gloria Dei) Church, which was completed in 1700. It was the home to Philadelphia soul in the 1960s and was influential in the spread of hip-hop and gangsta rap.

As you would expect from somewhere with Philadelphia's rich history, the city is dotted with important monuments celebrating the foundation of the USA and its cultural life.

*Swann Memorial Fountain*

# New York City

New York's five boroughs – Brooklyn, the Bronx, Manhattan, Queens and Staten Island – and its surrounding metropolitan area make up one of the largest cities in the world. It would be possible to spend a year here on holiday and still not run out of things to do: it is home to some of the world's best museums, its greatest tourist attractions, best entertainment and nightlife and fantastic food, garnered from one of the most culturally diverse populations of any city.

First visited by Europeans in 1524, settled as New Amsterdam in 1614 and renamed New York in 1644 after being captured by the British, New York has long been one of the most important cities in the United States, and was capital from Independence until 1790. Its harbour has seen the arrival of millions of immigrants, who from 1866 onwards were welcomed by the sight of the Statue of Liberty. Their history can also be seen in the Immigration Museum on Ellis Island.

Other iconic structures in the city are the Brooklyn Bridge, the Empire State Building, the United Nations building, the Rockefeller Center and the interior of Grand Central Station.

Shopping is a way of life to New Yorkers, and the must-visits include Macy's, Bloomingdale's, Tiffany's, Chinatown, SoHo, Greenwich Village and the Meatpacking district, although this is just the tip of the iceberg. Greenwich Village, SoHo and the East Village are full of character, as are Little Italy and Chinatown.

Museums include the The Cloisters on Manhattan Island, the Brooklyn Museum of Art, the Museum of Modern Art, the Frick Collection, the Metropolitan Museum of Art, the Solomon R. Guggenheim Museum and the Pierpoint Morgan Library, which between them should keep culture lovers busy for weeks.

Broadway is, it almost goes without saying, the heart of New York's theatreland: if you can't get tickets to the latest hit musical, head for an off-Broadway theatre for something different or experimental. Classical music lovers should head for Carnegie Hall, the Lincoln Center, the New York State Theater or the Avery Fisher Hall in the Lincoln Center.

**POPULATION:**
21,976,000 (2006)
**WHEN TO GO:**
Any time of year.
**DON'T MISS:**
Time Square.
Groud Zero.
Taking in a Broadway show.
Central Park.
Radio City Music Hall.
The Empire State Building.
**YOU SHOULD KNOW:**
Visitors need to reserve tickets in advance to access the Promenade and Observatory in the Statue of Liberty.

*The Empire State Building (left) and the Chrysler Building*

*The old State House*

# Boston

One of the most significant places in the history of the United States of America, Boston is the capital of Massachusetts and the largest city in New England. Founded on the Shawmut Peninsula, as the Massachusetts Bay Colony by Puritans in 1630, the colony was originally called Trimountain, but later became known as Boston after the town in Lincolnshire. Within six years, they had created Boston Latin School and Harvard College, the latter in the outlying area of Cambridge and by the end of the decade some 20,000 people were living in the colony.

The city is equally renowned as having been the cradle of the American Revolution: by the 1770s, the colonists were straining against British control and taxation. The quartering of British troops in American houses led to the Boston Massacre, while the decision to allow the British East India Company effectively to undercut prices on tea led to the Boston Tea Party, when protesters dumped the cargoes of three British ships into Boston Harbor. The first major battle of the American Revolution – the Battle of Bunker Hill was fought on the Charlestown Peninsula. Several of the important sites make up the Boston National Historical Park.

For visitors today, Boston is as important for its culture as for its history: despite extensive redevelopment, the downtown area retains older Federal-style buildings, while the South End Historic District has an extensive area of well-preserved Victorian buildings.

As well as the obvious contribution to learning of its world-famous institutions, Boston is home to the Boston Museum of Fine Arts, the Isabella Stewart Gardner Museum, the Institute of Contemporary Art, the Boston Symphony Orchestra (housed in the stunning Symphony Hall designed by McKim, Mead and White), the Boston Pops, two opera companies, the Boston Children's Museum and the Museum of Science. The John F. Kennedy Library is at the Columbia Point campus of the University of Massachusetts and the art museums in Harvard College are a short ride away.

The large student population, spread among some of the best colleges and institutes on the planet, means that there is a lively night life and music scene, varying from hard-core punk to world music, as well as comedy clubs and theatre.

Although there is plenty to keep visitors occupied in the compact centre of the city, the 'Greater Boston' area is also full of historic connections, beautiful buildings and sights to see. Boston is no longer the quaint enclave of the Boston Brahmins, but a modern city that is both respectful of its past and looking to its future.

**POPULATION:**
4,400,000 (2006)
**WHEN TO GO:**
Spring to autumn.
**DON'T MISS:**
Following the Freedom Trail – the Trail takes visitors to 16 historical sites in the course of two or three hours and covers two and a half centuries of America's most significant past. A red brick or painted line connects the sites on the Trail and serves as a guide. Seeing the Boston Red Sox at Fenway Park.
**YOU SHOULD KNOW:**
Contrary to popular belief, the Pilgrims did not found Boston; they founded the Plymouth Colony some ten years earlier.

# Portland

Straddling the Willamette and Columbia rivers, Portland is a port and industrial city that for more than 150 years has served as a major gateway to the Pacific Northwest. It is known as one of the greenest cities in the US (in both senses) and prides itself on its beautiful parks, including Mt. Tabor, built on the extinct volcano of the same name, and many city-centre parks such as the Portland Japanese Garden and Portland Classical Chinese Garden. Tom McCall Waterfront Park is a popular area and venue for events during the year.

Not all of the volcanoes in the area are as benign as Mt Tabor – Mt St Helens can be seen to the north-east and Mt Hood looms over the city.

The Arlene Schnitzer Concert Hall is the scene of many of the city's cultural events while the Portland Art Museum has a decent art collection. Other galleries include the Portland Art Center and the Portland Institute for Contemporary Art and many small galleries in the downtown area. The Meier and Frank Building is, basically, a department store, but it is beautiful, with glazed terracotta tiles cladding the walls. For a completely different type of architecture, head for the Equitable Building, the first to be built completely clad in aluminium. A popular attraction is the Pittock Mansion. The Oregon Museum of Science and Industry is always popular with children.

Downtown Portland's skyline is gradually rising as more high-rise buildings are added, and it is now a vibrant place in the evenings. The Pioneer Courthouse Square is a popular area, and the surrounding streets have a multitiude of restaurants and shops. The city is also well known for its micro-breweries and brewpubs.

Although Portland is in the far north-western corner of the US, its lively, friendly feel, cultural life and spectacular surrounding scenery make it well worth a visit.

**POPULATION:**
2,338,000 (2006)
**WHEN TO GO:**
Spring, summer or autumn.
**DON'T MISS:**
The Portland Rose Festival – held annually in June to promote Portland, the main event is a floral parade.
The Oregon Brewers Festival in July, serving over 73 different beers from 14 states.
Trips to Mt St Helens or Mt Hood.
**YOU SHOULD KNOW:**
Portland is known as 'the city of roses'.

*Portland with Mt Hood in the background*

# Seattle

**POPULATION:**
3,263,000 (2006)
**WHEN TO GO:**
Spring, summer and autumn.
**DON'T MISS:**
The Space Needle.
The Seattle Underground Tour.
The Seattle Aquarium.
**YOU SHOULD KNOW:**
Seattle is the home of Starbucks,
Microsoft and Amazon.

There is evidence of settlement here since the end of the last Ice Age, but Seattle was not reached by Europeans until the 1850s, after which it became a trading port, a centre for the timber industry and in the last years of the 19th century, a centre for transport and supply for the men heading north to the Klondike gold fields.

On the coast of Puget Sound and backed by the Cascade Range, particularly Mt Rainier, Seattle is in an active geological region and has suffered minor earth tremors from the Seattle Fault and the Cascadia Subduction Zone. The city's reputation for always being wet is undeserved – it can be grey, and the Puget Sound suffers from fog, but it gets less rain than many other American cities.

The city's skyline is dominated by several tall buildings, including the 76-storey Columbia Centre, the Smith Tower, the Washington Mutual Tower and the Space Needle.

*A ferryboat crosses Elliot Bay.*

Seattle is well known for its flourishing arts scene, from the Seattle Symphony Orchestra to Nirvana, Jimi Hendrix, Pearl Jam and the Foo Fighters. The city's theatres also host a wide range of performance poetry, including the Seattle Poetry Slam, and fringe events. Other events include the annual Seattle International Film Festival and the Greek Festival. The visual arts are catered for in the Henry Art Gallery, the Seattle Art Museum, the Frye Art Museum and the Seattle Asian Art Museum, as well as many smaller contemporary art galleries.

As well as providing a beautiful backdrop to the city, the Cascades are popular for hiking and skiing, while Puget Sound and other waterways in the region are a must for sailors and kayakers.

# San Antonio

*The Alamo Mission*

San Antonio is home to one of the most evocative sites in American history – the Alamo, where 198 volunteers held off the forces of the Mexican leader Antonio López de Santa Anna in early 1836, eventually succumbing after thirteen days, but the heroism of such men as Davy Crockett and Jim Bowie inspired Sam Houston's men to defeat the Mexicans a month later. The little mission church is one of the most visited sites in America.

The River Walk (Paseo del Rio) is another popular area of the city, and is home to many of San Antonio's festivals, including the festival of lights in winter and the Fiesta Noche del Rio and Cinco de Mayo. It winds along the riverbank, with woodland areas interspersed with lively areas such as the River Square and South Bank where there are pavement cafés, bars, shops and gourmet restaurants. Among the best of the Central Business District's buildings is Dillard's, a five-storey Art Deco store.

The culture of San Antonio has a mixture of Spanish and German roots so you can find both rodeos and oompah bands, as well as Rejano music, flamenco, and folklorico. The city's earlier buildings are also a reflection of this mixed heritage, including the Spanish Governor's Palace and the Menger Hotel.

The city's military heritage is explored in the San Antonio Cavalry Museum, while other attractions include the Tower of the Americas and the Institute of Texan Cultures in HemisFair Park and San Fernando Cathedral.

**POPULATION:**
1,942,000 (2006)
**WHEN TO GO:**
Any time of year.
**DON'T MISS:**
The Alamo.
The River Walk.
Listening to the Mariachi bands.
The Mission Trail, a short drive out of town.
**YOU SHOULD KNOW:**
Saint Anthony of Padua is the namesake of San Antonio. Spanish explorers stopped here on his feast day and so named the city after him.

*The Old State Capitol building*

# Baton Rouge

Although most people assume that New Orleans is the capital of Louisiana, this honour has, in fact, belonged to Baton Rouge, city sitting on high bluffs inland from the Mississippi Delta, since 1846. Its height above sea-level, its distance inland and the fact that the levees protecting its lower outlying areas held prevented it suffering anything approaching the same level of damage from Hurricane Katrina in August 2005 as New Orleans did. Baton Rouge, in fact, became the centre of rescue operations and provided refuge for hundreds of thousands of the displaced.

Even though Baton Rouge is a major port and industrial and petrochemical centre, it is in parts a lovely old place, with historic areas full of beautiful houses, such as the Garden District and Sherwood Forest, as well as Broadmoor's collection of Mid-Century Modern homes. Beauregard Town has many historic buildings.

The city is home to several good museums, including the Art, Natural Science and Rural Life museums of Louisiana State University, as well as the Louisiana Arts and Science Museum, the Louisiana Museum of Natural History, the Shaw Center for the Arts and the Old State Capitol (housed in a quirky neo-Gothic building).

One of the best old homes is the Magnolia Mound Plantation House, a rare survivor of a late 18th-century building type, while other historic monuments include USS *Kidd* and the Old Arsenal Powder Magazine.

Baton Rouge is a laid-back place, where it is easy to relax and just take in the ambience while enjoying the best that the Deep South has to offer, including Mardi Gras parades in such areas as Spanish Town and Southtown.

**POPULATION:**
224,000 (2005, pre Hurricane Katrina)
**WHEN TO GO:**
Spring, autumn or winter.
**DON'T MISS:**
The rides at Blue Bayou Waterpark or the Dixie Landin' Amusement Park.
**YOU SHOULD KNOW:**
The new Louisiana Capitol building is the tallest capitol building in America.

# Santa Fe

Properly called La Villa Real de la Santa Fé de San Francisco de Asis, Santa Fe was founded in 1515 in a remote area of the Sangre de Cristo Mountains. It is famous both for its architecture and its artistic connections.

Among the oldest buildings here are the San Miguel Mission and the Palace of the Governors, both of which date from the very beginning of the 17th century. The chapel's adobe walls are stunningly simple. The later Cathedral of Saint Francis of Assisi has touches reminiscent of the Alhambra in Spain's Granada.

The central part of the city has a unified look because in the early 20th century the city governors decided to promote a unified version of the region's architectural styles: this has come to be known as the Spanish Pueblo Revival look, and derives chiefly from the older buildings such as the adobe homes and the local churches, with their earth-toned walls.

One exception, because it was built earlier, is the Loretto Chapel – a pretty French-style Gothic revival monument, with a peculiar story about how the staircase to the choir loft was completed by a mysterious stranger.

In order to attract tourism the governors also decided to attract artists to the city, which was not difficult because of the area's natural beauty and the quality of the light here. Among the most famous artists to make their home here was Georgia O'Keeffe, and the museum here is devoted to her works and those of her associates. Santa Fe is third only to New York and Los Angeles as an art market, especially for work that reflects the regional traditions. The city's museums include the Museum of Fine Arts, the Wheelwright Museum of the American Indians, the Museum of New Mexico, the Museum of Indian Arts and Culture/ Laboratory of Anthropology, and the Museum of Spanish Colonial Art.

**POPULATION:**
72,000 (2006)
**WHEN TO GO:**
Spring, summer or autumn.
**DON'T MISS:**
The San Miguel Mission.
The Santa Fe Indian Market
in August.
The Fiesta de Santa Fe in September.
The amazing variety of New
Mexican food.
A visit to one of the local pueblos
open to tourists.
**YOU SHOULD KNOW:**
Take it easy for a day or so when you
arrive, the city is quite high up and
you may take a while to adjust to the
thinner air.

*The San Miguel Mission*

# San Francisco

**POPULATION:**
4,180,000 (2006)
**WHEN TO GO:**
Any time of year.
**DON'T MISS:**
The 49-mile Drive.
Colt Tower.
Pier 39.
The drive across the bay to Oakland.
**YOU SHOULD KNOW:**
Don't call it Frisco: the locals don't
like it.

Whatever image you have of San Francisco before you get here, you will find that it doesn't match up to the reality. Golden Gate Bridge is just as spectacular as you thought it would be, the hills are as steep as you imagined and, yes, there are still tie-dyed teenagers looking to find themselves around Haight-Ashbury. It's no surprise that San Francisco is always among the top tourist destinations in the world.

Despite being densely populated, the city's location on the waterfront, parks and the way that the hills ensure you can never see more than a few blocks make it seem more like a small town rather than the centre of a metropolis of more than 4 million people.

Among the highlights of a trip here is the obligatory visit to Alcatraz Island's 'inescapable' prison, as well as a drive across the Golden Gate Bridge, a trip that must be reserved for a sunny day. Golden Gate Park is home to the M.H. de Young Museum and one of the best botanical gardens in the world, as well as a great place for a picnic. It's also home to a herd of bison.

*San Francisco at dusk*

Neighbourhoods that are worth seeking out include North Beach (also known as Little Italy) and Chinatown. The Castro, is home to a thriving café culture and plenty of small art galleries, as well as being one of the focal areas for the city's gay population.

Fisherman's Wharf is the place to go for the regional speciality, Dungeness crabs, which you can eat while watching the sea lions lazing around in the sunshine.

The Museum of Modern Art is housed in an amazing building in South of Market, while the Palace of Fine Arts is in Pacific Heights, overlooking the Golden Gate and has a popular science museum. The Palace of the Legion of Honour in Lincoln Park has mainly European paintings. Other museums explore the African Diaspora, San Francisco's own history, craft and folk art, Mexican, Chinese and Jewish culture, among many other things.

A ride on the cable cars is a must – take a trip from Fisherman's Wharf or Union Square up to Nob Hill, home to the rich. It's also worth the trip to see the Grace Cathedral.

San Francisco has some of the best in sightseeing, dining, culture, history and scenery, and truly does have something to offer everyone.

# Charleston

*The mansions of the East Battery shoreline*

On the Atlantic coast of South Carolina, Charleston was originally named after Charles II, some four years afer his restoration to the thrones of England and Scotland. It was originally a walled city, and was home to two forts famous for their pivotal roles in America's history: Fort Moultrie withstood the British in the Revolutionary Wars and Fort Sumter is thought to be the location of the first shot of the American Civil War. The only part of the original walls to remain is the Powder Magazine. Its site on a peninsula between the Ashley and Cooper rivers made it an ideal location for a defence and the blockade of its port was a pivotal – if not always successful – part of the North's strategy during the American Civil War because it was a vital source of revenue for the South. The port is still among the largest and busiest in the world.

The downtown area is home to the central business district and many cultural and historic sites. The revenue from surrounding plantations made the city rich and the surviving buildings from this era include St Michael's Episcopal Church, the Old Exchange and Customs House (scene of the ratification of the US Constitution in 1788), the City Hall and the County Court House. There are also many pretty houses in 'historic Charleston', the epitome of Southern colonial charm, with grand houses on tree-lined streets that drip with Spanish moss. Rainbow Row, by the waterfront, has a collection of pastel-coloured historic homes.

In some ways similar to New Orleans, Charleston's culture is a mixture of French, West African and traditional southern American. The French influence can be seen in the dainty red-and-white Huguenot church.

The area's plantation past can be seen in the Boone Hall and Magnolia Plantations, Drayton Hall and Middleton Place, while Charleston Museum was the first museum on the American continent and the Gibbes Museum is home to more than 10,000 works of art. There are many other museums and historical attractions lurking around almost every corner. Each district of the city has its own unique character and charm with dozens of gardens and parks to chill out in and plenty of marinas.

**POPULATION:**
603,000 (2006)
**WHEN TO GO:**
March to November
**DON'T MISS:**
The Battery – Battery Park is where the Copper and Ashley Rivers meet. It is home to White Point Gardens, a large grassy area shaded by oaks and fringed with cannons, monuments and historical statues.
The Audubon Center at Beidler Forest.
The Charles Towne Landing – walk on the very spot where English colonists in 1670 established the first European settlement in the Carolinas.
USS *Yorktown* – go on board to explore the Congressional Medal of Honor Museum.
The Charleston Tea Plantation (the only tea plantation in America).
The French Quarter.
**YOU SHOULD KNOW:**
Many buildings were damaged in 1886 by an earthquake.

# St Louis

**POPULATION:**
2,801,000 (2006)
**WHEN TO GO:**
Spring or autumn.
**DON'T MISS:**
The mosaics of the Cathedral Basilica of St Louis.
The ride to the top of the Gateway Arch, the tallest man-made monument in the world.
The St Louis Zoo.
A St Louis Cardinals game.
The Museum of Transportation in Kirkwood.
The Mardi Gras festival in Soulard.
The Cahokia Mounds in Collinsville – the site of one of the largest pre-Columbian cities north of Mexico.
**YOU SHOULD KNOW:**
The Eads Bridge was the first to cross the Mississippi River, in 1874.

Among St Louis' nicknames are 'The Gateway City' and 'The Gateway to the West', and these describe perfectly both its location and character, where the Oregon Trail met the Missouri. It sits near the confluence of the Mississippi and Missouri rivers and so was an important river port when the rivers were plied by steamboats carrying goods. It is also where Lewis and Clark set off from on their expedition to find an overland route to the Pacific, a return trip that took them nearly two-and-a-half years and which is among the themes explored in the Missouri History Museum.

St Louis has splendid architecture, both old and modern, including the Basilica of St Louis, King of France and the St Louis Abbey; the St Louis Union Station is a destination in itself, the Fox Theatre on Grand Boulevard is special, and there are beautiful mansions in such areas as Hortense Place. The Pulitzer Foundation for the Arts is located in a building which is worth a visit on its own merits, while the St Louis Art Museum has a large range of both ancient artefacts and modern art.

The Riverfront area, especially to the north of the Eads Bridge, is renowned for its eateries and clubs, while the Hill is the best place to go for the area's renowned Italian food.

The Saint Louis Symphony Orchestra resides at the Powell Symphony Hall, but when most people think of music in the context of St Louis, they think of blues, jazz and ragtime, but there is also a thriving rock 'n' roll and rock scene.

Forest Park, even larger than New York's Central Park, is not only an important green space in the city, but home to the Zoo, the Municipal Theatre, the Science Center, the Art Museum and the History Museum.

Perhaps the most iconic place in St Louis is the Jefferson National Expansion Memorial, which commemorates the westward expansion of the United States after the Louisiana Purchase. The stainless steel Gateway Arch was designed by Eero Saarinen and is one of the city's most popular attractions.

*The Gateway Arch*

# Savannah

*One of Savannah's many magnificent squares*

One of the most beautiful cities in the Americas, Savannah is the epitome of what the United States' deep south ought to look like. It is one of the most historically significant places in America. It retains significant numbers of buildings that date back to the early and mid-19th century and beyond, with typical verandahs and balconies dripping with Spanish moss and surrounded by lush oak and tropical woodland. It is also known for the typical laid-back southern charm of its inhabitants.

The settlement was founded in 1733 by General James Edward Oglethorpe and a group of 120 like-minded individuals and it became the capital of the thirteenth British colony in America, Georgia.

Sadly, Savannah's wealth came on the back of the slave trade – through both the import of slaves and the export of cotton, deerskin and rice.

The historic area of the city has been declared a National Historic Landmark. Oglethorpe had laid it out in a grid form, envisaging broad streets interspersed with parks and shaded public squares, of which the majority survive to this day. In the 19th century, the growth, production and export of cotton became increasingly important to the southern parts of America and Savannah became one of the main centres of the industry.

Other early buildings that survive, if in a restored condition, include the Herb House, the oldest building to survive in Georgia, dating back to the year after the colony was founded, the Pirates' House from the 1750s and the Pink House from the 1780s, as well as the Owens-Thomas House, Wormsloe Plantation, and the Sorrel Weed House.

Unlike so many other southern cities, much of the historic area of Savannah survived the Civil War, chiefly because General Sherman was so impressed by its beauty he decided to spare it. Many freed slaves remained in the area, forming one of the most significant African-American communities in the country.

The middle of the 20th century was not so kind to the historic areas, and after various important buildings were demolished, the Historic Savannah Foundation was set up to stop the destruction, and eventually led to the city's emergence as a tourist destination.

The city is not just about the historic district: the City Market and the River Street area are filled with popular shops and restaurants while Tybee Island is a popular beach resort. Fort Jackson was important during the Civil War and the Laurel Grove and Bonaventure cemeteries are worth visiting.

**POPULATION:**
293,000 (2006)
**WHEN TO GO:**
Any time of year.
**DON'T MISS:**
Forsyth Park – home to Forsyth Fountain; a large, ornate, two-tiered cast iron icon of Savannah.
The Savannah Film Festival.
The Second African Baptist Church on Greene Square.
Johnson Square – the first and largest square in the city.
The jazz and blues clubs.
The Telfair Museum of Art.
**YOU SHOULD KNOW:**
Eli Whitney invented the cotton gin near here in 1793. The Cotton gin is the machine that separates the cotton fibres from the seeds.

# Washington

**POPULATION:**
8,207,000 (2006)
**WHEN TO GO:**
Spring to autumn.
**DON'T MISS:**
A tour of the Capitol buildings.
The 4th of July celebrations or
Emancipation Day.
A show at the Lincoln Theatre.
**YOU SHOULD KNOW:**
Getting on one of the White House
tours is incredibly complicated even
for US citizens.

The capital of the United States, Washington, DC, sits between Maryland and Virginia. It is home to some of the most iconic buildings and monuments in America, but is also full of areas of charm and some of the best museums on the planet.

The National Mall, is an area of parkland which joins the White House and the buildings of the Capitol. At its heart is the Washington Monument, while the Vietnam Veterans Memorial is in nearby Constitution Gardens and other monuments include the Lincoln Memorial, the Franklin Delano Roosevelt Memorial and Korean War Veterals Memorial and the United States Navy Memorial.

The Smithsonian Institution is a vast collection of museums, including the National Air and Space Museum, the Smithsonian American Art Museum, the National Museum of Natural History, the National Portrait Gallery, the National Museum of the American Indian and the National Zoo, among others.

Among Washington's historic districts, Georgetown is worth an especial mention for it's pretty brick town houses and cobbled streets. It is also a good place for fine dining and upmarket boutique shops. The Adams Morgan district is another good place to head for, with a wide variety of places to eat.

Among the green areas of the city are the US National Arboretum, Rock Creek Park, Theodore Roosevelt Island and the areas near the Potomac River, especially the Potomac Gorge. After years of work, the last is now once again providing a breeding ground for America's national bird, the Bald Eagle.

Arlington National Cemetery, just across the border in Virginia, is the resting place of tens of thousands of Americans, from casualties of the American Revolutionary Wars onwards, as well as explorers, astronauts, writers and presidents.

Washington DC is a rich cultural and friendly city filled with historical and political stories in a beautiful waterfront landscape.

*The Capitol Building*

# San Diego

In the far south-west of the continental United States, San Diego lies at the south of the Gulf of Catalina not far north of the border with Mexico. For a large city, it has an unexpected friendly, small-town feel. It is sprinkled with parks, forest areas and farms, and is backed by the coastal ranges which lead to the desert beyond.

San Diego has retained a surprising number of its older buildings, including the Spanish missions. Many of the city's attractions are grouped in Balboa Park, including San Diego Zoo, the Museum of Art, the San Diego Museum of Man and the Natural History Museum, while the Museum of Contemporary Art is located in upmarket La Jolla. This last area is also home to a number of smaller art galleries.

The city's beaches are favourites with surfers and sunbathers alike, both for the great surf and their spectacular beauty, while on land the skateboard culture rules. Mission Beach Boardwalk is a great place to hire blades or just find something to eat. Nearby Pacific Beach is also a good place to enjoy the eclectic food on offer and is one of the best places in the evenings, unless you want to head up to La Jolla.

The Navy have an important base here, as the port has long provided access to the Pacific Ocean, and many of the local industries provide support services for the Navy. Miramar, in the northern part of the city, was the location of the film *Top Gun*, while the San Diego Aircraft Carrier Museum in the Colombia district houses the USS *Midway*.

Whether you want to surf, explore the beautiful beaches, visit SeaWorld or even take the children to Legoland, San Diego has something for everyone.

**POPULATION:**
2,942,000 (2006)
**WHEN TO GO:**
Any time of year.
**DON'T MISS:**
Pacific Beach.
La Jolla for shopping and eating.
Mission Beach Boardwalk.
San Diego Zoo.
**YOU SHOULD KNOW:**
May and June can be foggy.

*The San Diego skyline at sunset*

*The Belles Artes Theatre*

# Mexico City

**POPULATION:**
19,200,000 (2005)
**WHEN TO GO:**
Spring and summer, although the air pollution can be bad at these times, the weather is better.
**DON'T MISS:**
The Angel of Independence.
The Templo Mayor.
Xochimilco, to see the remnants of what the city was like before the Spanish arrived.
The Casa Mural Diego Rivera.
The Aztec Calendar Stone in the National Museum of Anthropology.
The Torre Mayor or the Latinoamericana Tower for great views over the city.
**YOU SHOULD KNOW:**
Bear in mind that the Zona Rosa, although it is a great place for entertainment, has a reputation as a tourist trap.

High in the remote mountains, the Aztecs built a city on an island in Lake Texcoco in the early 14th century, and after the Conquest two centuries later, the Spanish rebuilt it and adopted it as the capital of New Spain. Three hundred years later, it became the capital of independent Mexico. The traces of the sophisticated construction and water-management techniques used by the Aztecs still live on in the layout of the modern city's principal thoroughfares.

Even after the damage of the 1985 earthquake, the historic centre of the city and the 'floating gardens' of Xochimilco to the south were deemed worthy of including on the UNESCO World Heritage List, and justifiably so. The centre has a unique mix of colonial and pre-Spanish monuments, which ought not to look good together, but somehow do.

The city is stuffed with museums which cover a wide range of subjects from archaeology to modern Mexican paintings and graphic arts. Particular highlights are the works of Frida Kahlo in the Museum of Modern Art, and the murals by her husband in the Casa Mural Diego Rivera. More of his work can be seen in the Palacio National (take ID).

Popular places for tourists, in addition to the historic centre and Xochimilco, are Condesa and Roma and San Angel for food, nightlife and shopping, Chapultepec de Lomas for its tourist sights, Ciudadela for the craft market and Polanco for upmarket shopping and people-watching.

The holiest place in America for Roman Catholics is the Basilica de Guadalupe, which is a major pilgrimage centre in a Spanish-era cathedral. An equally popular destination on the outskirts of the city are the Aztec ruins of Teotihuacán.

World-class museums and stunning archaeological remains, in a thriving city with amazing food and welcoming people. What more could you want?

# Oaxaca

Oaxaca is a lovely city on the Pacific coast with stunning sandy beaches for swimming, sunbathing and surfing, and gorgeous green seas. It is renowned for being peaceful and welcoming.

This area was long a centre for pre-Columbian peoples and some of the most important ruins lie high in the mountains above the city and together with the city's historic centre make up the UNESCO World Heritage Site of the Historic Centre of Oaxaca and Archaeological Site of Monte Albán. Native American culture and traditions are much more in evidence here than in other parts of the country. The Day of the Dead celebrations are reputed to be the best in the country.

The Conquistador Hernán Cortés had this area as his personal property but subsequent earthquakes mean that little remains from before the early 18th century. Like so many cities in Mexico, there are large numbers of religious buildings including the Cathedral de Oaxaca, Santo Domingo de Guzmán (the convent buildings of which house a museum of Oaxacan life), the Basilica de la Soledad, San Felipe Neri and San Juan de Dios – finished in 1703. Other museums include the Rufino Tamayo Museum, which specializes in pre-Columbian art, the Railway Museum and the Museum of Contemporary Art.

The historic city is a lovely place with colonial architecture and numerous plazas, courtyards and narrow streets, including the central square, the zócalo. Most of the important buildings are within easy reach on foot.

Oaxaca state is renowned for two drinks – hot chocolate and Mezcal – and the food here is great, with lots of restaurants specializing in seafood, although local dishes do include chapulines (grasshoppers).

**POPULATION:**
500,000 (2006)
**WHEN TO GO:**
Any time of year.
**DON'T MISS:**
The Day of the Dead Festival in early November or the Guelaguetza Festival in July.
Teotitlan del Valle village for its woven fabrics and artefacts.
The Zapotec ruins of Monte Alban, Mitla or Yagul.
A tour of the Mezcal distilleries.
The turtle beach at Escobilla.
**YOU SHOULD KNOW:**
Zipolite is a nudist beach.

*Pedestrianized Calle Alcala*

# San Miguel de Allende

**POPULATION:**
139,000 (2005)
**WHEN TO GO:**
Any time of year.
**DON'T MISS:**
A trip into the desert in the wet season (August to October), when the cacti are in bloom.
A trip to see the hibernating Monarch butterflies in January.
The Sanmiguelada bull run in September.
St Anthony's Day (17th January) when people take their animals to church to be blessed.
**YOU SHOULD KNOW:**
A decision on whether to award the city UNESCO World Heritage Site status is due in 2008.

Founded in 1542 by the monk Fray Juan de San Miguel, San Miguel el Grande was an important point on the route that brought silver from Zacatecas. It was renamed after General Allende, a national hero in the mid 19th century. After a period of decline during the first half of the twentieth century, it became a popular destination for American visitors, partly because of its beautiful architecture, which the long-sighted national government had chosen in 1930 to declare a national historic landmark in order to save it. Even today, the historic centre is free of neon signs and modern buildings, and wandering round its little cobbled streets is a fantastic way to spend a few hours, especially as restrictions on traffic are being brought into force.

The city is centred on the 'Jardin', the old town square. It is dominated by several old buildings, including the Templo de San Rafael Church and the Parroquia de San Miguel Arcangel, a beautiful 17th–18th-century Baroque church with a neo-gothic tower added in the late 19th century. According to rumour, the architect copied the design from postcards of European cathedrals. Next door, the Casa de Allende is a perfect example of the style of building favoured by Spanish nobles here in the 18th century.

The streets of the areas around the 'Jardin' have long been popular with painters and if you get here, you'll see why.

*A typical cobblestone street*

# San Juan

Thought to have been visited by Christopher Columbus in 1493, San Juan was founded by Spanish colonists in the early 16th century, and is the second oldest city in the Americas established by Europeans. Among the best monuments here are the forts of San Felipe del Morro and San Cristobal. They were very necessary: San Juan was an important port for Spanish merchant and military shipping and in its time the city has been attacked by the English (three times), the Dutch and the Americans, not long before the Spanish ceded the island to them at the end of the Spanish-American War.

*Plaza de las Monjas and San Juan Cathedral*

Old San Juan – which is a World Heritage Site – is on an island connected to the mainland by a causeway and bridges, and this historic area has more than 400 Spanish colonial buildings in little cobbled streets. It also has several delightful squares and parks, including the Parque de las Palomas (Pigeon Park), which is perched on the old city wall. The Fortaleza is a mixture of 16th-century fort and 19th-century governor's palace.

Among the most important buildings here is the Catedral de San Juan. It was built in the 1520s, rebuilt after a hurricane a few years later, was looted by the English in 1598 and then damaged by another hurricane in 1615, and finally restored in 1917. San José was a monastery church, and is the second oldest church in the western hemisphere. The area also has casinos, restaurants, nightclubs, arts venues, museums, expensive boutiques and spectacular beaches that encompass the neighbouring areas of the city, too. If all this takes too much energy, head for the Paseo de la Princesa, the perfect place to sit under a tree and watch the world go by.

**POPULATION:**
435,000 (2006)
**WHEN TO GO:**
Any time of year.
**DON'T MISS:**
The cobbled streets and pretty houses of Old San Juan.
The Pablo Casals Museum – enjoy hundreds of recordings and video footage of the world-famous cellist. Casals lived in Puerto Rico all his life until his death in 1973.
The Bacardi Distillery – offers tours in English and Spanish. Free samples of Bacardi on offer!
Isla Verde.
Ocean Park.
**YOU SHOULD KNOW:**
Puerto Rico is a self-governing commonwealth in union with the United States

497

# Kingston

Set on a protected harbour on the south-east coast of Jamaica, Kingston was founded in the 1690s after an earthquake destroyed the pirate haven of nearby Port Royal. The city has been ravaged by other earthquakes and fires since, but is still a joyous place to visit. The sound of reggae fills the air in this laid-back city by the sea.

Spanish Town, in the west of the city, was the capital for some two centuries and its surviving old buildings include St James' Cathedral and the Old King's House, among a mix of Spanish-style and Georgian architecture. The Jamaican People's Museum of Crafts and Technology is also here, and the Town Square has a lively local market.

The dilapidated old waterfront area of the city has been redeveloped into a modern, spacious commercial area with wide boulevards and open spaces. The National Gallery is in the Kingston Mall on Ocean Boulevard and is devoted to the works of Jamaica's best artists, while the most famous museum is, of course, that dedicated to Bob Marley, in his former home on Hope Road.

New Kingston is where the new upmarket areas and shopping malls are, but the downtown area gives a real feel of the city (although it should be avoided at night) with brightly coloured buildings, people who live their lives in the open. North of New Kingston are the really rich areas, with magnificent houses to stare at, against the backdrop of the stunning Blue Mountains.

When the colour and noise gets too much, head for the beaches of Lime Cay or Hellshire or up into the Blue Mountains themselves.

*Devon House, owned by one of Jamaica's first millionaires.*

# Santo Domingo

Formally Santo Domingo de Guzmán, the capital of the Dominican Republic, sits where the Ozama River meets the Caribbean Sea. It is the oldest European colonial city in the Americas, officially founded in 1498. The original settlement was damaged in a hurricane only a few years later, echoed by another that destroyed large swathes of the greater city in 1930. The area now known as the Colonial Zone (Zona Colonial) largely escaped the destruction and was declared a UNESCO World Heritage Site in 1990.

The most important buildings to survive include the Pantéon Nacional, the Cathedral (the Catedral Primada de América), the Alcázar de Colón, the first monastery and convent in the Americas, the Governor General's Palace (now the Museo de las Casas Reales), the Fortaleza Ozama and the historic square of the Parque Colón. Together the late Medieval buildings make a perfect collection and one of the best cityscapes you could wish to find, in a maze of cobbled streets.

A more recent architectural addition is the Faro a Colón, a lighthouse built to commemorate the five hundredth anniversary of Columbus' discovery of the Americas.

Behind the sea wall (the Malecón) is another favourite destination here, a long park that runs along the coast. Other highlights are the Museum of Modern Art, the Palacio de Bellas Artes, the Museum of Dominican Man and the Museum of Duarte. Art lovers should head for the Boulevard 27 de Febrero for the public displays of art.

Santo Domingo is, of course, also famous for its beautiful sandy beaches and amazing nightlife.

**POPULATION:**
2,253,000 (2003)
**WHEN TO GO:**
Any time of year.
**DON'T MISS:**
The beaches.
The Calle el Condo.
The Plaza de la Cultura.
Wandering through the Zona Colonial.
**YOU SHOULD KNOW:**
The area is prone to hurricanes.

*Santa Maria la Menor Cathedral*

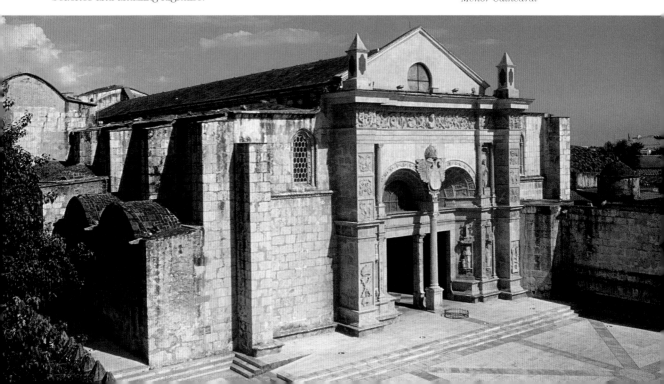

# Cienfuegos

**POPULATION:**
150,000 (2004)
**WHEN TO GO:**
Any time of year.
**DON'T MISS:**
A stroll along the bay or
the harbourfront.
Watching for whale-sharks in
December-February.
The best beach in the area at Playa
Rancho Luna.
**YOU SHOULD KNOW:**
Cienfuegos is also known as La Perla
del Sur – the Pearl of the South.

On Cuba's south coast, Cienfuegos is a city and port rich in history. The city was inscribed on the World Heritage List in 2005 because it is both the first – and outstanding – example of urban planning in Latin America. It is also beautiful, with an eclectic mixture of architectural styles in its public buildings, schools, churches and old houses.

The city sits within a protected bay, guarded at its entrance by the Castillo de Jagua, which dates from the Spanish era, but its chief claim to fame lies in the collection of neoclassical buildings, unrivalled in the Caribbean. The Catedral de la Purísma Concepción was built between 1833 and 1869 and has beautiful stained glass imported from France, while the Palacio de Valle, from 1913–1917, is neo-gothic on the outside, with inside a dining room that wants to be the Alhambra, and bedrooms done in an odd assortment of styles. The neoclassical City Hall, with its beautiful red-tiled domes, overlooks the Parque José Martí, named after Cuba's favourite poet. In one corner of the park, the Palacio Ferrer is the Casa de la Cultura, while the Teatro Tomás Terry – finished in 1890 and in wonderful condition – is on the north. If you think that there is a surprising French feel to many of the old buildings, you'd be right: the town was settled by the French in 1819.

The Prado, the main drag, is counted among the best in the island, probably just pipped by Havana's. This is the place to see and be seen.

*Jose Marti Park*

# Havana

The capital of Cuba, and for centuries its largest and most beautiful city, Havana's architecture – although its splendour is somewhat faded – gives a unique record of colonial buildings from several different centuries, from the defensive walls and the fortress of El Morro via the grand neo-classical houses in French or Spanish style and neo-baroque buildings such as the German-style Gran Teatro to the Art Nouveau Capitolio and Art Deco in the Edificio Bacardi.

*Vintage American cars outside Cuba's national Capitol*

The importance of the old city (Habana Vieja) and the fortifications were recognized in 1982 when they were inscribed on the UNESCO World Heritage List. Because of the country's political isolation, the historic areas have not been invaded by fast-food chains or identikit coffee shops, and they are all the better for this. In some places, the dilapidation veers from the picturesque to the pitiful, but even then it manages to be photogenic. Government-funded restoration programmes are managing successfully to bring buildings back into use without ruining their character.

The city's links with and importance to the region's trade with Europe are evident in the many treasures in its wonderful museums. Havana is the last place one would expect to find a marble bust of Marie Antoinette, but she is in the Museum of Decorative Arts, along with Meissen, Sevres, Imari and Worcester porcelain, English landscape paintings and furniture, Chinese screens and more than 33,000 European paintings. Among the other 50 or so museums there are those dedicated to fine arts, Afro-Caribbean religious artefacts and Arabic and Asian arts. The must-see museums, however, are the Museum of the Revolution, the former Presidential Palace, and the Hemingway Museum.

But Havana is not just about its beautiful buildings and its museums; this city and its people have a vibrant character, as you would expect from a nation whose national drinks are rum, daiquiris and the mojito and whose national dance is the samba. Even though poor in material terms, Havana's near-five centuries of existence have made it rich in history, music, culture and food.

**POPULATION:**
3,073,000 (2005)
**WHEN TO GO:**
Any time of year.
**DON'T MISS:**
The beaches.
A show at the Tropicana.
A concert at the Gran Teatro, a fabulous Baroque-style building.
The Museum of the Revolution – ironically, this opulent building was formerly the presidential palace of Batista and is now a museum housing such items as Fidel Castro's boat and the clothing worn by Che Guevara when he was killed.
The National Museum of Fine Arts.
The Hemmingway Museum – housed in Hemmingway's former home, this museum documents the author's life and works.
**YOU SHOULD KNOW:**
Che Guevara's 1960 Chevrolet is in the Automobile Museum.

# Belize City

**POPULATION:**
300,000 (2007)
**WHEN TO GO:**
Any time of year.
**DON'T MISS:**
Placencia.
The Cockscomb Basin Wildlife Reserve - trails have been created to give visitors a taste of the area's bio-diversity, offering impressive views and an ideal environment for plant and wildlife spotting.
The Mayan sites of Caracol and Xunantunich.
**YOU SHOULD KNOW:**
It is hot and humid here virtually all the time.

The former capital of British Honduras, Belize Town was founded in 1638 by shipwrecked British sailors on the site of the small Mayan city of Hulzuz and gradually expanded into a city. It was the main port in the region for the export of tropical hardwoods brought down to the coast on the Belize River. The government moved inland to Belmopan in 1970 as a consequence of the destruction wrought here by Hurricane Hattie in 1961. There are still areas remaining from colonial times, notably in the Fort George area. The river, canals and smaller waterways are crossed by an intricate network of bridges, from the Swing Bridge (the only manually operated one left), the Belchina Bascule Bridge (operating on the same principles as London's Tower Bridge but on a rather smaller scale) to the rickety individual walkways to houses.

St John's Cathedral was built in 1812 and stands opposite Government House, a lovingly preserved white-painted colonial mansion, built two years later. Overlooking the harbour is the Lighthouse, built for Baron Bliss, a major benefactor to the region, whose tomb lies in front of it.

In the Marine Terminal are the maritime and coastal museums, the Image Factory is the place to head for contemporary art and the Bliss Institute is the cultural centre. The National Handicraft Centre is outstanding for locally made crafts.

Even though it is no longer the country's capital, Belize City remains a bustling, lively city well worth taking time to explore.

*An aerial view of Belize City*

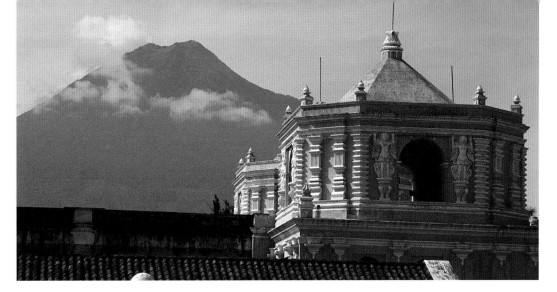

# La Antigua Guatemala

*The top of Volcán de Agua seen behind La Merced Church*

It is possible to sum up la Antigua Guatemala (commonly referred to as just Antigua or La Antigua) in just one word, Baroque. The third incarnation of the city of Santiago de los Caballeros, it was badly damaged by earthquakes and abandoned in favour of a new capital, in 1776. For the previous two centuries and more it had been the seat of the Spanish colony of Guatemala's governor and like its two predecessors – one of which was abandoned because of uprisings by the indigenous inhabitants and the other after flooding caused a mudslide that buried it – named after St James. It was declared a World Heritage Site in 1979.

The city is dominated by three peaks, the Volcán de Agua, Acatenango and the active Volcán de Fuego.

Architectural highlights here include the Palacio de los Capitanes Generales and the Catedral. The original of this building was completed in 1680, and it has been rebuilt several times. In its current form, it is only a fraction of the size of the orginal, and some of the ruins are open to the public. Similarly the Palacio de los Capitanes Generales is only part of what was originally a much larger complex. The Ayuntamiento (city hall) across the square was one of the few buildings to survive the 1773 earthquake more or less intact, and now houses the Museo de Santiago and the Museo del Libro, while the old university buildings by the Catedral house the Museo de Arte Colonial.

Elsewhere in the city are ruins of other old buildings – many of them draped in bougainvillea vines – including the old Capuchin convent, with its individual novices' cells and mysterious underground chamber. The Merced Church is one of the most beautiful, with ornate stucco decoration on the façade.

Antigua is a beautiful city, with large open squares, stunning architecture and beautiful ruins. It retains its old world atmosphere and is a must visit for anyone who loves Baroque architecture.

**POPULATION:**
33,000 (2002)
**WHEN TO GO:**
Any time of year.
**DON'T MISS:**
The Fountain of the Sirens in the Plaza de Armas.
The celebrations during Lent and Holy Week, especially the Good Friday procession.
The cloister of Santa Clara convent.
**YOU SHOULD KNOW:**
The area is still prone to destructive earthquakes and the city has been built and rebuilt time and time again.

*The rapidly developing modern city of Panama*

# Panama City

**POPULATION:**
1,063,000 (2000)
**WHEN TO GO:**
Any time of year.
**DON'T MISS:**
The view from Ancon Hill.
MARTA, the Museo Antropológico – the largest exhibition here focuses on Barriles culture, believed to be Panama's earliest civilization.
A boat trip along the canal – a 77 km (48 mi) journey from one end to the other, taking in stunning scenery and such landmarks as the Bridge of the Americas.
**YOU SHOULD KNOW:**
The city is increasingly becoming a retirement destination for Americans.

At the Pacific end of the Panama Canal, Panama City was founded in 1519 by Pedro Arias de Avila, destroyed in the 17th century by fire after an attack by the Corsair Henry Morgan and subsequently rebuilt a few miles away. It became the national capital in 1903. The completion of the canal in 1914 led to exponential growth. The ruins of the old city form the UNESCO World Heritage Site of the Archaeological site of Panama Viejo and Historic District of Panama, which was inscribed in 1997.

Even before the construction of the canal, Panama was an important gateway between the Pacific and the Caribbean because it was the shortest land crossing.

The old quarter of the city – the Casco Viejo – has the best of the old architecture, including the cathedral.

The modern city is rapidly developing, with one of the highest proportions of skyscrapers of any city. The former canal zone, once out of bounds to non-Americans, is rapidly becoming a tourist destination in itself. The city's nightlife, museums, shopping and culture are second to none in Central or South America.

Right on the doorstep is the rich rainforest, and the Parque Metropolitano has a wide range of wildlife including sloths, toucans and monkeys to marvel over.

# Medellín

Situated at 1,500 m (5,000 ft) in the heart of the Andes, Medellín is known as 'La Ciudad de la Eterna Primavera' (The City of Everlasting Spring) because of its benevolent climate. It is in a beautiful setting, winding along a valley, with trees and flowers everywhere and breathtaking views of the mountains. It would be a wonderful place to visit if it had not acquired a reputation as one of the most dangerous cities in the world.

Throughout the 1980s and 90s it was a narco-mafia centre, run by the cocaine king, Pablo Escobar, who had the city paralyzed with fear and caught in an economic stranglehold. It was only at his death that the government managed to re-assert control. Today Medellín has become an altogether safer place; the city is riding on a wave of optimism, experiencing an economic renaissance and is welcoming visitors with open arms.

For those with an adventurous streak, Medellín is an incredibly exhilarating city. There are busy markets, Baroque churches and a colourful street life, with hustlers and beggars and beautiful girls. The city is known for its parks where people congregate to hang out and there are many cultural attractions and beautiful buildings in the city centre. El Parque del Periodista is a bohemian square where the bars belt out alternative music. The Plaza de Cisneros, a formerly wealthy area that sank into decay through drugs and poverty, has some lovely 1920s buildings and is now on the up again, and the Prado neighbourhood in the heart of the city has some beautiful old houses, many of which are being renovated.

Medellín is still a city with an edge, where the wealthier residents live in well-protected suburbs away from the city centre but it is firmly back on the tourist map, as it should be.

**POPULATION:**
2,350,000 (2006)
**WHEN TO GO:**
December to January for Los Alumbrados – Christmas lights decorating the whole city, turning it into a fairyland. Late July/early August for The Festival de Flores – a gorgeous colourful display when thousands of *campesinos* (country farmers) parade through the city on horseback with massive garlands of flowers.
**DON'T MISS:**
La Candelaria Metropolitan Cathedral.
Museo de Antioquia.
The Museum of Modern Art.
Pedro Nel Gómez Museum – the house where this famous painter lived has more than 1,500 of his works on display.
Nutibara Hill and Pueblo Paisa – wonderful view and replica village.
Ermita de Veracruz.
**YOU SHOULD KNOW:**
The internationally renowned artist, Fernando Botero is a native of Medellin and his paintings and sculptures can be seen all over the city.

*Medellín at dusk*

# Barranquilla

**POPULATION:**
1,695,000 (2005)
**WHEN TO GO:**
Around Carnaval (just before Easter).
**DON'T MISS:**
The Customs Building – built in 1910 by English architect Leslie Arbouin, today it has many purposes, housing an historical archive, a library, the Chamber of Commerce to name just a few.
Montoya Station.
Teatro Amira de la Rosa – as its largest theatre this is the cultural heart of the city.
The Museum of Modern Art – most of the exhibits here focus on the works of Colombian artists.
Bocas de Ceniza – where the River Magdalena meets the Caribbean Sea.
The lovely Art Deco houses scattered around the city.
**YOU SHOULD KNOW:**
Barranquilla is the home city of singer/songwriter Shakira, and was home to Nobel Prize winner Gabriel Garcia Marquez in his youth. He frequented a bar called La Cueva that has been restored as an arty hangout.

Known as La Puerta de Oro de Colombia (the Golden Gate of Colombia), Barranquilla is a port city built on a promontory where the River Magdalena flows into the Caribbean Sea. The city is without any clear origins but has its own unique cosmopolitan heritage of tolerance and a multi-ethnic mix entirely different from anywhere else in Colombia. More than 50 per cent of its population are second-generation immigrants, for Barranquilla provided a refuge for people fleeing from Europe in both World War I and II and more recently from the Middle East and Asia. There is the largest Jewish community in Colombia here as well as Lebanese, Syrian, Italian, German and Chinese minorities, all of whom contribute to the city's international, dynamic atmosphere.

The annual Carnaval of Barranquilla has a tradition dating back to the 19th century and is one of the world's largest street carnivals – reputedly only outdone by that of Rio de Janeiro, but with none of the associated commercialization. It is a four-day event before Ash Wednesday, which has been designated a UNESCO Patrimony of Humanity for being a 'masterpiece of the oral and intangible heritage of humanity'. For several weeks beforehand the streets are filled with music and dancing as the carnival troupes come out to rehearse, and during the actual event the whole city goes wild. The cultural hotchpotch of music and dance is a wondrous spectacle of Caribbean revelry, and each year Carnaval becomes more spectacular.

The natives of Barranquilla call their city 'Curramba La Bella', a wordplay that loosely translates as 'beautiful party', and refer to themselves as Curramberos (literally: party people). The spontaneity and warmth of the people here is infectious and, even when it is not carnival time, the city has an upbeat atmosphere of optimism and enthusiasm for the good things of life.

# Bogota

**POPULATION:**
6,779,000 (2005)
**WHEN TO GO:**
December to March.
**DON'T MISS:**
Iglesia de la Concepción – 16th century Moorish influenced architecture.
Iglesia de San Agustin – noted for its woodcarving and frescoes.
Donación Botero – a huge collection of modern and impressionist art.
Museo de Arte Religioso – large

Founded in 1538 by a Spanish conquistador, Gonzalo Jiménez de Quesada on the site of the citadel of the Muisca king Bacata (from whom the city gets its name) Bogota grew into a significant cultural centre and was made the capital of the Viceroyalty of Nueva Granada in 1740. In 1810 the citizens rebelled against Spanish rule, and at independence in 1819 it naturally followed that it should be declared the capital of the Republic of Colombia.

The historic centre of the city, La Candelaria, has a bohemian ambience with its narrow streets of wooden-balconied colonial houses, small shops and family-run cafés. There are some

magnificent buildings in Plaza de Bolívar, including the Catedral Primada, a splendid Baroque edifice, and the neo-classical Capital, which took 79 years to build. A block to the south is the Casa de Nariño, the splendid Versailles-style presidential palace. Downtown, in the somewhat faded commercial centre, there are many interesting churches, museums and art galleries, including the fabulous Museo del Oro, stuffed with plundered treasure. The wealthier residential districts are to the north, where there are up-market restaurants, expensive shops and lively bars. El Parque de la 93 is one of the most exclusive areas, where the best hotels, restaurants and nightclubs are located. La Zona Rosa is perhaps the liveliest district of all – a small area packed with bars, clubs and shops.

At first sight Bogota may appear rather grim – you cannot doubt the existence of both pollution and poverty. But not for nothing is it known as the 'Athens of South America'. With an eclectic mix of some of the continent's finest architecture, a thriving intellectual scene, welcoming people, animated café culture and exuberant nightlife, Bogota rocks!

*The Baroque Catedral Primada in Plaza de Bolívar*

collection of religious artefacts, housed in the Biblioteca Luis Angel Arango, supposedly South America's largest library.
Museo Arqueológico – museum of pre-Colombian culture housed in colonial mansion.
Weekend antiques market in the cobblestoned district of Usaquen.
**YOU SHOULD KNOW:**
Bogota earned a bad reputation for itself at the end of the 20th century as a narco-mafia centre and was at one time considered too dangerous to visit. But now the city has been completely cleaned up and is as safe as anywhere else.

*The courtyard of a colonial era Franciscan monastery, now an upmarket hotel*

# Popayán

Popayán is known as the 'white city' because of its magnificent white architecture. It is one of Colombia's most beautiful colonial towns with a rich religious and cultural heritage, a prestigious university – Universidad del Cauca, and a reputation as a centre of literature and the arts.

In 1537, the city was captured by the conquistador, Sebastián de Belálcazar, who recognized its strategic importance to the Spanish. Its position in southwest Colombia, on the route from Quito and Lima to Cartagena, made it a perfect place for the transfer of gold and booty on its way out of Peru and Colombia to Spain. The wealth that Popayán accrued through this dubious enterprise is reflected in the beautiful religious and public buildings as well as the splendid private houses. A devastating earthquake in 1983 destroyed large parts of the city but it has been meticulously rebuilt, a reconstruction process that took twenty years.

Popayán is particularly famous for its colonial churches: Belen, perched on a hill overlooking the city, Iglesia de San Francisco – noted for its fine side altars, and Iglesia la Ermita – built in 1546, with some frescoes that came to light as a result of the earthquake. There is also a beautiful Romanesque bridge, Puente del Humilladero. The central square, Parque de Caldas has a lovely old clock tower known as 'the nose of Popayán'. Nearby is the city's cathedral, which, although very badly damaged in the earthquake, is still a remarkable building.

Popayán is famous for its Semana Santa celebrations. Every night during Easter Week there are huge processions and the streets are thronged with hordes of people watching the floats go by.

**POPULATION:**
259,000 (2005)
**WHEN TO GO:**
Easter for Semana Santa celebrations.
**DON'T MISS:**
Casa Museo Mosquera – collection of colonial art.
Iglesia and convent of San Augustín.
Iglesia de Santa Domingo.
Casa Museo Negret – contemporary art gallery.
Museo Guillermo Valencia – colonnaded building dedicated to the well known Colombian poet.
Puracé National Park – a thermal wonderland of hot springs, lakes and waterfalls.
**YOU SHOULD KNOW:**
Seventeen of Colombia's presidents have come from Popayán.

# Caracas

The capital and largest city of Venezuela, Caracas is located in the north of the country, following the contours of a narrow mountain valley close to the Caribbean Sea, though it is separated from the coast by 2,400-m (7,872-ft) high Mt Avila. Founded in 1567, the Spanish captain Diego de Losada managed to finally defeat the aborigine rebels and lay the foundations of the city of Santiago de León de Caracas.

During the 20th century, as the economy of oil-rich Venezuela grew steadily, Caracas was quickly modernized and soon became one of South America's economic centres. However, the rapid growth made the city a magnet for rural communities and immigrants from all over the continent who have moved to the city in an unplanned fashion, creating both the present-day cultural diversity and also the *ranchos* (slum) belt around the valley.

The traffic jams, slums and distinct contrasts in wealth between the city's inhabitants are relieved by the city's immense cultural wealth, whilst the long green valley, surrounded by lushly, forested mountains, blends the modern cityscape with a more tropical, ethereal feel. Caracas is most definitely Venezuela's cultural capital, boasting many fine restaurants, theatres, museums, bars and galleries. It has had great cultural aspirations throughout the course of history, to which institutions such as the old Atheneum bear witness. Visit the Casa Natal de Bolivar, the tranquil gardens and gorgeous colonial mansion of the Museo de Arte Colonial, the awe-inspiring Capitolio Federal or any one of Caracas's many parks, gardens and squares. Caracas is truly a mine of cultural heritage and certainly worth taking the time to see past the crowds.

**POPULATION:**
3,140,000 (2005)
**WHEN TO GO:**
With its proximity to the Caribbean, the city enjoys warm temperatures all year round, though the dry season is from December to April.
**DON'T MISS:**
Caracas Cathedral.
The National Library.
Shopping in Las Mercedes.
El Avila National Park.
The Teresa Carreno Cultural Complex.
Parque del Este.
**YOU SHOULD KNOW:**
Caracas is the birthplace of celebrated Simón Bolivar, leader of several independence movements throughout South America, collectively known as Bolivar's War.

*Caracas Cathedral*

# Coro

**POPULATION:**
140,000 (2006)
**WHEN TO GO:**
Any time as there is no real winter or rainy season. The area can get crowded during the North American holiday season (June to September).
**DON'T MISS:**
The House of the 100 windows – a beautiful red and white colonial building.
Museo Balcón de Los Arcaya - (Arcaya's Balcony Museum).
*Dulce de leche* – local sweets made from goats' milk.
The Waterfalls of Hueque and the Falcon Mountains – located to the south of Coro.
Urumaco – an important fossil site located to the west of the city.
**YOU SHOULD KNOW:**
Coro is an excellent base both for exploring Venezuela's Caribbean coastline and for island hopping in the Lesser Antilles.

Santa Ana de Coro is the capital of the Falcón State and was one of the first cities to be founded by the Spanish in Venezuela, in 1527. Lying some 32 m (105 ft) above sea level, Coro is 320 km (200 mi) northwest of Caracas, at the southern end of the isthmus that links the Paraguaná Peninsula to the mainland. Its inclusion on the UNESCO World Heritage list in 1993 has encouraged restoration of this fine city and has brought a halt to inappropriate and unrestricted new construction work.

A good way to approach the heart of the city is through the splendid arch at the entrance to the colonial centre. Walking through the town is like being transported back in time, as churches, elegant houses and tall trees rise above narrow cobblestoned streets. The city exhibits a unique blend of architectural styles; Spanish, Dutch, and traditional influences are apparent in more than 500 historic buildings. Prepare to be greeted by an explosion of colour, with houses variously painted in deep blues, reds and yellows.

The town's churches are worthy of a visit, from the Iglesia de San Francisco and the Iglesia de San Clemente to the massive whitewashed cathedral, the oldest surviving church in Venezuela (construction began in the 1580s). However, not everything is colonial. The city features museums dedicated to modern art, the Museo de Arte de Coro and the Museo de Arte Alberto Henríquez, both located in the centre of town. West of the centre is the Jewish Cemetery, the oldest of its kind on the continent.

One of Coro's most impressive and surprising spectacles is the Parque Nacional Médanos de Coro, situated 2 km (1.3 mi) outside the town. The Médanos (dunes) are an improbable environment so close to the city, and after a short walk the visitor is surrounded by desert.

*A beautiful example of colonial architecture*

# Georgetown

At the mouth of the Demerara River, on the Atlantic Ocean, lies Georgetown, Guyana's capital city. Not much visited by tourists, Georgetown has a somewhat dilapidated air, but look more closely and you'll discover that it contains a treasure trove of splendid, wooden, colonial buildings set on tree-lined streets and avenues.

Founded by the French in 1782, it was settled and designed to a grid pattern by the Dutch the following year, and renamed Stabroek. As the town was situated 2.1 m (7 ft) below sea level, canals were quickly built, and a seawall erected for protection. At that time the country's wealth lay in Demerara sugar and cotton, and large numbers of West African slaves were imported to work the plantations. Ceded to Britain in 1814, Guyana became independent in 1966.

*Wooden Cathedral*

St George's Cathedral (1889) was designed by the London architect, Sir Arthur Blomfield. This extraordinary Gothic construction, complete with flying buttresses, arches and vaulted ceilings is one of the tallest wooden buildings in the world. Like the Walter Roth Museum with its colonial style slate roof and 'Demerara windows' with louvred shutters, it is a fabulous building in desperate need of repair.

It's not only the architecture that makes Georgetown so attractive, but also the people: Amerindians, Europeans, Africans, East Indians and Chinese all live and work here. Visit Stabroek Market or window shop in Regent Street and Main Street where you will find some of the city's finest historic buildings. Sheriff Street hosts most of the bars, restaurants and nightlife, remaining lively until the small hours. The thriving port sees sugar, timber, bauxite, gold and diamonds leave the country, and a construction boom is underway that, with luck, may bring Georgetown to the attention of a wider audience than it enjoys today.

**POPULATION:**
214,000 (2002)
**WHEN TO GO:**
July to November, February and April.
**DON'T MISS:**
The marvellous Umana Yana building, built by Amerindians in 1972; it has no bolts, screws or nails.
The Red House, once the home of various governmental luminaries.
Austin House, home of the Anglican archbishop.
St. Andrew's Kirk, the oldest Presbyterian church in South America.
City Hall – Gothic architecture par excellence.
**YOU SHOULD KNOW:**
The balcony at St. Andrew's Kirk had a high wall built on it to prevent slaves, who could only hear the service, from seeing their masters kneeling below, which was considered 'unfitting'.

511

*Guayaquil Cathedral*

# Guayaquil

Situated on the Guayas River, near the head of the Gulf of Guayaquil, in the country's low-lying Pacific region, Guayaquil is Ecuador's largest city and its leading economic centre. Recent years have seen it transformed from a fishing and container port into a jewel of the Pacific Rim. In 1896 a fire destroyed large portions of the city and the old district Las Peñas is the only area where wooden houses survived.

A good way to get a feel of the city is to take a stroll along the Malecón 2000 promenade, a 3 km (2 mi) walk along the Guayas River. Here you will find the Palacio de Cristal, an international exhibition centre, originally designed and built by Eiffel in 1907 and the Hemiciclo de La Rotonda, a monument to the liberator Simón Bolívar. The promenade has many restaurants, parks and museums and offers free public shows on most nights from June to December. It also provides access to the spectacular Botanical Gardens.

The Urdesa district is famous for its restaurants where Encebollado (a seafood soup) is the local speciality. The Mercado Artesanal is the largest artisan market in the city selling indigenous crafts, jewellery, and paintings. The main centre for nightlife is the Kennedy Mall which offers a variety of bars and nightclubs. Guayaquil is within easy reach of Ecuador's most beautiful beaches, which are located along the Ruta del sol.

Often seen as a stopping off point on the way to the Galapagos Islands, this rapidly growing city is emerging as a destination in its own right. Churches, museums and gardens sit well with cafés, nightclubs and outdoor pursuits. Transport links are reliable and affordable.

**POPULATION:**
2,180,000 (2001)
**WHEN TO GO:**
The climate in the dry season is warm and pleasant; in the rainy season between January and April a hotel room with air conditioning is recommended.
**DON'T MISS:**
Palacio Municipal – the political hub of the city. Built in a neo-classical style, it is considered one of the most important architectural works in the country.
Las Peñas neighbourhood – the artistic centre of the city. Many of the area's 400-year-old houses have been converted into art galleries and several notable artists have studios in the area.
Parque Centenario – the city's largest park. It offers shady refuge from the sun, with tall trees arching over the walkways and lawns. A large Statue of Liberty dominates the central area of the park.
Bahia - the city's thriving market.
**YOU SHOULD KNOW:**
Most buildings in downtown Guayaquil include *soportales*, colonnades or arcades that provide protection to pedestrians from the equatorial sun.

# Quito

San Francisco de Quito lies in a verdant valley on the slopes of the Pichincha volcano, some 25 km (16 mi) south of the equator. At a height of 2,850 m (8,698 ft), making it the second highest capital city in the world (after La Paz in Bolivia), Quito lies in the midst of the Andes in a truly spectacular setting. Its name means 'centre of the world' in the language of the Tsáchila, some of the first people to have settled in this part of Ecuador.

The city is divided into two parts: the Old City being the heritage district situated to the north, while to the south, the New City boasts modern architecture, broad avenues and urban parks. The Old City contains a wealth of historical buildings; the New City is home to a wide variety of restaurants, cinemas and nightclubs.

The centre of the Old City became the first UNESCO World Heritage Cultural Site in 1978 and it is renowned for its colonial architecture. The most impressive example of this is the Government Palace, a mixture of Spanish and Moorish architecture. El Ejido is the park situated between the old part of the city and the modern section. Here you will find local handicrafts for sale every weekend.

Aside from its superlative setting, a major part of the charm of Quito lies in its numerous open spaces. Parque Metropolitano, located in the north of the city, is the largest urban park in South America. It offers trails through eucalyptus forest, ample picnic areas and many sculptures. La Carolina park is where the locals hang out. Lying in the middle of the business and shopping district, it provides a good focal point for the city. The park also contains the Quito Exhibition Centre and Botanical Gardens.

**POPULATION:**
1,866,000 (2001)

**WHEN TO GO:**
Due to its high altitude and position on the equator, Quito has a constant, mild to cool climate all year round. The typical high temperature at noon is 26 °C (79 °F) and the typical night-time low is 7 °C (45 °F). The city experiences only two seasons: the dry season, June to September, is referred to as summer and the wet season, October to May, as winter.

**DON'T MISS:**
The aerial tramway to Cruz Loma – it takes you from the city centre up the eastern side of the Pichincha volcano.
Museo del Banco Central – a showcase of Ecuadorian history, art and culture.
The view of Cotopaxi (the world's second highest active volcano) from the eastern part of Parque Metropolitano.
The Church of San Francisco – the oldest church in South America.
Plaza de la Independencia – home to many of Quito's finest buildings and breathtakingly stunning when illuminated at night.

**YOU SHOULD KNOW:**
The floor of the courtyard in the Archbishop's Palace is made from the spines of pigs. It is also home to Quito's best (though unofficial) craft market.

*The Monastery of San Francisco in the Plaza San Francisco*

# Cuenca

**POPULATION:**
400,000 (2005)
**WHEN TO GO:**
Cuenca enjoys a mild climate all year round; the heaviest rainfall occurs from October to December, though even then the mornings are typically bright with showers developing in the afternoons.
**DON'T MISS**
Museo de las Culturas Aborígenes – a private collection of some 5,000 pre-Colombian archaeological pieces.
The Panama Hat Factory – as any proud Ecuadorian will tell you, Panama hats originate here; they were first made in Cuenca in the 1830s. So, if you want authenticity, buy your hat from the factory shop.
The Church of Todos Santos – Cuenca's oldest church. Next to it is one of the four crosses that marked the city's original boundaries.
Plazoleta del Carmen – seldom open but many visitors come to view the outside of this church called El Carmen de la Asunción and look at the colourful flower market in the courtyard.
The Monastery and Museum of La Concepción – with 17th century tombs and a collection of religious art.
A day-trip to Sigsig, a remote agricultural village that is a key centre for Panama hat production.
**YOU SHOULD KNOW:**
The nearby community of Jima is a hiking hotspot. Hikes for all levels are available including a three-day hike from the peaks of the Andes mountains down into the rainforest of the Amazon basin.

Cuenca, or Santa Ana de Ríos de Cuenca to give it its full name, is the third largest city in Ecuador. Located in the southern part of the Ecuadorian Andean Mountain range at an altitude of 2,500 m (8,200 ft), the city is built on the ruins of the old Guapdondélig of Cañaris and Tomebamba Inca settlements.

The historical centre contains cobbled streets lined with churches and colonial houses with colourful facades, wrought iron balconies and red tiled roofs. Cuenca has 52 churches altogether (one for each Sunday of the year), with many dating back to the 16th and 17th centuries.

Plaza Abdon Calderón provides the hub around which Cuenca revolves. The Catedral de la Inmaculada (New Cathedral) with its huge blue domes is an impressive sight that dominates the plaza. Most places of interest can be found in the historic area between the River Tomebamba and the streets of Gran Colombia to the north, General Torres to the west, and Hermano Miguel to the east. This area's compactness, grid-like layout, and numerous readily identifiable monuments make it easy to navigate. Elsewhere the city can be confusing, as there are dozens of narrow colonial streets with similar buildings.

Inca Ruins may be found along Calle Larga, Avenida Todos los Santos, and along the river. Though the Spanish destroyed all the complete structures when they built Cuenca, some Inca stonework remains. Ingapirca, Ecuador's most important Inca ruin lies some 70 km (44 mi) north of Cuenca on the Pan-American Highway. Bus excursions can be booked at Terminal Terrestre.

Cuenca is home to eight universities – and this gives what is largely a conservative city a vibrant and youthful feel.

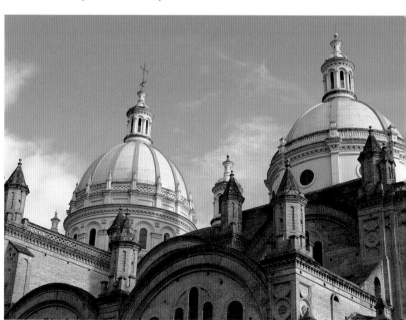

*The Cathedral of the Immaculate Conception dominates Plaza Abdon Calderón*

# Arequipa

Arequipa is a large city in southern Peru, just over 1,000 km (625 mi) from Lima, and capital of the Arequipa Province. Situated in the highlands at the foot of the snow-capped El Misti, it lies in the Valley of Volcanoes surrounded by 80 volcanoes. The fine colonial Spanish buildings constructed of sillar, a pearly white volcanic rock, give Arequipa its nickname La Ciudad Blanca ('the white city'). Archaeological findings indicate that the fertile valley of Arequipa city was occupied as far back as 5000 BC. In the 15th century the region, at the time occupied by Aymara Indians, was conquered by the Inca and soon became an important supplier of agrarian products to the Inca Empire. The modern city was founded in 1540 by Garci Manuel de Carbajal, an emissary of the Spanish conquistador Francisco Pizarro.

Stay in the city and visit the array of temples, convents, colonial mansions, palaces and museums – in particular, the striking Convento de Santo Catalina and the Museo de Arte Virreinal. Similarly, the city centre's bustling market places are worth exploring, as is the curious Juanita Mummy, an exhibition open from May to November, displaying frozen bodies of sacrificial victims found in neighbouring volcanoes.

However, arguably the real highlights of Arequipa can be found in the surrounding countryside where oasis-like valleys, thermal springs and outdoor camping attract the more active traveller. A visit to the Colca Canyon, once thought to be the world's deepest at 3,140 m (10,300 ft) and twice the size of the Grand Canyon, is strongly recommended and definitely worth the four-hour excursion. Walk, condor watch and explore the local towns whilst taking in the breathtaking views.

**POPULATION:**
800,000 (2006)
**WHEN TO GO:**
With an estimated 300 days of bright sunshine and warm temperatures, Arequipa is suitable to visit all year round.
**DON'T MISS:**
Claustrode de La Compania.
Yanahuara Church.
Colca's local dancers.
The Goyeneche Palace.
Casa del Moral.
**YOU SHOULD KNOW:**
In 2000 UNESCO declared the historic centre of Arequipa a World Heritage Site, stating 'The historical centre of Arequipa is an example of ornamented architecture, representing a masterpiece of the creative coalition of European and native characteristics'.

*The Cathedral in Plaza de Armas*

*Plaza Mayor and the Cathedral*

# Lima

**POPULATION:**
7,600,000 (2006)
**WHEN TO GO:**
December to May is the sunniest period, but to catch Lima at its best visit during the Carnival (last few days before Lent) or the Feast of Santa Rosa de Lima (30th August) with its major processions honouring the city's patron saint.
**DON'T MISS:**
Pachacamac – Inca ruins located in the valley of Lurín.
Chinatown.
Horse racing at Monterrico Hippodrome.
The Indio Market – bag yourself a bargain at this craft market located in Miraflores.
The Rafael Larco Herrera – housed in an 18th century vice-royal mansion, this museum contains Peruvian pre-Colombian art, including Inca pieces.
Archaeological Museum.
The beaches of Santa María del Mar and Punta Hermosa.
**YOU SHOULD KNOW:**
Many of Lima's shantytowns, known locally as *pueblos jóvenes*, are without the basic services of running water and electricity.

Peru's capital, Lima is on the coast overlooking the Pacific Ocean, located in the valleys of the Chillón, Rimac and Lurín rivers. Founded by Francisco Pizarro in 1535, as the 'City of Kings', it became the most important city in the Spanish Viceroyalty of Peru and, after the Peruvian War of Independence, the capital of the Republic. Today around one-third of Peru's population lives in the Lima metropolitan area.

This vast (800 sq km [309 sq mi]) and vibrant city is often noted for both its poverty and pollution, yet its notoriously friendly people and dream-like *garua* – a mist that settles over the city between May and October – make it truly unique. The historic centre of Lima was declared a UNESCO World Heritage Site in 1988, due to the large number of fine buildings dating from the Spanish colonial era. In particular, the Plaza Mayor, with its 16th century Cathedral, the Presidential Palace, and the catacombs of the Convento de San Francisco are bound to snare the curious traveller.

Equally, the city's many small beaches, the suburban district of Cieneguilla and the town of Chosica (in the Lurigancho District) provide attractive green landscapes and relief from the busy urban centres. The sprawling, seemingly endless districts give the city the feeling of being a cluster of smaller towns, whilst the slightly slower pace of more traditional rhythms gives Lima and its people a steadier, calmer constitution than in many South American cities. Explore the *peñas* (bars offering folk, jazz and creole music), shop at the open market places and dine at any one of Lima's celebrated restaurants that specialize in the popular local seafood.

# Cusco

Cusco (often spelled Cuzco in Spanish) is a high-altitude (3,500 m [11,500 ft]) city in south eastern Peru, near the Urubamba Valley (Sacred Valley) of the Andes Mountain range. South America's archaeological capital and oldest continuously inhabited city, it was officially founded in 1534 by the Spanish conquistador Francisco Pizarro, although its history goes back much earlier. Legend has it that in the 12th century the first Inca, Manco Capac, the 'son of the sun', was charged by Inti, the sun god, to find 'qosq'o' (the navel of the earth). Descendants argue that it was he who founded the city that was to become the thriving capital of the western hemisphere's greatest empire. After the city was sacked, the Spanish undertook the construction of a new city on the foundations of the old Inca site, replacing the temples with churches, and the palaces with colonial mansions. However, a major earthquake in 1950 destroyed many Spanish constructions, whilst the city's Inca architecture withstood the quake.

The mixed architecture, the remaining Palace of the Incas, the Temple of the Sun, the Temple of the Virgins, and the Quechua-speaking Incan descendents, crowding Cusco's stone-walled streets, are all testament to the legacy of the Inca Empire. Make a day trip to the amazing Inca city ruins of Machu Picchu (presumed to be legendary Inca leader Pachacuti's winter home), accessible by foot on the Inca trail or by train, the fortress at Ollantaytambo and the fortress of Sacsayhuaman. Alternatively stay in the city and visit Cusco's Cathedral, which is one of the city's greatest repositories of colonial art. The cathedral is combined with the Church El Triunto (1536), the oldest church in Cusco, to its right, and the church of Jesus Maria (1733) positioned to its left. The main structure is on the site of Inca Viracocha's Palace, and was built using blocks pilfered from the site of Sacsayhuaman.

**POPULATION:**
300,000 (2007)
**WHEN TO GO:**
May to September
**DON'T MISS:**
Plaza de Armas.
Iglesia de la Compania.
Museo Inka, with a collection of Inca mummies housed in a splendid colonial mansion.
Museo de Arte Religioso, housed in a handsome colonial palace.
San Blas Church, with an ornate pulpit considered one of the jewels of colonial art in the Americas.
The combined sacred sites of the Temple of the Sun at Koricancha and the Convent of Santo Domingo.
**YOU SHOULD KNOW:**
In 2006 this historic capital of the sun-worshipping Inca Empire was declared to be the city with the highest UV light level on earth.
Many believe that Cusco was planned to be in the shape of a puma.

*The main square in Cusco*

*Ver-o-Peso market*

# Belém

**POPULATION:**
2,009,000 (2006)
**WHEN TO GO:**
Any time of year.
**DON'T MISS:**
The Forte do Castelo – originally built in 1616 to protect Belém from French and Dutch invaders. Today it houses a small but excellent museum that focuses on the city's indigenous communites. There are great views of the city and the Amazon River from the top of the fort.
The Mangal das Garças park – enjoy the regional flora and fauna and spectacular views from the lighthouse located here.
The Plaçca Batista Campos – the square in the heart of the city.
**YOU SHOULD KNOW:**
It is also known as the Cidade das Mangueiras (city of mango trees).

Belém, Portuguese for Bethlehem, was founded as Feliz Lusitánia in 1616. In the remote north-east of Brazil and with easy access to the southern channel of the Amazon, it was ideally placed to prevent the British, Dutch and French from encroaching on Portuguese lands, and later to become a chief player in the export of rubber back to North America and Europe. There is still a strong Portuguese flavour to the city, especially in the older buildings such as the delightful Nazareth Basilica and the Forte do Castelo.

The heyday of the rubber industry was around the turn of the 20th centry, and many of the best buildings were constructed at this time, including the Palácio Antônio Lemos and the Colégio Gentil Bitencourt, as was the city's most visited tourist attraction, the Ver-o-Peso market. It is the biggest in Brazil and is particularly renowned for the quality of its fish and fresh produce.

A more modern attraction is the redeveloped warehouses by the river – known as the Docas – which house galleries, shops and restaurants.

Many of the city's attractions are near the shoreline, including the old docks and the fort. There are numerous old churches that are worth a detour. Guided tours of the splendid Teatro da Paz are a must, for its turn of the century decor and both the Museu de Artes de Belém and Museu Emilio Goeldi merit an hour or two.

With a bustling atmosphere and a character all its own, Belém is justifiably one of the most visited cities in Brazil.

# Brasilia

Designed from the start to be Brazil's capital and promote colonization of the country's interior, Brasilia's original construction started in 1956 and it was officially inaugurated just 41 months later in April 1960. The principal urban planner was Lúcio Costa and the principal architect was Oscar Niemeyer. The city was listed as a UNESCO World Heritage Site in 1987.

The basic layout is cruciform and from the air the city is variously described as looking like an aeroplane or a butterfly. It is possible only to mention a few of the city's iconic buildings here: the Palácio da Alvorada, the official presidential residence, the National Congress, the Complexo Cultural da República on the Monumental Axis and the more recent Juscelino Kubitschek bridge over Lake Paranoá are among the highlights. However, the building considered by most to be the best here is the cathedral. Also built by Niemeyer, the circular hyperboloidal structure represents a pair of hands praying.

The television tower is the spot to head for to get an overview of the city, while the Ermida Dom Bosco offers views across Paranoá Lake and gorgeous sunsets. Other open spaces include the Parque da Cidade and Brasilia National Park.

This young city, filled with stunning modernist architecture and public art, is a must-see for everyone.

**POPULATION:**
2,384,000 (2006)
**WHEN TO GO:**
Any time of year.
**DON'T MISS:**
The cathedral – the unusual shape of the building represents two hands reaching up towards heaven. A truly stunning building.
The Poço Azul waterfall.
Capada dos Veadeiros National Park – offers the best of Brasilia's natural fauna and wildlife. It also boasts crystal-clear springs and waterfalls that offer excellent bathing opportunities.
Watersports on Lake Paranoá.
**YOU SHOULD KNOW:**
In 1960 Brasilia formally became Brazil's capital.

*The National Congress building*

# Goiás

**POPULATION:**
27,000 (2006)
**WHEN TO GO:**
Any time of year.
**DON'T MISS:**
The local waterfalls with beaches –
head to Parque Nacional de Chapada
dos Veadeiros for beautiful waterfalls
and spectacular canyons. Check out
the amazing river beaches of the
mighty Araguaia River.
The Serra Dourada Mountains –
rugged and immense, these
mountains offer spectacular scenery.
**YOU SHOULD KNOW:**
In 1682 gold was discovered in the
gravel of a tributary of the Araguaia
River by the explorer Bartolomeu
Bueno da Silva.

Goiás is the former capital of the state of the same name, a role which it lost to the new city of Goiána in 1937. Named after the Goyaz Indians who were here before the Portuguese arrived, Goiás (now sometimes called Goiás Velho) was founded in 1727.

While tourism, ranging and farming are now the chief economic activities in the region, historically, the town's original foundation depended on a very different industry. Gold was found in this area and Goiás was an important mining town. The wealth the city gained during the gold rush era is reflected in the older buildings, including the Colégio Sant'Ana (1879), the Church of Nossa Senhora d'Abadia (1790), the Museu das Bandeiras (1761) and the Casa da Fundição (1752), the old foundry. The church has a beautiful altar painted in gold and blue. There are also pretty streets of old colonial-style houses.

Goiás' beautiful architecture was recognized in 2001 when UNESCO declared it a World Heritage Site because it represents a perfect example of the fusion between European building types adapted to the conditions of South America, and using local techniques and materials. The urban layout, the way the mining town developed naturally and the harmonious appearance within its natural setting were also considered important.

The mountains here are rugged and spectacular, and there are several beautiful waterfalls with beaches and rapids within easy reach.

# Armação de Búzios

**POPULATION:**
23,000 (2005)
**WHEN TO GO:**
Any time of year.
**DON'T MISS:**
A boat trip.
A meal in one of the pay-by-the-kilo
restaurants.
The reserves of Emerencias
and Taua.
The jazz festival in July.
**YOU SHOULD KNOW:**
The peninsula was popularized by
Brigitte Bardot.

Two hours away from Rio de Janeiro, this beautiful city, whose name is often shortened to Búzios, sits on the peninsula of the same name. It is one of Brazil's premier beach resorts but still retains some of the charm of the fishing village and (in the more distant past) haunt of pirates and slavers that it was before the advent of sun-seeking tourists.

It has more than 20 lovely beaches, each with its own special character and activities: Ferruda is great for snorkellers, Geriba for surfing and Ossos for people watching. There are several surf schools and a couple of dive schools that take advantage of the crystal-clear waters and good vision. In general, the east-coast beaches are the best for watersports as they face the open ocean, while the west-coast ones provide the better places for such activities as scuba and snorkelling.

This is serious celebrity territory and the prices of the best restaurants reflect this, but the sophisticated cuisine makes the expense worth it. The shops are clustered around the Rua das Pedras and the nightlife here is among the best outside Rio itself.

*Boats moored at Ossos*

# Rio de Janeiro

Not the capital of Brazil, but certainly its most important city, Rio is rightly one of the world's top tourist destinations. In Sugarloaf Mountain and the Cristo Redentor statue, it has two of the world's greatest iconic sights. Its fabulous beaches, music and renowned carnival celebrations add to the attraction. This is not a city for those who like peace and quiet as life is lived here at full throttle – even the beaches, such as Copacabana and Ipanema, are party zones rather than places to relax.

The Centro (downtown) area is the historic centre, and this is where the most old buildings survive and where the majority of the museums and historical attractions lie. The South Zone is home to the Atlantic beaches. Copacabana is the site of Rio's biggest New Year's Eve party and fireworks spectacular. The North Zone has the lovely Quinta da Boa Vista park, with the former Imperial Palace, which is now The Museum of Archaeology, Ethnology and Natural History. Other open spaces iinclude the botanical garden, the Passeio Público and the Parque Lage. Not only is the landscape around the city beautiful, but within the city limits are two of the largest urban rainforests in the world. Unusually for a city, there are also opportunities for both rock climbing and hang gliding.

Of course, the most famous thing about Rio is its carnival in the two weeks leading up to Mardi Gras, when the members of the samba schools outdo each other in the extraordinary costmes they wear and how much noise they can make. During the rest of the year, the nightlife is equally special, with clubs that attract the world's rich and famous.

If adrenaline-filled fun, set against a background of samba music, is for you then Rio is the only place to go.

*Sugarloaf Mountain sits in the bay*

# Ouro Prêto

**POPULATION:**
66,000 (2000)
**WHEN TO GO:**
Spring, summer or autumn, although
it can be wet in summer.
**DON'T MISS:**
Lavras Novas – an old slave town
located just outside the city. Full of
brightly coloured and charming
buildings, this is an ideal place to
sample traditional village life.
Itacolomi Peak and State Park for
stunning views across the city.
Wandering through the
cobbled streets, admiring the
Baroque buildings and absorbing the
atmosphere of this charming place.
**YOU SHOULD KNOW:**
Among the gems found here is
imperial topaz, which is unique to
the area.

Translating as 'black gold' Ouro Prêto (originally known as Vila Rica) was the centre of Brazil's gold rush in the 18th century and there are still important mineral resources being exploited in the area. The Museu Mineralógico da Escola de Mineras is an institution dedicated to these, and has a jaw-dropping collection of minerals and precious and semi-precious jewels on display. It is thought that gold was first discovered in the area in the 1690s, in the form of little nuggets covered in a layer of black iron oxide, which gave the city its name. This region truly was El Dorado, until the gold started to run out, the Portuguese rulers imposed higher and higher taxes and more and more stringent regulations, eventually provoking the Inconfidéncia Revolt. This was quashed but the town's prosperity was never regained. The period of wealth, however, has left a collection of Baroque buildings unequalled in their beauty and homogeneity, with different communities seeking to outdo each other in the construction and embellishment of their churches and public buildings. The site was inscribed on the World Heritage List in 1980.

There are few modern buildings to break the charm of the city, and its red-tiled roofs stretch across the little valley. The wealth of churches, red-and-white homes with painted doors and little cobbled streets are a perennial delight.

*Red-tiled roofs and beautiful
Baroque buildings*

# Recife

Recife is known for its beautiful urban beaches, including Boa Viagem, Candeias, Piedade and Pina. Sitting where three rivers meet the Atlantic Ocean, the city is set on a multitude of low-lying islands and is therefore known as the Brazilian Venice.

Founded in 1537, Recife has long been the main hub for the export of sugarcane from the region and the wealth that this brought resulted in the construction of the Baroque churches for which the city is famous, such as the Franciscan Convent, with its Golden Chapel, said by many to be the most beautiful church in Brazil. The ostentatious use of gold in its decoration is certainly striking. The cathedral – São Pedro dos Clérigos – is based on Santa Maria Maggiore in Rome, and each of the other dozen or so is equally worth visiting.

As in so many other areas, the plantations relied heavily on slave labour and this has given the region's culture unique elements such as the Frevo and Maracatu, as well as more recently the Mangue Beat.

The city museum in the Cinco Pontas Fort explores the history of the area, while the state museum – the Museu do Estado de Pernambuco – does the same through its art collections and the Northeastern Man Museum looks at its culture. There are dozens of other museums in the city, covering such diverse subjects as trains, archaeology, natural history, sociology, ceramics, military history, abolution, the sculpture of Francisco Brennand and modern and sacred art,

Several popular festivals here include the carnival events of Galo da Madrugada and the Noite dos Tambores Silenciosos, the Night of the Silent Drums, which comemorates slaves who died in jail. In midwinter, the Festa Junina lasts for more than two weeks and features fireworks, bonfires, folk dancing and dressing up in peasant costumes.

**POPULATION:**
3,646,000 (2005)
**WHEN TO GO:**
Any time of year
**DON'T MISS:**
The pretty buildings of Marco Zero Square in the old town.
Boa Viagem beach.
Carnival.
Diving one of the many reefs offshore.
The Instituto Ricardo Brennand.
The World Heritage Site of neighbouring Olinda.
**YOU SHOULD KNOW:**
Recife is Portuguese for reef.

*A view over a Baroque church in Olinda towards modern Recife*

# Manaus

*The Amazonas Opera House*

Originally founded in 1669 as a fort near the confluence of the Río Negra and Amazon, Manaus is today a cosmopolitan, buzzing city. At its height during the period when rubber was among the country's chief exports, it has several beautiful old buildings from those days, including the Mercado Municipal, which is a copy of Paris' Les Halles market halls, and the customs building. The highlight, however, is the Amazonas Opera House (Teatro Amazonas), a copy of the Opéra de Paris with a gorgeous coloured dome outside and dripping with chandeliers inside. It also houses a small museum.

The city has a wide variety of cultural events, including film, jazz, drama and opera festivals and is particularly known for October's samba festival. Late in the month is Boi Manaus, a local event in which Boi-Bumbá music forms the basis of a celebration of northern Brazilian culture. The Rio Negro Palace is a cultural centre and theatre, built by German farmers. One curiosity here is the Museu de Ciencias Naturais da Amazonia (the Natural Sciences Museum), a private museum dedicated to the wildlife of the area, while live specimens can be seen at the INPA reserve.

Manaus is a base for many tours of the Negro and the Amazon and the rainforest, which are just on the doorstep, from a few hours on the stretch near the city to three-week trips upriver. The CIGS Zoo is a place to see rescued animals, while there are good parks and reserves locally, such as the Bosque de Ciência. The grounds of the Federal University of Amazonas include a massive urban forest.

From wildlife to nightlife, and beautiful architecture to stunning rainforest species: Manaus has something to offer everyone.

**POPULATION:**
1,645,000 (2005)
**WHEN TO GO:**
Any time of year.
**DON'T MISS:**
A trip by boat or land into the Amazon rainforest – experience up-close the tropical birds, countless flowers, towering trees, reptiles and monkeys...a truly wondrous eco-system.
The CIGS Zoo for rescued animals.
A boat trip to Paricatuba Waterfall, situated on the Negro River.
The Boi Manaus annual festival – takes place on October 24th to celebrate the day that Manaus was granted city status. Enjoy the singing, dancing, local cuisine, grand costumes and savour the Latino spirit!
The Ponte Negra beach area.

# Salvador da Bahia

São Salvador da Baia de Todos os Santos is the third biggest city in Brazil, and renowned for its architecture, cuisine and music. Its historical centre – the Pelourinho was inscribed on the UNESCO World Heritage List in 1985 because of its 17th–19th-century monuments. It was the first colonial capital and has an interesting division between the commercial district in the lower town and the residential, governmental and religious centres in the upper town above the steep escarpment. The two have been linked by the Elevador Lacerda since 1873.

Although it is less famous than Rio's, carnival here is celebrated with just as much enthusiasm and has its own distinctive African-influenced flavour. The feast dedicated to Nosso Senhor do Bonfim is also important.

The church of Nosso Senhor do Bonfim, which houses the image of the same name is one of the best in the historic area. It is a delightful Rococo building with a neo-classical interior. The convent and church of São Francisco, on the other hand is very fine Baroque, while the Cathedral of Salvador is Mannerist. Many of the rich buildings here date from the period when the Portuguese imperial family lived here after escaping the ravages of Napoleon.

The fusion of African and Brazilian influences is particularly noticeable in the city's cuisine and in Capoeira, a dance-cum-martial art, which has its own music, songs and instruments that have their origins in sub-Saharan Africa.

Salvador is a beautiful city, welcoming and friendly, with a wealth of historical monuments and museums. Just one visit will not be enough.

**POPULATION:**
2,711,000 (2006)
**WHEN TO GO:**
Any time of year.
**DON'T MISS:**
Carnival.
Buying some of the local craftworks.
The beaches, especially those on the island of Itaparica, commonly described as paradise.
The Gastronômico da Bahia museum.
**YOU SHOULD KNOW:**
Candomblé is an African religion practiced in Brazil. It was originally taught by African priests who were brought over as slaves from 1549 onwards.

*Church of Nosso Senhor do Rosario dos Pretos in the Pelorinho*

# São Luís

**POPULATION:**
1,228,000 (2006)
**WHEN TO GO:**
Any time of year.
**DON'T MISS:**
Bumba Meu Boi.
**YOU SHOULD KNOW:**
São Luís has the largest and best-preserved heritage of colonial Portuguese architecture in all of Latin America.

Sitting on the island of the same name in the Baía de São Marcos, São Luís was the site of a fort built in 1612 by the French but conquered three years later by the Portuguese. The historic centre, which was declared a UNESCO World Heritage Site in 1997 for its cultural importance, retains an essentially Portuguese feel. The most distinctive features of its late 17th-century architecture are the beautiful patterned tiles that cover many of the buildings, like the blue-and-white tiles of Portugal, and the ironwork balconies and door grilles. An economic slump here in the early part of the 20th century fortutiously saved the buildings from the development that occurred in so many other cities and for the last 30 years there has been an active programme of restoration.

The region is well known for its Tambor de Mina – a local version of the Afro-Brazilian religious fusion called Candomblé. Tambor de Crioula is a popular group dance for women accompanied by drums and the form of Capoeira here is thought to be closest to its traditional roots.

A popular local event is the Bumba Meu Boi. Performances of a traditional comedic tragedy are staged all over the city between Easter and June, featuring evil settlers, witch doctors, Indians, slaves and other characters.

*Catedral da Sé*

*The Convento de San Felipe Neri*

# Sucre

Known as the 'Cradle of Liberty', this is where Bolivian independence was declared in 1825. In a valley surrounded by low mountains in the central highlands at an altitude of 2,800 m (9,184 ft), Sucre is Bolivia's most beautiful city, with a wealth of colonial architecture, flower-filled courtyards, dainty patios and proud, law-abiding citizens.

The 16th century Renaissance Cathedral on Plaza de Maya has a landmark bell tower and the museum next door contains a fascinating collection of religious relics. At the Convento de San Felipe Neri you can climb up to the top for stunning vistas of the 'White City of the Americas'. The monks used to meditate up here on the roof terraces as the scent of roses drifted up from the courtyards below.

The climate in Sucre is comfortably mild and it's an easy place to be. It has become a fashionable destination for students of Spanish and the university has the reputation of being the centre of progressive thought within the country. This is also Bolivia's chocolate capital, with chocolate shops (some offering free tastings) on every street.

In 1994 a mudstone face bearing over 6,000 dinosaur tracks (some 80 cm (32 in) in diameter) of over 150 species of dinosaur was discovered at Sucre's cement quarry, just outside the city. Sadly you are not allowed to get up close and personal but can gaze through your binoculars at the monster footprints from the Parque Cretácico, and wander amongst the life-sized models of diplodocuses, ankylosauruses and many others.

**POPULATION:**
247,000 (2007)
**WHEN TO GO:**
The Fiesta de Chu'tillos at the end of August features folk dancing from all over South America.
**DON'T MISS:**
The cemetery – the most beautiful in the country. A sign as you enter proclaims *Hodie Mihi Cras Tibi* (Today for me, Tomorrow for you).
The best view in town from the Café Mirador, attached to the Museo De Los Ninos Tanga-Tanga.
The venerable Cedar tree – Cedro Milenario – in the gardens of the Museo Recoleta.
The Inca Pallay, a weavers' and artisans' cooperative where you can buy intricately woven textiles and see weavers at work.
Iglesia De La Merced – with one of the finest church interiors in the country, including a filigree and gold inlay pulpit and Baroque-style altar.
**YOU SHOULD KNOW:**
Sucre is Bolivia's judicial capital and a UNESCO World Heritage Site.

527

# Cochabamba

A large sprawling city in the heart of Bolivia, Cochabamba is set at an altitude of 2,558 m (8,390 ft) in a green bowl in the central highlands, surrounded by low hills and fertile valleys – an area that is the country's bread basket.

The central business district of the city is compact. The town's Cathedral in Plaza 14 de Septiembre is the oldest religious structure in the area. Started in 1571, it has a fine gilded altarpiece and a grotto for the much-loved Immaculada (Virgin of the Immaculate Conception).

Cinema complexes and American restaurant chains have popped up around the city in recent years and there is a busy buzzy vibe with a distinct, almost Mediterranean, atmosphere.

Much of the city's population is poor but parts of town have a prosperous feel. The leafy new-town avenues have a big choice of restaurants, eagerly feasted at by the food crazy cochabambinos. This is a very affordable city, with prices far below those of Sucre or La Paz. The locals pride themselves on being the most food obsessed in Bolivia and are forever stopping to grab a pavement empanada or a special orchard/citrus juice.

Cochabamba is Bolivia's biggest market town – the main market is the vast La Cancha, one of the most chaotic, crazy and exhilarating places in the country. Thought to be the biggest open-air market in South America, you can find everything you need there, plus lots of things you never even knew existed. The fruit and vegetable section has had to move to the shore of Laguna Alalay in the southeast of town and the fascinating Mercado de Ganado livestock market happens at the end of Avenida Panamericana, far south of the centre.

**POPULATION:**
586,000 (2007)
**WHEN TO GO:**
May to October, when the days are dry and clear.
**DON'T MISS:**
The Convento de Santa Teresa, a beautiful cloistered convent.
Cristo de la Concordia, the statue of Christ that stands atop Cerro di San Pedro, the hill behind Cochabamba.
This Jesus is higher – by a few centimetres – than the famous statue of Christ in Rio de Janeiro. 1,250 steps up, or stay cool and take the cable car.
The Fiesta of Santa Vera Cruz Tatala, when local farmers gather at a chapel in a nearby valley to pray for good crops.
Chicha (a refreshing fermented drink made from maize), folk dancing and merrymaking.
The Museo Arqueologico, with an intriguing selection of artefacts and trepanned skulls.
**YOU SHOULD KNOW:**
In 2005 the eyes of the world turned to Cochabamba as its citizens protested against rises in water rates; 100,000 people from all walks of life took to the streets and forced the US giant water utility Bechtel out. Anti-globalization campaigners around the world saw this as a highly symbolic victory.

*Cochabamba is one of the wealthier and bigger cities in Bolivia and home to centuries of political activism.*

# La Paz

At 3,660 m (12,004 ft), Bolivia's capital La Paz is the highest city on the planet and visitors need to be careful to acclimatize gradually to its high altitude. Originally named La Ciudad de Nuestra Senora de la Paz (The City of Our Lady of Peace), La Paz lies in a huge canyon in the mountains, clinging to the vertiginous edges all around, with the enormous Mount Illimani, 6,402 m (21,000 ft), looming in the background.

This is one of Latin America's fastest growing cities and the centre for commerce, finance and industry in Bolivia. Moreover, tacked on to La Paz, high above on the lip of this canyon city, is El Alto, formerly a melting pot for subsistence farmers and people from all around the country, now with a population of 648,000 – a city in its own right.

There are plenty of historical and cultural museums down around the centre of La Paz but it is in the upper central regions of the city where the pace of life is most frantic. It's a maze of impossibly steep streets and alleyways, with men pushing heavy trolleys laden with street food dodging the traffic as they hawk their wares, while women with long black plaits and bowler hats stir steaming cauldrons of Plato Paceno – a bean and potato based stew. Looking up between the world's highest high-rises you can catch glimpses of Illimani's towering triple peak.

Formerly a big tourist draw, La Paz's San Pedro Prison must be the world's most bizarre jail – with no guards, no uniform and no curfew. The prisoners work to pay for their cells, some of which are extremely luxurious; they have unions and elect their leaders. The guided tours had to be stopped as too many visitors were coming on 'cocaine shopping sprees'.

**POPULATION**:
1,250,000 (2005)
**WHEN TO GO**:
May to October
**DON'T MISS**:
El Alto's delectable sprawling markets.
Seeing La Paz on a clear dark night with the glittering starry sky intermingling with the twinkling city below.
Enjoying a folksy show at the Teatro Municipal Alberto Saavedra Pérez - a rotunda theatre with curlicued balconies and elaborately painted ceiling mural.
Mercado de los Brujos (the 'witches market') where you can buy herbal remedies, magic potions and shrivelled llama foetuses.
Museo de la Coca - shows coca's role and uses in traditional life and society today.
The world's highest ski slope, 5,320 m (17,450 ft) down to 4,900 m (16,076 ft), 35 km (22 mi) north of La Paz at Chacaltaya on a retreating glacier.
**YOU SHOULD KNOW**:
Scams are rife – beware of fake tourist police, 'helpful tourists' and counterfeit banknotes.

*La Paz 'grows' amongst the mountains.*

# Tarija

**POPULATION:**
132,000 (2007)
**WHEN TO GO:**
The dry season is from
April to November.
**DON'T MISS:**
The daily siesta – from 1.00 pm till
3.00 pm the place is a ghost town.
Iglesia de San Juan – built in 1632 –
where the Spanish signed their
surrender to the liberation army; the
garden has a fine view over the city
with a dramatic backdrop of sand
coloured mountains.
A visit to a local winery to taste not
only the wine but also the local
distilled grape spirit – Singani – forty
per cent alcohol with a flowery
fresh fragrance.
Mirador Loma de San Juan, above
the tree-covered slopes of Loma de
San Juan, with great views of
the city.
Casa Dorada – a house once lived in
by a wealthy merchant. It has many
large and lurid rooms – kitsch for
the rich.
**YOU SHOULD KNOW:**
In the north-east corner of the
market, vendors sell various snacks
and pastries unavailable in other
parts of Bolivia, including delicious
crêpe-style *panqueques*.

*The views across the plaza from
the San Francisco Monastery*

Set close to the Equator but far from the sea, Tarija has a Mediterranean atmosphere, reminiscent of southern Spain. Luis de Fuentes, the city's founder, named the nearby river the Guadalquivir (after Andalucia's biggest river) and left the Chapacos – as residents of Tarija are known – with a lilting dialect of European Spanish.

The main plaza is planted with stately date palms and the surrounding landscape mixes cowboy country with lush grape-filled valleys – this is Bolivia's primary wine-producing region. The valley climate is idyllic, although winter nights can cool off a little. The student population is very lively so watch out for water balloons as you drink wine from the grapes of the world's highest vineyards and dance through the streets at Carnival season! The colonial architecture, sizzling Argentine barbecues, café terraces and Karaoke dives all add to the fun atmosphere.

The city is known too for its fiestas and unique musical instruments. Tarija's patron saint is St Roque (the Saint for good health and dogs), and at the Fiesta de San Roque every August canine beauties parade the streets dressed in outlandish outfits with feathers, sequins and flowing ribbons.

At the city's world-famous Paleantology Museum you can see the remains of a prehistoric armadillo (glyptodon) and a giant ground sloth (megatherium) as well as old hunting weapons, such as a *rompecabeza* (head-breaker).

# Buenos Aires

The capital of Argentina, on the Río de la Plata, was first settled as the Ciudad de Nuestra Señora Santa María del Buen Ayre in 1536, then refounded in 1580. It threw off Spanish rule in 1810 and became fully independent in 1816.

It is one of the most important cities in South America both economically and culturally, with world-class museums and galleries, orchestras, music and food.

Buenos Aires is, of course, synonymous with the tango, which grew in the poorer *barrios* (neighbourhoods) and the sound of it fills the air, especially on Sundays in San Telmo and La Boca, and on Tango Day in mid-December. As you would expect, the nightlife in the city is second to none, and there are specific establishments called Milongas where you will find tango at night, all night.

Most of the tourist areas are downtown (known as MicroCentro), and within easy walking distance, including San Telmo, Puerto Madero and La Boca, which is picturesque but expensive. Palermo has a beautiful large park that is a perfect place to people watch.

Buenos Aires is also renowned for its shopping opportunities. The main tourist shops in MicroCentro are in and around Florida Street and Lavalle Street, while Murillo Street specializes in leather goods. San Telmo has an excellent Sunday market and Francia Park in Recoleta has a craft fair at the weekends.

Beef, naturally, features large in the local cuisine, so head for one of the *parrillas*, which specialize in roast meats.

Buenos Aires is a lively city, filled with passionate people, proud of their cultural heritage, liberal attitudes, literary associations and history.

**POPULATION:**
13,349,000 (2003)
**WHEN TO GO:**
Spring, summer or autumn.
**DON'T MISS:**
A performance at the Teatro Colón.
Tango Day in December.
Buying some of the amazing
leather goods.
Eva Péron's tomb in the Cementerio
de la Recoleta.
**YOU SHOULD KNOW:**
Shop around: there are often two prices – one for locals and another for gringos and watch out for mass-produced items masquerading as hand made.

*The colourful La Boca
district in Buenos Aires*

# Mendoza

**POPULATION:**
130,000 (2006)
**WHEN TO GO:**
Any time of year.
**DON'T MISS:**
A taste of the region's
excellent wines.
The Puente del Inca Sulphur Springs.
The Vendimia festival in March.
The ice cream.
The view from the Cerro de la Gloria.
The Emiliano Guiñazú – Casa de
Fader museum.
**YOU SHOULD KNOW:**
The buildings here are built to
stringent earthquake-resistant
designs.

Mendoza is a beautiful city, with wide, tree-lined avenues and lovely plazas and parks and a European-style café culture. It was founded in 1561 by Pedro del Castillo and then rebuilt in its current form by the Frenchman Balloffet after an earthquake 300 years later. It is known as the Oasis City because of the network of irrigation canals that keep it green.

The vast Parque General San Martín, named after the national hero, is in the west of the city. There is a monument here to the general and his army's crossing of the Andes, as well as the city's football stadium, the zoo and the university. It has a large lake with watersports on offer and activities here include hang-gliding.

The city has several excellent museums, including the Museo Cornelio Moyano (natural history), the Museo del Area Funcacional (the history of the city, especially in relation to the 1861 earthquake) and in nearby Maipú, one dedicated to the wine industry. The national science museum is in the Parque General San Martin, while the museum dedicated to him is next to the Alameda walkway.

Because of its proximity to the Andes, Mendoza is popular with climbers and hill walkers in summer and with skiers in winter. It is one of the main bases for people aiming to climb Aconcagua, the highest mountain in the western hemisphere.

This is a lovely, laid-back city in beautiful mountain surroundings, with friendly people and is one of the most relaxing places to chill out, whether you want to wander through the streets and parks or head for one of the bars around the Aristides Villanueva Avenue.

*The beautiful tiled fountain in Plaza Espana*

# Salta

The capital of the province of the same name in the north-west of Argentina, Salta sits in the Andean foothills. Its chief claims to fame are its beautiful colonial architecture and the stunning scenery around. It was founded by the Spanish in 1582, but became an important stronghold against them during the war of independence in the early 19th century. Despite this, the people pride themselves on their Spanish heritage and keep up traditional dancing, music and cuisine.

The Spanish heritage is particularly evident in the city's skyline, where old rooftoops are punctuated by Baroque churches. The narrow cobbled streets near the Plaza 9 de Julio are dotted with pavement cafés and here you will come across the cathedral, the old city hall, the Convent of San Bernardo and the Church of San Francisco.

The area was, of course, inhabited long before the Spanish arrived and the MAAM museum has extensive collections on the Inca culture and heritage. The Museo de Alta Montaña houses the mummified bodies of three children found on Mount Llullaiillaco, the new Contemporary Arts Museum houses work by local artists while the Uriburu Museum and the Arias Rengel and Hernández houses explore the colonial era.

Nightlife tends to be concentrated in the area near the railway station – the Balcarce – where there is also a craft market at the weekend.

**POPULATION:**
465,000 (2005)
**WHEN TO GO:**
Any time of year.
**DON'T MISS:**
The April Culture Festival.
Looking for handicrafts in the Mercado Artesanal.
The view from the cable car up to San Bernardo Hill.
The Museo de Alta Montaña.
A trip on the Tren a las nubes (the train to the clouds).
**YOU SHOULD KNOW:**
Traditional forms of music here include *zambas* and *chacareras*.

*Salta Cathedral*

*Ushuaia reflected in the Beagle Channel*

# Ushuaia

The world's most southerly city, on Isla Grande, Ushuaia is backed by the Martial Mountains and overlooks the Beagle Channel. Its remote location made it an ideal place for a penal colony but it is now a popular stop for cruise liners on their way to Antarctica.

The old jail is now a museum, the Museo Maritimo y ex Presidio de Ushuaia, which includes displays on the history of the colony. The railway was among the constructions built by the convicts, and makes a really elegant way to see the area. A steam locomotive takes the carriages (which are heated, thankfully) mainly along the bank of the Río Pipo from the End of the world Station to the Tierra del Fuego National Park Station. Another old building that gives you an idea of the early days of settlement is the Beban House, with a reconstruction of the old town.

The national park is one of the area's major draws and includes the Martial Glacier and lakes Escondido and Fagnano. Wildlife in the area includes penguins, beavers and orcas and activities include horse-riding, trekking or mountain biking, as well as boat trips along the Beagle Channel.

This remote place is a testament to the determination of humans to survive in whatever conditions the planet can throw at them, although it is by no means as bleak here as you might think. Sheltered from the worst of the weather by the bay's islands, it is nevertheless usually windy here. The beauty and interest of this outpost at the foot of South America make even the long journey required to get here worth while.

**POPULATION:**
64,000 (2005)
**WHEN TO GO:**
Late spring to early autumn, or winter for the snow sports.
**DON'T MISS:**
The Tren del Fin del Mundo (the End of the World train).
The view from the peninsula across the Beagle Channel.
A visit to a traditional estancia.
**YOU SHOULD KNOW:**
Warm clothes are a necessity at any time of year.

# Santiago

In 1541 Pedro de Valdiva founded Santiago on an easily defended rocky island, called Huelen Hill. Here the Mapocho River divides around the island before rejoining further downstream to flow across a wide plain at the foot of the Andes, which form a stunning backdrop to the city.

Santiago's climate is mild, almost Mediterranean, and summer lasts from November to May. During winter, however, Chile's capital suffers from smog, as it is trapped between the Andes and the Pacific. Santiago is a city in which there is much to do and many places to explore, from quiet cobbled plazas in which to linger over coffee and snacks, to busy shopping arcades. It is a city where old colonial architecture stands amidst stunning modern skyscrapers.

There is probably no better place to start your exploration of Santiago than the Centro Historico, the action-packed heart of the city. In the cultural centre on the south bank of the Rio Mapocha there are art shows, concerts, an annual book fair and cafés, and in the arty Lastarria district there are several good museums, theatres and bookshops as well as the romantic Cerro Santa Lucia, a former Spanish fortification which is now a hilly and labyrinthine public garden.

Your next stop might be the Iglesia de San Francisco, with a good collection of macabre religious art and baroque paintings and the 19th century Republica is worth a look too. For something completely different, try the Barrio Brasil, with its cutting edge underground arts events, galleries and music venues.

If it's shopping that attracts you, the eastern areas of the city, Santiago Oriente, Victacura, Providencia and Las Condes, offer designer shopping, fine gastronomy and a busy night life on wide boulevards. Or for more traditional purchases there is the Mercado Central, Santiago's legendary wholesale market.

**POPULATION:**
201,000 (2002)
**WHEN TO GO:**
Summer is from November to May but the climate is good all year round.
**DON'T MISS:**
Barrio Bellavista, the area between the Mapocho River and San Cristóbal Hill that is famous for its bohemian nightlife, with many restaurants and clubs.
Santiago International Film Festival in August.
A visit to the opera at the Teatro Municipal.
Centro Cultural Palacio de La Moneda, the newest and largest cultural space, near the government palace of La Moneda.
*Paila marina* – an unidentifiable mix of small fish made into a salty soup.
**YOU SHOULD KNOW:**
The pollution can be difficult to contend with, especially at times of high humidity.

*The Plaza de la Ciudadanía and the stunning backdrop of the Andes*

*Valparaiso is Chile's most remarkable and atmospheric city.*

# Valparaiso

Perched on a dozen hills above a huge bay with its brightly painted houses spilling higgledy piggledy down towards the ocean, Valparaiso is Chile's most remarkable and atmospheric city. It used to be known as 'the Pearl of the Pacific' until a massive earthquake in 1906 almost razed the city to the ground.

Nowadays the city wears a slightly shabby bohemian air, although it is still Chile's most important working port, moving thousands of containers annually. The lower town, the narrow strip of land squeezed between the sea and the hills is a lively muddle of traffic-choked streets, jam-packed with shops, offices and crumbling warehouses, crowding around the quay and the port.

A few precipitous roads make it up the gradients to the high spots, but most people get up and down on the city's fifteen 'lifts' – *ascensores* – archaic looking funiculars that slowly haul you vertically to the fabulous viewpoints above. Built between 1883 and 1916, these 'lifts' provide a vital link between the lower town and the residential areas spread around the hillsides.

The city's main attraction lies in its crumbling romantic atmosphere and stunning setting on this rugged Pacific coastline. Pablo Neruda, Chile's Nobel Prize-winning poet, had a house here - La Sebastiana - perched atop a hill; it is a feast of bizarre and beautiful objects Neruda collected from all over the world.

In the hilltop residential area of Concepción, Paseo Atkinson, an esplanade with great panoramic views of the city and the ocean, is lined with pretty houses with tiny front gardens and window boxes, recalling their original English owners from the 1830s, when British businessmen flocked to the city where they ran trading empires built on copper and silver.

Valparaiso is widely considered to be one of the most intriguing urban areas on the continent, with a rich architectural and cultural legacy. The historic area of the city was declared a UNESCO World Heritage Site in 2003.

**POPULATION:**
263,000 (2007)
**WHEN TO GO:**
November and March are the best months – the weather is perfect and the beaches deserted.
**DON'T MISS:**
Ascensor Polanco on Calle Simpson, the most picturesque of the *ascensores*. Approached through a cavernous underground tunnel, it rises 80 m (262 ft) vertically through a yellow wooden tower to a balcony giving great views over the city.
The stock exchange, the oldest in Latin America.
The Museum of Fine Arts, housed in a splendid Art Nouveau building known as the Baburizza Palace.
Taking a boat ride round the harbour at sundown.
The handicraft market near the Muelle Prat Wharf.
The Palacio Lyon on Calle Condell – a splendid mansion built in 1881, one of the few to survive the earthquake, now housing the Museo de Historia Natural. Note the case of stuffed penguins.
**YOU SHOULD KNOW:**
Valparaiso hosts a hugely popular annual festival on the last three days of the year, culminating in the 'New Year by the Sea' fireworks show, the biggest in South America.

# Concepción

Concepción, known locally as Conce, sits astride the river Bio Bio in a fertile plain. The river, which separates the meadow pastureland of central Chile to the north from the lakes and volcanoes of the south, drains water from the Andes to the Pacific Ocean.

Chile's third largest city and the southern area's capital and economic centre, Concepción was founded in 1550 by Pedro de Valdivia but almost destroyed soon after in 1571 as well as badly damaged in subsequent centuries by earthquakes and tsunamis. It was relocated further upstream from its original position at the mouth of the Bio Bio to protect it but was again shaken by earthquakes in the 20th century, so today most of the city's buildings are of modern concrete design.

Concepción's advantages are that it has a mild climate with plenty of rain – the surrounding areas are very fertile, with many thriving farms and vineyards that produce some of Chile's best wines. For beaches there is a short 16-km (10-mi) trip to Talcahuano, the military area and fishing port, home to the famous Huascar monitor, a metal clad gunboat involved in the Chilean civil war, as well as the two sandy beaches Ramuncho and Rocoto.

The many students from the Universidad de Concepción inhabit the wide pavements and piazzas, giving the city a buzz of excitement with excellent nightlife and restaurants, where the local fare of *empanada* – meat, chicken or fish with onion, raisins and olives in flour pastry – or *bife a lo pobre* (steak and chips) can be enjoyed before looking at the outstanding Mexican mural in Casa de Arte, or strolling up to investigate the Galeria de la Historia.

*Concepción is Chile's third largest city.*

**POPULATION:**
212,000 (2002)
**WHEN TO GO:**
Summer season is November to May.
**DON'T MISS:**
Pisco – a powerful liqueur distilled from grapes after pressing.
The huge lobsters from the Juan Fernandez Islands – also abalone, clams and sea urchins.
The Municipal Market – for local foodstuffs.
Musem Cathedral of the Santísima Concepción.
The large and small lakes of San Pedro.
**YOU SHOULD KNOW:**
Its previous location was where the nearby town of Penco now stands. Somewhat confusingly, inhabitants of Concepción are known as *penquistas* while inhabitants of Penco are called *pencones*.

*Independence Square*

# Montevideo

Montevideo, positioned in the south of the country, is the capital, largest city and chief port of Uruguay. It was first discovered in 1516 by Spain's Juan Diaz de Solis who arrived only to be killed, along with his fellow travellers, by the natives already inhabiting the area. The Portuguese founded Colonia del Sacramento in the 17th century despite Spanish claims to the site due to the Treaty of Tordesillas. The Spanish and Portuguese conflict remained rife for years and Bruno Mauricio de Zabala, the governor of Buenos Aires, founded Montevideo in 1726 to prevent further incursions. In 1828 the town became the capital of Uruguay.

Home to almost 50 per cent of the nation's population, Montevideo is both a modern metropolis and a historical gateway. The city is slyly sophisticated and culturally diverse, boasting a picturesque blend of colonial, Spanish, Italian and Art Deco architecture. Surrounding the whole city is an uninterrupted stretch of white, sandy beach, which seduces many Argentinean and Brazilian holiday makers for their summer breaks.

Whilst Montevideo is often bypassed by North American and European travellers in favour of its more famous and flamboyant neighbours, the city is not only the largest in Uruguay but also one of the most interesting and lively. If you don't mind crowds then Montevideo's carnival, Uruguay's biggest party and most popular celebration, in February/March is a must. Alternatively enjoy the year-round good climate and explore the city's highlights at a quieter time. Visit Ciudad Vieja (the old town) with its 18th century architecture, the vibrant Mercado del Puerto, and the bustling commercial activity of Avenida 18 de Julio with its cultural offerings of theatres, museums and art galleries. On the intersection of this avenue stands the Palacio Salvo, a striking building designed by Italian architect Mario Palanti. Completed in 1925 the Palace stands 100 m (328 ft) high and was, at the time, the tallest building in South America.

# Colonia del Sacremento

Colonia del Sacremento, in the south west of Uruguay overlooking the Rio de la Plata, is the oldest town in the country and capital of the department of Colonia. Founded by the Portuguese in 1680, the town was a focus of struggle with the Spanish who established the settlement on the opposite bank at Montevideo in response. For years the colony changed hands between the two crowns until 1816, when it was claimed by the Brazilians and the entire Banda Oriental (Uruguay) was seized by the Rio de Janeiro government. Initially acting as a contraband port, evading the strictures imposed on trade by the Spanish crown, today Colonia is a resort city, a port and the trade centre for a rich agricultural region.

Whilst having expanded to the east, the old part of the city still keeps the irregular terrain-fitting street plan designed and built by the Portuguese. The winding, cobble-stoned streets and colourful Portuguese-style domestic architecture, so reminiscent of Lisbon, are a delight to explore and mark the city out from its Uruguayan neighbours.

Visit the Puerta de la Ciudadela, also called Puerta del Campo – a 1745 drawbridge built by the Portuguese governor to safeguard the walled city's only entrance. Now restored, it marks the beginning of the historic district, which was named a UNESCO World Heritage Site in 1995. Set on a small peninsula jutting out into the river, with its thick fortified walls and tile and stucco buildings, the site is definitely worth the walk. Alternatively you can amble through the relatively tourist-free streets and discover the small bars, the excellent restaurants, the art and craft shops and museums or explore the large yacht harbour.

**POPULATION:**
22,000 (2004)
**WHEN TO GO:**
Uruguay's pleasant climate makes any season a good time to visit Colonia, one of South America's least visited treasures, although the warmer months are from November to March.
**DON'T MISS:**
The Sunday market in the Plaza Mayor.
Bastión del Carmen, once a wharf and factory, today a theatre and cultural centre.
El Faro, a lighthouse constructed in 1857 with stones from the ruins of the Convento de San Francisco.
Iglesia Matriz – the oldest church in Uruguay.
A ferry trip to Buenos Aires.
**YOU SHOULD KNOW:**
Boat tours of the Parana River leave from Carmelo, north west of Colonia.

*A view of the harbour in Colonia del Sacremento*

# COUNTRIES

# CITIES

Alamy/Peter Adams Photography front cover picture 5, 463 inset 1, 471, 531; /Glen Allison 329; /allOver photography 130, 258; /AM Corporation 169; /Arco Images 24; /ArkReligion.com 58, 330, 458; /Jon Arnold Images 20, 39, 97, 141, 173, 230, 236, 254, 275, 293 inset 2, 368, 376, 384, 478; /Brian Atkinson 432; /Atmosphere Picture Library 116; /Authors Image 422; /Dan Bachmann 378; /Sandra Baker 485; /E.J. Baumeister Jr. 206, 212; / Pat Behnke 44, 391; /Simon Belcher 192; /BennettPhoto 400; /Roussel Bernard 538; /Bildarchiv Monheim GmbH 93, 351; /BL Images Ltd 104; /Black Star 429; /Tibor Bognar 21, 324, 399, 539; /Caro 264; /Charles O. Cecil 408; /Alan Copson City Pictures 168; /Corbis Premium RF 534; /Dennis Cox back cover picture 4, 355, 449; /Cro Magnon 151; /Jean Dominique Dallet 418; /Danita Delimont 152, 416; /DIOMEDIA 205; /dk 184, 419; /Andriy Doriy Travel Photography 224; /Paul Doyle 277; /Steven Dusk 450 inset 2, 454; /EDRaff 377; /Guy Edwardes Photography 102; /Chad Ehlers 371; /John Elk III 487; /eStock Photo 505; /Eye Ubiquitous 198; /f1 online 404; /face to face Bildagentur GmbH 81; / Malcolm Fife/zefa 181; /Michele Falzone 283, 379; /Leslie Garland Picture Library 11; /Oliver Gerhard 149; /Darryl Gill 109; /graficart.net 86 top; /Greenshoots Communications 441; /Alex Griffiths 171; /guichaoua 6 picture 4, 56; /Robert Harding Picture Library Ltd. 80, 115, 196, 321, 364; /Blaine Harrington III 316; /Hemis 304, 403 inset 1, 426; /Andrew Holt 108; /Michael Howell 120; /Matthew Jackson 122; /James Hughes 118; /Iconotec 417, 498; /Lily Idov 266; /imagebroker 79, 83, 174, 234, 260, 263, 410, 435; /Images&Stories 8 inset 1, 268; /ImageState 320; /Images Etc Ltd 466; /Images-of-france 54, 63; /IML Image Group Ltd 176, 201; /Indiapicture 317; /infocusphotos.com 295, 296; /Ingolf Pompe 25 523; /INTERFOTO Pressebildagentur 240; /isifa Image Service s.r.o 235; /Andre Jenny 36, 486; /Mark A. Johnson 463 inset 2, 477; /JTB Photo Communications, Inc. 51, 256, 350, 362, 372, 409, 512; /JUPITERIMAGES/Agence Images 67; /JUPITERIMAGES/Brand X 383; /Ali Kabas 276; /Wolfgang Kaehler 7 picture 6, 210, 402 inset 2, 424, 491; /Christian Klein 367, 373; /Russell Kord 536; /Art Kowalsky 23; /Stan Kujawa 220; /LMR Group 375; /Edward Longmire 185; /LOOK Die Bildagentur der Fotografen GmbH 167, 387; /Craig Lovell/Eagle Visions Photography 363; / Manor Photography 119; /J. Marshall - Tribaleye Images 530; /Iain Masterton 265; /Jenny Matthews 444; /Andrea Matone 200; /Neil McAllister 308, 393, 395; /mediacolor's 190; /Megapress 386; /Navin Mistry 25; /nagelestock.com 89; /Nikreates 248; /John Norman 7 picture 4, 451 inset 1, 459; /David Noton Photography 515, 516; /Mark O'Flaherty 532; /Bernard O'Kane 211; /Panorama Media (Beijing) Ltd 358; /Edward Parker front cover picture 4, 494; /Beren Patterson 514; /Dave Pattison 390; /PCL 241, 246, 251, 392, 414, 465, 519; /Douglas Peebles Photography 7 picture 5, 474; /Pegaz 226; /Nicholas Pitt 250, 332, 421; /Pixel 8 344; /Tony Pleavin 128; /Profimedia International s.r.o. 231; /Realimage 121; /Stephen Roberts Photography 13; /Stephen Saks Photography 229; /Scottish Viewpoint 124; /SCPhotos 247, 369, 448; /Alex Segre 6 picture 1, 46; /Selecta 110; /Mark Shenley 280; /Eitan Simanor 31, 403 inset 2, 438; /Trevor Smithers ARPS 111; /Keren Su/China Span 2, 33, 347; /John Ferro Sims 59, 154; /Gordon Sinclair 495; /South America Photos 527; /Jon Sparks 14; /Giffard Stock 357; /StockBrazil 520; /Johnny Stockshooter 274; /SuperStock 178; /Jane Sweeney 302; /Zalan Szabo 237; /Matjaz Tancic 189; /Paul Thompson Images 194; /Sergey Torockov 214; /travelstock44 133; /Ian Trower 300; /Bob Turner 29; /John Vahgatsi 208; /Genevieve Vallee 511; /Terence Waeland 262; /Richard Wareham Fotografie 209, 218; /Ken Welsh 49, 509; /Westend61 222; /Wilmar Photography 12; /Peter M. Wilson 252, 510; /Andrew Woodley 385; /Rawdon Wyatt 319; /Ariadne Van Zandbergen 428, 431; /Vlad Zisser 272.

Jon Arnold Images 202.

Emma Beare 165,166.

Corbis UK Ltd./Peter Adams 73, 132, 228, 290, 440, 529; /Peter Adams/JAI 223; /Peter Adams/zefa 136, 244; /O. Alamany & E. Vicens 131; /Archivo Iconografico, S.A. 381; /Jon Arnold/JAI 270, 273; /Atlantide Phototravel 445; /Ricardo Azoury 522; /David Ball 388; /Bruno Barbier/Robert Harding World Imagery 5 picture 4, 501; /Annie Belt 447; /Remi Benali 327; /Benelux/zefa 28; /Yann Arthur-Bertrand 177; /Walter Bibikow 472, 490; /Walter Bibikow/JAI 175; /Bilderbuch/Design Pics 221; /Alberto Biscaro 412; /Kristi J. Black 18; /Tibor Bognar front cover picture 3, 5 picture 2, 38, 52, 66, 155, 172, 292 inset 1, 293 inset 1, 322, 337, 361, 397, 462 inset 3, 467; /Christophe Boisvieux 326, 405; /Mark Bolton 153; /Charles Bowman/Robert Harding World Imagery 5 picture 5, 34; /S. Brendgen/A.B./zefa 84; /Lauren Victoria Burke 492; /Sebastien Cailleux 415; /Demetrio Carrasco/JAI 42, 142, 342, 346, 394; /Philip Coblentz/Brand X 7 picture 1, 186; /Ashley Cooper 148; /Alan Copson/JAI 40, 41, 143; /Joe Cornish/Arcaid 101; /Philip James Corwin 484; /Marco Cristofori 140; /Derek Croucher 126; /Richard Cummins 47, 48, 199, 452, 476; /Fridmar Damm/zefa 77, 451 inset 2, 460; /Howard Davies 443; /Julie Eggers 496; /Sophie Elbaz/Sygma back cover picture 2, 427; /Macduff Everton 128 bottom, 462 inset 1, 502, 535; /Eye Ubiquitous 144; /Michele Falzone/JAI front cover picture 1, 2 centre, 9 inset 1, 282, 289, 307, 309, 450 inset 1, 456, 525; /Werner Forman 430; /Michael Freeman 292 main picture, 315, 318, 433; /Franz-Marc Frei 91; /Paulo Fridman 3 right, 521; /Rick Friedman 396; /Sid Frisby/Loop Images 106; /Lee Frost/Robert Harding World Imagery 114; /Robert Garvey 453; /Roland Gerth/zefa 96, 207; /Ken Gillham/Robert Harding World Imagery 246; /Philippe Giraud 72; /Philippe Giraud/Good Look 197, 518; /Graeme Goldin/Cordaiy Photo Library Ltd. 328; /Louis Laurent Grandadam 360; /Uwe Gerig/dpa 253; /Paul Hardy 7 picture 3, 8 inset 2, 85, 107, 134; /Roger de la Harpe 446; /Blaine Harrington III 335, 473; /Brownie Harris 497; /Jason Hawkes 6 picture 5, 100, 125; /Chris Hellier 68; /Gavin Hellier/JAI 339, 374, 425; /Jon Hicks 8 inset 3, 26, 94, 145, 146, 191, 238, 243, 314, 323, 338; /Jeremy Horner 331; /Dave G. Houser 442, 503; /Jan Butchofsky-Houser 439; /Rob Howard 365; /JAI 513; /Mark A. Johnson 450 main picture, 455; /Martin Jones 225; /Ray Juno 6 picture 2, 61, 70; /Wolfgang Kaehler 267, 524; /Nicholas Kane/Arcaid 35; /Christian Kober/Robert Harding World Imagery 137; /Bernd Kohlhas/zefa 180; /Richard Klune 7 picture 2, 78, 86, 103, 112; /Bob Krist 489, 517; /Robert Landau 482; /Thom Lang 3 centre, 312; /Floris Leeuwenberg/The Cover Story 434; /Danny Lehman 499; /Frans Lemmens/zefa 336; /Charles & Josette Lenars 306; /Jean-Pierre Lescourret 5 picture 1, 45, 50, 488; /Michael S. Lewis 402 inset 3, 436; /Liu Liqun 349, 352; /London Aerial Photo Library, Ian 105; /Anatoly Maltsev/epa 216; /Lawrence Manning 420; /William Manning 6 picture 3, 64; /Gunter Marx/Gunter Marx Photography 469; /John McAnulty 483; /Mike McQueen 5 picture 3, 27, 398, 402 inset 1, 406; /MedioImages 507; /Gideon Mendel 382; /John and Lisa Merrill 139; /Mohamed Messara/epa 286; /Gail Mooney 74; /Bruno Morandi/Robert Harding World Imagery 279; /Masumi Nakada/zefa 389; /Richard T. Nowitz 480; /Diego Lezama Orezzoli 526; /Christine Osborne 411; /Matthieu Paley back cover picture 3, 299; /Doug Pearson/JAI 99; /Douglas Pearson 19, 60; /Paul C. Pet/zefa 292 inset 3, 325; /Bryan F. Peterson 69; /Sergio Pitamitz 402 main picture, 423, 462 main picture; /Sergio Pitamitz/zefa 504; /Louie Psihoyos back cover main picture, 366; /Jose Fuste Raga 8 main picture, 22, 43, 53, 98, 138, 162, 284, 292 inset 2, 340, 370, 383, 407, 461, 500; /Jose Fuste Raga/zefa 380, 413; /Redlink front cover picture 2, back cover picture 1, 353, 359; /Carmen Redondo 232; /Reuters 298; /Dietrich Rose/zefa 88; /Guenter Rossenbach/zefa 76; /Hans Georg Roth 150; /Bob Sacha 159; /Sybil Sassoon/Robert Hardy World Imagery 303; /Axel Schmidt/dpa 193; /Schmitz-Söhnigen/zefa 90 bottom; /Michel Setboun 55; /ML Sinibaldi 10; /Herbert Spichtinger/zefa 75; /Hubert Stadler 157, 158, 533; /Kurt Stier 288; /Ron Chapple Stock 470; /Hans Strand 2 left, 16; /Keren Su 30, 32, 95; /Rudy Sulgan back cover picture 5, 233, 242, 468, 481; /Murat Taner/zefa 92, 156, 182, 462 inset 2, 479; /Arthur Thevenart 281; /Paul Thompson 195; /Guy Thouvenin/Robert Harding World Imagery 62; /Upperhall Ltd/Robert Harding World Imagery 294; /Sandro Vannini 164; /Ivan Vdovin/JAI 170, 219, 278, 297; /Steven Vidler/Eurasia Press 82; /Patrick Ward 57; /Julia Waterlow/Eye Ubiquitous 354; /K.M. Westermann 37; /Nik Wheeler 311; /Adam Woolfitt 183; /Jim Zuckerman front cover main picture, 9 inset 2, 160.

Getty Images/Walter Bibikow 464; /Christian Science Monitor 528; /Jeremy Horner 291; /Yann Layma 356; /Andrea Pistolesi 537; /Randy Wells 493.

Lonely Planet Images/Krzysztof Dydynski 508; /Paul Harding 15.

Silk Road and Beyond 215.

Still Pictures/Knut Mueller/Das Fotoarchiv 310; /Voermans VanBree 6 picture 6, 437.